Citizen 2.0:

Public and Governmental Interaction through Web 2.0 Technologies

Kathryn Kloby
Monmouth University, USA

Maria J. D'Agostino
John Jay College of Criminal Justice, CUNY, USA

Information Science
REFERENCE

Managing Director:	Lindsay Johnston
Senior Editorial Director:	Heather Probst
Book Production Manager:	Sean Woznicki
Development Manager:	Joel Gamon
Development Editor:	Hannah Abelbeck
Acquisitions Editor:	Erika Gallagher
Typesetter:	Milan Vracarich, Jr.
Cover Design:	Nick Newcomer, Lisandro Gonzalez

Published in the United States of America by
Information Science Reference (an imprint of IGI Global)
701 E. Chocolate Avenue
Hershey PA 17033
Tel: 717-533-8845
Fax: 717-533-8661
E-mail: cust@igi-global.com
Web site: http://www.igi-global.com

Library of Congress Cataloging-in-Publication Data

Citizen 2.0: public and governmental interaction through Web 2.0 technologies / Kathryn Kloby and Maria J. D'Agostino, editors.
     p. cm.
  Includes bibliographical references and index.
   ISBN 978-1-4666-0318-9 (hardcover) -- ISBN 978-1-4666-0319-6 (ebook) -- ISBN 978-1-4666-0320-2 (print & perpetual access) 1. Internet in public administration. 2. Public administration--Technological innovations. 3. Communication in politics--Technological innovations. 4. Web 2.0--Political aspects. 5. Online social networks--Political aspects. 6. Public administration--Citizen participation--Technological innovations. 7. Decision making--Citizen participation--Technological innovations. I. Kloby, Kathryn, 1972- II. D'Agostino, Maria J. III. Title: Citizen two point zero.
  JF1525.A8C55 2012
  352.3'802854678--dc23
                                        2011044753

British Cataloguing in Publication Data
A Cataloguing in Publication record for this book is available from the British Library.

All work contributed to this book is new, previously-unpublished material. The views expressed in this book are those of the authors, but not necessarily of the publisher.

For Gerald, Orion and Atlin Kloby

In Loving Memory of Stanley E. Kloby

Table of Contents

Section 1
Defining Web 2.0 Technologies and Their Relevance to the Public Sector

Section 2
Applying Web 2.0 in the Public Sector

Section 3
Web 2.0 and the Potential for Transformation

Detailed Table of Contents

Section 1
Defining Web 2.0 Technologies and Their Relevance to the Public Sector

Public administrators must be prepared to select and apply relevant Web 2.0 technologies for public involvement in the policy process. This can be an overwhelming venture as much of the available information on Web 2.0 is generated by private sector managers or potential vendors who are presumably unfamiliar with the inner workings and complex relationships of government. This collection of chapters seeks to define Web 2.0 technology from the perspective of individuals working in government and in the public policy process. A detailed description of the different applications and tools that are currently available to public administrators and policy decision makers is presented to advance the understanding of the implementation challenges and potential for new opportunities to engage the public.

Chapter 1

This chapter examines recent developments on the use of social media in the public sector and explores current and emerging platforms, applications, and tools that can be used by the public sector in various settings. Social media best practices are presented, as well as initiatives from different regions and countries. The chapter concludes with an analysis of the critical challenges the public sector faces in embracing Web 2.0 technologies at the core of its processes and services.

Public comment processes in federal and state agency rulemakings are among the most substantial potential arenas for public input into government. Unfortunately, these processes have not been much used for thoughtful public input. This chapter explores whether online democratic deliberation and natural language processing tools, can empower participants to provide more informed input into an agency rulemaking. It also seeks to determine whether such an approach has other positive effects such as enhancing citizenship and increasing confidence in the pertinent agency. Results suggest that public deliberation can improve public comments into federal and state agency rulemakings while strengthening the citizenship qualities of participants. They also indicate that many of the desired effects of face-to-face deliberation with trained facilitators can also be obtained online without facilitators.

Chapter 3

Staci M. Zavattaro, University of Texas at Brownsville, USA

This chapter provides an overview of United States federal policies guiding citizen/government interaction on social media tools. Such an overview begins to fill the gap regarding how federal agencies make policies regarding records retention and privacy on these platforms. Records management, inherently linked with privacy concerns, also are explored to further ground the argument, and future recommendations are made based on a qualitative content analysis of social media policies from three U.S. government agencies. From analyzing these policies, along with bringing in relevant literature, a workable framework and recommendations emerge to guide future social media use within government.

Chapter 4

Julianne G. Mahler, George Mason University, USA

The term "virtual organization" is used in the literature to describe a range of public and private online work settings from telecommuting in traditional organizations to sophisticated arrangements for project members in different institutions and multiple locations to share information and interact online on a joint undertaking. Though virtual governmental organizations are increasingly common, the management challenges they pose are only beginning to be studied. Here, an exploration of management process in these virtual settings begins is conducted using primary and secondary case materials and published research on virtual organizations in the United States. The analysis is designed to answer questions about the use of information and communication technologies, the management of coordination, and leadership in two forms of virtual organizations.

Section 2
Applying Web 2.0 in the Public Sector

As Web 2.0 technologies are integrated into the everyday lives of citizens and the day-to-day operations of private organizations, many begin to question how such tools are utilized by government. These chapters present a survey of government jurisdictions to give some sense of the extent to which Web 2.0 technologies are used in the public sector. Findings of quantitative and qualitative research examine current adoption trends of Web 2.0 in the public sector with a discussion of different applications and how they can be used as engagement mechanisms.

Chapter 5

Aroon P. Manoharan, Kent State University, USA
Lamar Vernon Bennett, Long Island University, USA
Tony J. Carrizales, Marist College, USA

This chapter looks at technological inequities throughout the world within the context of e-government. The purpose of the study is to evaluate and highlight existing digital divides and current trends among the various divides. The concept of the digital divide, within the context of e-government, is often associated with the lack of access and resources to citizens for the purpose of utilizing technology in working with government. Utilizing survey data of international municipal Web portals as well as existing United Nations data, this chapter evaluates existing divides throughout the world. Opportunities for addressing such existing divides and modes of increasing e-government performance are presented. Specifically, mobile technology, or m-government, is examined as a medium for further connecting government and its citizens.

Chapter 6

Barbara L. Maclennan, West Virginia University, USA
Susan J. Bergeron, Coastal Carolina University, USA

This chapter explores how the development and implementation of a 3D digital city platform can be utilized in the context of solid waste management and sustainable planning in a small municipality or largely rural areas with limited resources. By leveraging 3D visualization and Web 2.0 functionality to allow stakeholders to collaborate on equal footing, digital city platforms can help with day-to-day management of solid waste assets and facilities, planning for solid waste and recycling facilities and drop-offs, mapping and planning efficient waste hauler routes, and identifying issues such as underserved populations and illegal dumping.

Chapter 7

Hua Xu, Auburn University at Montgomery, USA
Hugo Asencio, Auburn University at Montgomery, USA

The emergence of Web 2.0 technologies in recent years has the potential of allowing governments to move beyond simply disseminating information and providing more online services to citizens to the point of engaging them in policy-making and administrative processes. This chapter presents a survey study designed to find out the extent to which public officials in Alabama municipal governments utilize existing Web 2.0 technologies to engage citizens and to affect their attitudes toward e-government. The preliminary results indicate that although some progress has been made in terms of providing more online services to citizens, Alabama municipalities, particularly small ones, have yet to take advantage of the existing Web 2.0 technologies to make the transtition into e-governance. This chapter concludes with a discussion of the implications of the research findings for advancing e-government in local governments and future research on e-governmnent.

Chapter 8

Michael A. Brown Sr., Old Dominion University, USA

Mohamad Alkadry, Florida International University, USA

This chapter examines the relationship between social networking and individual performance and suggests a social networking participation model that takes advantage of innovation adoption and other important theories to help public organizations understand acceptance or rejection of participation. The chapter focuses the responses of 191 public administrators regarding the relationship between participation and five constructs: perceived usefulness, perceived ease of use, perceived improvement potential (PIP), intra-organizational trust, and type of use. The results of the examination demonstrate the potential of the survey instrument to serve as an adoption and participation methodology that can prove helpful for promoting social networking activities in public organizations.

Chapter 9

Guang-Xu Wang, National University of Tainan, Taiwan

The Civil Service E-mail Box (CSEB) is one of the windows that facilitate communication between Taiwan's government and its citizens. According to research, when a government has a user-friendly digital platform maintained by technologically literate public administrators, those public employees support using such an electronic system to increase governmental responsiveness. This chapter investigates how the perception of e-democratic administration and information and communications technology's (ICT) level of readiness influence public administrators' perception of CSEB effectiveness in facilitating communication with citizens. It does this by examining bureaucratic survey data gathered from Taiwan's Research, Development, and Evaluation Commission (RDEC). Findings show that an unfriendly digital platform, unskilled staff, low appreciation of e-democracy, and lack of readiness on the part of CSEB negatively affect public employees' enthusiasm in regarding ICT as an effective tool in raising governmental responsiveness in Taiwan.

Chapter 10

Kenneth L. Hacker, New Mexico State University, USA

This chapter explores the recent United States military policy changes regarding the use of social media by members of the services. It also discusses the use of these new policies for military public affairs. The chapter analyzes the policy changes in light of network theory in the studies of new media technologies and how users construct networks of influence by employing these new technologies. It is concluded that the military use of new media networking (NMN) is an effective way of both protecting the communication security of military information and optimizing the networking potential of the new media. It appears that the military can use its new social media policies to take advantage of NMN by generating news on their own sites, directing the public to more information, enhancing the morale of service members with families, and developing new methods of recruitment.

Section 3
Web 2.0 and the Potential for Transformation

Transformation refers to the ability of public administrators and policy decision makers to align policy actions with citizen expectations and preferences. Given the offerings of Web 2.0 technology, the mechanisms that government traditionally uses to engage citizens can be substantially revised with new, Web-based techniques to facilitate a more dynamic exchange. Such changes in outreach strategies present a number of implementation considerations and can potentially alter the relationship between government and citizens. In many cases, public managers and policy decision makers enter a virtually unexplored territory. These chapters address some of the unknowns, role changes, and potential for redefining how government can relate to its citizens with the aim of aligning policy actions with citizen preferences.

In this chapter, the use of Web 2.0 technology to engage citizens in the transportation decision making process is evaluated. It examines the potential of Web 2.0 technology to create effective participatory environments to enable authentic participation, provides an inventory of the current tools and technologies utilized, identifies barriers faced by administrators in the implementation of these tools, and summarizes universal lessons for public administrators. Based on a review of 40 cases of collaborations, the authors find that Web 2.0 technology is predominantly used as a complement rather than a substitute for traditional approaches. Furthermore, findings suggest that the full potential of Web 2.0 remains untapped, and additional tools and technologies can be utilized to overcome barriers to implementation.

Recent developments in social media allow people to communicate and share information instantly and have led to speculation about the potential for increased citizen participation in decision making. However, as with other developments in ICT, social media is not used by everyone and there is a danger of certain groups being excluded. Further, if social media tools are to be used by government institutions, there needs to be new internal processes put in place to ensure that the participation is meaningful. This chapter critically evaluates and analyzes the role of Web 2.0 tools (such as social networking services) for facilitating democratic participation, investigate and evaluate the development of Web 2.0 tools for eParticipation, and determine how they can be used to facilitate meaningful political participation.

Many forms of public communication are now mediated through technologies which challenge traditional models of civic engagement and the public's "right to know," including communication for disaster management. This chapter employs a comparative lens to look at how social media messages are pushed forward by different layers of government to reach their publics during times of calm and crisis. Specifically, the project studies how information is framed for public consumption, how it is made available, and how it is timely and relevant. Research methods include a triangulation approach, including interviews with officials from over 20 city, regional, state, and federal agencies to follow up on content and textual analyses of online content disseminated by over 40 public agencies. The chapter argues that public administrators must be engaged with citizens and prepared to use social media during emergencies as well as for routine news, and offers key goals for government departments to promote an agenda of increased citizen information and engagement.

With Congress approaching full adoption of the three major social media platforms – YouTube, Twitter and Facebook – this study gauges the performance of members' official channels in terms of building audiences. Despite the popularity of these platforms, a divide exists among a few high performing members and many low performers. Using an index to differentiate performance, this examination finds social media success is driven by several factors -- party affiliation and ideology being significant. Performance is also derivative of larger political and media forces, and the study shows that the issues confronting government can engage audiences that turn to social media for information, as demonstrated by the congressional debate over health care on YouTube. The chapter explores how the utilization of this technology could be an historical step as important as the advent of C-SPAN in connecting Congress to the American people.

This chapter is intended to introduce a new concept of Interactive Government (i-Government), provide an overview of current practices, and offer recommendations for development and implementation. i-Government is the use of smartphone applications to: a) connect citizens with resources; b) engage citizens in collaboration; c) empower citizens as volunteers; and d) enable citizens to serve as watchdogs. Smartphone applications enable government agencies to provide citizens with information and resources anytime (24/7), from anywhere. This anytime, anywhere feature, combined with smartphone technology such as a camera, GPS/location detection service, and an Internet browser, allows citizens to interact with government by accessing information and providing real-time data. Citizens become a new type of volunteer force, who serve as sensors in the community, and who provide information on anything from potholes, to graffiti, to suspicious activity. Because smartphones are always on, this chapter explores how government agencies can directly contact citizens who are also willing to serve their community.

Foreword

Kathryn Kloby and Maria D'Agostino have made a significant contribution to our understanding of Web 2.0 technologies and governance. It is easy for the average citizen, as well as the seasoned public administrator to feel overwhelmed by the new technologies that are introduced on a seemingly daily basis. Local governments have just gotten proficient with e-mail and websites and now there's Twitter and other social networking sites. Even the best public administrators, who are busy providing services and coping with the economic crisis, have precious little time to explore digital platforms and figure out which ones best meet their needs. Kloby and D'Agostino have done us all a favor in demystifying these emerging technologies and their relevance to the public sector.

Kloby and D'Agostino skillfully identified scholars and practitioners to contribute chapters to this edited volume. These contributors have extensive background in e-government, e-deliberation, and other digital platforms, and their shared expertise and experience helps us more clearly understand Web 2.0 technologies, how they can be applied to the public sector, and their potential for public sector transformation. Digital technologies have the power to not only enhance the performance of public sector agencies and institutions, but they also have the power to creatively engage and connect with citizens.

Of particular importance to the editors is the way Web 2.0 technologies can be adopted by the public sector to more meaningfully engage citizens in matters large and small. We learn about 3-D digital platforms and how they can be used for collaborative decision making in rural areas; we are introduced to Web 2.0 technologies and their ability to foster "authentic" participation; and we are also cautioned about transformational tweeting and the potential to devalue democracy.

Citizen 2.0: Public and Governmental Interaction through Web 2.0 Technologies is a must read for public administrators looking for new and cost effective ways to engage the public; for elected officials who want to increase their visibility and communicate more efficiently with their constituents; and for students of public administration, public policy, and communications as an introduction to emerging trends and digital strategies that have the potential to advance public discourse and engender broader civic participation.

Kathe Callahan
Rutgers, the State University of New Jersey, USA

Kathe Callahan, Ph.D. is Associate Director of the Center for Executive Leadership in Government at Rutgers, the State University of New Jersey. Dr. Callahan's research and teaching interests focus on civic engagement, public sector accountability, and performance measurement. She has published several books and numerous articles on these topics. Dr. Callahan is a board member of the Center for Accountability and Performance (CAP) for the American Association for Public Administration (ASPA). In addition, she is a member of ASPA's Action Team on International Outreach, a founding member of the South African Association of Public Administration and Management (SAAPAM) and a member of the Academic Senate for the African Democratic Leadership Academy (ADLA).

Preface

Goals of this Book

Citizen 2.0: Public and Governmental Interaction through Web 2.0 Technologies is intended to foster a better understanding of how technology can create opportunities for citizen engagement in the public policy process. The aim is to further define the role of Web 2.0 technologies in government as it relates to engaging citizens. The book begins with chapters that define Web 2.0 technologies and how they are relevant tools for public sector organizations. Providing hands-on illustrations and working examples, empirical research via large-scale projects, and case studies highlight strategies and concerns for implementation. It concludes with an analysis of how technology can provide new ways for supporting interaction and redefining how government can engage citizens. This book is relevant for working practitioners in search of new mechanisms to engage the public, as well as students of public administration and affairs, public policy, communications, and related disciplines, with instruction that focuses on emerging trends in the public sector and promoting strategies to advance how government relates with the public.

Why Examine Citizen Interaction with Government?

Determining how citizens should be engaged in the public policy process is an area of great interest for public administration theorists, scholars, and practitioners. Citizen engagement, for example, is considered a vital component of democratic governance that results in informed management decisions (Callahan, 2007; Berman, 2005), openness and fairness (Lukensmeyer & Tores, 2006), capacity to problem solve (Cuthill & Fein, 2005), and trust in government (Keele, 2007). Regardless of these virtues, the challenges of including citizens in the public policy process are well documented. Research, for example, illustrates how public administrators can be insulated from the very citizens they serve (Callahan, 2007), how bureaucratic processes are rigid and create disincentives for citizen engagement (Timney, 1998), and how elected officials and public administrators often rely on traditional engagement mechanisms, such as public meetings, as the primary means to engage the public (Adams, 2004). These encounters often fall far short of the ideals of citizen engagement, as they are sparsely attended gatherings that conflict with citizens' work schedules, child-care needs, or fear of public speaking (Adams, 2004; King, Feltey, & O'Neil, 1998; Berner, 2001). Despite these shortcomings, the overwhelming demands for public sector transparency and results in the policy context of economic crisis, large-scale public policy reforms, and fiscal constraints are considerable, leaving many public administrators in search of new techniques to capture the interest of citizens and include them more meaningfully in deliberative activities.

Technology holds the promise of providing innovative ways to engage the public – most notably, the World Wide Web. There has been some considerable progress with building a Web-based government presence through agency websites that provide information (e.g., downloadable reports or minutes) and transactions (e.g., supporting payments for fees). These are worthy accomplishments, yet the question of how this Web-based technology can stimulate *transformation* in the field of public administration and serve as a catalyzing agent for engaging citizens in the policy process remains unanswered (Garson 2006). Transformation, in this sense, refers to the ability of public administrators and policy decision makers to align policy actions with citizen expectations and preferences.

The potential for achieving transformation seems very likely with the advent of Web 2.0 technologies that support real-time or other innovative and web-based social interactions. Web 2.0 technologies such as wikis and blogs, or communication using Twitter, Facebook, and other venues for expression, such as YouTube, are ever more popular in leisure and business activities, and are increasingly present in government efforts. Trends indicate that Web 2.0 technologies are highlighted in key legislation and administrative reforms as a means to create a more transparent and accountable system of governance (Mullen 2005). How Web 2.0 technologies can be utilized by the public sector and which applications are appropriate for engaging citizens are some of the concerns raised in professional conferences and magazines such as *The Public Manager* and *PA Times*.

This book is crafted to answer the questions:

- What is Web 2.0, and how can government utilize these technologies to engage the public?
- How are governments using Web 2.0 technologies to engage citizens in the policy process? What should public administrators know about Web 2.0 technologies as they adopt and implement them?
- In what ways can Web 2.0 technologies transform government as they are used to engage citizens?

This book defines transformation as the extent to which citizen engagement via Web 2.0 technologies impacts management decision making and government performance. The editors use the term Citizen 2.0 in the title of the book, because the main thrust of the discussion focuses on how this technology is used for engaging and building relationships with citizens.

Overview

As with any new technology or management technique, there are many considerations to address before adoption and meaningful implementation. Without paying careful attention to the alignment between agency goals, democratic values, and organizational characteristics, for example, public administrators and staff run the risk of engaging in hollow exercises, window dressing, or symbolic gestures. In many cases, good intentions can simply run amok and fade like other passing management fads. To avoid these challenges, it is imperative to clearly define the role of Web 2.0 technology in the public sector and increase an understanding of how it can be successfully applied to engage citizens.

Addressing the leading questions highlighted above, authors contributing to this volume provide chapters that define Web 2.0 technologies and its potential applications in the public sector. Chapters include suggestions for adoption and implementation based on the lessons learned by scholars and practitioners in the field. Contributions address the potential for transformation providing chapters that examine how engaging the public with Web 2.0 technologies can impact the way public administrators make decisions.

The book is organized into three sections.

- Section 1: Defining Web 2.0 Technologies and Their Relevance to the Public Sector
- Section 2: Applying Web 2.0 in the Public Sector
- Section 3: Web 2.0 and the Potential for Transformation

Section 1: Defining Web 2.0 Technologies and Their Relevance to the Public Sector, describes the different applications and tools available to public administrators and policy decision makers. In chapter 1, *The Role of Social Media in the Public Sector: Opportunities and Challenges*, Anteneh Ayanso and Darryl Moyers discuss the meaning and attributes of Web 2.0, and examine recent developments and emerging platforms and how they might be used by various public sector organizations. How Web 2.0 applications can be employed as a means of improving the policy making process, specifically public comments, is further examined by Peter Muhlberger, Jennifer Stromer-Galley, and Nick Webb in chapter 2, *An Experiment in E-Rulemaking with Natural Language Processing and Democratic Deliberation*. Discussing the new terrain of employing Web 2.0 in practical terms, Staci M. Zavattaro, in chapter 3, *Records Management, Privacy and Social Media: An Overview*, examines the practical challenges associated with managing records, retaining employees, and privacy when working in an era of open and digital government. Finally, Julianne G. Mahler in chapter 4, *Managing Virtual Public Organizations*, uses primary and secondary case materials and published research to address questions about the use of information and communication technologies, coordination, and leadership in public organizations that are now relying on online work settings.

Section 2, Applying Web 2.0 in the Public Sector, presents large scale and case study research results that examine how jurisdictions are employing Web 2.0 and the extent to which they are using them to engage citizens in the policy process. In chapter 5, *M-Government: An Opportunity for Addressing the Digital Divide*, Aroon P. Manoharan, Lamar Vernon Bennett, and Tony J. Carrizales examine the concept of the digital divide within the context of e-government worldwide and suggest how the use of mobile phones can potentially increase governments' ability to access and engage citizens. Barbara Maclennan and Susan Bergeron bring this discussion to the local level in chapter 6, *3D Digital City Platforms as Collaborative and Decision-Making Tools for Small Municipalities and Rural Areas*, as they provide insight on how Web 2.0 can contribute to management decision making by allowing stakeholders in areas with limited resources to collaborate on equal footing. In chapter 7, *E-Government in Local Government in the Era of Web 2.0: Experiences of Alabama Municipalities*, Hua Xu and Hugo Asencio examine the extent to which municipal governments in Alabama utilize existing Web 2.0 technologies to engage citizens and how it impacts citizen attitudes towards government. Michael Brown and Mohamad Alkadry, in chapter 8, *Predictors of Social Networking and Individual Performance*, take into consideration the perceptions of public administrators and suggest a social networking participation model to facilitate Web 2.0 innovation in public organizations. Guang-Xu Wang in chapter 9, *E-Democratic Administration and Bureaucratic Responsiveness: A Primary Study of Bureaucrats' Perceptions of the Civil Service E-mail Box in Taiwan*, illustrates the importance of leadership and training for using technology to engage citizens and how these factors can influence the level of sophistication in agency engagement strategies. And finally, in chapter 10, *Social Media and New Military Public Affairs Policies*, Kenneth Hacker provides an analysis of how military agencies have responded to the availability of Web 2.0 technologies when reporting on agency activities and generating citizen interest in agency efforts.

Section 3, Web 2.0 and the Potential for Transformation, offers a more in-depth examination of how Web 2.0 can impact the relationship between government and its citizens. Colleen Casey and Jianling Li, in chapter 11, *Web 2.0 Technologies and Authentic Public Participation: Engaging Citizens in Decision Making Processes,* identify participation barriers faced by administrators in the implementation of Web 2.0 technologies and articulate some universal lessons for public administrators. Elizabeth Tait critically assesses the role of Web 2.0 tools for facilitating democratic participation, and evaluates the development of Web 2.0 tools and whether they can be used to facilitate meaningful political participation in chapter 12, *Web 2.0 for eParticipation: Transformational Tweeting or Devaluation of Democracy?* Tammy Esteves, Deniz Zeynep Leuenberger, and Danielle Newton examine how information is made available for public consumption and offer key goals for public organizations to promote an agenda of increased citizen information and engagement in chapter 13, *Reaching Citizen 2.0: How Government Uses Social Media to Send Public Messages during Times of Calm and Times of Crisis.* Exploring how Web 2.0 is realized for political purposes, Albert May and F. Christopher Arterton, in chapter 14, *Congress 2.0: Incumbent Messaging in Social Media,* investigate how the utilization of three major social media platforms-YouTube, Twitter, and Facebook-contribute to connecting Congress to the American people. In chapter 15, *i-Government: Interactive Government Enabling Civic Engagement and a New Volunteerism,* Linda-Marie Sundstrom examines the concept of *i*-government and illustrates how the relationship between citizens and government agencies transforms as they collaborate, as well as how agencies need to address managerial processes to accommodate these changing dynamics.

Examining the Potential of Technology to Engage the Public

This compilation of chapters from authors in the disciplines of public administration, public affairs, public policy, and communications shift the current focus of citizen engagement dialogue from implementation challenges and traditional engagement mechanisms, to exploring Web-based technologies and more innovative ways to connect with citizens and transform government. As a result, it strengthens the connective tissue between citizen engagement and technology as it explores the theory and practice of Web 2.0 technologies in government. These two areas are often treated as mutually exclusive from each other. Texts, for example, in the area of citizen engagement often focus on the traditional mechanisms for participation (e.g. public meetings). Texts in the area of Web 2.0 are largely written by and for private sector managers. Much of the emphasis is on technical aspects of Web 2.0 technologies with discussions of available products and their capabilities. In many instances the success of applying these technologies is measured by the number of visitors to a website, or the number of downloads, or length of time spent on a given site or page. Little analysis focuses on their utilization and their potential impact on management in the public sector and the relationship between citizens and government. Through this collective effort, chapters present a thorough overview of Web 2.0 technologies, their relevance to the public sector, and how they can be used to transform government so that its actions align with citizen preferences and expectations.

Potential Uses and Intended Audience

Fiscal constraints, a lagging economy, large-scale policy reforms, government cuts and spending, government reforms, and citizen demands for transparency and results are just a few of the compelling factors pushing government into a new era of citizen engagement. This new era is largely influenced and defined by the capabilities of Web-based technology, or Web 2.0 technologies. These pressures and technological advancements are leading public administrators to reconsider how they should engage citizens in the public policy process. This book works to build a theoretical understanding of Web 2.0 in the public sector as it relates to engaging citizens. Linking theory to practice, chapters highlight implementation considerations as demonstrated via case studies and other empirical works. Most importantly, it focuses on how the use of Web 2.0 technologies to engage citizens and impact management decision making, which aligns government actions with citizen expectations and preferences. Strategies for what works, challenges, and other considerations of adoption, modification, and implementation of Web 2.0 technologies presented in this book will be of interest to current public administrators at all levels of government and students of public administration and related disciplines.

The book can readily enhance graduate courses with students who are advancing in the field of public administration, public policy, public affairs, and communications. It is an attractive book for graduate public administration courses such as introduction to public administration, public management, civic engagement, e-government, technology and public administration, and citizen-driven performance improvement. It can be required for graduate public policy courses such as introduction to public policy, policy analysis and evaluation, public management and organizational behavior, citizen-oriented governance, and globalization. It is also relevant for graduate courses in communications such as communication in a digital age, changing relationships through communication, strategic communication and program management, using social and digital media, and grassroots political communication.

Kathryn Kloby
Monmouth University, USA

Maria J. D'Agostino
John Jay College of Criminal Justice, CUNY, USA

REFERENCES

Adams, B. (2004). Public meetings and the democratic process. *Public Administration Review*, 64(1), 43–54. doi:10.1111/j.1540-6210.2004.00345.x

Berman, B. (2005). *Listening to the public: Adding the voices of the people to government performance measurement and reporting*. New York, NY: The Fund for the City of New York.

Berner, M. (2001). Citizen participation in local government budgeting. *Popular Government*, (Spring): 23–30.

Callahan, K. (2007). *Elements of effective governance: Measurement, accountability and participation*. New York, NY: Taylor and Francis.

Cuthill, M., & Fein, J. (2005). Capacity building facilitating citizen participation in local governance. *Australian Journal of Public Administration, 64*(4), 63–80. doi:10.1111/j.1467-8500.2005.00465a.x

Garson, G. D. (2006). *Public Information Technology and e-governance*. Sudbury, MA: Jones and Bartlett.

Keele, L. (2007). Social capital and the dynamics of trust in government. *American Journal of Political Science, 51*(2), 241–254. doi:10.1111/j.1540-5907.2007.00248.x

King, C. S., Feltey, K. M., & Susel, B. O. (1998). The question of participation: Toward authentic public participation in public administration. *Public Administration Review, 58*(4), 317–327. doi:10.2307/977561

Lukensmeyer, C. J., & Torres, L. H. (2006). *Public deliberation: A manger's guide to citizen engagement*. Washington, DC: Center for the Business of Government.

Mullen, P. R. (2005). U.S. performance-based laws: Information Technology and e-government reporting requirements. *International Journal of Public Administration, 28*, 981–598. doi:10.1081/PAD-200064204

Timney, M. (1998). Overcoming administrative barriers to citizen participation: Citizens as partners, not adversaries . In King, C. S., & Stivers, C. (Eds.), *Government is us: Public administration in an anti-government era* (pp. 88–99). Thousand Oaks, CA: Sage.

Acknowledgment

A very special thank you for the critical support of Meghan Ryan, graduate assistant to the Department of Political Science and Sociology at Monmouth University. Megan's prompt response to project needs and deadlines, her attention to detail, and unwavering enthusiasm contributed substantially to the momentum and completion of this project.

We greatly appreciate the support of Mayuri Saxena, graduate student of public administration at the John Jay College of Criminal Justice, CUNY. Her keen editing skills helped us across the finish line.

We would like to thank the contributing authors, editorial board members, and chapter reviewers for all of their insights, efforts, leads, and guidance. This publication is a collective effort to explore the new frontier of technology and governance.

Kathryn Kloby
Monmouth University, USA

Maria J. D'Agostino
John Jay College of Criminal Justice, CUNY, USA

Section 1
Defining Web 2.0 Technologies and Their Relevance to the Public Sector

Public administrators must be prepared to select and apply relevant Web 2.0 technologies for public involvement in the policy process. This can be an overwhelming venture as much of the available information on Web 2.0 is generated by private sector managers or potential vendors who are presumably unfamiliar with the inner workings and complex relationships of government. This collection of chapters seeks to define Web 2.0 technology from the perspective of individuals working in government and in the public policy process. A detailed description of the different applications and tools that are currently available to public administrators and policy decision makers is presented to advance the understanding of the implementation challenges and potential for new opportunities to engage the public.

Chapter 1
The Role of Social Media in the Public Sector:
Opportunities and Challenges

Anteneh Ayanso
Brock University, Canada

Darryl Moyers
Brock University, Canada

ABSTRACT

Social media is promising new opportunities across a broad spectrum of public services. As the Internet and its ubiquitous applications extend globally, an increasing number of governments and their public service agencies are embracing social media as one of the major mechanisms to interact with the public. Social media provides a new wave of Web-based applications and channels for citizens to share constructive ideas and opinions and play active roles in various areas in the public sector. At the same time, social media helps government organizations and elected officials of different government levels to actively listen to citizens and constantly monitor their existing services as well as develop new initiatives. Effective integration of Web 2.0 technologies and applications into existing Internet infrastructure adds visibility and accountability in the public sector and enhances services to citizens.

INTRODUCTION

In this chapter, we examine recent developments on the use of social media in the public sector and explore existing as well as emerging platforms, applications, and tools that can be used by the public sector in various settings. We also review some of the social media best practices as well as initiatives from different regions and countries and discuss their values to various groups of users. Finally, we examine the critical challenges the public sector faces in embracing Web 2.0 technologies at the core of its processes and services.

DOI: 10.4018/978-1-4666-0318-9.ch001

The meaning of social media is closely linked to the concept of Web 2.0. The term Web 2.0 was first used in 2005 by Tim O'Reilly, a technology pundit who is recognized for being ahead of many Internet trends. O'Reilly initially classified Web 2.0 by identifying generally-accepted examples of Web 1.0 technologies, and then highlighting new tools and approaches that enhanced the features and functionalities of the web. For instance, O'Reilly classified Encyclopaedia Brittanica's Online Edition (a static version of the famous encyclopaedia's printed version) as an example of a Web 1.0 technology and then identified Wikipedia (a wiki-based encyclopaedia composed of collaborative and dynamic user generated content) as the successor that significantly improved the value to Internet users. Thus, the meaning of Web 2.0 covers not only the concept of the technology, but also demonstrates how the Web is currently used for various purposes. According to the pundit, "Web 2.0 applications are those that make the most of the intrinsic advantages of that platform: delivering software as a continually-updated service that gets better the more people use it; consuming and remixing data from multiple sources; creating network effects through an 'architecture of participation'; and going beyond the page metaphor of Web 1.0 to deliver rich user experiences" (O'Reilly, 2005). *Twitter, Wikipedia, Facebook*, and *YouTube* are shining examples of this "architecture of participation" in that users, without recognition or remuneration, commonly create and update contents to reflect current events and changes.

In defining the scope of Web 2.0, Osimo (2008) used a combination of technologies (e.g., AJAX, XML, open API, microformats, flash/flex), applications (e.g., blog, wiki, podcast, RSS feeds, tagging, social networks, Mashups), and values (e.g., user as a producer, collective intelligence, perpetual beta, extreme ease of use). Kaplan and Haenlein (2010, p. 61.) also defined Web 2.0 as "a group of Internet-based applications that build on the ideological and technological foundations of Web 2.0, and allow the creation and exchange of User Generated Content (UGC)." Web 2.0 also represents "social software" or "social computing" as it shifts computing to the edges of the network, and empowers individual users with lightweight computing tools to manifest their creativity, engage in social interaction, and share knowledge (Parameswaran and Whinston 2007a, 2007b).

The advent of smart phones, mobile networks, and seemingly constant Internet connectivity has created a culture where increasing portions of our lives are "lived" online. Following the prevalence of social media in our culture, the public sector is embracing Web 2.0 technologies and applications in an effort to raise performance and enhance transparency, accountability and citizen-engagement. These technologies are creating new, effortless mechanisms to foster online engagement and dialogues between government (or civil servants) and citizens (Reece, 2006). At the very least, Web 2.0 applications can be used to bridge the gulf between citizens and public institutions (Johnston et al., 2008). Strategic benefits from Web 2.0 initiatives are also becoming visible in many technology-based public services, such as eGovernment, eHealth, and eLearning. Web 2.0 tools can be used to improve internal collaboration and facilitate strategic knowledge-sharing among workers, managers, and partners in government organizations (Human Capital Institute, 2010). Government organizations are heavily involved with routine communications, information exchanges with internal units as well as other government organizations on a day-to-day basis. These activities constitute substantial part of administrative expenses which can be efficiently handled by integrating Web 2.0 technologies in their current administrative systems. In addition, Web 2.0 tools can help government organizations to share best practices and build communities of practice (Human Capital Institute, 2010).

WEB 2.0 VALUE PROPOSITION IN THE PUBLIC SECTOR

According to Howard (2001), electronic government (eGovernment) service maturity levels are classified into three major stages. These stages include 1) *publishing* information about government services online; 2) *interacting* with citizens through electronic means such as e-mails; and 3) *transacting* online such as applying for services, licenses, and permits. Web 2.0 tools such as Wikis, blogs, and microblogs not only enhance the depth and breadth of information that can be delivered to citizens, but allow near real-time interaction and dynamic content and service provision in all stages of the service maturity levels. Due to the impacts Web 2.0 tools and forums have on improving communications and the workings of government as well as citizen participation in government, new terms such as "Democracy 2.0", "Citizenship 2.0", and "Governance 2.0" have been coined (Wyld, 2007).

Web 2.0 applications are also increasingly shaping the political landscape and the democratic processes both in developed and developing nations. The participation of people from all walks of lives and demography in local, national, and international events through easily accessible tools is creating dynamic and interesting scenes in the mass media. Web 2.0 tools such as instant photo and video sharing, Tweets, blogs, and wikis provide new opportunities for inclusion and participation of different members of society in issues and forums that have not been traditionally popular or easy. The active involvement of the younger population in the 2008 presidential election in the U.S.A.; the speed of information flow from North Africa and the Middle East during the recent political uprisings; and the instant photos and videos being captured and shared for relief efforts during natural disasters in many corners of the world, are just a few examples to demonstrate how Web 2.0 applications are pervasive in today's society. As a result, several international, regional, and national initiatives are underway to guide progress as well as to develop policies for the effective utilization of these emerging technologies.

For example, in order to improve the monitoring efforts regarding the global digital divide, the International Telecommunication Union (ITU), a United Nations agency, commissioned the development of a single, comprehensive ICT Development Index (IDI) that is designed to consolidate useful information from previous measurement indices (ITU, 2009). One of the key uses of this measurement is to assess the adoption of existing and emerging technologies and how the digital divide among different regions and nations is evolving over time. In addition, the IDI incorporated a conceptual framework based on a basic three-stage information society model (readiness-use-impact) (ITU, 2009). Due to the cost-effectiveness and user-friendly nature of Web 2.0 technologies and applications, there exists tremendous potential for developing nations to bridge the disparity in ICT readiness (i.e., infrastructure and access), ICT usage (i.e., intensity) as well as ICT capability (i.e., skills) following the three-stage information society model.

In Europe, eGovernment has been a policy priority since the eEurope Action Plan in 1999 (Osimo, 2008). Under Europe's strategic framework for Information Society policy, Europe EU15 Heads of Government identified that achieving an inclusive European Information Society is one of the top priorities. In achieving this objective, the public sector is recognized as a key ICT application field, because of the impact that ICT-enabled public services can have on economic growth, inclusion, and quality of life (Osimo, 2008). A successor of this strategic framework is Digital Agenda for Europe which is Europe's strategy for a flourishing digital economy by 2020 (Digital Agenda for Europe, 2010-2020). The goal of this agenda is to bring stakeholders together to assess progress and emerging challenges, and work closely with national governments, concerned organisations and companies, and outline policies and actions to maximise the benefit of the Digital Revolution for all (Digital Agenda for Europe, 2010-2020).

In the United States, The Office of Citizen Services and Innovative Technologies and the Federal Web Managers Council jointly manage the Web site, *HowTo.gov* to help government workers deliver a better customer experience to citizens. They offer best practices, training, and guidance on strategic planning and coordinating customer service channels; federal Web requirements and policies; cloud computing, apps, data and Web infrastructure tools; online citizen engagement through social media and open government; Web content management, usability, and design; and contact center services (http://www.howto.gov).

In Canada, a comprehensive system for online collaboration and social networking projects by government departments was initiated. This project involves systems that can provide social networking capabilities for around 250,000 people and 58 government departments (Arellano, 2008). Recent media reports also indicate that the federal government is developing plans to make access to social media consistent across departments and agencies and give public servants more freedom to use social media, and encourage departments to engage more directly with the public and job candidates who expect the Web 2.0 environment (Mayeda, 2010).

In Australia, the Government 2.0 Taskforce (http://gov2.net.au) was established and is made up of policy and technical experts and entrepreneurs from government, business, academia, and cultural institutions. The purposes of the taskforce include increasing the openness of government through making public sector information more widely available to promote transparency, innovation and value adding to government information; encouraging online engagement; and funding initiatives and incentives which may achieve or demonstrate how to accomplish government 2.0 objectives.

There are also similar initiatives at a local level. For example, New York City recently released a report that contains a comprehensive strategy to make New York the nation's leading Digital City (NYC.gov, 2011). Informed by 90 days of research and over 4,000 points of engagement from residents, City employees, and technologists who shared insights and ideas, the "Road Map for the Digital City" outlines a path to build on NYC's successes and establish it as the world's top-ranked Digital City, based on indices of Internet access, Open Government, citizen engagement, and digital industry growth (New York City, 2011). This plan also involves partnerships with a range of social media companies including Facebook, Twitter, Foursquare and Tumblr in order to allow the City to engage with residents in a more efficient and unified manner using the latest advances in digital communication (NYC.gov, 2011).

The above initiatives all indicate that social media is among the top priorities of international forums, national, and local governments in order to enhance performance, achieve government transparency at all levels, and establish seamless connectivity and interactions with citizens

SOCIAL MEDIA APPLICATIONS IN THE PUBLIC SECTOR

Web 2.0 applications can be grouped in different ways depending on their scope and capability. For example, *Wikipedia, Facebook, MySpace,* and *SecondLife*, represent more than a single application and provide collaborative and networking platforms. *YouTube* and *Flickr* facilitate audio, video, and image content sharing. Blogs and Microblogs (e.g., *Twitter*) provide user-friendly channels for information disseminations. Mashups allow different groups of users to mix and remix contents and existing applications to create composite applications or generate customized information.

Regardless of the scope and the capabilities, Web 2.0 applications are now being used in different public administration settings. In the following sections we discuss some specific social media platforms and tools that are increasingly being used by the public sector in various settings.

Blogs and Microblogs

A *Weblog* (*blog* for short) is "an online journal that can be updated regularly, with entries typically displayed in a chronological order." (Wyld, 2007, p. 6). Blogging allows public administrators and elected representatives to directly communicate with their constituents. As opposed to pushing static information on websites maintained by webmasters, blogging provides an efficient channel for direct consultation, experimenting ideas, receiving comments, and engaging in continuous dialogue without being limited by time, Web design skills, and content formats. Anyone can simply create a blog by signing up with a blogging service provider at sites, such as www.blogger.com, http://wordpress.com, or www.sixapart.com. Due to their simplicity and cost-effectiveness, blogs have become commonplace in public sectors. In particular, bloggers have been very influential in elections in recent years and many politicians are using blogs for a more direct contact with their constituents (Osimo, 2008).

Wyld (2007) developed a typology of four different types of blogs for public officials, which is adapted from the Congressional Management Foundation, a nonpartisan non-profit dedicated to helping Congress and its Members meet the evolving needs and expectations of an engaged and informed 21st century citizenry (http://www.cmfweb.org/):

- *The Travel Blog*: Highlights elected officials' travels in and around their district or jurisdiction, or perhaps foreign trips.
- *The Blow-by-Blow Blog*: Emphasizes reports from elected representatives while their respective deliberative body is in session in order to update constituents on the status of pending bills and other actions.

- *The Personal Blog*: Provides elected officials' views on particular issues, perspectives on events, and/or updates on their activities as well as those of their families and friends.
- *The Team Blog:* Allows a caucus or group of elected representatives/officials to share a blog, reducing the burden on individual officials to administer the blog and encouraging more frequent updates from several contributors to the blog.

A *microblog* is a type of blog or blog post that is smaller in both scale and scope than a "traditional" blog site. While the medium is very useful for quickly sharing news and information, one of its greatest strengths is its ability to facilitate real-time communication between organizations, and members of the general population. This capability has been leveraged effectively by countless government agencies and representatives as a means to conduct quick opinion polling and to collect and respond to public comments, both solicited and unsolicited. In essence, microblogs facilitate constructive, though discrete, conversations between two parties, without either party experiencing a feeling of total anonymity. Microblog posts have many typical forms. While they may be used for "talking in a chattering fashion", many modern day microblog posts also allow the user to provide a link to further information with a small introduction or teaser about where the link will take the user. Some of the most popular microblogging platforms include *Twitter* and *Tumblr*.

Twitter (http://twitter.com/)

Microblogging in its present form first gained widespread-prominence in 2007 after Twitter (undoubtedly the world's most well-known microblogging site) was said to have reached critical mass. Though the service launched in 2006, frequent promotion at the 2007 South by Southwest Music Festival (SXSW) caused Twitter's usage to increase exponentially and set off its rise to power in the social media world (Mayfield, 2007). Twitter is a free social networking service that allows a person to receive and send short messages known as Tweets. The website is setup in such a way that anyone can create an account for free. Once an account is created, the user will be able to follow anyone who has a Twitter account. When people start posting Tweets and others find it interesting, they will follow this person. In this way a network is created in two directions. In one direction you have a number of people who you follow and there will also be a bunch of people who follow you. Anyone who follows you will be able to see the update. Someone who follows you and finds your information interesting can retweet (Twitter's way of saying "re-post" or "share") your information to his/her network of followers. Thus, your information has reached quite a few people in a short span of time through what Kaplan and Haenlein (2011) refer to as Push-Push-Pull communication. The advantage of Twitter is how fast the information is transferred from the sender to the receiver.

Tweets are famous for their brevity, but readers are often amazed to see how much information can actually be shared concisely within the confines of the site's 140 character-per-post limit. Interestingly, the motivation behind Twitter's character limit - an entire Tweet fitting inside one standard SMS (Short Message System) message - is also what drove the site to mass popularity (Boyd, Golder, and Lotan, 2010). Twitter's integration of text-to-tweet capitalized on the overwhelming popularity of texting. Twitter via SMS made it possible for users to post their own thoughts instantaneously, and to engage in Twitter conversations, while away from their computers.

Twitter is now not only a popular method of sharing information on the internet or mobile phones, but also a means of conducting quick opinion surveys, notifying users affected by emergencies, and running broad public relations campaigns. Several politicians in different coun-

tries and government levels use Twitter to build a more personal relationship with supporters. Due to their prominent public status, it is likely that government officials and public administrators who adopt social media will attract significant online followers (Boyd, Golder, and Lotan, 2010). In addition, politicians often follow each others' social media accounts to stay on top of their colleagues' and competitors' campaigns. Likewise, news agencies and reporters (further examples of accounts that garner a significant online following) also follow prominent politicians to cover issues that matter to the public. In this way, the network effect of social media dictates that these prominent accounts have the ability to reach a substantial number of influential users through just their first (direct followers) and second (followers of followers) connections. A perfect example was seen after the 2011 earthquake and tsunami that devastated Japan. Stephen Harper, the Prime Minister of Canada, used his Twitter account (@pmharper) to retweet a post by The Canadian Red Cross (@redcrosscanada) about how Canadians could donate to the relief efforts in Japan. While only 3000 users follow the Canadian Red Cross, Stephen Harper was able to amplify their message to the more than 100,000 users who follow his posts. This same concept is also increasingly being used by members of congress or parliament, governors, city mayors, and public managers across government to promote public services or provide information about places they'll be visiting or people they are meeting with.

Hashtags are one of the most popular features on Twitter and other microblogging platforms. However, the purpose of hashtagging is frequently misunderstood. A hashtag is a simple way of metatagging one's tweet by typing a word or phrase that is prefixed with the number sign, also known as the hash symbol ("#"). Hashtags can be used for humor or effect, such as when one tweets using an obscure hashtag, but the tag's greatest function is its ability to act as a message amplifier and to allow the user to take part in a broader conversation, often with users outside of their network of direct followers. If one uses the proper syntax in their hashtag on the Twitter platform, it is automatically converted into a hyperlink that will direct the user to a search for all tweets containing that hashtag (Boyd, Golder, and Lotan, 2010). In that search, users will see a real time chronological listing of their tweet with respect to all other posts that use that same hashtag.

Government officials and public administrators can participate in hashtagging as a means to facilitate and to be part of a topic-specific hyper-conversation via Twitter. When the same hashtag is used by hundreds or thousands of users, following the hashtag provides what is effectively an instantaneous, real-time cross-section of public sentiment on the topic. For example, consider the 2011 Federal Election in Canada. Since the election was Canada's 41st General Election since the country's Confederation, opinion leaders on Twitter began tagging all tweets about the election with the hashtag "#elxn41." The short form syntax of the word election was used as a means to save valuable characters in consideration of Twitter's 140 character-per-post limit. As the tag became more prominent, Federal Party Leaders, notable journalists, and members of the general public began adding the #elxn41 hashtag to all of their tweets about the election, so much so that the tag was being mentioned dozens of times per minute during peak Canadian usage hours.

Tumblr (http://www.tumblr.com/)

Following in the early success of Twitter, microblogging site Tumblr launched in 2007 and set out to integrate some of the most-popular features of Twitter, Facebook, and traditional blogging platforms into one, easy-to-use social-blogging platform. Tumblr is not a traditional microblog in that it does not have a character restriction. However, many of the site's posts are smaller than typical blogs (*aka* tumblelogs). One of Tumblr's main differentiating factors from Twitter is

that it encourages multimedia integration (such as photos and videos) and displays the content gracefully. It may be possible that as multimedia sharing becomes increasingly popular, Tumblr may eventually surpass Twitter as the world's most-popular microblogging platform.

The advent of Web 2.0 has conditioned avid Web users to expect extremely dynamic content in today's Internet age. While this expectation is manageable on social networking and microblogging sites, it is a much greater challenge to maintain primarily-static webpages so that the content seems fresh and up to date. As a result, social media accounts and metatags (such as Twitter hashtags) are increasingly being utilized as information dissemination tools with assistance from a number of free or low cost third-party applications and plugins. Other cost-free Web 2.0 tools include RSS feeds (Really Simple Syndication) that are used to "push" a running feed of updates from social media accounts and mix a website's static content with dynamic updates from social media platforms like Facebook, Twitter, and LinkedIn. Using such Web 2.0 tools helps government organizations, public service agencies, and political campaign managers to keep their websites reasonably dynamic without the need for frequent editing.

As part of its expansion of citizen-centric digital resources, the City of New York is embracing new social media channels and platforms that support City goals of transparency, engagement, participation, and access to information (New York City, 2011). For example, recognizing the growth of Tumblr, the City will unveil a new curated New York City government vertical that highlights stories, photos, videos, and more from New Yorkers and City agencies. In addition, building upon its Open Government architecture and API, the City in partnership with Socrata will launch data visualization tools that make the City's vast stores of public data portable and accessible through charts and graphs. This initiative also includes a streamlined Twitter feed for @nycgov as well as a new Facebook presence focusing on applets that support citizen engagement, transparency, crowdsourcing, and public service initiatives.

In an article titled, "smart political social media use changes Newark, NJ Election", Stephanie Noble, who served as the Director of Social Media Outreach in a local election in Newark, New Jersey, describes the role an array of social media tools played in getting an 'underfunded', underdog candidate a place on the city council (Paden Noble Consulting, 2010). According to her account, smart use of social media tools effectively battled the well-funded incumbent of the city. Their social media campaign strategy helped the candidate's Facebook friends to increase by 120%, fans by 320%, Twitter followers by 475%, and the Twitter hashtag mentions tally over 200 (Paden Noble Consulting, 2010). In addition, the campaign used FourSquare.com as a public relations tool to demonstrate the candidate's presence in the neighborhood and support of local businesses.

Wikis

A *wiki* is a website on which users can post contents and make changes to other contents through an "edit" link that may be available on individual pages of the site. Wikis promote collaboration and harness the collective intelligence of its collaborators, leading to better knowledge or information services for different application settings (Rainer et al., 2011). The largest wiki site in existence is Wikipedia with almost two million articles in English which are viewed almost 400 million times every day (Rainer et al., 2011).

Wikipedia

Wikipedia (http://www.wikipedia.org/) is a Web 2.0 platform that allows users to create and edit online documents. Its mission is to generate and distribute free content through the use of wiki tools. Wikipedia is open to a large contributor base, and its content is written by an open and transparent

manner. Wikipedia can be used to generate public knowledge bases to which multiple users from various communities can contribute. It offers an open and free platform for the public to contribute to ideas that incorporate multiple perspectives. The increasing viewership of Wikipedia, compared to other major news sources, makes it a popular source of information. It provides convenient and user-friendly access to various types of contents in a platform where there is no distraction from advertisements. This makes it a good candidate for organizations in the public sector to publish information about their roles, services, and links to other relevant resources. In the evolution of e-government infrastructure (publishing-interaction-transaction), the information publishing stage is an important step to establish significant online presence, attract the public interest, and provide information that serves the interests of different members of the public (Howard, 2001). As opposed to pushing static content on their websites, organizations can take advantage of platforms like Wikipedia to provide real-time information about their identities as well as encourage contribution of ideas and feedback about their services. In addition to the advantage on the depth and breadth of the information that can be provided, Wikipedia provides an evolving information hierarchy that includes category links, redirects, concepts and relationships between concepts.

Wikis are also used internally by organizations to facilitate team work among experts and promote knowledge-sharing from experienced workers to newly employed ones. For example, *Intellipedia* (www.intelink.gov) is a Wikipedia-like community networking website that allows free-flowing discussion about intelligence on topics such as terrorism or military missions. It is created by employees of the U.S. Office of the Director of National Intelligence (DNI) and the Central Intelligence Agency (CIA) as a response to the widespread criticism about a lack of intelligence-sharing that led to terrorist attacks and the Iraq war (Gross, 2006). The site is generally restricted to government employees with security clearance with different classification levels to create and access official intelligence-related documents. The site also facilitates knowledge-sharing between experienced intelligence analysts and the next generation of intelligence experts (Gross, 2006).

Mash-Ups

A *mashup* pulls content from several sources to create useful applications. The Google Maps API is an example of this Web 2.0 feature which is being used by community groups for purposes such as disaster relief, and to plot the location of educational facilities and healthcare services, etc. Examples of platforms that are used to create mashups include Microsoft Popfly (http://www. popfly.com/), and Yahoo pipes (http://pipes.yahoo. com/pipes/). Mashups turn various data sources into composite applications and services without the need to write complex coding. Don Tapscott, a Canadian business pundit and author, describes a number of real-life examples of government agencies using wiki-based mashups to increase collaboration in the book that he co-authored, "MacroWikinomics, How Mass Collaboration Changes Everything" (Frye and Crookall. 2010.). One such example came from the City of Edmonton, who made a significant amount of data about the city's busses and bus routes available to its citizens in 2004 and informed the residents that the busses had GPS tracking units built in. With that information, some citizens designed the first Edmonton Transit System (ETS) Trip Planner, a free mobile app to help other residents navigate the bus system and check the location of a bus they were waiting on. The initial system was improved upon and eventually replaced by the simplicity and customization available from Google's Transit Map feature. The ETS Trip Planner is a great example of how citizens could benefit from open and transparent e-governments willing to collaborate on innovative projects. There are also

several mashups in various application domains that are gaining popularity in different countries.

ElectionMap used Google maps to calculate the 2008 US Electoral votes, view standings, or load previous election results for comparison (http:// www.mapmash.in/election_map.html).

Data.gov is the United States Open Government Initiative whose purpose is to increase public access to high value, machine readable datasets generated by the Executive Branch of the Federal Government (http://www.data.gov). The website enables the public to participate in government by providing downloadable Federal datasets to build applications, conduct analyses, and perform research. Also in the United States, *DataMasher* is created to let citizens create mashups and visualize them in different ways and see how states compare on important issues (http://www.datamasher.org). Users can combine different data sets in interesting ways and create their own custom rankings of the states. The data is pulled from Data.gov, some of it directly from Federal Government sites, and from third parties who draw upon Federal Government or State Data.

Politwitter is a political twitter and social media site for Canadians to keep track of what politicians are saying on social media and what Canadians have to say about current politics from one location (http://www.politwitter.ca). The site allows users to search by indexing Canadian federal and provincial political twitter, facebook, blogs, youtube, flickr and more into one location. The site maintains a list of politicians and political tweeters as well as popular hash tags. Users can view tweets, narrowed down by MPs, partisan affiliation, province and more.

The Working in Canada (WiC) Tool is a mashup created by *Human Resources and Skills Development Canada* that pulls data from a variety of sources to help newcomers to the country make informed decisions about where to live and work and to get a more complete picture of the labour market in Canada (http://www.workingincanada. gc.ca/). There are also third-party customized versions of the WiC Tool for federal and provincial jurisdictions.

Healthmap is a mashup that pulls different data sources together to provide health professionals and other users a comprehensive view of the current global state of infectious diseases, and their effects on human and animal health (http://healthmap.org/). Healthmap combines the Google maps API, RSS feeds from different news sources, Google News, ProMED, the World Health Organization, and Euro Surveillance (HLWIKI Canada, 2010).

Interactive Traffic Map – a mashup provided by the city of Ottawa, Canada using Google Maps to display real-time information about construction delays, car accidents, traffic congestion, parking lots, red light cameras, traffic cameras, bus routes, and the geographical borders dividing the city's municipal wards (http://ww.traffic.ottawa.ca).

Havaria Information Services Alerts Map is a visualization tool to increase global disaster awareness (http://hisz.rsoe.hu/alertmap/). This interactive map pulls data relating to severe weather conditions, epidemic alerts, and seismic incidents around the world. Created by the National Association of Radio-Distress Signalling and Info-communications in Budapest, Hungary, the map draws from over 200 news sources for the information it displays (RSOE EDIS, 2004 - 2011).

National Public Toilet Map is a mashup developed by the Australian Government's Department of Health and Ageing that includes mobile apps, Google Maps and personalized user profiles to help citizens (especially those suffering from incontinence) locate the nearest public washrooms to their locations (http://www.toiletmap.gov.au/). The site shows the location of more than 14,000 public and private public toilet facilities across Australia and provides useful information about each toilet, such as location, opening hours, availability of baby change rooms, accessibility for people with disabilities and the details of other nearby toilets. Users who know the frequency of their urges can plan a route with scheduled pit

stops and they can access the site anytime using a mobile phone.

Appendix-1 summarizes other selected examples of mashups and related Web 2.0 applications and their use by different government levels and countries.

Online Virtual Worlds

An *online virtual world* is a game-like environment where any number of registered users (typically represented by a character or avatar) can communicate, explore, and interact with one another and with the virtual world's environment attributes. The exact origin of online virtual worlds is widely debateable however experts believe that the idea grew out of anonymous chat rooms which were popular in the 1990's (Mitchell, 1995). Today's online virtual worlds can generally be classified into one of two categories: Massively-Multiplayer Online Games (MMOGs) and Metaverses (Kumar et al., 2008). MMOGs involve a user who plays as a fantasy or fictitious character (such as a troll or warlock) that is often part of a larger team (also known as a clan) that completes missions (also known as quests). On the other hand, a Metaverse involves the user playing as a more life-like avatar interacting with other characters in the game as a means of online (often anonymous) socializing. Analysts predict that key opportunities exist for virtual worlds in the future. For example, as governments are pressured to reduce their costs and carbon emissions, online virtual worlds may be considered for digital meetings, etc. (Virtual Policy Network, 2009). Some of the most popular online virtual worlds include *Second Life* and *Habbo*.

Second Life

Second Life (http://secondlife.com/) is a Metaverse platform with more than 20 million registered users who represent themselves using avatars (ranging from real-life likenesses of themselves to more fantasy-based creations such as humanoid animals). This online virtual world is popular due to its expansive and highly-detailed, largely user-generated environment. The service's sophisticated and extremely-customizable interface and environment has made it a popular platform for public service agencies to represent and even offer their services in the online virtual forum (Hendaoui, Limayem, and Thompson, 2008). For example, a number of distance-education university programs facilitate their teaching through "classrooms" that they've built in Second Life and require all students enrolled in the class to have a Second Life account (Jin, Wen, Gough, 2010). Furthermore, government-supported tourism and immigration departments have begun to establish Second Life embassies, where they offer everything from information about passports and Visas, to simple tourism information (Handaoui, Limayem, and Thompson, 2008). Some politicians have also entered Second Life. For example, former Virginia Governor Mark Warner was one of the first politicians to enter Second Life (Gross, 2007). In France, the parties of the presidential candidates Le Pen, Royal and Sarkozy were also reported to have opened headquarters in Second Life (Osimo, 2008).

Habbo

Habbo (http://www.habbo.com/) is a virtual game world and chat site that bills itself as "the world's largest social game and online community for teenagers" (http://sulake.com/). The MMORLG was launched in Finland in the year 2000, but has since expanded to include a number of global sub-sites. The site allows users to represent themselves as digital avatars in a virtual world (known as a "Habbo Hotel") and encourages creative expression and safe interaction through a number of in-game features and destinations (known as "rooms"), many of which are created and maintained entirely by the user base. Habbo is free to play, but a number of users choose to purchase in-game add-ons such as digital furniture or accessories that allow them to further customize their avatar. Habbo is extremely popular among its target age range of thirteen to eighteen year olds (who make up 90% of the community's users) and the site indicates that it has greater than 200 million registered users and greater than 8.5 million monthly active users (users who sign on at least once per month) as of March 2011. Perhaps more important than the site's visitor statistics, Habbo indicates that the average user's visit lasts greater than 40 minutes, indicating that users are genuinely engaged in the experience.

Knowing that the majority of Habbo users are teenagers, there is an opportunity available to governments and public service agencies to reach this vulnerable and impressionable portion of the population through a medium that these users are both familiar and comfortable with. For example, a government-sponsored health agency could open a Habbo Room specifically to provide high-quality information and to answer anonymous questions on topics ranging from bullying and sexual orientation to teenage smoking and the dangers of alcohol abuse. In 2009, the British Government's Department of Health teamed up with a marketing agency to promote its "Talk to Frank" Campaign using Habbo (New Media Age, 2009). The Talk to Frank Campaign aimed to answer teens' questions about the effects of Cannabis and was based out of a Habbo room branded as a virtual manifestation of a cannabis user's brain. Government agencies that administer social programs for the youth could also consider opening simple Habbo Rooms to inform users about best practices for safe driving and to provide them information about how and where to obtain a driver's license (a rite of passage for many teenagers, depending on local regulations).

BEST PRACTICES AND NEW OPPORTUNITIES

Apart from the tools and applications that detailed in earlier sections of this chapter, there are a number of best practices and new opportunities for the public sector.

Crowdsourcing

Crowdsourcing is a means of gathering input on a question or issue from the parties that would be affected or potentially-affected by the decision. Typically done through the use of an app or third-party software, never has there been a greater opportunity for the use of crowdsourcing than in the recent global financial crisis. As governments at all levels struggle under tremendous debt loads, elected officials are being forced to implement sometimes-drastic fiscal austerity measures and unpopular service cutbacks to ensure that they remain financially stable. For example, The Government of the Borough of Sutton in London, England sought to realize a large cost savings from within the operational budget of their local library. The government used a software called Delib (http://www.delib.co.uk) which bills itself as "a Digital Democracy Company" to crowdsource input from citizens on what library services could be cut or changed to achieve their financial goal (Koehler, 2011). Additionally, the City of New York, as part of its road map for the Digital City, is leveraging crowdsourcing as it investigates the effective use of social media and Web 2.0 applications during emergency events. Software applications including Ushahidi, Google's People Finder, Ground-Crew, Frontline SMS, and CrisisCommons will be used to gather public input about what tools to use in crisis situations and how the public would like to see them used (New York City, 2011). As with any decision, not all parties may be happy with the end result of a crowdsourcing exercise, but at least the democratic nature of the experience allows individuals to feel as though they have an equal opportunity to speak about the decisions that affect them.

Open Data

As more people become tech-savvy, there exists a significant opportunity for governments who are willing to make some of their data available in an open form (Silicon Republic- Strategy, 2011). Similar to mashups, community-minded citizens can work with the openly-available government data to create useful apps for the public or for the internal use of the government or public service agency. In most cases, designers and developers will view the projects as a means of personal development and may even be willing to do the work for free (pro bono). Take, for example, the 18-Hour Open Data Challenge co-hosted by the Dublin (Ireland) City Council and the Fingal County (Ireland) Council in July, 2011. Over 100 competitors took part in the challenge and the winning entry was an application that helped businesses find an optimal location for their operations based on openly-available tax assessments and neighbourhood data (Silicon Republic –Innovation, 2011). Thus, the more-willing a government is to release non-sensitive data in an open format, the more access they'll have to a wide array of skilled citizens who can produce great tools and demonstrate more-effective ways of mining information and solving problems.

Law Enforcement

Although this concept is an ethical firestorm, there is a very real opportunity for the public service (including by-law enforcement agencies and police departments) to leverage social media and Web 2.0 applications in their enforcement efforts. Take, for instance, The City of Vancouver Riot in June, 2011 where hundreds of rioters caused millions of dollars in damage to city property. Throughout the rioting, these individuals were surrounded by curious onlookers who intended to capture the mayhem on their cell phones and cameras and then post pictures, videos, and status updates to social media sites. Within hours of the violence, thousands of social media users were actively trying to "help" the Police by identifying those who had caused the damage to their city and its reputation. Open-access Tumblr blogs and Facebook groups publicly accusing the rioters were started and used by Police in their post-riot investigations (Samuel, 2011). In the coming years, facial recognition software may even be used in conjunction with social media sites such as Facebook to track down wanted individuals whose images were captured on security cameras (Snyder, 2011). And, while the concept of scouring the internet for evidence of crimes already-committed has been around for a number of years, new efforts by these agencies are making it easier to predict and prevent planned crimes or by-law violations (Millich, 2008). The City of Boston Police Department, for example, uses keyword searches on Twitter to monitor "chatter" about crimes that may be planned or that may have already been committed. (Cohen, 2010).

Disaster Planning

Many of today's developed societies are interconnected through digital media, although this interconnectivity relies heavily on electrical power and physical infrastructure. Recent tragedies such as the Fukushima Disaster in Japan and Hurricane Katrina in Louisiana emphasized the need for public service agencies and relief groups to have disaster plans in place that are not exclusively dependant on electricity (Dvorak & Landers, 2011). Social media and Web 2.0 apps, many of which can function on battery-operated mobile devices and through wireless carriers' networks, present an opportunity for public service agencies to get critical information out to a large portion of the population in the event of a crisis involving a widespread power-outage. For example, New York City's Personal Localized Alerting Network (PLAN) will push emergency notifications to subscribers' mobile phones if there is an imminent threat to safety of life in their vicinity (New York City, 2011).

Analytics and Intelligence

Despite the number of public service agencies and individuals who are adopting Web 2.0 applications, there exists a massive opportunity in the area of analytics and data mining. Many of these applications include native tracking and analysis of visitors, trends, and entry/exit points to the site (for instance, what search term brought the user to land on the site). These capabilities, however, are not widely used in the public service sectors. For instance, in a survey conducted by *American City & County Magazine* in 2010 (Shark, 2010), more than 75% of respondents from the public service sector indicated that they did not actively review or use their sites' analytical data. Of the respondents who didn't review their metrics and analytics, only 20% indicated that they planned to implement metrics analysis in the 12 month period following the survey. Unlike the public service, business users have been utilizing their analytical data for years with generally successful results (Shark, 2010).If the public sector were to analyze trends about their visitors' location, they may be able to realize areas where they need more presence in order to reach their intended audience and demographic. Analytics provide insightful information and intelligence for effective utilization of social media tools. For example, one of the factors for the effectiveness of social media tools in the case of the Newark, New Jersey Central Ward Council political campaign was the use of analytics to constantly monitor relevant statistics and make informed decisions (Paden Noble Consulting, 2010).

SOCIAL MEDIA CHALLENGES IN THE PUBLIC SECTOR

Adopting social media technologies and interactions in the public sector involves several challenges. Despite the flexibility, scope and diversity of Web 2.0 applications, their influence can also be deemed as a double-edged sword. While there is no doubt that social media has given freedom of expression to society in all corners of the world, they also pose several controversial issues ranging from defamation to national interests. *WikiLeaks* has recently exemplified how far the Internet can expose the world and the complexity of the social, ethical and legal debates it raises.

Inappropriate Messages

Social media can be also used to promote any personal, social, and political views in various forms. Due to differences in social views, moral standards, ethics, and cultures, content that is acceptable to one individual or group may not necessarily be accepted equally by another individual or group. In particular, there is a greater risk for public administrators and government officials when posting views that can be easily interpreted by different segments of the society. For officials that are currently in office or running for office, any controversial idea can cost them their positions. Several instances of this situation (controversial Facebook, Twitter, or YouTube postings) have hit headlines in different countries in recent years.

Data Leaks

Social media also poses several challenges to organizations in their internal communications. For example, Proofpoint, Inc. found that US companies are increasingly concerned about a growing number of data leaks caused by employee misuse of email, blogs, social networks, multimedia channels, and even text messages (Marketwire, 2009). Such risks also exist, possibly in a greater

magnitude, in public organizations and government systems. In some cases, employees as well as administrators are unaware of the implications of engaging in social media activities.

Reliability

Social media contents are co-created by the community at large which may also raise issues on the quality and reliability of the contents for critical decision-making tasks. In some sectors, such as education, healthcare, and the military, information quality and reliability plays a significant role in achieving effective results. Contrary to this, any inconsistency, distortion, and misrepresentation of information could lead to costly and fatal mistakes. Mechanisms that can be employed to lower the negative effects of inaccuracies in information include using expert review of information posted, authentication, and moderation policies, particularly in internal application environments. For example, *Intellipedia* uses strong authentication linked to the organisation's network infrastructure (Osimo, 2008). Users also have different security classes and access privileges to access some categories of intelligence information.

Control of Information

Another challenge in the use of social media channels in the public sector is the possible conflict with traditional roles, power hierarchies, and even bureaucratic routes. Public administrators and government officials may resist the adoption of these technologies or even discourage their use in their environments in order to control the information channel (Johnson et al., 2008). Therefore, finding the right balance between traditional modes of interaction and the social media is critical. Regardless of their efficiency and convenience, Web 2.0 technologies should not be used as pure substitutes for all existing interactions and services. Doing so has the potential to isolate traditional followers who resist the adoption of these technologies or who are not anticipating any changes to their services.

Channel Conflict

In addition to the challenge with potential information control, channel conflict between social media and traditional media can cause problems for the public sector. Historically, a number of governments and government agencies have had a strong working-relationship with the traditional media and some like the United States Government even have highly-respected protocols and procedures for sharing information with these parties (Grossman & Kumar, 1979). The relationships between the government and the news outlets have often been fostered over many years. However, some parties argue that recent governments' forays into social media occasionally violate the established protocols (Lüfkens, 2011). If a newsworthy tweet or Facebook post is published before traditional correspondents have a chance to get the information from a formal press briefing, they may feel "scooped" (journalism slang for being beat to a story by a rival news outlet). Additionally, the advent of social media and push-to-publish news "as it happens" has been known to tempt journalists who are given the opportunity to get news first on the condition that they relay it to their counterparts before publishing (Parnes, 2011).

Legality

The use of social media by governments and public service agencies may be wrought with legal obstacles and gray areas depending on what laws exist and various interpretations of social media in the context of pre-existing laws (which tend to cover more-traditional media sources and communication mediums). In the State of Florida, for example, laws exist that prohibit elected officials from "using, giving, or lending their taxing power or credit to aid any private interest or individual" (Brody, 2009). This law exists to prevent against

public misuse of money or conflicts of interest whereby the elected official or their friend, family member, or ally can realize a benefit from the officials' clout or power that they wouldn't have otherwise had. In the context of business and traditional media, this law is relatively easy to interpret. However, Florida legislators are trying to decide whether this same law would to apply to seemingly harmless acts on social media such as providing an "@ mention" to another party on Twitter. Furthermore, the United States Federal Governments' Americans with Disabilities Act (ADA) covers accessibility and access to information and makes provisions for website content that is published by all levels of Government. There are again questions about legal statutes if a government agency or elected official uses a social media platform that does not, by default, comply with all elements of the ADA (Institute for Local Government, 2010).

Equality of Access

Social media challenges in the public also include whether or not all citizens have equal access to the technologies as well as the knowledge to effectively participate in these channels. The rapid growth of Web 2.0 technologies in developed regions and their absence in developing nations due to infrastructure may extend the already existing gap in access to or use of information and communication technologies (ICTs) between the developing and the developed parts of the world (de Kool and van Wamelen, 2008). Therefore, ensuring access to technology through low-cost alternatives and the development of the skills required to use these technologies should be part of the social media initiatives in the public sector.

Failure to Engage "Ordinary" Citizens

An article published by *New Media & Society* in 2010 indicates that the onslaught of a social media and Web 2.0 usage - especially in the political and public service sector – may be contributing to a widening gap between those citizens who are engaged and well-informed compared to those citizens who are disengaged and poorly-informed. With so much news coverage being done through social networks and online channels, traditional news outlets are moving more of their coverage from traditional mediums such as newspapers and television broadcasts into the digital realm (Davis, 2010). This has led to a situation where a portion of the population who was already quite informed has even greater access to information, whereas the portion of citizenry who were only moderately informed (through traditional news outlets) have become even less knowledgeable and engaged in the workings of their government (Davis, 2010).

CONCLUSION

Web 2.0 applications are already being used in a variety of government settings, ranging from public relations and public service announcements to core internal tasks such as intelligence services and enabling public participation in decision making (Osimo, 2008). This chapter reviewed several Web 2.0 applications and their current use and future potential in the public sector. Web 2.0 tools possess several value propositions to citizens, civil servants, public administrators, and elected government officials. Web 2.0 tools help to generate information that is based on the collective intelligence of its contributors. They facilitate creativity and participation and allow convenient exchange of information and knowledge-sharing among different groups of users.

We examined how public organizations and government officials use applications such as blogs, microblogs, wikis, mashups, and online virtual worlds, etc in various settings in the public sector. Some applications such as wikis encourage collaboration and increase general employee productivity. Others such as blogs and microblogs

help elected officials, public administrators, and civil servants engage with their constituents. Applications such as mashups pull relevant data from several sources and allow users make important decisions in various application settings, including healthcare, citizenship and immigration, traffic and transportation, education, politics, etc.

While social media provides tremendous opportunities for public administrators and government officials, the same technologies can be also exploited in a destructive way to invade privacy, and raise security issues. Most of the services such as Twitter are tied to a user's cell phone which can be more intrusive than PC-based networks. Since Web 2.0 platforms rely on connections and often encourage the user to provide personal profiles, these sites are easily susceptible to hackers. Users' online profiles may be also made available to the general public and attract unwanted attention. Thus, government officials and public administrators are confronted with the issue of striking a balance between the benefits of social media on one hand and the social costs on the other hand. Future academic research should address this trade-off in a broader framework that could overcome the limitations of existing Internet security and risk assessment tools and guidelines. Furthermore, the social costs of social media require time and resources to deal with. Adding to this resource requirement is maintaining the accuracy of information and the frequency of interactions. Therefore, public administrators and government officials need to pay serious attention to security measures towards new technologies and develop a policy framework towards social media and related activities (Serrat, 2010). Such policies must embrace all the channels employees are exposed to and be clearly communicated to employees to avoid serious consequences.

REFERENCES

Arellano, N. E. (2008). Canada embarks on major Web 2.0 initiative. *ITBusiness*. Retrieved March 30, 2011, from http://www.itbusiness.ca/it/client/en/home/news.asp?id=48569

Blogger Home Page. (n.d.). *Free weblog publishing tool from Google*. Retrieved from www.blogger.com

Boyd, d., Golder, S., & Lotan, G. (2010). Tweet tweet retweet: Conversational aspects of retweeting on Twitter. *43rd Hawaii International Conference on System Sciences-HICSS-43* (pp. 1-10).

Brody, C. E. (2009). Catch the tiger by the tail: Counseling the burgeoning government use of social media. *The Florida Bar Journal*, (December): 52–58.

Cohen, L. S. (2010). *6 ways law enforcement uses social media to fight crime*. Retrieved July 30, 2011, from http://mashable.com/2010/03/17/law-enforcement-social-media/

Congressional Management Foundation. (n.d.). Retrieved April 5, 2011, from http://www.cmf-web.org/

CrisisCommons Home Page. (n.d.). *A crowdsourcing app specializing in connecting and coordinating resources during crisis response scenarios*. Retrieved from http://crisiscommons.org/

Data.gov. (n.d.). *United States government*. Retrieved April 5, 2011, from http://www.data.gov

Datamasher. (n.d.). Retrieved April 5, 2011, from http://www.datamasher.org

Davis, A. (2010). New media and fat democracy: The paradox of online participation. *New Media & Society*, *12*(5), 745–761. doi:10.1177/1461444809341435

de Kool, D., & van Wamelen, J. (2008). Web 2.0: A new basis for e-government? *3rd International Conference on Information and Communication Technologies: From Theory to Applications (ICTTA)*, (pp. 1-7).

Dvorak, P., & Landers, P. (2011). Japanese plant had barebones risk plan. *The Wall Street Journal*. Retrieved July 30, 2011, from

ElectionMap. (2008). *United States electoral map, election 2008*. Retrieved April 5, 2011, from http://www.mapmash.in/election_map.html

European Commission. (2010). *Digital agenda for Europe*. Retrieved April 3, 2011, from http://ec.europa.eu/information_society/digital-agenda/index_en.htm

Frontline SMS Home Page. (n.d.). *A free, large-scale text messaging solution for NGOs and non-profit organizations*. Retrieved from http://frontlinesms.com

Fyfe, T., & Crookall, P. (2010). *Social media and public sector policy dilemmas*. Institute of Public Administration of Canada. Retrieved March 30, 2011, from

Government 2.0. (n.d.). *Best practices wiki*. Retrieved April 5, 2011, from http://government-20bestpractices.pbworks.com/w/page/10044431/Canada

Government 2.0 Taskforce. (n.d.). *Australia*. Retrieved April 5, 2011, from http://gov2.net.au

Gross, G. (2006). US intelligence community's wiki aids info sharing. *Infoworld*. Retrieved March 30, 2011, from http://www.infoworld.com/t/applications/us-intelligence-communitys-wiki-aids-info-sharing-673

Gross, G. (2007). U.S. House member gets Second Life. *Computerworld*. Retrieved March 30, 2011, from http://www.computerworld.com/s/article/9007218/

Grossman, M. B., & Kumar, M. J. (1979). The White House and the news media: The phases of their relationship. *Political Science Quarterly, 94*(1), 37–53. doi:10.2307/2150155

GroundCrew Home Page. (n.d.). *A group organization and dispatching application.* Retrieved from http://groundcrew.us/

Habbo Hotel. (n.d.). *A social networking website aimed at teenagers.* Retrieved from www.habbo.com/

Habbo Hotel. (n.d.). *Where else?* Retrieved April 5, 2011, from http://sulake.com/

Havaria Information Services Alerts Map. (n.d.). *National Association of Radio-Distress Signaling and Infocommunications (RSOE), Budapest, Hungary.* Retrieved March 30, 2011, from http://hisz.rsoe.hu/alertmap/

HealthMap. (n.d.). *Global health, local information.* Retived April 5, 2011, from http://healthmap.org/

Hendaoui, A., Limayem, M., & Thompson, C. W. (2008). 3D social virtual worlds: Research issues and challenges. *IEEE Internet Computing, 12*(1), 88–92. doi:10.1109/MIC.2008.1

HLWIKI Canada. (2010). *Mashups in medicine.* Retrieved April 5, 2011, from http://hlwiki.slais.ubc.ca/index.php/Mashups_in_medicine

Howard, M. (2001). E-government across the globe: How will "e" change government? *Government Finance Review, 17*(4), 6–9.

http://online.wsj.com/article/SB1000142405274 8703712504576232961004646464.html/

http://www.ipac.ca/documents/SocialMediaPublicSectorPolicyDilemmas.pdf

Human Capital Institute. (2010). *Social networking in government: Opportunities & challenges.* Human Capital Institute and Saba. Retrieved March 30, 2011, from http://www.hci.org/files/field_content_file/SNGovt_SummaryFINAL.pdf

Institute for Local Government. (2010). *Social media and public agencies: Legal issues to be aware of.* Retrieved July 30, 2011, from http://californiacitynews.typepad.com/files/technology-legal-issues.pdf

Intellipedia. (n.d.). *United States intelligence community.* Retrieved March 30, 2011, from www.intelink.gov

Interactive Traffic Map. (n.d.). *Ottawa, Canada.* Retrieved April 5, 2011, from http://ww.traffic.ottawa.ca

International Telecommunication Union (ITU). (2009). *Measuring the information society –The ICT development index.* Place des Nations, CH-1211 Geneva Switzerland. ISBN 92-61-12831-9 Retrieved March 30, 2011, from http://www.itu.int/ITU-D/ict/publications/idi/2009/index.html

Jin, L., Wen, Z., & Gough, N. (2010). Social virtual worlds for technology-enhanced learning on an augmented learning platform. *Learning, Media and Technology, 35*(2), 139–153. doi:10.1080/17439884.2010.494424

Johnston, P., Craig, R., Stewart-Weeks, M., & McCalla, J. (2008) *Realising the potential of the connected republic: Web 2.0 opportunities in the public sector.* Cisco Internet Business Solutions Group. Retrieved March 30, 2011, from http://s3.amazonaws.com/connected_republic/attachments/11/Government_2.0_WP_REV1126_NobelDraft.pdf

Kaplan, A. M., & Haenlein, M. (2010). Users of the world, unite! The challenges and opportunities of social media. *Business Horizons, 53*(1), 59–68. doi:10.1016/j.bushor.2009.09.003

Kaplan, A. M., & Haenlein, M. (2011). The early bird catches the news: Nine things you should know about micro-blogging. *Business Horizons*, *54*(2), 105–113. doi:10.1016/j.bushor.2010.09.004

Koehler, I. (2011). *Speak out Sutton!* Retrieved July 30, 2011, from http://socialgov.posterous.com/speak-out-sutton

Kumar, S., Chhugani, J., Kim, C., Kim, D., Nguyen, A., & Dubey, P. (2008). Second Life and the new generation of virtual worlds. *Computer*, *41*(9), 46–53. doi:10.1109/MC.2008.398

Lüfkens, M. (2011). *How world leaders use social media: Why the @WhiteHouse doesn't follow @BarackObama & other idiosyncrasies*. Retrieved July 30, 2011, from http://www.briansolis.com/2011/05/how-world-leaders-use-social-media-why-the-whitehouse-doesn't-follow-barackobama-and-other-idiosyncrasies/

Marketwire. (2009). *Social networking and reputational risk in the workplace*. Retrieved March 30, 2011, from http://www.marketwire.com/press-release/Proofpoint-Inc-1027877.html

Mayeda, A. (2010). *You have a friend request from Ottawa: Feds to expand use of social media*, PostMedia News. Retrieved March 30, 2011, from http://www.canada.com/technology/

Mayfield, R. (2007). *Twitter tips the tuna*. Retrieved April 5, 2011, from http://ross.typepad.com/blog/2007/03/twitter_tips_th.html

Microsoft Popfly. (n.d.). *A platform used to create mashups*. Retrieved from http://www.popfly.com/

Millich, G. (2008). Mich. police bust up party promoted on Facebook. [Radio transcript]. *NPR: All Things Considered* [Online]. Retrieved July 30, 2011, from http://www.npr.org/templates/story/story.php?storyId=89441570/

Mitchell, D. (1995). *From MUDs to virtual worlds*. Retrieved March 30, 2011, from http://web.archive.org/web/20051113010438/research.microsoft.com/research/scg/papers/3DV.htm

New Media Age. (2009). *Talk to Frank launches anti-cannabis activity on Habbo*. Retrieved March 30, 2011, from http://www.nma.co.uk/news/talk-to-frank-launches-anti-cannabis-activity-on-habbo/41819.article

NYC.gov. (2011). *Announcing the road map for the digital city: A plan to make NYC the nation's leading digital city*. Retrieved July 30, 2011, from http://www.mikebloomberg.com/index.cfm?objectid=f994fba2-c29c-7ca2-fbee94b-d47bd91a3

O'Reilly, T. (2005). *Web 2.0: Compact definition?* Retrieved March 30, 2011, from http://radar.oreilly.com/archives/2005/10/web-20-compact-definition.html

Office of Citizen Services and Innovative Technologies and the Federal Web Managers Council, USA. (n.d.). Retrieved March 30, 2011, from http://www.howto.gov

Osimo, D. (2008). *Web 2.0 in government: Why and how?* JRC Scientific and Technical Reports. Office for Official Publications of the European Communities, European Communities. EUR 23358 EN.

Paden Noble Consulting. (2010). *Smart political social media use changes Newark, NJ election*. Retrieved July 30, 2011, from http://www.padennoble.com/politics/darrin-sharif-newark-political-social-media

Parameswaran, M., & Whinston, A. B. (2007a). Social computing: An overview. *Communications of the Association for Information Systems*, *19*, 762–780.

Parameswaran, M., & Whinston, A. B. (2007b). Research issues in social computing. *Journal of the Association for Information Systems, 8*(6), 336–350.

Parnes, A. (2011). *White House press pool losing scoops to Twitter*. Retrieved July 30, 2011, from http://www.politico.com/news/stories/0611/58161.html

perspectives-on-social-media-the-vancouver-riots

Politwitter. (n.d.). *A Canadian non-partisan political twitter & social media aggregator & directory*. Retrieved April 5, 2011, from http://www.politwitter.ca

Rainer, R. K., Cegielski, C. G., Splettstoesser-Hogeterp, I., & Sanchez-Rodriguez, C. (2011). *Introduction to Information Systems*, 2nd ed. John Wiley & Sons, Canada, Ltd. ISBN: 978-0-470-67888-6

Reece, B. (2006). E-government literature review. *Journal of E-Government, 3*(1), 69–110. doi:10.1300/J399v03n01_05

RSOE EDIS. (n.d.). *Emergency and disasters information and monitoring services, hosted by the National Association of Radio-distress Signalling and Infocommunications*, Retrieved April 5, 2011, from http://hisz.rsoe.hu/alertmap/index.php?lang=eng

Samuel, A. (2011). *10 challenging perspectives on social media & the Vancouver riots*. Retrieved July 30, 2011, from http://www.alexandrasamuel.com/world/10-challenging-

Second Life Home Page. (n.d.). *A free 3D virtual world where users can socialize, connect and create using free voice and text chat*. Retrieved from http://secondlife.com/

Serrat, O. (2010). *Social media and the public sector*. Retrieved March 30, 2011, from http://www.asiandevbank.org/documents/information/knowledge-solutions/social-media-and-the-public-sector.pdf

Shark, A. (2010). Behind the curve. *American City & County Magazine*. Retrieved July 30, 2011, from http://americancityandcounty.com/technology/web-business-intelligence-201007/

Silicon Republic–Innovation. (2011). *Dublin councils launch 18-hour open data challenge*. Retrieved July 30, 2011, from http://www.siliconrepublic.com/innovation/item/22301-dublin-councils-launch-18-h/

Silicon Republic-Strategy. (2011). *The open data movement will be the people's choice*. Retrieved July 30, 2011, from http://www.siliconrepublic.com/strategy/item/21784-the-open-data-movement-will/

Six Apart. (6A). (n.d.). *Home page - Blog hosting service*. Retrieved from www.sixapart.com

Snyder, B. (2011). *Facebook facial recognition: Why it's a threat to your privacy*. Retrieved July 30, 2011, from http://www.cio.com/article/684711/facebook_facial_recognition_why_it_s_a_threat_to_your_privacy

The City of New York. (2011). *Road map for the digital city: achieving New York City's digital future*. Retrieved July 30, 2011 from http://www.mikebloomberg.com/NYC_Digital_Roadmap_05162011.pdf

The National Public Toilet Map (the Toilet Map). (n.d.). Retrieved April 5, 2011 from http://www.toiletmap.gov.au/

Tumblr Home Page. (n.d.). *A microblogging platform*. Retrieved from http://www.tumblr.com/

Twitter Home Page. (n.d.). *A social networking and microblogging platform*. Retrieved from http://twitter.com/

Ushahidi Home Page. (n.d.). *An open-source crowdsourcing and information democratizing application.* Retrieved from http://ushahidi.com/

Virtual Policy Network. (n.d.). *Best practice forum 235: Virtual worlds and public diplomacy in the digital age.* Department of Business, Innovation, and Skills, UK Government. Retrieved March 30, 2011, from http://www.virtualpolicy.net/_downloads/igf09/ukgov_tvpn-igf09-vw_publicdiplomacy.pdf

Wikipedia Home Page. (n.d.). *The free encyclopaedia.* Retrieved from http://www.wikipedia.org/

WordPress Home Page. (n.d.). *A semantic personal publishing platform.* Retrieved from http://wordpress.com

Working in Canada (WiC). (n.d.). *Government of Canada.* Retrieved April 5, 2011, from http://www.workingincanada.gc.ca/content_pieces-eng.do?lang=eng&cid=1

Wyld, D. C. (2007). *The blogging revolution: Government in the age of Web 2.0. E-Government Series.* IBM Center for the Business of Government.

Yahoo. Pipes Home Page. (n.d.). *A platform used to create mashups.* Retrieved from http://pipes.yahoo.com/pipes/

KEY TERMS AND DEFINITIONS

Blog: An online entry of personal thoughts (text, hypertext, images, or links) arranged in a reverse chronological order.

Citizen 2.0: Generally represents citizens' engagement with government or participatory government as a result of governments adopting social media and Web 2.0 technologies and applications.

Crowdsourcing: The practice of outsourcing a task to a group of people in order to take advantage of the collective intelligence of the public.

E-Government: Represents the use of information and communication technologies by governments for delivering services to citizens and conducting intra-government functions.

Hashtag: A tag embedded in a message posted on the Twitter microblogging service, which is used to mark keywords or topics in a Tweet.

Mashups: Interactive Web applications that combine data, presentation or functionality from multiple sources.

Microblog: A type of blog or blog post that is smaller in both scale and scope than a "traditional" blog site.

Open Data: Is the idea of making non-personal information held by government freely available to everyone to use and republish online.

Web 2.0: Used to describe second generation of the Web representing a cost-effective collection of technologies and applications, based largely upon user-generated content.

Wiki: A website on which users can post contents and make changes to other contents through a simple "edit" link.

APPENDIX

Social Media Engagement by Governments around the World: Selected Current Initiatives and Best Practices: *(Source: Government 2.0 Best Practices Wiki. Retrieved April 5, 2011 from http://government20bestpractices.pbworks.com/)*

Public Service Unit/ Department	Purpose	Country	Government Level	Social Media Platforms and Tools
(Various Health-Related Agencies) www.aids.gov	Aids.Gov – Providing frequent updates on research developments, awareness efforts, and prevention best practices in the fight against aids	United States	Federal	Blog, Twitter, MySpace, Facebook, RSS, Flickr, Podcasts
Department of Defence (Military Health System) www.health.mil/mhsblog	Military Health System Blog – Providing information relevant to armed forces personnel and their families about their health and wellness	United States	Federal	Blog
Department of Veterans Affairs www.blogs.va.gov/VAntage/	VAntage Point Blog – An integrated social media effort to foster engaging and informative, mutually-beneficial relationships between Veterans and the Department of Veterans Affairs	United States	Federal	Blog, Facebook, Twitter, Flickr, YouTube
Department of Homeland Security (Transportation Safety Authority) www.blog.tsa.gov	TSA Blog – Facilitating an ongoing dialogue on innovations in security, technology and the checkpoint screening process	United States	Federal	Blog
New York City Department of Health and Mental Hygiene www.facebook.com/NYC-condom	NYC Condom Service – Educating New York City on safe sex best practices and the prevention of sexually transmitted infections (STIs). Visitors can also download a mobile "condom finder" app that locates the nearest distributor of free condoms provided by the Health Department	United States	Municipal	Facebook, Mobile App
San Francisco Local Homeless Coordinating Board www.sfhomeless.net	San Francisco Homeless Resource Wiki – Providing a publically-editable "resource bible" about any and all topics related to homelessness in and around San Francisco, a collaboration between the municipal government and local shelters and support agencies	United States	Municipal	Wiki
Canadian Centre for Occupational Health and Safety www.ccohs.ca/products/webinars	CCOHS Webinar Series – Webinars aimed at efficiently helping organizations to raise awareness, assess risks, and improve workers' health and safety	Canada	Federal	Webinars
Healthy Canada http://healthycanadians.gc.ca/ra/mobile-eng.php	Healthy Canadians (Recall and Safety Alerts Website and Mobile App) – This app delivers real-time information on products that Health Canada has listed recall or safety alerts on to help shoppers avoid purchasing potentially dangerous products	Canada	Federal	Website, Mobile App

Chapter 2
An Experiment in E–Rulemaking with Natural Language Processing and Democratic Deliberation

Peter Muhlberger
Texas Tech University, USA

Jenny Stromer-Galley
University at Albany, USA

Nick Webb
University at Albany, USA

ABSTRACT

Public comment processes in federal and state agency rulemakings are among the most substantial potential arenas for public input into government. Unfortunately, these processes have not been much used for thoughtful public input. This chapter explores whether online democratic deliberation and natural language processing tools, can empower participants to provide more informed input into an agency rulemaking. It also sought to determine whether such an approach had other positive effects such as enhancing citizenship and increasing confidence in the pertinent agency. Findings indicate improvements in participant knowledge of the network neutrality rulemaking topic, systematic attitude change, improvements to citizenship measures, and increased confidence in the Federal Communications Commission. Results suggest that public deliberation under conditions needed to involve substantial numbers of people—namely, online deliberation without facilitators—can improve public comments into federal and state agency rulemakings while strengthening the citizenship qualities of participants. They also indicate that many of the desired effects of face-to-face deliberation with trained facilitators can also be obtained online without facilitators.

DOI: 10.4018/978-1-4666-0318-9.ch002

INTRODUCTION

E-government researchers and practitioners are increasingly interested in using online technologies not merely for transaction processing but also to open a public space for citizen-to-citizen and citizen-to-government interactions. One of the greatest potential spaces for meaningful public input into government is the domain of public comments on government agency proposed rules. Yet, research suggests that public comments tend to be of relatively low quality when it comes to their utility for government agencies (Shulman, 2006). Public and even expert comments in the rulemaking process might be improved by utilizing deliberative techniques that involve small group discussion. Held online, such discussion would permit large numbers of geographically dispersed individuals to participate. Deliberation is, however, typically conducted with trained facilitators. Agencies would be hard pressed to find trained facilitators for even a moderate number of small groups and face concerns about accusations of bias against these facilitators. A possible solution would be to combine Natural Language Processing (NLP) technologies to serve some of the functions of facilitators: answering questions, summarizing discussion, connecting people with common interests, eliciting comments from the quiet, and so forth. Thus, our project tested a combination of NLP technologies that would cover facilitator functions, in the hope of building a Discussion Facilitation Agent (DiFA).

This chapter describes the NLP technologies used and presents research from an experiment on the policy topic of network neutrality, which is the question of whether rules should be adopted to require internet service providers to treat all digital traffic equally. Our research question is whether online and unfacilitated deliberations and NLP technologies would lead to some of the positive outcomes of deliberation expected from theory and prior research on face-to-face deliberation with facilitation. The experiment showed that deliberation had impacts on a range of outcomes—such as increased topic knowledge, attitude change, positive changes in indicators of citizen engagement, and increased confidence in the FCC—but that the technologies deployed had limited effects. The chapter concludes with an examination of the limitations of the study and potential ways in which the NLP technologies could be further developed to enhance citizen deliberation on policy in the future.

E-DEMOCRACY AND RULEMAKING

The recent trend in open government initiatives in the United States and elsewhere has brought about noteworthy new opportunities for citizen engagement not only in interfacing with government but in participating more deeply in the policy process. The Obama administration's efforts on open government led to three principles: transparency, collaboration, and participation ("Transparency and Open Government," 2009). One of the ways that open government initiatives can manifest is through using the myriad of applications cast under the umbrella of "Web 2.0" (Chun, Shulman, Sandoval, Hovy, 2010). These technologies primarily include social media that enable collaboration and sharing among individuals, helping to facilitate the "wisdom of crowds" (Shirky, 2008). ICTs in general have been looked to for increasing efficiency and inter-agency cooperation as well as interfacing more effectively with the public (Margetts, 2009), in what Dunleavy, Margetts, Bastow and Tinkler (2006) refer to as a new "Digital Era of Governance".

Of particular relevance for the project at hand are the opportunities for increased participation by citizens in the policy process. Although there have been some limited efforts to engage the public in federal policy making (Heidinger, Buchmann, & Böhm, 2010), one of the underutilized and understudied opportunities is through the public comment process in government agency rulemakings.

Such rulemaking is the process by which agency officials seek to turn the often general language of legislation into specific rules that determine compliance with a law. Legislatures, such as Congress, make laws that are often abstract rather than specific guidelines. Agencies need to implement these laws by providing specific guidelines, that is rules. Before putting such rules in place, agencies typically seek public comment on proposed rules over a period of months or years. At the federal level, the Administrative Procedures Act (APA), which is the law governing how federal agencies can propose and enact regulations, requires the elicitation and consideration of public comments for significant rulemakings. The APA's Section 553 on rule makings stipulates that regulations proposed by government agencies must be published in the Federal Register, and section c explains, "After notice required by this section, the agency shall give interested persons an opportunity to participate in the rule making through submission of written data, views, or arguments with or without opportunity for oral presentation." The law also requires that the agency consider the "relevant matter presented." In brief, agencies must place proposed rules in the Federal Register, solicit public comments on them, and make a good faith effort to consider all comments. Agencies are motivated to follow this APA procedural format because if they do not, their rules will likely be challenged successfully in court. Because of their extensive use in federal and in many state agencies and their impact on actual rules enforced by government, the rulemaking comment process represents perhaps the most extensive arena within which the public could directly influence public policy. Rulemaking has great potential for substantive democratic engagement, though it is also an arena of which much of the public is unaware.

Although research suggests that the public comments agencies receive about a rulemaking have shaped final regulations (Yackee, 2005), there has been ongoing concern about the nature and content of public comments (Shulman, 2006), and the especially limited participation by citizens in providing comments (Kerwin, 2003). When citizens do involve themselves in the public comment process it is more commonly through the submission of form letters prompted by activist or lobbying groups of which citizens are members. In the efforts to motivate members to send comments, activist organizations frame the public comment process as a plebiscite, majority rule system where comments are perceived almost as votes (Shulman, 2009). Some research has examined the characteristic differences in form letters by activist groups versus original comments drafted by stakeholders, noting that original comments tend to provide more of the kinds of insight government agencies seek (Scholsberg, Zavestoski, & Shulman, 2007).

The advent of e-rulemaking in the U.S., through Regulations.gov, a one-stop portal for citizens to review regulations open for comment, and submit their comments electronically, led to optimism for increased citizen-involvement (Carlitz & Gunn, 2005). As e-mail campaigns and digital form letters have become more prevalent in the past decade, researchers have expressed concern that mass form letters are of limited utility for agencies seeking insight on the regulation (Shulman, 2009). On the other side of the debate is the position that the tactic by activist groups to mobilize members to send form letters is part of a complex public communication campaign and does not crowd out more original comments (Karpf, 2010). Other research suggests that the concern of interest or activist groups deluging agencies with public comments, either in the older print or newer digital forms, is misplaced. Instead, industry and stakeholder elites have been and continue to be significantly more likely to submit comments on environmental regulations over the past decade (de Figueiredo, 2006; Shafie, 2008). Put another way, the initial hope that moving the public comment process online would increase citizen involvement has not come to pass.

DEMOCRATIC DELIBERATION

Whether the public is swamping government agencies with meaningless form letters or is vastly outstripped in many rulemakings by elites, the public's overall impact on rulemaking outcomes is small at best. This raises concerns about the democratic legitimacy of agency rulemakings. While impartial experts should have final say on factual matters, in a democracy legitimacy for the values chosen in a policy decision comes from the public (Benhabib, 1994). A flourishing body of new work in deliberative democracy theory provides a compelling case for consulting the *informed* views of the public in making policy decisions (Bohman, 1996; Chambers, 1996; Dryzek, 2002; Gutmann & Thompson, 1996).

Public deliberation practice seeks to elicit more informed views of the public through a variety of methods. One widely used method is the Deliberative Poll® (Fishkin, 1997), in which a random sample of the public is recruited to participate in a one or two day deliberative event. Participants are provided with balanced information on the policy issue to read prior to the event, discuss the issue face-to-face in small groups of about 10 people with a trained facilitator, and question experts. Participants are also typically surveyed prior to and after discussion, allowing for pre- to post-discussion comparisons to determine the impact of deliberation on policy views, knowledge, and indicators of future engagement. The objective of using a representative sample of the public in a Deliberative Poll® is to determine what the general public would think about an issue if it were to collectively learn about and thoughtfully discuss the issue. While not permitted to call their work Deliberative Polls®, a number of researchers and deliberation practitioners utilize deliberation designs bearing some similarity.

Research on deliberation has arrived at a number of moderately firm empirical conclusions. Deliberations enhance the knowledge of participants with respect to the policies under discussion and generally result in significant and substantial changes in participant attitudes (Barabas, 2004; Farrar et al., 2010; Luskin, Fishkin, & Jowell, 2002). Somewhat more tentatively established, deliberation results in enhanced legitimacy for government policy decisions (Zillig, Herian, Abdel-Monem, Hamm, & Tomkins, 2010) and shifts in attitudes and predispositions that suggest greater propensity for future political engagement (Gastil, Black, Deess, & Leighter, 2008; Price & Cappella, 2002). Generally, these findings regard pre-discussion to post-discussion changes, with researchers only beginning to unpack what features of deliberation result in the changes (Muhlberger & Weber, 2006c; Stromer-Galley & Muhlberger, 2009d).

Importantly for this project, little or no research has been conducted to determine whether the positive changes resulting from deliberation can be obtained without trained facilitators. Also, much deliberation research has proceeded without an experimental control group. Arguably, in a one or two-day face-to-face deliberation there need not be a great concern with such threats to internal validity as history (outside factors, such as current events that may cause observed pre- to post-discussion changes) or maturation (changes in participants, such as growing cognitive complexity with maturation, that can cause pre- to post-discussion changes). For an overview of experimental and quasi-experimental methods and threats to internal validity see Campbell, Stanley, and Gage (1966). Because we introduce a control group here, the current study involves a higher standard of evidence than much deliberative research. Finally, comparatively little peer-reviewed literature exists regarding the impacts of online deliberation (Muhlberger & Weber, 2006c; Price & Cappella, 2002).

If deliberation is to become a more widely used process or even an everyday process in government, such as rulemaking, it will need to scale up. Such scaling is improbable for face-to-face deliberations with geographically dispersed groups because of the considerable cost of such events. In addition, as already noted, any substantial number of discussion groups would require a rare commodity in the Deliberative Polling® paradigm—trained facilitators. Thus, there is a need for research, such as presented here, on online deliberation in the absence of facilitators.

THE DELIBERATIVE E-RULEMAKING PROJECT

Natural Language Technology

The Deliberative E-Rulemaking (DeER) project was a three-year National Science Foundation project which sought to apply deliberation and NLP tools to federal and state agency rulemakings. The study described in the current paper is one of multiple efforts under DeER to test such e-rulemakings. Because federal and state agencies were ultimately not especially cooperative with the DeER project, the current data represents the largest body of data collected in the project. The technology deployed in the DeER project was chosen to address specific problems of multi-user deliberation among citizens. One problem is uninformed participants. Making available large amounts of contextual documentation that provides background research on the topic at hand places a large burden on the user. Some of the material may be already known to participants, while other information may be irrelevant to their concerns. Moreover, having vested parties to the deliberation put the documentation together can lead to concerns of bias in the material. Instead, using existing question-answering technology, we allowed users to explore the policy issue using natural language queries, resulting in paragraphs of information drawn from a pre-mined document base from the World Wide Web, that provided information relevant to the user and the deliberation.

We made use of the HITIQA (High-Quality Interactive Question-Answering) tool (Small &

Strzalkowski, 2009), developed at the University at Albany. HITIQA helps users find answers to complex analytical problems. That is, this system is not a factoid QA system, or one that returns solely single-fact answers to direct questions (such as "How tall is the Eiffel Tower?"), but rather is designed to answer difficult, compound questions ("What is the impact of the falling dollar on oil operations in the Caspian Sea?") by facilitating exploration through a series of returned paragraphs or subsets of complete documents. HITIQA uses the process of text framing to bring a level of semantic representation to open-domain data in order to facilitate meaningful dialogue with the user. In experiments using intelligence analysts, we demonstrated that HITIQA is more effective for research-based applications than using Google. Originally written with professional analysts in mind, HITIQA was designed with interactive features to help the user narrow extracted answers through a series of questions. Such use was unlikely for citizen users in a Web-based environment. Thus, we disabled the interactive capabilities of HITIQA, and focused on its use as a one-question retrieval mechanism for relevant data, with results presented in a list ordered by relevance.

A significant element of the evaluation process for HITIQA in the DeER project was to observe if users, with minimal training, would pose natural language queries to the HITIQA engine at all. There is a plethora of evidence (cf. HitWise report for 2010) that users are accustomed to posing short keyword queries. The average number of keywords to Google is between 2 and 3. In this environment, and told that HITIQA could answer their questions, how would users interact with the system?

This application of HITIQA was a 'pull' technology; it required users to be motivated to search the background documents. As the DeER project progressed, it became clear that few users were motivated to pose questions to the HITIQA system, preferring instead to opt for familiar search engines. This may partly be a function of having not highly motivated users or of users unfamiliar with NLP (something that will change with time). What was required was a 'push' technology that would present information more actively to the user. This involved answering non-rhetorical questions in individual postings *during a deliberation* and linking the question text to the result.

To determine which questions were non-rhetorical and meaningful and how to best answer them, it was necessary to classify discussion posting sentences. The technology we used is called dialogue act (DA) classification. Dialogue acts are simple labels applied to sentences that indicate the function each sentence is playing in the wider discourse. For example, we want to be able to differentiate statements of opinion from questions. Within questions, it is also useful to distinguish between wh-questions (who, what, where and so on), yes-no questions, ("Do you...?"), and rhetorical questions (which expect no particular answer). We employed a state-of-the-art dialogue act classifier (Nick Webb, Hepple, & Wilks, 2005), which is applicable to a wide range of dialogue types (Webb & Ferguson, 2010).

We applied DA classification to users' posts, with two aims. First, we automatically identified questions in the text, and directed them to the HITIQA system automatically. In the background, HITIQA retrieved paragraphs of data from our database, and linked them to the identified question. So, if a user asked, in a post "How many government agencies regulate the national parks?," such a question would be identified, sent to HITIQA, and then the material HITIQA retrieved would be linked to the question text in the post in which it occurred. Clicking this link opened a pop-up answer page containing the returned paragraphs from HITIQA. Thus, users did not have to actively explore the contextual material.

Second, we used DAs as a base mechanism to link users together. Another hypothesis of deliberation is that, once an active deliberation on an asynchronous message board (that is, not

real-time—posts are stored and people can participate at any time they prefer) of the type we were using becomes too large, it is difficult for users to track new messages in the expanding set of threads. We used DA classification to identify clear statements of personal opinion in posts, and then used keyword overlap of those utterances to automatically identify people expressing opinions on the same or similar topics. At this point, we did not pay attention to the valence of those arguments. What mattered was connecting users based on similarity of interests.

To encourage participation in the deliberation, regular emails were automatically created which contained links to posts with overlapping perspectives, indicating new postings in threads other than those in which the targeted user was active, in which topics similar to the user's postings could be found. In addition, to give all users some understanding of the development of the overall, on-going deliberation, we included a word cloud (automatically created from wordle. net), which shows the most frequently used words (we filtered typical stop words) by size, the larger being the more frequent.

Ultimately, for both citizen and agency consumption, we would want to make available large scale, multi-posting summarization systems. Initially, we had intended to employ such a summarization system (based on our existing, multi-document summarizer system, XDOX (Hardy et al., 2002)), but required a substantial body of textual data to tune the system, which we were unable to obtain.

The NLP technologies offered to users were a small step toward building a discussion facilitation agent (DiFA). Like a human facilitator, the system sought to answer factual questions and sought to connect the ideas of participants when these participants addressed similar issues but at different points in the discussion. The word cloud also served to summarize the main ideas in a discussion and rapidly refer the participant to the contents of each idea. The system can be enhanced in a variety of ways with existing technology, a point to which we return in the discussion.

Multi-Level Deliberation

The project utilized a Multi-Level Deliberation (MuLD) technique with a number of potential advantages, as suggested in prior theory and practice (Endenburg, 1998; Pivato, 2007). In MuLD, discussion groups eventually select one or a few persons to represent the group in a higher-level discussion group in which each member represents a lower-level group. In MuLD, participants discuss an issue in a small group—up to 30 people in an online setting. This group then elects, say, one of its members to represent the group in a second-level group of up to 15 people. Each member of that group represents a lower-level group. This second-level group discusses the issue, seeking to bring together the best ideas and reasoning from all the lower-level groups. If there are multiple second-level groups, each would elect a member for a third-level group. The process ends when there is one "top-level" group that represents all first-level discussants. Representatives of higher-level groups are also expected to return to their lower-level groups to explain what was decided in the higher-level groups and why.

It is possible for very large numbers of first-level discussants to share information efficiently among themselves in such a MuLD arrangement. In the example arrangement above, four levels of groups could encompass millions of discussants. Hypothetically, more informed and deliberative participants would flow to higher-level groups, improving the quality of discussion. The top-level group can, potentially, directly interact with policymakers as representatives of all discussants. Higher-level groups could utilize lower-level groups for such tasks as information processing, and potentially interact with agency officials in a meaningful way. Representatives relay the gist of their upper-level discussion back to their original groups, hopefully spreading good ideas from any group to all other groups and helping to legitimize higher-level decisions. MuLD could be crossed in many ways with online technologies to potentially improve communication, representation, and perceived legitimacy.

METHODS

Research Design

We conducted a partial 2X2 experimental manipulation—testing three of four crossed conditions, as depicted in Table 1. All discussion groups were online. Six of the discussion groups received access to our DiFA technology, including the question answering tool, and the email reminders with links to content-similar posts and a word cloud. These are depicted under "Technology Enabled" in Table 1. Another five groups were given only the opportunity to deliberate on an asynchronous message board, but without the additional tools. The number of groups per condition was unequal because of constraints to maintain a critical discussion mass in each group and uncertainty about the ultimate number of discussants. We also had three of the technology-enabled groups participate in a multiple level deliberation (MuLD), where they selected people to represent them in a higher-level group. The deliberations spanned a month.

Table 1. Research design—Number of discussion groups in each experimental condition

	Technology Enabled	Not Technology Enabled
Multiple Level Deliberation	3	
No Multiple Level Deliberation	3	5

Students in the MuLD condition were invited to vote for representatives two weeks into the deliberation. We did not test the fourth condition, with MuLD but no technology, out of concerns regarding sample size and, thereby, statistical power. This research can therefore clarify what impact MuLD has on top of or in interaction with technology, but not without technology.

We recruited 615 students from two public universities who participated in exchange for extra credit in several courses in communication. Students were randomly assigned to 11 online discussion groups that were hosted through an asynchronous, threaded message board system called VBulletin. Of the students that were recruited, 121 met the requirements for participation, including posting to the message board and answering pre- and post-discussion surveys. Another 63 students took the sign-up survey, but failed to take the pre-discussion survey and failed to participate in the discussions, but did take the "post-discussion" survey when allowed to do so for partial extra credit. These students served as a comparison group to determine whether changes observed among the discussion participants were really caused by the discussion and not some outside factors. We expected students in departments of communication to have at least a mild interest in the topic of network neutrality, which was the topic of the deliberation, and hoped that this interest would blossom as they discussed the issue. On the other hand, end of semester pressures might have dampened this possibility. In addition, it is unlikely that students would be as interested in the topic as the engaged public that would come to an agency rulemaking.

Network neutrality was presented to participants as the real issue of whether the Federal Communications Commission (FCC) should adopt a rule requiring all U.S. internet service providers (ISPs) to treat all digital traffic on their networks equally. Participants were told that proponents of the neutrality rule contend that without such a rule ISPs could throttle or block digital traffic in ways that would undermine free speech rights. Opponents, in contrast, contend that a network neutrality rule is unnecessary to protect free speech, but that such a rule would cause real problems for ISPs trying to offer such services as online phone calls or in protecting the internet access of average ISP user from the small number of people who use far more bandwidth. The network neutrality issue was selected because it was an important real issue at the time, with which the FCC was grappling, and because of its relevance for communications students. Participants were given access to a website with a "learn" page containing summaries of different pro and con arguments and links to the sources of these arguments. They also received access to our question-answering tool.

Measures

Participants answered two Web-based surveys: one before the deliberation began and another shortly after the deliberation concluded. The surveys were taken from any computer at the respondent's leisure. Because respondents were answering questions to a computer and without researchers present, responses should be relatively free of social desirability and demand effects. Survey items included standard demographic items and a wide variety of explanatory and outcome variables.

Direct Evaluation Measures

We adapted Schweiger, Sandberg, and Ragan's (1986) evaluation scales for work groups, measured with 7-point Likert-type scales. Participants were asked about their Satisfaction with Discussion (e.g., "I am committed to my discussion group's recommendations on net neutrality."), Future Participation Motivation ("I am motivated to participate in future public policy discussions."), and Reevaluated Assumptions ("Participating in this net neutrality policy discussion made me critically reevaluate the validity of the assumptions and recommendations that I held personally.").

Each of these three dimensions were measured with two questions and responses were averaged. Correlations within dimension were strong, and prior work establishes the presence of distinct factors (Stromer-Galley & Muhlberger, 2009d).

Respondents were also asked three questions regarding the perceived legitimacy of the deliberation and of FCC decisions. The variable "Impact Should Have On Officials" was measured with a question asking respondents to indicate how strongly FCC officials should weigh comments and conclusions from their discussion, with 0 meaning "have no effect on...the Officials' Decisions," 3 meaning "have moderate effect on...," and 6 meaning "determine...the Officials' Decisions." The "Impact On Officials – No Agree" variable asks much the same question but tells respondents to consider how much of an effect they would want on FCC officials' decisions if they personally disagreed with the comments and conclusions of other participants. The responses to the first and second question should clarify just how legitimate the deliberation process seemed to participants. The "Respect FCC" variable asks respondents to "Suppose the FCC does not end up taking the positions you do on net neutrality. If so, how strongly do you agree or disagree with the following statement: I will respect the FCC\'s decisions." The difference between the second and this third question should clarify how legitimate participants view FCC departures from their preferences in the absence of deliberation relative to deliberations that yield results different than the respondent would like.

A series of questions asked about the usefulness of such technological features as email links, the word cloud, and question answering. The basic structure of the questions was: "The 'Your Questions Answered' feature of the DeER website was useful." followed by a seven-point Likert scale. To measure the effectiveness of MuLD, two questions styled after the Schweiger measures asked respondents whether MuLD stimulated

their thinking or uncovered valid questions or assumptions they had not considered.

Outcome Measures

Policy Knowledge was measured as the summed number of correct answers to a seven question quiz about network neutrality. For each quiz question, respondents needed to select one of four possible answer options. An example question is: "What are 'common carriers'?" (Correct answer: "private companies that are required by law to carry information without discrimination"). Policy Attitude was measured as an average of three questions, such as: "Internet Service Providers (ISPs) should treat all information on the Internet the same." Higher scores indicate greater acceptance of network neutrality. Active Citizenship, which might also be considered a measure of deliberative conceptions of citizenship, was captured with four questions such as: "A good citizen should allow others to challenge their political beliefs." Active Citizenship involves a conception of good citizenship that includes willingness to allow others to challenge one's views, justifying views to others who disagree, and willingness to listen to and discuss politics with others who disagree. Prior research establishes active citizenship as a distinct factor (Muhlberger & Weber, 2006c), indicates that it is correlated with self-reported past participation, and shows that people with an active conception of citizenship acquire more objective knowledge during the course of a deliberation. In addition, three studies indicate that active citizenship grows in the course of deliberation (Muhlberger, 2007). Citizen Identity measures the centrality of politics to personal identity with such questions as: "Being politically conscious is important to who I am." Such Citizen Identity is strongly related to self-reported past participation (Muhlberger, 2005a).

A substantial literature suggests that right-wing authoritarianism (RWA) adversely affects citizenship (Muhlberger, 2011b). People high in RWA are less knowledgeable about important social facts, less politically active, and embrace forms of governance that minimize democratic input. RWA is measured with a shortened four-item scale with good factor properties (Muhlberger, 2011b), including such questions as "Obedience and respect for authority are the most important virtues children should learn." FCC Confidence was measured with an adapted government confidence question, "I approve of the way the Federal Communication Commission has been handling its job lately." Procedural Justice was captured with two questions adapted from Tyler's (2006) work, such as, "I have confidence that the Federal Communication Commission will take seriously the concerns of people like me."

RESULTS

We first explore the data to understand how engaged student participants were in the deliberation. This helps clarify expectations regarding the presence and size of deliberation effects, particularly relative to the engaged public of actual rulemakings. Second, we examine participant evaluations of the deliberation, the legitimacy of deliberative and FCC policy decisions, and evaluations of the DiFA technologies. These evaluations help clarify how participants experienced the deliberation, including their perceptions of deliberative quality. Third, we present results regarding the comparability of the comparison and experimental groups. With greater comparability, the comparison group can be relied upon to rule out the history and maturation threats to internal validity. Fourth, we present findings regarding pre- to post-discussion changes in policy knowledge, policy attitudes, and various indicators of engagement and citizenship, which may be strengthened via the deliberation. Finally, we consider whether participants who received more votes in the MuLD condition were more capable or engaged.

Engagement

One important consideration to put the current results into context is the degree to which participants in this study were engaged with the deliberation process. If students were highly engaged with the topic, we might expect to find more substantial effects of the deliberation, but, if not, weak or undetectable effects might be expected. Ideally, participants would either come to a deliberation interested in the topic or develop an interest during the discussion process.

A good measure of how engaged students were with the deliberation topic is how many times they posted. They were told that they would get class credit for participating, but only if they posted at least five thoughtful posts responsive to others on the bulletin board. Thus, a student seeking to do the bare minimum of work for the extra credit would post five times or perhaps a little more to provide some cushion in case the researchers decided that some of the posts did not qualify as thoughtful. We will examine only those students who posted two or more times because these students will be considered the group that deliberated in subsequent analyses. Participants who never posted cannot be said to have deliberated, and we will ignore those who posted only once because they constitute a gray zone.

Among participants who posted two or more times, 69% posted five or fewer times, thus either achieving the bare minimum requirement or less. Eighty-six percent posted six or fewer times, and 93% posted seven or fewer times. The vast preponderance of students, then, did not do more than the minimum amount of work, plus a small margin of one or two extra posts, likely to help insure they would receive extra credit. Few of the participants were sufficiently engaged in the process to suggest self-sustaining interest. This leads us to anticipate weak effects.

Table 2. Averages of participant evaluations of deliberation and of technologies, with t-tests

Variable	Mean (*s.d.* of mean)	Scale Range
Satisfaction with Discussion	1.00*** (.10)	-3 to 3
Future Participation Motivation	.77*** (.12)	-3 to 3
Reevaluated Assumptions	1.22*** (.10)	-3 to 3
Impact Should Have On Officials	3.79*** (.11)	0 to 6
Impact On Officials – No Agree	3.54*** (.10)	0 to 6
Respect FCC	.22 (.13)	-3 to 3
Email Links	.94*** (.18)	-3 to 3
Word Cloud	.65*** (.17)	-3 to 3
Question Answer System	.62*** (.16)	-3 to 3
Multi-Level Deliberation	.33* (.14)	-3 to 3

Notes: *N*=121 for all non-technology evaluation questions. *n*=63 for Email Links, Word Cloud, and Question Answer System, and *n*=38 for Multi-Level Deliberation. The mean is the mean value for each variable across all participants. *t*-tests are used to determine whether this mean is significantly different than zero—that is, whether respondents have significantly positive evaluations.

* is *p*<.05, two-sided; *** is *p*<.001, two-sided based on single-sample t-tests.

Evaluations

A weak but not ignorable form of evidence regarding the value of deliberation is participants' own evaluations of the experience. Table 2 shows a variety of evaluations participants in this project gave of the deliberations, the legitimacy of the deliberations, and of the technologies used. Included are the mean evaluation, standard deviation of the mean, information on whether the evaluation was significantly different than zero, and the scale of the variable. The full sample of 121 was used for all non-technology evaluations (other than MuLD). The technology evaluations could only be considered for those who were in the technology conditions, cutting the sample to 63. MuLD was tested on only 38 participants, so the numbers reflect only their responses.

The deliberation experience received modestly positive evaluations that are highly significantly above zero. General satisfaction and perceived reevaluation of assumptions due to the deliberation hover at or above one on a -3 to 3 scale. Motivation to participate in future deliberations averages to a modest but positive value (.77). The legitimacy of the proceedings appears

to be quite substantial. Respondents believe that government officials should take into account the deliberation's conclusions about the network neutrality at a moderate level (3.79), where 0 means the officials should ignore the deliberation results and 6 means official choices should be determined by the deliberation results. A second legitimacy question, in which the respondent was instructed to imagine that they personally disagreed with the deliberation results still shows only a slightly diminished legitimacy level. When asked whether they would respect an FCC decision opposed to their own wishes on the net neutrality issue, respondents average a small value (.22) on a -3 to 3 Likert scale—not significantly different than zero. While the scale is not strictly comparable to the legitimacy scales, it does appear the respondents privilege the outcome of a deliberation, even one that takes a position in opposition to their preferences, above that of an FCC decision contrary to their preferences.

Respondents evaluated the technologies and the MuLD deliberation design from modestly favorable to very modestly favorable, but nonetheless positively and quite significantly so. Email links to possible posts of interest were viewed most favorably, followed by the word cloud and QA system, and, least favored (but still positively favored), the MuLD deliberation design. The order of preference might be in terms of familiarity in prior experience.

Comparability of the Comparison Group

This study includes, as described earlier, a non-experimental comparison group—students who completed the first survey but never posted to the bulletin board. These students were asked to complete the post-discussion survey. While this comparison group is not a perfect control group, because it is self-selected and conceivably some of its members were exposed to some of the experimental manipulation, as online readings or exposure to messages about the discussion, they nevertheless may help build a case against some threats to internal validity.

To address the concern of self-selection, it is helpful to determine to what extent this non-discussant comparison group is self-selected. Does it differ significantly from discussants? In t-tests of differences on an array of variables, there were no significant or trend differences on: gender, ethnicity (Caucasian / non-Caucasian), need for cognition, citizen identity, or confidence in the FCC. There were non-significant trend differences ($.05 < p < .10$) on network neutrality attitude and knowledge, with discussants showing mildly more opposition to network neutrality (-.34 vs. -.06 on a 7-point scale, a difference of 4% of the scale range) and mildly more knowledge about the issue (3.74 vs. 3.41 on an 8-point scale). There were two significant differences. Discussants were modestly further along in school ($p=.02$, two-sided; 3.22 vs. 2.81, where 1=freshman, 2= sophomore, etc.) and had slightly higher levels of active citizenship ($p=.03$; 1.54 vs. 1.27 on a 7-point scale or 3.9% of the scale range). Besides the possibility that some of these differences may be due to chance variation across a substantial number of indica-

tors, it is implausible that such small differences between these two groups could account for significant outcome differences between the groups. For example, active citizenship might account for somewhat more learning among a split-half of people high in active citizenship compared to the half low in this quality, but the impact these differences have on learning is small even where both groups are exposed to an intensive learning environment (Muhlberger & Weber, 2006c). With only a 4% scale difference in active citizenship between discussants and non-discussants in the current study, it seems unlikely that the observed differences would noticeably affect outcomes.

Deliberation Outcomes

Table 3 shows the impact of the deliberation conditions on the average *change* in various outcome variables from the pre- to post-discussion surveys. Three discussion conditions were tested: no-technology and no MuLD, technology and no MuLD, and technology and MuLD. Due to limited sample size and the group nature of the data, MuLD was added on top of the technology condition rather than tested both with and without technology. The intercept indicates the average change in the outcome variable ("Change in Variable") among discussants in the no technology and no MuLD condition. Subsequent coefficients indicate what needs to be added to the intercept to obtain the average change of the outcome variable in that column's condition. For example, the average change in policy knowledge for non-discussants is .34 - .43 = -.09—or effectively zero. Also, discussants in the technology and MuLD condition had an average change of citizen identity of .22 - .33 + .41 = .30. Ideally, the intercept adjustment for non-discussants would be significant and of the opposite sign of the intercept (average change due to deliberation). This would indicate that discussants and non-discussants have significantly different average changes, suggesting that the deliberation manipulation had an effect that cannot

Table 3. Ordinary least squares regressions of post- minus pre- outcomes on deliberation conditions with cluster-robust standard errors

Change In Variable	Intercept (Avg. Change Due to Deliberation)	Intercept Adjust for Non-Discussants	Intercept Adjust for Technology Exposure	Intercept Adjust for Multi-Level Deliberation	N; R^2; s.e.
	Coefficient (standard error)				
Policy Knowledge	.34* (.17)	-.43* (.21)	-.03 (.23)	.15 (.22)	184;.044; 1.46
Policy Attitude	-.58*** (.11)	.22† (.17)	.13 (.15)	-.16 (.27)	184;.146; 1.22
Active Citizenship	.21** (.08)	-.34** (.13)	.04 (.15)	-.05 (.15)	184;.040;.93
Citizen Identity	.22** (.07)	-.03 (.15)	-.33* (.15)	.41** (.14)	184;.057;.90
Right-Wing Authorit.	.05 (.05)	-.12 (.08)	.05 (.08)	-30** (.09)	184;.035;.70
FCC Confidence	.29* (.13)	.05 (.19)	-.02 (.19)	-.03 (.19)	184;.027; 1.20
Procedural Justice	.11 (.14)	.09 (.21)	.02 (.19)	.10 (.19)	184;.054; 1.25

Notes: N=184 (deliberators plus comparison groups, N=121 and 63, respectively). Each row represents an OLS regression of the "Change in Variable" indicated in the left column on the conditions of deliberation listed in the remaining columns. The "Change in Variable" represents the difference in the variable from the pre-discussion to the post-discussion survey (post minus pre). The intercept is the constant for the model but also represents the average change in the outcome variable for participants in the no technology exposure and no multi-level deliberation condition. The remaining independent variables indicate what would have to be added to the intercept to obtain the average for that condition or combination of conditions. Reported R^2 values are corrected to include the variance explained by the intercept, which is an explanatory variable in this case. Each row of the table represents an OLS regression with the "Change in Variable" as the dependent variable and the remaining columns as independent variables. † is $p<.10$; * is $p<.05$; ** is $p<.01$, *** is $p<.001$. All p-values are two-sided, except for the non-discussant coefficient, which is expected to be in the opposite direction from the discussant coefficient and is therefore reported as one-sided. Errors are cluster robust (accounting for covariation of errors within discussion groups) and were estimated in R.

be dismissed as due to threats to internal validity such as history or maturation—for example, news events between the pre- and post-discussion surveys that may have resulted in a significant change in responses (history) or maturation of participants in this time period resulting in changes (maturation). This represents a higher standard of evidence than has been typical of deliberation research—that is, it is more difficult to establish both a change in the experimental group and no change in the comparison group. Because of imperfections of the comparison group—we cannot rule out that the group did not experience some of the experimental manipulations—it is possible for there to be real changes that will not be identified by this high standard.

Policy knowledge and active citizenship show the ideal pattern. Both show significant changes from pre- to post-surveys among discussants and also significantly less change for the comparison group. This provides strong evidence of an effect not clouded by potential internal validity threats.

Policy attitudes also significantly changed and the change for the comparison group was less but only shows trend significance. Citizen identity shows a significant improvement for discussants, though the value also appears to improve for the comparison group.

In general, this deliberation shows significant changes similar to those found in many face-to-face deliberations, particularly knowledge increases, attitude change, and some evidence for enhanced future citizenship, here measured as active citizenship and citizen identity. In addition, in contrast to literature critical of deliberation that predicts deliberation will undermine confidence in government, the evidence here regarding confidence (in the FCC) and procedural justice (the FCC respects and takes seriously the views of people like the respondent) indicates that these variables either show no change or significant improvement.

Technology exposure and exposure to MuLD does not increase objective knowledge nor change policy attitudes, contrary to expectations. Such exposure does appear to have some impact on variables that seek to capture future engagement and citizenship potential. Technology exposure significantly reduces citizen identity. Exposure to MuLD significantly counteracts the effect of technology on citizen identity and significantly decreases right-wing authoritarianism, an effect that may be beneficial for citizenship.

The Best and the Brightest

One of the hopes for MuLD is that the representatives elected by group members to represent the group at higher levels will be more knowledgeable and capable than the average group member. In effect, MuLD would allow leaders to emerge from among discussants and raise the level of discussion. Alternatively, critics might claim that those elected will overrepresent the already socially dominant. To test these hypotheses in the current study, ordered probit analysis was used to regress the number of votes each discussant received on the discussant's internal and external efficacy, network neutrality policy knowledge, active citizenship, citizen identity, need for cognition, political interest and demographics (university class level, gender, ethnicity, and family income). None of these variables show a significant impact on number of votes, even at trend levels of significance ($p<.10$).

DISCUSSION

This project sought to address a little studied issue—the feasibility of technology-enabled deliberations as regular rather than one-off processes in government. In particular, we tested the use of Natural Language Processing (NLP) technologies in the context of citizen deliberation of a federal rulemaking issue—whether the Federal Communication Commission should adopt a network neutrality rule requiring Internet Service Providers to treat all internet traffic equally. The federal and state agency rulemaking processes, which typically require public comment by law, promise a substantial, if underused, arena for direct public input into government in the U.S. We tested a deliberation under conditions that would likely prevail were such deliberations to become regular parts of the rulemaking process involving substantial numbers of geographically dispersed participants—namely, online discussion without facilitators, who are costly and unlikely to be available in substantial quantity. Such a test expands the meager research on online deliberation and the largely non-existent literature on deliberation in the absence of trained facilitators. Our hope was that a combination of NLP technologies, forming a Discussion Facilitation Agent (DiFA), would cover some of the functions of facilitators.

The results provide suggestive evidence for the value of online deliberation in the absence of facilitation. Participants gave significantly positive evaluations of the deliberation and its quality as well as of the NLP technologies tested (Table 2). With respect to legitimacy, participants believed that officials should moderately take into account the comments and outcomes of this deliberation—even supposing they personally did not agree with those comments and outcomes. On the other hand, they indicated little or no respect for unilateral FCC decisions running contrary to their personal views. For government agencies struggling to make decisions the public perceives as legitimate, this finding suggests some value in agencies using deliberative fora to enhance decision legitimacy. An interesting question for future research is whether members of the public who hear about an agency-held deliberation, rather than participating in it directly, will perceive the agency decision as more legitimate.

Importantly, this study finds significant pre- to post-discussion changes in a variety of deliberation outcome indicators that have been taken as the hallmarks of successful face-to-face deliberations with facilitation in prior research (Table 3).

Policy knowledge increases and policy attitudes systematically change. Two indicators of enhanced citizenship and likely future participation, Active Citizenship and Citizen Identity, show significant improvement. Also confidence in FCC decisions increases.

The current study improves on much past research by including a comparison group of participants who completed pre- and post- surveys but failed to post to the discussion. This non-discussant comparison group does not differ from the discussant experimental group in most respects. The two significant differences between the groups are small in size. On the other hand, it is conceivable that non-discussants were exposed to components of the experimental manipulation. They may have read some background materials on the topic of discussion or viewed some of the discussion. They were exposed to the "minimal manipulation" of being asked to consider themselves as part of a citizen deliberation on the issue. Still, the non-discussant group diverged significantly or nearly significantly from the experimental group on three of the five significant changes in outcomes. For policy knowledge and active citizenship, the non-discussant group showed significantly less change than the discussant group. For policy attitude change, the discussant group showed trend significance for less change than the discussant group. For these outcomes, then, there is some reassurance that history and maturation threats to internal validity likely can be discounted.

With respect to two other variables, Citizen Identity and FCC Confidence, the comparison group did not significantly differ in pre- to post-discussion change from the experimental group. Conceivably, the observed change in the comparison group might be wrought by the "minimal manipulation"—simply contemplating themselves in the role of citizen deliberator may have resulted in changes in both experimental and control groups. This, plus the merely trend significance on policy attitude change, indicate that

deliberation research may benefit from utilizing comparison or even control groups.

These significant outcome changes as well as positive evaluations are encouraging for the prospects for online deliberation in rulemaking. Nonetheless, it must be noted that, while positive, evaluations were not exuberant and outcome changes were small. Possibly, being online rather than face-to-face reduced the quality of the experience. Looming perhaps more heavily over this project was the low enthusiasm of the student participants, who showed little sign of self-sustaining interest in the deliberations beyond that required for receiving course extra credit.

The citizens who might volunteer to participate in an online deliberation in a real agency rulemaking would likely be more engaged with the issue of discussion. On the other hand, there remains the question of whether these citizens would take to online discussion as readily as college students. The longer-term trend, however, is for the public to become increasingly facile in the use of online technologies. More broadly, the citizens who participate in agency rulemakings are typically middle-class and well-educated, which suggests that voluntary rulemaking participants may not be less responsive, for reasons of education, to deliberation than our subjects. They may, instead, be rather more motivated because they self-select for interest in the rulemaking topic.

Certainly, researchers should seek to test online deliberation in real rulemakings. We sought to do so, but encountered widespread reluctance from multiple federal and state agency offices as well as more than 100 public interest groups—we suspect because citizen-based politics threatens established power brokers and power relationships (Muhlberger, Stromer-Galley, & Nick Webb, 2011). Perhaps the results of the current study will add to the weight of evidence suggesting agencies should consider such efforts. While the positive effects here were small, with more engaged participants those effects should be larger. Also, even small effects over large numbers of participants and repeated episodes of deliberation could help create a more informed and engaged public that grants agency decisions greater legitimacy. Perhaps as well, technologists should pay more attention to creating NLP applications that help agencies intelligently deal with their substantial information load from public comments, thus encouraging agencies to buy into these efforts.

Disappointingly, our NLP technologies had no significant effects on policy knowledge, policy attitudes, agency confidence, or perceived procedural justice. Also, with two of three indicators of improved citizenship the technology experimental condition had no significant effect. With respect to a third indicator, Citizen Identity, the technology condition showed a significant negative effect, though at only the .05 level. Perhaps this is a fluke consequence of looking at multiple indicators. There remains the concern, however, that something about the availability of the technology blocked the positive impact of deliberation on the centrality of citizenship to personal identity. Conceivably, NLP technologies that answer questions may give people less reason to consult others for information, thus reducing the stress on citizenship. Also, technologies that connect participants discussing similar topics might form subgroups of more like-minded individuals, again reducing opportunities to perceive a common citizenship. Either of these concerns would require additional research to establish firmly. Still, they suggest that technologists should be cautious about unintended consequences in complex social contexts. The MuLD technique more than reverses the negative impact of the technology, so it is possible to combine features to avoid negative effects.

Perhaps, the NLP technologies could have a positive effect with more engaged participants. In addition, improvements to the technology that would better help facilitate discussion may enhance positive effects. A full Discussion Facilitation Agent would include a variety of other technologies such as: summarization; argument maps; suggestions for additional lines of discus-

sion (for instance, summarizing the main points of a more successful discussion); feedback on discussion quality, possible miscommunication, and relevance; and requests that silent participants state what they think. Such functionality is within reach of existing NLP software, though such software would likely have to be tailored to and tested within the context of political discussion.

NLP technology could also be built to help agencies better cope with the large volume of public comments. Specifically, this includes an ability to highlight, list and potentially summarize all the arguments made in the deliberation. For instance, semantically similar comments could be clustered together to present an overview of all key points in the discussion. Along the same lines, software could classify the aspects of the discussion into the main areas covered during the deliberation. Finally, as previously indicated, technologists can apply polarity detection mechanisms commonly seen in opinion mining (Wiebe, Wilson, & Cardie, 2005) to determine the sides taken by participants in a deliberation. This would aid in automatically creating groups or units based either on similarity of opinion, or ensuring smaller groups reflect all opinions—as intended in MuLD.

Finally, the results here provide evidence for two positive effects of the MuLD technique. MuLD reverses the adverse effect of technologies on Citizen Identity. MuLD also significantly reduces right-wing authoritarianism, which has a number of negative effects on citizenship. MuLD did not result in more engaged participants being chosen to represent each group nor did it enhance policy knowledge, policy attitude change, or perceived legitimacy. These were the main effects expected, thus again suggesting that the low engagement of study participants may have insured minimal impacts of MuLD. The two significant effects observed may be "minimal manipulation effects." That is, simply by having participants undergo the MuLD technique, the researchers are suggesting that such arrangements and what they imply are normatively desirable. By directly electing their own leaders, MuLD participants may have inferred that authorities are chosen and thus should not be blindly obeyed—mildly undermining authoritarianism. Also, the MuLD election mechanism stresses the role of the participant as part of a collective, perhaps thereby enhancing Citizen Identity.

The results here are preliminary in nature with respect to the implications of citizen e-deliberations as a tool of government. This study presents various dimensions and measures of evaluation and outcomes that may be fruitful for such work. The results suggestive of impacts of minimal manipulations indicate that technologists and deliberation designers must be careful regarding the implications that participants might draw from their designs. In general, the findings here are sufficiently encouraging to recommend continued work in this area, particularly work with real agency rulemakings.

ACKNOWLEDGMENT

This material is based upon work supported by the National Science Foundation under Grant No. 0713143. We would like to thank Brian Tramontano and Mike Ferguson, who were our able assistants at the University at Albany, and the faculty at Texas Tech and the University at Albany who allowed us to recruit students in their classrooms.

REFERENCES

Barabas, J. (2004). How deliberation affects policy opinions. *The American Political Science Review*, *98*(4), 687–701. doi:10.1017/S0003055404041425

Benhabib, S. (1994). Deliberative rationality and models of democratic legitimacy. *Constellations (Oxford, England)*, *1*(1), 26–52. doi:10.1111/j.1467-8675.1994.tb00003.x

Bohman, J. (1996). *Public deliberation: Pluralism, complexity, and democracy*. Cambridge, MA: MIT Press.

Campbell, D. T., Stanley, J. C., & Gage, N. L. (1966). *Experimental and quasi-experimental designs for research*. Chicago, IL: R. McNally.

Chambers, S. (1996). *Reasonable democracy: Jurgen Habermas and the politics of discourse*. Ithaca, NY: Cornell University Press.

Dryzek, J. S. (2002). *Deliberative democracy and beyond: Liberals, critics, contestations. Oxford Political Theory*. Oxford, UK: Oxford University Press.

Endenburg, G. (1998). *Sociocracy: The organization of decision-making*. Delft, The Netherlands: Eburon.

Farrar, C., Fishkin, J. S., Green, D. P., List, C., Luskin, R. C., & Levy Paluck, E. (2010). Disaggregating deliberation's effects: An experiment within a deliberative poll. *British Journal of Political Science, First View*, 1-15.

Fishkin, J. S. (1997). *The voice of the people: Public opinion and democracy*. New Haven, CT: Yale University Press.

Gastil, J., Black, L. W., Deess, E. P., & Leighter, J. (2008). From group member to democratic citizen: How deliberating with fellow jurors reshapes civic attitudes. *Human Communication Research*, *34*(1), 137–169. doi:10.1111/j.1468-2958.2007.00316.x

Gutmann, A., & Thompson, D. (1996). *Democracy and disagreement*. Cambridge, MA: Harvard University Press.

Hardy, H., Shimizu, N., Strzalkowski, T., Liu, T., Zhang, X., & Wise, G. B. (2002). Cross-document summarization by concept classification. *SIGIR 2002: Proceedings of the 25th Annual International ACM SIGIR Conference on Research and Development in Information Retrieval*, August 11-15, 2002, Tampere, Finland (pp. 121-128).

Luskin, R. C., Fishkin, J. S., & Jowell, R. (2002). Considered opinions: Deliberative polling in Britain. *British Journal of Political Science, 32*(3), 455–488. doi:10.1017/S0007123402000194

Muhlberger, P. (2005). *Democratic deliberation and political identity: Enhancing citizenship.* International Society of Political Psychology 28th Annual Scientific Meeting. Toronto, Ontario.

Muhlberger, P. (2007). *Report to the Deliberative Democracy Consortium: Building a deliberation measurement toolbox.*

Muhlberger, P. (2011). (Manuscript submitted for publication). Stealth democracy: Authoritarianism and democratic deliberation. *Political Psychology.*

Muhlberger, P., Stromer-Galley, J., & Webb, N. (2011). *Public policy and obstacles to the virtual agora: Insights from the deliberative e-rulemaking project.* Information Polity.

Muhlberger, P., & Weber, L. M. (2006). Lessons from the Virtual Agora Project: The effects of agency, identity, information, and deliberation on political knowledge. *Journal of Public Deliberation, 2*(1), 1–39.

Pivato, M. (2007). *Pyramidal democracy.* Retrieved from http://mpra.ub.uni-muenchen.de/3965/1/MPRA_paper_3965.pdf

Price, V., & Cappella, J. N. (2002). Online deliberation and its influence: The electronic dialogue project in campaign 2000. *IT & Society, 1*(1), 303–329.

Schweiger, D. M., Sandberg, W. R., & Ragan, J. W. (1986). Group approaches for improving strategic decision making: A comparative analysis of dialectical inquiry, devil's advocacy, and consensus. *Academy of Management Journal, 29*(1), 51–71. doi:10.2307/255859

Small, S., & Strzalkowski, T. (2009). HITIQA: High-quality intelligence through interactive question answering. *Journal of Natural Language Engineering: Special Issue on Interactive Question Answering, 15*(1), 31–54.

Stromer-Galley, J., & Muhlberger, P. (2009). Agreement and disagreement in group deliberation: Effects on deliberation satisfaction, future engagement, and decision legitimacy. *Political Communication, 26*(2), 173–192. doi:10.1080/10584600902850775

Tyler, T. R. (2006). *Why people obey the law (illustrated edition.).* Princeton University Press.

Webb, N. Hepple, M., & Wilks, Y. (2005). Dialogue act classification based on intra-utterance features. *Proceedings of the AAAI Workshop on Spoken Language Understanding.*

Webb, N., & Ferguson, M. (2010). Automatic extraction of cue phrases for cross-corpus dialogue act classification. *Proceedings of the 23rd International Conference on Computational Linguistics (COLING-2010).* Beijing, China.

Wiebe, J., Wilson, T., & Cardie, C. (2005). Annotating expressions of opinions and emotions in language. *Journal of Language Resources and Evaluation, 39*(2-3), 165–210. doi:10.1007/s10579-005-7880-9

Zillig, L. P., Herian, M., Abdel-Monem, T., Hamm, J., & Tomkins, A. (2010). Public input for municipal policymaking: Engagement methods and their impact on trust and confidence. *ACM International Conference Proceeding Series: Proceedings of the 11th Annual International Digital Government Research Conference* (Vol. 292, pp. 41-50).

Chapter 3
Records Management, Privacy, and Social Media:
An Overview

Staci M. Zavattaro
University of Texas at Brownsville, USA

ABSTRACT

This chapter provides an overview of United States federal policies guiding citizen/government interaction on social media tools. Such an overview begins to fill the gap regarding how federal agencies make policies regarding records retention and privacy on these platforms. Records management, inherently linked with privacy concerns, also will be explored to further ground the argument and future recommendations based on a qualitative content analysis of social media policies from three U.S. government agencies. From analyzing these policies, along with bringing in relevant literature, a workable framework and recommendations emerge to guide future social media use within government.

INTRODUCTION

Many United States (U.S.) federal government agencies including the Department of State, Environmental Protection Agency (EPA) and Department of Defense (DoD) appear on social media websites. All three, for example, have presences on Facebook, an online social networking hub that allows users to be friends with or fans of people, products, places and more. Posts on State's Facebook page feature videos of Secretary of State Hillary Clinton's travels throughout the globe. A department-run weblog, akin to a digital journal, appears as a link on the Facebook page. "Friends" from anywhere in the world post replies on the State Department's Facebook page. The Environmental Protection Agency's Facebook page lists everything from organization position

DOI: 10.4018/978-1-4666-0318-9.ch003

openings to news updates to tips for improving personal and global environments. On the Department of Defense's Facebook page, there is a regular series called Warfighter Wednesday that highlights exemplary service members, along with pictures and news of latest DoD happenings. Each of these pages represents official communications from a government agency, similar to memoranda, meeting notes and electronic mail. The challenge facing government agencies using social media platforms is maintaining and archiving digital records produced on social media platforms, as well as maintaining personal privacy of social media followers. This chapter, then, explores the questions: How are federal agencies codifying records retention in social media policies? How are federal agencies codifying privacy requirements in social media policies?

The genesis for this chapter and research questions came from one Florida city, Coral Springs, that asked the state attorney general for legal counsel regarding records maintenance and retention before using social media platforms. To do so, the city sent a query to the state attorney general. In the letter, city legal counsel asked for guidance concerning public records, records retention and open meetings laws (McCollum, 2009). In answering the question, then-State Attorney Bill McCollum advised that, yes, content placed on the page is likely in accordance with state statutes regarding public records and official business. Therefore, records must be maintained according to the regular retention schedule. Further, if elected officials communicate on the page, such communication could represent a violation of the state's laws governing open meetings (McCollum, 2009). "Thus, to the extent that the information on the city's Facebook page constitutes a public record, the city is under an obligation to follow the public records retention schedules established by law" (McCollum, 2009, p. 2). After receiving this opinion, the city then became the state's benchmark for launching social media presences.

Though a city government spurred the idea for the chapter, exploring state public records laws and schedules such as in Florida would prove unwieldy and, ultimately, unhelpful, as each state in the U.S. has differing requirements and legislation. Therefore, attention turned toward the U.S. federal government where the playing field is more level, with federal agencies subscribing to the same set of (complicated yet related) laws. The purpose of this chapter, then, is to answer the research questions posed above by exploring social media guidance from three government agencies: Department of State, Department of Defense, and Environmental Protection Agency. Qualitative Media Analysis (Altheide, 1996) was used to find overarching themes and trends regarding records retention and privacy within department social media policies, Terms of Service agreements, and social sites themselves. Coupled with records management and privacy scholarship, the content analysis led to a workable framework for public administrators exploring social media technologies and how to manage records and privacy associated with such ventures. Moreover, unexpected patterns emerged, including directing people to other sources and proper branding of social media sites, so these trends also were included in final recommendations.

I should be clear at the outset that I am not a certified records manager, nor am I an attorney. What is presented here is not meant to be construed as legal advice in any way. Administrators venturing into social media technologies are strongly encouraged to consult legal counsel for clearer, case-specific advice. That acknowledged, the chapter proceeds with a brief overview of social media and the link to citizen participation. Next comes an overview of records management and privacy regulations at the federal level before detailing the three U.S. federal agencies listed above and their social media policies. The final section offers the results of the content analysis and a workable framework for practitioners exploring or even currently using social media.

BACKGROUND

The emergence and acceptance of digital government meant access to agencies 24 hours a day, 7 days a week. Most of these initial adopts used platforms also referred to as e-government portals, Web 1.0 or Government 1.0, which focused largely on one-way information and service delivery online (West, 2004). In other words, governments put information (meeting times/places, events, happenings, etc.) and services on the web and let people interact in an exchange-based manner, such as paying a fee online, applying for a building permit, reporting a pothole, etc. Government 1.0 included one-way communicative devices, with the agency pushing out information and having site users intake that information as they saw fit.

One-way platforms are making way to increasingly dialogic, interactive media choices within government, though the process is still developing. West (2004, p. 17) identified four stages of e-government transformation: "(1) the billboard stage; (2) the partial-service delivery stage; (3) the portal stage, with fully executable and integrated service delivery; and (4) interactive democracy with public outreach and accountability enhancing features." The first phase essentially is government using its web presence much like "highway billboards" (p. 17), leaving out two-way interaction. Government information is put out and consumed as is. In the second stage, citizens get slightly more interactivity, with the ability to search and parcel information. Transforming from this stage into the third gives rise to "fully executable and integrated online services" (ibid, p. 17). Finally, the fourth phase brings about citizen-government interactions. In this fourth phase, citizens can customize government websites, access information when and how they want, comment on government information, and interact with each other and administrators. It is in this fourth phase where social media should come into play. Social media platforms online that encourage user creation and co-creation of information and knowledge

should have realized this fourth phase of website interactivity, though research still is emerging on whether citizens engage in meaningful ways (Brainard & McNutt, 2010; Bryer, Forthcoming).

As citizens become more interconnected, they expect more from governments online, including interactive and participatory features West (2004) describes – e-mail, comments, complaints, search functions, government events/meetings online, etc. "E-government is no longer viewed as the simple provision of information or services via the internet but as a way of transforming how citizens interact with government and how government interacts with itself" (Rose & Grant, 2010, p. 26). Social media platforms, with inherent interactivity and co-creative capabilities, are now seen as the way to push governments toward achieving improved citizen-government interaction and, thus, increasing citizen participation. Social media, then, are viewed as Web 2.0 technologies, showcasing how static, one-way interactivity, though still in existence, are not the main foci within today's interactive society.

But what are social media? Within the federal government, the U.S. Federal Web Managers Council defines social media as tools which "[integrate] technology, social interaction, and content creation, using the 'wisdom of crowds' to collaboratively connect online information. Through social media, people or groups can create, organize, edit, comment on, combine, and share content" (Federal Web Managers Council, 2011, para. 1). It is through this definition that social media are joined to West's (2004) fourth phase of online government evolution – dialogic and interactive. Social media include a variety of platforms, most aimed at increasing integration and collaboration. Examples of social media include web publishing (blogs, wikis, Twitter, etc.), social networking (Facebook, LinkedIn, Social Life, etc.), and file sharing (Flickr, YouTube, Google Docs, etc.). "A key commonality between these technologies is their interactive nature. Content owners post or add content, but the audience also has the ability to contribute content" (National Archives and Records Administration, 2010, p. 5).

Utilizing social media platforms is seen as a way to increase citizen participation, government transparency and, perhaps, reduce corruption (Bertot, Jaeger & Grimes, 2010). The idea behind open government initiatives at the federal level is to improve quality of government information, institutionalize open government, and put government information online (McDermott, 2010). Each federal agency is required now to have an Open Government Plan in place to comply with President Obama's dictate to make government operations less mysterious and more transparent. "Using the internet to promote transparency is reasonable, not only in terms of the technological capacity, but also because it meets expectations of many members of the public" (Jaeger & Bertot, 2010, p. 372).

Keeping and maintaining paper records and digital records in the name of transparency and openness brings about its own challenges; social media adds another level to that process. Interactions online, permits filed digitally, water bills paid electronically – all these Web 1.0 operations produce records agencies must keep and store. Web 2.0 platforms also produce public records in terms of, say, blog posts, agency status updates on Facebook, Twitter posts, and more. Digital records usually mean digital electronic records management, which is different than traditional paper records maintenance. "Whereas the essential characteristics of paper records – content, structure and context – are clearly evident, this is not the case with e-records," (Mnjama & Wamukoya, 2007, p. 277). The authors continue, noting that an effective electronic records management system must embody elements of comprehensiveness, authenticity and fixity. By the first, the authors mean that essential information should be present about the document – who created the record and why (p. 277). Authenticity refers in this instance to maintaining the integrity of records, tracking who touched them, when, why and what they did

with them. Finally, fixity is keeping the record's integrity and not altering it in any way (Mnjama & Wamukoya, 2007). With social media, maintaining these vital characteristics is challenging because content is rapidly changing. The question remains how often an agency should capture socially generated records.

FEDERAL INFORMATION POLICY, RECORDS MANAGEMENT AND PRIVACY

Federal Information Policy: A Brief Overview

Before thinking about properly maintaining records, public organizations should know what constitutes a public record, how to keep that record and for how long, and when to destroy the record. Furthermore, practitioners also must be aware of privacy laws and protections in place that still apply to use within social media. In the United States, the U.S. Code dictates what constitutes a federal record. According to Title 44, section 3301, records include "all books, papers, maps, photographs, machine readable materials, or other documentary materials, *regardless of physical form or characteristics,* made or received by any agency of the United States Government under Federal law or in connection with the transaction of public business and preserved as appropriate for preservation by that agency…" (44 U.S.C. 3301, emphasis added). Furthermore, section 2901 of Title 44 defines records management as "planning, controlling, directing, organizing, training, promoting, and other managerial activities with respect to records creation, records maintenance and use, and records disposition…" (44 U.S.C. 2901). Section 3601 of the same Title applies to electronic government services, which include government agencies using web-based applications to enhance service and information delivery to citizens (44 U.S.C. 3601). The government's

Chief Information Officer ensures digital records are kept and disposed of properly. As social media come into play, records management is extended to those platforms as well, as the *type* of record does not matter, as long as it constitutes official documents from the federal government. The National Archives and Records Administration (NARA) remains the lead agency to give guidance regarding records management. Each individual federal agency, however, remains in charge of maintaining its own records.

Records management goes through a cyclic process: "creation, receipt, maintenance, use, disposition, accessioning, preservation and access" with records management coming in "*at the end* of the life cycle" (Sprehe, 2000, p. 14, emphasis in original). Because of its placement at the end of the so-called life cycle, records management is often neglected or forgotten (Sprehe, 2000). Record keeping is essential to the proper functioning of any organization. Records are kept for continuity, organizational knowledge, and to establish official procedures and precedents. Essentially, agencies keep records "because they believe they may need to access to records" (Sprehe, 2000, p. 15) for information, not simply to hang onto records because of a legal mandate.

In addition to the above-named statutes, other federal legislation (see Smith, Fraser & McClure, 2000 for examples), advisories and agencies govern records and privacy, including, but not limited to: Privacy Act of 1974; Government Performance and Results Act of 1993; Paperwork Reduction Act of 1995; Information Technology Management Reform Act of 1996; e-Government Act of 2002, Executive Order 13011; NARA; and the Office of Management and Budget. Other pieces of legislation related to federal information policy include the Freedom of Information Act and the Presidential Records Act of 1978 (Franks, 2010). The Freedom of Information Act governs availability of public records and guarantees public access to such information. The Presidential Records Act of 1978 details how presidential documentation

and records are maintained and made available. All these various pieces of legislation work together to created federal information policy.

It should be noted that, "it is a misnomer to discuss 'Federal Information Policy' as if it were an established system, because there is no single codified corpus of laws, regulations, guidelines, or judicial opinions on the topic of information policy" (Smith, Fraser & McClure, 2000, p. 275). Again, the above list is not exhaustive but gives an overview of the myriad avenues that govern federal records and records management. Each law or directive (save for the agencies) is briefly summarized here.

Privacy Act of 1974

The Privacy Act of 1974 does just as the name indicates – guarantees privacy for individuals by ensuring that any information released about them is the minimum necessary to accomplish the purpose of the records request. The act "codif[ies] principles of fair information use which agencies must meet in handling information, as well as rights for individuals who are subjects of that information. To ensure agency compliance to these principles, the Act enables individuals to bring civil and criminal suits if information is willfully and intentionally handled in violation of the act." (Regan, 1986, p. 629)

With social media, anything a person posts to his or her profile is public to that person's online network. Government cannot control what a person posts, so agencies grapple with guaranteeing privacy rights to online "friends" or "followers."

Government Performance and Results Act of 1993

Movement toward streamlined, efficient government took hold in the U.S. with the passage of the Government Performance and Results Act of 1993 (GPRA). The act (retooled in 2010) established performance measurement at the federal level and implemented mandatory strategic planning processes to achieve said goals. The idea was to better connect government with customer needs. The GRPA created additional records for federal agencies to keep – strategic plans, performance reviews, etc. As the digital revolution came into play, one way to connect with the government's customers and follow provisions of GPRA was through electronic means – instant feedback surveys, comments, etc. Again, these digital communications produce public records that agencies need to maintain.

Paperwork Reduction Act of 1995

This legislation meant to reduce waste within organizations of all types, including the federal government. At its core, the Paperwork Reduction Act aimed to reduce redundancies of information the federal government collects from people, as well as codifying proper maintenance, retention and disposal of federal records (44 U.S.C. 3502). The law also established the Office of Information and Regulatory Affairs within the Office of Management and Budget (OMB) to monitor the law's implementation. The office's administrator provides advice and assistance to the U.S. Archivist concerning records management, as well as oversees records management policies and principles concerning records in general and electronic records (44 U.S.C. 3504).

Information Technology Management Reform Act of 1996

Also called the Clinger/Cohen Act, the Information Technology Management Reform Act was part of the Defense Authorization bill that year and "introduced sweeping changes to federal information technology (IT) management by establishing agency chief information officers (CIOs) and calling for agencies to better manage IT by improving efficiency and effectiveness of IT in a range of government operations" (Smith,

Fraser & McClure, 2000, p. 275). The act also mentions performance reviews and the ability to use IT to see if the agency is achieving its performance goals (40 U.S.C. 11313).

E-Government Act of 2002

Passed in 2002, this act established the Office of Electronic Government within the Office of Management and Budget to improve government operations and interactions with citizens (or customers in the language of GPRA) by going online. The act required each federal agency head to establish and maintain an online presence, including the Supreme Court and lower courts. Little guidance is offered within the text of the legislation relating to records management, save for a mention of relevant U.S. Code sections, such as those referenced above, that must be followed. Either way, the act made it mandatory for federal agencies to create and maintain a digital footprint, which has now evolved into using social media platforms to enhance connectivity.

Executive Order 13011

Issued July 16, 1996, this Executive Order reaffirmed the federal government's commitment to a strong IT infrastructure. The order links federal legislation, including the GRPA, Paperwork Reduction Act and the Clinger/Cohen Act. In the order, cross-agency collaboration is stressed (section 4), along with using technology to achieve an agency's strategic directives (section 1) (Clinton, 1996). The order also "formalizes oversight of IT management by stressing the importance of performance-based planning and implementation of Federal IT" (Smith, Fraser & McClure, 2000, p. 275).

Moves toward Transparency

President Obama ushered in a renewed sense of transparency in government. To that end, the president issued a memo in 2009 relating to transparency and open government (Obama, 2009). In the memo, he called upon government to become more collaborative, interactive and, naturally, transparent. The OMB released several other memos relating to that directive. Specifically, some memos dealt with using social media to achieve a more open and transparent government. In an April 7, 2010 memo written by Cass Sunstein, the Office of Information and Regulatory Affairs (OIRA) administrator (OIRA is located within the OMB, as indicated above) at the time, guidance is given regarding social media as it relates to the Paperwork Reduction Act. Sunstein wrote that, "items collected by third party websites or platforms that are not collecting information on behalf of the Federal Government are not subject to the PRA" (Sunstein, 2010, p. 3). To illustrate, the Paperwork Reduction Act aims to minimize the amount of time people spend giving information to governments. According to the memo, several activities are excluded from falling under the PRA – general solicitations, public meetings and like items that are not information (Sunstein, 2010). Therefore, when someone posts to an agency's Facebook page or Twitter account, for example, that posting does not fall under the purview of information as the OMB defines because the person provided information voluntarily not at the behest of the government agency. (Twitter is what is known as a microblog site where users post updates in 140 characters or less.) If, for example, an agency posits a question for general discussion on its Facebook page and people respond, that counts as a general solicitation and is excluded from the PRA. Put differently, posts on many social media platforms do not count as official data-collection methods that would be subject to scrutiny aimed at reducing the public burden in providing such information.

In June 2010, then-OMB Director Peter Orszag released another memo concerning using third-party websites in federal agencies. Third-party websites relate directly to social media, as those platforms are naturally not government run but provided by said third party. In that memo, Orszag wrote about protecting privacy of those choosing to interact with the government on third-party websites. He further advised that agencies collecting information from the third-party websites should only collect that which is necessary regarding agency functioning (Orszag, 2010).

Records Management and Privacy: Meaning and Usage

All the laws, rules, regulations and recommendations discussed above make up part of federal information management policy. When government generates information, it must keep it for future agency use, as well as public use and scrutiny. "The ability to find, organize, use, share, appropriately dispose of, and save records – the essence of records management – is vital for the effective functioning of the federal government" (Powner, 2009, p. 4). Therefore, federal managers maintain records of all types. With the emergence and widespread embrace of social media, new records are created daily that also need preservation and retention.

According to National Archives and Records Administration officials, records management involves the "systematic control of the creation, maintenance, use and disposition of records" (National Archives and Records Administration, 2001, p. 1). Records also have what is called a life cycle, starting with creation/receipt, then maintenance/use, and finally disposition. NARA is but one component of federal records management; the General Services Administration spearheads efficiency regarding records management (44 U.S.C. 2904(b)). Effective records management is necessary for a top-functioning government (Sprehe, 2000; Sprehe, 2005) and pervades every aspect of governance, including but not limited to the judicial branch and discovery rules (Volonino, Sipior & Ward, 2007), food safety (Gessner, Volonino & Fish, 2007), risk management and cost savings (Sprehe, 2005), and knowledge sharing in communities of practice (Snyder, Wenger & Briggs, 2003).

On June 17, 2010, Carol Brock testified before a U.S. House committee regarding federal electronic records management. Brock, representing the Authority on Managing Records and Information (ARMA International), indicated that electronic records managers face several challenges. First, normal records management problems and issues do not go away; instead, issues migrate to the electronic realm. For example, she testified that "senior officials do not see records management as a vital agency function" (Brock, 2010, p. 1), despite indications otherwise from other government officials (see Powner, 2009). Second, technology challenges further complicate records management processes. Technology naturally changes quickly (the old saying is that as soon as you buy a computer and take it out of the box, it becomes obsolete). Records management must keep up with changing technology or founder in the agency's background. Brock identified several more challenges, including: unclear language governing what constitutes a federal record; limited staff resources; no imperative focus on records management; and lack of Chief Records Officers (Brock, 2010). Brock offered suggestions to improve electronic records management at the federal level: confirm and utilize benchmarks (including official policy guidance, as well as guidance from national associations); agency-wide commitment to records management; make NARA more visible and prominent within the government; and give NARA meaningful statutory authority (Brock, 2010).

Capturing digital records has been a learning process within the federal government. Digital records are as varied as a static e-mail to a dynamic satellite image or geographic information system (Powner, 2009). Naturally, the learning curve came when figuring out ways to capture digitally what was once paper, keeping in line with the Paperwork Reduction Act cited above.

Electronic records management (ERM) became its own field of practice. Social media fall under that general record-keeping purview. One problem with electronic records management "in federal agencies is that records management in general, let alone ERM, has not been an integral component of information technology (IT) planning and systems design" (Patterson & Sprehe, 2002, p. 308). Therefore, adequate training and agency integration is needed to ensure electronic records are captured and preserved (Patterson & Sprehe, 2002). Little policy and official guidance also makes it difficult to know which records to capture and when (Plocher, 1999).

To offer guidance, the Government Accountability Office released findings of a study concerning maintaining digital records (Powner, 2009). In that Congressional testimony report and statement, NARA originally proposed a program in 2001 to maintain digital archives. Such a system required hardware, software, and a vehicle for public access and information (Powner, 2009). Contracting with an outside company, NARA embarked upon an effort to maintain the growing number of federal records generated electronically. Full functionality is slated for 2012 (Powner, 2009), though delays occurred along the incremental implementation of the electronic records management system.

NARA also offered guidance concerning electronic records management, along with guidance in light of social media platforms. NARA noted that government agencies must maintain all documents that relate to carrying out the agency's mission, and this includes presences on the web. "It is NARA's view that much, if not all, documentation related to agency web site operations should be managed as Federal records. As such, they must be scheduled and can only be deleted with a NARA-approved disposition authority" (National Archives and Records Administration, 2005, p. 5). To that end, NARA listed types of digital footprints that should be kept: content pages; records generated through web interaction (forms filled out, for example); self-executing (graphics,

Java, etc.) and static (pictures, text) elements; program operation records; design records and blueprints; software information and more (see National Archives and Records Administration, 2005 for complete list). Like hard records, digital records also must maintain reliability, authenticity, integrity and usability (National Archives and Records Administration, 2005).

But what of social media? NARA released a 2010 bulletin from David Ferriero, U.S. Archivist as of this writing. In the bulletin (NARA Bulletin 2010-02), Ferriero wrote that "where and how an agency creates, uses, or stores information does not affect how agencies identify Federal records" (Ferriero, 2010, p. 1). He advised that while content created on social media sites does indeed indicate a federal record, provisions also govern maintaining duplicate records. If an agency uses Facebook to repost information it already released in, say, a press release, then maintaining as a record the repost on Facebook might not be necessary. He cautioned, though, that agencies still might have to worry about maintaining those non-records in compliance with federal law (see the NARA Code of Federal Regulations for more). Furthermore, Ferriero wrote that an agency "must ensure records management guidance is included in social media policies and procedures" (p. 1). The first step is to identify what constitutes a federal record relating to social media. Then, the agency decides what records retention and maintenance schedule to apply. He also suggested that agencies negotiate a records management clause in Terms of Service agreements to ensure records will exist even if the site shuts down or the agency chooses to remove its presence from the social media platform. These suggestions, then, made policies and Terms of Service agreements ripe for studying within this chapter's context.

Moreover, ARMA International created Generally Accepted Recordkeeping Principles®. GARP principles are accountability, integrity, protection, compliance availability, retention, disposition and transparency (ARMA International, 2009). Brock

(2010) recommended using GARP principles to guide overall electronic records management at the federal level. Franks (2010) took that a step further by linking GARP principles to social media. All citations in this following paragraph come from Franks (2010) unless otherwise noted or added. Regarding accountability, Franks recommended that records management rest with agency or department heads. Firm policies within organizations also must be set regarding social media use in general, along with retention of the socially derived records. The call for government transparency, Franks continued, also links to records retention. How those records are handled, along with types of comments permitted, should be made clear on the agency website and the social media site. Regarding the GARP principle of protection, Franks suggested designating certain people to be in charge of the agency's social media platforms. This way, messaging remains consistent. Finally, Franks advised tying retention and disposition of social media records to that of website records schedules to ensure fluidity and continuity from a records management perspective.

One problem the Government Accountability Office (GAO) identified with social media presences specifically was records management (Wilshusen, 2010). According to Gregory Wilshusen, Director of Information Security Issues for the GAO as of this writing:

Agencies may face challenges in assessing whether the information they generate and receive by means of these technologies constitutes federal records and establish mechanisms for preserving such records, which involves, among other things, determining the appropriate intervals at which to capture constantly changing Web content. The use of Web 2.0 technologies can also present challenges in appropriately responding to Freedom of Information Act (FOIA) requests because there are significant complexities in determining whether agencies control Web 2.0-generated content, as understood within the context of FOIA. (Wilsusen, 2010, p. ii)

Wilshusen (2010) continued, noting that initial difficult emerges when determining what exactly constitutes a record on social media. Even if a user generates the record, say a reply to an agency's Facebook post, that reply could constitute a federal record that needs preservation. The next challenge emerges when agencies have to preserve those digital records (Wilshusen, 2010), because "when information is collected via Web 2.0 technologies may not be clear" (p. 10). A third challenge regards compliance with the Freedom of Information Act (FOIA) noted above, which governs public access to federal information. Concerning social media, federal agencies might be unclear regarding a FOIA provision regarding agency control and what constitutes a record available for public consumption. Overall, problems relate to determining what are records, how to manage those records, and how to access the records later.

Privacy concerns are inter-related to records management in general. Personally identifying information (PII) is present on government-kept records, and anyone accessing those records also can examine a person's information. Electronic government and social media platforms add another layer to this puzzle. As noted before, the Privacy Act of 1974 is meant to safeguard such personal information on federal government records. But what about privacy protections not expressly related to the records themselves? What about privacy related to engaging in the online forum or discussion? McCarthy and Yates (2010) looked at this very problem, explaining the use of so-called tracking cookies associated with many websites, including and especially social media. According to the authors, "these cookies would allow the user to set preferences or settings while at the same time provide information for the cookie owner to use analytics to provide better web sites or conveniences for the public" (p. 231). In other words, whatever the website user chooses to put

on the site, the platform owner (in this case the government, but think of corporations that give personalized recommendations of what to buy or see) uses that information to analyze data and understand users. Such digital gatherings could indeed constitute federal records if above-mentioned legal conditions (i.e. – the definition of a record) are met. Overall, the federal government bans use of persistent tracking cookies (as of this writing), but has revisited implementing tracking cookies to allow users to customize experiences on federal websites and help administrators deliver better public services (McCarthy & Yates, 2010). Privacy is such a central concern that some scholars advocate creating a centralized privacy protection board for the federal government (Flaherty, 1984; Gellman, 1994; Jaeger, McClure & Fraser, 2002).

FEDERAL POLICIES: A CONTENT ANALYSIS

With federal agencies utilizing social media platforms, questions emerged regarding how those agencies are codifying privacy and records management, if at all. This chapter explores this question by examining documents from three government agencies that are prolific users of social media: State Department; Department of Defense; and Environmental Protection Agency. An online search for materials relating to social media policies from each of these agencies, along with Terms of Service (TOS) agreements and information from social sites themselves, specifically Facebook, were used within the analysis. The purpose of this content analysis is twofold: 1) to examine patterns within the policies, if any; and 3) to set the groundwork for recommendations presented in the conclusion. This section proceeds with brief overviews of the three departments selected (chosen because of their constant mentions as social media exemplars (Federal Computer Week, 2009)), then a presentation of content analysis findings.

The Three Departments

The State Department is the U.S. government's diplomatic arm, fostering ties with countries across the globe. Diplomatic relations in the U.S. date back to the American Revolution, with colonies sending people abroad to be colonial agents (Department of State, n.d.). As social and global conditions changed, so did the focus of the department. For example, during the time leading to the Civil War, expansion took place throughout the United States, and diplomatic efforts stepped up to foster and build the country's image abroad. Containment became the key priority, though, as the Cold War escalated.

The Department of Defense (DoD) is the government's branch responsible for overall national security. Both civilian and military personnel call this department home; according to the DoD's website, the 1.4 million men and women on active duty make this the nation's largest employer (Department of Defense, n.d.). DoD is as old as the U.S. itself, with the Army, Navy and Marine Corps created before the American Revolution. Though overall mission has remained the same since then: to provide for the national defense of the U.S.

Finally, the Environmental Protection Agency (EPA) is the agency charged with safeguarding the country's overall environmental health, including places and people. The EPA is the youngest federal agency under study, established in 1970 (Lewis, 1985) after conservation movements sprang up throughout the U.S. EPA initiatives and legislation include the Superfund law to clean up environmentally dangerous sites; the Clean Air Act to reduce and stop pollution; and various measures to tackle mercury emissions, water quality, air quality, recycling, etc. Essentially, anything environmentally related passes through this agency.

Content Analysis Process and Findings

The three cases are not meant to be blankets to cover the entire federal presence on social media platforms. Instead, each was selected based on pro-activity on the sites. The Department of Defense, for example, is perhaps one of the government's most prolific users of social media, even creating a social media hub on its webpage. Further, each of the agencies is listed as having the most followers on Facebook (Federal Computer Week, 2009). The methodology chosen was Qualitative Media Analysis, also called qualitative content analysis (Altheide, 1996). Qualitative Media Analysis (QMA) is a reflexive process that allows for research interaction with the documents, as well as research course correction along the way (if, for example, the original protocol is not working correctly). QMA also allows for patterns to emerge rather than looking for exact patterns at the outset. QMA includes 12 steps, each of which was followed here. The first step is to pick a problem to investigate (how federal agencies address privacy and records management in social media policies), then steps two and three are familiarizing oneself with the information source and choosing a unit of analysis, which are the agencies themselves. Steps four through six relate to drafting, testing and revising a research protocol. The protocol included introductory information, such as the agency being studied, and space for the relevant internet link. Some questions from the final protocol include:

1. How does this agency use social media?
    a. What sites are used?
    b. What media are selected?
2. Are there policies related to social media? If yes, provide link once again.
3. Are there mentions of records management within the identified policies?
4. Are there mentions of privacy within the identified policies?

5. How does the agency address records management? In other words, are policies express or short? What language is used regarding records management?
6. How does the agency address privacy? In other words, are policies express or short? What language is used regarding records management?
7. What other language appears often?

Using question seven allowed other patterns within the documents to emerge organically, as QMA recommends. Steps seven through nine in QMA involves collecting data, which in this case were the documents from each of the three agencies related to social media, as well as Terms of Service agreements. The social media sites themselves (Facebook) also were examined for mentions of policy provisions. To find documents related to social media, internet searches, as well as agency site searches, were done. An example of an internet search engine query included "State Department social media policy." Such a search was done because the policy was not easily found by looking at that agency's website, but the internet search turned up the policy in the first link. The Defense Department has its own social media page, as does the EPA, so information was taken from those sites. Links to relevant documents used within the analysis are provided in the Reference section of this chapter. Documents were collected from each site, saved digitally, then printed out. Different color bright markers were used to select language related to social media in general, records management, privacy and other language used often (branding, for example, emerged in this latter category). Notes within page margins also were made, as well as notes within the protocol, to give context to the language. For example, wording such as "expansive" was used when describing some records policies. The final three steps in QMA involved examining for outliers and reporting findings. No outliers emerged, and findings are reported within the chapter.

From that analysis, several findings emerged. The first two were expected because they were specifically search for, though the latter two emerged from the QMA and looking for patterns. Each is expounded upon below:

1. Records management gets attention in all agency policies, though the level of detail varies.
2. There are mentions of privacy and the Privacy Act of 1974, which shields peoples' personal information from public access.
3. Many of the policies refer readers to other agency policies, which could prove unwieldy.
4. Insistence on branding was evident in each.

Records Management in All Policies

As noted, records management has express mention in all three agency social media policies. The *degree* to which records management is addressed, however, varied. Within the EPA's guidelines (Environmental Protection Agency, 2010), there are two sentences addressing records management. To contrast, State Department' social media s policy is contained in its Foreign Affairs Manual (FAM) portion titled 5 FAM 790 (Department of State, 2010). Within those 15 pages are policies guiding use and maintenance of social media platforms. The policy covers everything from personal use, to branding, to privacy, to records management.

EPA's social media guidance offers the following about records maintenance: "Agency records created or received using social media tools must be printed to paper and managed according to the applicable records schedule in a recordkeeping system" (Environmental Protection Agency, 2010, p. 2). It is unclear why digital records must be printed as paper then put through the records cycle. A standard electronic record system is in place (Luttner & Day, 2003), so it is unclear why this system cannot capture social media records in a digital matter.

Within the Department of State, Section 5 FAM 794 specifically addresses both content and records management (Department of State, 2010). Within that section, the department identifies and explicitly notes two types of records that could be created on most social media sites. The first are "content records including entries, comments, blog posts, links, videos, and other social media communications," while the second type of records are "site management and operations records including design, policy and procedures, and other web management records" (ibid, p. 11). The policy dictates that records management cycles must be followed for documentation that is indeed a federal record. For non-records, such as duplications posted on social media sites of information that exists elsewhere, a retention schedule will not apply. Furthermore, the department or its subsidiary (a foreign office, for example) decides how long content will stay on the social media site, though it also could be contingent upon the external site's policies as well. Within this area, the policy is fuzzy – do the social media site's retention timeline trump federal guidelines? Policy writers addressed this question by noting that storage or disposal of content that is archived or removed must be addressed within the Terms of Service agreements. Finally, the policy also suggests contacting the agency's Archives Management staff for guidance.

The Department of Defense does not have an official social media policy, *per se*. Instead, the DoD issued Directive-Type Memorandum 09-026 regarding using Internet-based capabilities, which include social media. The memo as a whole dictates social media use, and mentions records management in a paragraph in section four (Department of Defense, 2010). The paragraph is short, so it is duplicated here in full: "Internet-based capabilities used to transact business are subject to records management policy in accordance with Reference (h). All users of these Internet-based capabilities must be aware of the potential record value of their content, including content that may originate outside the agency" (ibid, p. 6). Reference H directs readers toward the DoD's policy on records management. That policy (Department of Defense, 2000), governs all records created within the agency, including digital records. Even that policy is vague regarding exact records procedures and does not mention social media because of the date (2000). The policy does say a record is a record no matter the medium used.

In sum, each policy found did mention records management expressly, but the EPA and DoD seemed to give the issue passing mention as compared to the State Department, which had explicit recommendations included specifically within the social media policy. A related pattern, discussed later, involved agencies referring readers to other legislation relating to records management.

References to Privacy Protection

The second pattern revealed was references to privacy protections within documents studied. With social media, users who "follow," "friend" or "fan" a site share personal information with the government entity. For example, if someone becomes a fan of the Department of Defense on Facebook, the popular social networking site, then whoever controls the Facebook page for the DoD can click on that follower's entire profile. Information on the page no longer is private.

According to the Government Accountability Office (2003, p. 5):

The Privacy Act of 1974 is the primary act that regulates the federal government's use of personal information. The Privacy Act places limitations on agencies' collection, disclosure, and use of personal information in systems of records. A system of records is a collection of information about individuals under the control of an agency from which information is actually retrieved by the name of the individual or by some identifying number, symbol, or other particular assigned to the individual. The act does not apply when there is merely a capability or potential for retrieval by identifier, which is often the case with electronic records.

With the advent of social media, another layer was added to Privacy Act protections. In each of the three agencies presented here, there is mention of privacy protections, either explicitly or implied, and either in official policies or on social media platforms themselves (as in EPA). For example, the DoD's Facebook page contains the following statement: "You participate at your own risk, taking personal responsibility for your comments, your username and any information provided" (Department of Defense, 2011, para. 9). Deconstructed, this means the agency is warning people that any information they share, or have on their personal pages, could become subject to public records and Freedom of Information requests. Within the DoD's social media guidelines (Department of Defense, 2010), there is only a passing mention that social media sites shall comply with DoDD 5400.11, which the is the Department's overall privacy policy. Turning to that document (Department of Defense, 2007), there is guidance on: system of records maintenance, what records and information can be kept, what information must be redacted or destroyed, how records are released, and information collected within Privacy Act requirements. As the policy is from 2007, there is no mention of social media and privacy relations specifically. The link, as noted, comes from the DoD's social media guidance's note that social sites will comply with Privacy Act requirements.

State Department's policy (Department of State, 2010) is clearer relating to privacy protections for users. Section 795.1 details privacy protections, noting that State social media sites must have Terms of Use policies notifying users about tracking cookies (applications that can track someone's Internet patterns), collection of personally identifiable information (PII), and the risks in posting PII on social media. If a user voluntarily posts information that is covered by the Privacy Act (Social Security Number, for example), then "the Department does not take responsibility for or ownership of this information. By default, the user has granted permission to the Department to see this information by joining the Department's social media site" (Department of State, 2010, p. 13). The extensive mention of privacy in this policy provides more detail that the DoD and EPA. Looking to the Department's Facebook page, a user can click the "Terms" button to find the Department's social media rules for that site. There, readers see a link to Facebook's own privacy policy, as well as Department narrative regarding keeping information private. The statement warns users not to share information beyond what already is posted on Facebook, though the same statement notifies users that the Department does not store any of that personal information. Such an activity would violate the Privacy Act.

Finally, EPA's social media guidance does not mention aspects of privacy or the Privacy Act. That policy largely governs who can post to social media on behalf of the EPA and how those users should represent themselves to the public. There really is no policy detailing what protections are in place for external users of the sites when they interact with EPA on social media. Clicking onto the EPA's Facebook page, one can select "Policies" to find how EPA governs itself on that platform. There is a link to the EPA's overall policy statement, which advises users to "be aware that the privacy protection provided on social media and third party sites that are not part of the epa.gov domain may not be the same as the privacy protection described here" (Environmental Protection Agency, 2010, para. 16).

Reference to Other Policies

The third pattern to emerge, which came organically through the QMA, was referencing other policies within social media policies. While reading through each of the three agency's social media policies, one must dig through other online sources to find the references being made in each policy, as none of the references included digital hyperlinks. For example, within the DoD policy, there is constant pushing people to other documents – 12 references appear in front of the document and are noted inside the guidance itself. DoD makes reference to policies governing privacy, records management, intelligence components, public affairs operations, computer networks and more. If someone (either a DoD employee or citizen concerned with information placement on social media) wants to gather specific information relating to, say, his or her privacy on DoD social media platforms, that person has to find the external document instead of receiving guidance in one place.

EPA provides readers with links to outside policies such as ethics standards, public information requirements, records management, and the department's social media blog. As the EPA's social media documents are found online, links are active and take readers directly to those sites. The State Department also makes reference to outside policies in its Foreign Affairs Manual, but that department's references include some brief explanation rather than writing "see policy X" without context. To wit, the document refers readers to 5 FAM 772 when dealing with protecting children in social media environments. 5 FAM 772 is State's privacy policies, which can be discerned from its explanation within the social media policy to "comply with applicable provisions of the Children's Online Privacy Protection Act of 1998" (Department of State, 2010, p. 13). Without context (such as the DoD example), readers of the social media policies could be unsure of what documents are referenced and why.

In sum, this pattern revealed that each of the social media policies studied sent users to other existing agency policies. Some, such as the EPA, provided easy hyperlinks. The DoD, to contrast, tells readers about other policies, then people are on their own to find them. State splits the difference by providing references to other policies

with context so readers can at least understand what policy is being referenced. State, though, also does not provide direct hyperlinks to these other policies.

Insistence on Branding

The final pattern to emerge was mentions of branding in the policies related to social media. Each government agency using social media recognizes that these platforms represent a visible, often-accessed front for citizens. Social media sites are extensions of their organizations' overall image. Maintaining said image is vital across all platforms to demonstrate consistency and have users know quickly that they are looking at on official government website. Branding is important, as it can build user satisfaction and cut down on search time (i.e. – Is this really an official department website?) (Chiang, Lin & Wang, 2008; Rowley, 2004).

EPA's guidance in this area (Environmental Protection Agency, 2010) encourages EPA employees to represent themselves and the agency in a professional, ethical manner. "It is important that you remember that you are participating in your official capacity and not in your personal capacity. Make sure that your online activities and online content associate with you while you are officially representing EPA are consistent with you job responsibilities at EPA" (ibid, para. 2). While the policy does not mention specific EPA logos or colors, it does urge its employees to act professionally to foster a positive image of the agency.

DoD guidance (Department of Defense, 2010) offers this brief statement: "Use official DoD and command seals and logos as well as other official command identifying material per ASD(PA) guidance" (p. 5). Here ASD(PA) refers to the Assistant Secretary of Defense for Public Affairs. Again, there is a reference to an external source – ASD(PA) guidance, though there is no document or place noted. It seems DoD social media administrators are to ask this person for direction on representing DoD correctly on social media sites.

Finally, State Department's policy (Department of State, 2010) makes brief reference to branding. Section 5 FAM 793 details branding policies, noting that "official Department social media sites and content must be clearly labeled and identifiable as such" (p. 7). The definition section of the policy elucidates what the department means by branding, which, in this case, is the use of official department seals or markings to let users know this is an official department website.

How does this carry over into practice? Looking at the Facebook pages of each organization, branding elements are present. To illustrate, the State Department's page has the official Department seal and a photo of current Secretary of State Hilary Clinton. The DoD's seal appears prominently on its page, as does the EPA's logo on its page. Brand elements are present, and much of the content posted to these pages would count as public relations material aimed at building and fostering an image (Moon, 2002) and limiting citizen-government interaction (Norris, 2010).

CONCLUSION

With the emergence and acceptance of social media within government, administrators have the ability to interact with citizens and the public rapidly and repeatedly. Citizens, for their part, have a sense of involvement with the agency. Web presences are seen as ways to build a positive organization-public relationship (Kent & Taylor, 1998). As social media change the way governments and people interact, traditional information procedures such as record keeping and privacy cannot be forgotten. This chapter examined social media at the federal level to see how three agencies – State Department, Department of Defense, and Environmental Protection Agency – understand and utilize records management and privacy protections within social media policies.

Records management in social media platforms is difficult (Franks, 2010), as there is uncertainty about what constitutes a record, how to capture that record, and process it through retention schedules (Wilshusen, 2010).

In terms of records management, each policy mentioned the process, but the degree varied, either in detail (State Department) or as a brief passing sentiment (EPA and DoD). Privacy protections were present in all policies, again to varying degrees. Referring to other agency policies means that within social media policies, readers are instructed to seek guidance elsewhere, making citizens do extra work. For example, when mentioning privacy, an agency might send a reader searching for a privacy policy already in place. In other words, existing policies were simply referenced instead of repeated, either in detail or briefly to foster reader understanding. Finally, branding elements were implicit or explicit in each policy to ensure continuity among all digital presences.

Based on policy patterns, as well as the scholarly literatures noted above, several recommendations are offered regarding social media implementation, records management and privacy. The recommendations can be useful for practitioners exploring social media platforms within government agencies, as well as public administration scholars who want to theoretically or empirically examine the suggestions. Recommendations could help practitioners draft social media plans and policies with express attention to records retention and privacy protections, the latter of which could go a long way toward ensuring citizens are comfortable interacting with government entities online.

1. Explicitly mention records management and privacy protections in detail within social media policies
2. Place records management and privacy language on the social media platforms directly
3. Provide links when offering outside sources within the social media policy

4. Develop social media brand standards specifically

The final two – providing links and developing branding strategies – are briefly expounded upon here. As noted above, a commonality of the social media policies studied as referencing other policies and procedures. There is no need to reinvent the wheel and develop entirely new policies, but this recommendation has two parts. First, within social media policies, agencies should not simply say: "Please refer to Policy X." Context is important; even adding a few sentences could assist those implementing the policies to implement them correctly. Second, links to those referenced sources should be provided on all digital documents. This way, someone interested in finding, say, the privacy policy referenced within the social media policy can click the link and go directly to that content area.

Developing brand strategies should go beyond the definitional and superficial to detail how exactly brands are depicted on social media sites. Again, agencies can take guidance from existing web-based branding policies, but social media platforms should have a uniform look congruent with the agency's website – and express policies to govern that look so citizens know they are indeed interacting with an official government site. Policies governing social media could answer questions such as: What is the agency's brand? What elements must be present to have users identify our brand? How often are those elements used, how and where? What is the policy on posting comments? What colors can be used? What fonts can be used (if there is a blog or some other media that allows for creativity)? These questions and more would expand branding mentions within existing social media policies, making them more than a sentence or definition.

Returning now to the first recommendation, records management was mentioned in each policy, though some policies were not clear enough regarding what exactly is a record, how

it is retained, then how it is managed. Therefore, government agency social media policies should mention records management *in detail*. This cuts down on administrator's time usage, as they do not have to go from policy to policy looking for help. Addressing the following questions could help administrators developing social media policies:

- What is a record? (Offer a brief version of the federal definition)
- What is *not* a record? (Offer a brief version of the federal definition)
- How does the agency capture the records (printing screen shots, digital capture, etc.)?
- How long are records maintained and where?
- Who is specifically in charge of maintaining these records? (Chief Information Officer, others)
- What is the records schedule? (Periods of storage, deletion, etc.)
- How can the public access the records? (Freedom of Information Act)

Answering these questions would go a long way toward addressing challenges of records management in social media others have identified (Franks, 2010; Wilshusen, 2010). Furthermore, privacy protections must also come to the level of detail recommended for records management language. Some policies mentioned privacy protection in fleeting ways, or referred readers to other policies. Again, this could be corrected with an explicit detailing of privacy protections afforded users of social media, as well as potential pitfalls of participating in a social media setting and losing that privacy. (The Department of Defense did with its explanation on its Facebook page that participants participate at their own risk.)

As to the second recommendation, it is suggested that agencies place records retention and privacy language on social media platforms themselves. This can be achieved in several ways.

First, once the agency has its overall social media policy in place, that can be easily placed as a link or PDF file on the social media sites. Any content such as this should be placed in an obvious location. For example, the government sites studied here have links to policies or terms of use on the Facebook pages. On other platforms, similar links and spaces can be provided. If that overall social media policy contains, as suggested, a detailed accounting of records management and privacy procedures, then agencies are covered with this recommendation. Users might not be aware that information they voluntarily post to the site is likely subject to public records law because of its presence on an official government website. Though no personally identifiable information is allowed to be used (the Privacy Act of 1974 prevents that), people still need to be aware of how their posts are read, maintained, stored and destroyed. There is a possibility a person's comment can be used (again without his or her name) off the site – such is the nature of social media.

Additionally, social media administrators should look carefully at Franks' study (2010) for further suggestions. Franks advised establishing a Chief Records Officer for the federal government; implementing extensive records training; and integrating records management into information technology infrastructure. At the core, Franks (2010) advocated for elevating records management to an essential governance function that deserves express, lasting attention, not just another side job.

FUTURE RESEARCH DIRECTIONS

Literature on social media in public administration is still developing, and this book certainly does a long way to fill that gap. All one has to do is log onto any U.S. federal government agency website to know these organizations are indeed using this technology. Anecdotally, the White House's webpage has a space called Stay Con-

nected with links to Facebook, Twitter, YouTube, Flickr, MySpace, Vimeo, iTunes and LinkedIn, all various social networking and file-sharing sites to showcase citizen engagement. The mere presence of so many sites shows the importance social media re taking in the U.S. federal government – as well as the importance of understanding how social media are used.

From the perspective of records management, work still remains both practically and theoretically. As noted, Franks (2010) provided a nice foundation for tackling records management issues in the public sector. This chapter, too, scratched the surface by looking for how *policies* address records management and privacy. One avenue for future research is to speak with practitioners to gather best practices for records management policies regarding social media to develop a realistic, workable benchmark that tackles this issue. The scholarly community can do the same by examining existing literature, in-place best practices, and melding the two to develop something workable. A related study would be asking practitioners about best practices regarding privacy protections.

A second future research endeavor could include longitudinal studies of government agencies implementing social media records management and privacy policies. To illustrate, a researcher could examine existing records management policies and tools used before social media implementation, then examine how the policies/procedures changed through time. In addition, charting the amount of records generated via social media platforms through time would be another study. Just how often do citizens engage? How? Why? When? For what use? What happens with the comments? Finally, a researcher could implement some of the suggestions in this chapter then examine how those work in practice.

There are many other research paths to undertake regarding social media within public administration in general – privacy, ease of use, accessibility, citizen participation, administrator/personnel time devoted to platform maintenance, quality of citizen participation, citizen engagement versus participation, and more. Some research suggestions might be time consuming at the outset, such as providing digital hyperlinks to cited policies, or beefing up policies in place to expressly address records management. If accessibility and transparency are key goals of embracing social media, those same goals and values should apply to the organization's entire public face.

REFERENCES

Altheide, D. L. (1996). *Qualitative media analysis*. Thousand Oaks, CA: Sage Publications.

ARMA International. (2009). *Generally accepted recordkeeping principles*. Retrieved from http://www.arma.org/garp/garp.pdf

Bertot, J. C., Jaeger, P. T., & Grimes, J. M. (2010). Using ICTs to create a culture of transparency: E-government and social media as openness and anti-corruption tools for societies. *Government Information Quarterly*, *27*(10), 264–271. doi:10.1016/j.giq.2010.03.001

Brainard, L., & McNutt, J. G. (2010). Virtual government-citizen relations: Informational, transactional or collaborative? *Administration & Society*, *42*(7), 836–858. doi:10.1177/0095399710386308

Brock, C. (2010). *Testimony of Carol Brock, Certified Records Manager on behalf of ARMA International*. Retrieved from http://democrats.oversight.house.gov/images/stories/Hearings/Information_Policy/06.17.10_Electronic_Records/061510_IP_Carol_Brock_061710.pdf

Bryer, T. A. (in press). Public participation in regulatory decision making: Cases from Regulations.gov. *Public Performance and Management Review*.

Chiang, I., Lin, C., & Wang, K. M. (2008). Building online brand perceptual map. *Cyberpsychology & Behavior*, *11*(5), 607–610. doi:10.1089/cpb.2007.0182

Clinton, W. J. (1996). *Executive Order 13011 of July 16, 1996*. Retrieved from http://www.cio.gov/documents/federal_it_jul_1996.html

Department of Defense. (2000). *DoD records management program*. Retrieved from http://www.defense.gov/webmasters/policy/dodd50152p.pdf

Department of Defense. (2007). *Department of Defense privacy program*. Retrieved from http://privacy.defense.gov/dod_regulation_5400.11-R.shtml

Department of Defense. (2010). *Directive-type memorandum (DTM) 09-026 – Responsible and effective use of Internet-based capabilities*. Retrieved from http://www.dtic.mil/whs/directives/corres/pdf/DTM-09-026.pdf

Department of Defense. (2011). *Department of Defense info*. Retrieved from http://www.facebook.com/home.php#!/DeptofDefense?sk=info

Department of Defense. (n.d.). *About the Department of Defense*. Retrieved http://www.defense.gov/about/

Department of State. (2010). *5 FAM 790: Using social media*. Retrieved from http://www.state.gov/documents/organization/144186.pdf

Department of State. (n.d.). *A short history of the Department of State*. Retrieved http://history.state.gov/departmenthistory/short-history/origins.

Disposal of Records. 44 U.S.C. § 3301. (2006).

Environmental Protection Agency. (2010). *Privacy and security notice*. Retrieved from http://www.epa.gov/epafiles/usenotice.htm

Federal Computer Week. (2009). *Top 10 agencies with the most Facebook fans.* Retrieved from http://fcw.com/articles/2009/09/14/government-facebook-friends-list.aspx

Federal Web Managers Council. (2011). *Types of social media.* Retrieved from http://www.howto.gov/social-media/social-media-types

Ferriero, D. S. (2010). *Guidance on managing records in Web 2.0/social media platforms.* Retrieved from http://www.archives.gov/records-mgmt/bulletins/2011/2011-02.html

Flaherty, D. H. (1984). The need for an American privacy protection commission. *Government Information Quarterly*, *1*(3), 235–258. doi:10.1016/0740-624X(84)90072-8

Franks, P. (2010). *How federal agencies can effectively manage records created using new social media tools.* Retrieved from http://www.businessofgovernment.org/sites/default/files/How%20Federal%20Agencies%20Can%20Effectively%20Manage%20Records%20Created%20Using%20New%20Social%20Media%20Tools.pdf

Gellman, R. M. (1994). An American privacy protection commission: An idea whose time has come… again. *Government Information Quarterly*, *11*(3), 245–247. doi:10.1016/0740-624X(94)90043-4

Gessner, G. H., Volonino, L., & Fish, L. A. (2007). One-up, one-back ERM in the food supply chain. *Information Systems Management*, *24*(10), 213–222. doi:10.1080/10580530701404561

Government Accountability Office. (2003). *Privacy act: OMB leadership needed to improve agency compliance.* Retrieved from http://www.gao.gov/new.items/d03304.pdf

Information Technology Management and Reform Act of 1996. 40 U.S.C. §11313. *(2006).*

Jaeger, P. T., & Bertot, J. C. (2010). Transparency and technological change: Ensuring equal and sustained public access to government information. *Government Information Quarterly*, *27*(4), 371–376. doi:10.1016/j.giq.2010.05.003

Jaeger, P. T., McClure, C. R., & Fraser, B. T. (2002). The structures of centralized governmental privacy protection: Approaches, models and analysis. *Government Information Quarterly*, *19*(3), 317–336. doi:10.1016/S0740-624X(02)00111-9

Kent, M. L., & Taylor, M. (1998). Building relationships through the World Wide Web. *Public Relations Review*, *24*(3), 321–334. doi:10.1016/S0363-8111(99)80143-X

Lewis, J. (1985). *The birth of EPA.* Retrieved from http://www.epa.gov/history/topics/epa/15c.htm

Luttner, M., & Day, M. (2003). *Electronic records and document management system.* Retrieved from http://epa.gov/records/policy/erdms-memo.htm

McCarthy, L., & Yates, D. (2010). The use of cookies in Federal agency web sites: Privacy and recordkeeping issues. *Government Information Quarterly*, *27*(3), 231–237. doi:10.1016/j.giq.2010.02.005

McCollum, B. (2009). *Advisory legal opinion AGO 2009-19.* Retrieved from http://coralsprings.org/fb/Advisory%20Legal%20Opinion%20-%20Records,%20municipal%20facebook%20page.pdf

McDermott, P. (2010). Building open government. *Government Information Quarterly*, *27*(4), 401–413. doi:10.1016/j.giq.2010.07.002

Mnjama, N., & Wamukoya, J. (2006). E-government and records management: An assessment tool for e-records readiness in government. *The Electronic Library*, *25*(3), 274–284. doi:10.1108/02640470710754797

Moon, M. J. (2002). The evolution of e-government among municipalities: Rhetoric or reality? *Public Administration Review, 62*(4), 424–433. doi:10.1111/0033-3352.00196

National Archives and Records Administration. (2001). *Frequently asked questions about records management in general.* Retrieved from http://www.archives.gov/records-mgmt/faqs/general.html

National Archives and Records Administration. (2005). *NARA guidance on managing Web records.* Retrieved from http://www.archives.gov/records-mgmt/pdf/managing-web-records-index.pdf

National Archives and Records Administration. (2010). *A report on federal Web 2.0 use and record value.* Retrieved from http://www.archives.gov/records-mgmt/resources/web2.0-use.pdf

Norris, D. F. (2010). E-government 2020: Plus ça change, plus c'est la meme chose. *Public Administration Review, 70*(Supplement), S180-S181. McDermott, P. (2010). Building open government. *Government Information Quarterly, 27*(X), 401–413.

Obama, B. (2009). *Memorandum for the heads of executive departments and agencies: Transparency and open government.* Retrieved from http://www.whitehouse.gov/the_press_office/TransparencyandOpenGovernment/

Orszag, P. R. (2010). *Guidance for agency use of third-party websites and applications.* Retrieved from http://www.whitehouse.gov/sites/default/files/omb/assets/memoranda_2010/m10-23.pdf

Paperwork Reduction Act of 1995. 44 U.S.C. §3502. *(2006).*

Paperwork Reduction Act of 1995. 44 U.S.C. §3504. *(2006).*

Patterson, G., & Sprehe, J. T. (2002). Principal challenges facing electronic records management in federal agencies today. *Government Information Quarterly, 19*(10), 307–315. doi:10.1016/S0740-624X(02)00108-9

Plocher, D. (1999). The digital age: Challenges for records management. *Government Information Quarterly, 16*(1), 63–69. doi:10.1016/S0740-624X(99)80016-1

Powner, D. A. (2009). *National archive: Progress and risks in implementing its electronic records archive initiative.* Retrieved from http://www.gao.gov/new.items/d10222t.pdf

Public printing and documents. 44 U.S.C. § 2901. (2006).

Public printing and documents. 44 U.S.C. §3601. (2006).

Records management by the archivist of the United States and by the Administrator of General

Regan, P. M. (1986). Privacy, government information and technology. *Public Administration Review, 46*(6), 629–634. doi:10.2307/976229

Rose, W. R., & Grant, G. G. (2010). Critical issues pertaining to the planning and implementation of e-government initiatives. *Government Information Quarterly, 27*(1), 26–33. doi:10.1016/j.giq.2009.06.002

Rowley, J. (2004). Online branding. *Online Information Review, 28*(2), 131–138. doi:10.1108/14684520410531637

Services. 44 U.S.C. § 2904(b). (2006).

Smith, B., Fraser, B. T., & McClure, C. R. (2000). Federal information policy and access to Web-based federal information. *Journal of Academic Librarianship, 26*(4), 274–281. doi:10.1016/S0099-1333(00)00128-2

Snyder, W. M., Wenger, E., & Briggs, X. D. (2003). Communities of practice in government: Leveraging knowledge for performance. *Public Management*, *32*(4), 17–21.

Sprehe, T. J. (2000). Integrating records management into information resources management in U.S. government agencies. *Government Information Quarterly*, *17*(1), 13–26. doi:10.1016/S0740-624X(99)00022-2

Sprehe, T. J. (2005). The positive benefits of electronic records management in the context of enterprise content management. *Government Information Quarterly*, *22*(2), 297–303. doi:10.1016/j.giq.2005.02.003

Sunstein, C. (2010). *Social media, Web-based interactive technologies and the Paperwork Reduction Act*. Retrieved from http://www.whitehouse.gov/sites/default/files/omb/assets/inforeg/SocialMediaGuidance_04072010.pdf

Volonino, L., Sipior, J. C., & Ward, B. T. (2007). Managing the lifecycle of electronically stored information. *Information Systems Management*, *24*(3), 231–238. doi:10.1080/10580530701404637

West, D. M. (2004). E-government and the transformation of service delivery and citizen attitudes. *Public Administration Review*, *64*(1), 15–27. doi:10.1111/j.1540-6210.2004.00343.x

Wilshusen, G. C. (2010). *Challenges in federal agencies' use of Web 2.0 technologies*. Retrieved from http://www.gao.gov/new.items/d10872t.pdf

ADDITIONAL READING

Baker, K. H. (1997). The business of government and the future of government archives. *The American Archivist*, *60*(2), 234–252.

Barry, R. (2004). Websites and recordkeeping and "recordmaking" systems. *The Information Management Journal*, *38*(6), 26–32.

Bozeman, B., & Bretschneider, S. (1986). Public information management systems: Theory and prescription. *Public Administration Review*, *46*(Special Issue), 475–487. doi:10.2307/975569

Cammaerts, B. (2008). Critiques on the participatory potentials of Web 2.0. *Communication, Culture & Critique*, *1*(4), 358–277. doi:10.1111/j.1753-9137.2008.00028.x

Caudle, S. L., Gorr, W. L., & Newcomer, K. E. (1991). Key information systems management issues for the public sector. *Management Information Systems Quarterly*, *15*(2), 171–188. doi:10.2307/249378

Chang, A., & Kannan, P. K. (2008). *Leveraging Web 2.0 in government*. Retrieved from http://www.businessofgovernment.org/report/leveraging-web-20-government

Chief Information Officer Council. (2009). *Guidelines for secure use of social media by federal departments and agencies*. Retrieved from http://www.cio.gov/Documents/Guidelines_for_Secure_Use_Social_Media_v01-0.pdf

Dawes, S. S. (2008). The evolution and continuing challenges of e-governance. *Public Administration Review*, *68*(Supplement 1), S86–S102. doi:10.1111/j.1540-6210.2008.00981.x

Department of Energy. (2010). *Managing social media records*. Retrieved from http://cio.energy.gov/documents/Social_Media_Records_and_You_v2_JD.pdf

Department of the Interior. (2010). *Notices – Social media policy*. Retrieved from http://www.doi.gov/notices/Social-Media-Policy.cfm

Gagnier, C. M. (2008). Millenial-generated change to American governance. *National Civic Review*, *97*(3), 32–36. doi:10.1002/ncr.222

Golub, B., & Jackson, M. O. (2010). Naïve learning in social networks and the wisdom of crowds. *American Economic Journal: Microeconomics*, *2*(1), 112–149. doi:10.1257/mic.2.1.112

Hoover, J. N. (2009). Government wrestles with social media records retention policies. *Information Week*. Retrieved from http://www.informationweek.com/news/government/policy/showArticle.jhtml?articleID=217700689.

Ind, N., & Riondino, M. C. (2001). Branding on the Web: A real revolution? *Brand Management*, *9*(1), 8–19. doi:10.1057/palgrave.bm.2540048

Jaeger, P. T. (2005). Deliberative democracy and the conceptual foundations of electronic government. *Government Information Quarterly*, *22*(4), 702–719. doi:10.1016/j.giq.2006.01.012

James, R. (2010). Records management in the Cloud? Records management IS the Cloud! *Business Information Review*, *27*(3), 179–189. doi:10.1177/0266382110377060

Kalish, B. (2010). Social media presence tests agency records management. *NextGov*. Retrieved from http://www.nextgov.com/nextgov/ng_20101220_1267.php

Kozinets, P. S. (2010). Access to metadata in public records: Ensuring open government in the Information Age. *Communications Lawyer*, *27*(2), 1–30.

Kundra, V. (2010). *25 point implementation plan to reform federal Information Technology management*. Retrieved from http://www.cio.gov/documents/25-Point-Implementation-Plan-to-Reform-Federal%20IT.pdf

Lamont, J. (2009). *Managing the Web 2.0 lifecycle*. Retrieved from http://www.kmworld.com/Articles/Editorial/Feature/Managing-the-Web-2.0-life-cycle--54976.aspx

McCarthy, L., & Yates, D. (2010). The use of cookies in federal agency websites: Privacy and recordkeeping issues. *Government Information Quarterly*, *27*(3), 231–237. doi:10.1016/j.giq.2010.02.005

McClure, D. L. (2010). *Statement of Dr. David L. McClure*. Retrieved from http://www.gsa.gov/portal/content/158009

Melvin, V. C. (2010). *Information management: Challenges of electronic records management*. Retrieved from http://www.gao.gov/new.items/d10838t.pdf

Rubin, B. M. (1986). Information Systems for public management: Design and implementation. *Public Administration Review*, *46*(Special Issue), 540–552. doi:10.2307/975576

Sprehe, J. T., & McClure, C. R. (2005). Lifting the burden. *Information Management Journal*, *39*(4), 47–52.

Swartz, N. (2008). A new ERA for NARA. *Information Management Journal*, *42*(3), 24–28.

Thomas, J. C., & Streib, G. (2003). The new face of government: Citizen-initiated contacts in the era of e-government. *Journal of Public Administration: Research and Theory*, *13*(1), 83–102. doi:10.1093/jpart/mug010

Web Content Managers Forum. (2010). *Terms of service agreements*. Retrieved from https://forum.webcontent.gov/Default.asp?page=TOS_agreements

Weinstein, A. (2005). NARA enters new "ERA" of electronic records management. *The Information Management Journal*, *39*(5), 22–24.

Welch, E. W., & Pandey, S. K. (2006). E-government and bureaucracy: Toward a better understanding of intranet implementation and its effect on red tape. *Journal of Public Administration: Research and Theory*, *17*(3), 379–404. doi:10.1093/jopart/mul013

KEY TERMS AND DEFINITIONS

Branding: Creating an identity for an organization and promoting that at each avenue.

Content Analysis: Using words to generate patterns within documents, in this case federal government policies.

E-Government: One-way, transactional presences of government organizations online.

Federal Records: Legally defined documents the United States federal government must keep and manage based on a set schedule.

Privacy: Right to protect personal information.

Records Management: The process by which agencies control hard and electronic records

Social Media: Two-way, transformational, collaborative platforms that allow for user content creation.

Chapter 4
Managing Virtual Public Organizations

Julianne G. Mahler
George Mason University, USA

ABSTRACT

The term virtual organization is used in the literature to describe a range of public and private online work settings from telecommuting in traditional organizations to sophisticated arrangements for project members in different institutions and multiple locations to share information and interact online on a joint undertaking. Though virtual governmental organizations are increasingly common, the management challenges they pose are only beginning to be studied. Here, an exploration of management process in these virtual settings begins by distinguishing among forms of virtual organizations based upon whether members represent single or multiple organizations and whether their contact is continuous or intermittent. While the literature on virtual organizations suggests that all virtual organizations will be decentralized and self-organizing, here, differences in the forms of virtual organization are expected to be associated with differences in management practices. Citizens are engaged by these new forms both as clients and as members, with a range of anticipated advantages. Primary and secondary case materials and published research on virtual organizations in the United States are used to answer questions about the use of information and communication technologies, the management of coordination, and leadership in two forms of virtual organizations. The differences found are not entirely as expected. Actual patterns of management are complex; both hierarchical and self-organizing managerial patterns can co-exist.

DOI: 10.4018/978-1-4666-0318-9.ch004

INTRODUCTION

The term virtual organization is used in the literature to describe a range of public and private online collaborative activities from telecommuting in traditional organizations to sophisticated arrangements for project members in different institutions and multiple locations to share information and interact online on a joint undertaking. When the work performed virtually is governmental, they represent another challenge for electronic public management. The Telework Enhancement Act signed by President Obama in 2010 encourages the use of virtual workplaces in the federal government, and other forms of virtual organizations are emerging as an important new institutional form of organization at all levels of government. Public safety and intelligence information is collected and shared securely among many U.S. agencies online. Citizen services are offered in some cases by a virtual network of state, local and non-governmental organizations, much as corporations like Amazon assemble businesses into virtual shops. In science and technology realms these arrangements combine government actors at the National Aeronautics and Space Administration (NASA), the Department of Energy and the National Oceanographic and Atmospheric Administration (NOAA), for example, with their partners in academia, non-profit organizations and the business world. They link government organizations with each other and with other institutions in funded and unfunded partnerships.

Though virtual governmental organizations are increasingly common, the management challenges they pose in practice are only beginning to be studied. While some research has been conducted on the potential advantages of virtual organizations and their management (Green and Roberts, 2010; Ahuja and Carley, 1999; Cascio, 2000) there is much more to be learned about "the basic organizational abstractions, communication models, trust mechanisms, and technology infrastructure required to form and operate effective

[virtual organizations] across a broad range of target domains" (National Science Foundation 2008, 7). This chapter aims to make a contribution by investigating two of the variety of forms of virtual public organizations and the ways in which they manage the coordination of work. What communication and information technologies are in use? Do managers use traditional hierarchical design and coordination logics, or do lateral, self-organizing principles dominate? How does leadership direction and culture management proceed in virtual settings? Answers to these questions even for a limited array of virtual organizations will help clarify the management challenges of virtual organizations and suggest hypotheses for future research about this increasingly common public organization form.

This chapter is concerned with the ways government agencies use Web 2.0 and other information and communication technologies to manage the agencies that provide public services. The use of web technologies within agencies to make telework and distributed work teams possible is the focus. Thus this chapter focuses mainly indirectly on the ways interactive web technologies serve and engage citizens. More specific ways that citizens are affected by these developments are discussed below.

DEFINING AND CLASSIFYING VIRTUAL ORGANIZATIONS

The virtual organization has been defined as "a geographically distributed organization whose members are bound by a long-term common interest or goal, and who communicate and coordinate their work through information technology (Ahuja and Carley, 1999, p.743). Common characteristics of all of the forms of virtual organization that fall under this definition are that members are separated by distance and time and interactions occur using a variety of communication and information technologies. These technologies may be as simple as telephone, email and fax, or they may rely on interactive, joint authoring techniques such as wikis. Alternatively, they may depend upon more sophisticated online meeting software that allow member to share desktop views or converse while viewing the same website. In some agencies teleconferencing and videoconferencing capacities permit members to hold webinars and collaborate in real time. Podcasts and Webcasts allow meeting events to be viewed later or archived for public access. As we see below, some communication in virtual organizations is carried out with highly specialized software systems designed to simulate laboratory collaboration conditions.

A close examination of the literature on virtual organizations reveals that a variety of quite different arrangements fall under this definition, however. Organizations that are termed virtual may be composed of workers from the same conventional organization, or they may include members from different organizations and different sectors working to collate information, advance research, or integrate public service elements. These organizations also vary in terms of the continuity of interactions. Some virtual organizations are ongoing collaborations among members, while others are more loosely confederated arrangements linked by informal understandings or formal contractual relationships that trigger cooperative action only when needed. Other forms of virtual organizations include those whose members seldom or never interact directly, but share access to data files to which they all contribute on a system maintained

by one of the partners. All of these organizational forms are increasingly common in the public sector, reflecting the growth of knowledge work and the need to access talents across traditional organizational boundaries as well as efforts to reduce energy and transportation costs and balance work-life commitments.

These differences among virtual organizations illustrate the range of entities collected under the term. A typology of these forms offers a first step in examining the ways that work is managed in these online environments. Distinguishing the patterns of contact among the members and whether the members belong to the same organization suggests four types of virtual organizations. These forms might be labeled: virtual workplaces, virtual multi-organizational teams, virtual enterprises, and virtual data libraries. Virtual workplaces use information technologies to link workers from the same organization who operate in different locations. They include distributed organizations with offices and workers spread around the world. Also included are telework arrangements in which employees perform some or all of their work from home or in technology-equipped centers apart from the central workplace. Virtual multi-organizational teams involve staff from different organizations, typically geographically distant, interacting on an ongoing basis on the same short or long term project. Virtual enterprises link workers from a network of different organizations who interact intermittently on an as-needed basis to serve clients. And, virtual data libraries are composed of

Table 1. Forms of virtual organization

	Forms of Organization:			
	Virtual Workplace	Virtual Multi-organizational Team	Virtual Enterprise	Virtual Data Library
Number of traditional organizations whose member participate:	One	Multiple	Multiple	Multiple
Contact patterns:	Ongoing	Ongoing	Intermittent	Intermittent/None

members from multiple organizations who share a mutually useful assembly of information and technology resources but may rarely or never interact directly.

Each of these forms is seen in government. Telework options at all levels of government constitute virtual workplaces, and are growing in response to commuting costs and the mandate to ensure continuity of operations in emergencies, among other pressures. Federal legislation in 2010 provides strong encouragements for telework arrangements. Virtual multi-organizational teams are particularly common in science and technology research (Finholt and Olson, 1997) as illustrated in the NASA's Astrobiology programs and the B-2 "Stealth" bomber design program described below. The management of collaboration in these two continuously interacting forms provides a good opportunity to observe managerial activity and is the subject of the analysis below. The other two forms, virtual enterprises and virtual data libraries, are also important emerging kinds of virtual organizational arrangements, and research on their management constitutes an area for future study.

Virtual enterprises are exemplified in some human services networks and intergovernmental public safety systems with intermittent, online collaboration. The architecture of the enterprise arrangements have been studied extensively for collaborating firms, and is portrayed as "a continually evolving network of independent companies—suppliers, customers, even competitors—linked together to share skills, costs and access to one another's markets" (Dess et al., 1995, p. 10). These enterprises may be ongoing but the episodes of collaboration are usually temporary and trust is essential to maintain the relationship (Blecker & Neuman, 2000). In the public sector, a similar architecture is found in some networks of public and private health and human service providers at the state level. These networks are emerging to create service delivery "switchboards" (Deloitte, 2009) that allow citizens to select service

through a central online portal, but behind these service portals are as-needed linkages among service providers, not continuous interaction or collaboration. Massachusetts' Virtual Gateway and ACCESS Florida are examples of steps toward this form (Deloitte, 2009). Syndication is another form of commercial online integration that packages services for distribution and manages the relations between originators of services and distributors such as might be offered for human services (Regio, 2002) on one-stop websites. A slightly different version of this form is the Capital Wireless Integrated Network, which links first responders and transportation authorities in Virginia, Maryland and Washington DC to handle regional emergencies (Fedorowicz, Gogan and Williams, 2006). The work of the network is not a continuous process, but wireless collaboration is initiated when needed.

Virtual Data Libraries are the creation of members from different organizations who contribute to the collection of information available to all of them In some cases, such as the World-Wide-Telescope project (Szalay and Gray, 2001) which compiles astronomical observations from many sites for the use of professionals and amateurs, the data are publically accessible. In other cases, such as Intellipedia (CIA, 2009), the CIA-supported wiki that allows agents from 16 intelligence organizations to compile information, the sites are highly secure. The site operates like Wikipedia with over 3,600 registered users contributing to what has become a collaborative effort to compile up-to-date information for the intelligence community. The aim is to avoid past barriers to the integration of information (CIO Central, 2006). Diplopedia offers a similar forum for the diplomatic community. The Environmental Information Exchange Network provides an online repository for the EPA and state environmental agencies to upload environmental data created in a variety of formats into a form that can be accessed by all the members, saving a great deal of redundant reporting. The eventual goal is to generate collaborative environmental policies and projects across the states (Mahler and Regan, 2010). Plans for even more integrated data sharing across science domains are in process (Butler, 2007). An extended form of these data compilations are grid virtual organizations, defined as a "set of resources (computers, storage systems), distributed among participating organizations, available for use by a group of users... under mutually acceptable governing rules" (Doyle 2003, p. 3). Thus there is a range of types of Virtual Data Libraries from relatively simple information banks to complex cloud computing arrangements.

EFFECTS ON CITIZENS

The impact of these arrangements on citizens is mainly indirect. Virtual workplaces provide more robust citizen contact in time of emergencies and extended work hours across time zones. They offer real improvements in convenience and access for the public using the services. Virtual enterprises support online portal entry points for services from taxation to social services and often provide improved coordination and coherency for services. Virtual multi-organizational teams and virtual data libraries are often associated with science and technology projects that offer opportunities for public education and participation. Each of the NASA-based virtual organizations described below have made special efforts to involve the public in their work as professional observers and as interested amateurs. Their websites have entry points for teachers and students. The Principal Investigators at the Astrobiology Institute volunteer to put on virtual symposia of their findings for the public to disseminate findings and spur interest in the work of the Institute. Other organizations at NASA and NOAA have created virtual worlds to introduce the public to the work of the agencies and to generate interest in science education. (http://www.nasa.gov/offices/education/programs/national/ltp/home/index.html and http://www.esrl.

noaa.gov/gsd/outreach/secondlife.html). NASA's Kepler project makes its findings available at several levels: for professionals and amateur observers under its guest observer program (http://keplergo.arc.nasa.gov/index.shtml). For students and amateur astronomers, the MY Kepler website allows observers to "to join NASA's search for habitable planets" (http://www.mykepler.com).

The public also benefits as part of the workforce of virtual organizations. Those members of the public who telework for virtual governmental organizations, for example, gain from the greater freedom of work time and place, and enjoy reduced commuting costs. These and other advantages are described in much greater detail below.

INVESTIGATING VIRTUAL ORGANIZATION MANAGEMENT

Two forms of virtual organization will be examined to answer questions about their management: virtual workplaces and virtual multi-organizational teams. The dimensions of managerial practice to be explored include: the kinds of communication and information technologies in use, the ways in which work coordination is achieved when workers are geographically distributed, and the role of leadership in directing work and managing culture and cohesion. By far the most literature is concerned with virtual workplaces and the advantages or management challenges associated with this form, especially now in the wake of the 2010 legislation encouraging telework. Much of the literature presupposes that virtual organizations will be non-hierarchical and self-organizing, emphasizing lateral coordination by committed, professional employees (Fountain, 2001) DeSantis and Monge assume as much when they define virtual organizations as "a collection of geographically distributed, functionally and/or culturally diverse entities that are linked by electronic forms of communication and rely on lateral, dynamic relationships for coordination"

(1999, p. 693). This may be an over-generalization more appropriate for some of the virtual forms than others, however. -

This research is designed to explore the possible differences in management practices associated with different forms of virtual organization. These preliminary findings from a small number of cases can then be used to build hypotheses for more systematic examinations of the differences among forms. The initial expectation that guides this inquiry is that virtual workplaces where workers are geographically dispersed but still under one organizational authority will largely share management processes with their traditional counterparts. Gulick (1936) famously identified these management tasks to include: planning, organizing, staffing, directing, coordinating, reporting and budgeting. There is of course a great deal of variety in the ways of undertaking these tasks (Rainey, 2009) from classical to contingent approaches. But the conventional approach is to rely upon hierarchical direction, rule-following, and centralization for coordination and direction. As noted above, much of the virtual organization literature assumes a decentralized, laterally-coordinating, self-organizing model of management generally. Here I suggest that this is more likely in virtual multi-organizational settings than in virtual workplaces.

Virtual multi-organizational teams (as well as virtual enterprises and data libraries) could be expected to look more as the literature on virtual organizations suggests they will. As noted above, some suggest that self organization (Galbraith, 1973) and auto-adaptive management (Comfort and Kapucu, 2006) would emerge, meaning that members would accept responsibility for solving problems, spontaneously assemble and share information, and learn from experience. Plowman et al. find that in complex, self organizing systems, "leaders enable rather than control the future" (2007, p.341) by encouraging innovation, disrupting conventional patterns and interpreting events to participants. An example of this pattern emerges in the cases below. Alternatively, virtual multi-organizational teams might look more like their inter-organizational network counterparts, with various forms of self-organization or direction by lead organizations in which participating organizations must deal with problems of managing organizational commitment, conflict resolution, governance and decision making (Milward and Provan, 2006). Settling questions of authority and legitimacy and resolving differences in priorities and goals among members from different organizations would require the negotiation of agreements and the establishment of new governance structures. However, these expectations might be tempered by Agranoff's findings regarding the management of networks. While acknowledging that networks are of necessity voluntarily self-organized and must depend on trust in the absence of a formal legal hierarchy (2007, p.230), he also finds that they do replicate many features of traditional organizations as described above. Thus there is real ambiguity in the literature about what the management of virtual organizations, especially as the distinct type identified here, would look like. This exploratory research begins to examine these ambiguities.

This investigation of the virtual organizations begins with an analysis of management practices in two forms of virtual organization: virtual workplaces and virtual multi-organizational teams because these forms are the most common and they illustrate the key difference between shared and separate organizational foundations. The detailed examination of virtual enterprises and virtual data libraries, both less common in the public sector and more difficult to isolate and investigate, is reserved for a future research project.

A variety of sources are used here. Published research, including results from a large-sample government survey, answer some of the questions posed here especially for virtual workplaces. Much less published research is available specifically on the management of virtual multi-organizational teams. Thus to answer questions about the management of this form, case studies and interviews with program staff are used. Two published cases of projects for U.S. military and aerospace engineering are examined, and two other examples are based on author interviews with management staff from two NASA research programs and documentation from those programs.[1] Science and engineering projects were selected because of the interest in the management of these types of virtual organizations (NSF, 2008) and because such projects typically involve multi-institutional partners and online work. The published cases were selected because of the level of detail they offered about work processes and the information about management they reported. The observations offered below are drawn directly from the cases as reported. The interview questions posed to NASA project staff[2] similarly were targeted to uncover the means by which the core management tasks described in the research questions listed above were accomplished.

VIRTUAL WORKPLACES

The form of virtual organization closest in most respects to traditional organizational arrangements is the virtual workplace. Telework allows workers in an agency to work away from their offices with the appropriate information and communication technology, but it may also offer an opening for changing the design of jobs and work processes (Offstein, Morwick and Koskinen, 2010). For, example, the ability to switch key members between projects may make the organization more dynamic and effective. Telework is seen by some as a broader and more forward-thinking concept than telecommuting, which refers more directly to off-site work arrangements. In both cases, however, employees work from home, in telecenters[3] furnished with the necessary computers and connections, from mobile locations, or from the worksites of clients, sometimes called "hot desking." Other arrangements include "hoteling," or

reserving desk space for employees at the traditional office site for one or more days a week and allowing them to work off site at other times. At the Patent and Trademark Offices, a recognized leader in this last arrangement, 55% of the total employee population are regular teleworkers (Office of Personnel Management, 2011).

Underlying these various arrangements is the fact that the employees are still members of the same organization, with the same mission, legitimate leadership team, command structure, organizational culture and administrative structures for personnel and budget functions. As we will see, these management elements are still important in virtual workplaces, and operate with only some adaptations to their virtual settings.

Telework has long been a staple in the private sector but has gained adherents in the public sector at all levels. In December of 2010 the Telework Enhancement Act was signed into law. Behind the legislation is a push to shift the culture of agencies toward the presumption that a worker is eligible to telecommute unless there is a compelling impediment to telework, such as security or service concerns. The act requires agencies to revise their telework policies in line with best practice findings, to inform employees about their telework status, to provide employees and managers with telework training, and to formalize telework agreements.

A wide range of advantages are expected from telework. First, telework improves the capacity of the government to function during emergencies. Recent natural and man-made crises have demonstrated the vulnerability of all governments to chaos following disaster or failures in the transportation system. Pandemic flu concerns in 2009 prompted the Office of Personnel Management (OPM) to create plans for more telework (OPM, nd). Record snowfalls in Washington, D.C. in the winter of 2010 led to the $71 million in lost federal worker productivity a day (CBS, 2010). Representative John Sarbanes, who sponsored the telework bill in the House, noted that losses would have been much higher had large numbers of people not worked from home. This is an important rationale, and in a 2010 survey OPM found that "72% of Federal agencies have integrated telework into their COOP [Continuity of Operations] planning (2011, p. 2).

Furthermore, as commuting times increase even in the absence of catastrophe, the advantages of shorter trips or none at all become clearer. A decrease in air pollution, especially in areas dense with government workers like the Washington capital region, is an associated benefit. The often very significant reduction of government real estate costs when employees work from home or when they can take advantage of hoteling or shorter commutes to telecenters in less costly labor and real estate markets is also cited as an advantage.

The federal Office of Personnel Management, tasked with implementing the legislation, also sees virtual workplaces as offering an advantage for "recruiting and retaining the best possible workforce - particularly newer workers who have high expectations of a technologically forward-thinking workplace" (nd, p. 1). Many of these young workers are used to communicating online and have come to expect the more informal work settings characteristic of telecommuting. Private sector firms have found that telework expands the pool of potential recruits of talented individuals to include those who chose to live outside major governmental centers, and it allows disabled employees to work in settings already well-adapted to their needs (Offstein, Morwich and Kroskinen 2010). For them the human resource advantages outweigh even the facility savings.

Job satisfaction is also a plus. OPM found, "Compared with employees not able to telework, more teleworkers report greater levels of job satisfaction (76% versus 68%) would recommend their organization as a good place to work (75% versus 66%), and are less likely to express an intention to leave their current organizations (74% versus 68%) (2011, p. 6). Working some of the time from home is also often associated with more flexible

working regimes which make intermittent care for dependents or scheduling of personal time easier, though as noted below this advantage poses problems from managers' perspectives.

The OPM survey also found that the number of federal employees teleworking grew from 102,900 to 113,946 between 2008 and 2009, and for at least two-thirds of these workers, telework was a regular part of their weekly schedule. However, OPM also uncovered evidence of some level of resistance to telework, especially by managers, and their reasons were directly linked to issues of work coordination and accountability. They found that "The most frequently cited barriers to telework continue to be office coverage (64%), organizational culture (49%), and management resistance (47%) (2011, p. 5). The Government Business Council investigated these issues in interviews with 25 federal managers about the challenges of telework. Managers expressed concern about diminished oversight of employees and the security of information online. They also resisted telework based on the equipment costs and the cost of developing an "online portal where teleworkers could easily, remotely and securely access important documents, databases and guidance" (Newell, 2010, p. 34).

These constraints are not unique to governmental settings, and are found in private sector efforts to enlarge the use of telework as well (Green and Roberts, 2010). Costs for telework equipment to the employee or the government are compounded by the loss of economies of scale for such equipment and the cost of duplicating equipment. The possibility of lost productivity from less oversight and accountability has again been cited as sources of management apprehension (Green and Roberts, 2010). Cascio (2000) also identifies the cost of equipment as well as concern about employee isolation, culture clashes among widely dispersed workers, and lack of trust as impediments to telework.

Findings from a major OPM study contradict some of these management concerns about telework, however. OPM compared federal teleworkers with those whose jobs made them ineligible to participate or whose agency did not support telework even though they were eligible. As noted earlier, they found that compared to non-teleworkers, teleworkers were more likely to think their organizations were good places to work, less likely to be contemplating leaving, and more likely to see their superiors as supportive of work-life balance. Teleworkers were also more likely to feel they had clearer work expectations, were held more accountable, and had a clearer sense of control over their work processes. These views may be partly the result of the kind of work likely to be handled by teleworkers—work more easily defined and individuated. But employees were also more likely to think that their work arrangements allowed them to develop their skills, to showcase their talents, and to engage in knowledge sharing with colleagues (OPM, 2011).

Managing in Virtual Workplaces

The forms of management and the actual degree of lateral vs. hierarchical direction and coordination in virtual workplaces were expected to resemble traditional organizations based on the distinctions among virtual organizational forms outlined earlier. But the evidence suggests more complex conclusions. The management of communication and coordination for teleworking employees uses a combination of traditional and virtual approaches.

Forms of Communication

The forms of communication associated with successful application of telework blend traditional approaches and the tactics ascribed to virtual forms. The most successful virtual leaders used a variety of means of communication including face-to-face presence, telephone, email and web conferencing (Offstein, Morwick and Koskinen, 2010, p. 35). The warmth of voice communication was identified as particularly important for creat-

ing a social context for work. Successful leaders worked on establishing a sense of cohesion and social support within the team. This was most often accomplished by including some physical meetings over the year. Interestingly, the same pattern emerges for multi-organizational teams.

Leader Roles

Leadership is seen as essential for extracting benefits from telework arrangements. Offstein, Morwick and Koskinen examining both public and private organizations found that the key to successful telework "is more of a function of leadership than technology" and in particular, "creative, innovative and progressive leadership" (2010, p. 32). The traditional leader oversight presence, prized as Management by Walking Around (Peters and Waterman, 1982), is replaced in the Treasury Department's Tax Administration program, for example, with a focus on what is produced rather than what is done. "In a virtual world, where it is difficult, if not impossible to monitor or micromanage processes, leaders must focus instead on results" (p. 36). Reinforcing this lesson, Cascio notes, "Learning to make the transition from managing time to managing projects is critical and will determine the success of an organization's telework program (2000, p. 86). While results or performance-based management is touted everywhere as a hallmark of progressive public management, in the case of virtual workplace management, it appears to be essential.

Leader roles in shaping group cohesion are also important. Concerns that employees will become isolated and detached from the organization have also been raised, but echoing some of the points about leadership just noted, other researchers suggest that this is not inevitable. Green and Roberts argue that virtual workers can overcome the potential for worker isolation and loss of group cohesion. Trust, goal consensus, a strong group culture and leaders who are both technical experts and participative managers are all necessary (2010). These are many of the same organizational traits associated with high rates of information-sharing and collaboration in traditional organizations (Reagans and McEvily, 2003; Willem and Beulens 2007).

Coordination

The blend of hierarchical and lateral coordination practices in virtual workplaces is illustrated in an exploratory case study of remotely located Department of Energy engineers and scientists who supervise environmental contractors in the field (Green and Roberts, 2010). The authors found that communication with agency managers tended to be mainly conventional, with email and the grapevine being the most common means, and meetings, a newsletter and direct supervisory contact less common. In contrast to assumptions in much of the literature about virtual organizations, team members expressed a desire for more direct contact with supervisors because of the greater perceived reliability of information, and they favored the clarity of synchronous connections that permitted two-way conversations (Green and Roberts, 2010). They also found that team members identified traditional leader traits as important (decision making, initiative, communication skill) but also identified the need for computer literacy as a basis for supervisor selection. The authors recommended based on this case that leaders should assemble the team periodically to enhance group cohesion and provide opportunities for team members to get clarification of their understanding of work issues. The benefits from gathering additional information about team member views with surveys, focus groups or performance reviews were also suggested by the case findings. Peer interaction was viewed as an important source of professional learning, but the researchers found that members had a difficult time staying connected to each other (p. 54). Some of these recommendations have been

put into practice in the cases of interactive multi-organizational teams described next.

In sum, the telework form of virtual organization has grown quickly into a major government emphasis. Along with increases in the numbers of government teleworkers has come a growing recognition of the special managerial requirements of these arrangements. These include a managerial focus on results rather than the oversight of the work process itself and desire for face-to-face and synchronous as well as asynchronous communication. In general, coordination appears to be the result of leader direction, not lateral coordination or self-organizing. In fact some report finding coordination difficult. The means of communication were less specialized than the literature generally predicts, with email and telephone most commonly mentioned in studies of the form. Management attention to generating trust and team cohesion was important here as in other settings where information-sharing is important. Members often expressed a desire for greater face to face leader contact to clarify expectations. Opportunities for some level of physical group meetings are needed to gain the most from the new work-force arrangements.

VIRTUAL MULTI-ORGANIZATIONAL TEAMS

In contrast to telework, in which the employees linked by information technologies are members of a single organization, virtual collaboration refers to arrangements of employees from different organizations at different locations working together. Like telework in one organization, the virtual multi-organizational workforce offers flexibility in the timing and place of work that make it possible to put together teams who are widely spaced geographically, reducing travel or commuting costs and allowing members to remain in their home institutions. In addition however, virtual teams allow for the combination of specialized competencies and skills from different organizations and sectors, public, non-profit and private. Such an arrangement may be ongoing and relatively permanent or it may be used for shorter-term undertakings. In research projects, in which this form is often seen, these features make it possible to use of the full or part time efforts of experts from across the country or the world.

Because of the multi-organizational character of these forms, however, an additional and more complex set of management problems arise. Instead of the single mission and leadership seen in telework arrangements, virtual collaborations must create a new basis of legitimacy for establishing direction and goals. Leadership, work coordination, decision making and oversight become more problematical. Conflict resolution and finding agreement on the ways that communication technologies will be used also become problematic. Because much of the literature on virtual public organizations focuses principally on varieties of telework, case examples of virtual multi-organizational teams will be used to explore managerial requirements. These examples of the functioning of virtual organizations reveal that new patterns of management evolve in response to the task characteristics, member predilections, the interests of the home institutions and the capacities of the information technologies in use. In some cases the structure and management of the group evolves in response to these features in gradual or disjointed series of steps toward a working relationship (Majchrzak et al., 2000).

Examples examined here of these collaborative, multi-organizational virtual forms in the public sector include the research project teams sponsored by the NASA Astrobiology Institute, devoted to the study of the " origin, evolution, distribution, and future of life in the universe" (NASA 2008) by looking for life forms on other planets and studying Earth-based extremophiles, highly unusual life forms that may offer clues to what to expect and look for in space. The Institute evaluates and supports proposals from teams of researchers, currently 14 teams, each headed by a Principal Investigator or a group of Co-Investigators from NASA, universities and independent research institutes. A second NASA group, the Kepler Project includes a roster of 200 researchers who examine astronomical data transmitted monthly from the Kepler Telescope Spacecraft. "Kepler's primary science objective is exoplanet detection with emphasis on terrestrial planets located within the habitable zones of Sun-like stars" (NASA 2010). Researchers hunt for planets in a near region of our galaxy by examining light variations in stars when planets pass before them (NASA 2011). The project is directed by a large group of Co-Investigators from NASA, universities in the U.S., Canada, and Europe, and independent astronomical institutes. It is organized into a number of working groups and supports other proposals from participating scientists and guest observers. Two other cases involve scientists and engineers working on advanced design projects for the US government. The team of aerospace scientists and engineers from four firms who designed the "Stealth" B-2 bomber (Argyres, 1999) and the engineers from three corporations working on an innovative rocket engine (Majchrzak et al., 2000) described below also exhibit this virtual arrangement.

The underlying forms of relationships in these research organizations are contractual, including variable-year government grants from NASA for the investigation of high priority research questions and contracts between the government and firms for project design. In both of these design cases the virtual organization was composed of a prime contractor working with subcontractors. All of these virtual organizations are temporary, though one of the Astrobiology teams has been working successful in getting multiple grants and has gotten support for twelve years. Most of the members of the NASA teams from universities and independent institutes are part-time. That is, members have other assignments in their home organizations in addition to the work on the project.

All these conditions affect the management of the teams as noted below.

Three features of these arrangements of particular interest here are (1) the forms of communication and information technology they employ, (2) the means of coordination among members, whether traditionally hierarchical or self-organizing, and (3) the role of leaders in task direction and culture management.

Forms of Communication

The electronic communication technologies in use include the same array found in telework, ranging from email to video conferencing. The NASA Astrobiology Institute staff reported that they worked hard to make online meeting programs easy to use and reliable by listening to the team and what they found to be useful. They found that even for team scientists adopting new software presented challenges and required training and encouragement. The respondent from the Kepler team also reported improvements in the team's capacity to meet virtually without the cost and environmental impact of travel. But virtual collaboration can also opens the door to miscommunication. Email in particular was noted to be prone to misunderstanding depending on writing quality.

In addition to more standard electronic communication technologies, however, more specialized collaborative tools designed to support the particular research process were used in these cases. The engineering team designing a rocket motor piloted a new commercial cloud computing resource restricted to members only as a kind of "Internet Notebook" for recording conversations, the results of analyses, and multimedia information and making them accessible to the whole team (Majchrzak et al., 2000). In the "Stealth" B-2 Bomber case, after some serious negotiations, members agreed on standards for data transmission and storage and for the format for a common database. They also agreed to adopt the digital design program in use by the prime contractor as a joint working tool since programs to translate among their existing tools were not accurate enough for the extreme design requirements of the Stealth (Argyres, 1999). These negotiations were apparently lengthy and difficult, however, since only threats by the prime contractor to take legal action against the subs and the intervention of the Air Force to help support training and conversion costs ended the resistance of the subs to adopting the new design tools. The result was the creation of a common 'technical grammar" that made it possible for members to integrate their findings. The Kepler team also uses project-specific software developed at the Ames Research Center for data analysis and system management, but the individual scientists on the team have their own analysis tools as well. Teams supported by the Astrobiology Institute have used specially designed three dimensional visualization systems to allow remote communication and online analysis of data.

In each of the cases, however, it was also found that a degree of face-to-face meeting time was important to the success of the project, especially early in the relationship, to allow some measure of personal acquaintance and to set the ground rules for later interactions. The Principal Investigators for the Astrobiology teams meet face to face once a year and on the Kepler team twice a year, and in both cases they hold monthly teleconference meetings. A retreat on a riverboat before the launch of the Kepler telescope spacecraft was held to get the teams off to a good start. Face-to-face meetings are seen as essential for building trust based on the reassurance of facial expression and comprehension based on body language. In the rocket design case, the collaboration began with a face-to-face meeting to set the ground rules for the interactions and to determine how they would use their "Internet Notebook."

A special characteristic of the two NASA research organizations was that many of the members were already well known to each other, being part of the relatively small scientific communities associated with these specialties. The astrobiology community was actually to some degree a creation of the NASA program, as students and faculty researchers were drawn together and supported by the program to establish a previously undefined field. Prior personal acquaintance, except among members of the same traditional organizations on the virtual teams, was not identified as common in the engineering design organizations.

Lateral Coordination

A point upon which many researchers of virtual organizations typically agree is that lateral communication and coordination among members should be more common in virtual than traditional organizations. This characteristic takes on special importance in virtual collaborative arrangements that lack the legitimizing authority of a single chain of command within one organization. The case examples illustrate the complexity of coordination in this form of virtual organization.

In the Kepler and Astrobiology organizations the work of the teams was characterized by respondents as self- organizing. This means that coordination among members arises out of a technical and professional understanding of what is needed to accomplish the work (Galbraith, 1973). Members step in as needed based on this understanding and their commitment to the task. To do so however requires high levels of timely project information and members with considerable autonomy and dedication. These conditions emerged relatively easily in the science organizations because of the academic cultures from which they spring and the high value placed on being selected for the team, but evolved with more difficulty in the engineering teams. At the NASA Astrobiology Institute, teams of scientists propose research in response to an RFP (request for proposal), and successful teams break themselves down into interacting research groups. Annual reports and monthly video conferences among team members provide information needed for cooperative scientific problem solving. A three dimensional, online visualization system allows members to work together for data analysis. An added necessity in this case was for collaboration across disciplines within and among teams since the work combines astronomical and biological sciences. This led team members to retrain themselves and resulted in a gradual shift at conferences from disciplinary based presentations to plenary sessions that crossed disciplinary boundaries. Now members hold virtual, interdisciplinary seminars that bring the majority of teams together for "workshops without walls." This illustrates a form of self-organization that results from learning.

The Kepler team also holds yearly face-to-face meetings and monthly online meetings to report progress. Working subgroups collaborated more frequently. The ability of the team to debate and come to a decision about critical questions of measurement or how to cope with data gaps when the spacecraft computer experiences safemode episodes of interrupted transmissions has improved since the beginning of the program. Progress using virtual meeting technologies has so far been better than for virtual work collaboration. The incentives to work on the project are great, however, and most members are pleased with the opportunity to collaborate virtually. The Kepler team was characterized by a program participant as very cohesive, with members who have a "passion for planet hunting" and take great pride in their part in the mission.

Collaboration does not emerge without effort for either of these teams, however. The Astrobiology Institute requires that proposals for research support provide information about how the team will collaborate. In general, team supervision was characterized by staff as "fluid," with Principal Investigators themselves determining how to manage team relations and the disbursement of funds. But as noted, team members had to retrain themselves to make it possible for them to interact in interdisciplinary teams. Close relationships *among* teams has been slower to develop. To encourage collaboration among teams that had earlier competed for support, the Institute director initiated strategic workshops to strengthen team focus on the broader NASA science missions. They report success in this effort but note that the collaboration across teams has developed slowly as a cultural value.

Similar patterns can be seen for the Kepler team. The riverboat retreat held for the team at the launch of the spacecraft employed a human relations consulting group to help integrate the team. While in general the team works well together, there are said to be occasional professional tensions over technical and scientific issues. Strains also have emerged over questions of the authority of the Principal Investigators, what they can do autonomously and what decisions require democratic participation. Similar issues have emerged over decisions by sub-team chairs on determining team priorities. Concerns about trust surfaced over the possibility that individual team members might release news of planet finds independently. Team members must sign an agreement to reserve publication and release of new planets data until the formal team verification and release.

The rocket design group also expended considerable effort to find a workable collaboration process using a new Internet Notebook tool (Majchrzak et al., 2000). The team went through several phases of development and adjustment with the novel online design tools. They initially agreed in an open meeting of group members to record all of their work and conversations in the Notebook so that everything would be accessible to all members, including the executive project managers of the interacting organizations. They later scaled back this decision as data overwhelmed their ability to find and use what they needed. The typical project structure in which lead engineers act as a "communications hub" among the other team members was abandoned in favor of a "ubiquitous computing" mode that allowed all the team members to use the Notebook to communicate directly and immediately about their work, motivated by their conviction that

the work environment would be more productive (Majchrzak et al., 2000, p. 580). This reflects the decentralized, self-organizing pattern noted earlier. They later added audio teleconferencing to reproduce the reciprocally interactive work mode of brainstorming. While the chief engineer admitted he "missed being in control" (Majchrzak et al., p. 588) the increased interactive participation was credited with making the final innovative solution possible.

The B-2 design process was similar in some respects. The design tool the team finally adopted made it possible for team members to communication with a highly specialized "technical grammar," a precise set of communication codes for "transmitting informal and partly tacit knowledge from one engineer to another" (Argyres, 1999, p. 171). This system established rigid standards for design elements and reduced the ambiguity of communication among team members. The effect of this design system was to coordinate the efforts of team members without the intervention of a central authority, similar to the way the traffic signals coordinate the activities of strangers (p.172). This again illustrates a laterally coordinating, self-organizing design logic.

Leadership Direction

Though much of the literature on virtual organizing predicts that hierarchical direction and control of work will be less common, the cases illustrate the ways that leadership and hierarchy remain important, but at two different levels. Overall project direction, goal setting, and resolving major conflicts remains as essential in all the cases, but the extent to which leaders direct the coordination of work *within* the teams differed between the scientific research teams and the engineering project design teams. The former, surprisingly, appear to require more team level direction and management than the latter. This may be because of the more encompassing and specialized IT collaboration tools in use in the engineering project design teams. More likely these differences are linked to the different type of work in the teams, relatively open ended-research versus a defined and highly specified project.

Strong team leadership was identified in both the Kepler and the Astrobiology cases as essential for the success of the work. At the Astrobiology Institute, in the absence of strong leaders, "silos and pockets" or cliques can form within teams that interfere with the team's ability to do its best work because some contributions will be isolated or lost. Leaders may also have to spur contributions. In one instance, respondents report that a team leader blogged online on a scientific site to cajole dawdling team members, but most leaders were said to operate less publically. Leadership styles and cultures vary among teams, and show particular differences between the teams from NASA's centers and those based in universities. The personality of the Principal Investigator was said to influence the organization of work. The Institute staff manages inter-team collaboration from their birds-eye perspective, as noted earlier, and manage the overall direction of the projects. Though the Institute has limited leverage, they can steer the direction of the work over time by controlling the calls for proposals, though they consult with team leaders in identifying promising research directions.

At Kepler the team operates somewhat differently. Leadership at the Kepler mission level is vested in Principal Investigator and the Kepler Science council, a three-person elected group that works with the Principal Investigator to share the leadership responsibilities. Participation in the Kepler project is determined by the proposals submitted by individual scientists and by invitation from the Principal Investigator. The Kepler team is composed of a group of Co-Principal Investigators, members of the Science Work Group and other Participating Scientists. The work within the team as a whole is not as directly interactive as seen in the other cases. Findings from one group will affect the work on other projects, but not with

the immediacy that is found in the others cases, and thus the character of collaboration is different. However, the research does all rest on data from the Kepler telescope, so issues concerning the data from the telescope are of concern to all the members of the team and it is on these issues that frictions can arise. Occasional disagreements over priorities in the work and ways to deal with ambiguous data among other issue have been subject to "spirited debate" according to a Kepler investigator. Thus at Kepler, leadership of the project level is critical for resolving disagreement that remain. -

In the engineering design teams however, the role of lead engineers, supervisors and project managers in directing collaborative team activities was diminished. That is, the teams operated in a more self-organizing and autonomous fashion. This appears to have been principally because of the use of highly specialized design tools in both cases that allowed for synchronous and asynchronous interactive work. These tools replaced the need for managers to arrange the coordination of tasks. In the case of the B-2 design, information technology served as a substitute for hierarchy (Argyres, 1999, p. 164). In the rocket design case, the lead engineer said he missed being in control, and other members reported that "greater leader control might have been beneficial" (Majchrzak et al., 2000, p. 588), but the team operated collegially.

At the project leadership level, the cases are more mixed. In the rocket design case, the higher level project managers, who traditionally had used periodic reports to oversee the design work, initially agreed to play a different role in the "ubiquitous computing" environment by accessing the Internet Notebook tool on a continual basis. They abandoned this plan after a few weeks, however, saying they could not really follow the design results this way and reverted to receiving reports on a "need to know" basis. The flatter team structure also allowed a consensus to emerge among the engineers about the impossibility of meeting some of the design requirements. This led the team to successfully challenge management, and eventually resulted in a change in the requirements ((Majchrzak et al., 2000, p. 590). In the B-2 case, the Prime Contractor did exercise power and authority in requiring the use of their own online design tools and the Air Force, the contracting agency, intervened to help resolve the impasse over the extra training costs connected with the tools (Argyres, 1999, p.172).

Thus the patterns of hierarchy exhibit important differences among the cases and are more complex than expected. Hierarchy was clearly evident for top level decisions regarding directions and goals, because of differences in priorities and scientific judgments among team members and their home institutions. Leadership direction and hierarchical control at the team level was less evident, especially for the project design teams with highly specified products.

Another widely expressed expectation for virtual collaborative organizations is that they will exhibit more decentralized and participative decision making than their traditional counterparts. This appears to be true in the cases observed here. In the Kepler and Astrobiology organizations many decisions are made with participation of other team members if not in a fully democratic manner. In the Kepler project, a Science Council of three elected members along with the Principal Investigator, make critical decisions with the input of other Co-Investigators. These decisions largely concern technical measurement and data collection issues affecting the team as a whole. At the Astrobiology Institute, a large face-to-face conference is held to identify themes for research, and the Principal Investigators of the 14 teams form the executive council to make decisions about directions for future research. Consensus among the engineers in the rocket design team made possible the two key decisions: first to adopt "ubiquitous computing" to work virtually with the Internet Notebook for all the work, and later to challenge the project requirements. Aided by the decentralized team structure, consensus appears

to have been the model of choice (Majchrzak et al., 2000). An exception is the B-2 case. There the main decisions were made in the traditional way, by the executives of the participating firms, though it took considerable negotiation to get to an agreement.

FUTURE RESEARCH DIRECTIONS

Several hypotheses for future study might be offered based on the overall finding that management in virtual workplaces and virtual multi-organizational teams differs in several ways. First, despite the characterizations of virtual organizations generally in the literature, exchanges in virtual workplaces do not appear to make particular use of advanced Web 2.0 communication and information processing technologies, while the virtual multi-organizational teams described here use both conventional and advanced technologies. The difference seen in this small group of examples suggests a hypothesis to be examined for a larger set of cases. It might also be hypothesized that this difference in communication and information processing technologies are associated with greater requirements for collaborative work in the multi-organizational teams. That is, the work deemed appropriate for telework in virtual workplaces may be selected to require less collaboration. The work may represent the kind that Thompson (1967) described as exhibiting pooled or sequential rather than reciprocal interdependencies. The differences in level of collaboration might also be associated with differences in levels of self- organizing. Wide variability in the use of lateral coordination and self-organizing are seen in the cases described here, and further research to understand the sources of these differences is called for. The differences in leadership roles and reliance on hierarchical direction seen in the examples here also suggest hypotheses for future research about the prevalence of performance based management over more directive oversight of work processes in all forms of virtual organization. While the literature prescribes performance management, it is not at all clear how prevalent it is. Finally the cases suggest that virtual multi-organizational teams may exhibit a two-level leadership model in which executive decisions about contracts or budgets are made hierarchically while decisions about work processes emerge from self-organizing processes.

These cases only begin to scratch the surface of the questions about the management of virtual organizations and the managerial practices and requirements across the different types of virtual public organizations. Virtual workplace arrangements have received the greatest attention of the forms described here, but relatively few empirical studies of their management are available. More systematic inventories not only of virtual science and technology teams, but also of virtual multi-organizational teams in other fields such as human services and public safety are needed to determine how these multi-organizational teams are functioning. Research on cooperative network strategies has been plentiful in the past decade (Agranoff 2007; Milward and Provan, 2006; Fedorowicz, Gogan and Williams, 2006; Agranoff and Maguire, 2001), but research on the management of the virtual forms of these networks is relatively rare. Investigations of intermittent cooperative connections among virtual partners in public services are similarly uncommon. A great deal of research on the computing and data transfer requirements of virtual data libraries has emerged that make them possible, but much less is known about on the management of those arrangements (Mahler and Regan, 2010). The managerial and collaborative characteristics of all of these arrangements deserve further study given the expectations for their role in future government work from planning for public safety to the provision of services. The need for such research can only increase as expectations grow for telework and intergovernmental and inter-departmental teams to solve public service problems and provide services online.

CONCLUSION

The differences between the management of virtual workplaces and virtual multi-organizational teams are greater than anticipated in some areas and less marked in other areas. Since the sample of cases is so small, these conclusions must stand as suggestions for further study. However, based on the literature on telework and the cases of collaborating, multi-organizational teams, several observations can be offered. Both of the types of virtual organization studied here are using an array of online communication and information technologies, from email to videoconferences and webinars. But the use of more specialized, program-specific software and computing resources is more typically for the data analysis and design needs of the virtual multi-organizational teams. This software made the intra-team collaboration feasible for these science and technology projects at a level that does not appear in the telework literature. These resources do not replace the need for face-to-face relationships, however. This contact is needed by both types of virtual organizations to generate team trust, cohesion and understanding of the needs of the organization. In the NASA teams special interdisciplinary workshops and conferences reinforce these relations.

The management of collaboration also differs between virtual workplaces and multi-organizational teams. In virtual workplaces neither lateral task coordination nor self-organizing systems were reported. Hierarchical direction was more often indicated. Management by results was identified as a valuable approach, but work oversight was still reported to be a major concern of public sector telework managers. OPM research on the motivation and productivity of teleworkers and experience with virtual workplaces may put some of these concerns to rest.

The virtual teams in the science and technology organizations illustrated much more self-organization based on personal knowledge in the NASA cases, as well as the reciprocal interdependencies built into the research enterprises. Disagreements emerged in all the virtual multi-organizational teams over substantive work matters such as the use of online communication tools, project priorities, and technical data problems and were largely resolved by members themselves, attesting to the commitment and professionalism of the team. Leader intervention and group process consultants were necessary in some cases.

Hierarchical control is still important in all cases, but at different levels in single and multi-organizational arrangements. In the telework form, hierarchical control appears at the team level *and* at the level of program or project direction. For multi-organizational teams, however, the intervention of virtual team leaders and Principal Investigators was needed on occasion to manage controversies *among* teams or between teams and contractors. Like lead organizations in networks (Milward and Provan, 2006), hierarchies in virtual multi-organizational teams help resolve disagreements and manage relations. Executive managers for the Prime-Contractors and NASA staff provide it, to a limited degree. Others have also found more hierarchy than expected in virtual multi-organizational teams. Ahuja and Carlry report, "High-level planning regarding resource allocation takes place among the few key members of the group. While most design discussions are decentralized and take place over e-mail, resolution of issues often takes place at a higher level" (1999, p.752).

The expectation with which this research began, that virtual multi-organizational teams will follow more closely than virtual workplaces the assumptions in the literature about lateral and self-organizing coordination, has thus found mixed support. The need for face to face communication arises in all virtual organizations, including virtual teams. Despite the use of more sophisticated collaborative software in virtual multi-organizational teams, some degree of hierarchical direction is needed for some kinds of decisions. Top level governance structures arise in virtual multi-organizational teams to manage the differences in institutional priorities and judgments, supporting ideas borrowed from the network literature about the need for governance of virtual, multi-organizational forms. All this suggests that there is more variability in what we call virtual organizations than is generally acknowledged, and they cannot be treated as a universal form.

In sum, the patterns of communication, collaboration and leader control in virtual workplaces and multi-organizational teams differ from each other in some ways that are important for their design and management. Distinguishing among forms of virtual organization appears to be a useful strategy for investigation given the differences uncovered in the preliminary research. These differences open up a number of questions about the management of different forms. Is greater lateral collaboration actually needed in virtual workplaces but blocked because of structural or technical impediments? Do the task requirements of virtual workplaces differ from their traditional counterparts? What conditions foster lateral collaboration in virtual multi-organizational teams? Do human service and public safety teams operate similarly to the science and technology teams studied here? What models of management are most likely to lead to effective virtual organizations? This research takes a step toward answering these questions by distinguishing among type of virtual organizations and identifying some of the dimensions of difference in their management.

REFERENCES

Agranoff, R. (2007). *Managing within networks*. Washington, DC: Georgetown University Press.

Agranoff, R., & McGuire, M. (2001). Big questions in public network management research. *Journal of Public Administration: Research and Theory, 11*(3), 295–326.

Ahuja, M., & Carley, K. (1999). Network structure in virtual organizations. *Organization Science, 10*(6), 741–757. doi:10.1287/orsc.10.6.741

Argyres, N. S. (1999). The impact of Information Technology on coordination: Evidence from the B-2 "Stealth" bomber. *Organization Science, 10*(2), 162–180. doi:10.1287/orsc.10.2.162

Blecker, T., & Newman, R. (2000). Interorganizational knowledge management: Some perspective for knowledge oriented strategic management in virtual organizations. In Malhodra, Y. (Ed.), *Knowledge management and virtual organizations* (pp. 63–83). Hershey, PA: Idea Group Publishing.

Butler, D. (2007). Agencies join forces to share data: US to create a universal database of all its research results. *Nature, 446*(7134), 354. Retrieved April 12, 2011, from http://www.nature.com.mutex.gmu.edu/nature/journal/v446/n7134/full/446354b.html

Cantwell, P. (2011). When telework really isn't: GSA's closure of telework centers raises a question. *Federal Computer Week Online*. Retrieved April 12, 2011, from http://fcw.com/articles/2011/03/03/telework-centers-are-not-true-telework-paul-cantwell-argues.aspx

Cascio, W. F. (2000). Managing a virtual workplace. *The Academy of Management Executive, 14*(3), 81–90. doi:10.5465/AME.2000.4468068

Central, C. I. O. (2006). *Intellipedia: The intelligence Wikipedia*. Retrieved April 12, 2011, from www.ciocentral.org/.../intellipedia-the-intelligence-wikipedia/

CIA. (2009). *Intellipedia celebrates third anniversary with a successful challenge*. Retrieved April 12, 2011, from https://www.cia.gov/news-information/featured-story-archive/intellipedia-celebrates-third-anniversary.html

Comfort, L. K., & Naim, K. (2006). Inter-organizational coordination in extreme events: The World Trade Center attacks, September 11, 2001. *Natural Hazards, 39*(2), 309–327. doi:10.1007/s11069-006-0030-x

Deloitte. (2009). *Integrating health and human services delivery: Making services citizen-friendly*. Retrieved April 12, 2011, from http://www.deloitte.com/view/en_US/us/Industries/us-state-government/Big-Issues-in-Government/improving_human_services/63ae11eef03a4210VgnVCM100000ba42f00aRCRD.htm

DeSantis, G., & Monge, P. (1999). Communication processes for virtual organizations. *Organization Science: Special Issue: Communication Processes for Virtual Organizations, 10*(6), 693–703.

Dess, G., Rahsheed, A. M. A., McLaughlin, K., & Preim, R. (1995). The new corporate architecture. *Academy of Management Review, 9*(3), 7–20.

Doyle, A. (2003). *Certificates, monitoring, & firewall working group on Information Systems and services*. Retrieved April 12, 2011, from http://wgiss.ceos.org/meetings/wgiss16/Monday/Doyle_Grid_Toolkit.ppt

Environmental Information Exchange Network. (2010). *Return on investment*. Retrieved on May 2, 2010, from http://www.exchangenetwork.net/benefits/roi.htm

Environmental Protection Agency. (2010). *Central data exchange benefits*. Retrieved on May 2, 2010, from http://www.epa.gov/cdx/benefits/index.htm

Federal Computer Week. (2011). *12 telework centers shuttered: GSA cuts funding to telework centers*. Retrieved April 12, 2011, from http://fcw.com/articles/2011/03/02/12-telework-centers-shuttered.aspx

Finholt, T., & Olson, G. M. (1997). Laboratories to collaboratories: A new organizational form for scientific collaboration. *Psychological Science, 8*(1), 28–36. doi:10.1111/j.1467-9280.1997.tb00540.x

Fountain, J. E. (2001). *Building the virtual state: Information Technology and institutional change.* Washington, DC: Brookings Institution Press.

Galbraith, J. (1973). *Designing complex organizations.* Reading, MA: Addison-Wesley.

Grabowski, M., & Roberts, K. (1999). Risk mitigation in virtual organizations. *Organization Science, 10*(6), 704–721. doi:10.1287/orsc.10.6.704

Green, D., & Roberts, G. (2010). Personnel implications of public sector virtual organizations. *Public Personnel Management, 39*(1), 47–57.

Gulick, L. H. (1936). Notes on the theory of organization. In L. Gulick & L. Urwick (Eds.), *Papers on the science of administration* (pp. 3–35). New York, NY: Institute of Public Administration. Fedorowicz, J., Gogan, J., & Williams, C. (2006). *The e-government collaboration challenge: Lessons from five case studies.* Arlington, VA: IBM Center for the Business of Government.

Mahler, J., & Regan, P. M. (2010). Implementing virtual collaboration at the environmental protection agency. In Garson, G. D., & Shea, C. (Eds.), *Handbook of public Information Systems* (3rd ed.). Boca Raton, FL: Taylor and Francis.

Majchrzak, A., Rice, R. E., Malhotra, A., King, N., & Ba, S. (2000). Technology adaptation: The case of a computer-supported inter-organizational virtual team. *Management Information Systems Quarterly, 24*(4), 569–600. doi:10.2307/3250948

Meadows, V. (2007-2008). Versatile bureaucracy: A telework case study. *Public Management, 36*(4), 33–37.

Milward, H. B., & Provan, K. G. (2006). *A manager's guide to choosing and using collaborative networks.* Arlington, VA: IBM Center for the Business of Government.

NASA. (2008). *About AstroBiology.* Retrieved on April 13, 2011, from http://astrobiology.nasa.gov/about-astrobiology/ accessed 3-27-2011

NASA. (2011). *Kepler: Search for habitable planets.* Retrieved on March 27, 2011, from http://kepler.nasa.gov/Mission/QuickGuide/

National Science Foundation. (2008, May). *Beyond being there: A blueprint for advancing the design, development, and evaluation of virtual organizations, final report from Workshops on Building Effective Virtual Organizations.* Retrieved on April 13, 2011, from http://www.ci.uchicago.edu/events/VirtOrg2008/VO_report.pdf

Newell, E. (2010). Homing in on telework. *Government Executive, 42*(11), 33–40.

Office of Personnel Management. (2011). *Status of telework in the federal government: Report to the Congress. A Guide to Telework in the federal government.* Retrieved on April 13, 2011, from http://www.telework.gov/Reports_and_Studies/Annual_Reports/2010teleworkreport.pdf

Office of Personnel Management. (n.d.). *A guide to telework in the federal government.* Retrieved on April 13, 2011, from http://www.opm.gov/pandemic/agency2a-guide.pdf

Offstein, E. H., Morwick, J. M., & Koskinen, L. (2010). Making telework work: Leading people and leveraging technology for competitive advantage. *Strategic HR Review, 9*(2), 32–37. doi:10.1108/14754391011022244

Peters, T., & Waterman, R. (1982). *In search of excellence: Lessons from America's best-run companies.* New York, NY: Harper & Row.

Plowman, D. A., Solanksy, S., Beck, T., Baker, L., Kulkarni, M., & Travis, D. V. (2007). The role of leadership in emergent, self-organization. *The Leadership Quarterly, 18*, 341–356. doi:10.1016/j.leaqua.2007.04.004

Rainey, H. (2009). *Understanding and managing public organizations*. San Francisco, CA: Jossey-Bass.

Reagans, R., & McEvily, B. (2003). Network structure and knowledge transfer: The effects of cohesion and range. *Administrative Science Quarterly, 48*(2), 240–267. doi:10.2307/3556658

Regio, M. (2002). Government virtual service networks. *Proceedings of the 35th Hawaii International Conference on System Science IEEE*. Retrieved on April 13, 2011, from www.hicss.hawaii.edu/HICSS_35/HICSSpapers/PDFdocuments/ETEGV04.pdf

Szalay, A., & Gray, J. (2001). The world-wide telescope. *Science, 293*(5537), 2037–2040. doi:10.1126/science.293.5537.2037

Thompson, J. (1967). *Organizations in action*. New York, NY: McGraw Hill.

Willem, A., & Buelens, M. (2007). Knowledge sharing in public sector organizations: The effect of organizational characteristics on interdepartmental knowledge sharing. *Journal of Public Administration: Research and Theory, 17*(4), 581–606. doi:10.1093/jopart/mul021

KEY TERMS AND DEFINITIONS

Collaboration: Organizational or inter-organizational cooperative effort to produce a jointly created result.

Continuity of Operations: Capacity of an organization whose members can function during emergencies from home or off-site locations.

Hierarchy: A system of superior and subordinate relations for directing the work of subordinates and resolving their disagreements or uncertainties.

Self-Organizing: Lateral coordination by committed, professional employees with the knowledge and autonomy to direct themselves and work collaboratively.

Telework: Work by members of the same organization who work off-site and use information and communication technologies in the conduct of their work.

Virtual Multi-Organizational Team: A geographically dispersed organization whose members belong to different cooperating organizations and who work interactively online with clients or each other.

Virtual Organization: A geographically dispersed organization whose members belong to the same or cooperating organizations and who use information and communication technologies to conduct their work.

ENDNOTES

[1] Inquiries into the use of this virtual organizational form to a series of federal agencies resulted in volunteers from the two NASA project teams described below.

[2] A senior staff member at NASA's Astrobiology Institute, a collaboration specialist, and a Co-PI for the Kepler project were interviewed. A great deal of information on program structure is also available on the websites for the projects, including http://www.kepler.nasa.gov/Mission/team/ and http://astrobiology.nasa.gov/about-astrobiology/.

[3] The General Services Administration will close twelve of these centers, however, because of funding and because they still require workers to commute (Federal Computer Week, 2011; Cantwell, 2011). Working from home is seen as preferable for reasons discussed presently.

Section 2
Applying Web 2.0 in the Public Sector

As Web 2.0 technologies are integrated into the everyday lives of citizens and the day-to-day operations of private organizations, many begin to question how such tools are utilized by government. These chapters present a survey of government jurisdictions to give some sense of the extent to which Web 2.0 technologies are used in the public sector. Findings of quantitative and qualitative research examine current adoption trends of Web 2.0 in the public sector with a discussion of different applications and how they can be used as engagement mechanisms.

Chapter 5

M–Government:
An Opportunity for Addressing the Digital Divide

Aroon P. Manoharan
Kent State University, USA

Lamar Vernon Bennett
Long Island University, USA

Tony J. Carrizales
Marist College, USA

ABSTRACT

This chapter looks at technological inequities throughout the world within the context of e-government. The purpose of the study is to evaluate and highlight existing digital divides and current trends among the various divides. The concept of the digital divide, within the context of e-government, is often associated with the lack of access and resources to citizens for the purpose of utilizing technology in working with government. Utilizing survey data of international municipal Web portals as well as existing United Nations data, this research evaluates existing divides throughout the world. Through these findings, the authors underscore opportunities for addressing such existing divides and modes of increasing e-government performance. Specifically, mobile technology or m-government is examined as a medium for further connecting government and its citizens.

INTRODUCTION

The use of technology by governments to provide services and communicate with its citizens – e-government – depends on the ability of the public to have access and competencies to utilize these technologies. The inability to access technologies or barriers to online government services have resulted in a divide between those who can utilize these online services and those who cannot. The "digital divide" has long been a concern with the ever-increasing use of online technologies by government entities. Research continues to review the emergence of a divide

DOI: 10.4018/978-1-4666-0318-9.ch005

among municipalities and regions throughout the world. Recently, Holzer and Manoharan (2009) had attempted to determine whether the divide between the "haves" and "have-nots" is merely an extension of the existing inequalities. Existing social and economic divides may be a critical factor in the existing technological divides that arise throughout the world.

There is a wealth of national and international research studies, which have been able to track the continued progress and performance of e-government (UN, 2008; Holzer & Kim, 2008; West, 2008); however the need to underscore the digital divide against e-government performance is critical. The data for this paper are drawn from a study of global municipal Web portals conducted by the E-Governance Institute at Rutgers University, Newark. The study ranked municipalities worldwide based on their scores in the following five e-government categories; privacy, usability, content, services and citizen participation. Initial surveys (2003 & 2005) indicated a growing digital divide between cities across the globe. However, recent surveys (2007 & 2009) point toward a stabilizing but a digital divide that remains. In this international perspective, we define the digital divide as the difference in the average e-government scores between developed (OECD members) and developing (non-OECD) nations included in the Digital Government in Municipalities Worldwide Surveys.

A review of international e-government data will underscore an overview of digital divide worldwide. Although various digital divides may be stabilizing, our primary research question focuses on what can be done to address existing divides. To this end we will conclude this paper with the role that m-government or mobile technology can do to address digital divides among e-government efforts. This research paper begins with an overview of the existing data and a literature review of e-government and the digital divide and m-government to provide a framework for the research.

LITERATURE REVIEW

E-Government Data

The key questions of public management research have often sidelined the focus on social consequences of public administration in a democratic society (Kirlin, 1996). Under such circumstances, the emerging study of e-government introduces the risk of a digital divide between the digital 'haves' and 'have-nots'. The definition of the digital divide is often associated with the lack of access to technology by certain sections of the public. The digital divide is not only confined to people's access, but it can also be applicable to the online public service delivery by national governments. There clearly exists a divide among nations, particularly between the developed and developing nations, in terms of e-government functionality and performance. According to a United Nations report, "the network society is creating parallel communications systems: one for those with income, education and literal connections, giving plentiful information at low cost and high speed; the other for those without connections, blocked by high barriers of time, cost and uncertainty and dependent upon outdated information" (United Nations Development Program, 1999, p.63). In this research, we examine the divide in online services and functionality, among large municipalities throughout the world and also attempt to further understand the relationship of this digital divide to other divides - social, political, economic and literacy divides among nations, particularly those between OECD and non-OECD nations.

The Digital Divide

Digital divide, in general refers to the gap between those who have access to information and communication technologies (ICTs) and those without such access. Based on a study conducted by the United States Department of Commerce (1999, p. 16), there existed a digital divide between "the information rich (such as Whites, Asians/Pacific Islanders, those with higher incomes, those more educated, and dual-parent households), and the information poor (such as those who are younger, those with lower incomes and education levels, certain minorities, and those in rural areas or central cities)". The major issue with the prevalence of the digital divide is the potential for a widening gap in the society, resulting in a fourth world as predicted by Castells in his book, End of Millennium. The fourth world represents a population experiencing inequality, poverty, and disempowerment and exuberated by the lack of access to technology (Castells, 2000). Moreover, the digital gaps had become increasingly smaller by the turn of the 21st century. The divide had stabilized with regard to computer ownership, but Internet access still continues to be an issue, especially with the advent of high-speed access (United States Department of Commerce, 2000). The design barriers of government websites also have significant implications on the problem of digital divide (Becker, 2004). Online accessibility of government websites still falls short of expectations, including federal websites where being accessible is mandated (Stowers, 2004).

According to Mossberger et al. (2003), the definition of the digital divide should move beyond its traditional focus on "access" to a broader concept that addresses the lack of skills and economic opportunities for effective technology use. Kuttan and Peters (2003) associates the digital divide to other divides based on IT usability, computer access, and Internet and broadband access. In terms of IT usability, a government's website should be easy to navigate and user-friendly. Usability refers to the degree of comfort of citizens using the websites. According to Brinck et al. (2001), a website is considered usable if it enables the users to accomplish their goals quickly, efficiently and with simplicity. According to Cappel and Huang (2007), usability of a website represents the aspects of clarity, simplicity, consistency and ease of use. Website usability is important for both public

and private organizations to establish channels of communication and enhance the relationship between government and citizens. A website with appropriate levels of usability reduces the necessity for training, support, and maintenance costs (Verma & Ornager, 2005).

Bridging gaps in access is not enough to bridge the digital divide, as there are also often gaps in computer skills that present an obstacle for an individual to navigate the Internet. The Sipior and Ward (2005) case study of increasing citizen engagement through e-government shows that computer literacy is a prerequisite for bridging the digital divide. Their work presents a highly compelling argument that as residents become more comfortable navigating the Internet, it is more likely that they will visit government websites. Their work highlights the importance of including technical literacy in any definition of digital divide. Nevertheless, not every user can be expected to have the appropriate IT training or experience to effectively navigate a government website.

Apart from usability and accessibility, website privacy protection and channels for online participation are increasingly growing in expectations. The recent decade has seen tremendous increase in the adoption of e-government across the world, however not every initiative is completely trusted and embraced by citizen users. Many citizens and advocacy groups are very skeptical of the privacy protection efforts on government websites that requires users to submit their personal information apart from making use of tracking tools and cookies. According to the Hart–Teeter national survey conducted by the General Accounting Office (2001, p. 14), a significant section of the population have "concerns about sharing personal information with the government over the internet, fearing that the data will be misused and their privacy diminished."

According to Keniston and Kumar (2004), the digital divide can be broadly classified into four categories. The first category refers to a "massive digital divide based on income, related to education and urban residence, and correlated with economic, political and cultural power" (Keniston & Kumar, 2004, p. 13). The second divide, referred to as the "Anglo-Saxon linguistic and cultural hegemony" (Keniston & Kumar, 2004, p. 16) can be witnessed between nations with residents more comfortable in English language and nations without such comfort level. These refer to the English-speaking nations of US, UK Canada, New Zealand, Australia, as well as those nations with large English-speaking populations like India, South Africa, Singapore and Hong Kong and those nations where the English language is more prominent. The third divide is between the information-rich nations in the North and the information-poor nations in the South. The final divide is between those citizens who are experiencing the immediate effect of IT revolution and those left out of the boom. This new professional elite, made up of computer engineers and professionals have reaped huge benefits from the computerization phenomenon (Keniston & Kumar, 2004, p. 17). Jones (2003) agrees on such classifications by proposing the following dimensions: social divide between the information rich and information poor; global divide between developed and developing nations; and democratic divide between those who use internet for civic participation and those who do not.

According to Tichenor et al. (1970, p. 159) "segments of the population with higher socio-economic status tend to acquire information at a faster rate than the lower segments so that the gap in knowledge in these tends to increase rather than decrease". This association of ICT access to one's socio-economic status is not new to the Internet age. Jan van Dijk (2005) considers the digital divide as more of a social and political problem, rather than a technological one. He stated that rather than a simple division, a 'tripartite' division occurs in society, in terms of the access to information technology. The digital divide is a direct consequence of inequitable distribution of technology, compounded by poverty, illiteracy and other social problems (Gorla, 2008).

The most cited solution to bridging the digital divide, regardless of its cause, is to increase Internet access and to educate citizens about how it functions. Once the country implements e-government, citizens will be ready to utilize the services, and hence will be more engaged with the government. Bridging the digital divide may be cost prohibitive for many countries, especially those in the developing world. While the cost of communication has drastically decreased in the Internet age, the cost of purchasing a computer and Internet service may be outside the reach for a majority of citizens in the developing world. What further complicates this situation is the fact that many parts of the developing world are not wired for the telephone or the Internet. One technology that has gone a long way to bridge the digital divide is the use of mobile devices in the provision of governmental services.

M-Government

M-government or mobile government is defined as the "strategy and implementation of governmental services through a mobile platform to provide its users, both citizens and civil servants, the benefits of getting services and information from anywhere at any time" (Kushchu & Borucki, 2004, p. 4). Kushchu and Kuscu (2003, p. 3) view m-government as a "strategy and its implementation involving the utilization of all kinds of wireless and mobile technology, services, application, and devices for improving benefits to the parties involved in e-government including citizens, businesses, and all government units." According to a United Nations report, m-government is "subset of e-government where ICTs are limited to mobile and/or wireless technologies like cell or mobile phones, and laptops and personal digital assistants (PDAs)) connected to wireless local area networks (LANs)" (Ahmed, 2003, p. 14). Snellen and Thanes (2008, p. 1) define m-government as "the application of mobile devices, such as mobile telephone, Personal Digital Assistant (PDA) and hand held PCs in the exchanges between officials, citizens (organizations), and public administration as such."

There has been an increase in the use of m-government by state and local governments with the aim of improving the quality of services and meeting service needs (Moon, 2004). In addition to flexibility and mobility, another advantage of using m-government in the developing world is that it allows people who do not have the experience, training, or access to the Internet to engage government on their mobile devices. In addition, using mobile technologies to bridge the digital divide is more cost effective than traditional means. In many developing countries, there is more advanced mobile infrastructure as compared to telephone and Internet. In a case study of m-government in China, Gang (2005) showed how m-government improved citizens' overall perception and trust of government through closer interactions and improved service delivery. M-government is advantageous as "[c]itizens don't need to find a telephone or Internet access to complain or solicit a public service through virtual interaction" (2005, p. 6).

In this study we hope to provide ample evidence that while the digital divide may follow other societal divides mobile technology does not follow this pattern. This would indicate that utilizing m-government would be a more feasible and cost effective way to bridge the digital divide and engage citizens in government.

DESIGN AND METHODOLOGY

In our research, we review the potential for a digital divide by reviewing the differences between the average e-government scores between the cities belonging to the OECD and non-OECD nations evaluated in the Digital Government in Municipalities Worldwide Survey conducted in

2003, 2005, 2007 and 2009. These differences did not necessarily constitute the existence of a digital divide in these selected countries, but rather provide a place for focused attention and research. Any divide may already have begun to get addressed through m-government and other non-internet-based technologies. The Digital Government in Municipalities Survey was conducted by the E-Governance Institute at Rutgers-Newark, USA and the Global e-Policy e-Government Institute at Sungkyunkwan University in Seoul. The e-government measure combines five aspects – privacy, usability, content, services, and citizen participation – all of which play a role in the digital divide. The OECD consists of 28 nations and the largest municipality in each nation was evaluated including those of 59 non-OECD nations.

This research evaluates the digital divide, defined as the differences in performance scores between OECD and non-OECD nations as compared to the societal and economic divides of human development, education level, GDP, life expectancy, number of online users and number of mobile users. These various divides are evaluated over six years, beginning with the first e-government survey in 2003 and continuing every other year until 2009. The potential direction of the divides among OECD and non-OECD nations is assessed. The data used for human development, education level, life expectancy and GDP are obtained from the UN Human Development Report (2009). This report ranks nations based on a combination of factors - healthy life, access to knowledge, and standard of living - measured by life expectancy, literacy rates, and levels of education. In addition, the life expectancy measures are obtained from the World Population Prospects database prepared by the United Nations Department of Economic and Social Affairs Population Division.

The International Telecommunication Union (ITU), a United Nations (UN) affiliated organization, produces the data on the number of mobile users and Internet users for nations throughout the world. These same figures served as the bases for

Table 1. Worldwide e-government average scores of OECD and Non-OECD nations

	OECD	Average	Non-OECD	Difference
2009 Overall Averages	46.69	35.93	30.83	15.86
2007 Overall Averages	45.00	33.37	27.46	17.54
2005 Overall Averages	44.35	33.11	26.50	17.85
2003 Overall Averages	36.34	28.49	24.36	11.98

selecting the municipalities utilized in the Rutgers E-Government Survey. The top 100 municipalities were selected using ITU data for which telecommunications data was reported. Nations with an online population over 260,000 were selected for the Rutgers study. The top 100 online user nations were identified and studied in each of the past Rutgers E-Government worldwide studies. As a proxy for the nation and region, the most populous municipality was selected for each of the 100 nations. In all, 87 municipalities were surveyed as these cities had available official websites.

DATA ANALYSIS AND RESULTS

Overall, the average e-government score for OECD nations in 2009 was 46.69 while that of the non-OECD nations was 30.83, resulting in a gap of 15.86 points. This gap represented a decrease from a 17.54-point gap in the 2007 survey (table 1). This is also a more significant decrease from the previous two-year gap observed from 2003

and 2005. Among the OECD and non-OECD countries, the digital gap between the two scores increased from 11.98 in 2003 to 17.85 in 2005, but decreased to 17.54 in 2007 and 15.86 in 2009. The significance of this slowing of the digital divide can be attributed to greater gains in e-government by non-OECD nations. Additionally, the increase for OECD member countries from 2007 was only 1.69 points, and for non-OECD member countries, there was an increase of 3.37 from 2007. Table 2, below, highlights how these gaps are represented in each of the five e-government categories in 2009. The largest gap is in the category of usability (5.39) and the smallest gap is in content (2.11).

When we evaluate the digital divide against other societal divides, we find that there is a stabilization of existing divides or in some cases, have began to increase after a period of decline. The human development index highlights an overall increase among OECD and non-OECD nations. The human development index is a combination of various factors and variables which, when looked at independently, also reflect a sta-

Table 2. Average scores and gap of e-government categories in OECD and Non-OECD nations (2009)

	Usability	Content	Service	Privacy	Citizen Participation
OECD Member Countries	9.23	13.39	10.72	8.31	5.03
Average Score Gap	5.39	2.11	3.70	2.40	2.26
Non-OECD Member Countries	3.84	11.28	7.02	5.91	2.77

Table 3. Digital and societal divide of OECD and Non-OECD nations

Year	Digital Divide[1]	Human Development[2]	Life Expectancy[3]	Education Index[2]	GDP Index[2]	Mobile Cellular Subscribers (per 100 inhabitants)[3]	Internet Users (per 100 inhabitants)[4]
2009	15.86	0.162	0.143	0.121	0.222	23.06	38.40
2007	17.54	0.155	0.128	0.116	0.219	28.89	36.35
2005	17.85	0.175	0.146	0.145	0.233	39.50	37.05

bilized divide. For example, the gap in human development between OECD and non-OECD nations increased from 0.155 in 2007 to 0.162 in 2009. Even though there was an increase this gap is still lower than the human development gap in 2005 (0.175). Similarly, the gaps in education and GDP among non-OECD nations increased but remain below 2005 levels.

In addition to societal factors, technological divides have begun to show some significant changes. In terms of overall Internet users within non-OECD nations, there has been an increase in the divide. Most notably, the divide among mobile cellular users continued to decrease from 39.5 per 100 users in 2005 and 28.89 per 100 users in 2007 to 23.06 per 100 users in 2009. The increase in mobile use in non-OECD countries reflects the most significant change among all the societal and technological divides discussed here. It is this aspect that we look to explore further with our research as the decreasing divide among mobile users may provide an opportunity for addressing issues of e-government.

Moreover, the 2009 survey results show that only 31% of the municipalities have websites utilizing wireless technology such as messages to a mobile phone, a Palm Pilot, or a PDA (Personal Digital Assistance) to update about applications, events, etc. Among these cities, 57% of those in OECD nations provided such features online compared to only 14% of the cities in non-OECD nations.

Therefore, we should consider looking at mobile use as a medium for improving e- government performance. Especially when we take

into account that the existing divides associated with mobile use is decreasing consistently over time. The following section will examine the opportunity of m-government and the means for increasing the citizen-government relationship in areas where divides are minimal and can have the most impact.

DISCUSSION

Traditionally Internet access through the use of personal computers requires a strong, stable technological infrastructure. The basic telecommunication network of a nation highlights the potential Internet infrastructure, and other advanced communication infrastructure, for that nation. Investing in technology infrastructure will help reach not only the upper levels of society in developing nations but also set the foundation for reaching out to all parts of the nation's society. However, not all nations possess such infrastructure for personal computers, and this gap is being filled by the increasing use of mobile technology.

According to a recent CNN report, about 24 million Americans are yet to experience access to broadband Internet, especially in the rural areas of the country. Also any immediate possibility of such access seems ruled out, as the high-speed Internet providers claim that it is not economically feasible for them to install broadband in these areas with very few potential subscribers (Griggs, 2010). However, a more recent survey conducted by the Pew Research Center found that about 59% of all American adults have accessed the Internet through wireless technology as of May 2010. The study conducted as part of the Internet and American Life Project defined such wireless access as including access through cell phone or using a laptop with a Wi-Fi connection or mobile broadband card. Compared to their previous survey in 2009, cell phone ownership has remained the same, but their users are increasingly utilizing the Internet and other applications on their cell phones.

Thus the effort to bridge the digital divide should involve innovative technologies, especially by the cities of non-OECD nations striving to catch up with their OECD counterparts on the ICT scale. Recently many cities in both OECD and non-OECD nations have began creating smart communities by utilizing emerging technologies to improve the quality of public service. In response to increasingly online populations, governments are striving to improve the standard of living of its residents by "disseminating knowledge, strengthening social cohesion, generating earnings, and finally, ensuring that organizations and public bodies remain competitive in the global electronic marketplace" (Lambrinoudakis et al., 2003, p.1). Urban areas are gradually becoming venues of more interactions between physical and virtual environments, resulting in the phenomenon of 'digital cities' (Craglia, 2004). This transformation is also fueled by the increasing use of mobile phones and mobile technology.

Among the five categories in the index, the gap between the average scores of OECD and non-OECD cities is highest in usability (5.39), followed by service (3.70) and privacy (2.26) with comparatively lower differences. Bridging the digital divide will need to focus specifically on improving the usability aspect of information technology, which is significantly possible with the use of mobile devices. Being easily accessible and usable by illiterate populations as well, mobile technology encourages two-way communication, especially among previously neglected communities. Gradually, mobile phones are transforming

into full-fledged computers with their differences reducing due to advances in mobile devices such as mobile printers, thin folding screens, and gesture keyboards. These developments along with reduced costs, and reduced electricity requirement exhibit great promise to bridge the digital divide (Dholakia, 2002). This adoption has expanded the boundaries of the Internet from computers to mobile carriers, enabling the possibility of mobile government or m-government. M-government holds tremendous potential in bridging the digital divide, due to its unique advantages of "mobility" and "wirelessness" (Sheng & Trimi, 2008). A successful implementation of m-government will involve certain potential barriers relating to infrastructure, privacy and security issues, and usability issues. One of the major factors influencing m-government in developing nations is the cost related to infrastructure development, which can often be addressed through public-private partnerships (PPP) (Karan & Khoo, 2009). The governments could harness the potential of the private mobile technology companies in expanding the necessary infrastructure across the nation, especially the rural areas. The development of a suitable infrastructure needs to be followed by promoting the awareness and advantages of mobile government among citizen users as well as government agencies, and one of the major challenges in this direction is the issue of privacy and security. Mobile phone usage does not provide the anonymous environment as those using public computers and wireless network signals are susceptible to being hacked. With regard to usability, mobile phone users can access only those websites that are capable of being translated from HTML to WML, along with the issue of fitting appropriate information into the smaller mobile screens (Trimi & Sheng, 2008). Additional challenges such as interoperability between operators, roaming between countries, compatibility and difference in platforms also need to be addressed in the process of implementing m-government.

CONCLUSION

The use of technology by governments to provide services and communicate with its citizens is continually evolving as both governments and citizens expect increased quality of service delivery. As mobile technology continues to evolve, so will the opportunities of m-government to address the concerns of existing digital divides. The ability of the public to have access and competencies to utilize these technologies is not new and will continually resurface with every passing generation – but the methods to address the digital divide can help minimize them. This research study has reviewed the digital divides among municipalities and regions globally as well as their current trends.

Based on these findings, we provide three key recommendations for practitioners and future research. First, the research has underscored the opportunities of m-government as a critical avenue for the potential reduction in these existing divides. M-government holds countless opportunities and as future innovative ways are being developed for the use of mobile technologies, so should the means by which these innovations and services are made accessible. Second, an area where research and focus can begin in addressing potential divides is among nations outlined as non-OECD countries. Finally, initiatives that look to address the digital divide can and should look at societal divides when predicting areas of concern and potential areas of focus. As this research has shown, there are existing divides among nations that are at times reflected digitally.

The introduction of mobile technologies enables a natural transformation from an era of e-government to the era of m-government. Nowadays, m-government is not just viewed as a parallel phenomenon to e-government but as a necessity to complete e-government. M-government results in a deeper and more intensive utilization of e-government applications. This paradigm shift is more than simply a change in technology, but also a change in attitudes and approaches of both the citizens and government officials. However, most government agencies, especially at the local level are yet to utilize mobile technologies to their full potential in providing services to their residents, especially to those at the lower half of the digital divide.

The research study has certain limitations that should be noted. First, the methodology of surveying the largest municipalities throughout the world as proxies for the country and region and using national UN data for comparison is a key limitation to the study. Future research would ideally utilize national e-government scores or increased municipal data to reflect more than one municipality per country. Finally, the survey instrument does not specifically measure the use of m-government technologies to capture the e-government score. Therefore, future research would aim to include specific analysis of m-government scores among municipalities.

REFERENCES

Ahmed, N. (2003). *An overview of e-participation models*. New York, NY: United Nations Division for Public Administration and Development Management.

Becker, S. A. (2004). E-government visual accessibility for older adult users. *Social Science Computer Review*, *22*(1), 11–23. doi:10.1177/0894439303259876

Brinck, T., Wood, S., & Gergle, D. (2001). *Usability for the Web: Designing web sites that work*. San Francisco, CA: Morgan Kaufmann.

Cappel, J. J., & Huang, Z. (2007). A usability analysis of company websites. *Journal of Computer Information Systems*, *48*(1), 117–123.

Castells, M. (2000). *End of millennium: The rise of the fourth world: Capitalism, poverty and social exclusion*. Oxford, UK: Blackwell.

Craglia, M. (2004). Cogito ergo sum or non-cogito ergo digito? The digital city revised. *Environment and Planning B, 31*(1), 3–4. doi:10.1068/b3101ed2

Dholakia, N., & Kshetri, N. (2002). The global digital divide and mobile business models: Identifying viable patterns of e-development. In S. Krishna & S. Madon (Eds.), *Proceedings of the Seventh IFIP WG9.4 Conference*, (pp. 528–540). Bangalore, India.

Gang, S. (2005). Transcending e-government: A case of mobile government in Beijing. *The Proceedings of the First European Conference on Mobile Government*. Brighton, England.

General Accounting Office. (2001). *Electronic government: Challenges must be addressed with effective leadership and management*. Retrieved August 11, 2005, from http://feapmo.gov/links.asp

Gorla, N. (2008). Hurdles in rural e-government projects in India: Lessons for developing countries. *Electronic Government, an International Journal, 5*(1), 91-102.

Griggs, B. (2010, July 21). U.S. not getting broadband fast enough, FCC says. *CNN*. Retrieved August 15, 2010, from http://www.cnn.com/2010/TECH/web/07/20/fcc.broadband.access/index.html

Holzer, M., & Kim, S. T. (2008). *Digital governance in municipalities worldwide, a longitudinal assessment of municipal web sites throughout the world*. The E-Governance Institute, Rutgers University, Newark; & The Global e-policy e-government Institute, Sungkyunkwan University.

Holzer, M., & Manoharan, A. (2009). Tracking the digital divide: Studying the association of the global digital divide with societal divide, in e-government development and diffusion. In Sahu, G. P., Dwivedi, Y. K., & Weerakkody, V. (Eds.), *Inhibitors and facilitators of digital democracy* (pp. 54–63). Hershey, PA: IGI Global. doi:10.4018/978-1-60566-713-3.ch004

Jones, S. (2003). *Encyclopedia of new media*. Thousand Oaks, CA: Sage Publications.

Karan, K., & Khoo, M. (2009). Mobile diffusion and development: Issues and challenges of m-government with India. In J. S. Petterson (Ed.), *Proceedings of 1st International Conference on M4D 2008, General Tracks*, Karlstad University Studies, (p. 61).

Keniston, K., & Kumar, D. (2004). *Experience in India: Bridging the digital divide*. Thousand Oaks, CA: Sage Publications.

Kirlin, J. (1996). What government must do well: Creating value for society. *Journal of Public Administration: Research and Theory, 6*(1), 161–185.

Kushchu, I., & Borucki, C. (2004). *Impact of mobile technologies on government*. Mobile Government Lab. Retrieved August 19, 2010, from http://www.mgovlab.org

Kushchu, I., & Kuscu, H. (2003). From e-government to m-government: Facing the inevitable. *The Proceedings of European Conference on E-Government*, Trinity College, Dublin.

Kuttan, A., & Peters, L. (2003). *From digital divide to digital opportunity*. Lanham, MD: The Scarecrow Press, Inc.

Lambrinoudakis, C., Gritzalis, S., Dridi, F., & Pernul, G. (2003). Security requirements for e-government services: A methodological approach for developing a common pki-based security policy. *Computer Communications, 26*(16), 1873–1883. doi:10.1016/S0140-3664(03)00082-3

Moon, M. J. (2004). *From e-government to m-government? Emerging practices in the use of mobile technology by state government. E-government Series*. Washington, DC: IBM Center for the Business of Government.

Mossberger, K., Tolbert, C. J., & Stansbury, M. (2003). *Virtual inequality: Beyond the digital divide*. Washington, DC: Georgetown University Press.

Sheng, H. & Trimi, S. (2008). M-government: Technologies, applications and challenges. *Electronic Government, an International Journal, 5*(1), 1-18.

Sipior, J. C., & Ward, B. T. (2005). Bridging the digital divide for e-government inclusion: A United States case study. *The Electronic Journal of E-Government, 39*(1), 137–146.

Snellen, I. T. M., & Thaens, M. (2008). From e-government to m-government. In Pennella, G. (Eds.), *European cases, administrative innovation and growth* (pp. 211–256). Formez, Italy: Gianni Research.

Stowers, G. (2004). *Measuring the performance of e-government*. Washington, DC: IBM Endowment for the Business of Government.

Tichenor, P. J., Olien, C. N., & Donahue, G. A. (1970). Mass media flow and differential growth in knowledge. *Public Opinion Quarterly, 34*(2), 159–170. doi:10.1086/267786

Trimi, S., & Sheng, H. (2008). Emerging trends in m-government. *Communications of the ACM, 51*(5), 53–58. doi:10.1145/1342327.1342338

United Nations Development Program. (1999). *Human Development Report 1999*. New York, NY: United Nation Development Program/Oxford.

United Nations Human Development Report. (2009*). Overcoming barriers: Human mobility and development*. Retrieved April 2, 2010, from http://hdr.undp.org/en/reports/global/hdr2009

United Nations Public Administration Network (UNPAN). (2008). *Global e-government survey: From e-government to connected governance*. Division for Public Administration and Development Management. Retrieved March 16, 2010, from http://www.unpan.org/egovkb/global_reports/08report.htm

United States Department of Commerce. (1999). Falling through the net: Defining the digital divide. Washington, DC: United States Department of Commerce. Retrieved November 12, 2007, from http://www.ntia.doc.gov/ntiahome/fttn99/FTTN.pdf

United States Department of Commerce. (2000). *Falling through the net: Toward digital inclusion.* Washington, DC: United States Department of Commerce. Retrieved November 12, 2007, from http://search.ntia.doc.gov/pdf/fttn00.pdf

van Dijk, J. A. G. M. (2005). *The deepening divide: Inequality in an information society*. Thousand Oaks, CA: Sage Publications.

Verma, N., & Ornager, S. (2005). *E-government toolkit for developing countries.* Retrieved August 5, 2010, from http://www.unescobkk.org/fileadmin/user_upload/ci/documents/UNESCO_e-Govt_Toolkit.pdf

West, D. M. (2008). *Global e-government survey*. Retrieved March 16, 2010, from http://www.insidepolitics.org/

KEY TERMS AND DEFINITIONS

Citizen Participation: The active involvement of the public in issues of governance and decision-making.

Digital Divide: The divide between those who have access to information and communication technology tools and those who do not have such access.

E-Government: The use of information technologies by governments to enhance effectiveness and efficiency.

M-Government: The use of mobile technologies by governments to enhance communications with citizens.

Municipalities: Local designated government entities.

ENDNOTES

1. Data for the digital divide reflects the difference between the average scores of OECD and Non-OECD nations surveyed in Rutgers 2009, 2007 and 2005 Surveys.

2. Data for the social divides of OECD and Non-OECD nations for the Human Development Index, Life expectancy Index, Education Index, and GDP index represents the two most recent accessible data years from the UN Human Development Reports 2003, 2006, and 2009.

3. The Mobile Cellular and Internet Users data taken from the ITU Reports for 2005, 2007 and 2008 highlights the divide between OECD and Non-OECD nations.

Chapter 6

3D Digital City Platforms as Collaborative and Decision-Making Tools for Small Municipalities and Rural Areas

Barbara L. Maclennan
West Virginia University, USA

Susan J. Bergeron
Coastal Carolina University, USA

ABSTRACT

This chapter explores how the development and implementation of a 3D digital city platform can be utilized in the context of solid waste management and sustainable planning in a small municipality or largely rural areas with limited resources. By leveraging 3D visualization and Web 2.0 functionality to allow stakeholders to collaborate on equal footing, digital city platforms can help with day-to-day management of solid waste assets and facilities, planning for solid waste and recycling facilities and drop-offs, mapping and planning efficient waste hauler routes, and identifying issues such as underserved populations and illegal dumping.

INTRODUCTION

Initiatives to develop digital city models, or 'smart cities', have been gaining prominence within the past several years, as more people become aware of the power of GIS coupled with 3D visualiza-

tion to allow government officials and managers to manage assets and perform day-to-day operations, develop sustainable planning initiatives, and collaborate between expert and non-expert groups. However, much of the focus of this new research and implementation has been on large cities, which already possess many of the tools and experts necessary to implement such digital city

DOI: 10.4018/978-1-4666-0318-9.ch006

models. This paper will explore how the digital city platform can be utilized in the context of solid waste management and sustainable planning in a small municipality or largely rural area with limited resources.

By leveraging 3D visualization and GIS functionality to allow stakeholders to collaborate on equal footing, digital city platforms can help with day-to-day management and long-range planning of solid waste assets and facilities, planning for solid waste and recycling facilities and drop-offs, mapping and planning efficient waste hauler routes, and identifying issues such as underserved populations and illegal dumping. 3D visualization can be utilized by community environmental courts and other efforts to engage citizens, by providing non-experts to interact with their community in the way that they understand it. Recent developments in the areas of software, cloud computing, and open web-enabled technologies have lowered the barrier of entry for regional and rural organizations to begin experimenting with these technologies.

This chapter discusses the potential of 3D digital city platforms as collaborative and and outlines the development of a pilot 3D digital city platform for the small municipality of Star City, West Virginia. The main goal of the Star City pilot project was to demonstrate how geospatial technologies, such as GIS and 3D geovisualization, can be integrated with Web 2.0 collaborative technologies to create a digital city platform for local government decision-making, planning, and collaboration with citizens. The Star City digital city platform[1], built upon a GIS database generated for Star City and integrated with Web 2.0 based tools for public input on issues related to trash and recycling pickups, clearly demonstrated how such digital technologies can serve as a platform for more open and effective government in small municipalities.

BACKGROUND

At the heart of the movement to leverage the social media aspects of Web 2.0 for open government and public participation, known as Government 2.0 (Gov 2.0) is the belief that the relationship between government and citizen is a two way dialogue or a collaborative, transparent effort to create good government (O'Reilly, 2010). Technology, specifically Web 2.0, plays an integral role in establishing and encouraging this dialogue, making it accessible to anyone with access to the Internet at home, the public library, or increasingly on mobile phones. The central focus of Gov 2.0 is to build on the concept of government as a platform by leveraging the social networking aspects of Web 2.0 to develop data structures and applications that allow a dynamic, transparent relationship between government and its constituents (O'Reilly, 2010).

However, involving citizens in government does not begin when a technological application is launched to the public; it starts with the act of wanting to involve citizens in the government process. The more transparent a local government, the more likely that local government wants the public to actively participate in its policy process and in turn the more likely the public will want to participate. Internally, when local government officials support innovation and transparency, government employees feels more comfortable in extending the resources to do so. Externally, when the public feels wanted in the policy process, it strengthens their trust in the legitimacy of policy decisions. Quinn (2002) found that "The closer people are to the culture of the knowledge being transferred, the easier it is to share and exchange." If the willingness to involve the public in government processes does not exist, then technology cannot create it.

Geographic Information Systems (GIS) are often the first crucial step towards Gov 2.0 because local governments are already used to collecting geospatial data about their assets and citizens, and the demand for geospatial data by citizens has also spurred the adoption of GIS as a management and planning tool (Curtin & Meijer, 2006; Otenyo & Lind, 2004; Pina et al., 2007). Since the early 2000s, GIS has increasingly been seen as an integral part of the e-government process because it facilitates the exchange and analysis of large amounts of data. The bulk of this data has always been held local government authorities, but the problem in the past has been how to use it effectively. The public's increased awareness and use of geospatial technologies in their everyday lives, through Web 2.0 mapping applications such as Google maps, has given them the skills to be involved not just as an end player in the local government process but an integral part of it. Citizen 2.0 is a reflection of the fact that technology has caught up to the desires of the public to take a more active role in government (Higgs & Turner, 2003; Jou & Humenik-Sappington, 2009).

Geospatial Technologies and Web 2.0

Geographic Information Systems (GIS) are a set of technologies that are used for the storage, mapping, and analysis of geographic information, and are increasingly used by government agencies at all levels as management and planning tools. The first GIS systems were developed in the early 1970s as land management systems, but the adoption of GIS technology has broadened into many fields and disciplines within the past few decades. GIS is now an increasingly important tool in emergency management, urban and regional planning, utility and infrastructure management, transportation, public health, and law enforcement (Maguire, 1991). However, implementing and maintaining a GIS is often a costly process, requiring the purchase and maintenance of computer hardware and GIS software, as well as staff with GIS expertise to utilize the system. In addition, the collection and maintenance of the geographic data sets, such as transportation networks, utilities, structures, and other urban features, that are required for the GIS can add significantly to the cost of a project. As a result, access to GIS technology and data has generally been limited to those public and private entities who can afford the costs to deploy and maintain such systems.

Since the early 1990s, the issues surrounding open access to geographic information and GIS technology have been a research focus within Geographic Information Science (GIScience). A series of debates within the discipline of Geography at this time raised a number of issues related to the use of GIS technology in government and planning, including questions of community empowerment, data access, public participation and the incorporation of local knowledge into expert-driven systems such as GIS (Weiner et al., 2002; Harris and Weiner, 1998). These "GIS and Society" meetings and publications led to initiatives in Public Participation GIS, which has since evolved into the more precisely termed Participatory GIS (PGIS) (Sieber, 2006). Essentially, the main focus of PGIS research is the empowerment of communities by enabling greater community input and access to geospatial data and technologies, to develop community mapping and spatial analysis in support of project decision making (Elwood, 2006; Rouse et al., 2007).

As the Internet infrastructure and the World Wide Web matured in the late 1990s, researchers began to explore the potential for Web-based PGIS to broaden community access to GIS mapping and analysis. However, these systems still required substantial expertise and technology to implement, as Internet based GIS applications are often built on proprietary Web mapping platforms. For example, the Community Mapping Network project utilized commercial GIS software to develop online mapping tools that integrated Web mapping and local knowledge to support collaborative community planning in British Columbia, Canada (Mason & Dragicevic, 2006). While community groups can effectively utilize such tools, they require a general awareness of GIS and its functions, as well as partnerships with software providers. Consequently, while a number of expert-driven Web-based PGIS projects have been successful in broadening access to GIS information and increasing community collaboration in planning and decision-making, they are limited in number due to the resources and expertise required (Rouse et al., 2007).

In the summer of 2005, the web mapping landscape changed dramatically when Google released its Google Maps application. Not only did Google Maps and other competing services offer the public the opportunity to interact with geographic information through an intuitive and easy-to-use online mapping viewer, but these applications were also driven by the Web 2.0 elements of user-generated content and collaboration. Google, Yahoo!, and Microsoft all released Application Programming Interfaces (APIs) that allowed users to fairly easily combine their own data with the mapping application's background mapping layers. The ability to create these personalized maps, or mashups, meant that anyone with a computer, an Internet connection, and data they wanted to share could become a mapmaker (Boulton, 2010; Turner, 2007; Rouse et al., 2007; Goodchild, 2007). An important consequence of this Web 2.0-driven mapping explosion was the upsurge of awareness of the power of mapping and visualizing geographic information.

While the technologies themselves, such as Google Maps and other web mapping applications are often the focus of discussion, in reality the driving force behind the Web 2.0 movement is the information and the dynamic connections between data across the Internet (O'Reilly, 2007). The idea behind web services and mashups in Web 2.0 is to bring together data sources to aggregate content, create visualizations, and conduct real time analyses to create information that is relevant to the audience. While many of the data sources come from government, commercial, and NGO sources, a wealth of data has come about through the use of Web 2.0 technologies that allow users

to create data. This user-generated data ranges from individual data creation that is used to share information to large peer reviewed data projects that is intended to provide a robust base data set. Within the expert GIS community, there has been tension between the use of these authoritative/formal (government or commercial) and non-authoritative/informal (user generated) data sources that revolve around a perceived difference in rigor (Goodchild, 2008). In the case of Web 2.0 mapping initiatives for government, authoritative data is often used to build the representation of streets, structures, and infrastructure that provide the platform, while user generated data is used to mark changes, add detail, and provide associated content or public input.

An excellent example of the development of web mapping tools to facilitate public input and participation can be seen in Montgomery County, Maryland's Snow Map interactive web mapping application (Montgomery County, 2011). A local Montgomery County politician was concerned because the perception of local citizens was that snow removal in the county was not adequate despite increased efforts by the county to meet these needs. The Montgomery County GIS Team was approached to find a way to convey to residents the status of snow removal in their area. Because Montgomery County had the resources, expertise, and support necessary, what started out as the desire to create greater transparency became an award winning example of citizen and government working together to create a better system for everyone. The interactive snow map allows citizens to report issues such as lack of snow removal, downed trees, or even property damage caused by plowing. Citizens who do not have access to the Internet can still contribute to the system by calling a County-wide 311 number to report issues. The snow map interactive web mapping application is part of a larger integrated GIS system for police, fire, facility, and infrastructure that enables local government agencies to view data such as tax parcels, building preplans and floor plans, live feed for traffic, and real-time events like snow removal reports, maintenance issues, and crime incidents. (Gong et al., 2011).

Montgomery County's GIS services demonstrate how GIS and geospatial technologies have become an essential component of government at all levels, from local municipalities to national government agencies (Jou & Humenik-Sappington, 2009; Greene, 2000). Within the last decade, the role of GIS within the e-government process has continued to expand, as government agencies, local governments, and community stakeholders increasingly recognize the potential of GIS technology in the integration and analysis of large amounts of geographic data. The bulk of these data sets are held by local government authorities, but the problem has always been how to effectively use such geospatial data in decision-making and planning processes involving public input and community stakeholders. (Higgs & Turner, 2003).

Web 2.0 and the Digital City

There is a growing movement to develop 3D digital cities, or 'smart cities' as powerful visualization and collaborative tools to aid in daily operations and decision-making (Hudson-Smith, 2008, 2007; Tan & Wong, 2006). Combining a strong GIS database and analysis capability with 3D modeling and visualization, digital city models allow multiple stakeholders to collaborate effectively by displaying data and analysis results within a 3D environment. Much of the work currently being done to develop and implement these digital city models has been undertaken in large urban areas, including a number of large cities in Europe and Asia (Hudson-Smith, 2008, 2007; Dollner et al., 2006; Shiode, 2001; Ranzinger & Gleixner, 1997). While these projects and others continue to demonstrate the growing utility of 3D digital cities as platforms for the synthesis, analysis and display of information, their focus on large urban environments excludes the even greater potential

for these technologies to help small municipalities and rural areas.

A 3D digital city platform that combines GIS datasets and analysis capabilities, 3D visualization, and the collaborative and user-driven functionality of Web 2.0 can be a powerful tool for government decision-making, long-range planning, information dissemination to the public, and community collaboration. Such a 3D digital city concept builds on the Gov 2.0 notion of government as a platform (O'Reilly, 2010), whereby the 3D digital representation of the city serves as the base upon which data is organized, displayed, and analyzed. Since 3D representations of the physical landscape are intuitive and less abstract than other types of expert knowledge representation, the digital city platform can reduce miscommunication, improve decision-making and management workflows, and provide better

When combined with the collaborative power of Web 2.0, which allows users to access and interact with such applications via the Internet, 3D digital city models have the potential to serve as an integrative platform for a participatory local Gov 2.0 (Howard & Gaborit, 2007). In addition, the accessibility and low cost of implementing Web 2.0 based technologies addresses some of the challenges faced by municipalities with limited resources to allocate to such projects. As these technologies become even more prevalent in many public agencies and municipal governments around the world, public expectations of the availability of maps and other geographic information products are also rising.

3D DIGITAL CITY INITIATIVES FOR SMALL MUNICIPALITIES

As the adoption of GIS and 3D visualization technologies as tools within government and other organizations at the national, regional, and metropolitan levels has grown tremendously within the last decade, there is now increasing pressure on smaller municipalities to develop and deploy such systems in order to keep up with standards in data collection, management, and availability, and to improve local management and planning practices. In addition, the level of awareness of these technologies has also grown rapidly among tech-savvy citizens, who are beginning to advocate for the use of such technologies within their communities.

While larger cities are more likely to initiate innovative policies and rural areas imitate or follow policy trends, this is often an artifact of budget constraints or lack of expertise (Shipan & Volden, 2008). Currently, the belief is that highly concentrated urban areas will develop and utilize digital cities, however the researcher and associates have found that smaller municipalities can not only go from non-documented knowledge to digital city fairly quickly, they can do so in a way that is more flexible and cheaper than large urban areas. Thus it is not necessary for rural and developing areas to wait for the technology. The diffusion of digital technology, specifically free easy to use tools for developing digital city platforms now makes the digital divide less of an obstacle (Matisoff, 2008).

By integrating multiple stakeholder communities, from policy makers to citizens, a digital city platform allows both expert and non-expert users to interact in a dynamic and digital environment that can be accessible by all citizens in some capacity. Small cities and towns often find it difficult to leverage new and innovative technologies such as GIS and 3D modeling due to limited access to resources and expertise to design and implement such tools. In addition, local government is often comprised of mature citizens who are committed to serving their community but may be wary of unfamiliar new technologies. Utilizing 3D digital city models, which visualize geographic information in an environment that is closer to the visual look of the real world, allows stakeholders from government and the community to collaborate more effectively by sharing information within the

3D environment (Wu & Isaksson, 2008; Vajjhala, 2006). Such models can also leverage the collaborative functionality of Web 2.0, by utilizing web-based applications to allow stakeholders and the general public to view and explore the 3D digital city platform, and offer input and feedback. There are a number of free or low-cost commercial 3D virtual globe applications that can be utilized as viewing and collaborative platforms for a 3D digital city project, such as Google Earth and Esri's ArcGIS Explorer, as well as open source options.

Star City 3D Digital City Platform

In order to demonstrate how a 3D digital city platform can go beyond expert-driven GIS as a management, collaborative, and decision-making tool, this research focused on solid waste management issues in the small municipality of Star City, West Virginia. As a small community, Star City has a small staff of full and part-time employees that work alongside the mayor and elected officials, and most of their data and procedures are paper-based. City officials, including the mayor and members of the city council, recognized that digital technologies such as GIS could go a long way toward modernizing operations and maximizing scarce city resources. However, they also recognized that the lack of expertise within the city government, as well as limited funds to purchase computer hardware and software and secure outside professional consultation and services with GIS expertise, makes the implementation of such technologies difficult.

Consequently, the city partnered with a local NGO, the Monongalia Solid Waste Authority, to leverage their expertise in developing a GIS database for the city, focusing at first on base infrastructure layers and on solid waste management and recycling data sets. Solid waste management and recycling is a useful mechanism for examining the increasing role of geospatial Web 2.0 technologies in the context of an emerging concept of Citizen 2.0 due to its visibility and impact on a broad scale, from individual households to local, county, and even regional government. Because a citizen's trash is still picked up from the front of their home, it is a highly personal social and cultural issue, and a visible form of government in action. Issues related to proper (or improper) solid waste management are also important to the community as a whole, as the visibility of trash can have a strong impact on perceptions of the community.

The Star City GIS that was first developed as a tool to map solid waste management assets and procedures is an excellent example of how a small municipality can utilize geospatial technology to help improve its ability to meet the needs of its constituents. However, building and using a GIS requires expert knowledge and resources, and can often prevent such systems from being used to their full capability by local officials and interested citizens. In order to bridge that gap, a digital city model uses 3D visualization to display the expert GIS data in a way that is easier for stakeholders of all levels of technical skill to understand and engage (Harvey, 2009). In the case of the initial Star City GIS project, many citizens and even city workers were not familiar or comfortable with computer technology and, while the visualization of GIS data helped them understand the process of trash collection and recycling to some extent, they remained wary of the technology. Consequently, the Star City 3D Digital City pilot project was proposed to create a platform that would provide a more intuitive 3D visualization of the urban landscape of Star City.

The extension of Star City's GIS to include the 3D data and visualization capabilities of a 3D digital city platform centered around the modeling of the structures within the city limits. The footprints of these structures were digitized and updated to reflect the most recent aerial imagery. These data layers were then imported into a 3D virtual globe application, with Star City's structures extruded as 3D shapes (Figure 1). This simplified 3D representation of the Star City urban

landscape serves as the base for the 3D digital city platform, and allows for multiple variables to be symbolized within the virtual landscape.

To highlight various attributes related to each structure, color symbology was used to indicate different values. Since solid waste management issues in Star City were the focus for this pilot study, demonstrations of the 3D digital city platform focused on these data sets. For example, commercial cardboard recycling pickup days were each assigned a different color, allowing users to immediately see where pickups were occurring on a given day (Figure 2). By utilizing such easily interpreted visual symbology, the digital city application allows the expert data stored in a GIS to become a dynamic visualization that can be utilized in day-to-day operations, as a collaborative tool when officials and staff from different agencies and parts of city government must come together to address issues, and as an effective presentation tool when issues such as planning and development that require public input are discussed. When the Star City 3D digital city prototype was presented to local government officials and city employees, it was well-received and employees especially noted the ease with which they could manipulate the 3D visualization and readily interpret the symbology in the context of the 3D virtual landscape.

Public input is an important aspect in utilizing a digital city platform for open government and, by leveraging custom notes functionality in the 3D viewer and in other integrated mapping applications, citizens were able to view and add notes about issues that relate to trash pickup and recycling. These notes can then be reviewed by city staff, and appropriate action taken or dialogue started. The notes can also be updated to acknowledge receipt of the comment and display the status. This Web 2.0 functionality is familiar to users of Google maps or Google Earth and other online mapping applications, and is fairly intuitive for most users. The initial implementation of collaborative input via the 3D viewer interface was

Figure 1. Star City virtual globe application

Figure 2. Commercial cardboard recycling pickup days in Star City virtual globe application

well-received, and future versions of the Star City Digital City will expand upon the collaborative and real-time interaction aspects of the platform, including the integration of social media.

FUTURE RESEARCH DIRECTIONS

The prototype Star City 3D Digital City platform clearly demonstrates the potential for such systems as tools for citizen government in an emerging Gov 2.0 framework, using the issue of solid waste management and recycling as an example. Responses of local government officials and citizens who were able to test the digital city platform were positive, and they were excited about the possibilities of implementing the platform. In the near future, the authors hope to continue working with local government and community stakeholders in Star City to expand the geospatial data layers available for access within the digital city platform to include other aspects of city management, such as zoning, utility asset management, and parcel information. In addition, the collaborative functionality of the Star City digital city platform will be further tested by the deployment of enhanced public participation capabilities, in the form of commenting and public input on other city issues.

More broadly, the development of the 3D digital city concept as a platform for collaborative open government is still a fairly new avenue of research, and offers exciting possibilities for exploring the engagement of an increasingly tech-savvy citizenry in participatory government. One of the most exciting areas of research in this movement is the integration of geospatial technologies and Web 2.0 technologies through the development of 3D digital city platforms which combine expert GIS data sets with 3D visualization capabilities. These 3D virtual landscapes can serve as a platform for users of all levels to view and explore data about their cities and towns, and collaborate with local government to identify and address concerns about day-to-day management

and decision-making and even long-range planning for their communities. However, a number of challenges still remain in broadly implementing such digital city platforms, including 1) cultural and social barriers to utilizing technology in local government; 2) limited resources and awareness of such technologies and how they might benefit small communities; and 3) lack of infrastructure or expertise to support the deployment and maintenance of Web 2.0-based platforms.

CONCLUSION

This chapter has briefly outlined how the development of Web 2.0-enabled 3D digital city platforms have the potential to fundamentally change both in-house decision making within municipal agencies and interaction with community stakeholders as part of an emerging movement toward government as a platform, or Gov 2.0. Policymakers, government officials, and community stakeholders can easily display and manipulate information through the 3D city model interface, which provides an intuitive visualization of the urban landscape and associated geographic information. Collaboration through Web 2.0 technologies, such as user contributions or feedback displayed on the 3D digital city model also provides an innovative mechanism for citizen involvement and community participation in municipal government.

To date, many 3D digital city initiatives have been focused on large urban areas, where financial resources, technology and expertise are more readily available. However, small municipalities and even rural areas could also benefit greatly from the development of 3D digital city initiatives, which could serve as a platform for decision-making, planning, and community participation in government. Where resources are scarce, such local governments can often partner with NGOs and universities to fill the gap in technical expertise required for implementation. The pilot Star City 3D Digital City project demonstrated this potential using the essential, but often overlooked, municipal responsibility of solid waste management. More importantly, this pilot project illustrated how digital technologies can provide a platform for local government to fulfill its responsibilities of day-to-day management, decision-making, and planning, as well as provide a collaborative platform for citizen and community participation.

REFERENCES

Boulton, A. (2010). Just maps: Google's democratic map-making community? *Cartographica, 45*(1), 1–4. doi:10.3138/carto.45.1.1

Curtin, D., & Meijer, A. (2006). Does transparency strengthen legitimacy? A critical analysis of European Union policy documents. *Information Polity, 11*, 109–112.

Dollner, J., Kolbe, T. H., Liecke, F., Sgouros, T., & Teichmann, K. (2006). The virtual 3D city model of Berlin – Managing, integrating, and communicating complex urban information. *Proceedings of the 25th International Symposium on Urban Data Management*, Aalborg, Denmark, 15-17 May 2006.

Elwood, S. (2006). Critical issues in participatory GIS: Deconstructions, reconstructions, and new research directions. *Transactions in GIS, 10*(5), 693–708. doi:10.1111/j.1467-9671.2006.01023.x

Gong, Y., Teng, A., & Galic, I. (2011). Integration of geospatial Web services with the 311 call center operations. *ESRI Federal User Conference Proceedings 2011*, Washington, DC.

Goodchild, M. (2007). Citizens as sensors: The world of volunteered geography. *GeoJournal, 69*, 211–221. doi:10.1007/s10708-007-9111-y

Goodchild, M. (2008). Spatial accuracy 2.0. *Proceedings of the 8th International Symposium on Spatial Accuracy Assessment in Natural Resources and Environmental Sciences*, Shanghai, China, June 25-27, 2008.

Greene, R. W. (2000). *GIS in public policy: Using geographic information for more effective government*. Redlands, CA: Esri Press.

Harris, T., & Weiner, D. (1998). Empowerment, marginalization and community-integrated GIS. *Cartography and Geographic Information Systems, 25*(2), 67–76. doi:10.1559/152304098782594580

Harvey, P. (2009). Between narrative and number: The case of ARUP's 3D digital city model. *Cultural Sociology, 3*(2), 257–276. doi:10.1177/1749975509105534

Higgs, G., & Turner, P. (2003). The use and management of geographic information in local e- government in the UK. *Information Polity, 8*(3-4), 151–165, 1570–1255.

Howard, T. J., & Gaborit, N. N. (2007). Using virtual environment technology to improve public participation in urban planning process. *Journal of Urban Planning and Development, 133*(4), 233–241. doi:10.1061/(ASCE)0733-9488(2007)133:4(233)

Hudson-Smith, A. (2007). Digital urban – The visual city. *UCL Centre for Advanced Spatial Analysis Working Paper Series*, Paper 124. London, UK: UCL.

Hudson-Smith, A. (2008). The visual city. In Dodge, M., McDery, M., & Turner, M. (Eds.), *Geographic visualization: Concepts, tools, and applications* (pp. 183–196). London, UK: Wiley & Sons. doi:10.1002/9780470987643.ch9

Jou, C. T., & Humenik-Sappington, N. (2009). *GIS for decision support and public policy making*. Redlands, CA: Esri Press.

Maguire, D. J. (1991). An overview and definition of GIS. In Maguire, D. J., Goodchild, M., & Rhind, D. W. (Eds.), *Geographic Information Systems: Principles and applications* (pp. 9–20). London, UK: Longman/Wiley.

Mason, B., & Dragicevic, S. (2006). Web GIS and knowledge management systems: An integrated design for collaborative community planning. In Balram, S., & Drageicevic, S. (Eds.), *Collaborative Geographic Information Systems*. Hershey, PA: IGI Global. doi:10.4018/978-1-59140-845-1.ch014

Matisoff, D. C. (2008). The adoption of state climate change policies and renewable portfolio standards: Regional diffusion or internal determinants? *Review of Policy Research, 25*(6), 527–546. doi:10.1111/j.1541-1338.2008.00360.x

Montgomery County. (2011). *MCDOT storm operations*. Retrieved from http://www5.montgomerycountymd.gov/snowmap/

O'Reilly, T. (2007). What is Web 2.0: Design patterns and business models for the next generation of software. *Communications & Strategies, 65*, 17-37. Retrieved from http://ssrn.com/abstract=1008839

O'Reilly, T. (2010). Government as a platform. In Lathrop, D., & Ruma, L. (Eds.), *Open government: Collaboration, transparency, and participation in practice*. Sebastopol, CA: O'Reilly Media.

Otenyo, E. E., & Lind, N. S. (2004). Faces and phases of transparency reform in local government. *International Journal of Public Administration, 27*(5), 287–307. doi:10.1081/PAD-120028811

Pina, V., Torres, L., & Royo, S. (2007). Are ICT's improving transparency and accountability in the EU regional and local governments? An empirical study. *Public Administration, 85*(2), 449–472. doi:10.1111/j.1467-9299.2007.00654.x

Quinn, S. (2002). *Knowledge management in the digital newsroom*. Oxford, UK: Focal Press.

Ranzinger, M., & Gleixner, G. (1997). GIS datasets for 3D urban planning. *Computers, Environment and Urban Systems, 21*(2), 159–173. doi:10.1016/S0198-9715(97)10005-9

Rouse, L. J., Bergeron, S. J., & Harris, T. M. (2007). Participating in the geospatial Web - Collaborative mapping, social networks, and participatory GIS. In Scharl, A., & Tochtermann, K. (Eds.), *The geospatial Web*. London, UK: Springer. doi:10.1007/978-1-84628-827-2_14

Shiode, N. (2001). 3D urban models: Recent developments in the digital modeling of urban environments in three-dimensions. *GeoJournal, 52*, 263–269. doi:10.1023/A:1014276309416

Shipan, C. R., & Volden, C. (2008). The mechanisms of policy diffusion. *American Journal of Political Science, 52*(4), 840–857. doi:10.1111/j.1540-5907.2008.00346.x

Sieber, R. (2006). Public participation and geographic Information Systems: A literature review and framework. *Annals of the Association of American Geographers. Association of American Geographers, 96*(3), 491–507. doi:10.1111/j.1467-8306.2006.00702.x

Tan, S., & Wong, O. (2006). Location aware applications for smart cities with Google Maps and GIS tools. *Proceedings of the Fourth International Conference on Active Media Technology (AMT06)*, Brisbane, Australia.

Turner, A. J. (2006). *Introduction to Neogeography. O'Reilly Short Cuts Series*. Sebastopol, CA: O'Reilly Media.

Vajjhala, S. P. (2006). Ground truthing policy: Using participatory map-making to connect citizens and decision makers. *Resources, 162*, 14–18.

Weiner, D., Harris, T. M., & Craig, W. J. (2002). Community participation and geographic Information Systems. In Craig, W. J., Harris, T. M., & Weiner, D. (Eds.), *Community participation and Geographic Information Systems* (pp. 3–16). New York, NY: Taylor & Francis.

Wu, C. J., & Isaksson, K. (2008). *Participatory mapping as a tool for capturing local perspectives on cultural landscapes*. Stockholm, Sweden: KTH – School of Architecture and the Built Environment.

ADDITIONAL READING

Aurigi, A. (2006). New technologies, same dilemmas: Policy and design issues for the augmented city. *Journal of Urban Technology, 13*(3), 5–28. doi:10.1080/10630730601145989

Bojórquez-Tapia, L. A., Cruz-Bello, G. M., Luna-González, L., Juárez, L., & Ortiz-Pérez, M. A. (2009). V-DRASTIC: Using visualization to engage policymakers in groundwater vulnerability assessment. *Journal of Hydrology (Amsterdam), 373*(1/2), 242–255. doi:10.1016/j.jhydrol.2009.05.005

Brandes, U., Kenis, P., Raab, J., Schneider, V., & Wagner, D. (1999). Explorations into the visualization of policy networks. *Journal of Theoretical Politics, 11*(1), 75. doi:10.1177/0951692899011001004

Chadwick, A. (2009). Web 2.0: New challenges for the study of e-democracy in an era of informational exuberance. *I/S: A Journal of Law and Policy for the Information Society, 5*(1), 9-41.

Cogburn, D. L., & Espinoza-Vasquez, F. K. (2011). From networked nominee to networked nation: Examining the impact of Web 2.0 and social media on political participation and civic engagement in the 2008 Obama campaign. *Journal of Political Marketing, 10*(1/2), 189–213. doi:10.1080/15377857.2011.540224

Dockerty, T., Lovett, A., Appleton, K., Bone, A., & Sünnenberg, G. (2006). Developing scenarios and visualisations to illustrate potential policy and climatic influences on future agricultural landscapes. *Agriculture Ecosystems & Environment, 114*(1), 103–120. doi:10.1016/j.agee.2005.11.008

Downey, E., Ekstrom, C. D., & Jones, M. A. (Eds.). (2010). *E-government website development: Future trends and strategic models*. Hershey, PA: Information Science Reference. doi:10.4018/978-1-61692-018-0

Dykes, J., Andrienko, G., Andrienko, N., Paelke, V., & Schiewe, J. (2010). Editorial - GeoVisualization and the digital city. *Computers, Environment and Urban Systems, 34*(6), 443–451. doi:10.1016/j.compenvurbsys.2010.09.001

Ebenezer, J., Kaya, O. N., & Ebenezer, D. L. (2011). Engaging students in environmental research projects: Perceptions of fluency with innovative technologies and levels of scientific inquiry abilities. *Journal of Research in Science Teaching, 48*(1), 94–116. doi:10.1002/tea.20387

Esnard, A. (1998). Cities, GIS, and ethics. *Journal of Urban Technology, 5*(3), 33–45. doi:10.1080/10630739883822

Goodchild, M. F. (2007). Citizens as voluntary sensors: Spatial data infrastructure in the world of Web 2.0. *International Journal of Spatial Data Infrastructures Research, 2*, 24–32.

Hoyt, L., Khosla, R., & Canepa, C. (2005). Leaves, pebbles, and chalk: Building a public participation GIS in New Delhi, India. *Journal of Urban Technology, 12*, 1–19. doi:10.1080/10630730500116479

Hudson-Smith, A., Evans, S., & Batty, M. (2005). Building the virtual city: Public participation through e-democracy. *Knowledge, Technology & Policy*, *18*(1), 62–85. doi:10.1007/s12130-005-1016-9

Jacobs, K., Garfin, G., & Buizer, J. (2009). The science-policy interface: Experience of a workshop for climate change researchers and water managers. *Science & Public Policy*, *36*(10), 791–798. doi:10.3152/030234209X481969

Janssen, M., Chun, S. A., & Gil-Garcia, J. R. (2009). Building the next generation of digital government infrastructures. *Government Information Quarterly*, *26*(2), 233–237. doi:10.1016/j.giq.2008.12.006

Jude, S. (2008). Investigating the potential role of visualization techniques in participatory coastal management. *Coastal Management*, *36*(4), 331–349. doi:10.1080/08920750802266346

Liao, E., Shyy, T. K., & Stimson, R. J. (2009). Developing a Web-based e-research facility for socio-spatial analysis to investigate relationships between voting patterns and local population characteristics. *Journal of Spatial Science*, *54*(2), 63–88. doi:10.1080/14498596.2009.9635179

Lorimer, J. (2010). International conservation volunteering and the geographies of global environmental citizenship. *Political Geography*, *29*(6), 311–322. doi:10.1016/j.polgeo.2010.06.004

Luton, L. S. (1996). *The politics of garbage: A community perspective on solid waste policy making*. Pittsburgh, PA: University of Pittsburgh Press.

Maisonneuve, N., Stevens, M., & Ochab, B. (2010). Participatory noise pollution monitoring using mobile phones. *Information Polity: The International Journal of Government & Democracy in the Information Age*, *15*(1/2), 51–71.

Malecki, E. J. (2006). Cities in the Internet age. In B. Johansson, C. Karlsson & R. Stough (Eds.), *The emerging digital economy: Entrepreneurship, clusters, and policy* (pp. 215-237). Advances in Spatial Science series. Berlin, Germany: Springer.

Mendes, L. D., Bottoli, M. L., & Breda, G. D. (2010). Digital cities and open MANs: A new communications paradigm. *IEEE Latin America Transactions*, *8*(4), 394–402. doi:10.1109/TLA.2010.5595129

Mersky, R. (Ed.). (2011). Solid waste and recycling section. In R. A. Meyers (Ed.), *Encyclopedia of sustainability science and technology*. Springer.

Mostashari, A. L. I., & Sussman, J. (2005). Stakeholder-assisted modelling and policy design process for environmental decision-making. *Journal of Environmental Assessment Policy and Management*, *7*(3), 355–386. doi:10.1142/S1464333205002110

Neves, B. B. (2009a). Are digital cities intelligent? The Portuguese case. *International Journal of Innovation and Regional Development*, *1*(4), 443–463. doi:10.1504/IJIRD.2009.022732

Nuojua, J. (2010). WebMapMedia: A map-based Web application for facilitating participation in spatial planning. *Multimedia Systems*, *16*(1), 3–21. doi:10.1007/s00530-009-0175-z

Ojo, A., Estevez, E., & Janowski, T. (2010). Semantic interoperability architecture for Governance 2.0. *Information Polity: The International Journal of Government & Democracy in the Information Age*, *15*(1/2), 105–123.

Ostergaard, S. D., & Hvass, M. (2008). eGovernment 2.0 - How can government benefit from Web 2.0? *Journal of Systemics Cybernetics & Informatics*, *6*(6), 13–18.

Paskaleva, K. A. (2009). Enabling the smart city: The progress of city e-governance in Europe. *International Journal of Innovation and Regional Development, 1*(4), 405–422. doi:10.1504/IJIRD.2009.022730

Petrizzo-Páez, M., & Palm-Rojas, F. (2010). Ways of citizen learning: Political deliberation on the Internet. In Cordoba-Pachon, J. R., & Ochoa-Arias, A. E. (Eds.), *Systems thinking and e-participation: ICT in the governance of society*. Hershey, PA: IGI Global.

Pickles, J. (Ed.). (1995). *Ground truth: The social implications of geographic Information Systems*. New York, NY: Guilford.

Salter, J. D., Campbell, C., Journeay, M., & Sheppard, S. R. J. (2009). The digital workshop: Exploring the use of interactive and immersive visualization tools in participatory planning. *Journal of Environmental Management, 90*(6), 2090–2101. doi:10.1016/j.jenvman.2007.08.023

Sheppard, S. R. J. (2005). Landscape visualisation and climate change: The potential for influencing perceptions and behaviour. *Environmental Science & Policy, 8*(6), 637–654. doi:10.1016/j.envsci.2005.08.002

Sheppard, S. R. J., & Cizek, P. (2009). The ethics of Google Earth: Crossing thresholds from spatial data to landscape visualisation. *Journal of Environmental Management, 90*(6), 2102–2117. doi:10.1016/j.jenvman.2007.09.012

Sirakaya-Turk, E., Ingram, L. J., & Hung, K. (2011). Testing the efficacy of an integrative model for community participation. *Journal of Travel Research, 50*(3), 276–288. doi:10.1177/0047287510362781

Soon Ae, C., Shulman, S., Sandoval, R., & Hovy, E. (2010). Government 2.0: Making connections between citizens, data and government. *Information Polity: The International Journal of Government & Democracy in the Information Age, 15*(1/2), 1–9.

Stich, B., & Holland, J. H. (2011). Using a multiple criteria decision-making model to streamline and enhance NEPA and public participation processes. *Public Works Management & Policy, 16*(1), 59–89. doi:10.1177/1087724X10390227

Tolbert, C. J., Mossberger, K., & McNeal, R. (2008). Institutions, policy innovation, and e- government in the American States. *Public Administration Review, 68*(3), 549–563. doi:10.1111/j.1540-6210.2008.00890.x

van Lammeren, R., Houtkamp, J., Colijn, S., Hilferink, M., & Bouwman, A. (2010). Affective appraisal of 3D land use visualization. *Computers, Environment and Urban Systems, 34*(6), 465–475. doi:10.1016/j.compenvurbsys.2010.07.001

Van Lieshout, M. J. (2001). Configuring the digital city of Amsterdam: Social learning in experimentation. *New Media & Society, 3*(2), 131–156. doi:10.1177/14614440122226029

Weiner, D., Warner, T., Harris, T. M., & Levin, R. M. (1995). Apartheid representations in a digital landscape: GIS, remote sensing, and local knowledge in Kiepersol, South Africa. *Cartography and Geographic Information Systems, 22*(1), 30–44. doi:10.1559/152304095782540537

KEY TERMS AND DEFINITIONS

Government 2.0: Government 2.0 is the immediate inclusion of the public in the political management process. It gets its roots in some of the participatory GIS literature when the state includes the expert knowledge of the local citizenry in their governing functions. Citizens are not expected to be experts in the roles and functions of government but may or may not be experts in a domain in which the government is seeking input.

Web 2.0: Web 2.0 was a term coined in 2004 to describe the second (2.0) generation of Internet technology which facilitated interoperability, geo-spatial capabilities, social networking, dynamic, collaborative content and applications.

ENDNOTE

[1]   The design and development of the Star City 3D digital city platform prototype was supported by the incumbent Star City mayor and officials, but subsequent turnover and uncertainty in the municipal government has put further implementation on hold

Chapter 7
E–Government in Local Government in the Era of Web 2.0:
Experiences of Alabama Municipalities

Hua Xu
Auburn University at Montgomery, USA

Hugo Asencio
Auburn University at Montgomery, USA

ABSTRACT

The emergence of Web 2.0 technologies in recent years has the potential of allowing governments to move beyond simply disseminating information and providing more online services to citizens to the point of engaging them in policy-making and administrative processes. This survey study attempts to find out the extent to which public officials in Alabama municipal governments utilize existing Web 2.0 technologies to engage citizens and to affect their attitudes toward e-government. The preliminary results indicate that although some progress has been made in terms of providing more online services to citizens, Alabama municipalities, particularly small ones, have yet to take advantage of the existing Web 2.0 technologies to make the transtition into e-governance. This chapter concludes with a discussion of the implications of the research findings for advancing e-government in local governments and future research on e-governmnent.

DOI: 10.4018/978-1-4666-0318-9.ch007

INTRODUCTION

Information and communication technologies (ICTs) have been extensively applied in local governments since the 1990s, when the Internet became widely available. In an attempt to enhance their services to the public and to increase transparency and citizen participation, governments at all levels have taken advantage of these new technologies to engage in what scholars now call "electronic-government," or "e-government" for short.

The emergence of Web 2.0 technologies (social media) in recent years has the potential of allowing governments to move beyond simply disseminating information and providing more online services to citizens ("e-government") to engaging them in policy making and administrative processes ("e-governance"). That is, the ability of public officials to engage citizens through the existing Web 2.0 technologies has the potential of improving not only the perceptions citizens have of their government (Berman, 1997) but also the quality of public service delivery in general since through their feedback citizens can play a more active role in the administrative process. Unfortunately, as some scholars point out, the implementation of Web 2.0 technologies for promoting transparency and participation in government settings has lagged (D'Agostino et al., 2011; Weber 2002); governments at all levels have yet to take full advantage of such technologies to engage citizens in a more interactive way ("e-governance").

In an effort to contribute to the existing dialogue about the use of Web 2.0 technologies in local-government settings, this study attempts to find out the extent to which public officials in Alabama municipalities utilize existing Web 2.0 technologies to engage citizens. The purpose is to obtain an accurate picture of the status of e-government in Alabama, as well as to shed some light on the challenges public officials face when implementing e-government programs. The

following section reviews the relevant literature. Next, discussions of the research design and a summary of the key findings are provided. The paper ends with a brief conclusion and some suggestions for future research.

LITERATURE REVIEW

Digital Government: From E-Government to E-Governance

The application of ICTs in the public sector in the last decade of the 20th century created what we now call "e-government," a phenomenon in which governments take advantage of ICTs to provide a wide variety of public services to citizens through the Internet, ranging from services that allow them to make tax payments, to services allowing them to hold web-based conferences and to voting. In this regard, many scholars observe that the use of ICTs in government has evolved from simply disseminating information and supporting online transactions ("e-government") to engaging citizens in policy-making and administrative processes ("e-governance") (Moon, 2002; Norris and Moon, 2005; Scott, 2006; Dawes, 2008).

According to Carrizales (2008), there are four distinct functions of e-government: e-organization (for internal management), e-services (to citizens), e-partnering (with other organizations), and e-democracy (for citizen participation). Although the adoption of e-government, which can be defined as the creation of websites, was fairly rapid toward the end of the 20th century, the transition from transaction-oriented e-government to democracy-oriented e-government has been relatively slow (Norris and Moon, 2005). In this regard, research finds that among the factors influencing the adoption and use of e-government are both internal organizational factors, such as leadership and organizational capacity, and institutional and demographic factors, such as city size and form of government. (Moon, 2002; Moon and Bretschneider, 2002; Jun and Weare, 2010).

It is important to mention that although research finds that the use of ICTs in the public sector can reduce the cost of services and improve the quality of services, thus, resulting in improved efficiency, productivity, and responsiveness of public organizations and programs (Pirog and Johnson, 2008), its benefits transcend the economic realm. That is, e-government can also have a significant positive impact on government transparency, accountability, public trust in government, and digital democracy (Holzer et al., 2005; Tolbert and Mossberger, 2006; Scott, 2006; Mergel, Shweik, and Fountain, 2010; Morgenson, Van Amburg, and Mithas, 2010). Further, the emergence of the new generation of e-government, which is defined as Government 2.0, in which the new Web 2.0 technologies (social media) are being applied to engage citizens, is expected to have a global impact and to further shape the way in which governments interact with citizens and run government business (Chang and Kannan, 2008; Mergel, Schweik, and Fountain, 2010; Chun et al., 2010; Abdallah and Khalil, 2009).

Web 2.0 and E-Governance

What is Web 2.0? There have been different definitions in the recent years (see, for example, DiNucci, 1999; O'Reilly, 2005). Although it may be difficult to reach a consensus on what the concept Web 2.0 refers, the definition given by Chang and Kannan (2008) seems to adequately capture the key features of Web 2.0 technologies. They write:

The Web 2.0 platform is a networked world supporting individual users creating content individually and collectively, sharing and updating information and knowledge using sophisticated, diverse sharing devices and tools, and remixing and improving on content created by each other. It is a network platform that allows high levels of user interactions, resulting in content and updates that are in the 'permanent beta' stage, which in turn enables rich user experiences that go much beyond the Web 1.0 era (p.10).

Examples of Web 2.0 applications include blogs, mash-ups, peer-to-peer computing, RSS, social networks and online communities, podcasts, wikis, tagging and bookmarking (Chang and Kannan, 2008). Compared to Web 1.0 technologies, Web 2.0 applications have a greater potential for engaging citizens, since they emphasize a more interactive process for generating and sharing user-defined contents. Web 1.0 technologies are most applicable to e-organization, e-services, and e-partnering, whereas Web 2.0 applications are especially conducive to e-democracy, since as they can create multimodal, non-hierarchical, collaborative and deliberative networks. A more detailed comparison between Web 1.0 technologies and Web 2.0 technologies, and their implications, can be found in Ferro and Molinari's work (2010).

In the context of the United States, in recent years not only the Federal Government has started to use Web 2.0 applications, or social media, to engage citizens in more interactive ways (Chun et al., 2010), and the potential of these media for promoting more citizen participation has been demonstrated with the 2008 election of President Barack Obama. The potential of Web 2.0 technologies has been further demonstrated in more recent international political events, such as the pro-democracy movements in the Middle East, particularly in Egypt and Bahrain, in which these technologies have enabled citizens to self-organize and mobilize, to disseminate ideas, and, more importantly, to circumvent censorship by undemocratic governments. This shows that Web 2.0 applications are effective in promoting political participation not only in the American and European contexts but also in different social and cultural settings, such as those in the Arab world (Abdallah and Khalil, 2009).

Compared to e-government, the concept of e-governance accentuates several key aspects of e-government, including citizen participation and empowerment, collective intelligence and local knowledge, decentralization of decision/policy-making, and transparency and openness of government. It concerns "not only [public] services and administration but also democratic processes and the relationships among citizens, civil society, the private sector, and the state" (Dawes, 2008). A recent effort to study e-governance, for example, identified 20 e-governance website features, including comments or feedbacks; newsletters; online bulletins or chat capabilities; online discussion forums on policy issues; scheduled e-meetings for discussion; online surveys/polls; synchronous video; citizen-satisfaction surveys; online decision-making; and performance measures, standards, or benchmarks (D'Agostino et al., 2011). In this regard, however, it is important to mention that some of these e-governance features, such as newsletters, are not Web 2.0 technologies, while others are contents rather than new modes of communicating with citizens. It is obvious that, while e-government mainly emphasizes efficiency, effectiveness, and responsiveness of public services, e-governance attaches far more importance to openness and transparency of government and to citizen engagement in the policy-development and administrative process.

Potentially, the key features of Web 2.0 technologies can enhance e-governance by creating additional ways for citizens and government to interact with each other. In fact, the principal advantage of Web 2.0 is that it allows citizens to engage conveniently and informally in policy discussions. Some evidence indicates that the government-initiated Web 2.0 is effective in engaging citizens in American and European contexts (Parycek and Sachs, 2010; Ferro and Molinari, 2010). Some even assert that "[by 2015] Government 2.0 tools will become even more intensely embedded and integrated into all aspects of governance and daily life, indistinguishable in

practice from other tools and channels and often hidden from sight" (Millard, 2010).

Despite the benefits of Web 2.0 technologies, these technologies, like Web 1.0 technologies, also face some key challenges and obstacles when it comes to their application in the public sector. For example, privacy and security issues are cited as two of the main concerns in the use of Web 2.0 technologies. Other issues, such as how to distinguish the right information from the noisy information, are yet to be addressed (Chun, et al., 2010). Indeed, it is a reasonable fear that the public may be disturbed by, and may subsequently suffer from, the spreading of misinformation on controversial or sensitive public issues on the social media. Moreover, some other research seems to give valid reasons for cynicism regarding the actual impact of Web 2.0. For example, Osimo (2010) regards the current impact of Web 2.0 technologies on government as being far less noticeable than what in many areas might have been expected, and while there are anecdotes indicating successful applications of Web 2.0 technologies in the public sector, various studies show that there are more "hoped for" or "hyped up" benefits and strengths than realized ones (Kuzma, 2010; Bianchi and Cottica, 2010). In fact, some authors even argue that e-participation in political processes actually amplifies the existing problems while creating a set of new problems for democracy (Ostling, 2010).

Furthermore, the culture and attitude of a government have been two of the factors that determine the adoption of Web 2.0. Even in the highly profiled political movements facilitated by Facebook, a sober assessment shows that traditional media still played an important role. For instance, the independent media in Egypt, such as *Al-Masry Al-Youm*, played a vital role not in "triggering the revolution but in preparing the way for it" (Bloomberg Businessweek, 2011, p.64). Clearly, political and legal guarantees such as freedom of the press and freedom of association are the key to realizing the potential power of social-network media. Further, in some countries, the lack of press and association freedoms inhibits the healthy development of social media. A recent reversal of the progressive movement took place in some countries controlled by authoritarian regimes. For instance, the pro-democracy Jasmine Revolution, which was largely inspired by the Facebook-facilitated political movements in the Middle East, was forestalled by the Chinese government; despite the enormous potential power of Web 2.0 in promoting democracy, authoritarian regimes tightened up their online censorship in an attempt to maintain their control of social-network media and to prevent public unrest.

This illustrates that using e-government and social media to promote transparency and openness in different political, cultural, and social contexts can face a number of potential barriers both from inside and outside government (Bertot, Jaeger, and Grimes, 2010). Without necessary institutional changes to buttress the Web 2.0 technologies, the applications of social- network media in public affairs are "tokenism" for citizen participation, at best (Arnstein, 1969). Some other necessary conditions for Web 2.0 include availability of government documents (Bertot et al., 2009), a willingness of government to share data, neutrality in moderating Web 2.0 technologies, access to information technology, and a more informed and educated citizenry.

When it comes to the factors that lead to e-governance, it seems that managerial factors are still the main determinants and, in many cases, the key obstacles for fostering e-governance. That is, as Carrizales's (2008) survey of New Jersey municipalities shows, the practices of municipal e-government, including e-democracy, are partly determined by the attitudes of municipal administrators toward the different uses of ICTs. Further, as Aikins and Krane's (2010) survey of the municipalities of five Midwestern states (Missouri, Kansas, Iowa, Nebraska, and Minnesota) also shows, a high proportion of city officials still may prefer traditional ways of citizen participa-

tion, including postal mail, television, radio, and newspaper.

Too, other factors may also impede the development of e-governance. For example, in their study of the websites of 20 of the largest cities in the United States, D'Agostino et al. (2011) find that while the development of e-government has made rapid progress, the progress of e-governance has been fairly limited. The reasons for this include the scarcity of resources for local governments, the necessity of finding a balance between the needs for administrative efficiency and the values of citizen participation, and the limited mechanisms for citizen participation.

An Assessment of Prior Empirical Studies

The survey approach to the study of e-government largely includes three categories: citizen surveys, public-official surveys, and website evaluations by outsiders and users. Some examples in the first category include studies by Tolbert and Mossberger (2006) and by Morgenson et al. (2010). The second group includes studies by the International City/County Management Association (ICMA), by Carrizales (2008), and by Aikins and Krane (2010). The third group includes studies by Scott (2006) and by Holzer et al. (2008).

In terms of research design, some studies are cross-sectional while others are longitudinal. The former group includes the studies on public trust in government by Tolbert and Mossberger (2006) and by Morgenson et al. (2010), and the local survey study by Carrizales (2008). The latter group includes the study by Jun and Weare (2010) of the adoption of e-government by American municipalities during the period 1994-2003.

In terms of research methods, prior studies can be divided into three broad categories: qualitative methods, quantitative methods, and mixed methods. In particular, qualitative methods can be subdivided into case studies, content analyses, interviews, observational studies, etc. An example

Figure 1. Conceptual framework for e-government, government 2.0, and e-governance

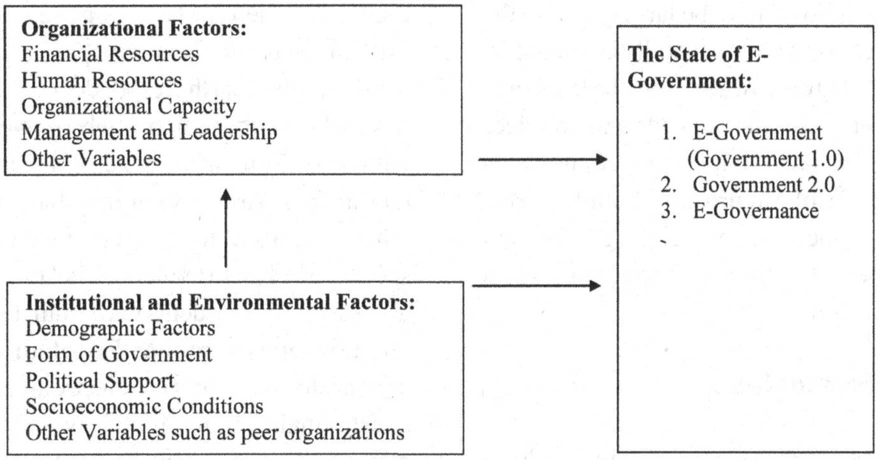

```
┌─────────────────────────────────┐
│ Organizational Factors:         │
│ Financial Resources             │          ┌──────────────────────┐
│ Human Resources                 │          │ The State of E-      │
│ Organizational Capacity         │ ───────▶ │ Government:          │
│ Management and Leadership       │          │                      │
│ Other Variables                 │          │  1. E-Government     │
└─────────────────────────────────┘          │     (Government 1.0) │
               ▲                              │  2. Government 2.0   │
               │                              │  3. E-Governance     │
┌─────────────────────────────────┐          │                      │
│ Institutional and Environmental │          │                      │
│ Factors:                        │ ───────▶ │                      │
│ Demographic Factors             │          │                      │
│ Form of Government              │          │                      │
│ Political Support               │          │                      │
│ Socioeconomic Conditions        │          │                      │
│ Other Variables such as peer organizations │ └──────────────────────┘
└─────────────────────────────────┘
```

of qualitative methods is the study by Ho and Ni (2004). Quantitative studies include descriptive statistics, such as studies by Holzer et al. (2008); linear-regression analysis, such as that of Moon and Bretschneider (2002) and Tolbert and Mossberger (2006); non-linear multivariate analyses, such as logistic regressions, cox regression, structural-equation modeling, etc., which include Carrizales (2008), Jun and Weare (2010), and Morgenson et al. (2010). Third, Schwester's study (2010) can be regarded as an example of a mixed method, if the effort to rate municipal websites, which employed content analysis during the prior stage of the survey, is included.

Finally, most e-government surveys have been conducted on state or large-to-medium-sized municipal governments, and fewer studies focus on small municipal governments, especially those of cities with populations less than 25,000. This study attempts to fill this gap in the literature by conducting a comprehensive study of all the municipalities in a selected state.

Based on the literature review on e-government, this study posits that the development of e-government, including Government 2.0, is jointly affected by organizational, environmental, and institutional factors. Furthermore, this study assumes that environmental and institutional

factors affect organizational factors, and this fact, in turn, further complicates the relationship between organizational factors and the practice of e-government (see Figure 1 for illustration).

RESEARCH DESIGN

E-Government in Alabama

The development of e-government in Alabama local governments as a whole seems to lag behind that of many other states. In one of the influential surveys of municipalities conducted by Rutgers-Newark, two of the largest cities of each U.S. state were selected for evaluation in terms of usability, privacy and security, content, services, and citizen participation (Holzer et al., 2008). In the case of Alabama, the cities of Birmingham and Montgomery were selected and their overall development of e-government was ranked 89th and 58th, respectively, out of 101 cities surveyed. In comparison, the website of Alabama's state government was once rated as one of the top five websites among the U.S. state governments (Center for Digital Government, 2010).

This shows there is a considerable gap between the state and local governments in Alabama when it comes to their level of e-government. This disparity, or "digital divide," may be largely due to the fact that state governments generally can dedicate more resources to ICTs. In addition, there seem to be large discrepancies in the needs and practices of e-government among local governments in Alabama. The city of Auburn, for example, seems to have one of the best municipal government websites in the state, whereas some cities do not even have a website.

Research Strategies

The authors do not find any state-wide study of e-government in Alabama municipalities, except for the e-government surveys by the International City/County Management Association (ICMA). The data used in this study come from a specific survey instrument developed by the authors. It includes 96 questions, which were used to operationalize the concepts/variables depicted in the theoretical framework of the study. The questions generally concern the extent to which local-government officials use existing ICTs; the amount of resources dedicated for creating more responsive e-government and ICTs; applications of ICTs; use of intranet; attitudes and perceptions of officials regarding the benefits of, and barriers toward, adopting more innovative ICTs; and the demographics of the respondents. Further, because we believe that a survey on Government 2.0 cannot be separated from a survey on general e-government, since Government 2.0 is a sophistication of existing Web 1.0 technologies, a number of questions on generic e-government were also included in the survey.

The survey was administered online to the members of the Alabama League of Municipalities (ALM). Each of the 458 municipalities in Alabama has one mayor and one city/town clerk, and several council members. In addition, the survey was also distributed to 13 administrators and 7 managers on the membership list, resulting in a total of 2,287 potential respondents. However, because most of the municipalities are medium or small–sized, in most cases there was only one response from an official in a particular municipal government. It is safe to assume that the respondent is the person who has the best information or who is most concerned with e-government in his/her own jurisdiction and that his/her participation may have discouraged other officials of the same municipality from responding. A link to the survey-hosting website was given to the respondents via e-mail. In some cases, questionnaires were e-mailed to the respondents if they preferred to receive electronic copies of the questionnaire. In the future, we will also mail a paper version of the survey to those who prefer it as well as make accommodations for employees with disabilities. Participation in the survey was completely voluntary; participants were informed that their answers would be confidential and would be reported anonymously in publications. It is apparent that the nature of an online survey can discourage many respondents who might otherwise participate in a survey. There may be some level of discomfort and inconvenience for some respondents in taking an online survey as compared to taking a paper-based survey. This may result in some sample-selection bias.

To supplement our online survey, we randomly sampled 46 municipal websites to evaluate the e-government status of those municipalities by conducting content analysis. The evaluation includes determining whether the municipal website provides, and it identifies several other key features of websites, such as what kinds of information and online services are available through the websites. Some demographic information, such as population and population density were also collected. These variables are subsequently analyzed in tandem with the results of the website evaluations.

As compared to some other studies, which have included administrators, mayors, or city managers, the current survey was distributed to mayors, city council members, city managers, and city/town clerks. The intended respondents are more diverse, and for a good reason; because it can be argued that the adoption and implementation of Web 2.0 technologies is affected not only by organizational resources, but also by the support (or lack thereof) of council members, the survey was distributed to all members of the ALM. We hoped that this distribution would allow us to examine the impact of such a new generation of e-government on local governments in a comprehensive manner, as well as to increase the response rate and thus, the sample size.

FINDINGS AND DISCUSSION

Within one week after distributing the survey online, we received a total of 23 responses from different municipalities. After we made a second wave of requests for participation, the responses increased to 41, with 39 valid responses. The low response rate can be largely attributed to factors such as the online nature of the survey, the lengthiness of the survey, etc. The sample is likely to be biased by the fact that respondents who work in municipalities with more advanced e-governments tend to answer the survey. One case in point, for example, is a person who works in a municipal government that does not have a city website and simply did not answer the online survey. However, thanks to a follow-up search, we found that the information of this particular municipality was actually available in the website of the local chamber of commerce. This indicates an additional way in which municipal governments get involved in e-government indirectly.

The respondents include mayors, council members, city/town clerks, assistant city managers, and IT personnel. It is important to recognize that clerks may tend to view e-government from an administrative perspective whereas elected officials, including council members and mayors, who have to be more responsive to the needs of local citizens, tend to view e-government from a political perspective or from the perspective of the needs of constituents (at this stage, we do not compare the differences in their views on e-governments).

Even after we made two rounds of requests for participation in the online survey, the response rate ended up being below 10%, which is low by many standards. If all the respondents in a particular municipality are counted as one unit, the response rate is about 8.7%. However, considering the online nature of the survey, we think this is not terribly low. Furthermore, comparing the sample with the total number of municipalities in Alabama, we consider our sample fairly representative of the composition of municipal governments of Alabama (see Table 1). As indicated earlier, one of the often-overlooked areas of e-government research relates to small municipalities. Our sample contains 18 municipalities with a population less than 2,500, or 45% of the entire sample, whereas the municipalities included in the often-used ICMA survey data do not include any municipality with a population less than 2,500. Thus, our research particularly addresses some of the e-government issues of small municipalities. Of course, there are other practical limitations of our survey instrument. For example, the paper version of the survey looked shorter than the online one (although the same number of questions were included in both) since the survey-hosting software does not allow us to transfer the entire format of the survey to the online site in which the survey is located; this fact, in turn, increased the length of the online survey and could have discouraged people from answering it.

The responses overwhelmingly came from small municipalities, except for one that came from a municipality with a population over 250,000. Some would assume that large municipalities may tend to have favorable conditions for developing e-government and have a better e-government, and, thus, tend to participate in the survey. To our surprise, this was not the case for the sample we obtained from the survey. As indicated above, our sample actually includes a large number of small municipalities, a fact that

Table 1. A comparison of the current sample with Alabama statewide municipalities and ICMA national survey

Population group	Municipalities included in current sample	Sample Distribution by Size	Alabama Municipalities	Distribution by Size	Municipalities included in ICMA sample	Sample Distribution by Size
Over 1,000,000	0	0.00	0	0.00	9	0.00
500,000-1,000,000	0	0.00	0	0.00	23	0.01
250,000-499,999	0	0.00	0	0.00	36	0.01
100,000-249,999	1	0.03	4	0.01	179	0.04
50,000-99,999	1	0.03	5	0.01	405	0.07
25,000-49,999	1	0.03	11	0.02	776	0.12
10,000-24,999	8	0.20	41	0.09	1,819	0.25
5,000-9,999	7	0.18	42	0.09	1,875	0.24
2,500-4,999	4	0.10	48	0.10	1,973	0.25
Under 2,500	18	0.45	309	0.67	0	0.00
Less than 1,000 (included in under 2,500 group)	5	0.13	202	0.44	0	0.00
Total	40		460		7,095	

is very helpful in improving our understanding of e-government of small municipal governments. In other words, this research contributes to our understanding of e-government of local governments in the United States, especially the municipalities that tend to be under-studied in national surveys.

This statewide survey research allows us to draw conclusions and present the descriptive statistics, and discuss the implications of the findings on the practice of, and research regarding, e-government. The following are the main findings from the survey of municipal governments:

Finding 1: E-Government as an Efficient Tool

All respondents have positive views with respect to efficiency gains and cost-saving of e-government, despite the fact that about half of their local governments do not even have an official website. The fact that municipal officials have this point of view undoubtedly is critical for the initiation

Table 2. Profile of Respondents as of July 31, 2011

Positions	Number of Respondents	Percentage
City/Town Clerk	19	49
Mayor	8	20
City Council Members	7	18
City Manager	3	8
Others (Network Administrator, CIO, etc.)	2	5
Total	39	100

and development of e-government, given that the support of local elected officials and administrators is essential.

Finding 2: E-Government as a Beneficial Tool for Citizens

The vast majority of respondents believe that e-government is beneficial to citizens in terms of accessibility and convenience. They also believe that there is a large demand for e-government from citizens. Again, this recognition of the needs of their constituents among municipal government administrators and elected officials is vital to any efforts at developing e-government.

Finding 3: Perceived Effectiveness of Online Communication with Citizens

While the respondents unanimously indicate that e-government promotes transparency, they are more skeptical about whether communicating online with citizens is more effective and honest. This is somewhat contradictory to the research findings based on citizen surveys, which indicate that e-government increases trust and confidence in government. According to some studies, it is expected that e-government initiatives would promote transparent and honest government. However, public officials' skepticism is not surprising, given recent studies on e-government that are more critical of the actual impact of e-government in terms of realized benefits and unintended consequences.

Finding 4: E-Government Adoption to Address Citizens' Needs

Very few respondents (5/33) indicated that their local governments created a website and provided more online services to citizens because of a recommendation from their IT department/personnel. In comparison, fewer than 1/6 of the respondents (5/32) believe that their government provides online services because other governments are doing so. This gives some idea of the driving forces behind IT innovations in local government. Our survey indicates that many of these local governments adopt e-government initiatives not because their peers do so, but largely because of other factors, such as perceived needs of citizens and perceived benefits of e-government.

Finding 5: Noble Ideas and Pragmatic Considerations in E-Government Adoption

The survey responses confirm that administrators recognize the democratic values and benefits of e-government in terms of transparency and participation. They also recognize other positive effects of e-government, such as an increased visibility of the local governments via a website. This demonstrates both the noble ideas and the pragmatic considerations of local officials in dealing with e-government in government business.

Finding 6: Barriers to and Concerns about E-Government Adoption

The survey responses indicate that public officials believe that financial and human resources are the major barriers to the advancement of e-government. Internet security is regarded by most respondents as one of the major issues of concern. On the positive side, it seems that they believe there is strong internal and external support for e-government. Taken together, these barriers and concerns demand that local officials find creative ways to overcome these constraints by taking advantages of the local support.

Finding 7: Web 2.0 Usage in Alabama Local Governments

The survey responses show that almost half of the respondents (municipalities) used at least one form of social-media technology for themselves, but that only a very few of them (3/37) used it for online policy deliberation and political participation. This "gap" is not unusual, given the complexity of protocols and learning required to use these technologies for policy deliberation. There may be other political and institutional reasons as well. It can be argued that while the private use of social (network) media is generally safe, the use of social media for public (government) affairs can involve a great deal of risk for public officials. A wide variety of social media are used by the respondents, including Facebook, Linkedin, Twitter, and YouTube. Texting and AIM are also mentioned as alternatives to these social media in interacting with citizens. Given the fact that many local governments use traditional media such as postal mail, local newspapers, bulletins, radio, television, public postings, e-mails, and even face-to-face meetings, at this point we are unable to conclude which medium is more effective in engaging citizens. There is a good argument that over-reliance on Web 2.0 technologies may potentially make the political process more exclusive rather than inclusive, as compared to traditional means of interacting with citizens. Interestingly, one innovative means is to distribute city newsletters by enclosing them with water bills. It is evident that there are additional means for communicating with citizens. For instance, some Alabama local government websites use an online submission form ("Action Center") to allow residents to file any service requests or complaints.

Finding 8: Web 2.0 and E-Government Implementation

The supplemental website evaluation indicates that only 24 out of 46 municipalities in the random sample maintain an official website; this figure is extremely low when compared to the figures from local governments in some other states. Further, municipalities with official websites tend to own those websites and to make their email contacts available on their websites. Creating and maintaining a website is the first step in the development of e-government, and a large number of small municipalities have yet to take this first step. On the other hand, many of the municipalities with websites have yet to acquire and implement the several mainstream Web 2.0 technologies used in promoting citizen participation and government transparency.

Finding 9: E-Government, Population Size, and Population Density

Related to Finding 8, the existence and the complexity of municipal online services correlate with the size of population and the population density. Specifically, the larger the population of a municipality is, or the higher its population density, the higher the likelihood that it will have an official website and that its e-government will be more advanced. It is plausible that a sufficient size of population and the economy of scale are good predictors for the development of e-government for Alabama's municipalities, including small ones.

Finding 10: Web 2.0, E-Government and E-Governance in Alabama Local Governments

Because there are already some local governments using Web 2.0 technologies, it is tempting to conclude that some municipal governments have already reached the relatively advanced stage of e-government. However, the results of the research indicate that transaction orientation still dominates the current stage of e-government in most of Alabama municipalities. In other words, the majority of municipalities in Alabama are stagnant in their application of Web 1.0 technologies and many of them have a lot of catching-up to do before they can capitalize on the benefits of Web 2.0 technologies.

CONCLUSION

This study contributes to the existing dialogue about the use of Web 2.0 technologies in local government-settings by examining the latest generation of e-government practices and studying the attitudes of local public officials in Alabama. The results indicate that a significant number of small municipal governments in Alabama started using Web 2.0 technologies to promote e-governance while some others are still in the early stages of e-government and rely heavily on traditional means to interact with local citizens. That is, there are glaring disparities among these municipalities in terms of their adoption and implementation of e-government.

There are some important implications for Alabama local governments. For example, although officials in municipal governments generally are aware of the benefits of e-government and Web 2.0 technologies and support e-government initiatives, as suggested by Moon (2002), the results of this study indicate that the implementation of e-governance and Web 2.0 technologies in Alabama faces financial, technical, personnel, and legal barriers. The dilemma is that, on the one hand, e-government seems to be the solution for problems created by the spreading-out population in Alabama, while on the other hand, the development and implementation of e-government in many Alabama local governments seem to be lagging. Those municipalities without e-government tend to face more resource constraints.

In light of this situation, local governments in Alabama need to find innovative ways to overcome the above-mentioned constraints. In addition, the role of government needs to be adjusted during the Government 2.0 era. That is, as governments make the transition into e-governance through the implementation of Web 2.0 technologies, creating an enabling environment that fosters user-generated content and, thus, e-democracy, and formulating an updated legal framework that ensures online security and privacy should be two of the major new roles of governments in the future.

Despite the above-mentioned challenges that many local governments are facing, there are several good reasons for optimism concerning the future of e-government in Alabama local governments. First, some of the initiatives in Alabama are conducive to the development of e-government in local governments. For instance, the best-practice-awards program managed by Auburn University Montgomery's outreach team regularly promotes innovations in local government by identifying and recognizing local governments that are exemplars in using technologies. Second, the increased availability of affordable ICTs in Alabama and many other states bodes well for them in the long run. Third, local governments in Alabama and in other states can learn a lot from a recent success story in local government transition from Web 1.0 to Web 2.0. For example, the City of Auburn has one of the best e-governments in the state. Auburn's success can be attributed to a host of factors, such as the relatively high social-economic conditions in Auburn, the existence of a major university there, and a highly trained labor force. While some of these factors do not exist in many other local governments, some municipalities with similar conditions and environments, such as Troy, can certainly benefit from increased exchanges with a local exemplar in e-government.

Even more encouraging is the fact that the disparities among the small municipalities identified by this research are indicative of the ways that local governments can overcome the constraints and become more proactive in developing e-government. For instance, our research suggests that population size is closely correlated with the availability of online government information and services. This may lead some to argue that population size is critical for achieving the economy of scale for adopting e-government. However, it is puzzling that a closer examination shows that some municipalities with fewer than 500 people have their own websites and offer services online, while about one quarter of the municipalities with over 1,000 residents that were randomly selected for the website evaluation have no website or online services. Future research should take a closer look at these "outliers" in developing e-governments, in order to generate more insights. It will not be surprising if in-depth case studies find more conclusive evidence showing the institutional and organizational factors, other than financial resources and IT personnel that have actually played a key role in the planning, adoption, and implementation of e-government initiatives.

Last, future research should, in a more comprehensive way, investigate the connections between the practice of e-government and the social and economic factors of local communities, particularly small communities. As in some European countries, it is evident that minority populations in Alabama, including those in the Black Belt, are among the "unplugged" ones (Ferro and Molinari, 2010). International experiences suggest that the development of e-government highly correlates with the status of social and economic development. In other words, those experiences indicate that "digital divide" is the result of social and economic disparities (Manoharan and Carrizales, 2010). It is quite plausible that it is the same case for the "digital divides" between individual Alabama local governments and between Alabama local governments and the local governments of other states. Recent research in this direction that focuses only on large municipalities (Schwester, 2010) seems inadequate.

REFERENCES

Abdallah, S., & Khalil, A. (2009). Web 2.0 and e-governments: An exploration of potentials & realities in the Arab world. *Proceedings of the European and Mediterranean Conference on Information Systems*, Izmir, Turkey.

Aikins, S., & Krane, D. (2010). Are public officials obstacles to citizen-centered e-government? An examination of municipal administrators' motivations and actions. *State and Local Government Review*, *42*(2), 87–103. doi:10.1177/0160323X10369159

Arnstein, S. (1969). A ladder of citizen participation. *Journal of the American Institute of Planners, July*.

Berman, E. M. (1997). Dealing with cynical citizens. *Public Administration Review*, *57*(2), 105–112. doi:10.2307/977058

Bertot, J., Jaeger, P., & Simmons, S. (2010). Using ICTs to create a culture of transparency: E-government and social media as openness and anti-corruption tools for societies. *Government Information Quarterly*, *27*, 254–271. doi:10.1016/j.giq.2010.03.001

Bertot, J., Jaeger, P., Simmons, S., & Shuler, J. (2009). Reconciling government documents and e-government: Government information in policy, librarianship, and education. *Government Information Quarterly*, *26*, 433–436. doi:10.1016/j.giq.2009.03.002

Bianchi, T., & Cottica, A. (2011). Harnessing the unexpected: Public administration interacts with creatives on the Web. *European Journal of E-Practice*, *9*, 82–90.

Bloomberg Newsweek. (2011, June 6). *Not just the Facebook revolution*, (pp. 63-66).

Carrizales, T. (2008). Functions of e-government: A study of municipal practices. *State and Local Government Review*, *40*(1), 12–26. doi:10.1177/0160323X0804000102

Center for Digital Government. (2010). *Digital government achievement awards*. Retrieved from http://www.centerdigitalgov.com/survey/88

Chang, A.-M., & Kannan, P. K. (2008). *Leverage Web 2.0 in government. IBM Center for the Business of Government*. Washington, DC: Government Printing Office.

Chun, S. A., Shulman, S., Sandoval, R., & Hovy, E. (2010). Government 2.0: Making connections between citizens, data, and government. *Information Polity*, *15*, 1–9.

D'Agostino, M., Schwester, R., Carrizales, T., & Melitski, J. (2011). A study of e-government and e-governance: An empirical examination of municipal websites. *Public Administration Quarterly, 35*(1), 3–25.

Dawes, S. (2008). The evolution and continuing challenges of e-governance. *Public Administration Review*, (December): S82–S106.

DiNucci, D. (1999). Fragmented future. *Print, 53*(4), 32.

Ferro, E., & Molinari, F. (2010). Framing Web 2.0 in the process of public sector innovation: Going down the participation ladder. *European Journal of E-Practice, 9*, 20–34.

Ho, A. T.-K., & Ni, A. (2004). Explaining the progressiveness of e-government: A case study of Iowa county treasurers' offices. *American Review of Public Administration, 34*(2), 164–180. doi:10.1177/0275074004264355

Holzer, M., Manoharan, A., Shick, R., & Stowers, G. (2008). *US municipalities e-governance survey 2008: An assessment of municipal websites. E-Governance Institute*. Newark: Rutgers University.

Holzer, M., Melitski, J., Rho, S.-Y., & Schwester, R. (2005). *Restoring trust in government: The potential of digital citizen participation. IBM Center for the Business of Government*. Washington, DC: Government Printing Office.

Jun, K.-N., & Weare, C. (2010). Institutional motivations in the adoption of innovations: The case of e-government. *Journal of Public Administration: Research and Theory, 21*(3).

Kuzma, J. (2010). Asian government usage of Web 2.0 social media. *European Journal of E-Practice, 9*, 69–81.

Manoharan, A., & Carrizales, T. (2010). Technological equity: An international perspective of e-government and societal divides. *Electronic Government: An International Journal, 8*(1), 73–84. doi:10.1504/EG.2011.037698

Mergel, I., Schweik, C., & Fountain, J. (2010). *The transformational impact of Web 2.0 technologies on government*. Retrieved from http://ssrn.com/abstract=1412796

Millard, J. (2010). Government 1.5 – Is the bottle half full or half empty? *European Journal of E-Practice, 9*, 35–48.

Moon, J. (2002). The evolution of e-government: Rhetoric or reality? *Public Administration Review, 62*(4), 424–433. doi:10.1111/0033-3352.00196

Moon, M. J., & Bretschneider, S. (2002). Does the perception of red tape constrain IT innovativeness in organizations? Unexpected results from simultaneous equation model and implications. *Journal of Public Administration: Research and Theory, 12*(2), 273–291.

Morgenson, F. III, Van Amburg, D., & Mithas, S. (2011). Misplaced trust? Exploring the structure of the e-government-citizen trust relationship. *Journal of Public Administration: Research and Theory, 21*(2), 257–283. doi:10.1093/jopart/muq006

Norris, D., & Moon, J. (2005). Advancing e-government at the grassroots: Tortoise or hare? *Public Administration Review, 65*(1), 64–75. doi:10.1111/j.1540-6210.2005.00431.x

O'Reilly, T. (2005). *What is Web 2.0: Design patterns and business models for the next generation of software*. O'Reilly Media. Retrieved August 24, 2011, from http://www.oreillynet.com/pub/a/oreilly/tim/news/2005/09/30/what-is-web-20.html

Osimo, D. (2010). Hype, hope or reality? *European Journal of E-Practice, 9*, 2–4.

Ostling, A. (2010). ICT in politics: From peaks of inflated expectations to voids of disillusionment. *European Journal of E-Practice, 9.*

Parycek, P., & Sachs, M. 2010. Open government – Information flow in Web 2.0. *European Journal of E-Practice, 9.*

Pirog, M. A., & Johnson, C. (2008). Electronic funds and benefits transfers, e-government, and the winter commission. *Public Administration Review*, (December): S103–S114. doi:10.1111/j.1540-6210.2008.00982.x

Schwester, R. (2010). Socio-demographic determinants of e-government adoption: An examination of major U.S. cities. *Journal of Public Management and Social Policy, 16*(2), 21–32.

Scott, J. (2006). E" the people: Do U.S. municipal government web sites support public involvement? *Public Administration Review, 66*(3), 341–353. doi:10.1111/j.1540-6210.2006.00593.x

Tolbert, C., & Mossberger, K. (2006). The effects of e-government on trust and confidence in government. *Public Administration Review, 66*(3), 354–369. doi:10.1111/j.1540-6210.2006.00594.x

Weber, L. M. (2002). *A survey of the literature on the Internet and democracy*. Paper presented at the Prospects for Electronic Democracy Conference, Carnegie Mellon University, September 20-22, Pittsburgh, PA.

Chapter 8
Predictors of Social Networking and Individual Performance

Michael A. Brown Sr.
Old Dominion University, USA

Mohamad Alkadry
Florida International University, USA

ABSTRACT

Public organizations that can successfully predict participation and understand the value propositions that drive performance can be very effective in social networking, which is a process and practice by which people and organizations are drawn together by family, work, or hobby to interact via websites. This chapter examines the relationship between social networking and individual performance and suggests a social networking participation model that takes advantage of innovation adoption and other important theories to help public organizations understand acceptance or rejection of participation. In a recent study, responses from 191 public administrators were analyzed using structural equation modeling (SEM) to focus on the relationship between participation and five constructs: perceived usefulness, perceived ease of use, perceived improvement potential (PIP), intra-organizational trust, and type of use. The study found favorable model fit statistics that support positive correlations between the latent variables examined and the dependent variable, participation. The results demonstrate the potential of the survey instrument to serve as an adoption and participation methodology that can provide public organizations with knowledge that predicts and promotes social networking activities as they relate to perceived performance improvement. This approach arms organizations and leaders with a new lens with which to focus on the value proposition regarding perceived improvement potential based on social networking participation.

DOI: 10.4018/978-1-4666-0318-9.ch008

INTRODUCTION

Several studies examine social networking in the workplace (Hendrix, 1984; Kwon & Wen, 2010; Leaman & Bordass, 2000; Mazman & Usluel, 2009; Nakata et al., 2008; Venkatesh, 2000; Warshaw & Davis, 1985), but research is scarce when it comes to what drives participation in social networks, especially in the public sector. Employees accept or reject participation in social networking activities. They determine who they want to connect to while participating, and they decide how much time and effort they are willing to commit to the activity. This chapter theoretically and empirically examines a model of social networking participation that can improve an organization's ability to enhance employee participation in social networking.

Social networking goes beyond widely-used tools or applications of choice, such as Facebook, Twitter, LinkedIn, or MySpace. Understanding social networking behaviors is necessary to evaluate acceptance or rejection of participation. Innovation adoption theory promotes evaluation of internal decision processes and leads to an understanding of how users are attracted to a system, how their behavior is affected, and how they make decisions.

Social networking provides vital opportunities to build and enhance social capital. Organizations and people are involved in a daily struggle to understand and manage social networking. In building social capital through social networking, it is important to provide evidence of a return on the investment of time. If employees perceive a return on the investment of their time, they may be more inclined to participate, or they may participate at higher levels. Even if there is simply a perception of a benefit, users may be more inclined to participate or may be moved to increase their participation levels. In this chapter, we propose a social networking and performance model based on an examination of the relationships involved in predicting participation in organizations.

BACKGROUND

The lack of research and discovery in social networking as it pertains to social networking and individual performance constructs is primarily caused by the relative newness of the social networking phenomenon. The lack of research also indicates the need to examine social networking with a particular focus on perceived performance improvement. As many organizations work to create social media policies, performance is neglected or reserved for later consideration. Organizations do not tend to inquire about return on investment or performance implications until they are well into social networking activities. This article offers ways to understand participation in the beginning stages of social networking activities and policy decisions. It offers organizations tools with which to impact online interactions as they happen, and to affect behaviors that support the organization's goals and objectives.

The newness of social networking leads to limitations in the body of research in terms of available data and depth of examination of the construct. There appear to be no direct examinations of social networking as it pertains to individual improvement potential, whether one considers productivity, performance or some other aspect of personal- or organizational-driven improvement possibilities. Further, a review of the literature does not reveal much in terms of organizations that evaluate individual improvement, skill, capacity, time, etc., in concert with innovation adoption prior to making the decision to engage in social networking. Studies show that it is relatively easy to convince individuals, and organizations, about the benefits of social networking activities (Boyd & Ellison, 2008; Brandyberry et al., 2010; Pallis et al., 2011; Preece & Shneiderman, 2009).

Social networking is important to organizations because there is a "digital conversation" that is constantly going on around the world. Organizations can improve their chances for success and explore new opportunities by employing social networking strategies that influence the conversation about their organizations (Safko & Brake, 2009, p. 14). Monitoring the digital conversation also provides insights into what competitors, partners, and even governments are doing. The success of any organization depends on its employees, and social networking activities that have a positive effect on behavior may create positive perceptions of individual performance improvement. Those positive perceptions can have a significant impact on social networking participation.

All organizations, particularly public sector ones, need help particularly in two areas. The first requires understanding and appreciating the value of social networking to the work process and its effect on the responsiveness of administrators. Second, organizations need an understanding of why people participate and of what predicts their acceptance or rejection of social networking activities. This chapter helps develop an adoption and participation model for social networking activities. The basis for the model is innovation adoption theory, which evaluates internal decision processes, attraction to a networking system, and behavioral implications. Knowledge of social networking adoption behavior provides vital information and opportunities to build social capital. Evaluation of the model proposed herein is important because little work has been done in public sector organizations to examine social networking and relevant behaviors that can lead to improved performance.

Performance may be influenced or improved when people are presented with evidence of a return on the investment of their time. To what extent do individual perceptions of usefulness and type of use predict social networking levels of participation? This chapter examines the effects of six constructs – perceived usefulness, perceived improvement potential (PIP), perceived ease of use, perceived encouragement, intra-organizational trust, and type of use – on the level of participation in social networking activities.

Many models and theories have been offered to examine social networking as it relates to adoption, diffusion, and acceptance of innovation. The theoretical basis for examining social networking involves adoption of innovation at the individual level. Literature on innovation adoption (J.P. Hatala & Fleming, 2007), the technology acceptance model (F. D. Davis, 1989; Kwon & Wen, 2010), governing by network (Goldsmith & Eggers, 2004), social capital theory (Putnam, 1993), and intra-organizational trust (Grey & Garsten, 2001) contribute to a theoretical basis for the model proposed in this chapter. A review of relevant literature provides a closer look at social networking and suggests a framework to identify determinants and opportunities that affect levels of acceptance and participation.

The review begins with literature on innovation adoption theory – which is the most critical aspect of an organization's ability to manipulate the social networking behavior of employees. Innovation adoption, or connectivity, is based on the ability of an organization to become connected at a level where performance is seen as optimal and where leadership has created an atmosphere capable of maintaining the necessary structural support mechanisms for information sharing and knowledge management (J.P. Hatala & Lutta, 2009a).

Diffusion of innovation is the process through which some innovation is communicated within a social system (Perry, 2006). Perry's innovation-decision process has three main components: the innovation-decision process, the characteristics of an innovation, and adopter characteristics.

Figure 1 is a domains of connectivity model that shows information sharing adoption within an organization (J.P. Hatala & Lutta, 2009b, p. 15).

An organization's connectivity position is constantly changing. Placing the organization in one of the quadrants depends on three factors: density levels, social structure and demographic characteristics. Social network analysis (J.P. Hatala, 2006) can identify density level, which is

Figure 1. Domains of connectivity within an organization

	Sharing Within Groups	**Limited Sharing Between Groups**
Sharing Between Groups	Connected (Open)	Interconnected (Dysfunctional)
Limited Sharing Between Groups	Intraconnected (Control)	Disconnected (Entropy)

connectivity among and between various network groups. An organization's social structure is identified by examining the position of actors (centrality) in the network, and by examining the formal structure (Scott, 2000; Wasserman & Faust, 1994). Current state of social networking, company records and traditional surveys and interviews are demographic characteristics that can be examined to assist with connectivity (J.P. Hatala & Lutta, 2009b).

The two columns in the chart represent whether information sharing occurs or does not occur within a group, and the two rows represent whether information sharing is occurring or not occurring between two or more groups:

Column 1: Optimal information sharing within a work group.
Column 2: Minimal information sharing within a work group.
Row 1: Optimal information sharing between work groups.
Row 2: Minimal information sharing between work groups.

The upper left quadrant shows a high level of density within and between work groups. This is

the quadrant where an organization should strive to be, where information is exchanged openly and freely and the culture of the organization supports the concept of information as a tool. This is the optimal position for an organization because it is characterized by social support mechanisms that promote information sharing and knowledge management. The upper right quadrant shows a high level of density between groups within an organization but not within a group. The desired density level is based on the level of information sharing required for optimal performance. Information sharing within a group is limited, but access to information across groups, departments, units and divisions is promoted and carried out.

The lower left quadrant illustrates minimal information sharing between groups. This is where we find organizational development silos, and information is not shared within the organization even though it may flow freely within groups. The lower right quadrant features little connectivity in a minimally dense organization that is drifting apart. Little to none of the potential of the organization is achieved because information is not shared freely and is not easily accessible.

The governing by network approach (Goldsmith & Eggers, 2004) is also important to the discussion of social networking. It involves helping governments ensure their network-based partnerships are administratively effective and politically accountable. Governments should move away from having employees view themselves as doers and instead try to create a culture where employees view themselves as facilitators, conveners, and brokers of how to engage the community's talents to accomplish the task at hand. This approach requires less reliance on public employees in traditional roles and more on a web of partnerships, contracts and alliances to do the public's work.

Network initiatives can therefore help in accomplishing public objectives with measurable performance goals, assigned responsibilities to each partner, and structured information flow. The ultimate goal of these efforts is to produce the greatest possible value proposition, greater than the total of what each player could accomplish on his or her own without collaboration (Goldsmith & Eggers, 2004).

Effective network governance that enhances performance first requires leaders who can master the challenges of goal alignment, provide oversight, avoid any communications meltdown, coordinate multiple players, manage the tension between competition and collaboration, and overcome data deficits and capacity shortages. Next, the organization needs to address issues of mission and strategy.

Leaders can assist with individual performance improvement by starting with mission and then determining the process; a much-needed change from the tradition of deciding on a process and then trying to fit it to a mission. This allows the destination, not the path, to be the focus around which the components and interactions of the network are built (Goldsmith & Eggers, 2004). It's also important to address what members of the network ought to do. Ask the right question in terms of what outcome-based value proposition, or public value, the organization is trying to cre-

ate. Once those decisions are made, it important to communicate those intentions to employees.

Leaders must always pay attention to cultural compatibility when selecting network partners. This is essential for fostering long-standing, mutually beneficial relationships. The key is shared values across the culture. Creating ties that bind is related to cultural compatibility, and it requires that effective network ventures establish dependable communication channels, coordinate activities between network participants, and build trusting relationships. The challenge, however, goes beyond simply using the technology to manage relationships. Social networking still requires vigilance in addressing people issues, examining processes, aligning values, and building trust. Finally, network integrators must create and maintain the infrastructure and conditions that support long-term relationship building. Network governance, knowledge sharing, value and incentive alignment, trust building, and overcoming cultural differences are challenges every good integrator must face head on.

When responsibilities are managed effectively, they can open the door to the enormous value available to participants. The value is available because of the varied and unlimited points of employee contact that can be translated into useful responses by the many employees involved in the network, allowing each to adjust their responses appropriately. Governing by network is a way to address the limitations we find in social networking research.

The current evaluation of social networking and individual perceptions of performance would not be complete without social capital theory (Putnam, 1993). Social capital theory is a prominent consideration in all social media applications, and is important to any view of performance or behaviors that drive it. The theory's central ideas are that relationships matter and that social networks are a valuable asset (Field, 2003). People derive benefits from interaction that builds communities and commitment that creates ties as they knit a kind of "social fabric." Social capital theory suggests that trust relationships are essential for social networking experiences that build strong ties and a sense of belonging.

Social capital exists between individuals and is all about establishing relationships purposefully and employing them to generate intangible and tangible social, psychological, emotional and economical benefits in short or long terms. Social capital can be examined in terms of five dimensions: networks or lateral associations between individuals and/or groups, reciprocity and expectation, trust and risk based on assumptions, social norms, and personal and collective efficacy.

Social capital and organizational learning have been studied to understand knowledge transfer and perceived organizational performance. Rhodes et al (2008) examined these relationships, integrating organizational learning capability with social capital to shape a holistic knowledge sharing and management enterprise framework. They argued that an integrative model can produce a significant strategy to achieve organizational success. Their results indicate that these dimensions are distinct and have different effects on knowledge transfer.

Examining social capital in the online era requires different sets of scales than have been historically used for these purposes. Researchers argue that existing approaches to studying social capital online have been stymied by importing measurements from older, functionally different media (Williams, 2006). Williams (2006) attempts to theorize, create, and validate a series of scales to measure social capital in online and offline contexts, finding 10-item scales that are valid and reliable. The confirmatory factor analysis in that research was primarily concerned with bridging and bonding as two distinct but related dimensions of social capital.

Research by Sabatini (2009) contributes to social capital literature in three ways. The first is with a new framework for measurement of social capital and social networks, then with a single, synthetic measure dealing with the configuration of social capital and, finally, with an empirical assessment of the relationships between different types of social capital.

Trust is important to any social media or social networking examination because it is a construct that has a relationship to dependence, satisfaction and commitment. Trusting relationships in organizations involves an ongoing decision to give most people the benefit of the doubt, and it can be extended even to people one does not know from direct experience. McEvily, Perrone and Zaheer, serving as guest editors, answer the question "Why Trust?" in a special issue on trust in an organizational context (2003). The authors discuss the importance of trust and examine why it is so important "now." They find that a part of the trend is explained by the fact that changes in technology had, at that point, reconfigured exchange and the coordination of work across distance and time. Those changes continue today. Focusing on, among other organizational forms, knowledge-intensive organizations, they write:

A distinguishing feature of these new organizational forms is that they alter the patterns of interdependencies and the nature and extent of uncertainty. The consequence being that the individuals working in the new organizational forms become more dependent on, and more vulnerable to, the decisions and actions of others – both preconditions and concomitants of trust (McEvily et al., 2003, p. 1).

The authors point out that organizational science has made some important advances that promote understanding of the meaning of trust and how it relates to certain factors that characterize organizations. They mention examples of an increasing number of journal articles and special issues (Bachmann et al., 2001; Rousseau et al., 1998) and books (Gambetta, 1988; Kramer, 1996; Lane & Bachmann, 1998) devoted to the topic of trust in and between organizations. The special issue published seven papers that represent a wide range of methodological approaches, a diverse set of theoretical disciplines, a variety of levels of analysis, and a blend of empirical models (McEvily et al., 2003).

Two of the papers in the special issue are important for the current focus on trust. Becerra and Gupta (2003) probes the influence of organizational context on trust, emphasizing how the influence of social structure in an organization is contingent on communication frequency. They argue that frequency of communication is related to emphasis, in that as frequency increases the emphasis shifts from the trustor's to the trustee's individual and contextual characteristics. The relationship among senior managers of a multinational organization is the basis for testing the hypotheses. Findings point to a view of trust production in organizations that consists of individual, dyadic and contextual components.

Another paper in the special issue argues that people tend to trust members of their own organizations more than they trust people from outside of the organization (Huff & Kelley, 2003). The authors also argue the notion that the effect of this trust is greater in collectivist than in individualistic societies. Trust on average is lower for people from collectivist society, a prediction that runs counter to conventional wisdom (McEvily et al., 2003). The authors generally find support for their hypotheses using data from a large sample (Huff & Kelley, 2003).

Examining the trust construct as it relates to performance in organizations requires an examination of two issues that seem central. The first involves trust as a means for dealing with uncertainty. The second focuses on trust and acceptance of vulnerability (Newell & Swan, 2000). Luhman (1988, p. 103) argues that trust occurs in situations of risk and uncertainty: "A system requires trust as an input condition in order to stimulate supportive activities in situations of uncertainty or risk."

Trust is also a multi-dimensional concept where values, attitudes and emotions or moods

interact (Newell & Swan, 2000). There are three reasons someone may be able to develop trust (Sako, 1992):

1.   Because of a contractual agreement that binds the parties in the relationship;
2.   Because of a belief in the competencies of those involved; and
3.   Because of a belief in the goodwill of those involved.

There are other dimensions to consider as well. The research of Dirks and Ferrin has a wide focus and great applicability here, covering trust in organizational settings (2001), using rewards to increase and decrease trust (2003), and examining the effects of third-party relationships on interpersonal trust (2006). A typology distinguishing between deterrence-based trust, knowledge-based trust and identification-based trust was developed in 1992 (Shapiro et al.). Zucker (1986) argues for a developmental focus, establishing three central mechanisms of trust production: process-based, characteristic-based and institutional-based. Process-based focuses on reciprocal, recurring exchange, characteristic-based is defined by social similarity, and institutional-based is determined by expectations embedded in societal norms and structures.

The proposed social networking and individual performance model requires a tighter focus on trust, one that leads to an examination of intra-organizational trust Intra-organizational trust concerns interactions and activity within organizational relations (Grey & Garsten, 2001). Grey & Garsten argue that most literature gives more emphasis to inter-organizational trust, between-organization trust, but there are a number of researchers interested in what happens "within" organizations (Li & Betts, 2003; Mayer et al., 1995; Steinfield et al., 2009; van de Bunt et al., 2005).

A 2010 study concerning building trust in nonprofit networks (Lambright et al., 2010) reveals factors influencing interpersonal trust in networks:

propensity to trust, perceived trustworthiness of the trustee, the relationship between the trustee and trustor, and third-party relationships. The findings support the argument that trust between a trustor and trustee positively influences expected future cooperation. The study can be related to strength of ties (bonding, bridging, or linking) in the network (J.P. Hatala & Fleming, 2007; Ivancevich, 2008), focusing on successful past cooperation and frequency of interactions as two of the most important factors influencing interpersonal trust in networks (Lambright et al., 2010).

There is also some relevance to trust in social learning theory, which indicates that behavioral change in organizations can be the result of vicarious learning through modeling and, if the learning is successfully accomplished, trust can be achieved. In vicarious learning, the nature of the observed model can influence the probability that an observer will imitate the modeled behavior and have a chance to be successful (Manz & Sims, 1981). People will normally seek out the model who possesses the greatest interpersonal attraction (A. Bandura, 1977a). Credible models are people perceived as being successful and who exert greater influence than non-credible models (A. Bandura, 1969, 1977a). Relevant literature supports the notion that modeling-based training programs will be more effective if the models presented have achieved high status and competence (Goldstein & Sorcher, 1974; Rosenbaum, 1978; Weiss, 1978). One study reports that subordinates showed greater similarity in behavior to superiors who were viewed as being competent and successful, indicating great possibilities for building trust.

In 2009, researchers analyzed the importance of trust and its consequences for management (Gursakal et al., 2009). A network analysis was conducted to determine which employees trust other employees on a personal level. Based on the findings, the researchers argue that trust can create effective cooperation within enterprises, thereby having a positive influence on performance, growth and survival.

There is much more information available for social networking and performance examinations and discovery can and should go beyond innovation adoption, governing by network and social capital. The growing volumes of information include more on social networking (Cerulo, 1990; Chung et al., 2007; Fowler et al., 2004; Zack & McKenney, 1995), trust (Newell & Swan, 2000; Nyhan, 2000), measuring performance or productivity (Akdere & Roberts, 2008; Bearman et al., 1985; T. R. V. Davis & Luthans, 1980; Otis, 2007), capacity or skill building (Eastin & LaRose, 2000; Erickson & Jacoby, 2003; Segrest et al., 1998; Shetzer, 1993) and other constructs. However, the social networking literature is primarily descriptive and categorizing without providing value-creation and value-capturing strategies.

The literature does not contain information about linkages between social networking and performance in the manner that is suggested here. Similarly, the literature does not specifically address individual performance or relevant perceptions, so there is no sufficient body of knowledge in this area. The lack of research and discovery in social networking as it pertains to the constructs addressed herein is primarily caused by the relative newness of the social networking phenomenon. The aforementioned lack of research clearly suggests a need to examine social networking with a particular focus on perceived performance improvement.

MAIN FOCUS

Problem

The model proposed in this chapter links social networking to individual performance, searching for perceptions that enable organizations to understand participation and to examine whether there are tangible benefits involved in that participation. Leaders are just now beginning to ask difficult questions about social networking, but not much is being done to understand the value proposition involved. The questions are about the effect of social networking on the work process and on the responsiveness of administrators. The questions are also about understanding predictors of accepting and rejecting participation in social networking. This chapter proposes a conceptual model to provide an understanding of the "moving parts" in social networking and how they affect performance.

The challenge is to use the vital source of information available through social networking to address the impacts of participation (Igbaria & Tan, 1997). Employees may be more inclined to participate in the organization's social media tool of choice if they perceive that there is some return on the investment of their time or attention. This return may be in the form of improved skills, availability of new challenges or increased standing in the firm.

In getting people to believe that an action will lead to improvement of their performance, organizations face a two-fold challenge. The first part involves understanding the dynamics of change processes. Management problems are created when people are reluctant to move from the status quo and accept new methods (Lasden, 1981). There are four negative reactions to the introduction of a new system: sense of awkwardness, fear and suspicion, misunderstanding and resentment (Lasden, 1981). Leadership can circumvent these negative reactions by taking the critical first step of developing understanding. The keys to success involve improving participation through education and information programs, and beginning the change with mild participatory measures and then moving to tactics that are more forceful.

The second part of the challenge involves addressing an individual's determination of whether the change will result in some level of performance improvement. For instance, a study conducted among 100 international senior executives involved in technological innovation within their firms examines barriers to in-house diffusion of new ideas (Vandermerwe, 1987). First among the barriers listed was the difficulty of making observable benefits clear to others.

Linking social networking and perceptions of performance is limited by the lack of available data and depth of examination because social networking has been only recently introduced to organizations. There appear to be no direct examinations of social networking as it pertains to individual improvement potential, whether one considers productivity, performance or some other aspect of personal- or organizational-driven improvement possibilities. There is also a lack of research that shows development of social networking beyond that point in the direction of performance improvement or return on the investment of time.

The large, and growing, numbers of people and organizations involved in social networking make further research and analysis imperative for social science and management disciplines. A key question for leaders might be, "Are my employees better off because we expended money or effort in social networking?" Employees who have limited participation, or those who do not participate, might ask, "Will my participation make me a more skilled or more productive worker?"

Igbaria and Tan (1997) suggest information technology applications should focus on the impacts of accepting or rejecting tools and capabilities. That examination also indicates that system usage and user satisfaction can be used to indicate a performance impact. The researchers suggest that their results support prior research, suggesting that indicators of computer system acceptance, such as satisfaction and usage, may produce performance value and operational effectiveness. In addition, they argue that IT acceptance helped individuals accomplish tasks more effectively and more efficiently. This significant link between acceptance, participation and impact on productivity has important implications for building the model we are proposing in this chapter.

The recommended approach to link social networking and individual performance appears to be the first-ever attempt to examine the constructs of interest and their relationships in this grouping. This initial examination is necessary because organizations require even informal benchmark evidence that social networking is able to establish a personal focus prior to implementation.

Solutions and Recommendations

While there is no reason to believe that people won't continue to participate in social networking, there are concerns that those who accept participation could benefit from a higher level of activity and that their productivity might be improved. That's why there is a need to develop a model that allows public organizations to plan and successfully implement social networking programs in a way that addresses individual values, attitudes and lifestyles at every step of the process. In a dissertation on social networking and individual performance predictors, Brown (2011) addressed value propositions for participation that are clear to users. Currently, organizations wait for people to participate, and then leaders begin to seek individual-level benefits that promote greater participation. At the heart of the issue is the need for a line of questioning concerning whether organizations and their employees are better off because of social networking activities, and that line of questioning is needed at the beginning of the social networking process instead of while it's already in progress. The large, and growing, numbers of people and organizations involved in social networking requires this analysis.

Research is needed to define the most relevant methodologies at the individual level to allow public organizations to successfully deal with improvement concerns prior to making a decision to participate in social networking. This avoids the return on investment concern that is voiced at some point after the organization has made the commitment to network. There is also

value in attempting to understand the difference between those who accept and those who reject participation, so it seems beneficial to add perceptions of individual improvement to widely-used determining constructs in the social networking/social media field. The research by Brown (2011) found favorable model fit statistics that support positive correlations between the constructs of interest and participation. Those results demonstrate the potential for further research to develop a survey instrument that organizations can use to evaluate a person's intent to participate in the desired behavior, to actually exhibit the desired behavior, and to participate at a level that is personally and professionally significant. The proposed evaluation has the potential to provide public organizations with a formal process that would allow the greatest return on investment.

The need for research can be addressed by helping organizations decide on embracing or rejecting social networking. A decision to embrace social networking recognizes that success is driven by more than simply beginning activities. Organizations need to understand how the constructs in the model (Figure 2) relate to social networking, performance and participation.

The primary purpose of the model is to use a new focus to test determinants of social networking participation. This type of research will extend social networking knowledge by presenting a new model that identifies factors organizations can consider in advance of making a decision to participate in these activities. A second purpose is to continue to identify the psychological process of participating in social networking, an area where additional inquiry is needed. The perceived impact of social networking is widely supported, evidenced by the ease with which organizations sign up for these activities and from the ever-increasing number of social network services. There continue to be dramatic increases in the number of people who benefit from social networking; however, the speed of the "social networking sign

Figure 2. Social networking and individual performance model

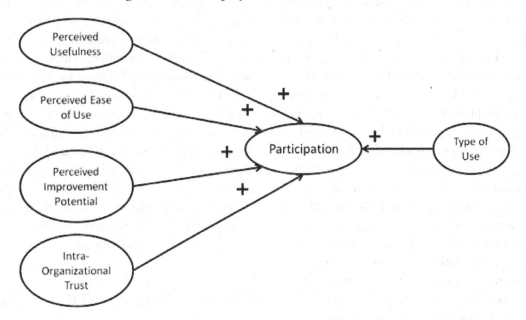

up process" leaves potential individual benefits, or PIP, as an after-thought in many cases.

Prior studies form the basis for perceived usefulness, perceived ease of use, perceived encouragement and intra-organizational trust. PIP is based on self perception in social networks and type of use characterizes individual involvement.

Davis (1989) argues that perceived usefulness and perceived ease of use are fundamental determinants of user acceptance. Perceived usefulness refers to capabilities that reinforce good performance in various ways within an organizational context; these capabilities can be used advantageously. Therefore, a system that is high in perceived usefulness reinforces the user's belief in the existence of a positive use-performance relationship.

The perceived usefulness scale from the Technology Acceptance Model (TAM) (F. D. Davis, 1989; F. D. Davis et al., 1989) refers to the degree to which the user believes that using the technology will improve his or her work performance. TAM, the most widely applied model of user acceptance and usage, was adapted from the Theory of Reasoned Action (Ajzen & Fishbein,

1980; Fishbein & Ajzen, 1975). Perceived usefulness and perceived ease of use are two specific beliefs that, according to the TAM, determine one's behavioral intentions to use a technology, which has been linked to subsequent behavior (Venkatesh, 2000).

Bandura (1989) argues the significance of perceived ease of use through extensive research, defining it in terms of people making judgments as to how well they can execute courses of action required to deal with prospective situations. Perceived ease of use refers to a person's perception of how effortless use of the technology will be. Perceived ease of use is a construct that is linked to an individual's assessment of the effort involved in the process of using the system (Masrom, 2007; Venkatesh, 2000).

Perceived encouragement refers to the organizational support and assistance to participate that is important for affecting human performance. Kwon and Wen (2010) argue that expressing encouragement could be literal as well as verbal, and that encouragement is perceptional. The way one person perceives the other's encouragement is a critical consideration.

Kwon and Wen (2010) argue that encouragement is a sort of intangible social support that provides a specific individual with psychological wellness. People can avoid negative stimuli or recover from undesired states based on perceived encouragement. The researchers focused on literal encouragement through a blogging concept, examining how people perceive others' encouraging expression and analyzing whether that distinction was more critical than how the person expressed his or her willingness to encourage a different person.

Trust is crucial to any social networking activity. Intra-organizational trust is the trust people have in one another that creates and nurtures social bonds and collaboration in organizational social networking activities. It is included in this framework because researchers have consistently argued its necessity for organizational effectiveness. Intra-organizational trust is a vital part of achieving collective receptivity to and exploitation of computer technologies (Barney, 1991; Dedrick et al., 2003; Kramer, 1996; Nakata et al., 2008). Intra-organizational trust is defined as the positive expectations that workers across the organization have about one another's abilities, actions, and motives. It consists of cognitive, affective, and moral dimensions and describes the perceived intent and behaviors of organizational members (Chowdhury, 2005; Hosmer, 1995; McAllister, 1995; Nakata et al., 2008).

PIP is a construct based on a person's self-perception of effectiveness. PIP has a two-fold purpose; to predict a person's intention to behave in a certain way and to determine whether they will actually exhibit that behavior. PIP can be measured using a factor analysis of a set of 5 items regarding the respondents' personal intentions and attitudes toward social networking: (1) personal quality of output, (2) work group quality of output, (3) performance in comparison to others, (4) assistance with high priority tasks, and (5) identification of available resources (e.g. personnel and materials).

Participation refers to the level, type and duration of a person's participation. This examination can be based on gratifications (Anderson & Harris, 1997): cognitive, which refer to an individual's desire for information; interpersonal utility, which reflects the individual's need to establish a "social location" in relation to others in society; and diversion, which includes relief from boredom, entertainment, and arousal. Evaluating the proposed model may lead to a methodology organizations can use to address the challenges of understanding the social networking change process and of the individual's determination of the usefulness of these activities.

FUTURE RESEARCH DIRECTIONS

Social networking will continue to be an important tool for organizations far into the future. The Social Networking and Individual Performance Model has potential to provide real benefits for future organizational endeavors. Several actions are recommended to take advantage of that potential. First, empirically testing the model will demonstrate the value of the constructs by allowing evaluation of predictor variables against participation criteria. Second, conducting surveys in public and private organizations would be helpful in showing the difference in participation in those populations, and may shed light on other social networking considerations that have not been identified. Third, the creation of an assessment tool with automated scoring affords organizations an ability to add measurement and feedback to their social networking efforts.

CONCLUSION

This chapter establishes a recommended linkage between social networking and perceptions of individual performance improvement. Addressing the challenges of predicting the relationship between social networking and performance provides insight into the value proposition that can lead to enhanced participation. Success in this endeavor would be found in providing a clear view of the dynamics of change processes, and in affecting an individual's view of the performance implications of social networking activities.

Improved social networking participation then allows organizations to take full advantage of the "digital conversations" that are so vital in today's technological, online world. Perfecting the model proposed in this chapter, and using it to create an assessment tool, can allow organizations to take full advantage of the social networking capability.

REFERENCES

Akdere, M., & Roberts, P. B. (2008). Economics of social capital: Implications for organizational performance. *Advances in Developing Human Resources, 10*(6), 802. doi:10.1177/1523422308325007

Anderson, S. E., & Harris, J. B. (1997). Factors associated with amount of use and benefits obtained by users of a statewide educational telecomputing network. *Educational Technology Research and Development, 45*(1), 19–50. doi:10.1007/BF02299611

Bachmann, R., Knights, D., & Sydow, J. (2001). Special issue: Trust and control in organizational relations. *Organization Studies, 22*(2). doi:10.1177/0170840601222007

Bandura, A. (1969). *Principles of behavior modification.* New York, NY: Holt, Rinehart and Winston.

Bandura, A. (1977a). *Social learning theory.* Englewood Cliffs, NJ: Prentice-Hall.

Bandura, A. (1989). Human agency in social cognitive theory. *The American Psychologist, 44*(9), 1175–1184. doi:10.1037/0003-066X.44.9.1175

Barney, J. (1991). Firm resources and sustained competitive advantage. *Journal of Management, 17*(1), 99. doi:10.1177/014920639101700108

Bearman, T. C., Guynup, P., & Milevski, S. N. (1985). Information and productivity. *Journal of the American Society for Information Science American Society for Information Science, 36*(6), 369. doi:10.1002/asi.4630360605

Becerra, M., & Gupta, A. K. (2003). Perceived trustworthiness within the organization: The moderating impact of communication frequency on trustor and trustee effects. *Organization Science, 14*(1), 32. doi:10.1287/orsc.14.1.32.12815

Boyd, D. M., & Ellison, N. B. (2008). Social network sites: Definition, history, and scholarship. *Journal of Computer-Mediated Communication, 13*(1), 210–230. doi:10.1111/j.1083-6101.2007.00393.x

Brandyberry, A. A., Li, X., & Lin, L. (2010). *Determinants of perceived usefulness and perceived ease of use in individual adoption of social network sites.* Paper presented at the AMCIS 2010, Paper 544.

Brown, M., Sr. (2011). *Social networking and individual performance: Examining predictors of participation.* Unpublished Ph.D., Old Dominion University, United States -- Virginia.

Cerulo, K. A. (1990). To err is social: Network prominence and its effects on self-estimation. *Sociological Forum, 5*(4), 619–634. doi:10.1007/BF01115394

Chowdhury, S. (2005). The role of affect- and cognition-based trust in complex knowledge sharing. *Journal of Managerial Issues, 17*(3), 310–326.

Chung, K. S. K., Hossain, L., & Davis, J. (2007). *Individual performance in knowledge intensive work through social networks.* Paper presented at the 2007 ACM SIGMIS CPR Conference on Computer Personnel Research: The Global Information Technology Workforce, St. Louis, Missouri, USA.

Davis, F. D. (1989). Perceived usefulness, perceived ease of use, and user acceptance of Information Technology. *Management Information Systems Quarterly*, *13*(3), 319–340. doi:10.2307/249008

Davis, F. D., Bagozzi, R. P., & Warshaw, P. R. (1989). User acceptance of computer technology: A comparison of two. *Management Science*, *35*(8), 982. doi:10.1287/mnsc.35.8.982

Davis, T. R. V., & Luthans, F. (1980). A social learning approach to organizational behavior. *Academy of Management Review*, *5*(2), 281–290.

Dedrick, J., Gurbaxani, V., & Kraemer, K. L. (2003). Information Technology and economic performance: A critical review of the empirical evidence. *ACM Computing Surveys*, *35*(1), 1–28. doi:10.1145/641865.641866

Dirks, K. T., & Ferrin, D. L. (2001). The role of trust in organizational settings. *Organization Science*, *12*(4), 450. doi:10.1287/orsc.12.4.450.10640

Eastin, M. S., & LaRose, R. (2000). Internet self-efficacy and the psychology of the digital divide. *Journal of Computer-Mediated Communication*, *6*(1).

Erickson, C. L., & Jacoby, S. M. (2003). The effects of employer networks on workplace innovation and training. *Industrial & Labor Relations Review*, *56*(2), 203. doi:10.2307/3590935

Ferrin, D. L., & Dirks, K. T. (2003). The use of rewards to increase and decrease trust: Mediating processes and differential effects. *Organization Science*, *14*(1), 18. doi:10.1287/orsc.14.1.18.12809

Ferrin, D. L., Dirks, K. T., & Shah, P. P. (2006). Direct and indirect effects of third-party relationships on interpersonal trust. *The Journal of Applied Psychology*, *91*(4), 870–883. doi:10.1037/0021-9010.91.4.870

Field, J. (2003). *Social capital*. London, UK: Routledge.

Fowler, S. W., Lawrence, T. B., & Morse, E. A. (2004). Virtually embedded ties. *Journal of Management*, *30*(5), 647–666. doi:10.1016/j.jm.2004.02.005

Gambetta, D. (1988). *Trust: Making and breaking cooperative relations*. New York, NY: B. Blackwell.

Goldsmith, S., & Eggers, W. D. (2004). *Governing by network: The new shape of the public sector*. Washington, DC: Brookings Institution Press.

Goldstein, A. P., & Sorcher, M. (1974). *Changing supervisory behavior*. New York, NY: Pergammon.

Grey, C., & Garsten, C. (2001). Trust, control and post-bureaucracy. *Organization Studies*, *22*(2), 229–250. doi:10.1177/0170840601222003

Gursakal, N., Oguzlar, A., Aydin, Z. B., & Tuzunturk, S. (2009). Measuring trust in an intra-organisational context using social network analysis. *International Journal of Management and Enterprise Development*, *6*(4), 494–512. doi:10.1504/IJMED.2009.024238

Hatala, J. P. (2006). Social network analysis in human resource development: A new methodology. *Human Resource Development Review*, *5*(1), 45. doi:10.1177/1534484305284318

Hatala, J. P., & Fleming, P. R. (2007). Making transfer climate visible: Utilizing social network analysis to facilitate the transfer of training. *Human Resource Development Review*, *6*(1), 33. doi:10.1177/1534484306297116

Hatala, J. P., & Lutta, J. (2009a). Managing information sharing within an organizational setting: A social network perspective. *Performance Improvement Quarterly*, *21*(4), 5. doi:10.1002/piq.20036

Hatala, J. P., & Lutta, J. G. (2009b). Managing information sharing within an organizational setting: A social network perspective. *Performance Improvement Quarterly, 21*(4), 5. doi:10.1002/piq.20036

Hendrix, W. H. (1984). Development of a contingency model organizational assessment survey for management consultants. *Journal of Experimental Education, 52*(2), 95–105.

Hosmer, L. T. (1995). Trust - The connecting link between organizational theory and philosophical ethics. *Academy of Management Review, 20*(2), 379–403.

Huff, L., & Kelley, L. (2003). Levels of organizational trust in individualist versus collectivist societies: A seven-nation study. *Organization Science, 14*(1), 81. doi:10.1287/orsc.14.1.81.12807

Igbaria, M., & Tan, M. (1997). The consequences of Information Technology acceptance on subsequent individual performance. *Information & Management, 32*(3), 113–121. doi:10.1016/S0378-7206(97)00006-2

Ivancevich, J. M., Konopaske, R., & Matteson, M. T. (2008). *Organizational behavior and management* (8th ed.). New York, NY: McGraw-Hill/Irwin.

Kramer, R. M. (1996). *Trust in organizations: Frontiers of theory and research.* Thousand Oaks, CA: Sage Publications.

Kwon, O., & Wen, Y. (2010). An empirical study of the factors affecting social network service use. *Computers in Human Behavior, 26*(2), 254–263. doi:10.1016/j.chb.2009.04.011

Lambright, K. T., Mischen, P. A., & Laramee, C. B. (2010). Building trust in public and nonprofit networks: Personal, dyadic, and third-party influences. *American Review of Public Administration, 40*(1), 64–82. doi:10.1177/0275074008329426

Lane, C., & Bachmann, R. (1998). *Trust within and between organizations: Conceptual issues and empirical applications.* New York, NY: Oxford University Press.

Lasden, M. (1981). Turning reluctant users on to change. *Computer Decisions, 13*(1), 92.

Leaman, A., & Bordass, W. (2000). Productivity in buildings: The killer variables. In Clements-Croome, D. (Ed.), *Creating the productive workplace.* London, UK: E & FN Spon.

Li, F., & Betts, S. (2003). Between expectation and behavioral intent: A model of trust. *Allied Academies International Conference. Academy of Organizational Culture, Communications and Conflict Proceedings, 8*(1), 33.

Luhmann, N. (1988). Familiarity, confidence, trust: Problems and alternatives. In Gambetta, D. (Ed.), *Trust: Making and breaking cooperative relations.* New York, NY: Basil Blackwell.

Manz, C. C., & Sims, H. P. Jr. (1981). Vicarious learning: The influence of modeling on organizational behavior. *Academy of Management Review, 6*(1), 105–113.

Masrom, M. (2007, 21-24 May 2007). *Technology acceptance model and e-learning.* Paper presented at the 12th International Conference on Education, Sultan Hassanal Bolkiah Institute of Education, Universiti Brunei Darussalam, Universiti Teknologi Malaysia City Campus.

Mayer, R. C., Davis, J. H., & Schoorman, F. D. (1995). An integrative model of organizational trust. *Academy of Management Review, 20*(3), 709–734.

Mazman, S. G., & Usluel, Y. K. (2009). The usage of social networks in educational context. *World Academy of Science Engineering and Technology, 49*, 404–408.

McAllister, D. J. (1995). Affect-based and cognition-based trust as foundations for interpersonal cooperation in organizations. *Academy of Management Journal, 38*(1), 24–59. doi:10.2307/256727

McEvily, B., Perrone, V., & Zaheer, A. (2003). Introduction to the special issue on trust in an organizational context. *Organization Science, 14*(1), 1. doi:10.1287/orsc.14.1.1.12812

Nakata, C., Zhu, Z., & Kraimer, M. (2008). The complex contribution of Information Technology capability to business performance. *Journal of Managerial Issues, 20*(4), 485.

Newell, S., & Swan, J. (2000). Trust and interorganizational networking. *Human Relations, 53*(10), 1287–1328.

Nyhan, R. C. (2000). Changing the paradigm: Trust and its role in public sector organizations. *American Review of Public Administration, 30*(1), 87–109. doi:10.1177/02750740022064560

Otis, B. (2007). *Factors in social computing related to worker productivity.* Unpublished Capstone Report, University of Oregon, Portland.

Pallis, G., Zeinalipour-Yazti, D., & Dikaiakos, M. D. (2011). Online social networks: Status and trends. In *New directions in Web data management (Vol. 331*, pp. 213–234). Heidelberg, Germany: Springer Verlag. doi:10.1007/978-3-642-17551-0_8

Perry, R. (2006). Diffusion theories. In E. F. Borgatta & R. J. V. Montgomery (Eds.), *Encyclopedia of sociology* (2 ed., Vol. 1, pp. 674-681). New York, NY: Macmillan Reference USA.

Preece, J., & Shneiderman, B. (2009). The reader-to-leader framework: Motivating technology-mediated social participation. *AIS Transactions on Human-Computer Interaction, 1*(1), 13–32.

Putnam, R. D. (1993). *Bowling alone.* New York, NY: Simon & Schuster Paperbacks.

Rhodes, J., Lok, P., Hung, R. Y.-Y., & Fang, S.-C. (2008). An integrative model of organizational learning and social capital on effective knowledge transfer and perceived organizational performance. *Journal of Workplace Learning, 20*(4), 245. doi:10.1108/13665620810871105

Rosenbaum, B. L. (1978). New uses for behavioral modeling. *The Personnel Administrator*, 27–28.

Rousseau, D. M., Sitkin, S. B., Burt, R. S., & Camerer, C. (1998). Not so different after all: A cross-discipline view of trust. *Academy of Management. Academy of Management Review, 23*(3), 393. doi:10.5465/AMR.1998.926617

Sabatini, F. (2009). Social capital as social networks: A new framework for measurement and an empirical analysis of its determinants and consequences. *Journal of Socio-Economics, 38*(3), 429–442. doi:10.1016/j.socec.2008.06.001

Safko, L., & Brake, D. K. (2009). *The social media bible: Tactics, tools, and strategies for business success.* Hoboken, NJ: John Wiley & Sons.

Sako, M. (1992). *Prices, quality, and trust: inTerfirm relations in Britain and Japan.* Cambridge, UK: Cambridge University Press. doi:10.1017/CBO9780511520723

Scott, J. (2000). *Social network analysis: A handbook.* London, UK: SAGE Publications.

Segrest, S. L., Domke-Damonte, D. J., Miles, A. K., & Anthony, W. P. (1998). Following the crowd: Social influence and technology usage. *Journal of Organizational Change Management, 11*(5), 425. doi:10.1108/09534819810234841

Shapiro, D. L., Sheppard, B. H., & Cheraskin, L. (1992). Business on a handshake. *Negotiation Journal, 8*, 365–377. doi:10.1111/j.1571-9979.1992.tb00679.x

Shetzer, L. (1993). A social information processing model of employee participation. *Organization Science, 4*(2), 252. doi:10.1287/orsc.4.2.252

Steinfield, C., DiMicco, J. M., Ellison, N. B., & Lampe, C. (2009). *Bowling online: Social networking and social capital within the organization.* Paper presented at the Fourth International Conference on Communities and Technologies, University Park, PA.

van de Bunt, G. G., Wittek, R. P. M., & de Klepper, M. C. (2005). The evolution of intra-organizational trust networks: The case of a German paper factory: An empirical test of six trust mechanisms. *International Sociology, 20*(3), 339–369. doi:10.1177/0268580905055480

Vandermerwe, S. (1987). Diffusing new ideas in-house. *Journal of Product Innovation Management, 4*(4), 256. doi:10.1016/0737-6782(87)90029-4

Venkatesh, V. (2000). Determinants of perceived ease of use: Integrating control, intrinsic motivation, and emotion into the technology acceptance model. *Information Systems Research, 11*(4), 342. doi:10.1287/isre.11.4.342.11872

Warshaw, P. R., & Davis, F. D. (1985). Disentangling behavioral intention and behavioral expectation. *Journal of Experimental Social Psychology, 21*(3), 213–228. doi:10.1016/0022-1031(85)90017-4

Wasserman, S., & Faust, K. (1994). *Social network analysis: Methods and applications.* Cambridge, UK: Cambridge University Press.

Weiss, H. M. (1978). Social learning of work values in organizations. *The Journal of Applied Psychology, 63*(6), 711–718. doi:10.1037/0021-9010.63.6.711

Williams, D. (2006). On and off the 'Net: Scales for social capital in an online era. *Journal of Computer-Mediated Communication, 11*(2), 593–628. doi:10.1111/j.1083-6101.2006.00029.x

Zack, M. H., & McKenney, J. L. (1995). Social context and interaction in ongoing computer-supported management groups. *Organization Science, 6*(4), 394. doi:10.1287/orsc.6.4.394

Zucker, L. G. (1986). Production of trust: Institutional sources of economic structure. In Staw, B. M., & Cummings, L. L. (Eds.), *Research in organisational behaviour* (*Vol. 8*). Greenwich, CT: JAI.

KEY TERMS AND DEFINITIONS

Governing by Network: Assist with individual performance improvement by starting with mission and then determining the process. This allows the destination, not the path, to be the focus around which the components and interactions of the network are built.

Innovation Adoption: This theory promotes evaluation of internal decision processes and leads to an understanding of how users are attracted to a system, how their behavior is affected, and how they make decisions.

Perceived Improvement Potential: Based on a person's self-perception of effectiveness. Purpose is to predict a person's intention to behave in a certain way and to determine whether they will actually exhibit that behavior.

Social Capital: This theory suggests that trust relationships are essential for social networking experiences that build strong ties and a sense of belonging.

Social Networking: A process and practice by which people and organizations are drawn together by family, work or hobby to interact via websites.

Chapter 9

E–Democratic Administration and Bureaucratic Responsiveness:
A Primary Study of Bureaucrats' Perceptions of the Civil Service E–Mail Box in Taiwan

Guang-Xu Wang
National University of Tainan, Taiwan

ABSTRACT

The Civil Service E-mail Box (CSEB) is one of the windows that facilitate communication between Taiwan's government and its citizens. According to research, when a government has a user-friendly digital platform maintained by technologically literate public administrators, those public employees would support using such an electronic system to increase governmental responsiveness. This chapter investigates how the perception of e-democratic administration and information and communications technology's (ICT) level of readiness influence public administrators' perception of CSEB effectiveness in facilitating communication with citizens. It does this by examining bureaucratic survey data gathered from Taiwan's Research, Development, and Evaluation Commission (RDEC). Findings show that an unfriendly digital platform, unskilled staff, low appreciation of e-democracy, and lack of readiness on the part of CSEB negatively affect public employees' enthusiasm in regarding ICT as an effective tool in raising governmental responsiveness in Taiwan.

DOI: 10.4018/978-1-4666-0318-9.ch009

INTRODUCTION

With the popularity of information and communication technology (ICT), the interaction in intra-organizational, inter-organizational, inter-governmental, and boundary-crossing relationships has gradually evolved from the use of traditional written documents to e-communication via ICT. Advances in ICT have impacted the public sector, resulting in original administrative procedures that are both faster and more convenient. With the emphasis on facilitating public relations, and with the increased degree of readiness inherent in e-governance, citizen participation in today's decision-making process has become more convenient and frequent (Shiang, 2002; Snellen, 2002). Facing increased dissemination of citizens' opinions, the public sector has found that the convenience brought about by ICT has opened a window of opportunity to increasing bureaucratic responsiveness.

The Civil Service E-mail Box (CSEB) is one of the public sector's most accessible venues for receiving public opinion. As an application of Web 2.0 techniques in a government setting, its significance is not only manifested in the rapid response to the populace's complaints, opinions and queries, but it can also enhance the populace's participation in public affairs. The public sector emphasizes processing and resolving complaints as a public relations management mechanism. In the future, CSEB can aid in the timely resolution of problems, constituting a modern, emphatic, responsive, and democratic administrative foundation. If the public's problems cannot be solved immediately, the administrative organ can at least promptly explain the reason for its inability to resolve the problem, thus achieving the mission of comforting and informing through ICT. The very existence of CSEB strengthens the effective use of ICT and emphasizes bureaucratic responsiveness as a key link in e-governance.

Past related research, however, mostly concentrated on discussing the developmental trend of new governance style in the era of e-governments (Milward & Snyder, 1996; Scavo & Shi, 2000; Peled, 2001; Welch & Wong, 2001; Danziger & Andersen, 2002; Roy, 2003; Grant & Chau, 2004; Pavlichev & Garson, 2004; Carrizales, 2008; Dawes, 2008); identifying the correlation between ICT application and service quality (Cohen & Eimicke, 2001; Bovens & Zouridis, 2002; Buckley, 2003; Gant & Gant, 2003; West, 2004; Norris & Moon, 2005; Pirog & Johnson, 2008), the populace's perception of e-democracy (Barber, 1998, 2001; Bryan, Tsagarousianou & Tambini, 1998; Hacker & van Dijk, 2000; Chadwick, 2003; Stanley & Weare, 2004; Morgenson, Van Amburg, & Mithas, 2010) and public trust (Moon, 2003, 2005; Parent, Vandebeek & Gemino, 2004; Tolbert & Mossberger, 2004), or relevant research on digital division (Compaine, 2001; Norris, 2001; Becker, 2004; Groper, 2004; Moon & Welch, 2004). There has been very little in-depth analysis focusing on the process of public administrators' resolving the issues relating to the use of ICT, especially in regard to bureaucrats' attitudes towards the utilization of CSEB to make their office routine more effective and efficient. Examination of whether it leads to an "effective increase in bureaucratic responsiveness, and specifically, if it does help to solve the public's complaints and problems" as a research subject, has been lacking. In Chen, Huang and Hsiao's (2006) and Ong and Wang's (2009) research regarding the operation of the Taipei City Mayor's Mailbox, it is discovered that coping with the populace's "snowflake-like" complaint mails frequently resulted in the internal customer[1] processing expiration and engendered accusations from the public for the public sector's low response efficiency. Chen, Huang and Hsiao's (2006) and Ong and Wang's (2009) research is thus considered to be of vital importance in facilitating the creation of an environment wherein the administrative worker is able to satisfy the public by providing a service via ICT. Three elements are necessary to create a friendly environment for transforming communication between the government and the public. To more thoroughly understand the similarities and differences of public relations management and customer relations management, the first step lies in pursuing effective internal customer relations management in the public sector. The second step is the use of a public and logical consideration for work division and appraisal in pursuing internal customer relations management. Finally, the circumstance of information revolution demand that knowledge management, information management, and the provision of related training courses be used to establish and maintain internal customer relations as well as provide the external customer with truly responsive services (Garson, 1995; Chen, Huang & Hsiao, 2006).

The above study referred to a very important governance problem, namely: although the development of ICT enhances public involvement in the policy process, it is also more costly to govern. By establishing a CSEB for improving the efficiency of government responsiveness, the government needs to allocate more resources to manage the system, as well. In addition to the public's perception of the government's responsiveness, the ability of the public administrator to serve as both participant and responder in the use of CSEB, while simultaneously facing an increased volume and complexity of information is an important issue needing further discussion. The questions of whether information processing skill encompasses the ability to process huge amounts of public opinion cannot be neglected. Nor can one ignore the perception of whether CSEB is valid to improve bureaucratic responsiveness. In other words, under the circumstance surrounding the implementation of the e-government policy, what are its real effects on governance activities? How effective is ICT in promoting bureaucratic response efficiency? Do public employees feel that CSEB can effectively address the populace's complaints and demands? This article uses the public administrator's perception of the effectiveness of CSEB in improving governmental responsiveness

as its dependent variable, and draws on clues and critical factors for explaining this perception, while using the perception of CSEB's readiness level as the intervening variable to test its causal relationship.

To sum up, this article's concrete research questions are as follows:

Primary issue: identifying the correlation between the e-democratic administration and bureaucratic responsiveness in Taiwan.

Secondary issues:

1. Identifying the correlation between a sector's ICT readiness and public servants' perception of CSEB to strengthen bureaucratic responsiveness.
2. Identifying the correlation between individual ICT accomplishment and public servants' perception of CSEB to strengthen bureaucratic responsiveness.
3. Identifying the correlation between individual perception of e-democratic administration policies and public servants' perception of CSEB to strengthen bureaucratic responsiveness.
4. Identifying the intervening effect of the perception of CSEB's readiness level between independent and dependent variables.

BACKGROUND

ICT and Bureaucratic Responsiveness

Improving responsiveness has always been one of the most essential missions in a democratic government. The invention and application of ICT not only changed the application and storage of information, but also simultaneously changed government structure, business and lifestyles. ICT has emerged in the political arena, urging government to attain greater efficiency and potential, while in the achievement of the goal of good governance, it has produced many important contributions. Through the Internet, the public can directly voice its personal opinions to the government, while simultaneously — directly or indirectly — joining in discussions relating to the formulation of policies. According to the public's utilization of ICT, the government's role and actions will also have to be transferred. Such a situation not only facilitates the public's involvement in the policymaking process but also motivates the government to be more effective. Thus, the use of ICT to improve government's bureaucratic responsiveness is an inevitable trend (Tapscott, 1997, p. 26).

According to previous research, the provision of services through e-government does not exhibit the anticipated improvement in services and citizens' trust (Toregas; 2001; Moon, 2002; West, 2004; Streib & Navarro, 2006), but helps government improve democratic responsiveness while giving the impression of efficient action (West, 2004). Based on the continuous development of ICT, government also pursues more efficient and effective ways to improve public relations by introducing new e-government or e-governance policies. The establishment of CSEB aims to satisfy the demands of the public with the goal of constructing an e-government. Using ICT allows the populace to enjoy faster and more convenient services, as the administrative sectors also utilizes this convenient channel to respond to and the resolve the public's problems and demands. In theory, the goal of e-government policy is related to the managerial skill "Customer Relationship Management" (CRM; Davidow, 1995) in business management. The government's original mission-driven operations have been reoriented to the CRM service concept under the stream of New Public Management (NPM). CSEB can be considered as one of the managerial skills for improving public relations in this arena.

To take one further step in discussing the in-depth internal link, we need to understand that the development of ICT will strengthen the populace's demands for democracy. The creation of an 'e-democracy' primarily lies in the formation of a CSEB. Apart from the readiness level of the administrative mechanism's ICT, the administrators' perception of ICT and their appreciation of the administrative function are important factors influencing the application of ICT. Heeks and Bhatnagar (1999, p. 49) concluded that the success or failure of administrative sectors' application of ICT rely on whether or not the public sector's administrator has the ability to cope with information. Otherwise, the e-government policy is restricted. Accordingly, the development of ICT satisfies the populace's need to participate in public affairs and challenges the traditional bureaucratic system's public affair decisions and response mechanism. In short, while the development of ICT has caused greater complications in public affairs, the establishment of CSEB enables the populace to express opinions in a swifter and more direct manner. It drastically shortens the time required for the administrative bureaucracy to respond to the populace as well. If the administrative unit is unable to produce an immediate response, this will inevitably create a bigger governance contradiction. It can be concluded that the development of ICT is a double-edged sword. It strengthens the populace's participation on the one hand, while potentially weakening the administrative sectors' responsiveness on the other hand.

Thus, the public administrator's ability to use ICT is a decisive factor influencing the implementation of e-democratic administration (Garson, 1995). Chen, Huang and Hsiao (2003, 2006) and Ong and Wang (2009) discovered that due to the establishment of the Taipei Government Mayor's E-mail service, the volume of public personal complaint cases increased approximately tenfold each year between 1996 and 2001. It is obvious that not only has the CSEB become a popular channel for the public to express their opinion, but it has also increased the public servant's workload. Nevertheless, it has been established that public servants in the Taipei Government regard the Mayor's Mailbox as being of help in enhancing service provision to citizens. However, in contrast, the study also revealed that the Mayor's Mailbox has led to some disadvantages, such as higher public expectations for government responsiveness, increased workload, difficulties in coordination between different facilities, impacts on work morale negatively and other negative effects.

Also, Hsiao and Huang (2005) used the Theory of Planned Behaviour (TPB) as their approach for investigating the perception of administrative staffs regarding the feasibility of an e-democracy. Their research discovered that CSEB is perceived as an institutionalised e-democracy mechanism that is helpful for facilitating the efficiency of public service while also strengthening public servants' will to put e-democracy into practice.

The participants in the above research were primarily public servants who were responsible for the e-mail service, while the studies discussed the difficulties encountered in processing the populace's mails and approaches to problem resolution. This article, on the other hand, investigates "whether or not there is effective creation of e-democracy perception" in the use of CSEB. Moreover, the perception of CSEB's effectiveness in enhancing e-democracy can influence public administrators' attitude towards the practice of bureaucratic responsiveness. If the participants lack confidence in CSEB effectively creating popular democratic results, or if they do not believe that the use of information and correspondence via ICT service can enhance civil participation in decision-making, CSEB might be seen as useless and dysfunctional. This article seeks the antecedents that influence the perception of CSEB's effectiveness. It also attempts to understand whether or not the intervening variable regarding CSEB readiness level perception affects bureaucratic responsiveness, thereby contributing to both theory and practice.

Analytical Framework and Hypothesis

This article's analytical framework primarily applies studies on e-government and bureaucratic responsiveness as its theoretical foundation. After conducting exploratory factor analysis, the resulting analytical framework includes six independent variables representing the perception of e-administrative democracy: "sector's recourse support," "sector's policy support," "individual electronic skills," "perception of e-democracy's feasibility," "appreciation of e-voting policy to improve democracy," and "appreciation for citizen's participation to improve democracy by ICT." "The perception of CSEB's readiness level" is taken as an intervening variable in the analytical framework. The dependent variable is "the perception of CSEB's effectiveness to strengthen bureaucratic responsiveness" (the perception of CSEB's effectiveness) which is this article's focus of discussion. Furthermore, the dependent variable includes such items as "the CSEB can cope with citizens' inquiries and complaints," "the CSEB can shorten the process time to respond to citizens' inquiries and complaints," and "the CSEB can be the channel to access citizens' opinions." Below provides further explanations of the analytical variables and research hypotheses.

(1) Independent Variables

1.1 Organizational Factors

Many studies have demonstrated that in order to develop a practical relationship between e-government and democracy, the first step would be to construct a complete ICT architecture. In other words, the readiness of ICT is the premise for developing an e-government. However, the ICT readiness level can either be derived from the sector's resource support, or, conversely, from the sector's policy support. This article combines the previous two organizational factors to study

Figure 1. Analytical framework

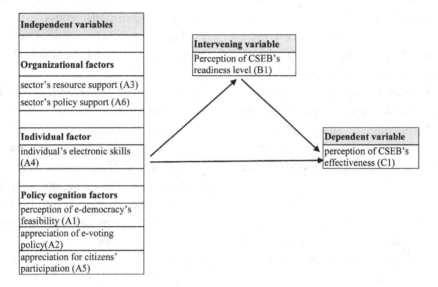

the policy environment for CSEB promotion. It is reasonable to assume that if the sector's policy can fully support the impetus of the e-government and its related activities and adopts the compulsory rule to enhance the employee's use of ICT, there will be greater effectiveness in the impetus of ICT utilization (Joyce, 2002). Also, if there is an increase in support resources, the maturity level of ICT in the sector will also increase. ICT also has increased usability, so naturally it can strengthen bureaucratic responsiveness. Based on the above, two hypotheses can be discussed:

Hypothesis 1: The correlation between sector resource support and the perception of CSEB's validity is statistically positive.
Hypothesis 2: The correlation between sector policy support and the perception of CSEB's effectiveness is statistically positive.

1.2 Individual Factor

From the discussion of related literature on e-government, it is evident that many scholars believe that the electronic skills of the administrative staff can positively influence the promotion of e-government, the possibility of using ICT to

handle routine, and the achievements of e-services (Moon, 2002; Tseng, 2003, p. 99). Therefore, this article takes individual electronic accomplishment as an independent variable in order to measure the participant's ability to use ICT. If an individual's electronic skills improve, this means that his/her ability to utilize ICT or operate CSEB will also improve. Relatively, it can be said that the existence of the CSEB has positive influence on government's ability to respond to the populace's needs. Based on the above discussion, this article proposes the hypothesis below:

Hypothesis 3: The correlation between individual's electronic skills and the perception of CSEB's effectiveness is statistically positive.

1.3 Policy Cognition Factors

It has been widely verified in social psychology research that staff perception, ideas, organizational culture, and organizational climate can have an impact on the application of ICT or e-government (Heeks & Davies, 1999). In addition, how individuals and organizations regard the application value of ICT may influence the support level towards the expected results of ITC application.

(Tseng, 2003, p. 98). This article divides the policy cognition factor into three aspects: perception of e-democracy's feasibility, appreciation of e-voting, and appreciation that the government should employ ICT to strengthen citizen participation. When these three factors become more positive, they will influence the bureaucrats' perception of CSEB's effectiveness in strengthening bureaucratic responsiveness. Based on the above discussion, this article proposes the following hypotheses:

Hypothesis 4: The correlation between the perception of e-democracy's feasibility and the perception of CSEB's effectiveness is statistically positive.

Hypothesis 5: The correlation between the appreciation of e-voting policy and the perception of CSEB's effectiveness is statistically positive.

Hypothesis 6: The correlation between the perception that government should employ ICT to strengthen citizen participation and the perception of CSEB's effectiveness is statistically positive.

(2) Intervening Variable

In Tseng's research (2003), the public sector's ICT application condition is taken as the intervening variable for the analysis of whether or not e-governments can increase administrative effectiveness, namely focusing on the influence of convenient ICT's utilization. This article postulates that the influence of previous independent variables on the perception of CSEB's effectiveness might be felt in the perception of CSEB's readiness level. In other words, if the CSEB can gain all necessary resources and policy support from sectors, the ICT readiness level will be higher. A high level of ICT readiness might increase the working performance of the administrative staff. It also can be anticipated that the perception of CSEB's readiness level can have a positive im-

pact on the perception of CESB strengthening bureaucratic responsiveness.

Based on the above discussion, this research proposes the hypotheses below:

Hypothesis 7: The perception of ICT's readiness level has an intervening effect between organizational factors (Hypothesis 7-1 (A3) and Hypothesis 7-2 (A6)) and the perception of CSEB's effectiveness.

Hypothesis 8: The perception of ICT's readiness level has an intervening effect between individual factors and the perception of CSEB's effectiveness.

Hypothesis 9: The perception of ICT's readiness level has an intervening effect between policy cognition factors [Hypothesis 9-1 (A1), Hypothesis 9-2 (A2), and Hypothesis 9-3 (A5)] and the perception of CSEB's effectiveness.

Research Methodology

This article uses secondary data from Research, Development and Evaluation Commission's (RDEC) investigation of bureaucratic perception of the feasibility of e-democracy in Taiwan. The questionnaire and data that this research uses were designed from the viewpoint of the internal customer (the public administrators working in the public sector) to understand the impetus of e-democracy in the public sector. Furthermore, the questionnaire was constructed according to the plan's behavioural theory to test these public administrators' perception of implementing e-democracy and its administrative feasibility. The questionnaire can be divided into five different parts, from the internal customer's perception of e-democracy as its core, while paying attention to bureaucrats' administrative behaviour, the perception of democracy, and the experience of using ICT. Apart from this, based on the research demand, the questionnaire took into account individual personal information, including: "gender," "educational background," "age," "public department service period and duty," "managerial or other position," "work time and place and involvement in multiple services."

In addition to individual background data, this questionnaire also uses a five-point Likert-type scale for other items, including a section in which subjects can add their opinion at varying degrees of agreement, specifically "extremely agree," "slightly agree," "neither agree nor disagree," "slightly disagree," and "extremely disagree." In the fourth part of the questionnaire, which was designed to measure bureaucrats' feasibility perception of e-democracy, the five-point scale is changed to "extremely feasible," "slightly feasible," "neither feasible nor unfeasible," "slightly unfeasible," and "extremely unfeasible."

In executing the test process, the research team obtained the government workers' population information (248,991 government workers in total, 2004), separating the population into the two large groups, namely central and local government, and obtaining 6,073 samples by means of a systematic random sampling method. The period of study was from December 2004 to February 2005, with a total of 6,073 questionnaires mailed and 995 returned. Deducting 33 invalid response samples, the total valid sample was 882, and the actual effective return ratio was 14.7%. However, this research obtained a secondary data of equal ratio, condensing 400 samples from 882 successful samples with the RDEC's permission. After conducting the chi-Square test, it is clear that the sample's composition and characteristics (gender, chi-Square=0.136, p=0.713 and education, chi-Square=1.423, p=0.698) are statistically no different from the original sample in comparison. The 400 samples can thus be used to represent the composition of original 882 samples.

ANALYTICAL RESULTS

Demographic Analysis

The population size indicated previously includes all workers working in the public sector in Taiwan. As shown in Appendix One, 61.8% (247) of the population are female and 37.5% (150) are male; 0.5% (2) hold a doctorate degree, 11.8% (47) hold a master's degree, 40.3% (161) completed college, 34.5% (138) finished vocational school, and 11.8% (47) finished high school or below. A majority at 79.8% (319) hold a non-managerial position, while those holding managerial positions make up 18.3% (73). Taken a step further, in terms of the participant's period of service and duty, appointed civil officials account for 24.8% (99), first-grade civil officials numbered 48% (171), and second-grade civil official's account for 3.5% (14). With regard to office duty, those in central authority offices account for 38.3% (153), those in municipal governments account for 11.3% (45), and those in county municipal governments account for 46.5% (186). In the scope of business, the information department and research department with higher correlation in the promotion of e-government number 6.8% (27) and 4.8% (19) respectively, while human resources, civil service ethics, and others constitute 77.8% (311). The population concurrently handling services, the information and research departments, separately account for 7.5% (30) and 3.01% (12). Human resources, civil service ethics and others account for 34.3% (137).

Factor Analysis and Naming

After performing factor analysis (Appendix Two), eight factors with eigenvalues higher than 1 were selected, which were used for the theoretical explanation of this research. Independent variables altogether brought out six factors, and explain the total variance of 60.321%, namely, "sector's resource support (A3)," "sector's policy support

(A6), " "individual's electronic skills (A4), " "perception of e-democracy's feasibility (A1), " "appreciation of e-voting policy (A2), " and "appreciation for citizens' participation can facilitate democracy (A5)."[2] With regard to the factors representing dependent variables, two factors were extracted from the 18 items in the section "the experience of coping with the CSEB" in the questionnaire, named separately as "perception of CSEB's readiness level," and "perception of the CSEB's validity to strengthen bureaucrats' responsiveness." Although the Cronbach alpha of the perception of the CSEB's validity is 0.79, other factors' Cronbach alphas reach as high as 0.8 or above. Moreover, the factors named "perception of e-democracy's feasibility" and "sector's policy support" reach as high as 0.93 and 0.94, respectively. Based on above results, the validity and reliability of the questionnaire design can be accepted.

According to the analytical framework, the eight factors discussed above can be further divided into three major analytical aspects. The factors related to organizational aspects can be categorized by two factors, namely the sector's resource support and policy support. With regard to individual factors, an individual's electronic skills can be extrapolated and identified to represent individual factors. With regard to bureaucrats role in policy cognition, three factors were identified as "perception of e-democracy's feasibility," "perception of e-voting policy" and "perception of citizens' participation facilitating democracy." In the part of the intervening variable, "the perception of CSEB's readiness level" can be extracted and then named, while the dependent variable is constructed from "the perception of CSEB's effectiveness."

Validation of Hypotheses

(1) Correlation Analysis

As shown in Table 1, all independent variables and the intervening variable correlate positively with the dependent variable "perception of CSEB's effectiveness to improve bureaucrats' responsiveness." The correlation coefficients for different items are determined as follows: the sector's resource support (.47**), the sector's policy support (.44**), individual electronic skills (.29**), perception of e-democracy's feasibility (.57**), appreciation of e-voting policy (.40**), appreciation for citizens' participation (.53**) and perception of CSEB's readiness level (.67**).

Each of above results can verify Hypotheses to 6. However, by merely conducting correlation analysis, there is insufficient evidence to clearly reveal the true correlation among each independent and dependent variable, as well as explaining the intervening effect of the perception of CSEB's readiness level. Therefore, it is necessary to carry out regression analysis and path analysis to detect the causal relationships between indepen-

Table 1. Correlation analysis

Factor	Perception of CSEB's effectiveness (C1)
Perception of CSEB's readiness level (B1)	.67**
Perception of e-democracy's feasibility (A1)	.57**
Appreciation of e-voting policy (A2)	.40**
Sector's resource support (A3)	.47**
Individual's electronic skills (A4)	.29**
Appreciation for citizens' participation (A5)	.53**
Sector's policy support (A6)	.44**

Correlation is significant at the $\alpha=0.01$ level (2-tailed)

Table 2. Dependent variable: Perception of CSEB's readiness level (B1)

Model	Independent Variables	B value	Std. Error	Std. β	t	Sig.	R²	Adj-R²	F
1	A1	.399	.027	.63	14.606	.00	.402	.40	213.33
2	A2	.511	.050	.501	10.168	.00	.251	.24	103.38
3	A3	.736	.051	.650	14.426	.00	.422	.42	208.12
4	A4	.480	.119	.217	4.020	.00	.047	.04	16.16
5	A5	1.057	.094	.531	11.284	.00	.282	.27	127.33
6	A6	1.171	.090	.592	12.967	.00	.351	.34	168.15

Correlation is significant at the α=0.05 level (2-tailed)

dent and dependent variables and test the research hypotheses.

(2) Simple Regression Analysis and Intervening Effects

The test of intervening effects is conducted through regression analysis and based on the method suggested by Baron and Kenny (1986). According to this method, the method of testing intervening effects can be divided into three steps, namely: (1) checking whether the independent variable is statistically significant on the intervening variable; (2) checking whether the independent variable is statistically significant on the intervening variable; and (3) verifying that adding the intervening variable in the regression model in step two is statistically significant on the dependent variable. If the independent variable's coefficient decreases, it means that the intervening effect between independent and dependent variables is partial. By contrary, if the original significance of the independent variable dissolves while adding the intervening variable between the independent and dependent variables, we can conclude that the intervening effect is perfect (Baron & Kenny, 1986). Each independent factor relating to the intervening variables' effects is presented in Table 2.

Based on the above analytical results, all the independent factors showing the analytical result of significance on the intervening variable sat-

isfy the first condition presented by Baron and Kenny (1986). Also, with regard to the second and third conditions, the use of regression analysis is illustrated in Table 3.

As can be seen in Models 1 and 1-a, the independent variable "perception of e-democracy's feasibility" is statistically significant on the dependent variable (β=0.631, p<0.05), which further verifies Hypothesis 4. Again, after adding the intervening variable to the original regression model, the standardized coefficient of the perception of CSEB's readiness level is significant (β=0.47, p<0.05); the original independent variable "perception of e-democracy's feasibility" is still significant even though the value decreased (β=0.334, p<0.05). The analytical result demonstrates that the intervening variable "perception of CSEB's readiness level" has a partial intervening effect on the dependent variable "the perception of CSEB's effectiveness to improve bureaucrats' responsiveness." Therefore, Hypothesis 9-1 is verified.

As can be seen in Models 2 and 2-a, the independent variable "perception of e-voting policy" is statistically significant on the dependent variable (β=0.5, p<0.05), which means that Hypothesis 5 is true. Again, after adding the intervening variable into the original regression model, the standardized coefficient of the perception of CSEB's readiness level is significant (β=0.56, p<0.05). The original independent variable "perception

Table 3. Dependent variable: Perception of the CSEB's validity (C1)

Model	Independent Variables	β value	Std. Error	Std. β	t	Sig.	R^2	Adj-R^2	F
1	A1	.396	.028	.631	14.375	.00	.398	.39	206.65
1-a	A1	.210	.031	.334	6.787	.00	.538	.53	180.74
	B1	.74	.07	.47	9.67	.00			
2	A2	.501	.050	.500	10.042	.00	.250	.24	100.84
2-a	A2	.251	.045	.251	5.526	.00	.503	.50	152.21
	B1	.88	.07	.56	12.36	.00			
3	A3	.718	.051	.642	14.043	.00	.412	.41	197.19
3-a	A3	.459	.050	.411	9.247	.00	.581	.57	194.16
	B1	.73	.06	.47	10.61	.00			
4	A4	.531	.118	.243	4.499	.00	.059	.05	20.24
4-a	A4	.076	.095	.035	.799	.42	.455	.45	133.80
	B1	1.04	.06	.66	15.25	.00			
5	A5	1.033	.095	.520	10.876	.00	.270	.26	118.28
5-a	A5	.432	.096	.218	4.502	.00	.481	.47	147.56
	B1	.86	.07	.55	11.37	.00			
6	A6	1.143	.091	.583	12.516	.00	.339	.33	156.66
6-a	A6	.677	.086	.345	7.852	.00	.541	.53	179.44
	B1	.79	.06	.50	11.57	.00			

Correlation is significant at the α=0.05 level (2-tailed)

of e-voting policy" is still significant even if the value decreased (β=0.251, p<0.05). The analytical result demonstrates that the intervening variable "perception of CSEB's readiness level" has a partial intervening effect on the dependent variable "the perception of CSEB's effectiveness to improve bureaucrats' responsiveness." Therefore, Hypothesis 9-2 is proven.

As can be seen in Models 3 and 3-a, the independent variable "sector's resource support" is statistically significant for the dependent variable (β=0.642, p<0.05), which further verifies Hypothesis 1. Again, after adding the intervening variable into the original regression model, the standardized coefficient of the perception of CSEB's readiness level is significant (β=0.47, p<0.05); the original independent variable "sector's resource support" is also significant, but the value decreased (β=0.411, p<0.05). The analytical result indicates that the intervening variable "perception of CSEB's readiness level" has partial intervening effect on the

dependent variable "the perception of CSEB's effectiveness to improve bureaucrats' responsiveness." Therefore, Hypothesis 7-1 is accepted.

As can be seen in Models 4 and 4-a, the independent variable "individual's electronic skills" has statistical significance with regard to the dependent variable (β=0.243, p<0.05), which proves Hypothesis 3 to be true. Similar to above analyses, after adding the intervening variable into the original regression model, the standardized coefficient of "perception of CSEB's readiness level" is significant (β=0.66, p<0.05), while the original independent variable "individual's electronic skills" is not significant (β=0.35, >0.05). The analysis demonstrates that the intervening variable "perception of CSEB's readiness level" has perfect intervening effect on the dependent variable "the perception of CSEB's effectiveness to improve bureaucrats' responsiveness." Therefore, Hypothesis 8 is accepted.

As can be seen in Models 5 and 5-a, the independent variable "appreciation for citizens' participation" is statistically significant with the dependent variable (β=0.52, p<0.05), which demonstrates that Hypothesis 6 is acceptable. Similarly, after adding the intervening variable into the original regression model, the standardized coefficient of "perception of CSEB's readiness level" is significant (β=0.55, p<0.05). Also, the original independent variable "appreciation for citizens' participation" is significant, though its value is lower (β=0.218, p<0.05). The analytical results demonstrate that the intervening variable "perception of CSEB's readiness level" has partial intervening effect on the dependent variable "the perception of CSEB's effectiveness to improve bureaucrats' responsiveness." Therefore, Hypothesis 9-3 is accepted.

As can be seen in Models 6 and 6-a, the independent variable "sector's policy support" is statistically significant on the dependent variable (β=0.583, p<0.05), which further verifies Hypothesis 3. Again, after adding the intervening variable into the original regression model, the standardized coefficient of "perception of CSEB's readiness level" is significant (β=0.5, p<0.05). The original independent variable "sector's policy support" is also significant, but the value dropped (β=0.345, p<0.05). The analytical result demonstrates that the intervening variable "perception of CSEB's readiness level" has partial intervening effect on the dependent variable "the perception of CSEB's effectiveness to improve bureaucrats' responsiveness." Hence, Hypothesis 7-2 is accepted.

(3) Multiple Regression Analysis

In order to further verify the research question regarding which factors impact the perception of CSEB's effectiveness in improving bureaucrats' responsiveness, three factors can be identified that have positive effects on the dependent variable by performing multiple regression analysis[3] under the 95% confidence interval. As shown below, Model 3, which contains three significant independent variables, has a unified explanation variance of 43.3%. Model 3 has the highest forecast ability to the dependent variable among all the studied models. In contrast, Model 2, which includes two independent variables, has a total explanation variance of 41.5%; Model 1, which has only one significant independent variable in the regression model, possesses 36.5% of the total explanation variance. In sum, Model 3, having the highest variance, is the best regression model to explain the dependent variable. Hence, the standard regression model can be presented as such:

The perception of CSEB's effectiveness = 4.43 + 0.38 identification of citizens' participation + 0.12 perception of e-democracy's feasibility + 0.12 sector's resource support.

In addition, according to the β value in Table 4, it is found that the independent variables such as "identification of citizens' participation," "perception of e-democracy's feasibility" and "sector's resource support" have statistically positive effects on the dependent variable "the perception of CSEB's effectiveness to improve bureaucrats' responsiveness" (β values are 0.38, 0.12, and 0.12 accordingly), which further verify Hypotheses 1, 4 and 6 in this research.

(4) Path Analysis

In order to understand the influence path between the independent variables and the dependent variables, the structure of the pathways is shown as below:

Based on Figure 2, the possible causal pathways are described below.

There are three possible pathways for the organizational factors influencing "the perception of CSEB's effectiveness to improve bureaucrats' responsiveness:" (1) the organizational factors directly influencing the perception of CSEB's effectiveness, (2) the organizational factors im-

Table 4. Multiple regression analysis

Independent Variables	Model 1	Model 2	Model 3
Perception of e-democracy's feasibility	.24 (.02) **	.15 (.02) **	.12 (.02) **
Appreciation of citizens' participation		.42 (.08) **	.38 (.08) **
Sector's resource support			.12 (.04) **
Constant	7.59 (.97) **	4.82 (1.09) **	4.34 (1.09) **
Adj. R²	.36	.41	.43
S.E.E.	2.69	2.58	2.54
VIF	1.00	2.006 2.006	2.252 2.048 1.433

Correlation is significant at the $\alpha=0.05$ level (2-tailed)

Figure 2. Original pathway model

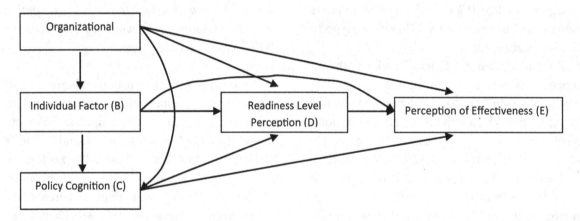

pacting the perception of CSEB's effectiveness via the perception of CSEB's readiness level, and (3) the organizational factors influencing the perception of CSEB's effectiveness via improving policy cognition factors.

There are four possible pathways for the individual factors influencing "the perception of CSEB's effectiveness to improve bureaucrats' responsiveness:" (1) the individual factor directly impacting the dependent variable; (2) the individual factor influencing the factor "the perception of CSEB's readiness level" and further influencing the dependent variable "the perception of CSEB's effectiveness;" (3) the individual factor influencing the factor of policy cognition,

then influencing the perception of CSEB's readiness level; and finally influencing the perception of CSEB's effectiveness; and (4) the individual factor influencing the factor of policy cognition, then influencing the factor of "the perception of CSEB's effectiveness".

There are two pathways for the factors of policy cognition to influence the factor of perception of CSEB's effectiveness: (1) the factors of policy cognition directly influencing the factor of the perception of CSEB's effectiveness and (2) the factors of policy cognition influencing the factor of perception of CSEB's readiness level, then influencing the dependent variable of the perception of CSEB's effectiveness.

Table 5. Multiple regression analysis[4]

	Perception of CSEB's effectiveness (E) Model 1		Perception of CSEB's Readiness level (D) Model 2		Policy cognition Model 3 (C)	
	Std. β	VIF	Std. β	VIF	Std. β	VIF
A	-.02	2.40	.45**	2.000	.66**	1.123
B	.12**	1.14	-.04	1.122	.05	1.123
C	.33**	2.27	.38**	1.998		
D	.41**	2.22				
Adj. R²	.50		.55		.44	
S.E.E.	2.36		3.54		10.61	

Correlation is significant at the 0.05 level (2-tailed)

Figure 3. Modified pathway model

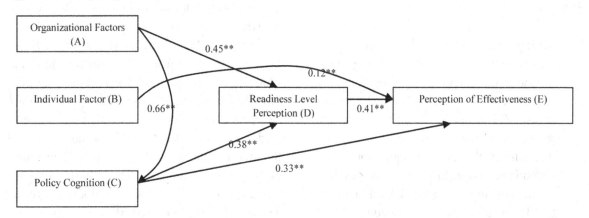

The result of multiple regression analysis is shown below in Table 5. The model in Figure 2 can be modified into the one in Figure 3 to illustrate the best model to explain the perception of CSEB's effectiveness to improve bureaucrats' responsiveness.

Regarding the direct effect, the organizational factor (A) has direct significant effect on the factor of perception of CSEB's readiness level (D) (β=0.12, P<0.05) as well as on the factor of policy cognition (C) (β=0.66, P<0.05); the individual factor (B) exhibits direct effect on the factor of perception of CSEB's effectiveness (E) (β=0.12, P<0.05). In addition, the perception of CSEB's readiness level (D) (β=0.41, P<0.05) and the factors of policy cognition (C) (β=0.33,

P<0.05), also directly influence "the factor of perception of the CSEB's validity" (E). This not only demonstrates that individual factor (B) can directly influence the factor of perception of the CSEB's validity (E), but also that organizational factor (A) can strengthen the bureaucrats' perception of appreciation for citizens' participation and the perception of CSEB's readiness level (D).

Regarding the partial and total effects, it is worth noting the correlation between the organizational factor (A), policy cognition (C), perception of CSEB's readiness level (D) and perception of CSEB's effectiveness (E). The seven pathways discussed above can verify that the perception of CSEB's readiness level (D) is an intervening dependent in this model, but also that the factor of policy cognition (C) can become an intervening variable. The organizational factor (A) has no direct pathway to influence the perception of CSEB's effectiveness (E), and must pass through the perception of CSEB's readiness level (D) and policy cognition (C). It indicates that the influence of organizational factor (A) on the perception of CSEB's effectiveness (E) is indirect, thus making it suitable as an independent variable.

Solutions and Recommendations

As discussed above, two recommendations can be suggested to strengthen bureaucratic responsiveness:

1. Setting up a suitable and friendly organizational environment, strengthening information training, and inculcating the policy cognition of e-democracy are the best ways to use ICT concepts to put bureaucratic responsiveness into practice.
2. According to the results of regression analysis, bureaucrats can put e-responsiveness into practice by improving the perception of the CESB's readiness level. The readiness level of the ICT or CSEB and other related regulations and procedures should be combined to make it easier for government workers to cope with their routine through ICT.

FUTURE RESEARCH DIRECTIONS

Two specific topics can be identified on this theme for further study. First, the issues discussed in this study can be applied to countries investing considerable resources in building an efficient and effective e-government. It is widely known that ICT innovation has changed the landscape of interaction between governments and citizens. However, e-government is not a simple and easy matter (Toregas; 2001; Moon, 2002; West, 2004; Streib & Navarro, 2006). The easy, low cost and two-way nature of CSEB opens a new agenda for communication between governments and citizens. In other words, adding an email access on the governmental website is technologically easy, but efficient management and response to incoming email even more critical. It can be anticipated that CSEB will become a costly governance mechanism which not only requires more human resource investment, but also training for public administrators to handle the various types of requests and complaints. The agenda mentioned above has been little discussed in the literature dealing with the broader scope of e-governance.

Second, the most important limitation of this paper is that it does not put the variable related to "whether dealing with CSEB is a burden" into the analytical framework. In fact, a primarily exploratory research from Chen, Huang and Hsiao (2003, 2006) and Ong and Wang (2009) regarding how the internal staff copes with the Taipei City Mayor's E-mail Box indicated that ICT has created a greater burden for workers and influenced the mood in the workplace. Thus, ICT provides both positive advantage and negative pressure for bureaucratic responsiveness in Taipei City's case. The variable can be put to further investigation to present a complete picture of this theme.

DISCUSSION AND CONCLUSION

This research discusses the correlation between e-democratic administration and bureaucratic responsiveness. With regard to the factor of e-democratic administration, factor analysis exacts three factors from independent variables: (1) organizational factors such as sectors' resource and policy support; (2) individual factor for individual electronic skills; and (3) policy cognition of the perception of e-democracy's feasibility, the appreciation of e-voting policy, the feasibility of e-democracy and the appreciation for citizens' participation. In addition, with regard to the experience of using CSEB, the perception of

Table 6. Hypothesis verification list

Independent variables	Hypotheses	Dependent variable	Results
Sector's resource support	Hypothesis 1	Perception of CSEB's effectiveness	+
Sector's policy support	Hypothesis 2		+
Individual's electronic skills	Hypothesis 3		+
Perception of e-democracy's feasibility	Hypothesis 4		+
Appreciation of e-voting policy	Hypothesis 5		+
The perception that the government should employ ICT to encourage citizen participation	Hypothesis 6		+

Table 7. Intervening effect results

Independent variables	Hypothesis	Dependent variable	Intervening variable	Results
Sector's resource support	Hypothesis 7-1	Perception of CSEB's effectiveness	Perception of CSEB's readiness level	+(Partial)
Sector's policy support	Hypothesis 7-2			+(Partial)
Individual's electronic skills	Hypothesis 8			+(Partial)
Perception of e-democracy's feasibility	Hypothesis 9-1			+(Perfect)
Appreciation of e-voting policy	Hypothesis 9-2			+(Partial)
The perception that the government should employ ICT to encourage citizen participation	Hypothesis 9-3			+(Partial)

CSEB's readiness level and perception of CSEB's effectiveness can be exacted. This article uses the perception of CSEB's effectiveness in strengthening bureaucrats' responsiveness as the dependent variable to measure bureaucratic responsiveness and the perception of CSEB's readiness level as the intervening variable to discuss whether or not they influence the coloration between independent and dependent variables. The verified results of the hypotheses are shown in Table 6 and table 7.

As shown in Table 6, all independent variables towards the perception of CSEB's effectiveness exhibited significant positive influence results. Strategically, in order to improve bureaucratic perception of CSEB's effectiveness in strengthening bureaucratic responsiveness, it can be an effective and feasible method to increase sector resource and policy support for e-democratic administration in organisational factors designed to promote CSEB. On the individual factor side,

the electronic skills of individuals also play a significant role in the perception of CSEB's effectiveness in strengthening bureaucratic responsiveness. If the sector can invest resources to improve the staff's electronic skills, the bureaucratic perception of CSEB's ability to effectively strengthen bureaucratic responsiveness will be improved as well. It also means that the public sector can try to strengthen the bureaucrats' information education or provide some useful training programmes. In addition, the identification of e-democratic administration policy also has a positive influence on the perception of CSEB's ability to strengthen bureaucratic responsiveness. In other words, the more positive the identification of e-democracy's feasibility, the higher the perception of e-voting policy and the higher the appreciation for citizens' participation are, the greater the perception will be of CSEB's ability the strengthen bureaucratic responsiveness.

In sum, setting up a suitable organizational environment, strengthening staffs' information training and inculcating the policy cognition of e-democracy are the best ways to put the concept of ICT improving bureaucratic responsiveness into practice.

Furthermore, we can continue to discuss the effect of intervening variables and further consider more advanced strategies to improve bureaucratic responsiveness. The analytical result is shown in Table 7 below.

As can be seen in Table 7, the perception of CSEB's readiness level has perfect intervening effect between the perception of e-democracy's feasibility and the perception of CSEB's effectiveness. The perception of CSEB's readiness level and others merely has partial effects between independent and dependent variables. It obviously shows that the perception of CSEB's readiness level can influence government workers' perception of CSEB's effectiveness in strengthening bureaucratic responsiveness, and also has an intervening effect between other independent and dependent variables. In other words, if the goal is to encourage bureaucrats put e-responsiveness into practice by improving the perception of the CESB's readiness level, the readiness level of the ICT or CSEB and other related regulations and procedures should be combined to make it more convenient for government workers to cope with their ICT routine.

If we take a further step to see the explanation model using multiple regression analysis, it can be seen that the factors "the perception that the government should employ ICT to encourage citizen participation," "the perception of e-democracy's feasibility" and "sector's policy support" have positively significant effects on the dependent variable with a total explanation variance of 43.3%. However, based on each model's regression calculation std. β value, the factor of "the perception of e-democracy's feasibility" has the best explanation power on the dependent variable. In addition, the factors "the perception that the

government should employ ICT to encourage citizen participation" and "sector's resource support" are also significant and correlate positively with the perception of CSEB's effectiveness. Based on the above results, the regression analysis is unified with the result of previous correlation analysis.

Lastly, after further testing by path analysis, the original model can still be maintained. The analytical results show the following about the seven pathways: (1) of these three pathways, the perception of CSEB's readiness level serves as the intervening variable, and (2) the two other pathways are based on the factor of policy cognition as their intervening variable. It is obvious that these two factors can be seen as an intervening variable in the original model. In addition, it can be seen that among the independent variables, only the organizational factors are unable to directly influence the perception of CSEB's effectiveness. However, the organizational factor has a strong impact on the perception of CSEB's readiness level and policy cognition. As an antecedent variable, the organizational factor cannot be neglected.

To sum up, this research has already sufficiently answered all the research questions. The independent and intervening variables have positively influence the dependent variable. From the perspective of practical strategy, all factors can be used as enhancement to strengthen the bureaucrats' responsiveness via CSEB. In particular, the organizational resource and policy support can help to build an impetus organizational culture, strengthen the e-democracy perception of bureaucrats and construct complementary measures for running CSEB. Increased confidence in the perception of ICT can facilitate democracy, which in turn would encourage administrators to become more willing to put policy into practice.

Two specific topics can be identified on this theme for further study. First, the issue discussed in this study can be applied to countries investing substantial amounts of resources in building an efficient and effective e-government. It is widely known that ICT innovation has changed the landscape for interaction between governments and citizens. However, e-government is not a simple and easy matter (Toregas; 2001; Moon, 2002; West, 2004; Streib & Navarro, 2006). The easy, low-cost and two-way nature of CSEB opens a new agenda for communication between governments and citizens. In other words, adding e-mail access to a governmental website is technologically easy, but managing and responding to incoming email is even more critical. It can be anticipated that CSEB will become a costly governance mechanism which not only requires more human resource investment but also training for public administrators in how to handle the various types of requests and complaints. The agenda mentioned above has been little discussed in the literature about the broader scope of e-governance.

Second, the most important limitation of this paper is that it does not put the variable related to "whether dealing with CSEB is a burden" into the analytical framework. In fact, a primarily exploratory research from Chen, Huang and Hsiao (2003, 2006) and Ong and Wang (2009) regarding how internal staff copes with the Taipei City Mayor's E-mail Box indicated that ICT has created a greater burden for workers and influenced the mood in the workplace. Thus, ICT provides both positive advantage and negative pressure for bureaucratic responsiveness in Taipei City's case. The variable can be investigated further to present a complete picture of this theme.

REFERENCES

Barber, B. (1998). Three scenarios for the future of technology and strong democracy. *Political Science Quarterly, 113*(4), 573–589. doi:10.2307/2658245

Barber, B. (2001). The uncertainty of digital politics: Democracy's uneasy relationship with Information Technology. *Harvard International Review, 23*, 42–47.

Baron, R. M., & Kenny, D. A. (1986). The moderator-mediator variable distinction in social psychological research: Conceptual, strategic and statistical considerations. *Journal of Personality and Social Psychology, 51*(6), 1173–1182. doi:10.1037/0022-3514.51.6.1173

Becker, S. A. (2004). E-government visual accessibility for older adult users. *Social Science Computer Review, 22*(1), 11–23. doi:10.1177/0894439303259876

Bovens, M., & Zouridis, S. (2002). From street-level to system-level bureaucracies: How information and communication technology is transforming administrative discretion and constitution control. *Public Administration Review, 62*, 174–184. doi:10.1111/0033-3352.00168

Bryan, C., Tsagarousianou, R., & Tambini, D. (1998). Electronic democracy and the civic networking movement in context. In Tsagarousianou, R., Tambini, D., & Bryan, C. (Eds.), *Cyberdemocracy: Technology, cities, and civic networks* (pp. 1–17). New York, NY: Routledge.

Buckley, J. (2003). E-service quality and the public sector. *Managing Service Quality, 13*(6), 453–462. doi:10.1108/09604520310506513

Carrizales, T. (2008). Functions of e-government: A study of municipal practices. *State and Local Government Review, 40*(1), 12–26. doi:10.1177/0160323X0804000102

Chadwick, A. (2003). Bringing e-democracy back in: Why it matters for future research on e-governance. *Social Science Computer Review, 21*(4), 443–455. doi:10.1177/0894439303256372

Chen, D. Y., Huang, D. I., & Hsiao, N. I. (2003). The management of citizen participation in Taiwan: A case study of Taipei city government's citizen complains system. *International Journal of Public Administration, 26*(5), 525–547. doi:10.1081/PAD-120019234

Chen, D. Y., Huang, D. I., & Hsiao, N. I. (2006). Reinventing government through on-line citizen involvement in the developing world: A case study of Taipei City Mayor's E-mail Box in Taiwan. *Public Administration and Development*, *26*, 409–423. doi:10.1002/pad.415

Cohen, S., & Eimicke, W. (2001). The use of the Internet in government service delivery. In Abramson, M. A., & Means, G. E. (Eds.), *E-government 2001* (pp. 9–43). Oxford, UK: Rowman and Littlefield.

Compaine, B. M. (Ed.). (2001). *The digital divide: Facing a crisis or creating a myth?* Cambridge, MA: MIT Press.

Danziger, J. N., & Andersen, K. (2002). Impacts of Information Technology on public administration: An analysis of empirical research from the golden age of transformation. *International Journal of Public Administration*, *25*(5), 591–627. doi:10.1081/PAD-120003292

Davidow, M. (1995). *A conceptual framework of customer communication handling and management*. Paper presented at the Marketing and Public Policy Conference. Atlanta, GA, US.

Dawes, S. (2008). The evolution and continuing challenges of e-governance. *Public Administration Review*, (December): 82–106.

Gant, D. B., & Gant, J. P. (2003). Enhancing e-service delivery in state government. In Abramson, A. M., & Morin, T. L. (Eds.), *E-government 2003* (pp. 53–80). Oxford, UK: Rowman and Littlefield.

Garson, G. D. (1995). *Computer technology and social issues*. Hershey, PA: Idea Group Press. doi:10.4018/978-1-87828-928-5

Grant, G., & Chau, D. (2004). Developing a generic framework for e-government. *Journal of Global Information Management*, *13*(1), 1–30. doi:10.4018/jgim.2005010101

Groper, R. (2004). Digital government and the digital divide. In Pavlichev, A., & Garson, G. D. (Eds.), *Digital government: Principles and best practices* (pp. 291–305). Hershey, PA: Idea Group Press.

Hacker, K. L., & van Dijk, J. (2000). What is digital democracy? In Hacker, K. L., & van Dijk, J. (Eds.), *Digital democracy: Issues of theory and practice* (pp. 1–9). Thousand Oaks, CA: SAGE.

Heeks, R., & Bhatnagar, S. (1999). Understanding success and failure in information age reform. In Heeks, R. (Ed.), *Reinventing government in the information age: International practice in IT-enabled public sector reform* (pp. 49–74). London, UK: Routledge. doi:10.4324/9780203204962

Heeks, R., & Davies, A. (Eds.). (1999). *Reinventing government in the information age: International practice in IT-enabled public sector reform*. London, UK: Routledge. doi:10.4324/9780203204962

Hsiao, N., & Huang, D. J. (2005). *The feasibility of e-democratic government: The perception of public officials' behavior*. Paper presented at the 5th Political and Information Science and Technology Academic Conference at Fo Guang University, Ilan, Taiwan. (in Chinese)

Joyce, P. (2002). E-government, strategic dependent and organizational capacity. In Milner, E. M. (Ed.), *Delivering the vision-public services for the information society and the knowledge economy* (pp. 157–171). London, UK: Routledge.

Lewis, N., & Mawson, C. O. S. (1964). *The new Roget's thesaurus*. New York, NY: G. P. Putnam's Sons.

Merriam-Webster, Inc. (1986). *Webster's ninth new collegiate dictionary*. Springfield, MA: Author.

Milward, H. B., & Snyder, L. O. (1996). Electronic government: Linking citizens to public organizations through technology. *Journal of Public Administration: Research and Theory, 6*(2), 261–275.

Moon, M. J. (2002). The evolution of e-government among municipalities: Rhetoric or reality? *Public Administration Review, 62*(4), 424–443. doi:10.1111/0033-3352.00196

Moon, M. J. (2003, January 6-9). *Can IT help government to restore public trust? Declining public trust and potential prospects of IT in the public sector.* Paper presented at 36th Annual Hawaii International Conference on System Sciences. Big Island, Hawaii. Retrieved from http://csdl2.computer.org/persagen/DLAbsToc.jsp?resourcePath=/dl/proceedings/&toc=comp/proceedings/hicss/2003/1874/05/1874toc.xml&DOI=10.1109/HICSS.2003.1174303

Moon, M. J. (2005). Linking citizen satisfaction with e-government and trust in government. *Journal of Public Administration: Research and Theory, 15*(3), 371–391.

Moon, M. J., & Welch, E. W. (2004). Same bed, different dreams? A comparative analysis of citizen and bureaucrat perspectives on e-government. *Review of Public Personnel Administration, 25*(3), 243–264. doi:10.1177/0734371X05275508

Morgenson, F. III, Van Amburg, D., & Mithas, S. (2010). Misplaced trust? Exploring the structure of the e-government-citizen trust relationship. *Journal of Public Administration: Research and Theory, 21*(2).

Norris, D. F., & Moon, M. J. (2005). Advancing e-government at the grassroots: Tortoise or hare. *Public Administration Review, 65*(1), 64–75. doi:10.1111/j.1540-6210.2005.00431.x

Norris, P. (2001). *Digital divide: Civic engagement, information poverty, and the Internet worldwide.* Cambridge, UK: Cambridge University Press.

Ong, C. S., & Wang, S. W. (2009). Managing citizen-initiated email contacts. *Government Information Quarterly, 26*, 498–504. doi:10.1016/j.giq.2008.07.005

Ostrom, V. (1989). *The intellectual crisis in American public administration.* Tuscaloosa, AL: The University of Alabama Press.

Parent, M., Vandebeek, C. A., & Gemino, A. C. (2004). Building citizen trust through e-government. Retrieved from http://csdl.computer.org/comp/proceedings/hicss/2004/2056/05/205650119a.pdf

Pavlichev, A., & Garson, D. G. (Eds.). (2004). *Digital government: Principles and best practices.* Hershey, PA: Idea Group Press.

Peled, A. (2001). Centralization of diffusion? Two tales of online government. *Administration & Society, 32*(6), 686–709. doi:10.1177/00953990122019622

Pirog, M. A., & Johnson, C. (2008). Electronic funds and benefits transfers, e-government, and the winter commission. *Public Administration Review,* (December): 103–114. doi:10.1111/j.1540-6210.2008.00982.x

Roy, J. (2003). The relational dynamics of e-governance: A case study of the City of Ottawa. *Public Performance & Management Review, 26*(4), 391–403. doi:10.1177/1530957603026004006

Scavo, C., & Shi, Y. (2000). The role of Information Technology in the reinventing government paradigm: Normative predicates and practical challenges. *Social Science Computer Review, 18*(2), 166–178. doi:10.1177/089443930001800206

Shiang, J. (2002). Digital democracy. In Shiyi, L. (Eds.), *Popular government* (pp. 69–91). Taipei, Taiwan: Open University Press. (in Chinese)

Snellen, I. (2002). Electronic governance: Implications for citizens, politicians and public servants. *International Review of Administrative Sciences, 68*(2), 183–198. doi:10.1177/0020852302682002

Stanley, J., & Weare, C. (2004). The effects of Internet use on political participation: Evidence from an agency online discussion forum. *Administration & Society, 36*(5), 503–527. doi:10.1177/0095399704268503

Streib, G., & Navarro, I. (2006). Citizen demand for interactive e-government: The case of Georgia consumer service. *American Review of Public Administration, 36*(3), 288–300. doi:10.1177/0275074005283371

Tapscott, D. (1997). *The digital economy: The digital economy: Promise and peril in the age of networked intelligence.* London, UK: McGraw-Hill.

Tolbert, C., & Mossberger, K. (2004). *The effects of e-government on trust and confidence in government.* Retrieved from http://knowlton.osu.edu/ped/Egov/TolbertMossbergerOSU1.pdf

Toregas, C. (2001). The politics of e-gov: The upcoming struggle for redefining civil engagement. *National Civil Engagement, 90*(3), 235–240. doi:10.1002/ncr.90304

Tseng, D. I. (2003) *E-government's influence on administrative governance: A case study of economic department's international trade bureau.* Doctoral dissertation in Public Administration at National Chengchi University.

Waldo, D. (1952). Development of theory of democratic administration. *The American Political Science Review, 46*(1), 81–103. doi:10.2307/1950764

Welch, E. W., & Wong, W. (2001). Global information technology pressure and government accountability: The mediating effect of domestic context on website openness. *Journal of Public Administration: Research and Theory, 11*(4), 509–538.

West, D. M. (2004). E-government and the transformation of service delivery and citizen attitudes. *Public Administration Review, 64*(1), 66–80. doi:10.1111/j.1540-6210.2004.00347.x

Wu, M. (2002). *SPSS statistics and application.* Taipei, Taiwan: Song Gang Press. (in Chinese)

ADDITIONAL READING

Barber, B. (2001). The uncertainty of digital politics: Democracy's uneasy relationship with Information Technology. *Harvard International Review, 23*, 42–47.

Beierle, T. C. (2002). *Democracy on-line: An evaluation of the national dialogue on public involvement in EPA decisions.* Retrieved from http://www.rff.org/reports/PDF_files/democracyonline.pdf

Best, S. J., & Krueger, B. S. (2005). Analyzing the representativeness of Internet political participation. *Political Behavior, 27*(2), 183–216. doi:10.1007/s11109-005-3242-y

Bovens, M., & Zouridis, S. (2002). From street-level to system-level bureaucracies: How information and communication technology is transforming administrative discretion and constitution control. *Public Administration Review, 62*, 174–184. doi:10.1111/0033-3352.00168

Brown, M. M. (2003). Technology diffusion and the "knowledge barrier": The dilemma of stakeholder participation. *Public Performance & Management Review, 26*(4), 345–359. doi:10.1177/1530957603026004003

Browning, G. (2002). *Electronic democracy: Using the internet to transform American politics.* Medford, OR: CyberAge Books.

Chadwick, A. (2003). Bringing e-democracy back in: Why it matters for future research on e-governance. *Social Science Computer Review, 21*(4), 443–455. doi:10.1177/0894439303256372

Chen, D. Y., Huang, D. I., & Hsiao, N. I. (2006). Reinventing government through on-line citizen involvement in the developing world: A case study of Taipei city mayor's e-mail box in Taiwan. *Public Administration and Development, 26*, 409–423. doi:10.1002/pad.415

Coleman, S. (1999). Cutting out the middle man: From virtual representation to direct deliberation. In Hague, B. N., & Loader, B. D. (Eds.), *Digital democracy: Discourse and decision making in the information age* (pp. 195–210). London, UK: Routledge.

Danziger, J. N., & Andersen, K. (2002). Impacts of Information Technology on public administration: An analysis of empirical research from the 'golden age' of transformation. *International Journal of Public Administration, 25*(5), 591–627. doi:10.1081/PAD-120003292

Garson, G. D. (2000). Information systems, politics, and government: Leading theoretical perspectives. In Garson, G. D. (Ed.), *Handbook of public Information Systems* (pp. 591–609). New York, NY: Marcel Dekker.

Garson, G. D. (2004). The promise of digital government. In Pavlichev, A., & Garson, G. D. (Eds.), *Digital government: Principles and best practices* (pp. 2–15). Hershey, PA: Idea Group Press.

Grant, G., & Chau, D. (2004). Developing a generic framework for e-government. *Journal of Global Information Management, 13*(1), 1–30. doi:10.4018/jgim.2005010101

Klein, H. K. (1999). Tocqueville in cyberspace: Using the Internet for citizen associations. *The Information Society, 15*(4), 213–220. doi:10.1080/019722499128376

Locke, T. (1999). Participation, inclusion, exclusion and netactivism: How the internet invents new forms of democratic activity. In Hague, B. N., & Loader, B. D. (Eds.), *Digital democracy: Discourse and decision making in the information age* (pp. 211–221). London, UK: Routledge.

London, S. (1995). Teledemocracy vs. deliberative democracy: A comparative look at two models of public talk. *Journal of International Computing and Technology, 3*(2), 33–55.

Milward, H. B., & Snyder, L. O. (1996). Electronic government: Linking citizens to public organizations through technology. *Journal of Public Administration: Research and Theory, 6*(2), 261–275.

Moon, M. J. (2002). The evolution of e-government among municipalities: Rhetoric or reality? *Public Administration Review, 62*(4), 424–433. doi:10.1111/0033-3352.00196

Moon, M. J. (2003, January 6-9). *Can IT help government to restore public trust? Declining public trust and potential prospects of IT in the public sector.* Paper presented at 36th Annual Hawaii International Conference on System Sciences. Big Island, Hawaii. Retrieved from http://csdl2.computer.org/persagen/DLAbsToc.jsp?resourcePath=/dl/proceedings/&toc=comp/proceedings/hicss/2003/1874/05/1874toc.xml&DOI=10.1109/HICSS.2003.1174303

Moon, M. J. (2005). Linking citizen satisfaction with e-government and trust in government. *Journal of Public Administration: Research and Theory, 15*(3), 371–391.

Moon, M. J., & Welch, E. W. (2004). Same bed, different dreams? A comparative analysis of citizen and bureaucrat perspectives on e-government. *Review of Public Personnel Administration, 25*(3), 243–264. doi:10.1177/0734371X05275508

Moon, M. J., & Welch, E. W. (2005). Same bed, different dreams? A comparative analysis of citizen and bureaucratic perspectives on e-government. *Review of Public Personnel Administration, 25*(3), 207–224. doi:10.1177/0734371X05275508

Norris, D. F., & Moon, M. J. (2005). Advancing e-government at the grassroots: Tortoise or hare. *Public Administration Review, 65*(1), 64–75. doi:10.1111/j.1540-6210.2005.00431.x

Ong, C. S., & Wang, S. W. (2009). Managing citizen-initiated email contacts. *Government Information Quarterly, 26*, 498–504. doi:10.1016/j.giq.2008.07.005

Panagopoulos, C. (2004). Consequences of the cyberstate: The political implications of digital government in international context. In Pavlichev, A., & Garson, G. D. (Eds.), *Digital government: Principles and best practices* (pp. 116–132). Hershey, PA: Idea Group Press.

Parent, M., Vandebeek, C. A., & Gemino, A. C. (2004). Building citizen trust through e-government. Retrieved from http://csdl.computer.org/comp/proceedings/hicss/2004/2056/05/205650119a.pdf

Peled, A. (2001). Centralization of diffusion? Two tales of online government. *Administration & Society, 32*(6), 686–709. doi:10.1177/00953990122019622

Roberts, N. (2004). Public deliberation in an age of direct citizen participation. *American Review of Public Administration, 34*(4), 315–353. doi:10.1177/0275074004269288

Roy, J. (2003). The relational dynamics of e-governance: A case study of the city of Ottawa. *Public Performance & Management Review, 26*(4), 391–403. doi:10.1177/1530957603026004006

Scavo, C., & Shi, Y. (2000). The role of Information Technology in the reinventing government paradigm: Normative predicates and practical challenges. *Social Science Computer Review, 18*(2), 166–178. doi:10.1177/089443930001800206

Shi, Y., & Scavo, C. (2000). Citizen participation and direct democracy through computer networking. In Garson, G. D. (Ed.), *Handbook of public Information Systems* (pp. 247–264). New York, NY: Marcel Dekker.

Stanley, J., & Weare, C. (2004). The effects of Internet use on political participation: Evidence from an agency online discussion forum. *Administration & Society, 36*(5), 503–527. doi:10.1177/0095399704268503

Tolbert, C., & Mossberger, K. (2004). The effects of E-government on trust and confidence in government. Retrieved from http://knowlton.osu.edu/ped/Egov/TolbertMossbergerOSU1.pdf

Welch, E. W., & Wong, W. (2001). Global information technology pressure and government accountability: The mediating effect of domestic context on website openness. *Journal of Public Administration: Research and Theory, 11*(4), 509–538.

Yang, K. (2003). Neo-institutionalism and e-government: Beyond Jane Fountain. *Social Science Computer Review, 21*(4), 432–442. doi:10.1177/0894439303256508

KEY TERMS AND DEFINITIONS

Bureaucratic Responsiveness: Dictionary definitions give us a clear meaning of responsiveness although "responsiveness" might be a problematic concept in public administration. "Responsive" means "quick to respond or react appropriately or sympathetically, sensitive" (Webster's Ninth New Collegiate Dictionary, 1986). Synonyms include "sentient, answering, passible [capable of feeling or suffering], respondent, reactive" (The New Roget's Thesaurus, 1964). Democracy would seem to require public administrators who are responsive to the popular will, at least through legislatures and elected chief executives if not directly to the people. Thus, the idea of bureaucratic responsiveness emphasizes that the bureaucratic system in democratic countries is expected to be responsive to the public's needs.

Civil Service E-Mail Box (CSEB): Civil service e-mail box (CSEB) is an official channel for the public sector to receive public opinion and provide the people with a more convenient way to express their needs and inquiries online. The establishment of CSEB can be seen as one of the policies to complete the readiness of ICT under the policy of e-government. It can be anticipated that the establishment of CSEB can not only enhance the people's involvement in decision-making process but also improve government responsiveness.

E-Democracy: E-democracy (a combination of the words electronic and democracy) refers to the use of information technologies and communication technologies (ICT) and managerial strategies in political and governance processes. Democratic actors and sectors in this context include governments, elected officials, the media, political organizations, and citizens/voters and these stakeholders can communicate and interact without difference through e-platform. E-democracy aims for broader and more active citizen participation enabled by the internet, mobile communications, and other technologies in today's representative democracy, as well as through more participatory or direct forms of citizen involvement in addressing public challenges. In comparison to the idea of e-government, e-democracy is a two-way interaction between government and the public.

E-Democratic Administration: As Waldo (1952: 102) indicates, the central problem of democratic administrative theory, as of all democratic political theory, is how to reconcile the desire for democracy with the demands of authority. A rational bureaucratic system is necessary to maintain the operation of a state and satisfy the public's need. However, the public administrator in a democratic country is expected to have neutral competence to

be more responsive, responsible, and accountable. According to Ostrom (1989: 146), on the other hand, democratic administration is about fragmentation of authority and overlapping jurisdictions, perhaps an opposite of the competing bureaucratic model that was built around unitary command of authority structures. For Ostrom, an overreaching executive and centralization of power created conditions for mistrust of citizens in government. It is obvious that democratic administration can be seen as a bureaucratic model which is more appreciative of the people's right for participation and concerned more about public fairness as the core value for governmental activities. E-democratic administration (a combination of the words electronic, democratic and administration) means that the democratic administration can be taken into practice more effectively and efficiently on the platform of ICT.

E-Government: E-government (a combination of the words electronic and government, also known as e-gov, digital government, etc.) is digital interaction between a government and citizens (G2C), government and businesses/commerce/ ecommerce (G2B), and between government agencies (G2G). This digital interaction consists of governance, information and communication technology (ICT), business process re-engineering (BPR), and e-citizen at all levels of government (city, state/province, national, and international). More specifically, e-government usually explains how the government utilizes IT, ICT and other telecommunication technologies to enhance the efficiency and effectiveness in the public sector and to make the public sector become more transparent. In the context of public administration literature, e-government emphasizes service and information provision rather than civil participation. It is more similar to a one-way policy implementation.

Information and Communications Technology (ICT): Information and communication technology, usually called ICT, is often used as an extended synonym for information technology (IT) but is usually a more general term that stresses the role of unified communication and the integration of telecommunication and internet (telephone lines and wireless signals), intelligent building management systems and audio-visual systems in modern information technology. ICT consists of all technical means used to handle information and aid communication, including computer and network hardware, communication middleware as well as necessary software. In other words, ICT consists of IT as well as telephony, broadcast media, all types of audio and video processing and transmission and network based control and monitoring functions. The expression was first used in 1997 in a report by Dennis Stevenson to the UK government and promoted by the new National Curriculum documents for the UK in 2000.

ENDNOTES

[1]   An internal customer refers to administrative staff working in the public sector, while an external customer refers to the public (Chen, Huang & Hsiao, 2006).

[2]   With regard to the factor analysis of independent variables, 10 factors can be exacted based on eigenvalues larger than 1. However, from the seventh factor, there is just one item exacted into one factor, which therefore cannot be used as factors for the analysis.

[3]   In running multiple regression analyses, it should be noted whether or not there is multicollinearity within independent variables. It also means that there is high correlation within independent variables, which leads to the lower explanation power of regression analysis. Regarding the test of multicollinearity, it is possible to run SPSS's tolerance degree and VIF test. For tolerance degree, the tolerance value is between 0 and 1. A value closer to 0 demonstrates that the independent variables are more likely to have multicollinearity. In addition, a higher VIF (as high as 10) reflects multicollinearity problems in the independent variables, indicating that they are not suitable to conduct regression analysis (Wu, 2002:8-4-5; Chen, Huang & Hsiao, 2006). This article demonstrates independent variables' VIF, showing that each independent variable does not clearly present the problem of multicollinearity. Therefore, it is suitable for regression analysis. Furthermore, the multiple regression analysis's P-P chart presenting 45-degree direct line, which clearly presents that this regression analysis, obeys the rule of normal distribution.

[4]   The VIF values of these three models' variables are not higher than 10, and do not have the problem of multicollinarity. The P-P figures present in 45-degree direct line, indicating that the sample is distributed normally.

APPENDIX 1

	Item	Number	Percentage
Gender	Male	150	37.5
	Female	247	61.8
	Miss	3	0.8
Educational Level	Junior School and Below	0	0
	High School	47	11.8
	Vocational School	138	34.5
	College	161	40.3
	Master's	47	11.8
	Doctorate	2	.5
	Blank	5	1.3
Duty	Junior	99	24.8
	Associate	171	42.8
	Senior	14	3.5
	Others	82	20.5
	Blank	34	8.5
Post Held	Manager	73	18.3
	Non-manager	319	79.8
	Blank	8	2.0
Age	20 or below	0	0
	20-25 years	6	1.5
	26-30 years	34	8.5
	31-35 years	79	19.8
	36-40 years	68	17.0
	41-45 years	78	19.5
	46-50 years	80	20.0
	51-55 years	34	8.5
	56-60 years	13	3.3
	61-65 years	6	1.5
	65 or above	6	1.5
	Blank	2	0.5
Length of Service Period	5 years or below	57	14.3
	6-10 years	79	19.8
	11-15 years	84	21.0
	16-20 years	57	14.3
	21-25 years	66	16.5
	26-30 years	31	7.8
	30 years or above	25	6.3
	Blank	1	0.3

continued on following page

	Item	Number	Percentage
Present Office	Central Authorities	153	38.3
	Municipal Government	45	11.3
	County Government	186	46.5
	Blank	16	4.0
Sponsor Services	Information	27	6.8
	Research	19	4.8
	Accounting	15	3.8
	Human Resource	19	4.8
	Ethic	6	1.5
	Others	311	77.8
	Blank	0	0
Concurrently Held Services	Information	30	7.5
	Research	12	3.0
	Accounting	8	2.0
	Human Resource	10	2.5
	Ethic	11	2.8
	Others	137	34.3
	Blank	0	0

APPENDIX 2

Intervening Variable

Factor 1: The perception of CSEB's readiness level (B1)	Factor Load	Explain Variance Measures	Alpha
1-17 In general, CSEB has complete resource and policy support	.896	48.97	.8835
1-16 In general, CSEB has complete information for staffs	.871		
1-18 In general, CSEB has complete administrative support	.847		
1-11 The processing procedure for using CSEB is easy	.698		
1-10 CSEB is consistent to the common administrative principles of public servants	.674		
1-15 In general, CSEB can promote civil participation in decision-making	.652		
1-12 My sector has had the experience of accepting public opinion submitted through CSEB	.610		
Dependent Variable			
Factor 1: The perception of CSEB's Validity (C1)	Factor Load	Explanation of Variance Measures	Alpha
1-2 CSEB can effectively respond to the populaces' problems	.825	11.58	.7903
1-3 CSEB can efficiently respond to the populaces' problems	.810		
1-4 CSEB is user-friendly	.701		
1-1 CSEB can effectively collect people's opinions	.696		
1-9 I am used to handling people's opinions through CSEB	.662		

KMO is 0.90

Independent Variables

Factor 1: Perception of e-democracy's feasibility (A1)	Factor Load	Explanation of Variance Measures	Alpha
4-7 Promotes e-forum for interaction with the public	.829	33.911	.9320
4-9 Conducts e-surveys to collect the public's opinion	.820		
4-6 Promotes CSEB	.818		
4-10 Promotes public consultancy to enhance civil participation	.811		
4-2 Issues e-newspapers	.808		
4-4 Handles citizen inquires	.797		
4-3 Promotes government information transparency	.792		
4-5 Establishes e-search mechanisms for the public to find information easily	.787		
4-11 Establishes public hearings/forums to collect the public's opinion	.771		
4-8 Establishes online chat space for communication with populace	.740		
4-12 Holds e-meeting with the public to reach consensus	.729		
4-1 Promotes government information renew	.712		
Factor 2: Appreciation of e-voting policy (A2)	Factor Load	Explanation of Variance of Measures	Alpha
4-14 Establishes e-voting system	.851	7.560	.8844
4-13 Promotes referendum on line	.838		
4-15 Allows citizens to vote for political candidates electronically	.823		
2-6 Allows citizens to vote for political candidates on line	.802		
2-5 Provides the public with a platform to express their thoughts on line	.727		
Factor 3: Sector's resource support (A3)	Factor Load	Explanation of Variance Measures	Alpha
2-17 I believe that the sector will invest resources to promote the e-government	.829	6.059	.8587
2-18 I believe that the sector will provide related training courses	.805		
2-12 I expect that more resources will be allotted to the promotion of e-democracy in the future	.790		
2-11 The resource to support e-democracy in my sector is sufficient	.788		
2-16 I can get resource assistance when I meet difficulties in using ICT	.713		
2-10 I have sufficient resources to promote e-democracy in my duty	.635		
Factor 4: Individual's electronic skills (A4)	Factor Load	Explanation of Variance Measures	Alpha
2-15 I often use ICT in my daily life	.891	5.091	.8443
2-13 I have enough skills to use ICT	.863		
2-14 My duty requires me to cope with ICT routinely	.857		
Factor 5: Appreciation for citizens' participation (A5)	Factor Load	Explanation of Variance Measures	Alpha
2-1 The government should invest resources to provide e-administrative services	.825	4.17	.8267
2-2 The government should announce information on line for transparency	.788		
2-4 The government should interact with the public on line	.784		
2-3 The government should invite the public to express their opinions on line	.779		
Factor 6: Sector's policy support (A6)	Factor Load	Explanation of Measures	Alpha
2-8 E-democracy is consistent with my sector's policy goal	.832	3.52	.9403
2-9 E-democracy is consistent with my unit's policy goal	.819		
2-7 E-democracy is consistent with my higher competent authority's policy goal	.805		

KMO is 0.92

Chapter 10
Social Media and New Military Public Affairs Policies

Kenneth L. Hacker
New Mexico State University, USA

ABSTRACT

This chapter explores the recent United States military policy changes regarding the use of social media by members of the services. It also discusses the use of these new policies for military public affairs. The chapter analyzes the policy changes in light of network theory in the studies of new media technologies and how users construct networks of influence by employing these new technologies. It is concluded that the military use of new media networking (NMN) is an effective way of both protecting the communication security of military information and optimizing the networking potential of the new media. It appears that the military can use its new social media policies to take advantage of NMN by generating news on their own sites, directing the public to more information, enhancing the morale of service members with families, and developing new methods of recruitment.

INTRODUCTION

This chapter explores the demands of the military for traditional public affairs concerns such as demands for operational security or keeping information and communication secure ("information assurance"), in relation to new social media policies and military encouragement of personnel to use the new media. Policy changes made in the past two years are considered in relation to network theory principles of social networking dynamics. The first objective here is to clarify the changes in military new media and social media policies that have been made in recent years, along with reasons for the changes. A second objective is to describe the tension within the military regarding how communication is kept secure while social networking is allowed to expand. Third, the efforts

DOI: 10.4018/978-1-4666-0318-9.ch010

by the military to employ new and social media to be more open with the public are explained in terms of traditional and strategic military communication goals. Administrators in other sectors of society may find the changes in military public affairs instructive as they also are confronted by the challenges of an age of new media.

The basic work of public affairs in the United States military affairs involves the dissemination of factual information to external and internal audiences in ways that protect the military services and also facilitate strategic communication goals of the services. The military acknowledges a responsibility to provide the public with timely and accurate information. It has a continual focus on trust and credibility (U.S. Army, 2009). The goals of public affairs include explaining events that have caused concern in the news, educating people about military capabilities, and helping the public to learn more about certain accomplishments (U.S. Army, 2009).

Controlling military public affairs and news about military events was once a straightforward process in days of old media (TV, radio, print). A public information officer or public affairs officer stood in front of journalists and presented the official narrative and then answered questions. Another major public affairs action was sending out press releases to newspapers and broadcast stations. That situation changed dramatically after 2004 and the emergence of YouTube, Twitter, viral messaging, buzzworthy news, Facebook, Meetup, Second Life, RSS feeds, the blogosphere, and smart phones. It continues to get more complicated as new waves of connection technologies increase the social media tools available to everyone using the Internet or smartphone communication. While the new media and social media provide many platforms for many military voices, there is a principle of public affairs which says that the services should speak with one voice on certain matters (U.S. Army, 2009). However, the age of new media did not see military personnel communicating directly with members of the public.

In past times, this was done with letters sent home, diaries, and handwritten journals.

Some communication theorists postulate an age of "hypermedia" today in which communication chaining is a process of messages moving quickly from one form of new media to another with variations of old and emerging media involved in the chaining. Communication chaining can been seen in many world events such as the recent "Arab Spring" use of new media and social media for organizing protest movements. Such uses of social media were in play earlier in Lebanon in 2005 and then recently after the presidential re-election in Iran. In communication chaining, messages from the old media merge with messages from what are called emerging media (connection technologies like smart phones used for social networking). The resulting communication space is far different than the old media space of passive listeners/viewers simply receiving content (Kraidy & Mourad, 2010). In the emerging media spaces, people produce messages as well as receive messages (Kraidy & Mourad, 2010). Communication chaining involves the use of emerging media in ways that elude control by political or journalistic authorities. In 2009, in Iran, when the young woman Neda was shot during post-election protests, a video clip of her dying was uploaded to YouTube where it went viral. From there, it went into social media like Facebook and Twitter, and then onto the mainstream old media (Kraidy & Mourad, 2010). Twitter users were providing observations to mainstream media and also demanding more attention from them. Five months later, the BBC made a documentary about Neda. The reason for this being important to an analysis of military public affair is that official communication faces the challenges of a) getting out factual information rapidly through expanding social networks, and b) correcting errors in messages which have already been disseminated through those networks.

New media (post-TV communication technologies) and social media (social networking technologies) have brought new interaction capabilities to their users. These include wider networks by geographic location of users, easier group formation and discussion, and rapid dissemination of ideas (Carafano, 2011). Web 2.0 communication changes the relationship between government and citizens by giving citizens more opportunities to locate and disseminate information that may challenge government information. This includes capabilities of open-source information retrieval, refuting mainstream news, and forming political movements. On the other hand, government also develops new capabilities of quickfire public opinion measurement, largescale distribution of official documents explaining and defning policies, and conducting strategic communication, public diplomacy, and information operations.

Along with general realizations by military leaders that there is a great deal of knowledge at the "boots on the ground" level of analysis, has come the recognition that new media and social media can draw information upward while other information continues to flow top-down in traditional military style. A Pentgon spokesman for social media policies notes that social media is an information source for the military because warfighters in places like Iraq and Afghanistan are sending messages that informs people back home about the problems and successes of their efforts in real time (Floyd, 2010).

Prior to Web 2.0 communication, government systems followed policies which focused on intranets and proprietary software (Carafano, 2011). These systems operated independently of each other and many were independent of the Internet (Carafano, 2011). After 9-11, there was a new effort among government agencies to begin sharing information about possible terrorist planning and activities. Web 2.0 brought many challenges to the military which was generally used to mass communication strategies for public affairs. The United States government (USG) in general and the military specifically, has to deal with a twenty-four hour news cycle that keeps expanding in content. This includes the fact that disinformation from enemies and misinformation from a variety of sources could contribute to rapid and negative framing (Paul, 2011). The military has harnessed the power of visual images for public affairs by establishing Combat Camera (COMCAM) teams to capture images and visual footage of combat and enter them into a distribution system (Paul, 2011). This is just one example of how the military seeks to keep pace with expanding networks of information created by social media.

Social media encourage networking, interactivity, and messages that can go viral through the interlinkages of emerging new channels of communication. The military realized that communication policies designed in the age of typewriters cannot be effective in age of Twitter and other connection technologies. The pattern of dealing with information and communication from a Web 2.0 paradigm has affected all of the armed forces including Air Force, Army, Marines, Navy, and Coast Guard.

The miltary viewed social media as threatening to communication security in 2007, but went through various policy shifts that led to not only accepting, but also promoting miliary use of social media. There was no official DOD social media policy in 2007, but YouTube and MySpace were blocked from military networks (Gohring, 2010). In 2007, the Army put strict limitation on what soldiers could do with blogs. The military was concerned about sensitive information getting out in the soldiers' messages. The Army required that a commander be consulted before each blog update could be published (Shachtman, 2007). Examples of soldiers being told to change their blogs include one soldier posting pictures of how well body armor stand up to bomb attacks and another soldier being told that she should not have personal family information posted (Shachtman, 2007).

At times, the services had opposing views on the value of social media to the military. In 2009, the Department of Defense (DOD) considered a total ban on social media sites like Twitter and Facebook. This is because some DOD professionals considered Web 2.0 a threat to internal military security (Ackerman, 2011). The military knew that social networking sites do not protect their user accounts from malicious software. A malware program entering a Facebook account could then spread messages to a user's friends, encouraging them to take actions that give entry to harmful software (Shachtman, 2009).

At the time of the proposed ban, the Army was already embracing social media. In 2009, the Army stopped blocking Facebook for its soldiers (Perry, 2010). The Army put out the order to allow soldiers access to certain Web 2.0 sites including Twitter, Facebook, Flickr, Delicious, and Vimeo (Shachtman, 2009). In 2009, the Army initiated the Online and Social Media Division of the Office of the Chief of Public Affairs. In the same year, the Department of Defense was debating issues of cyber security while also perceiving a need to take advantage of the social media appearing to be useful for public relations and recruiting (Dao, 2009). The latter view also saw social media as useful for shaping public opinion about the war in Afghanistan (Dao, 2009b). At the same time, high-ranking military officers such as Gen. Ray Oierno (commander of forces in Iraq) and Adm. Mike Mullen (chairman of the Joint Chiefs of Staff) were using social media themselves (Dao, 2009b). In the same year, the Pentagon unveiled its blogs, Flickr, Facebook, Twitter, and YouTube sites (Dao, 2009b).

In 2008, the Department of Defense launched a webite called Defense Media Activity for the purpose of providing service members around the world with news, information, and entertainment in all possible media forms. Before the DOD announced a social media policy in 2010, each service in the military had its own guidelines for emerging media usage. The Army perceived social media a good means of telling the Army story and disseminating important unclassified information (Shachtman, 2009). Sites that remained blocked by the Army were YouTube, Pandora, MySpace, MTV, Metacafe, Live 365, and others (Shachtman, 2009).

The Marine Corps banned Web 2.0 sites from its computer networks in 2009 (Hodge, 2010). The Marines viewed Twitter, Facebook, and MySpace and other social networking sites as susceptible to dangerous information exposure and attacks from adversarites (Shachtman, 2009). As was the U.S. Strategic Command, the Marine Corps was concerned with the fact that social networking sites do not scan messages and thus leave pages users susceptible to viruses, worms, and trojan horses. In constrast to the Marines, the Army ordered its bases to allow soldiers Facebook access (Shachtman, 2009). While the Army was moving toward accepting social media in 2009 and the Marine Corp had banned any social media usage on its network in 2009, the Pentagon studied the social media in an effort to formulate a DOD policy in the fall.

The DOD policy announced in 2010, allowed the services and their members to access social media with some restrictions. The DOD knew that Facebook had nearly 500 million users, Twitter had about 200 million users, and that there would be advantages for the military to be present where the public is present (Ackerman, 2011). The new permissive policy change of 2010 had restrictions such as possible bandwidth limits, protection of operational security and banned access to gambling, hate crimes sites, and pornography (Gohring, 2010; Miles, 2010). Concerns with malicious code, operational security, and communication security continue. The 2010 DOD policy is the first official Pentagon social media policy (Gohring, 2010). Before this policy, services issued their own policies about social networking. The DOD policy forced a reversal of the social media policy of the Marines (Gohring, 2010). By March of 2011, the Marines Facebook site had over one million fans (See Appendix A). The Marines plan to expand their new media efforts with content suitable for Android tablets, Nooks, Kindles, and many other mobile devices. They were the first service to make their official magazine an app for the iPad (Schmidt, 2011).

All of the U.S. military services had to change their public affairs policies to accomodate the fact that more service members are using social media to stay connected with family members and friends and to also tell their stories to people both in and out of the military. The main challenge to the military is to allow the freedom for service members to use social media in ways that maintain public affairs goals, a task that brings on the dynamic of balancing traditional hierarchy with new norms of dialogue and freedom. Essentially, the military appears to be attempting to maintain top-down information and communication control while also allowing and steering horizontal conversations of service members with each other, with publics, and with news media. In an interview on National Public Radio in 2010, Price Floyd, thje Principal Deputy Assistant Secretary of Defense for Public Affairs, noted that miliary concerns for operational security continue despite increasing social media usage. He noted that the military does not simply make decisions about social media use but also provides information to personnel to educate them on possible dangers. For example, they recommend that service members learn how to use social media services responsibly and safely (Floyd, 2010). There are numerous websites, policy manuals, and online courses to help them with this. Floyd argues that the many ways that military families use social media to stay in touch is a good morale booster for the service members deployed overseas.

There are at least three major concerns that the military has regarding social media. First, there is control over information and messages. Military communication is more constricted than civilian communication because of security concerns. Second, there are issues about bandwidth because there are millions of service members and limited resources. Third, there are issues about how time is spent. For the military, information and communication are never only about facts and descriptions. They are also concerned with information warfare (information operations, civil affairs, psychological warfare, public relations, etc.) and strategic influence. At first blush, one might wonder why a hierarchical organization grounded in rules, discipline, and following orders would be interested in non-hierarchical communication platforms such as social media new media networking. Analysis done by both military and non-miltary experts shows that there are many reasons for the acceptance of social media. These include changes in military leadership patterns that bring about more participation from followers into leadership actions, clear changes from old media to new media spheres of communication, and recognition of the influence potential of networked spheres of interests.

Social media involve relationships, conversations, and networking in forms never found before in the age of mass media and audience members who perceived media messages on their own and often in isolation from each other. The amount of available information just on websites is staggering. For example, a Google search on Army will call up over 200 million site links (Perry, 2010).

In allowing and encouraging service members to engage more in social media, the military hopes that sharing experiences and gaining feedback contributes to the positive impression management as members are encouraged to follow certain rules when they use Web 2.0 interaction. They are told, for example, to keep discipline and positive image development in mind when they use social media. While military personnel are freer to communicate openly when speaking as civilians, they are reminded that if they are speaking as military members, they are representing both their service and their nation. Additionally, they are told to sort out what they post as personal opinions and what might get construed as military statements.

Four major productive functions of social media for government have been identified. These are internal sharing of information, external sharing of information, obtaining information, and information sending (CIO Council, 2009). Internal sharing is organizational information distribution. External sharing consists of a government entity providing information to other organizations or individuals. Military communication with civilians with social media is one application of external sharing. Obtaining information, also known as inbound sharing, involves onlinine deliberation and polling. Information sending or outbound sharing entails government messages being distributed through social media (CIO Council, 2009).

Key Concerns of Military Public Affairs

There has always been a concern in the military for operational security. Key principles of military public affairs include releasing truthful information in a timely manner that does not jeopardize national security, providing consistent messages, and telling the military story. Friction can develop over the determination of what can be released versus what cannot in light of operational security (JCS, 2005). Despite such friction, public affairs professionals know they need to use whatever media are most effective in affecting perceptions and building influence networks (Keeton & McCann, 2005).

Public affairs professions work on community and media relations by addressing questions raised about military operations and structures. Until recently, the services did not embrace new media or social media as tools of public affairs. With recent changes of policy, however, the new media (Internet, websites, networking) and social media (connection technologies like social network sites) are now viewed as part of the information space that military analysts consider an inherent part of contempory battle space.

With the change in policy away from mass communication and toward new media, the military has also changed the roles of military personnel from people who relied solely on their public affairs officers (PAOs) to disseminate information to each person also being a disseminator of messages. This does not mean an end to chain of command organizational structure or public affairs officers, but it does open opportunities for new forms of lateral communication. The exigence in the reversal of military policies regarding new media are summed up well by this Air Force statement: "If the Air Force does not tell its own story, someone else will." (AFPAA, 2010).

For the military, information spaces are always related to national security. Thus, the embrace of new media is part of new strategies of military security and not just expression for personnel. Indeed, information is treated as an instrument of national power (AFPAA, 2010). Air Force experts believe that all airmen can become journalists by taking advantage of the fact that mainstream news media mine blogs for stories and news content (AFPAA, 2010). There is also a strategic influence angle to recent military embrace of new and social media. Because of the repeated recognition that terrorists like Al Qaeda successfully exploit new media, the military views the same technologies as means to work against the mispresentations of the terrorists.

Despite the freedom typically associated with social media and the Internet, military uses of new and social media are monitored and directed by policies and rules. As with all aspects of military communication, there are freedoms within contraints. Policies are determined by military authorities and then disseminated and explained as needed. Military personnel are reminded that when on duty or in uniform, they represent their service. When on active duty, they are expected to follow military rules and Uniform Code of Military Justice all year round and twenty fours per day. They are also expected to carry the values they learn in their service into the free spaces they find online.

The Changing World of Communication

Clawson (2009) describes three eras of information and knowledge which affected how societies were organized and how people related to each other in organizations and other contexts. The changes in what he calls the information age show some glimpses of what we know today as network society and the increasing uses of network technology platforms for many types of communication.

In the past two hundered years, the American society has moved from an agrarian to an industrial to and information-based system of economics and government. Argubly, the currrent emergence of "infocracy" and network society continue various trends in less centralized admininstration and work. Along with this come changes in how organizational members communicate with each other and with other people outside of their organization (Clawson, 2009).

In the agrarian epoch of our society, people believed that the best of society should run the society. Even in revolutionary America, there was an early distruct of democracy. Wealthy families and noble or aristoratic leaders control most the power in the society. This era was followed by the industrial age era. Bureacracies emerged along with the technological innovations of the industrial revolution. One reason for military leaders creating pyramid structures was to impose discipline and order on untrained troops. In other organizations, employees gained influence and position in relation to the skills they displayed (Clawson, 2009). As military personnel became more skilled, it was less necessary for the same amount of control as in earlier days when "micro-management" was more acceptable. Bureaucracies arose to have organizations run by rules,

hierarchical organization, appointments based on expertise, and decision-making made at the top levels of administration (Clawson, 2009).

In all contemporary organizational environments, quicker decisions have to be made at the point of action by the main workers, thus making more decentralized decision-making by some organizational members imperative. Thus, it appears that adminisrators or managers cannot manage every interface between an organization and its environments as was possible in the past (Clawson, 2009). For the military and military public affairs, this suggests that input is no longer sought only from commanders but also from personnel in the field and from their families.

Some observers note a trend today in the military toward what is known as adaptive leadership. Adaptive leadership includes the principles of being able to act quickly under circumstances of high uncertainty, keeping organizational interests as the highest priority, and giving subordinates opportunities to improvise rather than micro-managing them (Useem, 2010). Rather than being risk aversive, the adaptive leader is ready for unexpected changes (Whiffen, 2010). The adaptive leader is also flexible and read to deal with complex situations. Such leaders look at going into unfamiliar territory as a great way to obtain training (Whiffen, 2010). Perhaps this type of military leadership can handle the rapid and exponential changes typical of new media adaptation and not go back to more predictable ways of dealing with old media and try applying them to social media.

In the current age of new media networking (NMN), boundaries of organizations expand beyond traditional borders as employees are able act more indepedently. However, it should not be concluded, particularly for military organizations, that as traditional hierarchical power is accompanied by network power that the former disappears or that vertical lines of authority disappear. The picture is not that simple. To understand the changes, an understanding of network dynamics is necessary.

From Mass Media to Networking Media

We are now in a world of Bell's Law where every decade appears to bring a new generation of computer technology. While only about 25% of the world has Internet access, there about 3 billion cell phone users in a world of approximately 6 billion people. Twitter and micro-blogging emerged in 2006, just five years before the writing of this chapter. The IPhone came out in 2007. Social networking sites (SNSs) allow users to create public and private identies online within certain parameters. SNS formats vary are not limted to the most popular sites like Facebook. Twitter is one type of SNS which allows micro-blogging or the sending of short messages (limited to 140 characters) that function as news feeds to those who sign up to "follow" the account holder. Facebook, the most popular SNS, has over 400 million users today, a population that exceeds the population of the United States (Sauerbier, 2010). Mark Zuckerberg, the creation of Facebook, designed the site to help people extend their offline networks rather than to create new identities as he thought MySpace was doing (Vogelstein, 2007). With its gigantic social graph, Facebook became an engine of word-of-mouth communication. Information is not controlled by powerful point-to-many sources, but rather by numerous personal contacts or nodes in a personal network. Facebook has become a social hub or center of activity that brings people together for communication and sharing things like video links and invitations to use various online applications (Vogelstein, 2007).

Facebook began in 2004 and was the first SNS to offer a user news feed on their page (Sauerbier, 2010). Facebook differed from MySpace, which it surpassed in numbers of users, in that it offered micro-blogging in contrast to the traditional blogging offered by MySpace. Facebook status updates are limited to 420 characters (Sauerbier, 2010). LinkedIn, created in 2003, has different functions than MySpace and Facebook. Rather than reconnecting with old friends or making new ones, LinkedIn provides professional networking. It presently has over 60 million users (Sauerbier, 2010).

Today, new media, NMN, connection technologies, networking in general, and all of the new communication devices and systems offer multiple plaform communication which uses more than one type of communication channel or medium to increase social interaction. Smart phones, for example, provide a hub for personal communication networks that integrate phone, websites, SNSs, media like film, music, and TV, navigation devices, and other applications that use the Internet to enhance covergence and interoperability of communication capabilities. Today, about 30% of smart phone users access SNSs with their phones (Sauerbier, 2010).

An interesting function of Twitter that developed in recent times is its use as a news source. Photos of breaking events, for example, have been disseminated earlier than other sources at times on Twitter. When a user "twitters" or "tweets" a message, the "tweet" is disseminated over two networks – the SNS site and through text messaging (Sauerbier, 2010). This makes Twitter a significant component technology of NMN and one that can be used for the diffusion of accurate or inaccurate information.

Not only is Facebook larger than the U.S. in terms of population, but even the online multiplayer game World of Warcraft has a population larger than about 150 nations (Christakis & Fowler, 2009). Gaming aside, this is another example of a social site where users can work together, play together, collaborate, and chat with instant messaging. Studies of this kind of social media experience have shown how easy it is for users to employ Web 2.0 tools to interact in large-scale communication situations that would be difficult to arrange without such tools (Christakis & Fowler, 2009). Many of the contacts users have in Web 2.0 environments are weak ties rather than strong ties, but research has shown value to both types of connections. Second Life is another example of virtual environments providing social networking and social collaboration opportunities.

Studies of online communication have consistently shown that using Web-based social interaction tools facilitates the maintenance of offline relationships and both weak ties and strong ties (Christakis & Fowler, 2009). Social ties of those who are geographically distant can also be maintained with online communication. While some SNS are designed to facilitate extending relational communication such as Facebook, others are designe for users to create new relationships. These include the online dating sites like match.com. One important aspect of SNS is that the social networks of users can be viewed by people in those networks and sometimes by people simply visiting their social network page (Christakis & Fowler, 2009). The span of a person's personal communication and relational networks can be increased by the use of social media. In turn, the larger network allows greater diffusion of information and chances for influence.

Some organizations are concerned about how much time employees spent on activities such as updating their SNSs. Nearly half of the companies in the U.S. ban employees from using SNS during company time (Sauerbier, 2010). However, companies also use SNS themselves to investigate job applicants or to monitor current employee online activities (Sauerbier, 2010). One example of employer monitoring is a software package known as Social Sentry. In NMN there is in increating amount of porting data from one platform to another. For example, one can post on multiple SNS at the same time or have one SNS import information from another (Sauerbier, 2010). For technology developers, the goal appears to be the integration of multiple platforms.

At the same time, organizations will use NMN to monitor employees, screen applicants, promote their organizations, and attract recruits for new employment.

Humans have always relied on groups and networks for social organization. Today, new media networking (NMN) makes the organizing of groups and networks easier than ever before in history.

Using groups to accomplish tasks is the rule rather than exception in human actions. Shirky (2008) notes that even great artists like Michaelangelo had assistants to do part of their work, as did great inventors like Thomas Edison.

Shirky (2010) notes that there are interesting challenges for how new media users use their new opportunities for easier sharing. Practical considerations include making enough social value in NMN to attract more users and build a network of users with similar interests. To keep rules in place without too much moderation or censorship, effective social media platforms must encourage early culture formation that remind people of the most aceptable norms for the new media interactions (Shirky, 2010). To create more social value from social media, users should be encouraged to experiment, but in military contexts they can only experiment within public affairs parameters. In a relative few number of years, American society has moved from public information coming from mass media alone with some elements of interpersonal communication, to the network ecology today where public (mass) media and private media (social media) blend together (Shirky, 2010).

People have often heard about systems theory and the famous axiom that the whole is greater than the sum of its party. Yet, few can explain where such power originates. Network theory, a field of many disciplines including social sciences, physical sciences, and mathematics has found key structural and process principles of self-organizing systems known as networks. Networks may looks like small systems but they are less determined by authorities than by common interests of people who share interests and goals. The whole is greater than the sum of its parts in a network because networks involve increasing connectivity and interactivity. From the increasing density of communication is a network, more information flows through channels and more influence among members of the networks is facilitated.

Network theory had early starting points in findings like the one by psychologist Stanley Milgram that people in the United States are within six human connections from each other ("six degrees of separation"). Duncan Watts found later that the six degrees of separation finding applies the world as well as to the United States and that it also applies to the use of email (Barabasi, 2002). Network theorists observe that the reason why humans are so closely linked is that we confuse large numbers of people with an absence of close interconnections. In fact, people are more connected than they realize. Even pages on the Web are more connected that we suspect upon learning that there are billions of Web pages and sites. Despite the enormous quantity, any Web page is within 19 links from any other page (Barabasi, 2002).

Military Stategic Communication and Online Communication

Understanding the use of new media and social media by the military and the changes in policies described earlier requires a recognition of the larger context for military communication challenges. The USG and the military seek to use all available means of communication to facilitate their strategic communication, public diplomacy, public affairs, and information operations efforts. The problem is that these endeavors lack a basis in communication theory and a clear mission for emerging technologies. As James Carfano (2011) observes: "Government social networking has an even greater challenge because it is not clear if

Washington knows what it is trying to do online." (p. 77). More research is also needed to help guide decisions about what to do with social media since these new platforms of communication are most imporant for their networking dynamics.

Military commanders seek to understand and adapt to changes in warfighting, political conflicts, technologies of war including communication technologies, and various ways of keeping up with both actions of potential adversaries and present enemies. They also seek to understand networks of information, cognition, decision-making, and communication (Mayfield, 2011). Social media are viewed by the military as a means to more effectively use information is ways that support military operations (Mayfield, 2011). Some of the increasing acceptance of social media is due to the fact that the military realized how quickly information is disseminated against its operations with new media. One way to challenge misinformation was to engage the same technologies used to spread the negative content (Mayfield, 2011). Thomas Mayfield (2011) argues, "If military leaders do not fully understand these tools, they may miss their significant impact on the nature of future conflicts." (p. 80).

Actively using social media also provides the media with a tool for military civil affairs. Civil affairs involves the relationships between military forces and civilian populations in an area of operations. Social media can provide important information about local population perceptions (Mayfield, 2011). This can only enhance what military professionals call "situational awareness." Social media can also help military services learn more each other and to work with more unity. Military coordination with non-governmental organizations (NGOs), embassies, and local community organizations can also be enhanced with social media usage (Mayfield, 2011). Military public affairs and public relations professionals can also use social media to generate more persuasive messages about the government's objectives in various military operations. Another function of social media for military purposes involves intelligence gathering. Social media monitoring teams can look for useful information in any given area of responsibility.

The military is faced with a situation of both needing to increase sharing while also needing to assure operational security. Security officers are likely to deny certain expansions of social media usage (Mayfield, 2011). The services have clearly learned the necessity of rapid response communication when they are accused of behaviors such as killing innocent civilians. A case in point is Operation Vahalla which took place in Iraq in 2006. During a firefight, American and Iraqi soldiers killed numerous enemy fighters. By the time they returned to their base, the bodies have been re-positioned to make it look like the enemies had been shot while doing prayers. In less than one hour, photos of the new body positions were upoaded onto the Internet. U.S. soldiers had camera footage of the incident that they were later able to upload, but that was three days later. This delay is believed to have given force to enemy claims about what occurred (Mayfield, 2011).

Military Concerns with Security

As noted earlier, a major concern with military communication whether online or offline is operational security. Changes in government policies regarding social media are consistent with communication research on new media and social media, that is, the effects of these technologies are not determined by hardware or software but rather by user behaviors. Therefore, government policies do not focus on specific new media or social media but rather on guidelines that help users make good decisions about what they do with emerging technologies (CIO Council, 2009).

Specific threats to USG social media include spear phishing, social engineering and attacks on applications. Phishing is enticing a user to open a document or hyperlink that starts an attack action (CIO Council, 2009). The process begins with the phisher having information about the user. Interests and travel plans, for example, can be used in this way and such information can be gleaned from SNS. Social engineering is mining personal information from SNS such as addresses, family information, work information, and education, in order to build trust relationships with user and his/her friends. From there, various attacks can be launched (CIO Council, 2009). If one reads how this not only affects the military, but also the general public, it should be easy to appreciate the military concern for communication security while being committed to expanding social networking.

As the military frees up social media access to its personnel more, it also disseminates policy statements which remind personnel that what they do online can be viewed by their adversaries in the world as well as by their family and friends (U.S. Army, 2009). One recommendation is that personnel remind themselves that they represent their nation and values with all of their messages and behaviors. It is also made clear that any messages on government computers can be monitored (U.S. Army, 2009).

NETWORKING AND MILITARY PUBLIC AFFAIRS

As the study of new media networks has progressed, communication scholars have moved closer to network theory and network logic to explain how people use new communication technologies and computer networks for communication. Research about one user communicating with another user with channel differences (or one group with another) is giving way to studies about how groups organize, collaborate, etc. by the formation and usage of networks. This can also include how individuals develop personal networks of information and communication.

While the U.S. military created the Internet, it did not reserve it for national security alone. The decentralized nature of the Internet began with the technical nature of packet switching (Chadwick, 2006). The scientists developing the Net technology sought to maintain the direction of open design. There are many aspects of the Internet that make it unique. One is that the Net can be used for either interpersonal communication (email, chat, IM, social networking, twitter, etc.) or mass communication (websites, etc.). Additionally, the Net can be used for what is called many-to-many communication. In terms of political communication, the Internet offers much more political interactivity than previous communication systems – citizen-leader interaction, citizen-citizen interaction, and citizen-media interaction (Klotz, 2004).

Along with communication research examining online communication and how it works in tandem with offline communication, scholars have developed concepts and principles of networking involved in many-to-many communication. Network logic is not just about the technical nature of open systems or the technologies that form networks; it is also about how online networks are used as major and expanding means of social and political organization (Stalder, 2006). Physical geography is not assumed to vanish as an important factor in human affairs but becomes a factor operating along side of the expanding importance of online geography and new media networks. Network logic stresses social morphology. Networks are treated, in network theory, as systems which change by adapting to their circumstances. Their key characteristics emerge from their changing dynamics not from their static qualities (Stalder, 2006). A network cannot be understood by studying components alone because the network properties and dynamics are related to changing interactions of network components. This does not mean that components are not important but rather that they do not determine the ends of a network. An analogy is human DNA.

DNA will affect you health and other parts of your nature but, it along with many other factors, not alone by itself, will determine what you do with your life. Understanding networks requires understanding how network components interact (Stalder, 2006).

This brings the realization that studying communication networks involves systems thinking. It means that networks are greater than the sum of their parts and that people in a network work together for common goals and to keep the system succeeding in meeting its goals. A network is self-organized while a system may be determined by authorities. A network is an enduring form of organization that can be identified by its relational constancy of its members (Stalder, 2006). Nodes or network members do not produce the network. Instead, people in a system interact and create connections and relations which makes them nodes of members of the emerging network (Stalder, 2006).

Networks tend to be less hierarchical than other systems. Here is a great challenge for the military use of new media and social media. A traditionally hierarchical form of human organization is now experimenting with more lateral means of organizing and interacting. In a network, members can come and go and the structure and decisions keep changing in light of the absence of central control. This may sound like networks being random in their organization but this is not the case. They are self-organizing and distributed in terms of authority but they are not random. A network has a logic which develops from interactional patterns and the formation of accepted rules over time (Stalder, 2006).

While this may seem chaotic and unmanageable, there are forms of control in network that are explained by communication scientists who study interactivity and social structures. In general, what holds a network together is not authority but rather common purpose. Beyond that, networks also have centers of control which tend to regulate the network interactions of the peripheral nodes of the network.

Part of network logic is that coordination and flexibility can work together unless what was thought about them working against each other in the past. Social movement and protests can be seen as examples of networks in political communication. Such a movement like the anti-globalization movement, because of the vast differences among members, has to be flexible. Such flexibility makes coordination possible (Stalder, 2006).

New media networking (NMN), which is based on converging communication technologies with shared electronic (Internet) networks, is replacing the one-dimensional concepts of computer-mediated communication (CMC) such as email alone, cell phone alone and other genres where users have communciation devices dedicated to singe purposes without connections to other communication devices. With NMN, we see that cell phones become smart phones and the latter are becoming major hubs of personal communication technology intersections that are capable of affecting political communication.

Perhaps the single most dominant trend within emerging media is the move toward social networking. Social networking is done through email, websites, gaming, and cell phones (Grant & Meadows, 2008). Social networking increasingly occurs via particular platforms such as Facebook, Twitter, and MySpace. These sites have clearly allowed numerous individuals to increase their social links across a myriad of interest groups. While connectivity among members of a social network is enhanced, communication scholars are more interested in what and how new forms of communication are organized than in simple increases of social linkages. In other words, these emergent new media allow, and often require, different structures underlying communication practice.

Two fundamental characteristics of emerging media and NMN are self-organization and increases in collaborative relationships. The technological attribute of self-organization refers to the ability of users to generate their own communication networks. Barry Wellman and other scholars refer to this as networked individualism (Castells, 2001; van Dijk, 2006). Users are now able to create individualized profiles that are widely shared. However, in this sharing, a new community with new norms and rules of practice is instantiated and regulated. New media networks are characterized by mobile individuals that are no longer tethered to particular places as with telephones in the past (Grant & Meadows, 2008). This mobility undercuts a primary assumption of telecommunication of old in that no longer are communication partners able to employ schemata of place when interacting with others. Thus, a new self-organizing and (at times decreasingly) self-regulating system is created for communication, including political communication. The second characteristic shaping NMN is collaboration. Increasingly users are able to engage in "integrative collaboration" through audio, video, or on-line channels (Ogden, 2008, pg. 322). The collaborative characteristic is particularly important in e-government and e-democracy. NMN provides a platform for users to perceive that they are engaged in political discourse in a collaborative sense.

Going beyond multimedia, there are new forms of communication resulting from emerging and extended media and what are referred to as extensible media (Dallow, 2007). These changes are related to what are known as Web 2.0 developments and include trends that are both summative (communication technology convergence) and exponential (emerging media). (Dallow, 2007). Interactivity, convergence, and connectivity are all easily high in NMN and new forms of interrelationships are made possible (Dallow, 2007).

The Department of Defense (DoD) has a set of guidelines known as Principles of Information which include the following (JCS, 2005):

1. Information should be made readily available except for cases when national security is endangered.
2. There should be a free flow of information to military personnel and their dependents.
3. Information should not be classified in order to prevent criticism of the government.

Along with these basic principles are the ones which state that public affairs personnel are only to release truthful information. Public affairs professionals are also expected to disseminate messages that are consistent. This means that information should be reviewed and coordinated before releasing to the public (JCS, 2005). With social media, one might not immediately recognize the possible threat to such review by distermediating new platforms of information and social interaction. Military public affairs and other information professionals, on the other hand, are sensitized to such issues.

As noted earlier, one activity of public affairs specialists goes beyond message diffusion and includes message monitoring. This includes reviewing public opinion polls and news coverage (JCS, 2005). While disseminating factual information is a central goal of public affairs, an additional goal is helping to generate as many positive impressions of the military as possible while giving out truthful information. Until recently, public affairs officers could spend the greatest amount of attention on the old media (TV, radio, print). They would be ready to meet the journalists when they arrived for interviews. This operating environment has changed with new media and social media.

Social media and Web 2.0 platforms make information sharing and social interactions with friends, family members, and contacts easier than ever before. When the military first noticed the incredible proliferation of networking concerning it affairs, it observed that many platforms were telling the military story without being affiliated with the military. This raised red flags (Perry,

2010). The Army created its Online and Social Media division in its public affairs office (Perry, 2010). It was recognized that the new media and social media are largely about conversation and dialogue. This year, in 2011, the Army released its guidelines for social media usage. Even before the release of these guidelines, however, military leaders and personnel knew that their online communication was linked to the Uniform Code of Military Justice (UCMJ) and the commitment that soldiers have to operational security (Perry, 2010). Once the potential of public affairs online was recognized by the military, all major social media channels were tapped for military messages.

The Army policy manual on social media argues that expanding military social media increases information distribution that social media allow all soldiers to participate in telling the Army story (OCPA, 2011). It is also argued that soldiers have the freedom to talk about what they do as long as they do not violate key principles of operational security. User-generated content that does not threaten operational security guidelines can be distributed through military social media. One answer to a frequently asked question about social media is ended this comment: "Don't be afraid to experiment and have fun." (OCPA, 2011, p. 34).

Military social media, like other social media, allow content providers to use analytics to measure how content is being judged and which content is generating the most interest (OCPA, 2011). While the military views social media as a marketing mechanism, it also recognizes it as a tool for building community and networking. For example, the Army policy manual states, "Social media is more than just a platform to push command messages, it's a social community." (OCPA, 2011, p. 9). There is a recognition here of social media offering a method of stimulating dialogue and getting visitors interested in what is being discussed. To some extent, there is recognition of the importance of interactivity in social media as

Figure 1. A social media model for military public affairs

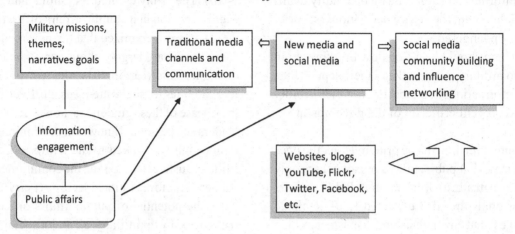

when the manual talks about getting user feedback and then acting on that feedback.

New Media and Military Information Engagement

The military does not view information as data or anwers to questions alone. Instead, the military sees information as a tool of war or preventing war (DSB, 2009). What is termed "information engagement" is used to shape operational landscapes, to build trust with populations and other actors, to promote support for United State actions and to foster strategic influence (DSB, 2009, p. 11). Part of the information engagement concept is gaining more understanding of target audiences. Building more understanding of both old media and new media uses and networking provides more knowledge about "influence networks" that can be used for persuasion.

The strongest goal thus far for military public affairs and social media is the objective of generating what we can call networks of influence. With governmental use of new media, what used to be called audiences and now are known as users are both targets and channels of strategic messages (Latar, Asmolov, & Gekker, 2010). As do other government agencies, the military seeks to sets news agendas and help along positive framing

of the military. The model offered here sums up some of the key strategies to military public affairs using social media.

Figure 1 assumes that military public affairs can expand its influence while retaining principles of communication security. It also assumes that the acceptance and promotional of social media for public affairs is making military communication both internally and externally, more consistent with theories of communication and networks.

Following the principles of information engagement that guide all of the forms of military communication described earliers, public affairs efforts are directed toward both old media and new media platforms. Agenda setting and framing are no longer simply set by mass media, but now are created by interactions of old media, new media, and social media. Thus, military affairs will attempt to use Web 2.0 to affect agenda setting and framing in the old media as well as the new media. Simultaneously, military public affairs will attempt to build identification of the public with the military and to build networks of influence through which military perspectives are diffused more widely.

One way for the military to set agendas is by using social media to write stories and narrative about military missions and objectives in addition to simply providing factual information to journalist and answering news media concerns. This is consistent with trends in public affairs by all sorts of other organizations whether they be in government, academia, or business. The basic premise is that new media encourage pull technologies and sites as well as push technologies and sites (Scott, 2010). This is why the Air Force has sites with many photos, videos and articles written by public affairs offciers. These materials can be found by the public and by journalists looking for materials for stories that they are writing (Scott, 2010). One Air Force officer says "Instead of pushing things out, people are finding our information." (Scott, 2010, p. 243). Along with the visual materiala and stories, the public affairs writers provide the journalists with contact information. This provision of materals online is joined with photos posted on Flickr, messages posted on Facebook, and information written in blogs.

There are many findings in studies of human networks that indicate that neworking increases diffusion of messages and also, up to three degrees of connectedness (friends, friends of frends, and friends of friends' friends), influence and persuasion (Christakis & Fowler, 2009). Network theorists note that when a social network is small, adding links may not look like it having much effect, but later addition of links begin forming clusters as some of the news links are already linked together (Barabasi, 2002). At a certain time, in that cluster of connections, it is possible for most people in the network to get information from anyone else in the network Barabasi, 2002).

The building of influence networks is a key objective of military 2.0 social media. By bringing private citizens and military professionals together in conversations, it is possible to increase network size, trust, and legitimacy (Latar, et al., 2010). Content in this type of networking is both organizational and user-generated content. One job of public affairs is crisis management. When a crisis occurs, public affairs officials speak for the military organization regarding the crisis.

With social media influence networks, diffusion of public affairs crisis messages becomes easier, faster, and more extensible.

Fears about operational security in social media are alleviated by the function of public affairs staff for monitoring messages disseminated by military personnel and by others participating in military communication via platforms like SNSs. While the military public affairs network is more inclusive that previous communication platforms and military personnel are encouraged to be creative, the social media related to military public affairs are both monitored and regulated. For example, posts that are determined to be threatening to either the military or national security are likely to be deleted.

As Perry (2010) observes, the military seeks to balance public awareness with operational security. It is commonly known that enemies of the U.S. seek to exploit online communication in various ways. Despite risks, the military embraces social media today because it perceive online communication as a good way to expand the networking the military messages. As more military personnel join the networks, the power of the networks increases in terms of disseminating positive information (OCPA, 2011).

Jan van Dijk (2006) notes that while networked social structures (societies or organizations) rely increasingly on communication and information networks for organizing and doing work, the center of the network increases its control function. This is contradictory to the fantasies of flattened hierarchies that some observers attribute to organizational adoption of network technologies (Mantovani, 1994). As van Dijk observes, the diffusion of activity and work at the periphery of networks makes the control of the center more important since it must hold together a diffuse network and ensure that that entire structure is serving the goals of the center. The center remains concentrated in terms of political, economic, and managerial power. What van Dijk calls the Scale Extension/Scale Reduction Principle says that you can have opposite direction effects with new communication systems such as social media. For the military, this is good news since there can be lateral and free communication at the periphery while there can the kind of control necessary for operational and communication security at the center.

Toward Networks of Influence for Military Communication

Since new media researchers began to challenge the concept of a single public sphere for political discourse, there have been many arguments asserting the importance of multiple digital public spheres. The military has been concerned with balancing security with taking advantage of social media interaction with its personnel and with the public. It appears that the newer policies are promising and no longer see security and information sharing as necessarily hurting each other. In fact, the policies appear to increase information assurance (security) while also expanding social networks.

A mutual network of influence approach to military public affairs could theoretically result from a new view of public affairs and how the military and public interact. Figure Two shows how using social media for increasing interactivity of the military and the public can replace the old linear model of public affairs which was one directional message sending from the military the public. Interactivity is a key dynamic to communication network formation and the formation of social structures.

While there is no reason for the military to lessen its concerns with operational security, there are good reasons, based on network society theories and network logic, to believe that military public affairs and members of the public (family members, concerned citizens, journalists, etc.) can build networks of shared concerns and influence.

Figure 2. Interactive model of military public affairs

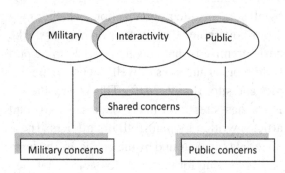

The military has come to see issues with social media as more behavioral than technological. Software and sites must be protected from cyber-attacks and users must be educated on responsible usage. The benefits to the military appear to outweigh the risks because the risks can be managed. The notion of digital public spheres comes from network and communication theories and has the potential to help the military network more with the public in ways that allow public affairs work of the military to be done more easily and for the public to become more capable of interacting with military leaders about policies, operations, and concerns. Researchers have noted that people using new media and social media are using a myriad of ways to locate and share information in ways that produce networks of interaction with others with whom they communicate (Drapeau & Wells, 2009). Networks offer increasing opportunities for creativity, collaboration; and working with others solve problems.

Military public affairs concerns the military explaining itself and its actions to the public. Social media provide a means of public affairs engagement with the public in which information dissemination through press releases and other one-way channels are augmented by interactive sessions on blogs and social networking sites like Facebook. An example of such public engagement is the Army Bloggers Roundtable. The Army says that this forum is deigned by provide transparency as well as an opportunity for audience participation. Another Army blog is Family Matters Blog. Dialogue is encouraged about deployments, family concerns, and problems of separation.

Applications of Social Media for Military Public Affairs

Web 2.0 public affairs in the military can be used for the building of networks and influence for bringing people normally outside of the military community into that community. In contrast to Web 1.0 communication, Web 2.0 communication involves social networking, collaboration, interactivity, and users of sites to add to site content or to challenge content (Drapeau & Wells, 2009). Military public affairs can take advantage of social media by expanding its message diffusion through social networks, helping families and service members stay in closer contact, and using the strong ties and weak ties of social networking to influence others about military concerns and accomplishments. Highlighted below are some illustrations.

- *The U.S. Army:* http://www.army.mil/media/socialmedia/

The U.S. Army has a website that invites service members to submit websites for approval. The Army finds social media for many uses including recruitment. YouTube is used by the Army for the posting of videos that present information about the experiences of soldiers and how committed they are to their missions. The Army has over 15,000 Twitter followers who receive links to stories on the Army website (Perry, 2010). The Army knows that many young people are heavily involved with social media and that it can connect to them easily with these channels. Social media are used to direct young people (18-24 yrs. old) to recruiting sites and to also answer their questions in low-pressure environments. The Army also encourages its soldier to post blogs and photos on its site Armystrongstories.com where soldiers can post content that expresses their feelings as long as they are not obscene, political commentary, or a threat to operational security.

- *The U. S. Air Force:* http://www.facebook.com/USairforce

The U. S. Air Force says that social media concerns collaboration. This service looks at new media as providing fast communication with very large numbers of user as they attempt to educate the public about their air, space, and cyberspace missions. One social media tool emphasized by this service is blogging. The Air Force states that Airmen bloggers function as Airmen journalists because mainstream jounalists mine blogs for stories or information. This service uses Facebook in the same way as done by the Army and other services.

- The U. S. Marines: http://www.marines.mil/unit/mcrc/Pages/MCRCFacebookPagepasses1millionfans.aspx

The U. S. Marines now lead the military services with their use of social media. Like the Army and Air Forces, the Marines use all of the major social media like Facebook, Youtube, and Twitter for public affairs. The Marines say that there are many conversations about the Marine Corps in online media and social networks and they seek to increase their participation in those conversations. Marines are allowed to use blogs and other social media for personal self-expression and also to help the public affairs objective of telling and explaining the Marine Corps story.

- Department of Defense Social Media Hub: http://www.defense.gov/socialmedia/

The DOD itself is today proactively promoting military social media. Former Secretary of

Defense Robert Gates had a section on the DOD website where he answered questions from the public. The Pentagon says that it seeks to have more open and two-way communication with the public in general. The services are not only allowing members to participate in civilian social media but are also creating many military social media platforms. On the military social media sites, there are many links to traditional websites. For the military today, social media present new opportunities for marketing and recruiting (Perry, 2010).

All of this effort appears consistent with research showing that social networking can aid message dissemination, relationship formation, and influence. It appears that military public affairs professionals seek to do what some might call fishing where the fish live, that is looking for the people they seek to recruit where they spend so much time – on the social networking sites. SNS like Facebook provide platforms for information updating, linking other websites, posting of photos and videos, and chatting with others about the services involved. Twitter provides a direct channel of information updating from public affairs to public and journalists as well as provision of links to information sources. With Flickr, a service can post thousands of photos to show the public what missions they are engaging. YouTube is useful for showing videos about service training, missions, and objectives.

Considering these and other examples of adoption in the field, there are many implementation challenges to consider. First, for example, how effectively the services balancing operational security with expanding channels of communication and networking? What restrictions stay constant in the domain of military communication when you allow service member to post opinions, blogs, and photos about ongoing missions? How effective is service member input to higher-ranking members when with social media as opposed to traditional channels of communication? Has the accuracy of news reporting increased as journal-

ists have become more interactive with members of the military? Despite these issues and potential challenges, efforts continue to adopt and evolve new techniques to promote more openness and engagement with the public.

CONCLUSION

The Internet was invented by the Defense Advanced Research Projects Agency (DARPA) which part of the U.S. Department of Defense. While the Internet and its network technologies follow trends of self-organization and open architecture, the military has never lost sight of the importance of the Internet and NMN to its missions and operations. In the 1990s, RAND, a military think tank, recommended that the United States have universal email. There are many reasons why the military changed its policies recently to embrace social networking. On one hand, these changes empower military personnel to diversify their channels of communication and enrich their jobs at the local levels where they accomplish them. On the other hand, the basic principles of network design also apply to military NMN. Thus, power at the center of the network controls the network while granting more freedom at the periphery of the networks. There should be nothing surprising about this as this pattern of networking can be found throughout history. However, changes in leadership in all organizations, including the military, may make it possible for personnel to have more input into centers of power and more freedom to communicate with larger spheres of contacts as they are trusted more and those in power realize the productivity boosts that can result from trust.

Over one half of people who serve in the military today were born after 1980 and many of them as known as "digital natives" -- people who grew up using the Internet and social media. They are used to getting their information through smartphones, email, websites, and social networking.

The military realizes this and seeks to keep with the current trends in comunication. The concept of influence in networks is not new. It is derived from diffusion theory which has proven useful in communication research for over fifty years. Quite simply, people learn a great deal through their social networks and are influenced most by people they trust, like, and share interests with on specific subjects.

It is natural and necessary for military leaders to be concerned with communication and operational security. Ironically, extending this concern into too much resistance to the use of social media by military members could lead to decreasing the overall effectiveness of military communication. The new policies in military public affairs appear to reflect a recognition of this fact. The analysis presented in this chapter indicates that the military use of new media networking (NMN) is an effective way of protecting the communication security of military information while simulteously optimizing the networking potential of the new media. The military has changed its social media policies to take advantage of NMN by generating news on their own sites, directing the public to more information, enhancing the morale of service members with families, and developing new methods of recruitment.

Administrators in other sectors of society may find the changes in military public affairs instructive as they also are confronted by the challenges of an age of new media. Future research should examine the precise ways in which military public affairs concerns and practices differ from public affairs in other types of organizations. It should also examine how more specific connections to network theory can help guide the development of social media for specific changes in public affairs and social media communication.

REFERENCES

Ackerman, S. (2011, January 14). Tweet away, troops: Pentagon won't ban social media. *Wired*. Retrieved from http://www.wired.com/danger-room/2011/01/tweet-away-troops-pentagon-wont-ban-social-media/

Air Force Public Affairs Agency/AFPAA. (2010). *New media and the Air Force*. Retrieved from http://www.af.mil/shared/media/document/AFD-090406-036.pdf

Army, U. S. (2009). *Army public affairs handbook, version 2.0*. Fort Meade, MD: Army Public Affairs Center.

Barabasi, A. (2002). *Linked: The new science of networks*. Cambridge, MA: Perseus Publishing.

Carafano, J. (2011). Understanding social networking and national security. *Joint Forces Quarterly*, *60*, 78.

Castells, M. (2007). Communication, power, and counter-power in the network society. *International Journal of Communication*, *1*, 238–266.

Cetron, M., & Davies, O. (2008). *Fifty five trends now shaping the future*. Washingon, DC: Proteus USA. Retrieved from http://www.carlisle.army.mil/proteus/docs/55-future.pdf

Christakis, N., & Fower, J. (2009). *Connected: The surprising power of our social networks and how they shape our lives*. New York, NY: Little, Brown, and Company.

Clawson, J. (2009). *Level three leadership*. Upper Saddle River, NJ: Pearson.

Council, C. I. O. (2009). *Guidelines for secure use of social media by federal departments and agencies*. Washington, DC: Federal CIO Council ISIMC NISSC Web 2.0 Secuirty Working Group. Retrieved from http://www.cio.gov/Documents/Guidelines_for_Secure_Use_Social_Media_v01-0.pdf

Defense Science Board/DSB. (2009). *Understanding human dynamics*. Washington, DC: Office of the Undersecretary of Defense for Acquisition, Technology, and Logistics.

Drapeau, M., & Wells, L. (2009). *Social software and security: An initial net assessment*. Washington, DC: National Defense University. Retrieved from http://www.dtic.mil/cgi-bin/GetTRDoc?AD=ADA497525

Federal, C. I. O. Council. (2009). *Guidelines for the secure use of social media by federal departments and agencies*. Retrieved from http://www.cio.gov/Documents/Guidelines_for_Secure_Use_Social_Media_v01-0.pdf

Floyd, P. (2010). *Social media and the U.S. military*. Interview with Neal Conan, National Public Radio, March 16, 2010.

Ford, C. (2011). Twitter, Facebook, and ten red balloons. *Homeland Security Affairs*, 7, 1–7.

Ghoring, N. (2010, March 1). U.S Defense Department Oks social networking. *PC World*.

Hodge, N. (2010, March 1). Will the Pentagon finally get Web 2.0? *Wired*. Retrieved from http://www.wired.com/dangerroom/2010/03/will-the-pentagon-finally-get-web-20/

Joint Chiefs of Staff/JCS. (2005). *Public affairs*. Joint publication 3-61. Retrieved from http://www.fas.org/irp/doddir/dod/jp3_61.pdf

Keeton, P., & McCann. (2005). Information operations, STRATCOM, and public affairs. *Military Review*, (November-December): 83–86.

Kraidy, M., & Mourad, S. (2010). Hypermedia space and global communication studies lessons from the Middle East. *Global Media Journal*, 9, 1–19.

Latar, M., Asmolov, G., & Gekker, A. (2010). *State cyber security*. A working paper in preparation for Herzliya Conference 2010. Lauder School of Government, Diplomacy, and Strategy. Retrieved from http://www.herzliyaconference.org/_Uploads/3035Newmediafinal.pdf

Lord, C. (2006). *Losing hearts and minds*. Westport, CT: Greenwood.

Mayfield, T. (2011). A commander's strategy for social media. *Joint Forces Quarterly*, 60, 79–83.

Miles, D. (2010). *New policy authorizes social media access, with caveats*. American Forces Press Services.

Office of the Chief of Public Affairs/OCPA. (2011). *U.S. Army social media handbook*. Washington, DC: Pentagon. Retrieved from http://www.carlisle.army.mil/dime/documents/Army%20Social%20MediaHandbook_Jan2011.pdf

Paul, C. (2011). *Strategic communication: Origins, concepts, and current debates*. Santa Barbara, CA: Praeger.

Perry, C. (2010). Social media and the Army. *Military Review*, (March-April): 63–67.

Sauerbier, R. (2010). Social networking. In Grant, A., & Meadows, J. (Eds.), *Communication technology update and fundamentals* (12th ed., pp. 292–304). New York, NY: Elesevier. doi:10.1016/B978-0-240-81475-9.50020-7

Scott, D. (2010). *The new rules of marketing and PR*. Hoboken, NJ: John Wiley and Sons.

Shachtman, N. (2009, July 30). Military may ban Twitter, Facebook as security "headaches." *Wired*.

Shirky, C. (2008). *Here comes everybody*. New York, NY: Penguin Books.

Shirky, C. (2010). *Cognitive surplus*. New York, NY: Penguin Books.

Shirky, C. (2011). The political power of social media. *Foreign Affairs (Council on Foreign Relations)*, *90*, 28–41.

Van Dijk, J. (2006). *Network society*. London, UK: Sage.

Vogelstein, F. (2007, October). Saving Facebook. *Wired*, 188-193.

Section 3
Web 2.0 and the Potential for Transformation

Transformation refers to the ability of public administrators and policy decision makers to align policy actions with citizen expectations and preferences. Given the offerings of Web 2.0 technology, the mechanisms that government traditionally uses to engage citizens can be substantially revised with new, Web-based techniques to facilitate a more dynamic exchange. Such changes in outreach strategies present a number of implementation considerations and can potentially alter the relationship between government and citizens. In many cases, public managers and policy decision makers enter a virtually unexplored territory. These chapters address some of the unknowns, role changes, and potential for redefining how government can relate to its citizens with the aim of aligning policy actions with citizen preferences.

Chapter 11
Web 2.0 Technologies and Authentic Public Participation:
Engaging Citizens in Decision Making Processes

Colleen Casey
University of Texas at Arlington, USA

Jianling Li
University of Texas at Arlington, USA

ABSTRACT

In this chapter, the authors evaluate the use of Web 2.0 technology to engage citizens in the transportation decision making process. They evaluate the potential of Web 2.0 technology to create effective participatory environments to enable authentic participation; provide an inventory of the current tools and technologies utilized, identify barriers faced by administrators in the implementation of these tools, and summarize universal lessons for public administrators. Based on a review of 40 cases of collaborations, the authors find that Web 2.0 technology is predominantly used as a complement rather than a substitute for traditional approaches. Furthermore, the review suggests that the full potential of Web 2.0 remains untapped, and additional tools and technologies can be utilized to overcome barriers to implementation.

DOI: 10.4018/978-1-4666-0318-9.ch011

INTRODUCTION

The objective of the chapter is to answer the following questions: What barriers are reported to *authentic* citizen participation? What is the *potential* of Web 2.0 technology to address the barriers to authentic participation? How are they currently used to *reduce the barriers* to authentic participation? And, what untapped potential exists?

We first consider the conditions of authentic participation. King, Feltey and Susel (2008) provide a critique of public participation, arguing that effective participation is participation that is sought early, often and ongoing and utilized at multiple phases of the decision-making process. When authentic participation exists, more effective and efficient decision-making can occur. The ideals of authentic participation resonate with the philosophy of Web 2.0 technology—to use Internet enabled tools to foster interaction and deliberation between multiple stakeholders. In addition to fostering more effective participatory processes, there is some evidence that the use of Web 2.0 technology has the potential to reduce the costs of citizen participation in the long run. For example, in 2009, the U.S. General Services Administration (GSA) recognized the Centers for Disease Control (CDC) for saving taxpayers $6 million dollars by consolidating several toll-free numbers into a single line and using a mobile version of its website, podcasts, videos and a MySpace page to promote the new toll-free number (GSA, 2009c).

Despite the potential of Web 2.0 technology, more remains to be known as to how it is used to enhance citizen participation. In this chapter, we evaluate the use of Web 2.0 technologies to foster authentic participation, focusing on the creation of effective participatory environments. To accomplish this, we define the components of effective participatory environments, identify actions administrators can take to achieve it, and evaluate the internet-enabled information and communication technologies (ICTs) administra-tors use to take action. We apply the criteria to 40 cases of collaboration in the transportation and public health communities, both of which have been targeted by federal legislation to engage in collaboration and engage citizens in the decision-making process. Using these cases, we identify a set of recommendations and generalizations applicable to administrators in a wide variety of organizational contexts.

Overall, we find that internet-enabled tools are rarely used alone, but rather they are used to complement the use of traditional tools and technologies such as face-to-face meetings, community events and small group workshops. The most comprehensive use of Web 2.0 technologies was found in the design of particular systems to enable flexibility in project decision-making between key stakeholders. However, while these have the potential to include citizen participation, gaps and barriers remain. We conclude the chapter with a set of lessons for administrators on how to create a set of tools and technologies to facilitate effective participatory environments.

AUTHENTIC PARTICIPATION AND WEB 2.0 TECHNOLOGIES

Authentic Participation and Effective Participatory Environments

Prior to a discussion of authentic citizen participation and an analysis of the potential of various tools to foster such conditions, it is necessary to define the word "authentic". We borrow the definition provided by King, Feltey and Susel (2008) and define authentic participation as "deep and continuous involvement in administrative processes with the potential for all involved to have an effect on the situation" (p. 388), and includes public engagement from the very beginning stage of issue framing and identification to the very end stage of decision-making.

Today citizens are involved in all stages of policy making, from analysis, initiation, formulation, implementation, and evaluation (Roberts, 2004, as cited in D'Agostino 2009). However, the mere engagement of citizens in government does not guarantee that participation is authentic. As D'Agostino (2009) summarized, "even though public participation is commonly accepted as part of public administration—and deliberative models that encourage collaboration have already been developed—there nonetheless remain some gray areas in the implementation of such models" (p. 660). Furthermore, debates continue over the potential of participation to enhance decision-making or to create additional burdens on the administrative state.

Supporters advocate for enhanced public involvement as a way to bridge traditional models of public administration (King et al., 2008) and furthermore see the decision-making process as inherently incomplete without the inclusion of citizen input. A major advantage of citizen participation for administrators includes an enlightened and educated citizenry, which can foster more effective and efficient implementation of policies and programs. As Irvin and Stansbury (2004) argued, active and engaged citizens are better able to understand policies and administrators are more aware of their concerns and interests, making it easier for the implementation of many policies.

Opponents on the other hand, see the engagement of citizens in the process as creating additional burdens on the administrative state, including additional red tape, greater delays, and in turn, reduced efficiency of government (Kettering Foundation, 1989, as cited in King et. al, 2008). Concerns include a need for time and money to inform citizens and even get their approval on policies and decisions before they are implemented. Also, by seeking citizen approval, if there is much opposition, this can slow down the process and even allow for poor decisions to be made.

One way to mitigate the concerns expressed by opponents of citizen participation is to ensure the conditions for an environment of effective participation exist. Even many proponents would argue that unauthentic participation provides little benefit to any governmental agency or organization. Conditions of an *effective participatory environment* include an empowered and educated citizenry, educated and trained administrators, and enabling administrative structures and processes.

Together these three conditions produce an environment conducive to more effective decision-making, as depicted in Figure 1. For example, administrators can engage in outreach to empower and educate citizens; however, if they do not utilize citizen participation to better understand key issues and potential solutions, the benefits of a participatory environment are not realized. Likewise, if administrators do desire to obtain citizen input on key issues, but the structures and processes do not enable learning, the result may be less than optimal.

Components of Effective Participatory Environments

Empowered and Educated Citizenry

The first condition of an effective participatory environment is an educated and empowered citizenry. Callahan and Yang (2007) found that individual citizens often lack expertise and feel powerless when facing bureaucratic regulations and government hierarchies. This in turn, can further fears of administrators that responding to individual citizens may decrease agency effectiveness, and hence administrators resort to achieving only citizen *buy-in*. Many administrators think that they are "best suited to make policy decisions for the community" (Stewart, 2007, p. 1068) because they are more knowledgeable of broad issues, have access to more information that help them make more informed decisions than regular participatory citizens, and because they serve full or part

Figure 1. Conditions necessary for effective participatory environments

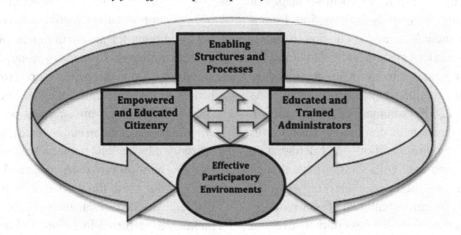

time in government positions, have the time to devote their attention to the difficult questions that community issues raise.

However, when citizens are educated, informed and empowered to participate, agency decision-making can be enhanced. Irvin and Stansbury (2004) found that educated, informed citizens are more capable of understanding policies, which not only aids the deliberation process but also eases the implementation process. As Innes and Booher (1999) argued, as citizens become more informed and engaged, and as this capital grows and spreads, the civic capacity of a society grows, and participants become more knowledgeable and believe more in their ability to make a difference. This capacity has the potential to create a more flexible, adaptive society, more welcoming or tolerant of change and more competent to address difficult, controversial issues.

Educated and Trained Administrators

In effective participatory environments, education and empowerment is a two-way street. It is equally important to have administrators that are educated about citizens needs, wants and the issues they face, as well as administrators that are empowered with the skills necessary to facilitate participatory efforts. Irvin and Stansbury (2004)

found that when government representatives were educated about citizen interests and concerns, the potential for the enactment of highly controversial policies were reduced or prevented, in turn, simplifying the implementation process.

However, a precursor to educating administrators is to ensure trust exists between administrators and citizens. If administrators do not establish trust with citizens, it can have a negative effect on participation, and in many cases, it can lead to biased information. First, a lack of trust of government can result in a lack of overall participation or participation by only a select few. Second, if administrators do not trust in the ability of citizens to effectively inform decision-making, administrators may be reluctant to engage citizens in the process, leading to either reduced opportunities to participate or limiting citizen participation to the later phases of decision-making (Lowndes, Pratchett, & Stoker, 2001).

Thus, to achieve the second condition, administrators must work to build and maintain trust with citizens, as well proactively take action against those forces that seek to destroy trust. A primary way to accomplish this is through open and transparent communication between citizens and administrators through a number of channels. Callahan and Yang (2007) found that local media can support or destroy efforts for citizen participation. Local media can play a positive role in citizen participation by reporting community problems, providing information, introducing participation opportunities and sometimes speaking on behalf of the public. However, the local media can also destroy trust particularly when they engage in government bashing. Likewise, relationships with community-based groups, private organizations and nonprofit organizations can be important catalysts for building trust and seeking input from citizens (Callahan & Yang, 2007; D'Agostino, 2009; Dekker, Volker, & Lelievelet, 2010; LeRoux, 2009). Not only does a negative relationship destroy trust, but it can also make administrators withdraw from opportunities to engage citizens in the process.

Enabling Structures and Processes

Finally, in order to make participation work, there is a need for administrative structures and processes that enable the process, rather than encumber the process. Administrative structures and processes are the formal and informal elements of organizations that can influence its rigidity or flexibility. For example, Innes and Booher (2004) attacked commonly used

structures such as public hearings that offer citizens one-shot to provide input on a particular decision. Rather, they argued there is a need for structures that promote collaborative participation at multiple stages of the process and utilize a variety of processes and mechanisms to interact with citizens. Structures and processes that are too rigid can prevent opportunities for adjusting project directions based on new evidence and knowledge provided by citizens, leading to meaningless and inefficient participation.

ADMINISTRATOR ACTIONS AND TOOLS TO CREATE THE ENVIRONMENT

The purpose of creating the conditions for an educated and empowered citizenry is to ensure that citizens have the opportunity to participate, understand how to participate, understand the value of participation, to ensure that citizens have timely and accurate knowledge and more generally build relationships among citizens. Specific actions that administrators can take to achieve this condition include: Workshops with citizens where administrators, experts and citizens are brought together to discuss issues; training sessions with citizens and community-based organizations to explain current project plans; provide opportunities for community members to gather and interact with each other; identify and recruit citizens to participate; and establish personal relationships with citizens and community-based groups (King, Feltey, & Susel, 2008).

In the second condition, while communication and outreach to a wide diverse group of citizens is important, even more important is that administrators engage in dialogue and deliberation with citizens and other relevant agencies or organizations. Educated administrators are those that are not only aware of the issues facing citizens, but those that are prepared and trained to facilitate the relationships necessary to work with citizens to identify potential responses. To accomplish this, administrators must take actions to interact with citizens and establish relationships; ensure that projects and opportunities to participate, as well as project updates, are advertised and accessible to a wide variety of groups; and be prepared to serve as a facilitator. Serving as a facilitator requires a broad set of skills including team-building, organizational development, interpersonal communication and discourse skills.

Finally, there are a number of actions administrators can take to enable administrative structures and processes. Actions include the following:

Figure 2. ICT components and administrator and citizen interactions

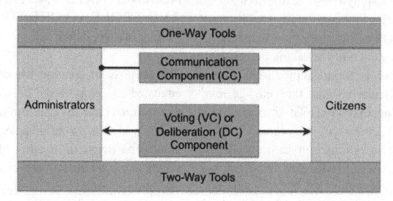

redesign current decision-making processes to bring citizens into the process early; seek citizen input at multiple points in the process; reorganize or allocate staff to serve as key contacts and liaisons; and adopt systems and tools that enable citizen input to be incorporated and shared with key project partners throughout the process. To meet the needs of a diverse citizenry, it is important to hold small group meetings or forums, encourage greater interaction between administrators and citizens in a personal manner, hold roundtable discussions and utilize outside, neutral facilitators to create a more level playing field and ensure group participation is not biased. Flexibility in location, access and modes of communication is important as well.

Tools and Technologies to Take Action

Administrators use different types of information and communication tools (ICTs) to interact with citizens. ICTs can be delivered through traditional methods or via the Internet. Kumar and Vragov (2009, p. 119) classified ICTs along the components they contain, communication, deliberation and voting. As depicted in Figure 2, these components can be further classified based on their ability to foster interactions between administrators and citizens.

ICTs can be classified based on their ability to enable one-way or two-way forms of communication.

Communication Component (CC)

Citizens are informed about policies. This is essentially a one-way dissemination of information and in traditional contexts mechanisms include TV, radio, newspapers, printed materials. Internet enabled ICTs include traditional and digitized information on the government or agency's web site, e-mail distribution lists, recorded audio and video.

Deliberation Component (DC)

Citizens can identify and deliberate on issues of importance. This component involves ICT tools that support two-way communication and deliberation. Traditional methods include telephone, fax, face-to-face meetings and town hall meetings. Internet enabled technologies include traditional plus feedback forms such as chat tools, interactive discussion boards, virtual worlds, electronic petitions and blogs.

Voting Component (VC)

Citizens make collective decisions on various issues. Traditional mechanisms include paper-based

Figure 3. Relationship between effective participatory environments and information and communication tools (ICTs)

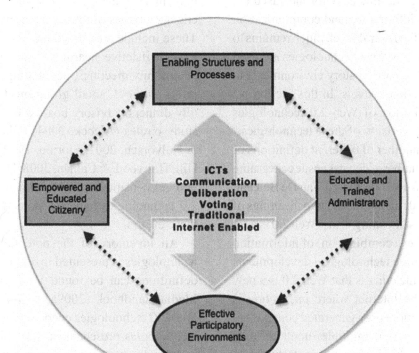

ballots and electronic voting systems designed for physical polling booths. Internet enabled technologies include traditional plus online or electronic voting systems.

The use of ICTs with varying components can foster the conditions for effective participatory environments. For example, ICTs with communicative components can educate and empower residents—administrators can provide information to residents and communicate timely and important information. ICTs with deliberative and voting components can help to educate administrators on citizen's perspectives, needs and concerns. Flexible structures and processes are necessary to maximize the potential of ICTs with communicative and deliberative components, to ensure the information exchanged influences decision-making. Figure 3 presents the relation-ship between ICTs and the actions administrators can take to achieve these conditions.

The Potential of Web 2.0 Technologies

Web 2.0 technologies have the potential to facilitate the creation of effective participatory environments and mitigate the second concern of opponents, and enhance the efficiency of citizen participation efforts. As noted by the GSA, Web 2.0 technologies can lead to agency savings, as evidenced by the CDC example, as well as make it easier for citizens to get information and services. For example, in 2008, the Social Security Administration (SSA) made dramatic improvements to its online filing system, iClaim, reducing processing time as well as providing a number of internet enabled tools to educate citizens on the process, including videos and podcasts (GSA, 2009c). However, despite calls for increased usage of Web 2.0 information and communication technologies at the federal level, much remains to be known as to how these technologies are used to create effective participatory environments at the local and regional levels. In this section we review the definition of Web 2.0 technologies and provide an overview of these technologies.

There are a number of different definitions of Web 2.0, and a number of debates ensue concerning whether or not Web 2.0 is "new". Van De Belt and colleagues (2010) distinguished two meanings of Web 2.0. The first meaning is that Web 2.0 is a set or "mashing" (i.e. a combination) of information and communication technological developments and the second meaning is that Web 2.0 is a new generation of the Internet where *interaction* is important, with more user-generated content that empowers people and multiple, nontraditional stakeholders. In this interpretation, technology, or the mashing of different technologies, are only tools, and the idea or philosophy of Web 2.0 is more than the technology—at its core is the creation of systems, conditions and processes that foster greater participation and collaboration. In this chapter, we adopt a definition of Web 2.0 as stated in the GSA's social media policy (2009b) that treats "social media" and "Web 2.0" as umbrella terms that encompass the various activities that integrate technology, social interaction, and content creation, or more simply, a collection of Web tools that facilitate collaboration and information sharing.

The technology used to achieve the ideas of Web 2.0 is not necessarily new, because technically, a number of the tools draw upon old techniques. However, what distinguishes Web 2.0 is the reliance upon multiple users, and the ability to foster *collaboration and information sharing* between users. Web 1.0 was mostly unidirectional, whereas Web 2.0 allows the user to add information or content to the Web, thus creating interaction, collaboration and information sharing.

Administrators use a wide array of traditional, non-Internet enabled tools and techniques to engage citizens in the decision-making process. These include area based meetings, public hearings, legislative hearings, town-hall meetings, community meetings, negotiating tables, citizen juries, surveys, small group meetings, community dinners, advisory boards, focus groups and study circles (Alcock, 2004; Baker, 2005; Carr & Halvorsen, 2001; Florino, 1990; Gooberman-Hill, Horwood, & Calnan, 2008; Heikkila & Isett, 2007; Luensmeyer, 2004; Plough, 1987). Web 2.0 technologies have the potential to enhance these efforts.

An inventory of the potential of Web 2.0 technologies is presented in Table 1 and detailed definitions can be found in the GSA's Social Media Handbook (2009a, p. 3-4). While most Web 2.0 technologies encourage interaction, the technologies presented in the table range from highly interactive tools that can replicate face-to-face interactions or group meetings that can be classified as fostering or enhancing deliberation to modes that facilitate basic information or communication exchange.

For example, social bookmarking, podcasts, RSS feeds, and widgets provide opportunities for administrators to share relevant information with citizens. *Social bookmarking* is a web-based service where users create and store links that can be stored in a publicly available online account. A *podcast* is a way of publishing MP3 audio files on the web so they can be downloaded onto computers or portable listening devices. Podcasts allow users to subscribe to a feed of new audio files using software that automatically checks for and downloads new audio files. A *RSS feed* is a web content format that when used with an RSS aggregator, alerts users to new or important content on a website. RSS feeds enable administrators to proactively push out timely and relevant information directly to citizens, rather than passively assuming they will find the relevant information and updates through conventional methods of

Table 1. Web 2.0 technologies and potential

Technology	Potential
Blogs	Provide information to new audiences; puts human face on government using an informal tone; opens public conversation; surface and solve issues
Wikis	Workgroup or public collaboration for project management, knowledge sharing, public input, contributions to third party sites
Video Sharing and Multimedia	Public outreach, education, training, other communication for "connected" and on-line audiences; how-to videos and audios to improve service and achieve mission; training and education of staff and administrators
Photo-Sharing	Cost savings potential; attract new audiences; issue awareness
Podcasting	Another tool to disseminate information; build trust with conversational voice; use for project updates; live deliberations; emergencies; how-to messages
Virtual Worlds	Public outreach; virtual town halls; education; training; ability to bring people together worldwide for meetings, lectures, etc.
Social Networking	Intranet use to cross internal stovepipes; cross government coordination; create public communities; viral impact; knowledge management; recruitment; event announcements
Syndicated Web Feeds	Expand reach; pull content together across government; authoritative source; reduce duplication and keep people up-to-date on project developments
Mashups	Expand government reach; provide service; integrate external data; make content available to others that use mashups; foster deliberation and issue identification
Widgets, Gadgets, Pipes	Increase awareness of what is happening in government or agencies; bring content and key information to the user's home page
Social Bookmark & News	Increase the popularity and use of particular governmental web sites; information; and services.
Micro-blogging, Presence Networks	Seek input; broadcast messages; emergencies; news; announcements; real time reporting.

Adopted from Goodwin (2008).

browsing or Internet searches. *Widgets, pipes and gadgets* are interactive tools with single-purpose services such as displaying the latest news and weather, construction updates, health alerts or a map program.

Blogs, micro-blogs, videosharing, photosharing, mashups, social networking sites, wikis, and virtual worlds are tools that administrators can use to foster deliberation. A *blog* is a web-based forum with regular entries of commentary, descriptions of events or other materials. The blog host posts materials on the website and others may provide comments. Administrators of blogs can elect to moderate the posts, maintaining greater control of content, or may allow any material to be posted. A *micro-blog* is an extremely short blog posting, very similar to text messaging. Again, the host can moderate these or allow any material to be

posted. A *mashup* is a web-based presentation of information that combines data and/or functionality from multiple sources. For example, a Google map showing average housing prices drawn from a city assessor's online database. *Photo sharing* and *video sharing* allow users to post and share digital photos or videos on web sites and often include options to allow others to comment on photos or allow meta-data to be attached to the photos. *Social networking* services are Internet enabled tools that can connect people who share the same interests and/or activities and who are interested in exploring the interests and activities of others. A *wiki* is a collection of web pages that encourages users to contribute or modify the content. Wikis use a simple web interface, which enables a community to collaborate on developing a document or web page, no matter where they are located. *Virtual worlds* are imagined places where users can socialize, deliberate and create using voice and text chat.

Web 2.0 technologies can be used to create deliberation opportunities between citizens and administrators in a virtual world environment; or through the use of social networking tools, blogs and wikis, citizens can share their concerns. Furthermore, in areas where there is a history of distrust between agencies and citizens, administrators may need to restore trust and keep citizens informed at all stages of the process and may need to consider Internet-enabled communication tools such as RSS feeds, widgets, pipes and gadgets. These can be used to alert citizens when key project decisions are on the horizon, update citizens on the status of key projects, and share with them how public input has influenced project development. However, despite the potential for deliberation technologies, Kumar and Vragov (2009) found that, in general, most governments rely most heavily upon internet-enabled technologies to disseminate information rather than technologies that foster deliberation.

APPLICATION OF WEB 2.0 TECHNOLOGY IN CREATING SUPPORTIVE CONDITIONS FOR AUTHENTIC PARTICIPATION

In this particular chapter, we consider how the transportation and public health communities have utilized Web 2.0 technology to create effective participatory environments towards the goal of building healthier communities. To answer our research questions, we identified 40 published transportation cases between 1998-2010 from multiple sources including peer-reviewed journal articles, project and case study reports and other professional reports that discussed the involvement or engagement of citizens in the decision making process. Given the history of federal legislation geared towards enhancing citizen par-

ticipation in the transportation planning process, a review of transportation cases will not only provide insight on the tools and technologies currently in use for transportation projects, but will also yield a set of valuable recommendations for other administrators, particularly those in agencies or organizations that to a lesser extent have faced legislative demands to engage citizens in the decision-making process.

The Case of Public Health and Transportation Decision Making

Historically, transportation choices have been made inside of policy silos, isolating decision-making from commuting patterns to decisions concerning how we live (Swanstrom, 2009), and have often relied upon top-down, expert driven processes. However, since the passage of the National Environmental Policy Act (NEPA) of 1969 and the subsequent major transportation and environmental legislation, much attention has been given to the broader environmental impacts of transportation planning and infrastructure development. There have been guidelines on processes, procedures, methods, and best practices to assist state Department of Transportation (DOTs) and Metropolitan Planning Organizations (MPOs) to consider environmental factors in transportation planning and to meet the NEPA conformity requirements.

However, despite greater attention to environmental factors, often discussions about the health impacts of transportation decisions on citizens are neglected. Most environmental factors have been limited to the impacts of transportation on air and water quality, noise, wildlife, wetland, and social equities. As Corburn and Bhatia (2007) argued, although NEPA directed the Council on Environmental Quality (CEQ) to issue guidance for analyzing environmental impacts and to consider human health impacts, no federal agency detailed guidance has been issued for human health analyses within environmental impact analyses nor are there specific methods or processes specified. The effects of which have led to what they call a fairly 'nonresponsive process' that reflects a decide-announce-defend model driven by expert agencies (Corburn & Bhatia, 2007).

Expert-based decisions disconnected from the local contexts and those impacted by the decisions may inhibit the ability to achieve the broader goals of building healthier, more livable communities. As Swanstrom (2009) stated,

The goal of making transportation more efficient is not to move people faster and farther but to give them wider access to all the things that are necessary for a good life: jobs, education, family, friends, recreation, culture, etc. ...But for it to happen requires a more democratic decision-making process in which all community stakeholders have input (p. 103).

In this chapter we review the Web 2.0 technologies used in transportation cases to foster deliberation between citizens, transportation planners and health care administrators, and offer transferrable recommendations to administrators.

The criteria for case selection included, (a) a case of a successful collaboration among multiple agencies in the transportation and public health communities and (b) citizens were engaged at some point of the process. The nature of the cases range from large-scale, motorized transportation projects, such as highway or bridge construction or planning, to nonmotorized projects such as trail and walkable transportation projects or plans. The cases were inventoried based on the actions administrators took and the tools and technologies employed to create effective participatory environments. For example, if a tool or technique was used to educate residents about governmental processes we categorized this as taking action to create an educated and empowered citizenry. We then inventoried the tools and technologies used to achieve the action. We used the model established by Kumar and Vragov (2009) and

classified the ICTs used along the dimensions of one-way (communicative) and two-way components (deliberative or voting) and traditional or Internet enabled.

In Table 2, we provide a summary of the communication and deliberation capacity of Web 2.0 technologies that have the potential to be utilized to achieve effective participatory environments. Table 3 presents a summary count of the cases utilizing one-way and two-way tools by technological capacity, traditional or Internet enabled. Table 4 is an inventory of the specific Internet-enabled tools used in the cases. Overall, our findings support Kumar and Vragov (2009)-- very few Web 2.0 technologies with deliberative or two-way communication components were employed alone. Rather Internet enabled tools were more commonly used *in conjunction with* traditional methods, *after* citizens are initially engaged, and as part of a deliberative process in a traditional setting. In the section that follows, we highlight key examples found in the cases.

Empowered and Educated Citizenry

In the case of public health and transportation, empowering and educating citizens on the interconnectedness between transportation decisions and health outcomes is a priority. In the review of cases, administrators and planners largely rely upon a combination of traditional and Internet bases ICTs with communication components to empower and educate citizens. As summarized in Table 3, in 39 of the 40 cases, some traditional form of one-way communication was utilized and in 17 cases traditional forms were only utilized to disseminate information. In 22 cases, Internet enabled technologies were used to disseminate information, complementing traditional approaches. Particularly in cases where a lack of participation existed, Internet enabled tools such as email listserves and electronic newsletters were only used after initial face-to-face gatherings. Web sites and list serves were utilized to post the proceedings

Table 2. Web 2.0 technology: Potential mix to ensure one-way and two-way communication

Web 2.0 Technology	One Way	Two Way	Used in Cases
Blogs	X	X	X
Wikis	X	X	
Video Sharing and Multimedia	X		X
Photo-Sharing	X		X
Podcasting	X		
Virtual Worlds	X	X	
Social Networking Sites	X	X	
Syndicated Web Feeds	X		
Mashups	X	X	X
Widgets, Gadgets, Pipes	X		
Social Bookmark & News	X		
Micro-blogging, Presence Networks	X	X	

from previous meetings as well as keep citizens up-to-date and informed on project progress.

There are a few notable cases were deliberative Internet enabled components were utilized to build community and relationships around particular interests or issues. For example, in an effort to encourage active transportation in Seattle, project blogs were used as part of a strategy to spur communication and deliberation among health care providers and administrators, the public, transportation planners and other officials around the issue of community walkability. In the case of an environmental assessment in Colorado, a geographic information systems (GIS) tool was converted into a web-based map called Geo-Map. The interactive tool combined multiple data sources and allowed users to review data and then provide comments that were made available to all participating users for comments and response (TRB, 2010a). Through the use of these tools, issues related to transportation and health were shared among multiple agencies and citizens and contributing to the building of a community interested in the intersection between health and transportation.

The Wasatch Front Regional Council (WFRC) engaged citizens in an 18 month visioning process to discuss transportation and environmental concerns related to growth (TRB, 2010c). A web site was created to educate and empower residents, which provided information about the council, its contacts, activities, projects, schedule and ac-

Table 3. Summary of one-way and two-way tools by technological capacity

	One-Way Tools		Two-Way Tools	
	Traditional	Internet Enabled	Traditional	Internet Enabled
Count of Cases Utilizing Traditional and Internet Enabled	39	22	31	13
Count of Cases Utilizing Only Internet Enabled Tools	--	0	--	1
Count of Cases Utilizing Only Traditional Tools	17	--	18	--

Table 4. Internet enabled ICTs utilized to achieve authentic participation in cases

Conditions	Actions Taken	Internet Enabled ICTs Utilized		
		Communication	Deliberation	Voting
Empowering and Educating Citizens	►One-on-one meetings ►Small group sessions ►Community gathering events ►Education and training workshops ►Partnering with community-based groups	►Listserves ►Email ►Web sites ►Electronic newsletters ►Photo sharing	►Blogs ►Mashups	
Educating Administrators	►Citizen recruitment ►Utilization of local media ►Visioning workshops ►Open house Meetings ►Administrator training	►Web sites	►Blogs ►Mashups Ex. MetroQuest Metroscope	►Electronic Polling
Enabling Administrative Systems and Processes	►Variable meeting arrangements ►Flexible project review processes ►Designated project personnel	►Listserves ►Email ►Web sites	►Blogs ►MashUps Ex: ProjectSolve2 CMART	

complishments, and other general organizational information. The WFRC website served as the public calendar, announcement board, contact sheet, and document repository. It also provided links to partner organizations, and other web resources and makes public project documents digitally available. The use of this tool allowed citizens to express concerns they had concerning growth and enabled health care administrators to educate citizens and planners of potential health impacts of growth.

In the case of the Eastern Neighborhoods Community Health Impact Assessment (ENCHIA), the San Francisco Health Department (SFHD), in conjunction with citizens and community-based groups, developed an internet-enabled Healthy Development Measurement Tool (HDMT) and trained citizens to utilize it to identify health concerns (Corburn & Bhatia, 2007). The tool, best described as a mashup, integrates multiple data sources to make neighborhood-level data available to citizens on a wide variety of indicators such as housing, socioeconomic and demographic, health outcomes and safety. Citizens can utilize the tool to learn more about the health of their neighborhood.

In another case in Colorado, citizens had little information or knowledge on technical aspects related to a highway projects. As part of the project, a decision had to be made concerning the selection of a retaining wall, a subject the citizens knew little about. In order to educate citizens on potential options, photos and video sharing tools were utilized to relay engineering issues and concerns to the citizens. Communication methods included visual simulation, both computerized and artist renderings, as well as displays of alternatives for retaining wall textures and designs. A participant summarized the effectiveness of the effort, "Using high-quality graphics, mostly aerial imagery with overlays, they brought engineering to the public" (TRB, 2010f, p. 8).

Educated and Trained Administrators

Another component of an effective participatory environment is educated administrators, which results as a function of intense outreach, the development of trust and opportunities for deliberation, calling for the utilization of ICTs with two-way communicative capacity, those with both communicative and deliberative functions. Overall, traditional tools such as workshops and meetings were more predominant in the cases, and

Internet-enabled tools when used in most cases were combined with traditional tools. As indicated in Table 3, in 31 of the cases traditional two-way tools were utilized and 14 utilized Internet enabled two-way tools. Although traditional two-way tools alone were utilized in 18 cases, Internet enabled two-way tools were only used alone in one case.

In a number of cases, emails, list serves and web sites were used to keep citizens up-to-date on project progress as well as announce any additional information or opportunities for participation. For example, in a highway expansion project in Colorado, a website was established for public input on a feasibility study that was conducted (TRB, 2010f). The project team gathered information on every aspect of potential impact, and themes of public concern were distinguished early in the process. Finally, blogs were commonly used in a number of cases to raise points or solicit feedback on particular issues or concerns.

In Oregon, the Oregon Department of Transportation (ODOT) held meetings in workshop format, going beyond the traditional open house meeting style to facilitate participation in an environmental assessment plan (TRB, 2010l). At these meetings, small groups worked together to discuss issues using maps and Post-it notes enabling the public to work through the issues collaboratively and record their ideas at different points in the process. To complement these efforts, ODOT also used an interactive project-specific web based forum, to provide opportunities for ongoing information exchange among stakeholders following the workshop. Specifically, ODOT asked interested persons to provide input on the problem statement, alternative evaluation criteria, the range of alternatives to be considered, the alternatives that should be forwarded for detailed analysis in the environmental assessment and the preliminary analysis of environmental effects of project alternatives.

Mashups were often used to facilitate deliberation. For example, in a town hall meeting in Idaho, a mashup was combined with a tool that enabled voting. The voting component allows residents to express their opinion without feeling pressure from others in the group. It was noted, "the department used town hall polling, mapping, and dynamic real-time scenario planning of alternative investment patterns to help participants visualize the different possibilities for Idaho's future" (TRB, 2010i, p.1). By utilizing MetroQuest, workshop facilitators were able to create on-the-fly scenarios for discussion. MetroQuest has the potential to be utilized in face-to-face workshop settings, on the web, or on kiosks distributed in public places. The benefit of the tool is that it enabled participants to quickly play out and score alternatives on a wide range of priority areas and through an iterative process, participants honed in on a preferred scenario that best met their collective priorities. A representative responsible for facilitating the process stated,

I can't imagine the process having gone even 50 percent of where it went without those tools. There were a lot of tools that were used: town hall polling allowed people to be citizens, to vote differently and anonymously. Scenario planning allows you to have insight and make connections between policy implementation, needs, priorities, from as wide an array of issues as you could ever imagine" (TRB, 2010i, p. 14).

Mashups were used in another case to discuss concerns and issues related to growth and congestion. A decision support tool, Metroscope, enabled facilitators to model changes in measures of economic, demographic, land use and transportation activity and testing a wide range of policy scenarios with workshop participants (National Policy Consensus Center, 2003g). The tool comprises four models (economic, travel and two real estate models) and combines a set of geographic information system (GIS) tools that keep track of the location of development activities and produce visual representations. In Utah, the Wasatch Front Regional Council (WFRC) combined GIS tools, urban simulations and travel demand models to facilitate deliberation and present different scenarios and uncover citizen concerns. The value noted in these tools overall is that it enables a much richer public discourse and dialogue as it allows citizens and administrators to see the potential effects of different scenarios as well as revealing concerns and issues not previously identified.

Enabling Structures and Processes

Creating enabling administrative structures and processes is the final component of effective participatory environments. Internet enabled tools used to enable administrative environments included blogs, listserves, web sites and mashups. Most notable was the use of Internet-enabled decision software to enhance process flexibility. Traditional tools included flexible meeting venues, offering daycare services, extensive outreach into the community and neighborhoods and to employers. In the cases reviewed, 29 exhibited some degree of structure or process flexibility and 11 maintained traditional forms of structure and process. In Tables 5 and 6, we present an inventory of all of the cases reviewed classified into those that adopted enabling structures or processes and those that resembled more traditional administrative structures and processes, The tables indicate evidence of the utilization of one-way and two-way tools and technologies and if traditional (T) or Internet enabled (I) tools were used.

Internet enabled tools were more often utilized in cases with flexible structures and processes than in cases without. As demonstrated in Table 5, one-way Internet enabled tools were utilized in 62 percent of the cases where flexible structures and processes were present. Compared to Table 6, cases with traditional processes and structures, one-way Internet enabled tools were only utilized in 36 percent of the cases. ICTs with two-way components were also more prevalent in cases that exhibited flexible structures and processes. Two-way Internet enabled tools were reported in

45 percent of the cases with flexible systems and processes compared to only 9 percent of the cases (one case) without flexible systems and processes.

There were several examples of how Internet enabled tools were utilized to enhance system and process flexibility. In Texas, a mashup with communication and deliberative components was developed and utilized by key stakeholders within collaborating organizations (TRB, 2010h). However, while the potential exists, the public cannot directly contribute information to the database at this time. Nonetheless, the adoption of this tool, ProjectSolve2, has been effective in allowing public feedback to be shared at multiple phases and enables administrators to enter public input into project reviews. When different parts of projects are posted and available, interested parties can request to be notified and they can submit comment and feedback. The functions of the application includes: GIS data set transfer and collection; deliberation through a message board; concurrence documentation; issues identification and tracking; project contacts database; significant meetings and public involvement events calendar; new information alerts; and related web links.

A similar tool and technology is employed in the Washington Puget Sound region to facilitate growth management planning (TRB, 2010m). The Comment Management Response Tool (CMART) is a web-based tool that has the ability to manage documents and comments and create a response and review chain, maintain response history, query comments/responses, track the status of "in process" responses, develop summary comments/responses for "like" comments, and produce the typical environmental impact statement side-by-side output report. Tools such as this not only provide the opportunity for immediate feedback and inclusion of feedback in real time, but also have the opportunity to foster a transparent decision-making process as citizens can see and track how their input is used in the process.

Table 5. Tools used in cases with enabling administrative structures and processes

	Cases	One-Way Tools		Two-Way Tools	
1	ENCHIA Marin County, CA	T	I		
2	Washington-Oregon Strategic Plan for I-5 Corridor: WA, OR	T	I	T	I
3	Bryan Park Interchange: Richmond, VA	T		T	
4	Utah 3500 South Partnering Agreement: UT	T		T	
5	Martin Luther King Jr. Boulevard Revitalization: Portland, OR	T		T	
6	Florida's Strategic Intermodal System: FL	T	I	T	
7	Sacramento Transportation and Air Quality Collaborative: CA	T	I	T	I
8	Transportation Vision: ID	T	I	T	I
9	Blueprint Project: Sacramento, CA	T		T	
10	Metropolitan Transportation Tomorrow Plan: Binghamton, NY	T		T	
11	Prairie Parkway Project: Northeastern IL	T		T	
12	I-69 Trans-Texas Corridor Study	T		T	I
13	Puget Sound Region TIP: WA	T	I	T	I
14	Woodrow Wilson Bridge: Greater Washington DC	T	I		
15	US-24: New Haven, IN to Defiance: OH	T	I	T	
16	I-5/Beltline interchange: Springfield-Eugene, OR	T	I	T	I
17	Regional Transportation Plan: Wasatch Front Region, UT	T	I	T	I
18	Regional Transportation Plan: Maricopa County, AZ	T	I	T	I
19	Colorado's STEP UP: Denver, CO	T	I	T	I
20	Get Active Orlando Partnership, Orlando, FL	T	I	T	I
21	Healthy Communities Initiative, Buffalo, NY	T	I	T	
22	Active Living Logan Square, Chicago, IL	T		T	
23	ACTIVE Louisville, Louisville, KY	T		T	
24	WALK Sacramento, Sacramento, CA	T	I	T	I
25	Active Seattle, Seattle, WA	T	I	T	I
26	Connecting Cleveland Communities Partnership, Cleveland OH	T		T	
27	US-285 Foxton Road to Bailey: Denver, CO	T	I	T	I
28	US-131 S-curve replacement: Grand Rapids, MI	T	I	T	
29	NJ-31 integrated land use and transportation plan: NJ	T		T	
Total Count		29	18	28	13
Percent of Cases		100	62	97	45

T=Traditional I=Internet enabled

Table 6. Tools used in cases with traditional administrative structures and processes

	Cases	One-Way Tools		Two-Way Tools	
1	Active Transportation Plan: Kirkland, WA				I
2	Colorado's Shortgrass Prairie Initiative: CO	T		T	
3	Corridor System Management Plan: CA	T			
4	Portland's Active Living by Design, Portland, OR	T		T	
5	Project U-Turn, Jackson, Michigan	T	I		
6	Building the Base, Kokua Kalihi Valley, Honolulu, HI	T			
7	Promoting and Developing a Trail Network, Wyoming Valley, PA	T		T	
8	Activate Omaha, Omaha, NE	T	I		
9	Music City Moves, Nashville, TN	T	I		
10	Somerville Active Living, Somerville, MA	T	I		
11	Bike, Walk, Wheel: Columbia, Missouri	T			
Total Count		10	4	3	1
Percent of Cases		90	36	27	9

T=Traditional I=Internet Enabled

BARRIERS TO ACHIEVING EFFECTIVE PARTICIPATORY ENVIRONMENTS USING WEB 2.0 TOOLS

In achieving and implementing Web 2.0 tools and technologies, administrators encountered a number of barriers. In this section, we focus only on the barriers related to the use of ICTs with deliberative components, as these are inherently more complex. The primary barriers we identified included *data and technical limitations*, *institutional barriers* and *resource barriers*. The solutions to these barriers often required greater organizational collaboration and flexibility, greater education among all entities involved and upfront planning and resource allocation.

Data and Technical Limitations

A limiting factor in the use of mashups, such as Metroscope, is that they require timely and reliable data. Through the process of deliberation, new issues were often identified, resulting in the need of additional data or consideration of factors beyond the models scope. For example, the facilitators in the Colorado project envisioned a fully populated database; however, they were unable to do this because they lacked full participation from the federal and state resource agencies for data. In other cases, participants raised issues for which the models did not consider, resulting in a lack of available data to facilitate deliberation. Coordination, collaboration and flexibility were necessary to overcome these challenges. For example, for issues left unaddressed by the models, planners sought out the participation of other agencies or organizations that could comment or provide information on the potential impact of the issue. In Portland, Oregon, the transportation agency's data resource center created a process for identifying and prioritizing data development efforts and providing new data to all stakeholders. Finally, in the MetroQuest case, planners made an effort to streamline federal and state data resources.

Institutional Barriers

The institutional barriers cited in the cases reviewed included resistance from key stakeholders, including administrators and citizens, a lack of trust between agencies and citizens, lack of history of collaboration and misalignment between citizen desires and federal and state level policies.

Silo-mentalities of organizing were found to contribute to the institutional barriers. For example, often collaboration was necessary yet there was a lack of history of collaboration among key agencies and as such, a lack of knowledge as to how other agencies or departments "do business" and debates over the level and specificity of the data and detail needed to facilitate efforts. For example, in an environmental assessment project in Colorado, the natural resource agencies did not understand the planning process and the planners did not understand the natural resource agencies' responsibilities. In other cases, there were disagreements over the level of detail and data necessary for modeling and simulation. In order to address this, time was spent on educating necessary project partners on the roles and responsibilities of other agencies and what they contribute to the project.

A history of low public involvement was evident in many of the cases. Communication, consistent and reliable updates, and dedicated project personnel were seen as key to fostering greater public participation and building trust. In many cases, it was necessary for administrators and planners to convince and educate the public on the value of participating in these activities, as well as demonstrate to the public that their input was utilized. Furthermore, a significant factor cited was the importance of the creation and availability of communication materials and dissemination techniques to reach a wide array of nonnative English speakers.

Finally, misalignment between federal and state level policies and the desires of citizens were found to hinder administrators' efforts to build trust. For example, in Oregon, local residents became frustrated with the process and felt local decision-makers were not considering their input. However, in a number of areas, administrators were constrained by state and federal rules and regulations. In order to address this, additional efforts were taken to educate and inform citizens of the existing rules, regulations and procedures that bind decision-making so citizens do not lose trust for local officials.

Resource Barriers

Fiscal and human resources were often cited as barriers to implementing technologies in the cases reviewed. The use of the tools discussed previously require both fiscal resources to purchase and develop data, software and necessary equipment, as well as human and staffing resources to prepare, monitor, update, and train citizens on their uses. Furthermore, a dedicated and consistent project staff is necessary to facilitate relationships with citizens and help to develop trust and provide key information as well as collaborate across agencies and departments. For example, in Portland, it was noted that the use of modeling software required one to one and a half full time persons just to prepare modeling runs.

Particular ways in which fiscal resource barriers were addressed included factoring data collection and quality assurance costs upfront into project planning and budget and identifying particular collaborators that could provide data or contribute resources to data and technology needs. To address human resource needs, it was equally important to dedicate and train staff personnel that could be responsible for facilitating citizen participation or hire outside facilitators if in-house expertise does not exist or there is a need for a neutral facilitator.

SUMMARY OF FINDINGS: UNIVERSAL LESSONS LEARNED

Evidence from the cases reviewed suggest that Web 2.0 technologies can be used to overcome the barriers to creating effective participatory environments, particularly if the right mix of tools based on their communicative and deliberative properties are matched to the right environmental context. In this section, we offer a few lessons learned for administrators.

Lesson #1: One-Way Internet Enabled Tools Can Help Build Trust

One-way internet enabled tools can be very effective in aiding administrators in building trust and communicating a consistent and timely message to residents as well as demonstrating their progress on particular issues or projects. Email listserves and web sites were often used to inform residents of progress made on key initiatives of interest to citizens, update them to any unexpected changes, and send a consistent message to citizens rather than relying on traditional means where by information dissemination takes much longer. However, the key in the cases reviewed is that the coordination of the message is very important, particularly in cases where there is a need to build trust. Web sites that are not maintained, email list serves that are not timely or are only utilized sporadically, or messages that are not consistent can do more harm than good.

Lesson #2: Administrators Should Consider the Use of Traditional and Internet Enabled Tools as Complements, Not Substitutes

We found it is very rare that one tool or technique is employed to create an effective participatory environment, and this is further demonstrated in Tables 4 and 5. In many cases, an integration of tools and technologies are used to reach a broad range of citizens, particularly in cases that lack a strong degree to trust between government agencies and citizens. Therefore, administrators need to consider their context and rather than considering the isolated, singular use of tools, should understand the application and mixture of tools that will facilitate participation in their current environment.

Overall, we found administrators in these cases largely relied upon traditional methods of engaging citizens in the decision making process through one-on-one meetings, small group sessions, community gathering events, education and training workshops. Internet-enabled tools were often employed in conjunction with traditional tools, rather than replacing traditional tools. For example, following face-to-face interactions, often internet-enabled communicative tools would be employed to facilitate information flow to citizens. Mashups were used in several cases to facilitate deliberation, typically in traditional settings such as project workshops or public meetings, or facilitate deliberation between key project partners and enable more flexible administrative structures and processes.

Lesson #3: There Remains Untapped Potential of Web 2.0 Technologies to Educate and Empower Citizens

Even though a number of applications of Web 2.0 technologies were utilized in the cases, Web 2.0 technologies have not been used to their fullest capacity to create effective participatory environments. Ninety-eight percent of all cases reported utilizing traditional one-way tools and 78 percent reported utilizing traditional two-way tools. Conversely, 55 percent reported utilizing Internet enabled tools with one-way components and 35 percent reported utilizing Internet enabled two-way tools.

This is particularly important when considering the barriers to creating effective participatory environments as a number of Internet enabled tools can be used to overcome the barriers. The need for greater education of citizens and administrators was mentioned often, yet, utilization of tools such as RSS feeds, podcasts and social bookmarks to overcome this barrier were not cited in any of the cases. Tools such as this can expand the reach of administrators and keeping citizens and other agencies informed of relevant changes in federal and state rules and regulations or provide project updates.

Lesson #4: There Remains Untapped Potential of Web 2.0 Technologies to Facilitate Coordination across Agency Boundaries

Web 2.0 technologies have the potential to foster collaboration across multiple agencies, which in turn can overcome many of the information gaps faced by administrators in different agencies. A major barrier cited in the cases reviewed was that often data and information from other levels of government or other governmental agencies were not timely or was not effectively communicated to administrators or the public. Greater coordination and sharing of information across agency boundaries is necessary to educate and empower citizens and to educate and train administrators. In a few of these cases, these challenges were overcome by utilizing Internet enabled administrative systems that facilitated deliberation across agencies and partners; however, Web 2.0 technologies have been underutilized in this area and much potential remains for administrators at multiple levels of government to use these technologies to further coordinate action.

Lesson #5: The Use of Deliberative Internet Enabled Tools Requires Flexible Administrative Systems and Processes

Although Internet enabled technologies are commonly used in conjunction with a variety of traditional tools and techniques, in the majority of cases, there were very few cases of usage of deliberative Web 2.0 technologies, such as virtual worlds. The use of virtual world such as Second Life requires administrators to move beyond traditional public hearing meeting formats and invite citizens into a virtual meeting space. In cases where the administrative environment was inflexible, Internet enabled tools and technologies with two-way components were rarely utilized. This could largely be attributed to the fact that an association exists between traditional forms of expert-citizen relationships and the willingness to adopt more flexible tools and technologies to bring citizens into the process at multiple points of the decision-making process or in unconventional formats. Therefore, the effective usage of two-way Internet enabled tools may not only require adaptation of the tools, but also may require a holistic revamping of the structures and processes by which citizen input and engagement is used to inform agency decision making. Administrators when selecting Internet enabled tools also need to consider existing agency structures and processes in place, and the ability of these structures and processes to facilitate or impede the effectiveness of Web 2.0 technologies.

Lesson #6: Dedicated Human and Fiscal Resources Are Important

Resources remain an important factor in the success of creating authentic participatory environments, and perhaps more important given the notion that often traditional and Internet enabled tools are used to create effective participatory environments. In most of the cases reviewed, it was acknowledged that resource barriers were faced and it was crucial to ensure there were dedicated human and fiscal resources to the facilitating the tools and technologies utilized.

Lesson #7: Citizens Should Have Access and Training

Administrators must coordinate the use and employment of Internet enabled tools to ensure that the tools are accessible to users with a wide variety of operating systems and levels of skill, knowledge and comfort. For example, the Metroscope tool can be included in kiosks in public places, allowing those that may not have the capacity or system specifications at home to access it in different locations throughout the city. In other cases, training and education is necessary so that citizens know where to obtain information, contribute feedback, obtain data and information on their community and inform decision-making. Administrators utilizing new tools should spend ample time and research piloting the tools as well as training and educating citizens on how to utilize the tools. Finally, administrators should both plan for a learning curve among users as well as an adjustment period for users to get comfortable interacting in web-based environments.

FUTURE CONSIDERATIONS FOR RESEARCH

In conclusion, there are two areas that deserve greater research and that should be priority considerations for public administrators. First, the use of Web 2.0 technologies to train and educate administrators on facilitation skills or to foster collaboration between organizations was not directly addressed in many of these cases. One component of an effective participatory environment is the training of administrators in facilitation skills, the training of administrators on each other's role and the training and education of administrators on actions taken at different levels of government. There is potential in Web 2.0 technologies to deliver this to administrators; however, the extent to which this is currently employed was only minimal in these cases.

Secondly, additional questions remain concerning the potential use of stand-alone Web 2.0 technologies and the outcomes of the usage of these tools on citizen participation and satisfaction. In this review, a number of technologies were often used as complements to traditional tools, instead of substitutes. Questions remain concerning the level of trust that needs to be present in a community before residents are willing to engage in virtual worlds or contribute to blogs and wikis. As Putnam (2000) suggested, dense relationships of trust, commitment, and reciprocity based on face-to-face relations -- may be "a prerequisite for, rather than a consequence of effective computer-mediated communication" (Putnam, 2000, p. 177; Wellman & Haythornthwaite, 2002). Furthermore, additional research needs to consider questions of access to Web 2.0 technologies and potential exclusionary elements of these technologies and their influence on citizen participation and satisfaction outcomes. Understanding the desirable mix between traditional and internet-enabled tools to build the conditions necessary for authentic participation is important for evaluating the effectiveness and efficiency of Web 2.0 technology in the long run.

ACKNOWLEDGMENT

This study is based on a research project sponsored by the U.S. Department of Transportation (USDOT). The authors wish to thank USDOT for its financial support and UTA for its research facilities. The authors would also like to thank the project manager Kenneth Petty, as well as representatives of our project partners – Lou K. Brewer from Tarrant County Public Health Department and Tamara Cook from North Central Texas Council of Governments for their leadership and guidance. The contents of this chapter reflect the views of the authors, who are responsible for the facts and the accuracy of the information presented herein. The contents do not necessarily reflect the official views or polices of the USDOT.

REFERENCES

Alcock, P. (2004). Participation or pathology: Contradictory tensions in area-based policy. *Social Policy and Society, 3*(2), 87–96. doi:10.1017/S1474746403001556

Baker, W., Addam, H., & Davis, B. (2005). Critical factors for enhancing municipal public hearings. *Public Administration Review, 65*(4), 490–499. doi:10.1111/j.1540-6210.2005.00474.x

Burke, N., Chomitz, V., Rioles, N., Winslow, S., Brukilacchio, L., & Baker, J. (2009). The path to active living: Physical activity through community design in Somerville, Massachusetts. *American Journal of Preventive Medicine, 37*(S62), S386–S394. doi:10.1016/j.amepre.2009.09.010

Carr, D., & Halvorsen, K. (2001). An evaluation of three democratic, community-based approaches to citizen participation: Surveys, conversations with community groups, and community dinners. *Society & Natural Resources, 14*, 107–126. doi:10.1080/089419201300000526

City of Kirkland. Washington. (2009). *More people, more places, more often: A plan for active transportation.* Retrieved February 13, 2011, from http://www.ci.kirkland.wa.us/depart/Public_Works/Transportation___Streets/Active_Transportation_Plan.htm

Corburn, J., & Bhatia, R. (2007). Health impact assessment in San Francisco: Incorporating the social determinants of health into environmental planning. *Journal of Environmental Planning and Management, 50*(3), 241–256. doi:10.1080/09640560701260283

Crosby, N., Kelly, J. M., & Schaefer, P. (1986). Citizen panels: A new approach to citizen participation. *Public Administration Review, 46*(2), 170–178. doi:10.2307/976169

D'Agostino, M. (2009). Securing an effective voice for citizens in intergovernmental administrative decision making. *International Journal of Public Administration, 32*(8), 658–680. doi:10.1080/01900690903000054

Deehr, R., & Shumann, A. (2009). Active Seattle: Achieving walkability in diverse neighborhoods. *American Journal of Preventive Medicine, 37*(S62), S403–S411. doi:10.1016/j.amepre.2009.09.026

Dekker, K., Volker, B., & Lelievelet, H. (2010). Civic engagement in urban neighborhoods: Does the network of civic organizations influence participation in neighborhood projects. *Journal of Urban Affairs, 32*(5), 609–632. doi:10.1111/j.1467-9906.2010.00524.x

Dobson, N., & Gilrow, A. (2009). From partnership to policy: The evolution of active living by design in Portland, Oregon. *American Journal of Preventive Medicine, 37*(6S2), S436-S444.

Florino, D. (1990). Citizen participation and environmental risk: A survey of institutional mechanisms. *Science, Technology & Human Values, 15*(2), 226–243. doi:10.1177/016224399001500204

Geraghty, A., Seifert, W., Preston, T., Holm, C., Duarte, T., & Farrar, S. (2009). Partnership moves community towards complete streets. *American Journal of Preventive Medicine, 37*(S62), S420–S427. doi:10.1016/j.amepre.2009.09.009

Gomez-Feliciano, L., McCreary, L., Sadowsky, R., Peterson, S., Hernandez, A., & McElmurry, B. (2009). Active living Logan Square: Joining together to create opportunities for physical activity. *American Journal of Preventive Medicine, 37*(S62), S361–S367. doi:10.1016/j.amepre.2009.09.003

Gooberman-Hill, R., Horwood, J., & Calnan, M. (2008). Citizens' juries in planning research priorities: Process, engagement and outcome. *Health Expectations, 11*(3), 272–281. doi:10.1111/j.1369-7625.2008.00502.x

Goodwin, B. (2008). *Matrix of Web 2.0 technologies*. Retrieved February 2011, from http://www.gsa.gov/portal/content/103597

Government Services Administration (GSA). (2009a). *GSA social media handbook*. Retrieved from http://www.gsa.gov/graphics/staffoffices/socialmediahandbook.pdf

Government Services Administration (GSA). (2009b). *GSA Social media policy*. Retrieved from http://www.gsa.gov/graphics/staffoffices/socialmediapolicy.pdf

Government Services Administration (GSA). (2009c). *GSA promotes best practice for citizen service*. Retrieved fromhttp://www.gsa.gov/portal/content/103597

Hamamoto, M., Derauf, D., & Yoshimura, S. (2009). Building the base: Two active living projects that inspired community participation. *American Journal of Preventive Medicine, 37*(S62), S345–S351. doi:10.1016/j.amepre.2009.09.025

Heikkila, T., & Isett, K. R. (2007). Citizen involvement and performance management in special purpose governments. *Public Administration Review, 67*(2), 238–248. doi:10.1111/j.1540-6210.2007.00710.x

Huberty, J., Dodge, T., Peterson, K., & Balluff, M. (2009). Activate Omaha: The journey to an active living environment. *American Journal of Preventive Medicine, 37*(S62), S428–S435. doi:10.1016/j.amepre.2009.09.024

Innes, J. E., & Booher, D. E. (2004). Reframing public participatory strategies for the 21st century. *Planning Theory & Practice, 5*(4), 419–436. doi:10.1080/1464935042000293170

Irvin, R. A., & Stansbury, J. (2004). Citizen participation in decision making: Is it worth the effort? *Public Administration Review, 64*(1), 56–65. doi:10.1111/j.1540-6210.2004.00346.x

Kettering Foundation. (1989). *The public's role in the policy process: A view from state and local policy makers*. Dayton, OH: Kettering Foundation.

King, C., Feltey, K., & Susel, B. (2008). The question of participation: Toward authentic public participation in public administration. In Roberts, N. (Ed.), *The direct age of citizen participation* (pp. 383–400). Armonk, NY: M.E. Sharpe. doi:10.2307/977561

Kumar, N., & Vragov, R. (2009). Active citizen participation using ICT tools. *Communications of the ACM, 52*(1), 118–121. doi:10.1145/1435417.1435444

LeRoux, K. (2009). Paternalistic or participatory governance? Examining opportunities for client participation in nonprofit social service organizations. *Public Administration Review, 69*(3), 504–517. doi:10.1111/j.1540-6210.2009.01996.x

Lowndes, V., Pratchett, L., & Stoker, G. (2001). Trends in public participation: Part 1- Local government perspectives. *Public Administration, 79*(1), 205–222. doi:10.1111/1467-9299.00253

Lukensmeyer, C., & Boyd, A. (2004). Putting the "public" back in management: Seven principles for planning meaningful citizen engagement. *Public Management, 86*(7), 10–15.

Mccreedy, M., & Leslie, J. (2009). Get active Orlando: Changing the built environment to increase physical activity. *American Journal of Preventive Medicine, 37*(S62), S395–S402. doi:10.1016/j.amepre.2009.09.013

Miller, E., & Scofield, J. (2009). Slavic Village: Incorporating active living into community development through partnerships. *American Journal of Preventive Medicine, 37*(S62), S377–S385. doi:10.1016/j.amepre.2009.09.023

National Environmental Policy Act of 1969, 42 U.S.C.A. § 4331. *(1969)*

National Policy Consensus Center. (2002). *Partnering program saves ADOT millions*. Retrieved February 16, 2011, from http://www.policyconsensus.org/casestudies/docs/AZ_transportation.pdf

National Policy Consensus Center. (2003a). *Bryan Park interchange- Richmond, Virginia*. Retrieved February 16, 2011, from http://www.policyconsensus.org/casestudies/docs/VA_bryanpark.pdf

National Policy Consensus Center. (2003b). *Colorado shortgrass prairie case study*. Retrieved February 16, 2011, from http://www.policyconsensus.org/casestudies/docs/CO_shortgrass.pdf

National Policy Consensus Center. (2003c). *Florida strategic intermodal system*. Retrieved February 16, 2011, from http://www.policyconsensus.org/casestudies/docs/FL_intermodal.pdf

National Policy Consensus Center. (2003d). *Martin Luther King Jr. Boulevard reviatalization- Portland, Oregon*. Retrieved February 16, 2011, from http://www.policyconsensus.org/casestudies/docs/OR_mlkBlvd.pdf

National Policy Consensus Center. (2003e). *Sacramento transportation and air quality collaborative case study*. Retrieved February 16, 2011, from http://www.policyconsensus.org/casestudies/docs/CA_AirQual.pdf

National Policy Consensus Center. (2003f). *Utah 3500 South partnering agreement*. Retrieved February 16, 2011, from http://www.policyconsensus.org/casestudies/docs/UT_3500south.pdf

National Policy Consensus Center. (2003g). *Washington-Oregon strategic plan for I-5 corridor*. Retrieved February 16, 2011, from http://www.policyconsensus.org/casestudies/docs/WA_OR_stratplan.pdf

National Policy Consensus Center. (n.d.a). *Negotiating transportation rules in Oregon*. Retrieved February 16, 2011, from http://www.policyconsensus.org/casestudies/docs/OR_transportation.pdf

National Policy Consensus Center. (n.d.b). *Case study: Florida DOT gains consensus on state transportation plan*. Retrieved February 16, 2011, from http://www.policyconsensus.org/casestudies/docs/FL_trans.pdf

National Policy Consensus Center. (n.d.c). *Mediating a highway dispute in Florida*. Retrieved February 16, 2011, from http://www.policyconsensus.org/casestudies/docs/FL_highway.pdf

Omishakin, A., Carlat, J., Hornsby, S., & Buck, T. (2009). Achieving built-environment and active living goals through Music City Moves. *American Journal of Preventive Medicine, 37*(S62), S412–S419. doi:10.1016/j.amepre.2009.09.005

Plough, A., & Krimsky, S. (1987). The emergence of risk communication studies: Social and political context. *Science, Technology, & Human Values, 12*(3), 4-10. doi:01622439/87/03/07/j.sthv.2011.02.04

Putnam, R. (2000). *Bowling alone: The collapse and revival of American community*. New York, NY: Simon and Schuster.

Raja, S., Ball, M., Booth, J., Haberstro, P., & Veith, K. (2009). Leveraging neighborhood-scale change for policy and program reform in Buffalo, New York. *American Journal of Preventive Medicine, 37*(S62), S352–S360. doi:10.1016/j.amepre.2009.09.001

Roberts, N. (2004). Public deliberation in an age of direct citizen participation. *American Review of Public Administration, 34*(4), 315–353. doi:10.1177/0275074004269288

Roof, K., & Glandon, R. (2008). Tool created to assess health impacts of development decisions in Ingham County, Michigan. *Journal of Environmental Health, 71*(1), 35–38.

Roof, K., & Maclennan, C. (2008). Tri-county health department in Colorado does more than just review a development plan. *Journal of Environmental Health, 71*(1), 31–34.

Roof, K., & Oleru, N. (2008). Public health: Seattle and King County's push for the built environment. *Journal of Environmental Health, 71*(1), 24–27.

Roof, K., & Sutherland, S. (2008). Smart growth and health for the future: Our course of action. *Journal of Environmental Health, 71*(1), 28–30.

San Francisco Department of Public Health. (n.d.). *Health, traffic and environmental justice: A health impact analysis of the Still/Lyell Freeway Channel in Excelsior District.* Retrieved December 8, 2010, from http://www.sfphes.org/HIA_PODER.htm

Schasberger, M., Hussa, C., Polgar, M., McMonagle, M., Burke, S., & Gegaris, A. (2009). Promoting and developing a trail network across suburban, rural, and urban communities. *American Journal of Preventive Medicine, 37*(S62), S336–S344. doi:10.1016/j.amepre.2009.09.012

Stewart, K. (2007). Write the rules and win: Understanding citizen participation game dynamics. *Public Administration Review, 67*(6), 1067–1076. doi:10.1111/j.1540-6210.2007.00798.x

Swanstrom, T. (2009). Breaking down silos: Transportation, economic development and health. In S. Malekafzali (Ed.), *Healthy, equitable transportation policy: Recommendations and research.* Retrieved March 2011, from http://www.policylink.org/site/apps/nlnet/content2.aspx?c=lkIXLbMNJrE&b=5136581&ct=8439979

Tenbrink, D., McMunn, R., & Panken, S. (2009). Project U-Turn: Increasing active transportation in Jackson, Michigan. *American Journal of Preventive Medicine, 37*(S62), S329–S335. doi:10.1016/j.amepre.2009.09.004

Thomas, I., Sayers, S., Godon, J., & Reilly, S. (2009). Bike, walk, and wheel: A way of life in Columbia, Missouri. *American Journal of Preventive Medicine, 37*(S62), S322–S328. doi:10.1016/j.amepre.2009.09.002

Transportation Research Board (TRB). (2010a). *Colorado Step Up environmental collaboration supported by Web-based technology.* Strategic Highway Research Program 2, Case Studies in Collaboration. Retrieved February 16, 2011, from http://onlinepubs.trb.org/onlinepubs/shrp2/SHRP2_CS_C01_CO-STEP-UP.pdf

Transportation Research Board (TRB). (2010b). *Maricopa County, Arizona: Regional transportation plan.* Strategic Highway Research Program 2, Case Studies in Collaboration. Retrieved February 11, 2011, from http://onlinepubs.trb.org/onlinepubs/shrp2/SHRP2_CS_C01_Maricopa.pdf

Transportation Research Board (TRB). (2010c). *Wasatch Front Region, Utah: Regional transportation plan.* Strategic Highway Research Program 2, Case Studies in Collaboration. Retrieved February 16, 2011, from http://onlinepubs.trb.org/onlinepubs/shrp2/SHRP2_CS_C01_UT-Wasatch.pdf

Transportation Research Board (TRB). (2010d). *Binghamton metropolitan transportation study.* Strategic HighwayResearch Program 2, Case Studies in Collaboration. Retrieved December 12, 2010, from http://onlinepubs.trb.org/onlinepubs/shrp2/SHRP2_CS_C01_NY-Binghamton.pdf

Transportation Research Board (TRB). (2010e). *CALTRANS: Corridor systems management plan: Using performanc emeasures to conduct analysis and make decisions.* Strategic Highway Research Program 2, Case Studies in Collaboration. Retrieved November 22, 2010, from http://onlinepubs.trb.org/onlinepubs/shrp2/SHRP2_CS_C01_Caltrans.pdf

Transportation Research Board (TRB). (2010f). *Colorado US-285: Foxton road to Bailey - Using a context sensitive solutions approach to highway capacity.* Strategic Highway Research Program 2, Case Studies in Collaboration. Retrieved Novemer 23, 2010, from http://onlinepubs.trb.org/onlinepubs/shrp2/SHRP2_CS_C01_Colorado.pdf

Transportation Research Board (TRB). (2010g). *Grand Rapids Michigan: US-131 S-curve replacement, collaborative design and construction closure of central urban access.* Strategic Highway Research Program 2, Case Studies in Collaboration. Retrieved November 22, 2010, from http://onlinepubs.trb.org/onlinepubs/shrp2/SHRP2_CS_C01_Michigan.pdf

Transportation Research Board (TRB). (2010h). *I-69 Trans-Texas corridor study: Using GISST, TEAP, Quantm, SAM, and ProjectSolve technologies.* Strategic Highway Research Program 2, Case Studies in Collaboration. Retrieved November 23, 2010, from http://onlinepubs.trb.org/onlinepubs/shrp2/SHRP2_CS_C01_Texas.pdf

Transportation Research Board (TRB). (2010i). *Idaho's transportation vision.* Strategic Highway Research Program 2, Case Studies in Collaboration. Retrieved December 12, 2010, from http://onlinepubs.trb.org/onlinepubs/shrp2/SHRP2_CS_C01_Idaho.pdf

Transportation Research Board (TRB). (2010j). *Illinois Prairie Parkway project: Developing comprehensive transportation system improvements using an in-depth screening process.* Strategic Highway Research Program 2, Case Studies in Collaboration. Retrieved November 23, 2010, from http://onlinepubs.trb.org/onlinepubs/shrp2/SHRP2_CS_C01_Illinois.pdf

Transportation Research Board (TRB). (2010k). *NJ-31 integrated land use and transportation plan.* Strategic Highway Research Program 2, Case Studies in Collaboration. Retrieved December 12, 2010, from http://onlinepubs.trb.org/onlinepubs/shrp2/SHRP2_CS_C01_NJ-31.pdf

Transportation Research Board (TRB). (2010l). *Oregon I-5/ beltline interchange: Structured decision making using community values as performance measures.* Strategic Highway Research Program 2, Case Studies in Collaboration. Retrieved December 12, 2010, from http://onlinepubs.trb.org/onlinepubs/shrp2/SHRP2_CS_C01_Oregon.pdf

Transportation Research Board (TRB). (2010m). *Puget Sound region, Washington: Regional TIP policy framework and Vision 2040 - Using paint the region to evaluate scenarios.* Strategic Highway Research Program 2, Case Studies in Collaboration. Retrieved December 12, 2010, from http://onlinepubs.trb.org/onlinepubs/shrp2/SHRP2_CS_C01_Washington-PugetSound.pdf

Transportation Research Board (TRB). (2010n). *Sacramento region, California: Blueprint Project.* Strategic Highway Research Program 2, Case Studies in Collaboration. Retrieved December 12, 2010, from http://onlinepubs.trb.org/onlinepubs/shrp2/SHRP2_CS_C01_Sacramento.pdf

Transportation Research Board (TRB). (2010o). *US-24: New Haven Indiana to Defiance, Ohio; The 9-step transportation development process.* Strategic highway Research Program 2, Case Studies in Collaboration. Retrieved November 22, 2010, from http://onlinepubs.trb.org/onlinepubs/shrp2/SHRP2_CS_C01_Ohio-Indiana.pdf

Transportation Research Board (TRB). (2010p). *Woodrow Wilson Bridge in Maryland and Virginia: FHWA leads the planning process for bridge redesign.* Strategic Highway Research Program 2, Case Studies in Collaboration. Retrieved November 22, 2010, from http://onlinepubs.trb.org/onlinepubs/shrp2/SHRP2_CS_C01_WilsonBridge.pdf

Van De Belt, T., Engelen, L., Berben, S., & Schoonhoven, L. (2010). Definition of Health 2.0 and Medicine 2.0: A systematic review. *Journal of Medical Internet Research*, 12(2). Retrieved February 12, 2011, from http://www.jmir.org/2010/2/e18/

Walfoort, N., Clark, J., Bostock, M., & O'Neil, K. (2009). ACTIVE Louisville: Incorporating active living principles into planning and design. *American Journal of Preventive Medicine*, 37(S62), S368–S376. doi:10.1016/j.amepre.2009.09.007

Wellman, B., & Haythornthwaite, C. (2002). *The Internet in everyday life.* Blackwell Publishing. doi:10.1002/9780470774298

Yang, K., & Callahan, K. (2005). Assessing citizen involvement efforts by local governments. *Public Performance & Management Review*, 29(2), 191–216.

Yang, K., & Callahan, K. (2007). Citizen involvement efforts and bureaucratic responsiveness: Participatory values, stakeholder pressures, and administrative practicality. *Public Administration Review*, 67, 249–264. doi:10.1111/j.1540-6210.2007.00711.x

KEY TERMS AND DEFINITIONS

Authentic Participation: Deep and continuous involvement in administrative processes with the potential for all involved to have an effect on the situation.

Communication Components: ICT tools that support one-way dissemination of information. Traditional mechanisms include TV, radio, newspapers, and printed materials. Internet enabled ICTs include traditional and digitized information on agency web sites, e-mail distribution lists, recorded audio and video.

Deliberation Components (DC): ICT tools that support two-way communication and deliberation. Traditional methods include telephone, fax, face-to-face meetings and town hall meetings. Internet enabled technologies include traditional plus feedback forms such as chat tools, interactive discussion boards, virtual worlds, electronic petitions and blogs.

Effective Participatory Environments: Environments characterized by an empowered and educated citizenry, educated and trained administrators, and enabling administrative structures and processes.

Information Communication Technologies (ICTs): Traditional and Internet-enabled tools used by administrators for communication purposes.

Voting Components (VC): Citizens make collective decisions on various issues. Traditional mechanisms include paper-based ballots and electronic voting systems designed for physical polling booths. Internet enabled technologies include traditional plus online and electronic voting systems.

Web 2.0: An umbrella term that encompasses activities that integrate technology, social interaction, and content creation to facilitate interaction, collaboration and information sharing.

Chapter 12
Web 2.0 for eParticipation:
Transformational Tweeting or Devaluation of Democracy?

Elizabeth Tait
University of Aberdeen, UK

ABSTRACT

Recent developments in social media allow people to communicate and share information instantly and have led to speculation about the potential for increased citizen participation in decision making. However, as with other developments in ICT, social media is not used by everyone, and there is a danger of certain groups being excluded. Further, if social media tools are to be used by government institutions, there needs to be new internal processes put in place to ensure that the participation is meaningful. This chapter will critically evaluate and analyse the role of Web 2.0 tools (such as social networking services) for facilitating democratic participation, investigate and evaluate the development of Web 2.0 tools for eParticipation, and determine how they can be used to facilitate meaningful political participation.

INTRODUCTION

The growing popularity of Web 2.0 technologies has led to intense speculation about the potential impact for engaging citizens and facilitating participation in politics (Saebø *et al.* 2009). New technologies have been developed includ-

ing: social networking services, location-based services, crowdsourcing, modelling and visualisation and semantic web tools (Millard, 2010). These developments have arisen at a time where there is a widely reported public disillusionment with formal political structures (Dalton, 2004) yet public participation in informal politics has increased. In particular, the growing popularity of cyberactivism has led some to think that Informa-

DOI: 10.4018/978-1-4666-0318-9.ch012

tion and Communication Technologies (ICTs) could be a solution to the problem of disengagement with politics (Anderson, 2003; Berman and Mulligan, 2003).

Social media technologies provide a platform for groups of citizens and Non-Governmental Organisations (NGOs) to share information, campaign and communicate with each other on issues that are important to them (Yang, 2009). It is recognised that online campaigns are more likely to be successful if a large number of people are engaged (Saebø *et al.*, 2009) and social media technologies can play an important role in this by facilitating the rapid 'viral' dissemination of ideas and issues and creation of networks for campaigns. Recent examples of the use of social media for political activism include anti-government protests in Iran whereby social networking technologies were used to coordinate protests and facilitate communication with reporters, human rights activists etc outside the country (Shangapour *et al.*, 2011). The apparent success of online activism has led to speculation that social media may facilitate democratic transition in authoritarian political systems (Xie and Jaeger, 2008) and during the 'Arab Spring' protests of 2011 social media was reported to have been crucial to the coordination of protests and raising awareness. It is important not to regard cyberactivism as a homogenous activity, however, boyd (2005) argues that online social networks attract collections of like-minded people who communicate with each other but that these networks may be virtually invisible to those who do not share their interests. Further, it is important to bear in mind that there are complex political, economic, social and cultural factors that influence political activity and that cyberactivism is one element of many that can contribute to political change.

While the radical claims made about the revolutionary capacity of social media are unproven, the use of web 2.0 technologies continues to grow and governmental organisations are increasingly utilising social media as a means of communi-

cating and engaging with the public. As these new technologies become more widely used by government organisations with ever increasing numbers of 'Apps', Twitter feeds and Facebook fan pages it is important to critically reflect on these technologies and determine what role they can play in facilitating meaningful participation between citizens and government organisations. As has been indicated so far in this chapter, the development of ICT and Web 2.0 technologies in particular has led to a great deal of speculation about the implications for political participation. However, few empirical studies have been undertaken (Schlosberg *et al.*, 2007) and there is a dearth of studies that try to make a meaningful contribution to theoretical developments of eParticipation within the context of public participation theory. Much of the literature on eParticipation examines the phenomenon in isolation rather than attempting to evaluate what role, if any, social media can play in the overall consultation and engagement strategy of government institutions.

Unlike some other research in this area this chapter does not contain original empirical research on the development of Web 2.0 systems, nor do I attempt to present an audit of all possible web 2.0 interventions. This is because the systems are developing so rapidly that it would be impossible to provide examples of all systems because the developments in ICTs have been so fragmented that it is difficult to find one system that is representative of democratic innovation (Smith, 2009). Instead this chapter addresses the gap in the literature about the challenges of integrating web 2.0 technologies into the broader governmental strategies for citizen engagement and participation. I will discuss the development of eParticipation with particular focus on those that utilise social media. An analytical framework will be outlined and the benefits and drawbacks will be discussed along with their potential impact on democratic institutions. The chapter will go on to propose solutions and recommendations for the successful adoption of web 2.0 in government institutions and proposals for future research will be outlined.

BACKGROUND

Much of the literature on Web 2.0 for eGovernment services claims that new technologies could have a transformative impact on Government-Citizen relations. Some believe that social media has the capacity to facilitate a more demand-led approach to governance to empower citizens, improve engagement, increase, transparency and allow government organisations to be more responsive to the needs of the public (Hui and Hayllar 2010, Millard 2010, Bertot *et al.* 2010). Chun *et al.* (2010) argue that social media could facilitate 'disruptive innovation' in digital government by forcing governments to adapt and change to accommodate the new technologies. Bertot and Jaeger (2010) identify opportunities for governments to use social media technology for activities such as:

- Democratic participation and engagement
- Coproduction, through which governments and the public jointly develop, design, and deliver government services
- Crowdsourced solutions, through which governments seek innovation through public knowledge
- Transparency and accountability
- Real-time location-specific information using apps (Bertot and Jaeger, 2010, p55)

The literature on the use of ICT in government and democracy and its development is huge and impossible to cover in a single chapter and so this chapter does not directly examine topics such as electronic voting nor online campaigning for election by political parties. The particular focus of this chapter is eParticipation.

Macintosh and Whyte (2006) define eParticipation as:

... the use of ICTs to support information provision and 'top-down' engagement', i.e. government-led initiatives, or 'ground-up' efforts to empower citizens, civil society organisations and other democratically constituted groups to gain the support of their elected representatives. (p. 2)

In this chapter, eParticipation is defined as being the use of ICTs (primarily but not exclusively web-based technologies) for facilitating engagement and participation in the policy making process. The term eParticipation is most appropriate because it has clear connotations of participative democracy as opposed to the term eDemocracy which has connotations of elective democracy, specifically online voting. The term eParticipation cannot be applied to all forms of electronic interactions between citizens and government. The generic term for the use of technologies for government to citizen interactions is eGovernment which is understood in this chapter to mean 'the delivery of government information and services online through the Internet or other digital means.' (West, 2004, p. 16) The focus of investigation is on participative mechanisms that have been developed rather than examining whether or not citizens can pay their council tax online or report street light faults. These are considered to be transactional or administrative rather than participatory actions. It is recognised that defining exactly what constitutes eParticipation can be difficult but for example, an online form on a government institution's website to report pot holes in the streets would be considered eGovernment. However, an online form for residents to give their views on the road network strategy or how the repairs service could be improved would be considered to be eParticipation.

It is important to consider the motivations for government institutions to adopt web 2.0 tools and determine whether they aim to provide channels for participation in policy making or whether the tools are used for service delivery or customer relations purposes. Studies have shown that many of the developments in ICT in government have focussed on service delivery or eGovernment rather than on public participation (Mahrer and Krimmer, 2005). The modernisation agenda which has driven developments in eGovernment is seen as having an ethos of the citizen as a consumer of services and hence promotes private sector ideologies of efficiency, value for money and responsiveness to customer feedback. This consumerist perspective is seen by some as being contradictory to the notion of the citizen being an engaged and politically active member of a society. It could be argued that by viewing people as consumers of services rather than democratic citizens (McLaverty, 2010) this demonstrates a devaluation of the role of citizenship and represents an erosion of the ideals of public participation. Orr and McAteer (2004), however, dispute the notion that citizenship and consumerism are necessarily mutually exclusive concepts and are also rather dismissive of the dichotomous view of participative and representative democracy arguing that the lines between the two are not as clear as some of the literature implies. Hui and Hayllar (2010) concur with the notion that there is not an inherent problem with the notion of citizen as a consumer of services and argue that Web 2.0 technologies have the potential to facilitate 'Citizen Relation Management' in a similar way that private sector organisations use these technologies for customer relations management. There are potential risks with using Web 2.0 technologies in this way, however. For example, in the private sector, some businesses have found that there have been negative consequences of social media such as poor reviews on websites such as Trip Advisor (Irvine and Anderson, 2008) and there is a potential for campaign groups who have been early adopters of social media to use these new channels for lobbying and campaigning and 'flood' the system which may overwhelm administrators or skew results of consultations.

The majority of examples cited in the literature are on administrative or procedural uses of web 2.0 technologies in government rather than participation in policy making. This may be because the use of ICT for policy making involves the development of new institutional processes as Bertot and Jaeger (2010) outline:

It's one thing to solicit participation and feedback but quite another to actually incorporate such public participation into government regulations, legislation, and services. This shift requires processes and mechanisms by which comments, feedback, and other forms of participation are incorporated into the government organizations, vetted, and acted upon in some way. (Bertot and Jaeger, 2010, p56)

As with all forms of eParticipation and participative processes in general, social media applications for eParticipation must be integrated into the decision making process in a formal and transparent way so that people can tell that their opinions are being taken into consideration. The rapid development of ICTs has outpaced the ability of governments to adapt to the changes (Bertot and Jaeger, 2010) and these tools have been adopted by governments without consideration of their effectiveness (Jaeger and Bertot, 2010). This could be due in part to lack of clarity about political goals during the planning of the initiative and low levels of impact on policy-making (Taylor-Smith and Linder 2010). In addition, a large number of projects that are developed for eParticipation are pilots rather than being embedded into political institutions for decision making. It is important for research in this field to determine the conditions that these new technologies can become formal parts of governance systems (Molinari 2010) and understand the relationship and interplay between technology, organisation and government values and the impact that this has on the integration (or not) of eGovernment processes (Grönlund, 2010), Lampe et al, 2011). This chapter will now briefly outline the theoretical background of public participation and eParticipation in order to provide a context for the discussion on the use of Web 2.0 for political participation.

The concept of public participation in policy making is not new but the development of participative mechanisms has accelerated over the last few years (McLaverty, 2002). Examples of participative mechanisms include: Citizens' Panels, Citizens' Juries, Community Planning, Planning for Real, Resident's surveys which are used alongside more offline forms of consultation such as public meetings and postal questionnaires (Smith, 2005).

Pratchett (1999) argues that the relatively recent trend towards participatory mechanisms can be attributed to three main factors:

1. The citizen-consumer agenda of the 1980s and attempts by public service managers to emulate private sector management techniques
2. Organisational politics that emerged when institutions threatened with reorganisation have sought to reassert their legitimacy by demonstrating close links with the communities which they serve
3. Initiatives that have emerged through party-political agendas and are associated with ideological predilections. (Pratchett, 1999, p. 617)

It is argued that the greatest advantage to government organisations for engaging the public in participatory initiatives is that if the public are consulted, policies will have greater legitimacy. Participative policies can also be argued to have a role in educating the public and making them aware of the work of government and the issues behind decision-making (Mehta and Darier, 1998). Theorists such as John Stuart Mill argued that public participation leads to better government (Hindess, 2000). Some believe that the public will be much more likely to comply with and respect new policies if they are involved in consultations and are allowed to express their views and concerns

about new proposals (Dryzek, 2000). It is argued that this is the case even when, ultimately, they disagree with the final policy provided they feel that the consultation was fair and their opinions were listened to (Grimes, 2006). Wilson (1999) disputes this claim, however, and posits that citizens believe that participative initiatives have failed if the decision goes against what they have asked for.

As well as having a positive impact on the legitimacy of policies and decision-making it is also argued that public participation may have a positive impact on the policies themselves making them more suitable to the needs of the people. This has been a driver behind the development of community planning initiatives such as 'planning for real' which aims to meet the needs of local people better than policies devised at the local authority level (Smith, 2005). The role of participation is seen as being more than just creating effective policies, however. There is also a broader issue of engagement that is being sought to overcome the problem of the democratic deficit and apathy towards politics within the general public that is perceived to be occurring at the local level in order to make the institutions of government more responsive and legitimate (Chandler, 2000). Participative governance strategies are promoted as being part of the solution to the problem of social exclusion and may broaden the base of participation (Newman, 2005). Of particular concern are the so-called 'hard-to-reach' groups such as young people, ethnic minorities and people from low income households (Pattie, Syed and Whitely, 2003).

Traditional methods of consultation such as public meetings are not perceived to have solved the problem of getting the 'hard to reach' to participate and leads to criticisms that participative initiatives are dominated by politically motivated groups or people who have mobilized over issues that they perceive as having a direct impact on their lives. Wilson (1999) believes that the widespread lack of interest allows small groups to dominate participatory activities and therefore the outcomes of participation initiatives are easy for politicians to dismiss because the participants are often not representative of the community as a whole. Ensuring that participative initiatives are representative of the local population is, however, very difficult to achieve in practice. Further criticisms of participative initiatives are that they can waste time and encourage procrastination in the development and implementation of policies (Shapiro, 2003). In addition, increasing participation leads to questions about the relationship between representative democracy and participative democracy and the extent that decision making should be devolved to the public (Albert and Passmore, 2008). Some argue that participatory initiatives could have negative democratic impacts as power is shifted away from elected representatives who are accountable to the public and that elected members may be unwilling to become involved in participatory exercises because they see them as a threat (Kiljn and Koppenjan, 2002).

Mechanisms for citizen participation are widely varied and the influence that can be exerted by citizens depends on which mechanism is being employed and the transparency of how the results are incorporated into the policy making process to ensure that the initiatives are having a genuine impact. An additional issue is 'control over the agenda' which means the extent to which the participants are allowed to set the agenda for the topic of the participatory exercise and conversely the extent to which the agenda for debate and participation are dictated by the authority. It could be argued that by participating in government initiated top-down participative exercises citizens are, in fact, subjecting themselves to different kinds of control (Hindess, 2000). Irvin and Stansbury (2004) argue that some participatory initiatives do not offer genuine opportunities for participation in policy making but are more akin to awareness-raising exercises 'where the participation process consists of government representatives guiding citizens towards decisions the administrators

would have made in the first place' (p. 57) and it is also argued that administrators only pick up ideas from participatory initiatives that fit with their own agenda (Mayer *et al.*, 2005). Newman (2005) argues that 'Public consultation is focused predominantly on changes at the margins of how public services are delivered, not on the consequences of the withdrawal of services or their shift to other sectors' (Newman, 2005, p. 134).

The development of eParticipation has been facilitated by the rapid development of communications tools and the adoption and acceptance of Internet technologies (Sanford and Rose, 2007). Some argue that new technologies can reduce the barriers to participation and lead to previously disengaged groups becoming active participants (Mitra, 2001). It is posited that by the creation of these 'new channels of democratic inclusion' (Kearns *et al.*, 2002, p. 13) that political participation can be both broadened and deepened by '… increasing the frequency and enriching the content of dialogue between citizens, elected representatives and all levels of government. ' (Kearns *et al.*, 2002, p. 13).

In the initial phase of Internet technology developments some believed that the Internet had the potential to transform the way that citizens interact with government creating a 21st version of ancient Greek politics (Kim, 2006). However, at the other end of the spectrum some have posited that ICTs will have a negative impact on democracy, reinforce social isolation and point to the dominance of corporate interests on the Internet (Rohlinger and Brown, 2009;). The dichotomous views of the potential of the Internet to either enhance or impede political activity is observed by Weare (2002):

Researchers have linked the rise of the Internet to greater citizen empowerment and to the reinforcement of existing divisions of power; to increased social fragmentation and to the rise of new forms of community; to reinvigorated democratic discourse and to Internet road rage that poisons civic engagement; to a new golden age of participatory democracy and to threats of ever greater surveillance and control of individuals; to an interactive age of democracy that overcomes voter apathy and to a commercialization of political life that marginalizes democratic concerns. (Weare, 2002, p. 663)

Some theorists have switched sides as time has passed. For example Barber was initially optimistic about the potential of electronic democracy in *Three Scenarios for the future of Democracy and Strong Democracy* (1999) but in other works such as *A Passion for Democracy* (2000) he has promoted face-to-face deliberation above computer mediated communication. There are concerns that, rather than being more inclusive, eParticipation initiatives may exclude people from less affluent backgrounds and older people who are regarded as having lower levels of ICT access (Sagle and Vabo 2005; Mehta and Darier, 1998). The relatively low cost of developing eParticipation initiatives also leads to concerns about information overload (Kampen and Snijkers, 2003) and technological determinism whereby officers may develop eParticipation initiatives without having carefully considered what the added value, if any, will be from these initiatives. While it may be simple to set up a Twitter account or to add a discussion forum to a website, if the participation is not linked to clear outcomes there will be a lack of transparency and accountability. Rather than increase engagement, a poorly conceived or implemented strategy will lead to further disengagement (Coleman and Gøtze, 2001; Coleman, 2004).

According to Wright (2006) there are three main schools of thought about the effect of the Internet on democratic politics:

1. The 'revolutionaries' who believe that the Internet will transform the democratic system.

2. A more moderate view that the Internet will re-invigorate representative democracy by providing technical solutions to challenges.
3. Those that believe that politics will normalise the Internet into established structures.

With so many claims and counterclaims about what impact, if any, developments in ICTs in general, and web 2.0 technologies in particular have on participation, the importance of conducting research to investigate these issues is clear.

EVALUATING WEB 2.0 TOOLS FOR E-PARTICIPATION IN GOVERNMENT

In order to critically evaluate the role of web 2.0 tools in citizen participation it necessary to develop 'theoretical lenses' which provide a useful framework for evaluation. Dahl's criteria for ideal democracy as a means of evaluating participation has been used by researchers such as McLaverty (2010) who utilised these criteria for evaluating deliberative initiatives and Smith (2009) developed an evaluative framework which were reflective of Dahl's criteria for ideal democracy.

Dahl's five criteria for ideal democracy are:

*   *Effective participation:*
*   *Equality in voting*
*   *Gaining Enlightened Understanding*
*   *Exercising final control over the agenda*
*   *Inclusion of adults*
    (Dahl, 1998, p. 38)

I believe that Dahl's criteria for ideal democracy lend themselves well to the development of a heuristic framework to develop a 'theoretical lens' for evaluating web 2.0 for eParticipation tools. The interpretation used is outlined below:

Effective Participation: how can web 2.0 be used in citizen participation and are these appropriate mechanisms for gaining views?

Enlightened understanding: how can the potential for providing information to citizens using web 2.0 be utilised to increase public understanding of the issues?

Equality in Voting: are there clear processes for including the results of web 2.0 participative exercises in the policy process?

Control of the agenda: do participants have the opportunity to influence the agenda for the participatory exercise or is this solely determined by the local authority?

Inclusion of Adults: what efforts are made to promote the project to include as many participants as possible and are there checks to ensure results are representative?

This chapter will now go on to discuss the benefits and drawbacks of using web 2.0 tools for eParticipation under the five headings proposed above.

Enlightened Understanding: Does Web 2.0 Increase Available Information to Help People Make Informed Decisions?

It is argued that eParticipation initiatives could be more effective than offline forms of participation because citizens have access to more information on which to base their decisions and come to an enlightened understanding (Jensen, 2003) and that in turn administrators can use the information gathered to create better policies (Chadwick, 2003). Web technologies allow for large amounts of information to be made available at a relatively insignificant cost compared with distributing information in hard copy which could facilitate citizens to scrutinise and monitor the authorities to hold them to greater accountability (Åström, 2004). Further, developments in technologies such as RSS feeds, email alerts etc are allowing users to access the information that they desire (Scott, 2006). However, the view that making large amounts of information available will have an in-

stant impact on accountability and empowerment of citizens makes certain incorrect assumptions about the way that people seek information.

The nature of web 1.0 based information means that people have to be actively seeking the information in order to find it and therefore some argue that, rather than acting as an equalising force for improving information access amongst citizens, it may increase the gap between the information haves and have nots (Cornfield, 2003). While web pages do potentially provide much greater access for citizens to find information, this assumes that they are interested in obtaining the information and that they have the skills to be able to interpret it (Polat, 2005; Wallis, 2005). It could be argued that it is unlikely that many members of the public will have the time or inclination to browse through the information and documents available on government websites to scrutinise them. Some writers also question the assumption that access to information is really empowering at all (Galusky, 2003).

Web 2.0 tools differ from the previous web 1.0 model as they place emphasis on a more active role for users who become content generators (Traunmüller, 2010; Osimo, 2008) as opposed to being restricted to being information receivers of information given out by governments etc in a kiosk fashion (Hui and Hayllar, 2010). It is argued that civil society organisations are able to develop social media apps that cross 'administrative silos' in ways that are difficult for public sector organisations to do themselves (Millard, 2010) and may be more in keeping with the realities of how people seek information which is done often in response to a 'major life need' as opposed to being 'articulated in terms on needing information from a specific government agency' (Jaeger and Bertot, 2010, p374).

In a significant development from previous eGovernment technologies, eGovernment 2.0 is much more reliant on externally developed platforms and apps. For example, Hui and Hayllar (2010) cite examples of Virginia using YouTube videos on their website and the San Francisco administration allowing registered users to tweet about problems such as street lighting.

Using YouTube, Twitter, Flickr, Second Life, or other social media sites to disseminate government information has the unusual characteristic of creating government information that is dependent on the existence of a particular company. Information is designed for a particular site, a site that controls the means of distribution and the materials distribute through the site. (Jaeger and Bertot, 2010, p374)

This development has the advantage of being able to capitalise on the success and popularity of these social media platforms and also allows for civil society organisations to also become producers of tools outside the control of government organisations (Osimo 2008). For example, in the UK Mysociety is a charitable project which develops digital applications such as www.write-tothem.com and www.fixmystreet.com '...that give people simple, tangible benefits in the civic and community aspects of their lives [and]... to teach the public and voluntary sectors, through demonstration, how to use the internet most efficiently to improve lives.' (mysociety.org, 2011)

While social media platforms provide relatively low cost opportunities for government organisations to develop new ways of communicating with their citizens there are concerns over the permanence of these new platforms. For example, in the UK over the last few years social networking sites such as Bebo, Myspace and Friends Reunited have all significantly declined in popularity as Facebook, Twitter and Flickr have risen in popularity (OFCOM, 2010). Content must be designed for a particular site and there have been concerns expressed regarding ownership of material (Jaeger and Bertot 2010). Also, while the rhetoric surrounding Web 2.0 often emphasizes the positive claims of democratisation of content production and empowerment, there are unintended consequences and concerns about the extent of personal information that people are sharing without considering fully the potential negative impact of doing so and the potential for surveillance and corporatization (Zimmer 2008). There are also concerns about security of government data and information and accuracy of the data available (Bertot and Jaeger, 2010).

From an analysis of the literature to date it appears that web 2.0 technologies have a great potential for increasing the amount of information available to citizens but that there are challenges in ensuring that information is compatible with the various platforms and a risk that time and money could be invested in developing tools for platforms that become obsolete. More research must be conducted on how people use social media for government information seeking.

Inclusion of Adults: Can Web 2.0 Increase the Diversity of Political Participants?

The perception that ICTs could be an effective way of broadening the base of participation has been cited for many years. Kurland and Egan (1996) claimed that the Internet will foster democratic participation because 'The Net is blind to gender, race, socioeconomic status, and other demographic characteristics. All persons have equal standing' (p. 390). It is suggested that eParticipation can broaden the appeal of political participation by engaging 'hard to reach' groups such as people from ethnic minorities and young people (Gibson *et al.* 2005, Macintosh *et al.* 2003, Chatterton and Style, 2001) and that the Internet provides a potential for giving marginalised people a real voice in government policy making (Eggers, 2005).

It has been argued that young people will be amongst those who benefit from eParticipation initiatives because they are more likely to utilise new technologies such as social media platforms. As they are also a group which has a traditionally low level of participation and are disengaged with formal politics (O'Toole *et al.* 2003), they have been the focus of many studies of eParticipation. Gibson *et al.* (2005) analysed data from a national opinion poll survey from the UK in 2002 and found that the claim that Internet use may have an impact on engaging young people may have some credence because while only 10% of young people participated in offline political activity, 30% of 15-24 year olds have engaged in online political activity. However, in their analysis, Gibson *et al.* (2005) point out that younger people tend to embrace new innovations but then abandon them and so it is too early to tell if the trend for digital participation will continue. Further, in an analysis of public participation in online and offline contexts in the UK using Oxford Internet Institute survey data from 2003 and 2005, Di Gennaro and Dutton (2006) found that younger people are more likely to seek political information online but also that they are not likely to use the Internet to contact public officials. Livingstone *et al.* 2005 found that younger children and those from a lower socio-economic background were more likely to be disengaged and argue that there are complex reasons behind take up of participative opportunities by young people.

The claim that the Internet can give a better voice to those who are marginalised from traditional political activity is unproven but it seems unlikely that simply creating a new medium for participation will change the traditional patterns of access to power and decision making (Rethemeyer, 2007). Some studies have tried to isolate the impact of the Internet on civic engagement usually by multivariate analysis of quantitative data. Gibson *et al.* (2005) found that the impact of the Internet on civic engagement was ambiguous but that there was no evidence that the Internet was transforming politically inactive people into active citizens.

It should also be remembered that technology adoption varies depending on cultural and social factors. Coco and Short (2004) examined a local government program in Queensland, Australia and found that there were established local patterns of interaction and communication that had positive and negative impacts on the adoption of eParticipation. This means that making broad generalisations about eParticipation facilitating greater participation simply because it is more convenient for people are simplistic and that existing patterns and norms of communication should be accounted for and that initiatives must be designed with the needs of the community in mind (Chadwick, 2006).

Further to the earlier concerns about the information seeking skills required to gain an 'enlightened understanding' there is also great concern that the level of information literacy required to participate in eParticipation initiatives and differing attitudes towards the technology may exclude certain demographic groups and lead to disempowerment (Shelley *et al.*, 2004). Older people and people from lower socio-economic groups are often used as examples of those who could be excluded by eParticipation (Sagle and Vabo, 2005; Mehta and Darier, 1998).

Web 2.0 technologies such as social media have greatly increased in popularity with a huge growth in the use of social networking sites such as Facebook in the UK (OFCOM, 2010). However, when Internet use is broken down by demographics it becomes clear that different age groups do not use the Internet in the same way with younger people more likely to use the Internet for leisure activities and older people for functional purposes to find out specific information or complete tasks (OFCOM, 2010). With any eParticipation initiative there is the potential for digital exclusion and that instead of broadening the base of participation, web 2.0 tools for eParticipation could end up simply giving the already engaged more opportunities to participate. For example, there was great speculation about the potential for Twitter to provide a new 'direct channel' for democratic participation but a study by Pew Internet revealed that only 8% of online Americans use Twitter (Smith and Rainie, 2010)

From the analysis of the literature on the potential impact of eParticipation and web 2.0 on the characteristics of those participating it is evident that there are predicted winners and losers from eParticipation including participation using web 2.0. Those who predict that eParticipation will broaden the base of participation mainly point to reasons of convenience, the anonymity of the medium and assumptions about the way that people use technology- for example that because young people are more technologically astute that eParticipation will automatically appeal to them. Studies to determine whether this is the case or not have demonstrated that the problem of political disengagement is complex and viewing eParticipation as being a solution in itself is dangerously simplistic and suggests that some writers' expectations of the impact of technology could be disproportionate (Kubicek, 2005). It could be argued, for example, that the reason people are not participating in politics is not through lack of opportunities but simply because it is not a primary concern in their lives (Mechling, 2002). If people do not wish to participate in local politics offline, there is little evidence to suggest that they will participate in local politics online either (Saglie and Vabo, 2005).

Effective Participation: Examples of Web 2.0 Tools for e-Participation

The chapter so far has largely discussed eParticipation as a single phenomenon. However, the development of eParticipation has evolved through a combination of several factors and has been largely experimental in nature. As a consequence a multitude of tools and ideas for their implementation have emerged which some claim offer the possibility of strengthening participation. There have been so many experiments and different tools and mechanisms created for eParticipation that a comprehensive analysis of all the different types of eParticipation is impossible and analysis of the different sub-types of eParticipation is rather

sparse in the literature. However, some of the main eParticipation tools will now be outlined briefly.

Some eParticipation tools such as basic electronic questionnaires are essentially the direct electronic equivalent of paper based surveys which are a very widely used tool for public participation. The use of questionnaires by local authorities are primarily associated with consultations on a specific issue or a user satisfaction survey to gain views on service provision (Berntzen and Winsvold, 2005).

As well as providing opportunities to collect views from individual citizens, eParticipation tools can also be created to facilitate dialogues. For example discussion forums can be set up for a specific issue or strategy or can be 'open' to allow citizens to set the agenda for discussion. They can be conducted between citizens and elected members and officers or could be developed to encourage dialogues between citizens (Kim and Holzer, 2006). The data from discussion forums is difficult to analyse and getting definitive conclusions by aggregating responses is much harder than with quantitative responses to a questionnaire (Kakabadse *et al.* 2003). The purpose of the discussion and the way that the results will be used must be clearly defined so that participants are aware the extent to which their contributions will impact on policymaking.

Online discussion forums require moderation which can be time intensive and has cost implications.

There are also concerns about the quality of online discussions and whether or not they facilitate genuine participation. Ferber *et al.* (2006), examined public discussion as found on NJ.com and its public forums. They found that there was a large amount of political dialogue and that politicians seemed to be participating but that the quality of the debate was poor. Another example is IDEAL-EU (www.ideal-deabte.eu) which was studied by Talpin and Wojcik (2010) to compare the results of online vs offline deliberation. The authors discovered that the subjective learning effect of deliberation appears to be stronger face to face than online (p. 86). The authors also noted that deliberation efforts are often not sufficient to change the minds of participants. There are further questions about the role of administrators such as web masters in the development and running of eParticipation initiatives.

...they foster electronic discussion, implement (and sometimes define) the rules of online debates and forward messages from the forum to politicians... and yet the webmaster has neither democratic legitimacy not legitimacy that is linked to technical or scientific expertise or knowledge. (Wojcik, 2009, p14).

Some researchers have conducted experiments with integrating novel computer science research with online discussions that seek to facilitate deliberation on policy issues. Cartwright and Atkinson (2009) for example give examples of a system called Paramedides which uses computational argumentation to support the debate.

... we can now not only see that a user disagrees with a particular statement, which part of this underlying evidence he or she disagrees with. This could help debate administrators further refine policy proposals and their choice of supporting statements.... It could even prompt a change for the policy proposal itself. (Cartwright and Atkinson 2009, p 50)

It is also argued that semantic web technologies can be utilised to 'match technical knowledge with 'popular' views of reality, in order to facilitate the interaction among stakeholders, administrative bodies and technicians.' (Tilio *et al.* 2009, p235). It is argued that future Web 3.0 developments which merge semantic web technologies with social media technologies will provide great opportunities for eParticipation utilising linked data and crowdsourcing (Peristeras 2009, Bizer 2009).

eParticipation initiatives can also include live chats with administrators and/or elected officials (Breindl and Francq, 2008). For example, these may take the form of online question and answer sessions arranged at specific times. Webchats can be difficult to manage and the rules must be established prior to the event such as whether the public can ask follow up questions or whether they are a straight question and answer session. As well as the participating elected member(s) or officer(s) there are also support teams required to assist with the technical side of managing the web chat.

Webchats can be seen as facilitating a more personal form of communication than online discussions and newer developments in technologies allow for the opportunity for using voice and video communication in addition to typing text. Webchats allow elected members and officers a direct form of communication with participants than some other forms of eParticipation. Web 2.0 tools such as Twitter and Facebook could be used as part of these chats or as supplementary tools to the discussion. For example, some participants 'tweet' from conferences or public debates. Analysis of the discussions is difficult, however, and it is difficult to determine whether or not participants are contributing to a policy process, in particular if there are supplementary social media discussions occurring that are not instigated by the organisers. There is also the danger that politicians can see webchats as being a marketing or PR exercise rather than a genuine attempt to engage the public in a dialogue.

The final tool that will be reviewed in this overview of eParticipation is ePetitions. ePetitioning has been used in the Scottish Parliament since 2000 and the Number 10 website introduced ePetitions in 2006. In order for an ePetition strategy to have credence there must be a commitment on the part of the government organisation to take into account petitions that meet a certain number of responses. This does not necessarily mean that new policies will be created as a direct result of the citizens but would demonstrate a willingness to devolve some degree of influence to the citizens. However, this raises questions of accountability. The parameters as to what can be included in an ePetition must be set, for example someone could set up an ePetition to abolish council tax which, while it may be popular, is not a feasible option. There have been high profile examples of ePetition strategies backfiring, most recently with the ePetitioning initiative on the Number 10 website where some 2 million people signed up for a petition protesting against the government's road pricing initiative which revealed a lack of transparency in how the results of the ePetitions were being used and a negative response in the media (Miller, 2008)

The 'viral' dissemination effect of social media technologies such as Facebook and Twitter can facilitate the distribution of ePetitions. There is also a concern amongst some that due to the ease that ePetitions can be signed up for and the impact of 'virtual chain letters' where requests to sign up for petitions can be passed around by email to potentially thousands or even millions of people, that respondents may not have carefully considered all the issues but have just signed because they were asked to by their friends.

ePetitions have been used as part of a pilot initiative for the local eDemocracy national project in Kingston upon Thames from 2004. Macintosh and Whyte (2006) found the initiative to be transparent because it established a process for publishing decisions and had strong political support but that it lacked integration with the wider consultative process and did not produce clear outcomes.

The diversity of tools available complicates research into the use of Web 2.0 for eParticipation. As has been mentioned earlier Smith (2009) argues that there is such little standardisation that analysing the effectiveness of eParticipation as a public engagement mechanism is extremely difficult. However, there is reason to be positive about the potential for utilising Web 2.0 for eParticipation as the nature of social media is to facilitate communication and collaboration between large groups of people. The challenge is how these can be integrated into the processes for democratic engagement and policymaking which will be outlined in the following sections.

Equality in Voting: Ensuring that Web 2.0 Tools are Integrated into Decision Making

It is argued that eParticipation can facilitate transparency of governance and make government organizations more responsive to public preferences (Baker and Panagopoulos, 2004). Chadwick (2003) suggests that developments in ICT could mean that 'Government becomes a 'learning organization' able to respond to the needs of its citizens, who are in turn able to influence public bureaucracies by rapid, aggregative feedback mechanisms such as e-mail and interactive web sites' Chadwick, 2003, p. 447).

However, as with any participative initiative, it will only succeed if it offers genuine opportunities for participation. The eParticipation initiatives must have clear objectives, processes for incorporating the results into the policy process so that the participants know that their participation will be worthwhile (Coleman and Gøtze, 2001; Coleman, 2004). This is particularly true given the climate of mistrust in government institutions where citizens feel disengaged. In order to build trust between citizens and governments, officers and administrators must demonstrate that citizens' views are genuinely being listened to and that power is being distributed (Yang, 2005).

It is argued the eParticipation may reduce the costs of consultation to the local authorities (Weare, 2002) and so may be seen as preferable to other forms of consultation. However, if eParticipation initiatives are just seen as a 'cheap and quick' way of ticking the consultation box to satisfy statutory requirements then this would not represent a genuine shift to more participative governance. Further, eParticipation is not 'cost free'- new systems have to be developed or purchased which will have cost implications. Once the systems are in place there needs to be monitoring for improper use and there must be new processes in place for collecting, collating and analysing the data produced (Baker and Panagopoulos, 2004, Kampen and Srijikers, 2003) and producing clear and transparent outcomes. For example, it is easy to set up a Twitter account or Facebook page. However, if this discussion is to be used as part of a policy-making process, the data retrieved from these would need to be collated, synthesised and analysed and could prove time consuming to manage and monitor for improper use.

There are also organisational culture issues that may act as a barrier to eParticipation in government organisations. In order for any organisation, whether in the public or private sector to effectively integrate e-solutions into their organisation their must be both the technological capability and the support of the members of staff (Levy, 2001; Sterling, 2005). It is argued that the majority of government IT spending is focused on the administrative process more associated with eGovernment rather than on democratic or participative uses of technology (Mahrer and Krimmer, 2005). In addition, social media websites are often blocked by government organisations as they are considered to be an inappropriate use of staff time and there are further issues of privacy and security that have to be addressed.

When eParticipation tools are developed they must not be seen as an 'add on' or as a way for a government organisation to appear more innovative and progressive or they will be doomed to failure. If people get the impression that their views are not taken into account (or at least acknowledged) then it will simply serve to further reinforce the perceptions of mistrust that the public have in government (Coleman and Gøtze, 2001). Clift (2002) states that eParticipation solutions should be incorporated into the official democratic processes in order to be effective which sup-

ports the argument advanced in this chapter that viewing eParticipation as being 'different' from other kinds of participation leads to a fragmented participation policy and inhibits the development of genuine participation.

Osimo (2008) identifies issues that may impede the success of eGovernment 2.0 initiatives:

...adopting only the technology, but not the values; not putting in place the appropriate governance mechanisms; focusing on developing a proprietary web 2.0 application, while most collaboration/ conversation happens outside government websites and/or across applications.

Utilising Web 2.0 technologies on third party platforms is rather paradoxical in terms of legitimacy and transparency. On the one hand, the development of these apps allows civil society organisations such as mysociety to facilitate 'bottom up' participation but if these are done externally to the processes being developed within government institutions they are unlikely to have a significant impact on the policy process. To date a great many of the apps tend to focus on rather low level environmental issues such as street lights, potholes in the roads or graffiti. While these issues are important to local populations it is not clear how these apps could be developed to tackle more complex and multi-faceted issues such as poverty, local economic development or climate change.

Control over the Agenda: Can Web 2.0 Tools Facilitate Greater Citizen Power?

This issue of the extent to which a participatory exercise devolves decision making is important with all participatory initiatives, as has been indicted in the last chapter Irvin and Stansbury (2004) argue that some participatory initiatives do not offer genuine opportunities for participation but rather are awareness-raising exercises where citizens are guided towards 'making decisions administrators would have made anyway' and it is also argued that administrators only pick up ideas from participatory initiatives that fit with their own agenda (Mayer et al., 2005). This section will primarily demonstrate that the institutional context that eParticipation tools are developed will have a bearing on how much control is devolved to the public and will also highlight some of the issues surrounding representative and participative democracy with eParticipation initiatives.

Despite the views held by some that web 2.0 eParticipation could devolve more power to the public than offline methods of consultation there is little evidence presented that this has happened to date. Parvez (2008) found that eParticipation strategies tend to be implemented from the top down, that the design of the tools tend to reflect existing practices for engagement and that there is little integration with online consultations and the traditional offline exercises. The institutional context within which the initiatives are developed will strongly influence the way that the eParticipation tools are developed and provide the norms and procedures surrounding their use (Parvez and Ahmed, 2006). Studies have shown that government websites are the product of technical, political and other choices and that the technical design of websites also has an impact on the level of participation by the public. For example, the design of online discussion forums has an impact on the deliberative quality of the debate (Wright and Street, 2007). Although web 2.0 eParticipation may utilise third party apps and may therefore overcome some of these problems, the decision regarding which apps to use and for what purposes will still be made according to institutional norms and policies.

While the idea of engaging the public in more participation to enhance the legitimacy of political institutions sounds appealing, it potentially creates the paradox of de-legitimising the institutions that it seeks to enhance. Power may be devolved from the elected representatives and more authority placed in the hands of the administrative side of government who are largely responsible for initiating eParticipation initiatives (Chadwick, 2003). Officers and civil servants may gain more power by gaining control over the information flows between citizens and elected members because they largely control the ICT resources and so can influence the agenda in more overt ways than with traditional offline consultations (Clift, 2003; Parvez and Ahmed, 2006).

Mahrer (2005) discussed findings from a survey of parliamentarians across Europe and found that politicians feel that they are more qualified to participate in decision making than ordinary citizens, that they fear a loss of power from eParticipation and a 'fear of change'. These findings also add credence to the notion that the drive for eParticipation is largely coming from the administration side of local authorities and that elected members were not playing a part in the development (Clift, 2003). Parvez (2008) also found that initiatives such as online consultations and discussion forums were created to provide support to and enhance representative democracy rather than being an attempt to devolve responsibility to citizens.

There are further concerns expressed in the literature about the erosion of representative democracy by participative mechanisms and that there is potential for eParticipation to 'dangerously overextend the sphere of democratic decision making into what should be the sphere of individual or corporate decision making because the institutional constraints that have been developed in 'analogue democracy' do not exist in the digital setting.'(Kakabadse *et al.* 2003, p. 51). However, as has also been identified, it must be borne in mind that members of the local populace may not want more input into decision making than they already have and that citizens may be happy for elected members to take on the majority of governing responsibility (Eggers, 2005, p. 156)

It is evident that there are issues of power and accountability with web 2.0 eParticipation initiatives and that, rather than devolving more power to the public, eParticipation tools may be devolving more power to administrators at the expense of elected members who can be disengaged from the development of eParticipation. While it could be argued that web 2.0 eParticipation tools could facilitate easier and more extensive devolution of power to citizens, the issue of whether the citizens actually want to shift the balance of representative and participative democracy is highly questionable.

SYNTHESIS AND ANALYSIS

As it has been established from the literature that there is a belief that offline participatory mechanisms are not successful at engaging a representative sample of the local population, the biggest selling point of web 2.0 eParticipation would be if more people from a greater variety of backgrounds than the 'usual suspects' participated. Participative exercises have a wider objective beyond consulting the public to validate policy decisions and also sought to foster more engaged communities in order to broaden involvement, achieve community capacity building and tackling social exclusion. The new opportunities created by web 2.0 technologies could make a contribution to overcoming the participation gap by offering more opportunities by making information more easily available and lowering the entry costs to participation by making it easier for people to participate. However, one of the primary barriers to public involvement in participatory mechanisms is that the issues being consulted upon were not of interest to the public as a whole. Much of the work conducted by government could be considered rather mundane and uninteresting to the general public and it is unlikely that social media could overcome this issue. Some public simply do not want to participate in government policy making and therefore developing innovative mechanisms

such as web 2.0 eParticipation will not transform the inactive into active citizens.

As stated at the start of the chapter it is important to consider web 2.0 for eParticipation within the broader strategy for citizen engagement as well as examining the novel technologies themselves. As web services increasingly become a core part of service delivery and communications for organisations, the online/offline dichotomy is becoming less useful for assessing citizen participation efforts as a mixed media approach can be used that encompasses both 'traditional' and online forms of participation. So, in the case of web 2.0 technologies, social media can be used in an enabling capacity to promote traditional forms of participation or to provide additional information rather than being utilised as a primary data collection tool, a 'bricolage' approach may be utilised whereby different forms of traditional and eParticipation tools could also be utilised, or a participatory exercise could be conducted entirely online utilising the 'dialogic' potential of eParticipation to facilitate online deliberative efforts.

Web 2.0 tools for eParticipation are likely to be more useful for certain participatory activities than others and eParticipation should play a part in the broader participation strategy along with other mechanisms such as postal questionnaires or meetings. Administrators should utilise a mechanism that is appropriate for the type of participation being undertaken taking into consider issues such as sampling, the demographics of the respondents being targeted and, where appropriate, ensuring that offline alternatives are provided so as not to exclude members of the public.

From the synthesis of the literature it seems it is too early to tell what the specific impacts of web 2.0 for eParticipation will be but that it is vital that there is clarity of purpose, procedures for the results to be fed into the policy process and for expectations of participants to be managed so that they understand what impact their participation will have and the stage of the policy cycle that they are feeding into.

SOLUTIONS AND RECOMMENDATIONS

This chapter has demonstrated that Web 2.0 technologies present new opportunities for engaging the public in active participation. However, with the new opportunities there are also challenges associated with selecting appropriate technologies that are sustainable, developing processes to incorporate the technology into the public policy process and ensuring that certain groups are not excluded. In order to move eParticipation beyond the 'experimental' stage into a mechanism that is an available tool in the 'participation toolbox' a number of policy recommendations can be made.

- Online forms of participation including those that employ web 2.0 technologies should not be viewed as distinct from 'traditional' forms of participation but should rather be integrated into the strategic public communications and participation strategies of government organisations. There should also be recognition of the different strengths and weaknesses of the various tools for participation and advice provided for selecting appropriate methods of participation depending on the topic, user group and purpose.

- It should also be recognised that different 'tools' (both online and offline) can be employed in a 'bricolage' approach to participation in order to maximise responses. For example, a consultation on a local plan may include traditional focus groups, online debates, electronic questionnaires and crowd sourcing of ideas via Twitter. In these circumstances, however, it is important to ensure that there are clear processes for incorporating the results into the policy process and to manage the expectations of participants.

- Government organisations should have internal public participation guidelines and quality monitoring procedures to ensure that best practice guidelines are followed. This would reduce duplicate consultations and also help to ensure standardisation of procedures and allow for better coordination and understanding of which public participation mechanisms (including eParticipation with web 2.0) are the most effective by allowing officers an overview of all consultation and engagement activities.

- Internal working groups involving elected members, ICT officers and officers involved in public participation in government organisations should be set up to review how ICTs should be used to engage the public and feed into the wider eGovernment strategies.

- Resources should be made available to provide staff training for officers and elected members to learn more about how web 2.0 can be effectively employed as a way to engage the public in participative activities. This would hopefully ensure that technologies selected are

- Government organisations should engage in knowledge exchange networks with each other, academics, NGOs and other organisations to conduct research with groups of citizens to share best practice and research into which participation tools including web 2.0 are most effective at engaging citizens, in particular those from 'hard to reach' groups.

SUGGESTIONS FOR FUTURE RESEARCH

As ICT is a rapidly evolving area it is inevitable that there will be more developments in web 2.0 technologies in the future. At this stage it is simply too early to tell what the future impact of these technologies will be and therefore there is great potential to conduct more research into this phenomenon. I propose that interesting future research could include:

- Comparative studies of the implementation of web 2.0 for eParticipation in different countries and also examination of variances between highly localised use of social media in communities vs national level initiatives.
- Studies of people who do not participate in public participation initiatives would be interesting to determine in more detail what the barriers to participation are and whether or not web 2.0 eParticipation mechanisms would make them more likely to participate.
- The development of impact indicators and ways of analysing if and to what extent public participation mechanisms in general (not just eParticipation) make a meaningful contribution to policy making to ensure that participative initiatives are transparent.
- Smith (2009) wrote that he believed more research was required to analyse whether online deliberative debates differed from those in the offline context. I believe that this would be beneficial but suggest that it should be broadened to examine whether or not responses to other forms of ePartcipation and from web 2.0 in particular differ from their offline equivalents.

In order to evaluate any eParticipation initiatives including those that utilise web 2.0 technologies it is necessary to examine the context in which the initiative is developed as well as the tools themselves. MacIntosh and Whyte (2008) have produced some evaluation criteria for eParticipation which have three components:

- The democratic perspective considers the overarching democratic criteria that the eParticipation initiative is addressing. Here one of the most difficult aspects is to un-

derstand to what extent the eParticipation affects policy.
- The project perspective looks in detail at the specific aims and objectives of the eParticipation initiative as set by the project stakeholders.
- The socio-technical perspective considers to what extent the design of the ICTs directly affects the outcomes. Established frameworks from the software engineering and information systems fields can be used to assess issues such as usability and accessibility. (Macintosh, 2008, p. 5)

External and internal factors that affect the development of participative policy making must also be examined such as local, regional and national statutory guidance. In order to gain a good understanding of how the eParticipation initiatives are being conducted it is necessary to gain insights into the workings of the particular institutions being examined through primary research conducted with elected members and officers and examination of internal working documents (Chadwick 2011). Methodological tools that can be used include the usual qualitative and quantitative methodologies employed in the social sciences but there are a number of new network analysis software tools that can also be used. For example, some researchers use software such as Node-XL to analyse online networks on Twitter and Facebook which can be used to map and graphically represent online networks indicating the strengths of network connections, how organisations and individuals are connected and how much interaction occurs between nodes on a network (Hansen *et al.*, 2011). These software tools could be used to provide a visual representation of interaction between government organisations and their 'followers' in order to analyse the extent to which government organisations are embracing them as a two-way communications tool by engaging in a dialogue. Of course there are limitations to what this software can tell researchers about the nature of the interaction and the impact that it is having on policy making but these tools could prove to be useful additions to a researchers toolkit for investigating eParticipation.

CONCLUSION

This chapter has outlined new developments in using ICT for political participation with particular focus on social media technologies. While there has been speculation about how new social media technologies can have a transformative impact on democracy there is little evidence to date that this will happen. However, there is evidence that web 2.0 tools could be effectively utilised for developing new opportunities for engagement. The base of participation could ultimately be widened by web 2.0 eParticipation initiatives to include those who would be willing to participate but are either not sufficiently inclined to invest the time in 'offline participation' or are unable to do so for reasons such as childcare or geographical location. However, there has been no evidence found that eParticipation would be effective in engaging those who do not want to participate or who feel that their contributions are not valued or that the topic of consultation is not relevant to them. More data would be required to investigate whether or not eParticipation actually increases the diversity of participants e.g. whether or not more responses are received from young people.

It is clear, however, that not only is the impact of eParticipation very ambiguous, but that there are also ambiguities of the impact of participation mechanisms in general. With this in mind it is believed that the debate about eParticipation vs 'offline' participation is framed in such a way that it overlooks these fundamental issues with public participation in government decision making. In order to effect genuine participation, when public participation mechanisms are employed they should be conducted with clear indications of how the results will be used to ensure that participants

have an impact. This should be the case whether the mechanism is online deliberation via social media, a postal questionnaire, public meetings or any other type of participation.

REFERENCES

Albert, A., & Passmore, E. (2008). Public value and participation: A literature review for the Scottish government. [online] The Work Foundation. Retrieved July 17, 2011, from http://www.scotland. gov.uk/Publications/2008/03/17090301/0

and sustained public access to government information. *Government Information Quarterly, 27*(4), 371-376.

Anderson, D. M. (2003). Cautious optimism about online politics and citizenship. In Anderson, D., & Cornfield, M. (Eds.), *The civic Web* (pp. 19–34). Lanham, MD: Rowman and Littlefield Publishers Inc.

Äström, J. (2004). *Digital democracy: Ideas, intentions and initiatives in Swedish local government* (pp. 96–115). Routledge ECPR Studies in European Political Science.

Auty, C. (2005). UK elected Members and their Weblogs. *Aslib Proceedings: New Information Perspectives, 57*(4), 338–355.

Baker, P. M. A., & Panagopoulos, C. (2004). Political implications of digital (e-) Government. In Pavlichev, A., & Garson, D. G. (Eds.), *Digital government: Principles and best practices* (pp. 78–96). Hershey, PA: Idea Group Publishing.

Barber, B. (1999). Three scenarios for the future of technology and strong democracy. *Political Science Quarterly, 113*(4), 573–589. doi:10.2307/2658245

Barber, B. (2000). *A passion for democracy*. Princeton, NJ: Princeton University Press.

Berman, J., & Mulligan, D. K. (2003). Digital grass roots, issue advocacy in the age of the Internet. In Anderson, D. M., & Cornfield, M. (Eds.), *The civic Web* (pp. 77–96). Oxford, UK: Rowman and Littlefield Publishers Inc.

Berntzen, L., & Winsvold, M. (2005). Web-based tools for policy evaluation. In *E-Government: Towards Electronic Democracy Proceedings*, *3416*, 13–24.

Bertot, J. C., Jaeger, P. T., & Grimes, J. M. (2010). Using ITCs to create a culture of transparency: E-government and social media as openess and anti-corruption tools for societies. *Government Information Quarterly*, *27*, 264–271. doi:10.1016/j.giq.2010.03.001

Bertot, J. C., Jaeger, P. T., Munson, S., & Glaisyer, T. (2010). Social media technology and government transparency. *Computer*, *43*(11), 53–59. doi:10.1109/MC.2010.325

boyd, d. (2005). Sociable technology and democracy. In J. Lebowsky & M. Ratcliffe (Eds.), *Extreme democracy Lulu*.

Breindl, Y., & Francq, P. (2008). Can Web 2.0 applications save e-democracy? A study of how new Internet applications may enhance citizen participation in the political process online. *International Journal of Electronic Democracy*, *1*, 14–31. doi:10.1504/IJED.2008.021276

Cartwright, D., & Atkinson, K. (2009). Using computational argumentation to support e-participation. *IEEE Intelligent Systems, Special Issue on Transforming E-government and E-participation through IT*, *24*(5), 42-52.

Chadwick, A. (2003). Bringing e-democracy back in: Why it matters for future research on e-governance. *Social Science Computer Review*, *21*(4), 443–455. doi:10.1177/0894439303256372

Chadwick, A. (2006). *Internet politics: States, citizens and new communication technologies*. Oxford, UK: Oxford University Press.

Chadwick, A. (2011). Explaining the failure of an online citizen engagement initiative: The role of internal institutional variables. *Journal of Information Technology & Politics*, *8*(1), 21–40. doi:10.1080/19331681.2010.507999

Chandler, J. A. (2001). *Local government today* (3rd ed.). Manchester, UK: Manchester University Press.

Chatterton, P., & Style, S. (2001). Putting sustainable development into practice? The role of local policy partnership networks. *Local Environment*, *6*(4), 439–452. doi:10.1080/13549830120091725

Chun, S. A., Shulman, S., Sandoval, R., & Hovy, E. (2010). Government 2.0: Making connections between citizens, data and government. *Information Polity*, *15*(1 & 2), 1–9.

Clift, S. (2003). E-democracy: Lessons from Minnesota. In Anderson, D. M., & Cornfield, M. (Eds.), *The civic Web* (pp. 157–165). Oxford, UK: Rowman and Littlefield publishers Inc.

Coco, A., & Short, P. (2004). History and habit in the mobilization of ICT resources. *The Information Society*, *20*, 39–51. doi:10.1080/01972240490269997

Coleman, S. (2004). Whose conversation? Engaging the public in authentic polylogue. *The Political Quarterly*, *75*(2), 112–120. doi:10.1111/j.1467-923X.2004.00594.x

Coleman, S., & Gøtze, J. (2001). *Bowling together: Online public engagement in policy deliberation* [online]. London, UK: Hansard Society.

Consultation Institute. (2009a). *Glossary*. Retrieved August 26, 2011, from http://www.consultationinstitute.org/resources/glossary/glossary-c/

Cornfield, M. (2003). Adding in the Net: Making citizenship count in the digital age. In Anderson, D., & Cornfield, M. (Eds.), *the civic web* (pp. 97–119). Oxford, UK: Rowman and Littlefield Publishers Inc.

Dalton, R. (2004). *Democratic challenges, democratic choices: The erosion of political support in advanced industrial democracies*. Oxford, UK: Oxford University Press.

Di Gennaro, C., & Dutton, W. (2006). The Internet and the public: Online and offline political participation in the United Kingdom. *Parliamentary Affairs, 59*(2), 219–313. doi:10.1093/pa/gsl004

Dryzek, J. (2000). *Deliberative democracy and beyond: Liberals, critics, contestants*. Oxford, UK: Oxford University Press.

Eggers, W. D. (2005). *Government 2.0: Using technology to improve education, cut red tape, reduce gridlock, and enhance democracy*. Lanham, MD: Rowman& Littlefield Publishers.

Ferber, P., Foltz, F., & Puhliese, R. (2005). The Internet and public participation: State legislature web sites and the many definitions of interactivity. *Bulletin of Science, Technology & Society, 25*(1), 85–93. doi:10.1177/0270467604271245

Fien, J., & Skoien, P. (2002). I'm learning… How you go about stirring things up- in a consultative manner: Social capital and action competence in two community catchment groups. *Local Environment, 7*(3), 269–282. doi:10.1080/1354983022000001642

Galusky, W. (2003). Indentifying with information: Citizen empowerment, the Internet, and the environmental anti-toxins movement. In Mccaughey, M., & Ayers, M. D. (Eds.), *Cyberactivism: Online activism in theory and practice* (pp. 195–208). New York, NY: Routledge.

Gibson, R.K., & Lusoli, W., 7 Ward, S. (2005). Online participation in the UK: Testing a contextualised model of Internet effects. *British Journal of Politics and International Relations, 7*(4), 561–583. doi:10.1111/j.1467-856X.2005.00209.x

Grimes, M. (2006). Organizing consent: The role of procedural fairness in political trust and compliance. *European Journal of Political Research, 45*, 285–315. doi:10.1111/j.1475-6765.2006.00299.x

Grönlund, Å. (2010). Ten years of e-government: The end of history and a new beginning. In M. A. Wimmer, J.-L. Chappelet, M. Janssen, & H. J. Scholl (Eds.), *Proceedings 9th IFIP WG 8.5 International Conference, EGOV 2010, LNCS 6228*, Lausanne, Switzerland, August/September 2010, (pp. 13-24). Springer.

Hansen, D. L., Shneiderman, B., & Smith, M. A. (2011). *Analyzing social media networks with NodeXL insights from a connected world*. Burlington, MA: Elsevier.

Hindess, B. (2000). Representative government and participatory democracy. In Vandenberg, A. (Ed.), *Citizenship and democracy in a global era* (pp. 33–50). Houndsmill, UK: MacMillan Press Ltd.

Horrocks, I., & Bellamy, C. (1997). Telematics and community governance: Issues for policy and practice. *International Journal of Public Sector Management, 10*(5), 377–387. doi:10.1108/09513559710180600

Hui, G., & Haylarr, M. (2010). Creating public value in e-government: A public-private-citizen collaboration framework in Web 2.0. *The Australian Journal of Public Administration, 69*(1), 120–131. doi:10.1111/j.1467-8500.2009.00662.x

Irvine, W., & Anderson, A. (2008). ICT (information communication technology), peripherality and smaller hospitality businesses in Scotland. *International Journal of Entrepreneurship Behaviour and Research, 14*(4), 200–218. doi:10.1108/13552550810887381

Jaeger, P.T., & Bertot, J. C. (2010). Transparency and technological change: Ensuring equal

Jensen, J. L. (2003). Virtual democratic dialogue? Bringing together citizens and politicians. *Information Polity, 8,* 29–47.

Kakabase, A., Kakabadse, N. K., & Kouzim, A. (2003). Reinventing the democratic governance project through Information Technology? A growing agenda for debate. *Public Administration Review, 63*(1), 44–60. doi:10.1111/1540-6210.00263

Kamarck, E. C., & Nye, J. S. (Eds.), *Governance. com: Democracy in the information age* (pp. 141–160). Washington, DC: Brookings Institution Press.

Kampen, J. K., & Snijikers, K. (2003). E-democracy. A critical evaluation of the ultimate e-dream. *Social Science Computer Review, 21*(4), 491–496. doi:10.1177/0894439303256095

Kearnes, I., Bend, J., & Stern, B. (2002). *E-participation in local government*. London, UK: IPPR. Retrieved April 15, 2011, from http://www.ippr.org.uk/members/download.asp?f=%2Fecomm%2Ffiles%2Fe_ participation_in_local_government.pdf

Kim, C., & Holzer, M. (2006). Public administrators' acceptance of the practice of digital democracy: A model explaining the utilization of online policy forums in South Korea. *International Journal of Electronic Government Research, 2*(2), 22–48. doi:10.4018/jegr.2006040102

Kim, J. (2006). The impact of Internet use patterns on political engagement: A focus on online deliberation and virtual social capital. *Information Polity, 11*(1), 35–49.

Klijn, E., & Koppenjan, J. F. M. (2002). Rediscovering the citizen: New roles for politicians in interactive policy making. In McLaverty, P. (Ed.), *Public participation and innovations in community governance* (pp. 141–163). Burlington, MA: Ashgate.

Kubicek, H. (2005). Scenarios for future use of e-democracy tools in Europe. *International Journal of Electronic Government Research, 1*(3), 33–50. doi:10.4018/jegr.2005070103

Kurland, N. B., & Egan, T. D. (1996). Participation via the Net: Access, voice and dialogue. *The Information Society, 12*(4), 387–406. doi:10.1080/019722496129369

Lampe, C., LaRose, R., Steinfield, C., & de Maagd, K. (2011). Inherent barriers to the use of social media for public policy informatics. *The Innovation Journal: The Public Sector Innovation Journal, 16*(1). Retrieved April 10, 2011, from http://www.innovation.cc/scholarly-style/lampe_social_media_v16i1a6.pdf

Levy, M. (2001). *E-volve-or-die.com: Thriving in the Internet Age through e-commerce management*. Indianapolis, IN: New Riders.

Livingstone, S., Bober, M., & Helpser, E. J. (2005). Active participation or just more information? Young people's take-up of opportunities to act and interact on the Internet. *Information Communication and Society, 8*(3), 287–314. doi:10.1080/13691180500259103

Macintosh, A., Robson, E., Smith, E., & Whyte, A. (2003). Electronic democracy and young people. *Social Science Computer Review, 21*(1), 43–54. doi:10.1177/0894439302238970

Macintosh, A., & Whyte, A. (2006). *Evaluating how e-participation changes local Democracy.* eGovernment Workshop '06 (eGov06) [online], September 11 2006.

Macintosh, A., & Whyte, A. (2008). Towards an evaluation framework for e-participation. *Transforming Government: People, Process & Policy, 2*(1), 16–30.

Mahrer, H., & Krimmer, R. (2005). Towards the enhancement of e-democracy: Identifying the notion of the middleman paradox. *Information Systems Journal, 15*(1), 27–42. doi:10.1111/j.1365-2575.2005.00184.x

Mayer, I., Edelenbos, J., & Monnikhof, R. (2005). Interactive policy development: Undermining or sustaining democracy? *Public Administration, 83*(1), 179–199. doi:10.1111/j.0033-3298.2005.00443.x

Mclaverty, P. (2002). Is public participation a good thing? In McLaverty, P. (Ed.), *Public participation and innovations in community governance* (pp. 185–198). Aldershot, UK: Ashgate Publishing Ltd.

McLaverty, P. (2010). Participation. In Bevir, M. (Ed.), *Handbook of governance.* London, UK: Sage.

Mechling, J. (2002). Information age governance: Just the start of something big? In

Mehta, M. D., & Darier, E. (1998). Virtual control and disciplining on the Internet: Electronic governmentality in the new wired world. *The Information Society, 14*(2), 107–116. doi:10.1080/019722498128917

Millard, J. (2010). Government 1.5- Is the bottle half full or half empty? *European Journal of ePractice, 9.* Retrieved December 15, 2010, from http://www.epractice.eu/files/European%20 Journal%20epractice%20Volume%209.3_1.pdf

Miller, L. (2008). E-petitions at Westminster: The way forward for democracy? *Parliamentary Affairs, 62,* 162–177. doi:10.1093/pa/gsn044

Mitra, A. (2001). Marginal voices in cyberspace. *New Media & Society, 3*(1), 29–48.

Molinari, F. (2010). On sustainable e-participation. *Proceedings of the IFIP ePart2010 Conference,* Lausanne (Switzerland).

Mysociety. (2011). *About us.* Retrieved April 15, 2011, from http://www.mysociety.org/about/

Newman, J. (2005). Participative governance and the remaking of the public sphere. In J.

Newman (Ed.), *Remaking governance, peoples, politics and the public sphere* (pp. 119-138). University of Bristol: The Policy Press.

O'toole, T., Marsh, D., & Jones, S. (2003). Political literacy cuts both ways: The politics of non-participation among young people. *The Political Quarterly, 74*(3), 349–360. doi:10.1111/1467-923X.00544

OFCOM. (2010). *Communications market research report.* Retrieved April 11, 2011, from http://stakeholders.ofcom.org.uk/market-data-research/market-data/communications-market-reports/cmr10/

Orr, K., & Mcateer, M. (2004). The modernisation of local decision making: Public participation and Scottish local government. *Local Government Studies, 30*(2), 131–155. doi:10.1080/0300393042000267209

Osimo, D. (2008). *Web 2.0 in government: Why and how?* Institute for Prospective Technological Studies (IPTS), JRC, European Commission, EUR 23358. Retrieved from http://ipts.jrc.ec.europa.eu/publications/pub.cfm?id=1565

Parvez, Z. (2008). E-democracy from the perspective of local elected members. *International Journal of Electronic Government Research, 4*(3), 20–35. doi:10.4018/jegr.2008070102

Parvez, Z., & Ahmed, P. (2006). Towards building an integrated perspective of e- democracy in practice. *Information Communication and Society, 9*(5), 612–632. doi:10.1080/13691180600965609

Pattie, C., Seyd, P., & Whitely, P. (2003). Civic attitudes and engagement in modern Britain. *Parliamentary Affairs, 56*, 616–633. doi:10.1093/pa/gsg106

Polat, R. K. (2005). The Internet and political participation. Exploring the explanatory links. *European Journal of Communication, 20*(4), 435–459. doi:10.1177/0267323105058251

Pratchett, L. (1999). New fashions in public participation: Towards greater democracy? *Parliamentary Affairs, 52*(4), 616–633. doi:10.1093/pa/52.4.616

Rethemeyer, R. K. (2007). The empires strike back: Is the Internet corporatizing rather than democratizing policy processes? *Public Administration Review, 67*(2), 199–215. doi:10.1111/j.1540-6210.2007.00707.x

Rohlinger, D., & Brown, J. (2009). Democracy, action and the Internet after 9/11. *The American Behavioral Scientist, 53*(1), 130–150. doi:10.1177/0002764209338791

Saebø, Ø., Rose, J., & Skiftenes, F. L. (2008). The shape of e-participation: Characterizing an emerging research area. *Government Information Quarterly, 25*(3), 400–428. doi:10.1016/j.giq.2007.04.007

Saglie, J., & Vabo, S. I. (2005). *Online participation in Norwegian local politics- The rise of digital divides?* Lokalpolitisk deltakelse,14th Nordic Political Science Association (NOPSA) Conference, 11 –13 August 2005.

Sanford, C., & Rose, J. (2007). Characterizing e-participation. *International Journal of Information Management, 27*(6), 406–421. doi:10.1016/j.ijinfomgt.2007.08.002

Schlosberg, D., Zavetoski, S., & Shulman, S. (2007). Democracy and e-rulemaking: Web-based technologies, participation, and the potential for deliberation. *Journal of Information Technology & Politics, 4*(1), 37–55. doi:10.1300/J516v04n01_04

Scott, J. K. (2006). 'E' the people: Do U.S. municipal government web sites support public involvement. *Public Administration Review, 66*(3), 341–353. doi:10.1111/j.1540-6210.2006.00593.x

Shangapour, S., Hosseini, S., & Hashemnejad, H. (2011). Cyber social networks and social movements. *Global Journal of Human Social Science, 11*(1)

Shelley, M. C., Thrane, L., Shulman, S., Lang, E., Beisser, S., Larson, T., & Muttiti, J. (2004). Digital citizenship: Parameters of the digital divide. *Social Science Computer Review, 22*(2), 256–269. doi:10.1177/0894439303262580

Smith, A., & Rainie, L. (2010). *8% of online Americans use Twitter.* Washington, DC: Pew Internet and American Life Project, Pew Research Centre. Retrieved from http://pewinternet.ord/Reports/2010/Twitter-update-2010.aspx

Smith, G. (2005). *Beyond the ballot: 57 democratic innovations from around the world.* ISBN: 0955030307.

Smith, G. (2009). *Democratic innovations: Designing institutions for democratic governance.* Cambridge, UK: Cambridge University Press. doi:10.1017/CBO9780511609848

Sterling, R. (2005). Promoting democratic governance through partnerships? In Newman, J. (Ed.), *Remaking governance, peoples, politics and the public sphere* (pp. 139–158). University of Bristol: The Policy Press.

Talpin, J., & Wojcik, S. (2010). Deliberating environmental policy issues: Comparing the learning potential of online and face-to-face discussions on climate change. *Policy & Internet, 2*(2).

Taylor-Smith, E., & Lindner, R. (2010). Social networking tools supporting constructive involvement throughout the policy-cycle. In *Proceedings of EDEM 2010 - Conference on Electronic Democracy, May 7-8, 2010, Danube-University Krems, Austria.* Vienna, Austria: Austrian Computer Society.

Traunmüller, R. (2010). Web 2.0 creates a new government. In. *Proceedings of EGOVIS, 2010,* 77–83.

Wallis, J. (2005). Cyberspace, information literacy and the information society. *Library Review, 54*(4), 218–222. doi:10.1108/00242530510593407

Weare, C. (2002). The Internet and democracy: The causal links between technology and politics. *International Journal of Public Administration, 25*(5), 659–691. doi:10.1081/PAD-120003294

West, D. (2004). E-government and the transformation of service delivery and citizen attitudes. *Public Administration Review, 64*(1), 15–28. doi:10.1111/j.1540-6210.2004.00343.x

Wilson, D. (1999). Exploring the limits of public participation in local government. *Parliamentary Affairs, 52,* 246–259. doi:10.1093/pa/52.2.246

Wojcik, S. (2008). *The three key roles of moderator in online discussions. The case of French local governments' forums.* Politics: Web 2.0: An International Conference, hosted by the New Political Communication Unit, Royal Holloway, University of London, April17-18, 2008.

Wright, S. (2006). Electrifying democracy? 10 years of policy and practice. *Parliamentary Affairs, 59*(2), 236–249. doi:10.1093/pa/gsl002

Xie, B., & Jaeger, P. T. (2008). Older adults and political participation on the Internet: A cross cultural comparison of the USA and China. *Journal of Cross-Cultural Gerontology, 23*(1), 1–15. doi:10.1007/s10823-007-9050-6

Yang, G. (2009). Online activism. *Journal of Democracy, 20*(3), 33–36. doi:10.1353/jod.0.0094

Yang, K. (2005). Public administrators' trust in citizens: A missing link in citizen involvement efforts. *Public Administration Review, 65*(3), 273–286. doi:10.1111/j.1540-6210.2005.00453.x

Zimmer, M. (2008). Preface: Critical perspectives on Web 2.0. *First Monday, 13*(3).

KEY TERMS AND DEFINITIONS

Consultation: Used in the broad sense to describe either: 1). The dynamic process of dialogue between individuals or groups, based upon a genuine exchange of views and, normally, with the objective of influencing decisions, policies or programmes of action; or 2). Where people are offered the opportunity to comment on what is planned, but are not able to develop and input their own ideas or participate in putting plans into action. (Consultation Institute website, 2009a)

Engagement: Is a less easily defined concept but can be seen as Actions and processes taken or undertaken to establish effective relationships with individuals or groups so that more specific interactions can then take place (Consultation Institute, 2009b).

eParticipation: Is defined as being the use of ICTs (primarily but not exclusively web-based technologies) for facilitating engagement and participation in the policy making process. The term eParticipation is most appropriate because it has clear connotations of participative democracy as opposed to the term eDemocracy which has connotations of elective democracy, specifically online voting.

Participative Democracy: Refers to the involvement of citizens in policy making and the running of government. It often involves a degree of decision making and responsibility being devolved directly to the people and the term 'direct democracy' is sometimes used as a synonym.

Participatory Mechanisms: Is used to describe all forms of public participation that contributes either directly into decision making or form part of a wider engagement strategy by government organisations

Representative Democracy: Refers to the more traditional model of democracy whereby citizen participation is limited to voting in elections while the main activities of governance are conducted by elected members.

Representativeness: Is used in this chapter to describe whether or not the respondents to participatory mechanisms constitute a valid sample of the wider population or whether or not certain groups dominate participatory initiatives while others are harder to reach.

Chapter 13
Reaching Citizen 2.0:
How Government Uses Social Media to Send Public Messages during Times of Calm and Times of Crisis

Nancy Van Leuven
Bridgewater State University, USA

Danielle Newton
Bennington College, USA

Deniz Zeynep Leuenberger
Bridgewater State University, USA

Tammy Esteves
Troy University, USA

ABSTRACT

Many forms of public communication are now mediated through technologies that challenge traditional models of civic engagement and the public's "right to know," including communication for disaster management. This chapter employs a comparative lens to look at how social media messages are pushed forward by different layers of government to reach their publics during times of calm and crisis. Specifically, the project studies how information is framed for public consumption, how it is made available, and how it is timely and relevant. Research methods include a triangulation approach, including interviews with officials from over 20 city, regional, state, and federal agencies to follow up on content and textual analyses of online content disseminated by over 40 public agencies. This chapter argues that public administrators must be engaged with citizens and prepared to use social media during emergencies as well as for routine news, and offers key goals for government departments to promote an agenda of increased citizen information and engagement.

DOI: 10.4018/978-1-4666-0318-9.ch013

INTRODUCTION

Blogs, tweets, real-time updates and Facebook's LIKE button. Social media is a critical communications tool in today's global conversations among citizens, non-governmental organizations, and public agencies, as seen in the explosion of blogging (e.g. the U.S. Department of State's DipNote), micro-blogging (e.g. Oxfam on Twitter), and social sites (including the British Embassy's presence on Facebook and former California Governor Schwarzenegger's YouTube channel). This is a huge shift from Web 2.0 – the shift from stationary websites to those with social networking and shared content—to reach Citizen 2.0, those people who rely on social media to share information.

For this project, "social media" includes technology-based media that allows individual and accessible postings and shared information, such as Twitter, Facebook, and WiserEarth, a social network for sustainability. These e-channels are increasingly recognized as a way of communicating that compels transparency and engagement, as evidenced in global dissemination of the Kenyan draft constitutions in local dialects. While much is now being studied about how public administrators are using social media to better connect for civic engagement, this project is more centered on message content and purpose that adapts to real-time needs. This is a critical time for public information, especially when various levels of government are trying to maintain balance and credibility amidst media and residence who regard government as a dirty word (Eliasoph, 1998).

Specifically, how are "routine" content and channels switched from "times of calm" to include timely, relevant public messages during "times of crisis"? After all, citizenry access to information is constantly shifting: During the three week coding timeframe for this project, a massive earthquake and resulting tsunami rocked Japan and first-hand horror stories (and photos) immediately zoomed throughout the social media sphere. West Coast cities in the U.S. prepared citizenry for after-effects and many other public and private groups launched massive campaigns about how to help Japanese victims. Whether analyzing how a municipality such as Portland, Oregon, posts updates on how its citizens can donate, or how tweets tracked the effects of the disaster on the global map, the larger study reveals how this inverted pyramid of information is reorganizing public voices and toppling silos of information.

While previous scholarship addresses the increase of "narrowcast" social media with multiple voices versus the traditional "broadcast" approach of singular news, this study seeks to clarify whether changes in media systems have increased the capacities of public groups to communicate both to targeted public audiences and among themselves. As social media is increasingly part of communication during crises, it is valuable to know how particular strategies help reach Citizen 2.0.

BACKGROUND

Research efforts about new media, and how it can be used by governments to more widely disperse knowledge as an accessible commodity, has steadily grown in the United States and elsewhere, particularly since 9/11. As noted by scholars of civic engagement, media plays a pivotal role in informing citizens, holding leaders accountable, and being a critical watchdog (Cammearts, 2009). From a participatory perspective, it is also increasingly part of crisis management plans prepared by agencies for potential natural disasters (flooding, earthquake, famines, etc.) as well as crises caused by humans (nuclear, environmental, and political uprisings, etc.). While public administrators might routinely use Twitter to publicize town halls, many are also crafting social media plans to include public relations best practices of engaging messages for internal and external audiences, especially in times of crises (Fearn-Banks, 2007). At the same time, previous scholarship notes that civic engagement is also increasing in areas of community volunteerism, consumer activism, and social justice causes (Bennet, 2008).

Before adding to such valuable discussions, it is important to agree on just what media is today and how public administrators define other terms. Much mediated information runs through mobile applications, which are software applications designed to run on hand-held computers such as PDAs and cell phones, including online citizen reporting (FixMyStreet, etc.). For the purpose of this project, e-government includes public efforts using Internet-based technologies for business and citizen Interaction, including recent Open Government websites and initiatives, but is considered a one-way delivery of information as opposed to the interactive capabilities of social media.

With the fragmentation of mass media channels and audiences, and the proliferation of new digital communication formats available to public administrators, it is difficult to draw sharp boundaries around separate media spheres. Which brings us to the subject of this chapter: The rise of social media aimed at bringing more than basic public information to citizenry is causing public agencies to loosen their hold on exclusive knowledge and entering traditions of common knowledge. This interactivity is contributes to the formation of networks with citizens who then become more bonded to the provider (Burnett & Marshall, 2003). A number of studies have emphasized perspectives of how public administrators produce and distribute knowledge for the betterment of civic engagement and democracy; specifically, as officials are increasingly tweeting and blogging to engage their publics, they are also creating horizontal flows of information that construct and move information. Thus, as today's public administrators share knowledge and facts, they are also creating personal relationships and building trust within the public sphere.

Information Technology in Public Administration: During Times of Calm and Crisis

Information technology and e-government are increasingly embedded in public administration structures and decision making, and serve several roles in the delivery of government services and public information. A classic role of information technology in public agencies is the accumulation of larger amounts of information and data about policy making and citizen needs and the management of data resources for service delivery (Sindelar, Mintz and Hughes, 2009). E-government services have been used for the purposes of notification, of gathering information, and of managing basic transactions such as paying taxes or fees (Susanto and Goodwin, 2010; Foley and Alfanso, 2009). Information technology is also increasingly used to build citizen participation and e-democracy opportunities for citizens. These are quite different from public channels of communication with one-way, top-down flows of information.

Citizen Participation and E-democracy

Citizen participation may be regarded as collaboration in public processes that include citizen voices, sometimes referred to as stakeholder engagement, such as town hall meetings. In order to maximize effectiveness and citizen participation, government agencies have the opportunity move beyond simply sharing information with citizens to meaningfully engaging them and with them (Power, 2002). This is especially important as vertically and hierarchically organized agencies use information technology to increase collaboration through e-democracy (Sindelar, Mintz,& Hughes). Citizen use of social media also follows particular models of public involvement: while a dutiful citizen rely on traditional uses of mostly one-way information, an actualized citizen uses social media for issues that reflect personal values and loosely networked activism (Bennett, 2007).

E-democracy not only allows for transparency in information sharing, but also directs input and influence by citizens on policy making (Jung Yun and Opheim, 2010; Kakabadse, Kakabadse, & Koluzmin, 2003). Robust communication systems can alter the relationship of citizens with their state, can enhance individual rights and improve service delivery, can expand civic engagement, and can provide opportunities to underserved communities (Thompson and Wilkinson, 2009, p.52; Austin and Callen, 2008, p.325; King and Cotterill, 2007, p. 333; Von Haldenwang, 2004, p.421).

Successful Design of E-Systems

This requires creating systems that integrate citizen beliefs and behaviors in relation to their information technology use (Susanto and Goodwin, 2010, p.62, Makadeo, 2007 p. 391). Several characteristics identify successful e-government initiatives, such as: perceived usefulness and relevance; perceived ease of use; compatibility; perceived value for the money; perceived responsiveness; perceived convenience; trust in the technology; and quality and reliability of information (Makadeo, 2007; Susanto and Goodwin, 2010; Wangtipatwong, Chutimakul, and Papasraton, 2008). Effective e-government systems are citizen-centered and results-oriented (Morgeson and Mithas, 2009, pp.740-742). Information technology can also be used to adapt to political, socio-economic, technological, and cultural changes (Bekkers, 2007, p.103). Therefore, public administrators should take an active role in designing and implementing systems that include democratic values and processes as designs are technical, administrative, and political acts (Brewer, Neubaen, and Geiselhart, 2006,pp. 473-474; Kim and Lee, 2006, p. 370).

Challenges in Public Communication

There are also several challenges in designing effective, efficient, and participatory systems of technology. One of these challenges is the management of privacy by government organizations. As there is a significant amount of personal information available through social networking sites and other e-based systems, government must be especially careful to protect citizen security and privacy by releasing identifying information that could compromise rights and welfare when combined with other privately and publicly held information (Wills and Reives, 2009, p. 279) Public agencies can build on existing trust and social capital with citizens by managing the risk associated with e-governance systems. Cyber trust can be improved through careful privacy, security, risk reduction, and identify protection (Dutton, Guerra, Zizzo, and Peltu, 2005, p. 15, Bannister, 2005, pp.74-76; Steeves, 2008, p.331). Additionally, access, security, authentication, and privacy in e-government systems need to be held in balance (Holden and Millett, 2005, p.367).

Another challenge of Information technology systems is that they can reduce, instead of enhance, human experiences and communication (Austin and Callen, 2008, p. 26; Jorgensen and Klay, 2007, pp. 303-304). If there is too much emphasis on artifacts and technical capabilities, instead of upon communication and collaboration with citizens and employees, then the effectiveness of information technology systems can be reduced (Lips, 2007, p.249). As the majority of information systems in the public sector are unsuccessful, agencies should explore low risk, low cost, and least disruptive systems when designing e-governance systems (Goldfinch, 2007, p.917). There is also a growing body of scholarship that portrays social media as lacking the critical interactivity needed to encourage public civic engagement in public (Brainard &McNutt, 2010).

Finally, information technology systems can change the social and physical environment of public organizations. The level of information technology adoption in public agencies impacts organizational performance and organizational structure (Heintze and Bretschneider, 2000, p. 827). Additionally, e-governance can change where and how citizens interact with public employees, how they exercise their vote and voice, and how they define what their role is in policy making. In designing e-governance systems, careful consideration of design impacts should be considered.

To that end, this chapter focuses on how four levels of government – cities, regional councils of governments, states, and federal departments – are using social media in 2011 to connect with publics. It attempts to offer the reader an aggregate of best practices and trends within Government 2.0, specifically focusing on engagement of respective audiences via social media for multiple purposes.

METHODOLOGY

To analyze Citizen 2.0 outreach, this research compares and measures the different strategies used to successfully (or not so successfully) bring real-time issues to the citizenry. It follows the methodological framework of the 2001 Pew Internet and American Life project (Pew, 2001). The chapter also updates information from cities studied in a 2009 Fels Institute Study, thus incorporating previous scholarship to include other platforms (Fels, 2009). Adhering to the same variables of Internet engagement as the Pew Study, this study compares the 2001 findings a decade later. The specific objects of study, such as specific cities and states, and ensuing recommendations come from these studies as a way to build upon previous scholarship.

For optimal rigor and appropriateness, the project's methodology included a triangulation approach using content analysis, textual analysis, and interviews (Scandura & Williams, 2000). Scholars recommend the selection of content

analysis as a valuable methodology for studying news culture and norms such as the use of social media, especially because the quantification of textual data in online texts can point to dominant and abstract patterns that include organizational norms and ideologies. In addition, the data obtained from textual and content analyses can be verified with interviews to clarify findings based on technological, organizational, or other variables that exist outside of the website text itself (Neuendorf, 2002). However, content analysis can also be used in conjunction with other methods of analysis, segmenting data sets based on organizational, technological, or other variables of importance that exist outside of the text itself (McMillan, 2000; Neuendorf, 2002). This study relies on content analysis as a qualitative research method to quantify communication data, combining those variables with textual analyses and interviews to construct categorical variables.

The chapter was organized by content analyzing all social media outlets from a representative sampling of cities, regional COGs, states, and federal levels of government as studied in the previously mentioned Pew and Fels studies.

As seen in Table 1, a total of 42 governmental agencies were examined for social media presence based on website content and textual analyses, as well as interviews from spokespeople.

All entities were content analyzed according to the instance, defined as the exact grouping of icons and words that could sustain the meaning of the coding category. Often the instance was a single social media icon (such as the Facebook symbol or Twitter bird), a small group of taglines or words, or a distinct phrase. When multiple instances of a coding category occurred in close proximity, they were counted as separate whenever distinct meanings could be identified. The coding categories for a period of "calm," between February 10 and February 24, 2011, were operationalized for instances of: 311 service; Blogs; Citizen training; Comments on official documents; Crowdsourcing; Email/contact us; Event registra-

Table 1. Objects of study

Level of Government	Number	Method of Selection	Specific Objects of Study
Cities	5	Pew Study	Austin, TX; Cleveland, OH; Nashville, TN; Portland, OR; Washington D.C
Cities	17	Fels Study	Ann Arbor, MI; Alexandria, VA: Boulder, CO; Boynton Beach, FL; Chandler, AZ; Huntsville, AL; Madison, WI; Mesa, AZ; Philadelphia, PA; Phoenix, AZ; Richmond, VA (Police Department); San Jose, CA; Santa Clarita, CA: Tampa, FL; West Palm Beach, FL; Winston-Salem, NC
Councils of Government	4	Evidence of social media activity and presence plus geographic sampling	Chicago Metropolitan Agency for Planning; Metropolitan Washington Council of Governments; Mid-Region Council of Governments of New Mexico; Southern California Association of Governments
States	10	Evidence of social media activity and presence plus geographic sampling	Alabama; California; Colorado; Kansas; Michigan; Ohio; Oklahoma; Tennessee; Vermont; Washington
Federal agencies	9	Evidence of social media activity and presence plus mentions on	Department of Defense; Department of Education; Environmental Protection Agency; Housing and Urban Development; National Aeronautics and Space Administration; National Oceanic and Atmospheric Administration; U.S. Department of State; White House

tion; Facebook; Flickr; LinkedIn; Live (online) chat; Mailing list; Mobile apps; News center; Newsletter; Press releases; RSS feeds; Survey; Text notification; TTY/ADA capabilities; Twitter; and YouTube. In contrast, the coding about the Japanese earthquake specifically focused on these words: Action; Aid; Community; Disaster; Emergency; Fundraisers; Radiation; Relief; Risk; and Safety. To best compare the two periods, we used the same websites studied during the time of "calm" to study how messages during this time of "crisis" changed public information; specifically, we coded from March 11, 2011, through March 25, 2011, to include two weeks of information after the initial earthquake and resulting tsunami.

As a first stage of research, nine graduate students coded for the above-mentioned terms and government organizations. Chapter authors ensured that all primary home pages were analyzed by at least two outside coders and inter-coder reliability coefficients were in the .95 range. A subset within the agencies was created to distinguish what were considered to be valuable case studies. As

mentioned in Table 1, criteria for inclusion were twofold: 1) Multiple instances of social media presence, and 2) geographical and other factors of representation.

Finally, a textual analysis of each website was undertaken to study interactivity within online content, including categories such as how website icons and text worked to build a platform for public information (How and what information is being sent out?), and whether public administrators also built a platform for interactivity (Can citizens send information back to the agency, or is the flow of information one-way?). And do these instances change when a disaster occurs? Once intercoder reliability was established and researchers could share common issues needing further study, the team created follow-up questions for opinion leaders associated with the public agency. This yielded an unstructured interview that allowed interviewers to "generate new questions, probe freely, and shift the order of questions" (Ferguson, 2000).

This triangulation of research methods – content analysis of websites, textual analysis of present social media, and interviews of those associated with the mediated messages, led to the following findings and ensuing goals and recommendations.

FINDINGS

While the initial research project timeline was bound by two dates in February 2011, to illustrate typical social media use, the March 11, 2011, earthquake in Japan during our follow-up research offered the opportunity to point out whether (and how) governments react after a crisis in terms of reaching the public.

Social Media during Times of Calm

Given the amount of content activity and engagement opportunities, the researchers expected to see robust dialogues on many public social media sites. However, some cities, regional councils of government, and states have no trace of social media, while others are as personable and engaging as Southwest Airlines (Twitter) and Starbucks (Facebook).One of the most surprising findings was the difference in content and tone between governmental groups, including neighboring cities or cities within a regional council of governments, or within a certain state. For the most part, the websites for regional councils seem to be underutilized and more about "appearance" of participation rather than actual invitations for it. Most requests for citizen feedback are solely within a mandated public review process for a specific document or project. This goes against one of the foundations of social media, which is to build an interconnectedness that is always in effect.

In terms of original content, regional councils of government were the most barren. Most did not provide content other than dates and times for meetings, and most of their fans are other public agencies. Two had an only three followers while others had more impressive numbers in the thousands. Some COGs included a "Discussion"

tab on their Facebook wall yet these were largely barren and inactive. During the two coding dates, researchers recorded the number of fans or likes on the first date but noticed that were only a handful of additional fans on the second date for all the COGs studied, indicating very little robust content and relevance to audiences.

What appeared to be links to original content were mostly forwarded articles, giving an impression of quantity over quality. With a 140-character count limit, most tweets from all studied websites are links to government blogs and other information. However, Twitter offers an extra element not found in Facebook; that is, while Facebook walls might allow comments from fans, Twitter has the added dimension of newspapers and broadcast stations sending tweet requests for information and interview subjects. And, since most traditional sources (such as newspapers and press releases) are still used in addition to social media, several agencies have ramped up their Twitter presence in order to follow journalists.

Facebook remains an anchor of social media, used by most entities to post news and events, often with room for public comment. Again, content and interactivity is key to public engagement, as seen in the Facebook pages of Reno, Nevada, which boasts over 10,000 fans and regular public comments (and city response). For instance, when a citizen grumbled at 10:42 p.m. about the use of public funds for City Hall energy efficiency measures, the City of Reno answered at 9:14 a.m. the next day and outlined funding sources. The entire thread was "liked" by four other citizens and the City was recently featured on a "Government Fun with Facebook" blog post about the need for humor in government channels. As of this writing, one of the most "liked" city pages award goes to Boston, MA, with over 144,000 people regularly posting new content (including 8 discussion boards) and also commenting on official posts such as, "Have you ever sat back and wondered how it is possible to have so much awesomeness in a single city? Really Boston, how do you do it?" This is a finding that reinforces previous scholarship about citizen models; that is, engaged citizens expect interactivity and response from public outlets.

One of the most-mentioned challenges in social media citizen engagement is the lack of resources in public offices. Several public administrators mentioned that social media requires resources beyond the funding for hard copy mailers and web design; effective Twitter, Facebook, and other messaging requires dedicated staff time to answer requests and post new content. Jeff Friedman, Director of IT for the City of Philadelphia, devotes only "15 to 20 minutes a day to social media" (Friedman, 2011). Lacking adequate staff to monitor, respond, and post to social media sometimes results in inconsistent messages across the platforms. The City of Riverside, CA, for instance, models top-down information sharing on Twitter because the City issues dry tweets ("Riverside Reaches Out to Sister City Sendai, Japan") and is not following anybody (thus discouraging public feedback), yet its Facebook page (with 789 likes) has much more frequent and engaging text ("Happy Friday, All! Venture out …or lounge on the couch in jammies and watch movies? What are your plans for this weekend?"). In addition, such data reflects the success of more consistent, united messaging.

It was interesting to note whether public agencies allow followers on Twitter, thus encouraging conversation and comments to their posts, and who was deemed worthy to follow. Although a model for other states in terms of developed operations in social media, Governor Christine Gregoire in the State of Washington has 5092 followers yet follows only 24. According to the Governor's social media director, social media is a means of communicating with the state's young people, especially issue-driven messages such as anti-texting while driving campaigns.

Social media efforts are also challenged by warring factions within a governmental group, such as when Public Information Officers disagree as to what types of information to send out and who is responsible for such messaging. Most governmental entities do not have tech-savvy leaders on board and one large city hired a social media consultant who quickly left because of an "outsider" status.

Several spokespersons asked for more collaboration between public agencies so that success stories (and failures) might be more readily available. For instance, FixMyStreet is open-source (free) software that was developed by mySociety.org, a U.K. nonprofit that serves as a middleman between local governments and citizens who report problems such as potholes, graffiti, and street lighting. Variations have popped up in U.S. cities such as Nashville, which uses the web application, and others are considering the mobile app. This indicates an increasing desire to reach Citizen 2.0 using interactive technologies that encourage two-way conversations.

Finally, the largest looming question remains how to encourage citizen comments without being overrun by demanding posts. According to Dionne Waugh, the Richmond, Virginia, Police Department public communications officer, agencies are changing strategies by not posting everything they can (Waugh, 2011). A discussion from a government web managers listserv run by a team that manages the home page for the Environmental Protection Agency included comments regarding, "Should government Facebook pages allow people to post?" According to Jeffrey Harvey, Director of Web Communications at EPA, comments are accepted on the main page, but citizens are not allowed to post their own threads for discussion.

I think of it this way: A social media presence is like a booth at a shopping mall. You're there so they can see you as people vs. an institution… you talk to people, you listen to what they say, they can hear each other's ideas and you catch casual conversations among people all around you whether they're talking directly to you or not. You might even hold a public discussion, where you put out a question and then invite people to share their thoughts. But you don't allow people to plaster their posters all over your booth and you don't hand them the microphone unchecked for 3 hours to say anything on any topic. - (Levy, 2011)

Although the District of Columbia does not allow independent posts, it does offer many social media channels to engage citizens, businesses, employees, and visitors to the nation's capital. As of this writing, the District operates: 16 Twitter accounts; 11 RSS feeds; 18 Facebook accounts, and blogs for various agencies to share information. Washington D.C. also offers its citizens text notifications, online newsletters, mobile apps, and Flickr as interactive tools for citizen inclusion and engagement.

With so much information flowing from an agency, a natural concern would be how to best determine and verify the message. NASA builds-in a vetting process for each page of its website: There is a page editor and NASA official responsible for web page content, which is guided by a communications policy for employees that offer specific guidelines about when it is appropriate to disseminate information. Ultimately, the Office of Communications is responsible for ensuring good communication from NASA to the public (Schierholz, 2011).

Social Media during Times of Crisis

In a final analytical component, this study looks back at organizations to see how social media and online strategies played into public conversations about issues in Japan following the March 11, 2011, earthquake and ensuing tsunami and nuclear emergencies. While some public groups chose not to post any information, such as the City of Austin, federal Housing and Urban Development Department, and Washington D.C., some focused solely on information about the crisis while others, like Portland, OR, included donation buttons or information about how the public could help Japan.

Federal agencies displayed mostly a top-down public information model, offering transparency but few opportunities for citizen participation. NASA displayed imagery of the environmental impact, sticking to information about topography and how the earthquake has shifted the Earth axis and reconfigured days. The Federal Emergency Management Agency tweeted "tsunami preparedness tips" to Smartphones, which was retweeted by the White House and hundreds of others. And the White House repeated emotional statements over multiple social media platforms about "standing with the people of Japan" and "the strength and spirit of the Japanese people."

State activity ranged from widespread emotional pleas for sympathy and condolences to no mention at all. The State of Washington used the public information strategy, delivering news about no radiation threats (including a FAQ about radiation and Potassium iodide) without information about donations to the Japanese people.

Most regional councils of government did not address the Japanese situation, with the exception of the Metropolitan Washington Council of Governments. This COG posted the same message on Facebook and Twitter: "The crisis in Japan has revived discussion on the pros and cons of nuclear energy. Should nuclear be part of a carbon-free energy mix?"

The City of Portland, OR, issued multiple blog posts by Mayor Sam Adams sending "thoughts and prayers" to the people of Japan on the day of the earthquake, followed by a more city-centered YouTube PSA about disaster preparedness on May 14, 2011, then a letter to Portland citizens on March 15, 2011, about how to aid Japan.

The City of Riverside, CA, quickly updated its home page to run a scrolling news and video column of updates, as well as condolences to those in its Sister City of Sendai. Officials also embedded a Relief Fund mechanism with a "Donate Now" icon for secure, tax-deductible donations directly to the City. And, to make it even easier for citizens to connect during the disaster, the

Table 2. Online content comparison during times of "crisis"

Tweets from federal agencies immediately following earthquake in Japan (March 11, 2011)	Website keywords and other media from City of Portland, OR., immediately following earthquake in Japan (March 11, 2011)
The President: "we will stand with the people of Japan as they contain this crisis, recover from this hardship & rebuild their great nation" <u>about 2 hours ago</u> via web President Obama: "Above all, I am confident that Japan will re-cover and rebuild because of the strength and spirit of the Japanese people" <u>about 2 hours ago</u> via web Starting soon: President Obama speaks on tragedy in Japan & US response, watch live: http://wh.gov/live <u>about 2 hours ago</u> via web Just announced: President will speak on situation in Japan at 3:30EDT. Watch here: http://wh.gov/live An update on US support for #Japan & links to how you can help: http://1.usa.gov/eQf4d7 <u>6:08 PM Mar 13th</u> via web from Washington, DC fema Get #tsunami preparedness tips on your smartphone http://m.fema.gov & pls cont to listen to local officials. <u>7:23 AM Mar 11th</u> via web Retweeted by whitehouse and 100+ others Obama: "Michelle & I send our deepest condolences to the people of Japan, particularly those who have lost loved ones" http://wh.gov/xMY <u>7:00 AM Mar 11th</u> via web	**Friday, March 11, 2011 4:03pm** Mayor Sam Adams released a paper to Consul General Okabe sending personal "thoughts and prayers" from the mayor to the people of Japan. Means for aid: Mercy Corps **Monday, March 14, 2011 3:03pm** Mayor Sam Adams released a YouTube PSA regarding local disaster preparedness. "Are you prepared if disaster strikes?" Keywords: horrific, tragic, earthquake, tsunami, disaster, anywhere, no warning, "reminded that an event on the other side of the ocean can impact lives-and livelihoods-here in Oregon," emergency, Neighborhood Emergency Team, public, residents, alerts, information, disruptions, resiliency, readiness, household, neighborhood, preparedness, and ongoing effort **Tuesday, March 15, 2011 1:03pm** "How to Help Our Friends in Japan," is a letter written from the Mayor to suggest to the Portland public how to aid Japan. Keywords: earthquake, tsunami, devastation, stunned, concerned, wellbeing, history, culture, business, response, team, Mercy Corps, assist, relief, survivor, disaster, team, organization, partner, supplies, donations, victims, grief, support, wishes, condolences, participate, public, recover, and rebuild.

homepage includes contact information for the U.S. Department of State, plus links to the Red Cross "Safe and Well" page for a family and friends location-finder.

Perhaps one explanation for this 'information and donation' cycle is that the public sphere is increasingly a place dominated by non-profit and non-governmental organizations, such as the Red Cross and others that became the focus for citizens to help others and lend support. While such partnerships help in the immediacy of a crisis, such as directing citizens to the Red Cross for donations, there is a need for governments to focus on earlier adoptions of social media applications to "get ahead of NGO passion." For instance, *TweetDeck* is a multi-platform tool that integrates and organizes contacts from Twitter, Facebook, LinkedIn, etc. *SwiftRiver* is a tool that was initially designed to allow the integration of multiple social network sites for emergency

managers to organize and utilize crisis information and, when partnered with the geographic mapping tool *Ushahidi*, provides a dynamic option for disaster response. Such tools were recently seen at work in situations like the earthquakes in Haiti and Japan, and Hurricane Katrina.

As seen above in Table 2, a sampling of online content showed a similar messaging strategy for both federal agencies and cities. However, researchers noticed a distinct shift in tone from West Coast public administrators (including the states of California and Washington) who initially echoed the "sympathy" tone of other agencies, yet quickly moved into a "disaster preparedness" tone. Much as the FEMA tweet about preparedness tips shows a strategy of social media use, the Portland YouTube video brought the global issue into local boundaries. This indicates an ability to shift content according to real-time circumstances and follows public relations models that call for crisis management before the crisis so that agencies are prepared to meet more challenges of e-information systems.

Solutions and Recommendations

Being in the "information age" with rapidly expanding mediums for sourcing information, governments have the opportunity to harness the cumulative power of citizens to make communities better. The internet and social media can heavily influence a government's ability to bring citizens to action, as seen in messaging content immediately following a global disaster that threatened the West Coast of the United States. Based on research findings, the following are areas of interest that public administrators should consider when building internet and social media connections to citizens as a means of enhancing information sharing and encouraging participation. We offer these recommendations to fill gaps in existing literature, that they may be used by government departments to push forward an agenda of increased social media for these purposes:

Public Participation

In order for the public to participate, they have to be informed about the opportunities for involvement. The internet and social media communication methods are currently the best way to relay information about participation opportunities, but make it easy for your publics to connect. For instance, the City of Reno hosts separate web pages about "Mobile Sites & Apps" as well as ways to connect, including: A blog with RSS feed; Facebook pages and Twitter names for both the City and Police Department; YouTube, LinkedIn, and Nixle (text message alerts) for the City; and Flickr for the City as well as the Reno Arts and Culture department. Simply, social media takes the comment process directly to citizens.

Public Access

In order for government to be accessible, government has to provide various means of participating. For example, the city of Nashville, Tennessee, highlights a mayoral "Community Matters" initiative for interlinked neighborhoods, as well as the common "Fix My Street" app for citizens to report potholes, overgrown bushes, and sunken drain covers. The internet and social media can bridge geographic and time gaps between citizens and government, allowing citizens to instantly report problems (and often keep track of the answering process).

Citizen (and Colleague) Engagement

Similar to the first two, in order for citizens to get engaged, they have to be informed and encouraged to participate. For instance, wheelchair-using citizens in Bristol, England, mapped out a color-coded map for "The Hills Are Evil" website, prompting public outcries for accessibility (Watershed, 2011). Social media can prompt citizens to engage in the issues they feel passionate about by providing specialized categories of interest. At the same time, public officials can use social media for government-talk and also crowd-source for creative ideas, such as the EPA's job postings and call for help to produce a map similar to one at Recovery.gov with information about where citizens live.

Citizen Governance

The political context of social media is most often linked to pressures of public spending cuts as well as public demands for increased transparency. As seen in Washington D.C., open source citizenry can use the wisdom of voters to save money and improve services, as well as embed participation within a more useful networked community. One EPA interviewee sees social media "playing a strong role in the future in true collaborative policy-making." And, in today's connected world where citizens want to vote for representatives as easily as they vote for the next American Idol, the internet and social media can provide citizens with the information they need to get involved with joining governing boards for true impact.

Community Building

Whereas some citizens are passionate about public participation in the political process and citizen governance, other citizens are more interested in community programs and activities that are more community based than government or politically based. Government can help to relay information about community based programs and initiatives that may not be government sponsored or direct information through social media and the internet as a way to promote community.

Volunteerism

Government should promote volunteer opportunities for citizens regardless if they relate to government sponsored initiatives. Increasingly referred to as "the third sector," volunteerism helps to build community and social capital within a community; for instance, studies have found that volunteer group members often carry higher levels of community orientation and morale, with much lower levels of alienation and apathy (Carmel & Harlock, 2008) and government can promote this aspect of a thriving community through information sharing via the internet and social media.

Disaster Management

Probably one of the most important aspects of information sharing through the government, disaster management planning, preparedness and real time instructions can be facilitated by government via the internet and social media. Building on the "window of opportunity" seen since 9/11 (and as evidenced in citizen support

during the 2011 crisis in Japan), network connections can help boost problem solving, community participation, and trust building (Kirlin &Kirlin, 2000). Additionally, government can help to connect neighborhoods to share best practices via the internet and social media because ultimately the more self reliant individuals and neighborhoods are to deal with disasters, the more functional the government can be in restoring normalcy.

Emergency Information

The government can help to relay information and warnings relating to any type of emergency situation from a missing child, precautions on how to protect pipes from freezing and bursting, to a gunman on the loose through messages via the internet and social media. Since the tragic shooting at Virginia Tech in 2007, for instance, most colleges and universities have implemented emergency plans where students will receive immediate text messages in the case of a crisis on campus.

Sustainability Programs

Sustainability and self-sufficiency are built at the personal and local level. Government can help to develop and implement some sustainability programs, i.e. waste management, smart grids, energy efficiency codes etc., but ultimately citizens should form bonds with their neighbors and learn best practices for their personal behavior and lifestyles. Although few cities are actively contributing to the #sustainability or other "green" feeds on Twitter or pages on Facebook, the better use of the internet and social media can help to connect citizens, inform them and allow them to share best practices.

Social Activity

Governments should support civic social activity and often government plays some part in the facilities or security aspects of social events, but government can also play a marketing role by providing information for events, government sponsored or not, through the use of social media and the internet.

FUTURE RESEARCH DIRECTIONS

While this study focused on government's use of social media, it is important to keep track of how platforms and technologies change and whether government is an early adaptor of such revisions. Most existing research focuses on Web 2.0, which was considered relatively new at the time of publications issued in 2009 and earlier, and is the primary platform of governments today. Future public administration studies might include an introduction to Web 3.0 and the possibilities it presents to municipalities; for instance, another model for stronger networked communities might be the Community of Practice, a foundation based on vigilance emerging as a sustainable and desirable post-9/11 behavior. Such research would underscore the potential of public agencies to build trust, educate stakeholders, and create grass-roots partnerships.

In addition, a parallel study of nonprofits would illustrate the strength of links between private and public partnerships, including those operating in the global arena. For example, many NGOs such as the Gates Foundation pair celebrities with social media for social good. Actress Alyssa Milano regularly raises money for charities through tweet challenges, asking her followers to donate to specific causes (Gates Foundation, 2011). The ONE Campaign debuted the "Living Proof" campaign in late 2010 to bring success stories to the public forefront in an effort to show progress in Africa and other developing countries (One Campaign, 2011).

Scholarship should also consider how administrators might cope with the "growing pains" of connections and transparency. As seen in interviews with public administrators admitting to the lack of time to properly deal with social media, the key to productivity is going to be about *managing* social media. According to William Davidow, public servants must avoid cultural lags and stay on top of technological advances. However, we must also prepare for instability and resulting emergencies in new media by creating stronger systems to handle accidents, buffers to mitigate feedback floods, and restructuring agencies to be less vulnerable and more effective and adaptable (Davidow, 2011). So, then, how should we avoid moving from the desirable state of highly-connected to the vulnerable state of over-connected?

Finally, additional research might look at the elephant in the room of a digital divide: Is social media reaching the neediest and deserving populations? Some municipalities highlight programs that bring technology skills and equipment to citizens, such as Portland's promotion of the national entity One Economy. This group funds broadband Internet services into communities; additionally, OneEconomy partners with others to offer free equipment for low-income citizens. However, with the economic downturn and reliance on private funding for technology, the question still remains whether meeting any mandated demands for Internet access in low-income communities are being met. Plus, public finance scholars might examine how budget cuts can kill even the most responsible e-government goals, as seen in the Office of Management and Budget plans to darken many of the Obama administration's top open government websites due to a 94% funding shortage (White House blog, March 17, 2011).

CONCLUSION

A common thread in existing literature and the "real-world" examples from this study is that social media is increasingly taking center stage in connecting multiple audiences with governmental messages and campaigns. This is a larger cultural shift wherein all organizations, public or private, define and redefine themselves in collaboration with communities and individuals, including with the use of social media. People are more likely to trust recommendations from their peers about voting and policy making, rather than a standard slate by traditional parties and public organization leaders. It has been stated that one word-of-mouth conversation has the impact of at least 200 TV ads. That word-of-mouth conversation is no longer limited to the one-on-one, face-to-face definition of conversation. Instead, social media itself is an organic and ongoing conversation occurring online between friends traditionally defined, and friends we have met with mutual interests (business or professional). We want to see social proof – real people talking about real experiences – consumers become the marketers for corporations. This is true also for governmental organizations, as evidenced throughout this chapter. There are four key goals as we move forward with social media in our public organizations:

1. *Investing and Planning*. While most sites like Facebook, Twitter, LinkedIn, etc. are free to users, there are transaction costs of managing and maintaining the social media presence. This cost can be expended to outside contractors or employees may have to be hired to manage e-governance resources and tools. As new technologies and tools emerge, upgrades and updates also have costs. Additionally, there are costs associated with policy development, planning, and establishing outcomes measures, Examples of social media policies describing how to monitoring and communication processes can be found at the City of Reno's "Social Media" page or the "Comment Policy of the U.S. Environmental Protection Agency" (City of Reno, 2011; EPA, 2011).

2. *Initiation and Inclusion*. The importance of building trust through the implementation process has been stressed throughout the paper. Social media, with appropriate design, allowing access to citizens with limited technological experience and resources, can act to build social capital. Citizen education, transparency, and negation of information symmetry can be included as a part of implementation. In the future, public agencies might encourage more opportunities for citizen reporting, taking care to outline how problems are ranked for receive faster and more meaningful responses. For instance, corporate networking leader Cisco advises cities to use public opinion to prioritize public requests and problems, perhaps asking citizens to rate the urgency of their problem during the reporting process (Cisco, 2009). Social media, in this case, can allow citizens not only to state the issues they would like to see addressed, but to weight the issues based on their preferences. Efficiency and effectiveness are maximized when resources can be aligned more directly to citizen demands not otherwise voiced to public agencies.

3. *Integration and Messaging*. In order to lead to strong outcomes, social media messaging and processes must be, at the same time, consistent and vibrant. Consistent message components repeated throughout websites, blogs, Facebook pages, and Twitter accounts send a message of stability that fosters citizen trust. Messages must also be careful to reflect the unique character of the agency and its programs, to translate information for targeted stakeholders, and to remain current and relevant.

4. *Reflection and Review*. We are in the middle of a true shift in communication paradigms, moving from a top-down standard to a horizontal flow of information. Old measurements don't apply when we move from a broadcast form of pushing out information to the newer model of narrowcasting, with individuals pulling what they need. So, monitoring the best use of resources to maintain an

active, effective presence without becoming overly-connected. Reflecting and measuring agency efforts to keep track of trends, citizen needs, and public resources is a valuable asset of e-governance and social media use.

As the saying goes, the only thing that is constant is change, and that is certainly true for social media and public administrators. The development of these new tools and processes provide opportunities for public agencies to foster citizen inclusion and democratic process. There is the potential for increased efficiency and effectiveness in policy making and program delivery. Thoughtful design that facilitates citizen and agency communication, and that builds on traditionally established mechanisms for trust and social capital, are key to the future of dialogue with Citizen 2.0.

REFERENCES

Austin, E., & Callen, J. (2008). Reexamining the role of digital technology in public administration: From devastation to disclosure. *Administrative Theory & Praxis, 30*(3), 324–341.

Bannister, F. (2005). The panoptic state: Privacy, surveillance and the balance of risk. *Information Polity: The International Journal of Government & Democracy in the Age, 10*, 65–78.

Bekkers, V. (2007). Modernization, public innovation and information and communication technologies: The emperor's new clothes? *Information Polity: The International Journal of Government & Democracy in the Information Age, 12*(3), 103–107.

Bennett, W. L. (2007). *Changing citizenship in the digital age.* OECD/INDRE Conference on Millennial Learners. Retrieved August 1, 2011, from http://spotlight.macfound.org/resources/Bennett-Changing_Citizenship_in_Digital_Age-OECD.pdf

Bennett, W. L. (2008). Civic learning in changing democracies: Challenges for citizenship and civic education. In Dahlgren, P. (Ed.), *Young citizens and new media: Learning and democratic engagement.* New York, NY: Routledge.

Brainard, L., & McNutt, J. G. (2010). Virtual government-citizen relations: Old public administration, new public management or new public service? *Administration & Society, 42*, 836–858. doi:10.1177/0095399710386308

Brewer, G., Neubauer, B., & Geiselhart, K. (2006). Designing and implementing e-government systems: Critical implications for public administration and democracy. *Administration & Society, 38*(4), 472–499. doi:10.1177/0095399706290638

Burnett, R., & Marshall, P. (2003). *Web theory* (pp. 108–115). New York, NY: Routledge.

Cammaerts, B. (2009). Civil society participation in multistakeholder processes: In between realism and utopia. In Stein, L., Kidd, D., & Rodriguez, C. (Eds.), *Making our media: Global initiatives toward a democratic public sphere* (pp. 83–101). Cresskill, NJ: Hampton Press.

Carmel, E., & Harlock, J. (2008). Instituting the third sector as a governable terrain. *Policy and Politics, 36*(2), 155–171. doi:10.1332/030557308783995017

Chicago Metropolitan Agency for Planning. (2011). Retrieved April 4, 2011, from http://www.cmap.illinois.gov/

Cisco Blog. (2009). *Ideas for state/local leaders: Fix my street.* Retrieved April 4, 2011, from http://blogs.cisco.com/localgov/fix_my_street/

City of Reno. (2011). *Social media policy.* Retrieved April 4, 2011, from http://www.reno.gov/index.aspx?page=2142#Facebook

Clinton, H. (2011). *Internet rights and wrongs: Choices & challenges in a networked world. Remarks.* Retrieved April 4, 2011, from http://www.state.gov/secretary/rm/2011/02/156619.htm

Davidow, W. (2011). *Overconnected: The promise and threat of the Internet.* Harrison, NY: Delphinium Books.

Dawes, S., Cresswell, A., & Pardo, T. (2009). From "need to know" to "need to share": Tangled problems, information boundaries, and the building of public sector knowledge networks. *Public Administration Review, 69*(3), 392–402. doi:10.1111/j.1540-6210.2009.01987_2.x

Dutton, W., Guerra, G., Zizzo, D., & Peltu, M. (2005). The cyber trust tension in e-government: Balancing identity, privacy, security. *Information Polity: The International Journal of Government & Democracy in the Information Age, 10,* 13–23.

Eliasoph, N. (1998). *Avoiding politics: How Americans produce apathy in everyday life.* New York, NY: Cambridge University Press. doi:10.1017/CBO9780511583391

Environmental Protection Agency. (2011). *EPA comment policy.* Retrieved April 4, 2011, from http://www.epa.gov/epahome/commentpolicy.html

Fearn-Banks, K. (2007). *Crisis communications: A casebook approach.* New Jersey: Lawrence Erlbaum.

Ferguson, S. (2000). *Researching the public opinion environment: Theories and methods* (pp. 180–182). Thousand Oaks, CA: Sage.

Foley, P., & Alfonso, X. (2009). E-government and the transformation agenda. *Public Administration, 87*(2), 371–396. doi:10.1111/j.1467-9299.2008.01749.x

Friedman, J. (2011). *Personal interview.*

Gates Foundation. (2011). *Social media for social good.* Retrieved April 3, 2011, from http://www.gatesfoundation.org/foundationnotes/Pages/alyssa-milano-101015-social-media-social-good.aspx

Goldfinch, S. (2007). Pessimism, computer failure, and Information Systems development in the public sector. *Public Administration Review, 67*(5), 917–929. doi:10.1111/j.1540-6210.2007.00778.x

GovLoop. (2011). Retrieved April 4, 2011, from http://www.govloop.com

Hansen, H., & Salskov-Iversen, D. (2005). Remodeling the transnational political realm: Partnerships, best-practice schemes, and the digitalization of governance. *Alternatives: Global, Local, Political, 30*(2), 141–164.

Heintze, T., & Bretschneider, S. (2000). Information Technology and restructuring in public organizations: Does adoption of Information Technology affect organizational structures, communications, and decision making? *Journal of Public Administration: Research and Theory, 10*(4), 801.

Hinson, C. (2010). Negative information action: Danger for democracy. *The American Behavioral Scientist, 53*(6), 826–847. doi:10.1177/0002764209353276

Holden, S., & Millett, L. (2005). Authentication, privacy, and the federal e-government. *The Information Society, 21*(5), 367–377. doi:10.1080/01972240500253582

Jorgensen, D., & Klay, E. (2007). Technology-driven change and public administration: Establishing essential normative principles. *International Journal of Public Administration, 30*(3), 289–305. doi:10.1080/01900690601117770

Jung Yun, H., & Opheim, C. (2010). Building on success: The diffusion of e-government in the American states. *Electronic Journal of E-Government, 8*(1), 71–81.

Kakabadse, A., Kakabadse, K., & Kouzmin, A. (2003). Reinventing the democratic governance project through Information Technology? A growing agenda for debate. *Public Administration Review, 63*(1), 44–60. doi:10.1111/1540-6210.00263

Kennedy, A. (2010). Using community-based social marketing techniques to enhance environmental regulation. *Sustainability, 2*, 1138–1160. doi:10.3390/su2041138

Kim, S., & Lee, H. (2006). The impact of organizational context and information technology on employee knowledge-sharing capabilities. *Public Administration Review, 66*(3), 370–385. doi:10.1111/j.1540-6210.2006.00595.x

King, S., & Cotterill, S. (2007). Transformational government? The role of Information Technology in delivering citizen-centric local public services. *Local Government Studies, 33*(3), 333–354. doi:10.1080/03003930701289430

Kirlin, J., & Kirlin, M. (2000). Strengthening effective government-citizen connections through greater civic engagement. *Public Administration Review, 62*, 80–85. doi:10.1111/1540-6210.62.s1.14

Levy, J. (2011). *Gov't FB pages: Allow fans to post or not? Government 2.0 Beta.* Retrieved April 4, 2011, from http://levyj413.wordpress.com/2011/03/09/govt-fb-pages-allow-fans-to-post-or-not/

Lips, M. (2007). Does public administration have artifacts? *Information Polity: The International Journal of Government & Democracy in the Information Age, 12*(4), 243–252.

Makadeo, J. (2009). Towards an understanding of the factors influencing the acceptance and diffusion of e-government services. *Electronic Journal of E-Government, 7*(4), 391–401.

Metropolitan Council of Governments. (2011). Retrieved from http://www.mweog.org/

Morgeson, F., & Mithas, S. (2009). Does e-government measure up to e-business? Comparing end user perceptions of U.S. federal government and e-business web sites. *Public Administration Review, 69*(4), 740–752. doi:10.1111/j.1540-6210.2009.02021.x

Neuendorf, K. (2002). *The content analysis guidebook* (pp. 9–23). Thousand Oaks, CA: Sage Publications.

Power, A. (2002). EU legitimacy and new forms of citizen engagement. *Electronic Journal of E-Government, 8*(1), 45–53.

Putnam, R. (2002). Bowling together. *The American Prospect, 13*(3). Retrieved April 1, 2011, from http://prospect.org/cs/articles?articleId=6114

Rushen, A. (2011). *Personal interview.*

Schierholz, S. (2011). *Personal interview.*

Shim, D., & Eom, T. (2009). Anticorruption effects of information communication and technology (ICT) and social capital. *International Review of Administrative Sciences, 75*(1), 99–116. doi:10.1177/0020852308099508

Sindelar, J., Mintz, D., & Hughes, T. (2009). The past is prologue: The Obama technology agenda. *Public Management, 38*(4), 24–27.

Southern California Association of Governments. (2011). Retrieved from http://www.scag.ca.gov/

Steeves, V. (2008). If the Supreme Court were on Facebook: Evaluating the reasonable expectation of privacy test from a social perspective. *Canadian Journal of Criminology and Criminal Justice, 50*(3), 331–347. doi:10.3138/cjccj.50.3.331

Susanto, T., & Goodwin, R. (2010). Factors influencing citizen adoption of SMS-based E-government services. *Electronic Journal of E-Government, 8*(1), 55–70.

Thompson, G., & Wilkinson, P. (2009). Set the default to open: Plessy's meaning in the twenty-first century and how technology puts the individual back at the center of life, liberty, and government. *Texas Review of Law & Politics, 14*(1), 48–89.

Von Haldenwang, C. (2004). Electronic government (e-government) and development. *European Journal of Development Research, 16*(2), 417–432. doi:10.1080/0957881042000220886

Wangpipatwong, S., Chutimaskul, W., & Papasratorn, B. (2008). Understanding citizen's continuance intention to use e- government website: A composite view of technology acceptance model and computer self-efficacy. *Electronic Journal of E-Government, 6*(1), 55–64.

Watershed. (2011). *Media sandbox: The hills are evil*. Retrieved April 1, 2011, from http://www.mediasandbox.co.uk/category/overlay-media/

Waugh, D. (2011). *Personal interview*.

White House Blog. (March 17, 2011). *Sunshine, savings, and service*. Retrieved April 1, 2011, from http://www.whitehouse.gov/blog/2011/03/17/sunshine-savings-and-service

Wills, D., & Reeves, S. (2009). Facebook as a political weapon: Information in social networks. *British Politics, 4*(2), 265–281. doi:10.1057/bp.2009.3

ADDITIONAL READING

Aaker, J., Smith, A., & Adler, C. (2010). *The dragonfly effect: Quick, effective, and powerful ways to use social media to drive social change*. San Francisco, CA: Jossey-Bass.

Couldry, N., Livingstone, S., & Marksham, T. (2008). *Media consumption and public engagement: Beyond the presumption of attention (consumption and public life)*. New York, NY: Palgrave Macmillan.

Cox, R. (2010). *Environmental communication and the public sphere*. Thousand Oaks, CA: Sage.

Eggers, W. (2007). *Government 2.0: Using technology to improve education, cut red tape, reduce gridlock, and enhance democracy*. New York, NY: Rowman & Littlefield.

Handley, A., & Chapman, C. (2010). *Content rules: How to create killer blogs, podcasts, videos, ebooks, webinars (and more) that engage customers and ignite your business*. Hoboken, NJ: John Wiley & Sons.

Hart, T., Greenfield, J., & Haji, S. D. (2007). *People to people fundraising: Social networking and Web 2.0 for charities*. Hoboken, NJ: John Wiley & Sons.

Herzog, D. (2003). *Mapping the news: Case studies in GIS and journalism*. Redlands, CA: ESRI Press.

Homberg, V. (2008). *Understanding e-government: Information Systems in public administration*. New York, NY: Routledge.

Kanter, B., Fine, A., & Zuckerberg, R. (2010). *The networked nonprofit: Connecting with social media to drive change*. San Francisco, CA: John Wiley & Sons.

Kotler, P., & Kartajaya, H. (2010). *Marketing 3.0: From products to customers to the human spirit*. Hoboken, NJ: John Wiley & Sons. doi:10.1002/9781118257883

Lathrop, D., & Ruma, L. (2010). *Open government: Collaboration, transparency, and participation in practice*. Sebastapol, CA: O'Reilly Media.

Li, C., & Bernoff, J. (2008). *Groundswell: Winning in a world transformed by social technologies*. Cambridge, MA: Harvard Business School Press.

Noveck, B. (2010). *Wiki government: How technology can make government better, democracy stronger, and citizens more powerful*. Washington, DC: Brookings Institute.

Scott, D. (2008). *The new rules of marketing & PR: How to use social media, blogs, news releases, online video, and viral marketing to reach buyers directly*. Hoboken, NJ: John Wiley & Sons.

Shark, A., & Toporkoff, S. (2008). *Beyond e-government & e-democracy: A global perspective*. Washington, DC: Public Technology Institute and ITEMS International.

Thielst, C. (2010). *Social media in healthcare: Connect, communicate, collaborate*. Chicago, IL: Health Information Press.

West, D. (2005). *Digital government: Technology and public sector performance*. Princeton, NJ: Princeton University Press.

KEY TERMS AND DEFINITIONS

Citizen Participation: Collaboration in public processes that include citizen voices, sometimes referred to as stakeholder engagement, such as town hall meetings.

E-Government: Public efforts using Internet-based technologies for business and citizen Interaction, including recent Open Government websites and initiatives.

GIS: Geospatial Information Systems is a technology mash-up of software, hardware, and data that helps government geographically reference information to help government provide public information as well as city and federal services.

Mobile Applications: Software designed to run on hand-held computers such as PDAs and cell phones, including online citizen reporting (FixMyStreet, etc.).

Social Capital: Connections between people that build benefits such as trust and sharing.

Social Media: Technology-based media that allows individual and accessible postings and shared information, such as Twitter, Facebook, and WiserEarth, a social network for sustainability.

Web 2.0: The shift from stationary websites to those with social networking and shared content.

Chapter 14
Congress 2.0:
Incumbent Messaging in Social Media

Albert L. May
George Washington University, USA

F. Christopher Arterton
George Washington University, USA

ABSTRACT

With Congress approaching full adoption of the three major social media platforms – YouTube, Twitter, and Facebook – this study gauges the performance of members' official channels in terms of building audiences. Despite the popularity of these platforms, a divide exists among a few high performing members and many low performers. Using an index to differentiate performance, the study finds social media success is driven by several factors, party affiliation and ideology being significant. Performance is also derivative of larger political and media forces, and the study shows that the issues confronting government can engage audiences that turn to social media for information, as demonstrated by the congressional debate over healthcare on YouTube. The chapter explores how the utilization of this technology could be an historical step as important as the advent of C-SPAN in connecting Congress to the American people.

INTRODUCTION

At the start of the House Energy and Commerce Committee's consideration of the Democrats' health care bill in July 2009, few would have expected the four-minute opening remarks of the tenth-ranking Republican to draw much attention.

Yet by late summer, as the historic health care debate began to unfold in Congress, Mike Rogers, a Republican representative from Michigan, became an improbable YouTube star.

Although neither flashy nor vitriolic, he delivered a succinct and a damning critique from the viewpoint of opponents of health care reform. Capturing the Republican theme, Rogers argued that the Democratic bill threatened to punish the

DOI: 10.4018/978-1-4666-0318-9.ch014

Figure 1. Track of daily views of Rep. Mike Rogers' YouTube video on health care reform from when it was posted on July 16 through November 2009.

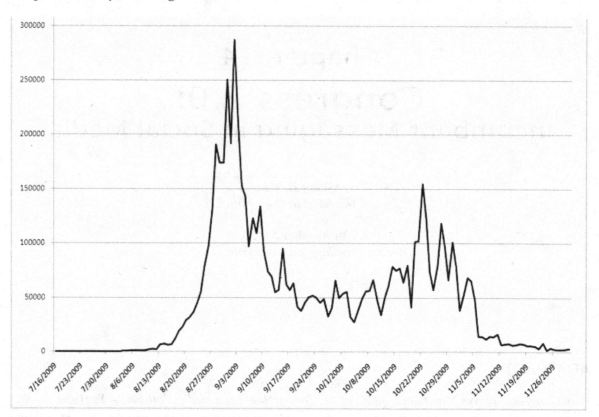

85% of Americans with health insurance to help the 15% of the uninsured. "Why would we punish the part that's working to cover the part that's not?" he asked. "It's like taking a queen sized sheet and trying to put it over a king sized bed. I will guarantee you the corners are going to come up (Rogers, 2009)."

Rogers' staff turned the comments into a video and posted it to his official House YouTube channel on July 16, 2009. Not much happened immediately; the video drew 1,200 views over the next two weeks. But in the August recess, as congressional town halls exploded in protest over health care reform and flooded YouTube and other Internet channels with the discourse, Rogers' video went viral, collecting 1.4 million views that month. In September as the House took up the legislation, the views jumped to 2.6 million,

followed by 2.2 million in October. By the time the House sent the bill to the Senate in November, the video had drawn 7.4 million cumulative views, according to the tracking analytic of TubeMogul. com, a pioneering online video firm.[1] Eventually, the views faded into the "long tail" of the Internet (Bremmer & Keat, 2009) through the remainder of the 111th Congress. (see Figure 1)

The popularity of Rogers' video surprised even his own staff (Plautz, 2009), but the roiling national debate kept people tuned into YouTube, which has become a personal version of C-SPAN for members of Congress.[2] By YouTube standards, however, Rogers' video would rank modestly in the largely entertainment medium. In comparison, the most-watched YouTube video of 2009 was Scottish singer Susan Boyle's appearance on *Britain's Got Talent*, which drew 120 million

YouTube views ("Boyle", 2009). The Boyle video drew more than double the entire viewership of Congress on YouTube, which as of July 2010 had posted 41,000 videos with 50 million in cumulative views, according to this study. By way of further comparison, in the same month, the *Associated Press*, the most successful news organization on YouTube (May, 2010, pp. 504-506) had posted 35,000 videos with 455 million cumulative views.

As an institution, Congress is a long way from YouTube stardom, but by congressional standards, the performance of Rogers' video was extraordinary. The tale of the Rogers video illustrates the potential reach of Congress on social media platforms, or what has come to be called *Web. 2.0* or *Gov. 2.0* in its government permutation, which is described below. Indeed, the adoption of the technology portends the largest expansion of unmediated communication between the Congress and the American people since the advent of C-SPAN in 1978.

In the 111th Congress, most of its members adopted some form of Web 2.0. That appeared to be accelerating in the 112th Congress: six months into its first session, all but two of the 114 new senators and representatives had launched official Facebook, Twitter or YouTube channels and three quarters of the freshmen had adopted all three. Despite the widespread adoption, however, the reach of members of Congress on social media platforms is far from uniform. The anomaly of the Rogers video exemplifies the pronounced divide that separates the handful of senators and representatives who dominate the space by drawing significant audiences from the bulk of members who attract only tiny audiences.

The objectives of this chapter are to describe Congress' participation in this first phase of the Web 2.0 revolution, identify important.variables that are shaping the adoption of these new media, and explore the ramifications of public officials' expanding use of social networking. The study presents a snapshot of social media use in the 111th Congress, using an index of "social media success" for members of Congress that combines their popularity on Twitter, Facebook and YouTube in enlisting followers and drawing video views. The index is the first step in identifying Congress' social media stars and laggards, and understanding the interplay of the factors that distinguish the two groups.

The findings suggest that success on social media is tied to several factors, with party affiliation being a major force in the 111th Congress. In a political season that favored the GOP, Republicans aggressively employed the technology and outstripped their Democratic counterparts. Thus, the findings suggest that the new media employed by Congress is derivative of the political climate and the larger media ecosystem.

The efforts of elected officials to connect can pay off by engaging citizens through out-bound communication, which presumably enhances electoral success. Certainly, Republican strategists saw their aggressive adoption of the technology as an ingredient in their success in the 2010 midterm election (Schaper, 2010). At the same time, this study shows that governmental leaders will be disappointed if they employ a "Field of Dreams" approach to the new technology, assuming that if they build it citizens will come. The findings suggest four factors which differentiate success in terms of building an audience through social media: (1) tapping into the larger media ecosystem; (2) adopting Web 2.0 values of vivid content; (3) using partisan appeals from the ideological extremes; and (4) working assiduously to engage citizens. Each of these factors is discussed below as well as other findings.

Growth may be occurring in stages, the first being a public relations push by elected officials designed to reach out to constituents. If, as Howard (2001) argues, there are three stages in the evolution of *e-government* -- publishing, interacting, and transacting--congressional offices have just begun to move onto the second stage. Unfortunately, the publicly available data measuring the response of constituents to these outreach efforts by elected officials is far from definitive. Even so, we will explore what the research to date can tell us about whether the technology is developing a two-way street between constituents and Congress.

Congress's adoption of Web 2.0 is changing the ways in which its members communicate, extending their reach to constituents and political elites. But adoption of these media by elected representatives also engages the question of whether, at this early stage of development, social networks will advance democratic values.

CONGRESS IN THE WEB 2.0 REVOLUTION

Web 2.0 has become a buzz word for a second generation of the World Wide Web ever since Internet pundit Tim O'Reilly coined the term in 2004. In the language of software developers the term denotes the evolution from a more static, service oriented web to a more dynamic user-empowering web. In a five-year retrospective of that first use of the term, O'Reilly and co-author John Battelle described the emergence of Google, Amazon, Wikipedia, craigslist and eBay as the first phase of Web 2.0 platforms that were "co-created by and for the community of connected users. Since then, powerful new platforms like YouTube, Facebook, and Twitter have demonstrated that same insight in new ways. Web 2.0 is all about harnessing collective intelligence (OReilly & Batelle, 2009, p. 2)." As it has been applied to government, Web 2.0 has become Gov. 2.0, and like its namesake the term means different things to different people. As O'Reilly (2010) put it:

Much like its predecessor, Web 2.0, "Government 2.0" is a chameleon, a white rabbit term that seems to be used by people to mean whatever they want it to mean. For some, it is the use of social media by government agencies. For others, it is government transparency, especially as

aided by government-provided data APIs. Still others think of it as the adoption of cloud computing, wikis, crowd sourcing, mobile applications, mashups, developer contests, or all of the other epiphenomena of Web 2.0 as applied to the job of government. (p. 914).[3]

More theoretically, O'Reilly argued that the transformative power of Gov 2.0 goes beyond government officials, politicians and other insiders using the channels to further their causes or even to hear the views of citizens. "Participation means true engagement with citizens in the business of government, and actual collaboration with citizens in the design of government programs (O'Reilly, 2010, p. 1344)."

From O'Reilly's menu, Congress has embraced the social media aspect and, at least rhetorically, the goal of greater transparency. But experimentation with the other tools outlined by O'Reilly has been limited and whether Congress – or any legislative body or any government – can achieve a new level of "actual collaboration" has yet to be demonstrated. However, O'Reilly and new media theorist Clay Skirky (2008) appear to have correctly predicted that Web 2.0 has lowered the transactional costs of organizing and communicating with heretofore dispersed and unengaged populations. Congress, or at least some of its members, is using social media to reach new audiences in direct ways simply not available through the old mediated communication channels.

While recognizing some risks, Shirky argues that this technology will be transformative in bringing citizens together: "Our electronic networks are enabling novel forms of collective action, enabling the creation of collaborative groups that are larger and more distributed than at any other time in history (Shirky, 2008, p. 660)." Following this logic, the issue isn't whether Congress, or government writ large, has a choice to make in whether to utilize the new technologies – at least not if the institutions want to remain relevant. Shirky's analogy (2008) is that society in adopting the technology is much like a kayaker navigating a torrent:

Our principal challenge is not deciding where we want to go, but rather in staying upright as we go there. The invention of tools that facilitate group formation is less like ordinary technological change, and more like an event, something that has already happened. As a result, the important questions aren't about whether these tools will spread or reshape society, but rather how they do so. (p. 3750)

However, sticking with Shirky's analogy of the kayaker, some scholars have warned of dangerous shoals ahead in adopting the new technology, which they argue exacerbates pre-existing tendencies in the political-media ecosystem, most significantly political polarization. No one has raised the connection between the new media and polarization more forcefully than legal scholar Cass Sunstein. In *Republic.com* in 2001, updated as *Republic.com 2.0* (2007), Sunstein argued that the online media could foster enclaves of like-minded people who reinforce their like-mindedness in an "echo chamber" effect, fueling dogmatism. He has more recently argued that "social networks can operate as polarization machines because they help to confirm and thus amplify people's antecedent views (Sunstein, 2009, p. 231)." A large literature has grown up around whether Sunstein's largely normative arguments hold up to empirical scrutiny. The debate has revived scholarly interest in selective partisan media exposure that traces its origin to cognitive dissonance theory in the 1950s (Stroud, 2011; Mutz, 2006). Most recently, the empirical evidence has been mixed.

Using largely survey research, Stroud (2011) found that with an explosion of media choices, citizens increasingly seek out like-minded partisan media sources, which reinforces those choices in a spiraling effect (Sunstein's echo chamber) and diminishes exposure to countervailing views. Using an experimental approach, Iyengar and

Hahn (2009) also found that media enhanced polarization in a similar way. At the same time, survey researcher Garrett found Sunstein's concerns "unnecessarily grave (2009, p. 694)" with findings that online users do seek opinion-reinforcing information but don't systematically shun competing opinions. And Gentzkow and Shapiro (2010), using Internet traffic data, found that not only was ideological segregation online only slightly higher than the segregation in off-line media consumption, but online media consumption can sometimes actually enhance exposure to diverse views.

Although conflicting in their findings, these scholars agree on one point. The link between the advent of the technology and polarizing effects, which can be profoundly important to governance, is an important question. This study comes at the question from a different direction. Do more polarized political actors who employ the new tools reach greater audiences than less polarized actors? And does that encourage behavior that gives incumbents advantage? These are old questions for Congress.

Trends in Congressional Communication

Technology has reshaped American political institutions from the dawn of the republic, starting with the explosion of newspapers in the late 18th century in what became known as the partisan press in the 19th century (Starr, 2004). As secretary of state and as president, Thomas Jefferson established and subsidized printers from the federal treasury, ostensibly so that official actions of the government could be communicated to the citizenry. Yet, as partisan politics emerged, many of these printers became the backbone of the Anti-Federalist party (Pasley, 2001, pp. 48 -78).[4]

In Congress, concern over how communications policies might influence the acquisition of political power has surfaced at various points, animating debates over the arrival of the telegraph in the 1830s, radio in the 1920s and television in the post WW II era (Pool, 1983, pp. 73-188). Before the proliferation of communication vehicles starting in the 1980s and the consequent deregulatory push, policies such as the *fairness doctrine* or the *equal time provision* were expressly designed, at least in part, to strike an appropriate balance between partisan advantage and the communications that incumbents, as elected officials, need to have with their constituents as part of the representative process (Simmons, 1978). More directly on point, the Congress early adopted and periodically modified long-standing internal policies over *franking* privileges governing the free usage of the U.S. mail through which members of Congress can communicate with constituents back home (Glassman, 2007).

C-SPAN Revolution

Enter the explosion of cable television beginning in the late 1970s. Scores and then hundreds of channels supplemented those available through broadcast stations. In 1978, an association of cable operators created the Cable-Satellite Public Affairs Network (C-SPAN) and petitioned the Congress for access to cover the floors and committee deliberations of the House and Senate. Though hotly debated, the House accepted C-SPAN's proposal to allow it full access to floor debates, under strict guidelines.[5] Coverage began on March 19, 1979 and was extended to the Senate in January of 1986 (Frantzich & Sullivan, 1996, p.23).

C-SPAN brought the deliberations of Congress into American homes through a gradually expanding network of cable systems. Those cable operators that did carry C-SPAN soon found that they had created an audience of "C-SPAN junkies," people who devoted hours each day to watching the network. When several local cable operators tried to eliminate this coverage during the 1980s in favor of more lucrative opportunities, they found themselves barraged by a small, but highly vocal community demanding preservation of C-SPAN

programming. Thus, as this story turns to social networking, it demonstrates that technology can both stimulate and satisfy a greater demand for access to public policy information.

Strong congressional partisans also seized upon C-SPAN coverage as a means to get their message to the public. Starting in the 1980s, House Republicans led by then Rep. Newt Gingrich began to take advantage of the *Special Orders* period at the end of the daily House session (Frantzich & Sullivan, 1996, p. 275). Using time when the mostly empty chamber was not readily apparent to the television audience, conservatives castigated the Democratic House leadership day after day. Their constant hammering from the House floor was one element in the Republican's eventual success in 1994 in capturing the House majority for the first time since the 1950s. As Frantzich and Sullivan (1996) argue of C-SPAN's partisan effect during this period, "with each technological change, political winners can usually be distinguished from political losers by their foresight and skill in using the new technologies (p. 257)."

Internet Brings New Challenges and Opportunities

The advent of the World Wide Web in the mid-1990s vastly expanded the information available to citizens about Congress. E-mail communications with constituents took off after the terrorist and anthrax attacks in September 2001 caused the U.S. Postal Service to slow down mail delivery to Congress by subjecting all incoming mail to x-ray inspection. The resulting overflow of e-mail has prompted most members to limit their responses only to constituents. As e-mail speeded up communications, members also ramped up their websites. Until quite recently, however, congressional websites were like libraries that citizens visited to retrieve information that interested them, what Howard (2001) would classify as the first stage of development in e-government: publishing. No longer. The advent of Web 2.0 technologies has ushered in an unprecedented number of interactive vehicles providing a two-way flow of communications over the Internet. And, with this new interactivity has come debates over both the values of democracy and the participatory goals of Web 2.0 proponents.

One dispute centers upon whether the barriers to citizen engagement in public life are technological or sociological. At stake is whether digital communications will markedly improve the ability of citizens to participate in policy making. The hope is that by giving them more information, Internet-based communications will give citizens a better understanding of the public policies that shape their lives, help them communicate more effectively with elected officials, and, as a result, hold those who govern more accountable. As Schacter (2010) points out, "groups of voters that know more about politics and policy overlap substantially with those that have also been able to obtain preferred policy outcomes (p. 647)."

Some argue that as technology increases the ways in which citizens can participate in public policy making, they increasingly will demand a greater role, as well as reforms of political institutions to make that possible (Sclove, 1995; Becker and Slaton, 2000). These proponents argue that the small percentage of citizens who participate actively in civic life, beyond occasional voting, is directly tied to the rather high transactional costs of political involvement and a low sense of efficacy. They argue that two-way communications with public officials through social networks will lessen the transactional costs and translate into greater participation (Shirky, 2008).

111th Congress Joins Web 2.0

The earliest use of social media by members of Congress was led by a handful of early adopters, including later Speaker Nancy Pelosi, who was the first member to launch a YouTube channel in May 2006 (Nylen, 2008). But it was President Obama's successful employment of the platforms in his 2008 campaign that spurred the adoption by members, particularly the House Republicans who created a New Media Caucus to aggressively promote adoption (Hart, 2009).[6]

This informal, and unauthorized, linkage of official websites to third-party providers, including YouTube, Facebook and Twitter, prompted both houses to re-examine their rules. Republicans, led by then Minority Leader John Boehner, pushed for permissive requirements on the linking and opposed a more restrictive policy advocated by House Democrats (Schaper, 2010). The chief issue in the debate was how to square the long-standing prohibition against mixing official communication with privately owned commercial communication (Hooper, 2008). In the fall of 2008, committees in both houses approved new rules to authorize the connections under terms acceptable to the Republicans. They took effect with the 111th Congress (Orr, 2008).[7]

With the rules in place for the 111th Congress, mass adoption of social media by Congress accelerated with the active encouragement of the service providers,[8] and by early 2009, congressional adoption of social media was in full swing, not only by members but also by House and Senate committees and caucuses. The Secretary of the Senate and the House Clerk's office began live Twitter feeds of floor action with each feed drawing about 100,000 *followers* by the end of the 111th Congress.[9] Several studies found that the Republicans jumped to an early lead in terms of adoption and audience on Twitter and YouTube (Glassman, Straus & Shogun, 2009; Senak, 2010; Rowland, 2009).[10] In late 2009, Boehner proclaimed:

Social media platforms like YouTube, Facebook and Twitter have become an indispensable component of House Republicans' efforts to communicate our better solutions to the American people. The Web allows us to not only deliver a clear, unfiltered message directly to the public, but also serves as an open forum where we can receive feedback from our constituents. (Hart, 2009)

Despite Boehner's nod to citizen engagement, outreach has been the main motivator. By the late spring of 2010, both parties in the House actually held contests to see who could build the largest social media audiences (Galloway & Guthrie, 2010).[11] The evidence is mixed that the new platforms have created a significant forum for constituent feedback.

A number of early studies (Glassman, Straus & Shogun 2009; Senak, 2010) anecdotally found the communication flowed in one direction, with Congress using the platforms to distribute press releases, links to news stories and television appearances, and announcements of their travel activities back home. Researchers at the University of Maryland conducted a content analysis of Twitter traffic that quantified the out-going nature of the communication as "vehicles for self-promotion (Golbek, Grimes & Rogers, 2010, p. 1612)."[12] Likewise, in reviewing Congress's outbound communications, Schacter (2010) wondered if greater accountability would be forthcoming and concluded that, so far, these communications constituted a "wasted transparency of abundant information, easily accessible but not known by many citizens (pp. 645-655)."

Those outbound communications need not be seen as merely self-serving, for citizens do need information about the actions of their elected officials and their policy prescriptions. But, in the longer run, a functioning democracy also requires that citizens be able to communicate back to their representatives. Nevertheless, as is true for the studies cited above, this study also will focus on communications originating from the Congress because the data on outbound communications is much more precise than measurements of citizen usage. Therefore, at this early point in the adoption of social media, the performance measures of necessity must focus on (1) the efforts congresspersons are putting into social media, and (2) the

size of audiences that they command through those efforts. There is little accessible data on the actual behavior of Twitter followers or those Facebook users clicking *like* or video viewers, including who they are, how detailed is their scrutiny of information provided by members, and whether they actively respond to the implicit requests for interaction coming from their representatives. It is also unclear how the inbound communication is affecting Congress' actions.

Congressional Management Foundation (CMF) studies have documented a surge in communication from citizens, largely Internet born, that has overwhelmed congressional staffs (Fitch & Goldschmidt, 2005). A CMF public opinion survey in 2008 found that almost half of Americans (44%) had contacted a member of Congress in the past five years, including all means of contact, not just through social networks (Goldschmidt and Ochreiter, 2008).

A survey of congressional staff members by CMF during the last two months of 111th Congress found that almost three-quarters said Web 2.0 was reaching previously disconnected citizens (Goldschmidt, 2011). Majorities of the practitioners said the tools were worth the time spent on them and the benefits outweighed the risks. Facebook particularly was rated as important in understanding the views of constituents by almost two-thirds of the respondents. However, the survey also found that social media ranked low when compared to other traditional communication channels, including local news media and face-to-face meetings with constituents. And overall, the staffers found social media more useful in communicating their members' views than understanding the views of constituents (Goldschmidt, 2011).[13]

In summary, as mixed as the studies have been, there is some evidence that Congress is moving toward interactivity, the second stage of adoption, and social media has joined the long progression of new communication vehicles that have increased the capacity of public officials to communicate with citizens.

HOW CONGRESS PERFORMS ON SOCIAL MEDIA

As of July, 2010, when most of the data for the study were collected, only four senators and 31 House members lacked an official presence on YouTube, Facebook or Twitter. Two-thirds of the Congress hosted Facebook pages, half were on Twitter, and nine in 10 individual members had YouTube channels. But the widespread adoption disguises a gulf separating highly successful members who have embraced the media and reached substantial audiences from those who have employed the tools but failed to reach more than a handful of Americans. The differences are stark: The top 10% of the most successful congressional users of the three platforms had half the Facebook likes, 80% of the Twitter followers, and almost 90% of the YouTube cumulative views.

Congressional Twitter accounts registered 2.6 million followers, but 1.8 million of them belonged to Sen. John McCain of Arizona. The median number of Twitter followers was 1,647. YouTube channels registered 50 million cumulative views, including the millions garnered by Rep. Mike Rogers' one video described above. The median congressional YouTube channel received 8,881 cumulative views. Facebook pages drew 832,547 likes, with the top Facebook performer in Rep. Michele Bachmann, Republican of Minnesota, with 56,513 likes. Contrast that with 1,190, the median number of congressional likes.

Using qualitative and quantitative means, this study explored a number of variables that might influence these varying rates of success or failure. The findings support the main hypotheses: that social media performance derives from, but also facilitates, larger forces in our political and media systems, including polarization by partisanship and ideology; and that success, at least measured in audience size, is also a function of members' effort and their sophistication in both tapping into the media ecosystem and conforming to the values that audiences expect to encounter on the

Web 2.0. The findings are incomplete in that they concentrate on YouTube, but they raise issues that will be important as Congress moves to the next stage of the digital age.

Methodology

The primary goals of the study were to gauge the performance of members' official channels on the three major platforms. Members not on social media as well as members' campaign and personal channels were excluded from the study to the degree they could be identified. The official hubs for YouTube and Facebook, the unofficial hub of TweetCongress.com, and the official websites of members were used to harvest the channels. Thus, the focus was on the use of taxpayer-supported Gov 2.0 communication channels between members of the 111th Congress and the public. The data from the three sites were collected from July 14 to Aug. 6, 2010.[14]

YouTube data were collected using the premiere tracking analytic of TubeMogul.com, which first built a database of official congressional YouTube channels in January of 2009 and periodically updated it as members joined.[15] The database was given to one of the authors in June 2010, who updated it again. Three forms of YouTube data are included in the study: cumulative views of videos on YouTube channels, daily tracking of views of videos, and the number of videos on each channel.[16] Data from the 2009 and 2010 *News Coverage Index* of the Pew Research Center's Project for Excellence in Journalism were used to compare news coverage of the health care debate in Congress with the tracking data of Congress on YouTube ("News Coverage," 2010, 2011).

Analytics to track Twitter and Facebook similar to those available on TubeMogul are being developed, but they were not available at the point of this data collection. Instead, a simple approach was followed for each of the other two platforms. For each Twitter channel, the numbers of followers were recorded, an approach that surely

Table 1. Social media index and average audience

Social Media Index	YouTube Views	Twitter Followers	Facebook Likes
Laggards	1,848	312	345
Muddlers	8,568	588	754
Strivers	37,859	2,215	1,722
Stars	349,747	5,993	5,736

underestimates the number of *tweet* recipients. Twitter can be accessed serendipitously without signing up to follow a feed, and a Tweeter feed also can be received through a *RSS* feed.[17] Facebook likes were also collected but exhibited the same problems of undercounting.

Although any index seeking to compare three disparate media is artificial by definition, an index was constructed to differentiate the performance of members of Congress on social media. YouTube, Twitter and Facebook operate differently and the metrics of a member's success or failure are different. But the data for each platform positively correlate with the others. Facebook likes and Twitter followers showed the strongest relationship ($p = .609, < .01$), followed by Facebook likes and YouTube cumulative views ($p = .359, < .01$) and Twitter followers and YouTube cumulative views ($p = .331, < .01$). Members were ranked by percentiles for each of three mediums, and given a score of 1 to 10 for each. The scores were added to create the index score of 1 to 30. Members were then grouped into quartiles using the standard deviation from the mean of the index and labeled "Laggards" (19.9%), "Muddlers" (20.5%), "Strivers" (40.4%) and "Stars" (19.3%). The effect of the index is to reward members who are on all three platforms but also to reward those who did particularly well on an individual platform. With outliers McCain and Rogers removed (as they were for the statistical analysis throughout), the distinctions between the groups are meaningful, although arguably the difference between Laggards and Muddlers is somewhat semantic. (see Table 1)

Party identification is self-evident, although Independents Sen. Joseph Lieberman of Connecticut and Sen. Bernard Sanders of Vermont, who caucus with the Democrats, were counted as Democrats. To assess ideology, the 2009 ratings of members of Congress by the American Conservative Union and Americans for Democratic Action were used ("Conservative.org," 2009; "ADA Today," 2010).[18]

Polarization

In the 111th Congress, Republicans outperformed Democrats on all three platforms almost across the board in terms of levels of adoption, effort and ability to draw an audience. As expected, senators, who have larger constituencies and larger staffs to produce social media content, generally outperformed House members. (see Figure 2).

Whether it was an out-of-power-appeal or technological innovation or both, the Republican effort paid off. The suggestion here is not that the new media causes the partisan divide, but it clearly reflected that divide, and possibly facilitated it by reaching the most motivated of political activists. Of all the variables that were tested, party identification appeared to be the most dominant. Indeed, to find meaningful relationships for other variables, it was necessary to control for party.

On the social media index, only 11% of all Democrats made it into the Star category, compared to 31% of all Republicans. The gap was most pronounced in the House. The party divide

Figure 2. Median audiences of members of Congress on Twitter, Facebook and YouTube in July 2010

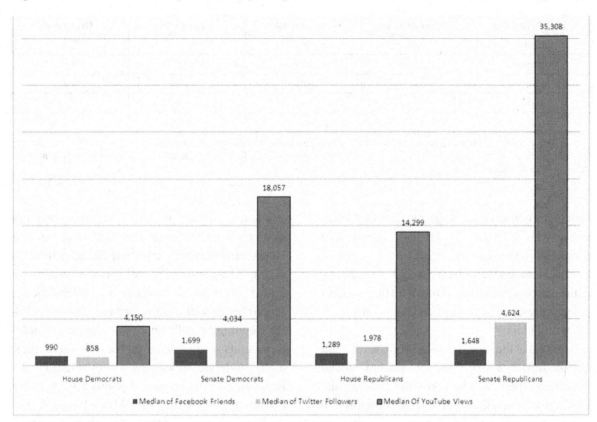

Table 2. How the parties performed on the index

Social Media Index	Democrats	GOP	House Democrats	House GOP	Senate Democrats	Senate GOP
Laggards	28%	9%	32%	10%	11%	8%
Muddlers	23%	17%	22%	17%	27%	18%
Strivers	38%	43%	37%	43%	43%	43%
Stars	11%	31%	8%	30%	20%	33%

Note. Comparing Democrats and Republicans, we find overall Republicans are more likely to use social media ($X = 49.26, p < .01$). The same is true when comparing Democrats and Republicans in the House ($X = 51.35, p < .01$); though the relationship is weaker in the Senate ($X = 2.18, p < .54$).

on social media among senators showed a similar pattern.[19] (see Table 2)

One only has to look at the biggest Stars in our index to find the point-persons in the partisan debates that shaped the 111th Congress. These "superstars" were not necessarily those at the very top of the party hierarchies who do tend to out-perform rank and file members. However, the top

of index, with the highest score of 30, was studded with partisan leaders such as Texas Sen. John Cornyn, chairman of the Republican Senatorial Campaign Committee, Rep. Darrell Issa of California, who leads Republican investigations on the House Oversight Committee, Rep. Paul Ryan of Wisconsin, the Republican leader on budget issues, and Rep. Thaddeus McCotter, then chair-

Table 3. House average scores on ACU and ADA

Social Media Index	Democrats ACU	Democrats ADA	GOP ACU	GOP ADA
Laggards	7.9	88.4	85.4	11.8
Muddlers	7.6	88.0	87.4	9.0
Strivers	5.0	91.6	91.4	8.9
Stars	2.6	94.7	94.4	5.3
All	6.3	90.1	91.1	8.1

Note. The correlations were appropriately negative and positive between the index and House Democrats on the ACU ($p = -.151 < .05$); the index and House Democrats on the ADA ($p = .139, < .05$); the index and House Republicans on ACU ($p = .281, < .01$); and the index and House Republicans on the ADA ($p = -.165, < .01$).

man of the conservative Republican Policy Committee who launched a short-lived presidential campaign in the summer of 2011 partly inspired by his success on Web 2.0 (Weinger & Barr, 2011). In the next tier below this group with near-perfect index scores, one begins to find Democrats, starting with Pelosi.

But two of the superstars stand out on the right and the left: "tea party" favorite Bachmann and liberal lion Sanders. The two, from the opposite ideological poles, drew considerable attention in the 111th as critics of the Obama administration. In late June 2011, Bachmann launched a presidential campaign, a decision likely encouraged by her rising popularity on social media. From July 2010 to July 2011, the Minnesota representative's likes on Facebook jumped fourfold to more than 240,000; her followers on Twitter rose threefold, and her cumulative views on YouTube increased by a third. The Vermont senator, who drew significant attention with a filibuster of the Obama tax compromise in the lame duck session of the 111th Congress, enjoyed similar gains, rising fourfold on Facebook (to more than 73,000 likes) and on YouTube and jumping nine fold on Twitter.

The strong performances by Bachmann and Sanders – neither of whom holds a party leadership posts but both of whom have national ideological constituencies – suggest that more than party affiliation is at play.[20] For empirical evidence of a link between social media performance and ideology, voting records were tested against the index.

While a significant relationship among senators did not appear, a relationship was observed among House members arrayed on the ideological scale of the ADA and ACU ratings of Congress in 2009.[21] The more conservative House Republicans scored better on the index than their more moderate Republican colleagues, and the more liberal Democrats scored better on the index than their more moderate colleagues. On average, House Republican Stars scored 10 points higher on the conservative ACU than Republican Laggards. On the Democratic side, Stars scored six points better than Laggards on the ADA and received less than half the ACU rating. (see Table 3).

Success Takes Effort

If only partisanship and ideology predict social media success, then it is hard to explain why someone like Sen. Claire McCaskill ranks so high on the index with a superstar score of 28 of 30. The Missouri Democrat is no partisan firebrand but a moderate who scored the highest among Democrats in the Congress on the conservative ACU ratings in 2009. In the study, she also ranked highest among Democrats on Twitter with 39,000 followers, which made her third in the Congress overall. She also scored in the top echelon on Facebook and well above average on YouTube. The answer to her success would appear to be that she works at it: McCaskill is personally involved in communicating on the platforms, not leaving it to staff. She has said she tweets four or more times a day on subjects ranging from college basketball to global warming (McCaskill, 2009). She personally answers some Tweets, particularly if the sender uses her home state's #MO *hashtag* (Warren, 2010), and she has been known to pull out a small digital camera to shoot footage for her YouTube channel (Messenger, 2009).[22]

The index supports the notion that sheer effort is an important factor in determining success. The metric is the number of videos posted to a congressional channel, which could be reliably gathered with the TubeMogul analytic. The variable is imperfect because there is a positive correlation ($p = .511 < .01$) between the number of videos and the cumulative views of videos, which is one of three components of the index. However, the size of the audiences drawn by videos varies considerably for a variety of reasons. At the time of our study, early adopter Pelosi had posted 1,931 videos, drawing 4.1 million cumulative views, which works out to 2,127 average views per video. Then Minority Whip Eric Cantor posted the next largest number of videos but only half the number as Pelosi (564). Yet Cantor drew 3.2 million views for an average per video of 5,651. The third most prolific video poster was Republican Rep. Ileana Ros-Lehtinen of Florida who posted 535 videos, which drew only 68,751 cumulative views for an average viewership per video of a paltry 129. Effort is clearly not the only variable at work, but serves as one broad indicator of success as our index showed, with Stars posting 153 videos on average, out-stripping everyone else by ratios of 7-1 for Stars over Laggards, 3-1 over Muddlers and 2-1 over Strivers ($p = .372 < .01$).

There is also some evidence that the personal commitment of members is generational, with younger and newer members more willing to participate in Web 2.0. The CMF survey of congressional staffers (Goldschmidt, 2011) found under age 30 staffers twice as positive about using the technology as their over 50 counterparts. Instead of age of members, length of service was tested

against the index and no statistically significant difference appeared between more veteran or more junior Democrats of both chambers. However, House Republicans, which have a young new leadership that aggressively pushed Web 2.0 adoption, showed an appropriately negative correlation ($p = -.293 < .01$). House Republican Stars averaged nine years of service, compared to 16 years for Laggards in the House GOP. Senate Republicans showed a similar trend but it was not significant ($p = -.143$).

A Closer Look at YouTube

In May 2010, Sen. Bill Nelson of Florida posted five videos on his Senate YouTube channel that propelled him to stardom in the index. All were video feeds of oil gushing from the broken Deepwater Horizon well at the bottom of the Gulf of Mexico. Within a month they drew more than 450,000 views (Nelson, 2010). There was no commentary from Nelson, only pictures worth a lot of traffic to his congressional site where none of his previous videos had topped more than a few thousand views. But two aspects of those videos were important in explaining the attraction online – they were highly visual and tied directly to the mega news story of the day, the BP oil spill.

A review of congressional YouTube videos also offers some impressions of how the platform is being used and the nature of the content. Although the review fell short of content analysis, the TubeMogul analytic was used to inspect almost 100 of the most popular congressional YouTube channels, noting the topics and watching those videos that drew significant audiences. There were many examples of how videos fit the entertainment culture of YouTube, which often rewards visually arresting raw footage, the off-beat, the amusing, and the dramatic or extreme (May, 2010, p. 504). Pet videos are big on YouTube, and they work for Congress too, including Pelosi's video of cats playing around her gavel (Pelosi, 2009) and Boehner hunting for stimulus dollars with a hound named Ellie Mae (Boehner, 2009).

Most of the congressional content, however, is closer to C-SPAN fare, such as excerpts of the members speaking from the floor or committee meetings. Unlike C-SPAN, the clips are self-selected and often reflect highly partisan congressional debate. Rep. Randy Forbes drew 3 million views to a video featuring the Virginia Republican attacking Obama for lack of commitment to the nation's Judeo-Christian heritage (Forbes, 2009). During the House health care debate, then Rep. Anthony Weiner, a Democrat from New York, launched an attack on the Republicans so fierce that his comments were struck from the record for violating House decorum. Wiener responded by putting the whole episode up on his House You-Tube channel (Weiner, 2010). Weiner's celebrated use of Twitter to send a lewd picture later led to his resignation from Congress.

Next to clips of speeches, the favorite YouTube fare of Congress is clips of television appearances by the members on often partisan cable talk shows. Such repurposing constitutes an interesting use of old media on Web 2.0, extending the reach of political discourse in the commercial media to a taxpayer financed communication channel. Members often post entire segments of shows on which they appear, stretching *fair use* under copyright laws.[23] We found examples such as an 11-minute segment of HBO's *Real Time with Bill Maher* on Issa's YouTube channel, featuring the congressman's appearance in May 2010 (Issa, 2010). Then Democratic Rep. Alan Grayson of Florida, a liberal firebrand, built a YouTube channel of more than 6 million views in part by airing his frequent appearances on cable talk shows, including a 10-minute segment on CNN's *Situation Room* to defend his charge that Republicans want "sick people to die quickly (Grayson, 2009)."

Tracking Congress on YouTube

According to a track of daily views to congressional YouTube channels, the 111th Congress did not sustain the audience that it had built on YouTube during the health care debate. Compressed into monthly views, Congress averaged 1.26 million views per month for the first six months, and averaged 1.23 million views per month for the last six months of its second session. In between, at the height of the health debate, Congress almost tripled those rates of monthly views in the last two quarters of 2009 (3.4 million monthly average) and increased them by more than half (1.9 million monthly average) in the first quarter of 2010. (see Figure 3). A separate YouTube track built for 112th Congress showed that as of the end of June 2011, the audience for the new Congress from the end of the 111th rebounded slightly, averaging 1.6 million views monthly, but once again the track showed a spike in March and April 2011 during the government shutdown debate, and a subsequent fall off in May and June.

Undoubtedly the track of the 111th Congress was influenced by several factors: most especially when Congress was in and out of session and the rate of adoption in the first half of 111th Congress. However, the timing of the health care debate corresponds closely to the peaks and valleys of YouTube views in the fall of 2009 and the winter of 2010, and suggests that a substantial number of Americans followed the historic debate on Web 2.0.

On September 9, 2009, the president addressed Congress on health care and the ensuing debates in the House led to that chamber's passage of the legislation on November 7. The House recorded its all-time YouTube high of about 5 million views in October.[24] The Senate passed the legislation on December 24 and hit its session high on its YouTube channels of 740,000 views in December. In February 2010, Obama renewed the effort that won final House passage on March 21. The Sen-

Figure 3. Daily tracking views of 111ᵗʰ Congress on YouTube and key dates in the passage of healthcare reform

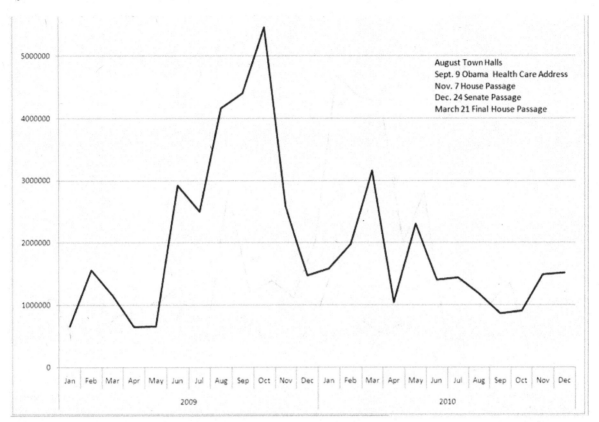

ate recorded its second highest monthly YouTube audience of 406,000 views in February and the House recorded it second highest monthly views of 2.8 million in March. And while Republicans drew considerably more views on YouTube in the 111ᵗʰ Congress, Democratic views followed the same pattern in the timing of views around the health care debate. (see Figure 4)

Web 2.0 does not operate separately from the larger media ecosystem. Technologists, practitioners in the traditional media and scholars have long debated which plays the larger role, legacy media or the newer online media. In one of most exhaustive content analyses to date of legacy media versus new media, the Pew Project for Excellence In Journalism found new online media is largely derivative of legacy media ("New Me-

dia," 2010). In 2011, computer scientists studying Twitter found that the content trending on Twitter drew largely from traditional media sources, which were then amplified by Twitter users to generate trends (Asur, Huberman, Wang & Szabo, 2011).

Accordingly, this study sought to compare the news coverage of the health care debate with the traffic to congressional YouTube channels. In its 2009 and its 2010 News Coverage Index, Pew tracked the health care story as it unfolded in the news. As the coverage increased in late summer and fall, so too did the views on congressional YouTube channels, spiking again for final passage of the legislation in March 2010. There is a strong positive correlation ($p = .767 < .01$) between the number of health care news stories and YouTube views to Congress. (see Figure 5).

Figure 4. Democrats and Republicans mirrored each other in drawing daily YouTube views in the 111ᵗʰ Congress

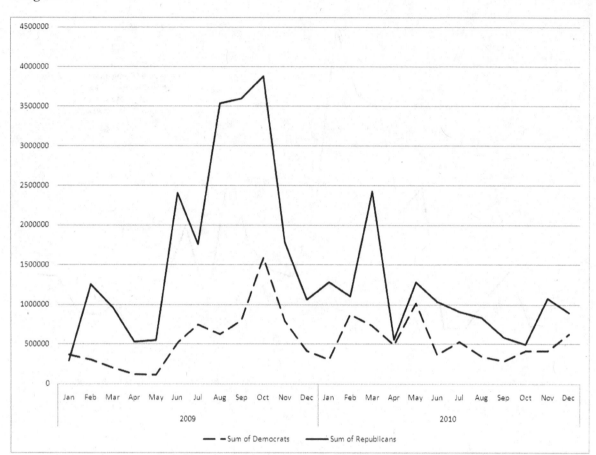

An Incumbent Advantage?

The ultimate consequence of employing a new technology for elected officials is, of course, winning re-election (Mayhew, 1974). The 111ᵗʰ Congress resulted in an historic turnover of the House to the Republicans and significant GOP gains in the Senate in the 2010 midterm elections. Did using the official social media channels improve the chances of winning and does social media performance signal electoral success? The findings are mixed.

Looking simply at members' margins of victory or loss regardless of party, social media Stars won with much larger margins than Laggards, roughly 12 points better ($p = .178 < .01$). This might initially suggest that social media stardom correlates with a larger margin of victory. However, the distinction fades when controlling for party identification, especially among Republicans, for whom there was no significant difference (actually negative) in the election margins and their performance on the index. ($p = -.057$). On average, Republicans won by large margins whether they were social media Laggards or Stars. Democratic Stars and Strivers, however, ran about six points better than Democratic Muddlers and Laggards ($p = .106 < .01$).

Looking at competitive contests within a 10-point spread also proved inconclusive in predicting performance on social media. Eighty members in the sample, of which 73 were Demo-

Figure 5. Health care reform news coverage appears to drive viewers to Congress on YouTube in the fall of 2009 into early 2010

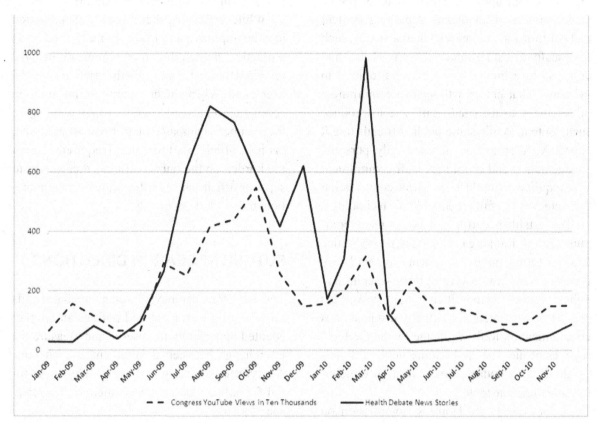

crats, had competitive races, rendering a comparison among Republicans meaningless. There was, however, no significant difference, although correctly positive, among the Democrats in competitive races when compared on the index ($p = .095$). The data also suggest that being in a competitive race did not prompt greater social media effort. Members in a competitive race averaged fractionally fewer social media platforms (2.0 on average) than members who were in noncompetitive contests (2.3 on average).

Solutions and Recommendations

Social media seem to thrive on bright colors, not the beige of bureaucratic discussion. The study found that there is a public audience for vibrant and unfiltered discourse on important issues facing

the nation. Indeed, Congress reached millions of Americans on YouTube alone during the health care debate. But as the debate showed, fleeting public attention will not necessarily build a sustained audience, and political tides are notoriously fickle. More sophisticated strategies for governing with the new technologies are needed to engage citizens more fully on issues of public policy. A pattern of ebb and flow may, however, be in accord with democratic values. One cannot expect a highly engaged citizenry all the time or in all policy disputes. As long as the barriers to participation are low enough for concerned citizens to enter the arena of politics when they desire, certain important democratic principles are satisfied.

Understanding the connection to the larger media ecosystem is critical to government's use of social media to reach sizeable audiences, whether one is focused upon elected officials or public administrators. That means deploying content that conforms to commercial media values, such as visually arresting material on YouTube, and doing so in a timely way when the topic is in the news. That in turn will mean a commitment of resources to technical staff able to produce such content. While some public officials might expect attention to flow automatically, personal engagement – and if not that, staff commitment – is required to build a two-way conversation that achieves the full potential of the technology.

The established rules of government communication – franking in Congress, proper notice and collecting public comments in regulatory procedures and laws governing record keeping and public access – were written in the pre-Web 2.0 eras. User-generated and virtually instantaneous communication tools challenge the hierarchical regimes of the past, and require public officials of all sorts to update communication policies. Consider one anecdote.

In June 2011, the House's Commission on Congressional Mailing Standards objected to language in a newsletter Democratic Rep. Gerald E. Connolly proposed to mail by frank to his Virginia constituents. The commission found Connolly's description of the Republican budget proposal "to eliminate Medicare was we know it" to be partisan misrepresentation (Shear, 2011). Yet, coincidentally, one could tune in Rep. Colleen Hanabusa's official, taxpayer supported YouTube channel to hear the Hawaii Democrat use almost exactly the same language, condemning "the Republican plan to do away with Medicare as we know it today (Hanabusa, 2011)." Her message in the new medium went out unmolested but the same message was restricted under the old rules. Over its history, Congress has confronted similar issues, such as rules governing franked mail or those banning C-SPAN footage in campaign advertisements. Web 2.0 technologies have called into question these carefully contrived formulas,

and Congress has yet to fully work out a set of uniform rules to fit the new medium.

While preserving these lines of demarcation may be important as a matter of public policy, as a practical matter, digital communications have rendered this distinction mostly a fiction from the user's end. When citizens search for information about their representatives, they may wind up on the member's campaign platform, a personal site, or on the official platform. Legal requirements put the burden on the public officials themselves to separate official and overtly political communication and mark them clearly.

FUTURE RESEARCH DIRECTIONS

The very transparency of social media affords scholars of government and politics an unprecedented opportunity to observe and measure the interchange between government and citizens. Analytic tools, similar to those used by TubeMogul for online video, are fast emerging for many social media.

Greater difficulty occurs on the other side of these relationships, namely the consequent actions of citizens. For this reason, deeper and more granular survey research is needed to understand the demographic characteristics of those who are connecting to government officials on social media, with particular emphasis on such variables as race, education levels and the urban and rural mix of the constituents represented.

Another fertile area for future research concerns the nature of the messages being transmitted through these various social media channels. Content analysis offers a fertile avenue, as the extensive review of YouTube videos found. A review of the studies found only one research team (Golbek, Grimes & Rogers, 2010) who was engaged in analyzing the content of the information being exchanged between citizens and Congress.

CONCLUSION

Congress has joined the Web 2.0 revolution and in the fall and winter of 2009-10, millions of Americans tuned in on congressional YouTube channels for the historic health care debate. The lower transaction costs of this new media allowed a single representative to reach a huge audience with his party's position on health care by catching a media wave with an inexpensively produced clip posted on a free online video platform. At the same time, hundreds of thousands of Americans have signed up to *follow* or *like* members of Congress on Twitter and Facebook. Just as C-SPAN engaged a new audience of citizens in the 1980s, social media has the potential to create another breed of congressional junkies and engaged citizens.

Despite the widespread adoption, the actual success of members of Congress in terms of building audiences by using social media platforms varies widely. For many, the reliance is minimal. This study showed that success in using social media correlates with several factors, party affiliation and ideology being the most important ones in the 111th Congress. This research supports the argument that social media employed by Congress are derivative of the political climate and the content available in the traditional media.

The study also found that it takes considerable effort on the part of public office holders to use social media to connect with citizens. Unless one is very lucky or very clever, as was Sen. Nelson in posting the live feed of the Gulf oil spill, just creating a Facebook page, loading videos onto YouTube or sending out tweets will not in itself draw an audience. The research also indicates that Web 2.0 values, such as presenting entertaining or visual content on YouTube, play a role.

Congress's adoption of Web 2.0 is rapidly transforming the way in which its members communicate. This changing media environment raises anew two fundamental issues as to where a balance should be struck among values in the American democracy that are, to some extent, contradictory.

The first relates to the interaction between elected officials and their constituents and the balance of power between them. While in this early stage, growth may be primarily seen in an outward public relations push by public officials designed to communicate with constituents, in the longer run, a functioning democracy also requires that citizens be able to communicate back to their representatives and be heard. This interactive stage of citizen engagement as yet falls short of the collaboration envisioned by O'Reilly and others, but that does not diminish its significance at this stage of development.

Related to the question of the interaction between leaders and citizens is one democracies inevitably confront: the enduring problem of providing elected public officials with sufficient means to communicate with their constituents without, at the same time, unduly advantaging incumbents in the electoral arena. Whether government supported social media channels will disturb this balance, is unclear. This study did not find a statistically significant and uniform relationship between the electoral successes of incumbents in the 2010 campaign and demonstrated successful use of social networking in the 111th Congress. It is likely that the tides of change toward Republican candidates in the 2010 elections were so strong that they eclipsed any advantage that the Stars and Strivers of the index might have otherwise achieved. But if history is a judge, a potential for abuse exists.

The second democratic value that is implicated concerns the widespread citizen engagement that Web 2.0 evangelists seek. The question is this: will increased mobilization inevitably be associated with enhanced partisanship? Here the data appear to support the conclusion that, at least in the short run, new technologies are first seized by political leaders and citizens who are ideologically intense. Mobilization and polarization emerge hand-in-hand. The more ideologically extreme members of Congress, particularly in the House, attracted the bigger audiences. The long term implications for the continued functioning of a healthy democracy, which requires compromise and consensus-building, are as unsettling as they are profound.

REFERENCES

Asur, S., Huberman, B., Wang, C., & Szabo, G. (2011, February). *Social media: Persistence and decay.* Social Computing Lab, Hewlett Packard Labs Palo Alto, CA. Retrieved from http://www.scribd.com/doc/48665388/Trends-in-Social-Media-Persistence-and-Decay

Becker, T., & Slaton, C. (2000). *The future of teledemocracy.* Westport, CT: Praeger.

Boehner, J. (2009, July 1). *Bloodhounds* [Video file]. Retrieved from http://www.youtube.com/watch?v=tl_q0afUl0E&feature=player_embedded

Boyle: The belle of the Web (2009, December 29). *The New Orleans Times-Picayune,* p. C1.

Bremmer, I., & Keat, P. (2009). *The fat tail: The power of political knowledge for strategic investing.* New York, NY: Oxford University Press.

Conservative.org. (2009). *Ratings of Congress.* American Conservative Union [Online archive]. Retrieved from http://www.conservative.org/congress-ratings/

Fitch, B., & Goldschmidt, K. (2005). *Communicating with Congress: How Capitol Hill is coping with the surge in citizen advocacy.* Congressional Management Foundation [Report]. Retrieved from http://www.cmfweb.org/index.php?option=com_content&task=view&id=63

Forbes, R. (2009, May 6). *Our Judeo-Christian nation.* Retrieved from http://www.youtube.com/watch?v=dpQOCvthw-o&feature=player_embedded

Frantzich, S., & Sullivan, J. (1996). *The C-SPAN revolution.* Norman, OK: University of Oklahoma Press.

Galloway, S., & Guthrie, D. (2010, August 18). *Digital IQ: U.S. Senate.* L2: A Think Tank For Digital Innovation. Retrieved from http://l2thinktank.com/research/u-s-senate-2010/

Garrett, R. K. (2009). Politically motivated reinforcement seeking: Reframing the selective exposure debate. *The Journal of Communication, 59,* 676–699. doi:10.1111/j.1460-2466.2009.01452.x

Gentzkow, M., & Shapiro, J. M. (2010, September 21). Ideological segregation online and offline. *Chicago Booth and National Bureau of Economic Research.* Retrieved from http://faculty.chicagobooth.edu/jesse.shapiro/research/echo_chambers.pdf

Glassman, M. (2007, December 5). *Franking privilege: Historical development and options for change.* Congressional Research Service, RL34274. Retrieved from http://www.fas.org/sgp/crs/misc/RL34274.pdf

Glassman, M., Straus, J., & Shogun, C. (2009, September 21). *Communication: Member use of Twitter during a two-week period in the 111th Congress.* Congressional Research Service, R40823. Retrieved from http://www.fas.org/sgp/crs/misc/R41066.pdf

Golbeck, J., Grimes, J., & Rogers, A. (2010). Twitter use by the U.S. Congress. *Journal of the American Society for Information Science and Technology, 61*(8), 1612–1621.

Goldschmidt, K. (2011, July 26). *Communication with Congress: Perceptions of citizen advocacy on Capitol Hill.* The Partnership for a More Perfect Union at the Congressional Management Foundation. Retrieved from http://www.congressfoundation.org/projects/communicating-with-congress/social-congress

Goldschmidt, K., & Ochreiter, L. (2008). *Communicating with Congress: How the Internet has changed citizen engagement.* Congressional Management Foundation [Report]. Retrieved from http://www.cmfweb.org/index.php?Itemid=50&id=64&option=com_content&task=view

Grayson, A. (2009, September 30). *Rep. Alan Grayson on the Situation Room.* Retrieved from http://www.youtube.com/watch?v=3H3gND4M9HA

Hanabusa, C. (2011, June 14). *One minute floor speech.* Retrieved from http://www.youtube.com/user/rephanabusa#p/u/7/3_deCQwOiPI

Hart, K. (2009, November 19). On technology. *The Hill,* p. 12.

Hooper, M. (2008, July 8). House rules on Web advertisements put video-sharing member offices in bind. *Congressional Quarterly Today.*

House Committee on House Administration. (2009). *Member's handbook* (pp. 44–45).

Howard, M. (2001). E-government across the globe: How will "e" change government? *Government Finance Review, 17*(4), 6–9.

Issa, D. (2010, May 15). *Issa gets real with Bill Maher.* Retrieved from http://www.youtube.com/watch?v=0TgKflkVfOE&feature=player_embedded

Iyengar, S., & Hahn, K. S. (2009). Red media, blue media: Evidence of ideological selectivity in media use. *The Journal of Communication, 59,* 19–39. doi:10.1111/j.1460-2466.2008.01402.x

Lovley, E. (2011, February 28). Social media not so hot on the Hill. *Politico.* Retrieved from http://www.politico.com/news/stories/0211/50299.html

Markey, E. (2007, May 10). *YouTube CEO Chad Hurley & Rep. Ed Markey discuss Web video.* Retrieved from http://www.youtube.com/watch?v=Fx1r8u_cmfs

May, A. (2009). The preacher and the press: How the Jeremiah Wright story became the first feeding frenzy in the digital age. In Johnson, D. (Ed.), *Campaigning for the Presidency 2008* (pp. 78–101). New York, NY: Routledge.

May, A. (2010). Who tube? How YouTube's news and politics space is going mainstream. *International Journal of Press/Politics, 15*(4), 499–511.

Mayhew, D. (1974). *Congress: The electoral connection.* New Haven, CT: Yale University Press.

McCaskill, D. (2009, April). *Why I Tweet.* Tumblr.com. Retrieved from http://clairecmc.tumblr.com/post/100898280/why-i-tweet

Messenger, T. (2009, March 16). McCaskill is all a-Twitter about politics in new age. *St. Louis Post-Dispatch,* p. A3.

Mutz, D. C. (2006). How the mass media divide us. In Pietro, S. N., & Brady, D. W. (Eds.), *Red and blue nation? Characteristics and causes of America's polarized politics* (Vol. 1, pp. 223–248). Washington, DC: Brookings Institution Press.

Nelson, B. (2010, May 20). *Never before seen footag.* Retrieved from http://www.youtube.com/watch?v=EXTcM2ntlkM

New media (2010, March). *The state of the news media 2010.* The Project for Excellence in Journalism, Pew Research Center. Retrieved from http://stateofthemedia.org/2010

News coverage index. (2010, July 1; 2011, July 1). *The Project for Excellence in Journalism,* Pew Research Cente. Retrieved from http://www.journalism.org/by_the_numbers/datasets

Nylen, L. (2008, September 29). Hill explores Net's worth. *Congressional Quarterly Weekly,* p. 2550.

O'Reilly, T. (2010). Government as a platform. In Lathrop, D., & Ruma, L. (Eds.), *Open government: Collaboration, transparency and participation in practice* (pp. 899–1777). Sebastopol, CA: O'Reilly Media, Inc.

O'Reilly, T., & Battelle, J. (2009, October). *Web squared: Web 2.0 five years on.* Paper presented at Web 2.0 Summit, San Francisco, CA. Retrieved from http://www.web2summit.com/web2009/public/schedule/detail/10194

Orr, J. (2008, October 19). Lawmakers now a click closer to constituents: Congressmen allowed to post on Internet sites after rule reversal. *Houston Chronicle*, A.16.

Pasely, J. (2001). *The tyranny of printers: Newspaper politics in the early American republic, Jeffersonian America.* Charlottesville, VA: University Press of Virginia.

Pelosi, N. (2009, January 13). *Speaker Pelosi presents Capitol cat cam.* Retrieved from http://www.youtube.com/watch?v=wtOW1CxHvNY&feature=player_embedded

Plautz, J. (2009, September 3). Mike Rogers, YouTube sensation? *NationalJournal.com.* Retrieved from http://healthtopic.nationaljournal.com/2009/09/mike-rogers-you-tube.php

Pool, I. (1983). *Technologies of freedom.* Cambridge, MA: Harvard University Press.

Ritchie, D. (1991). *Press gallery: Congress and the Washington correspondents.* Cambridge, MA: Harvard University Press.

Rogers, M. (2009, July 16). *Congressman Mike Rogers' opening statement on health care reform in Washington, DC.* Retrieved from http://www.youtube.com/watch?v=G44NCvNDLfc&feature=player_embedded

Rowland, K. (2009, March 20). GOP bests its rival for YouTube views. *Washington Times.* Retrieved from http://www.washingtontimes.com/news/2009/mar/20/gop-bests-its-rival- for-youtube-views/

Schacter, J. (2010). Digitally democratizing Congress? Technology and political accountability. *Stanford Law Journal*, No. 1565645.

Schaper, N. (2010). Entrepreneurial insurgency: Republicans connect with the American people. In Lathrop, D., & Ruma, L. (Eds.), *Open government: Collaboration, transparency and participation in practice* (pp. 5376–5562). Sebastopol, CA: O'Reilly Media Inc.

Sclove, R. (1995). *Democracy and technology.* New York, NY: Guilford Press.

Senak, M. (2010, January). Twongress: The power of Twitter in Congress. *Fleishman-Hilliard.* Retrieved from http://www.eyeonfda.com/files/twongress-white-paper-final-1-14-10.pdf

Senate Committee on Rules and Administration. (2008, September 19). *U.S. Senate Internet services usage rules and policies.* Retrieved from http://www.senate.gov/usage/internetpolicy.htm

Shear, M. D. (2011, June 16). House Democrat writes with GOP as editors. *The New York Times*, p. A24.

Shirky, C. (2008). *Here comes everybody: The power of organizing without organizations* [Kindle edition]. New York, NY: Penguin Press.

Simmons, J. (1978). *The fairness doctrine and the media.* Berkeley, CA: University of California Press.

Starr, P. (2004). *The creation of the media: Political origins of modern communications.* New York, NY: Basic Books.

Stroud, N. J. (2011). *Niche news: The politics of news choice*. New York, NY: Oxford University Press.

Sunstein, C. (2007). *Republic.com 2.0*. Princeton, NJ: Princeton University Press.

Sunstein, C. (2009). *Going to extremes: How like minds unite and divide*. New York, NY: Oxford University Press.

ADA Today. (2010). 2009 Congressional voting record inside. *Americans for Democratic Action, 65*(1).

Warren, C. (2010, March 16). How PR pros are using social media for real results. *Mashable.com*. Retrieved from http://mashable.com/2010/03/16/public-relations-social-media-results

Weiner, A. (2010, February 24). *Ever met a Republican not owned by the insurance industry?*. Retrieved from http://www.youtube.com/watch?v=KBqtyvn7OVw

Weinger, M., & Barr, A. (2011, July 7). McCotter finds friends on Hill. *Politico*. Retrieved from http://dyn.politico.com/members/forums/thread.cfm?catid=1&subcatid=1&threadid=5642494

ADDITIONAL READING

Abramowitz, A. (2010). *The disappearing center: Engaged citizens, polarization, and American democracy*. New Haven, CT: Yale University Press.

Ackerman, B., & Fishkin, J. (2003). Deliberation day. In Fishkin, J., & Laslett, P. (Eds.), *Debating deliberative democracy* (pp. 7–30). Malden, MA: Blackwell. doi:10.1002/9780470690734.ch1

Auletta, K. (2009). *Googled: The end of the world as we know it*. New York, NY: Penguin Press.

Bimber, B. A. (2003). *Information and American democracy: Technology in the evolution of political power*. Cambridge, UK: Cambridge University Press. doi:10.1017/CBO9780511615573

Burgess, J., & Green, J. (2009). *YouTube: Online video and participatory culture*. Malden, MA: Polity Press.

Castells, M. (1996). *The rise of the network society*. Cambridge, UK: Blackwell Books.

Chi, F., & Yang, N. (2010, June 20). *Twitter adoption in Congress: Who tweets first?* Social Science Research Network. Retrieved from http://papers.ssrn.com/sol3/papers.cfm?abstract_id=1620401

Cook, T. (1998). *Governing with the news: The news media as a political institution*. Chicago, IL: University of Chicago Press.

Cornfield, M. (2004). *Politics moves online: Campaigning and the Internet*. New York, NY: Century Foundation Press.

Cornfield, M. (2010). Game-changers: New technology and the 2008 presidential election. In Sabato, L. (Ed.), *The year of Obama: How Barack Obama won the White House* (pp. 205–230). New York, NY: Longman.

Delli Carpini, M., & Keeter, S. (1996). *What Americans know about politics and why it matters*. New Haven, CT: Yale University Press.

Ferejohn, J. (1990). Information and the electoral process. In Ferejohn, J., & Kulinski, J. (Eds.), *Information and democratic processes* (pp. 3–19). Chicago, IL: University of Illinois.

Gulati, G., & Williams, D. (2010). Congressional candidates' use of YouTube 2008: Its frequency and rationale. *Journal of Information Technology & Politics, 7*(2-3), 93–109. doi:10.1080/19331681003748958

Jenkins, H. (2008). *Convergence culture: Where old media and new media collide*. New York, NY: New York University Press.

Kirkpatrick, D. (2010). *The Facebook effect: The inside story of the company that is connecting the world*. New York, NY: Simon & Schuster.

Lathrop, D., & Ruma, L. (Eds.). (2010). *Open government: Collaboration, transparency and participation in practice*. Sebastopol, CA: O'Reilly Media Inc.

Noveck, B. S. (2009). *Wiki government: How technology can make government better, democracy stronger, and citizens more powerful*. Washington, DC: Brookings Institution Press.

Pariser, E. (2011). *The filter bubble: What the Internet is hiding from you*. New York, NY: Penguin Press.

Prior, M. (2007). *Post-Broadcast democracy: How media choice increases inequality in political involvement and polarizes elections*. New York, NY: Cambridge University Press.

Putnam, R. (2000). *Bowling alone: The collapse and revival of American community*. New York, NY: Simon & Schuster.

Reich, B., & Solomon, D. (2008). *Media rules! Mastering today's technology to connect with and keep your audience*. Hoboken, NJ: J. Wiley & Sons.

Shackler, E. (2001). *Disjointed pluralism: Institutional innovation and the development of the U.S. Congress*. Princeton, NJ: Princeton University Press.

Shane, P. M. (Ed.). (2004). *Democracy online: The prospects of political renewal through the Internet*. New York, NY: Routledge.

Turow, J. (1997). *Breaking up America: Advertisers and the new media world*. Chicago, IL: University of Chicago Press.

Zittrain, J. (2008). *The future of the Internet and how to stop it*. New Haven, CT: Yale University Press.

KEY TERMS AND DEFINITIONS

American Conservative Union: Founded in 1964, the umbrella organization encompasses conservatives on fiscal, social, national security and libertarian policy issues. It annually rates members of Congress on votes that it deems to be key conservative issues.

Americans for Democratic Action: Formed in 1947 to foster the legacy of the New Deal, the organization promotes liberal stances on social and economic justice, civil rights, women's rights, environmentalist and anti-war issues. It is best known for its annual ratings of members of Congress on what it deems to be key liberal issues.

Congressional Management Foundation: The nonpartisan organization has become a major source of research on the management of Congress since its founding in 1977. The foundation conducts training for congressional staff and conducts studies on how Congress can function better using sound management principles.

Facebook: Named after a guide to college classmates, the social networking site launched in 2004 was initially restricted to university students. By 2010, Facebook claimed a total worldwide membership of more than 500 million. The site allows users to create fan pages and personal profiles to share pictures, videos and comments with friends. Users can *friend* other users to create a community of interest and users can register *likes* on content they are sharing.

Project for Excellence in Journalism: Started in 1997, the nonpartisan think tank has conducted research on a range of media issues from economic to ethical. The project, which is housed in the Pew Research Center in Washington, is best known for its annual *State of the News* report.

The project's News Coverage Index compiles a weekly measure of the content of 52 news outlets in traditional media.

Twitter: A micro blogging service started in 2006, the platform shares text messages and links among users. By 2011, the service claimed 175 million users. The messages, or *tweets*, are restricted to 140 characters by authors who mark their usernames with the @ symbol. Users can subscribe to a Twitter feed to become *followers* and they can access the communications by subject areas, which are designated with a *hashtag* that precedes a subject name with the # symbol.

YouTube: Started in 2005, the website for sharing online video has emerged as the largest such platform in the world. A subsidiary of Google, the company reported in 2010 that it drew more than 2 billion views a day with 24 hours of video uploaded every minute. Users create *channels* to host videos, which can be shared, embedded and commented upon. Most of the content is user generated but the platform also hosts content from major media organizations.

ENDNOTES

[1] TubeMogul.com is headquartered in Emeryville, CA, and offers its commercial services to video producers and conducts research on the emerging world of online video at http://www.tubemogul.com/. One of the authors was given access to the firm's premiere analytic to track videos for research. It forms an important component of this study and the authors are grateful for the contribution of its service for research.

[2] YouTube videos normally have short shelf lives of peak viewing of a week or so (May, 2009, pp. 92-94), but the Rogers video had a solid run of more than three months. Almost 100 websites linked to the video, according to Google.

[3] API stands for an application programming interface, which is a set of specifications that allows different software programs to communicate with each other. Cloud computing is pooled computing and storage on the Internet that is not dependent on an individual client's server. A wiki is a website that allows users to create and edit content collaboratively. Crowd sourcing is using the Internet to engage an online community to solve a task. A mashup is the combination or aggregation of digital sources to create a new online entity.

[4] The partisan press was a commercial press that was subsidized by government through printing contracts and the 1792 Postal Act, which provided highly subsidized distribution of newspapers, many of which were party organs (Starr, 2004, pp. 83-94). The party in power in the Congress subsidized the Washington papers recording the actions of Congress by hiring the proprietors as official printers of the House or Senate (Ritchie, 1991, pp. 7-34).

[5] C-SPAN provides gavel-to-gavel coverage of the House and Senate floor debates under procedures set by the Congress. As described on C-SPAN webpage (http://www.c-span.org/About/About-C-SPAN/), the cameras are owned and operated by Congress but congressional policy does allow for C-SPAN's coverage of other congressional events, such as committee hearings and press conferences, produced by its own cameras.

[6] It took more than a year for Democrats to react to Republican embrace of social media. The House Democratic Caucus launched a New Media Working Group in the spring of 2010.

[7] The Senate rules allowed members to use third-party platforms with restrictions against employing them for commercial promotion, political purposes and in violation on pre-existing franking restrictions.

The Senate rules specifically prohibit the use of data gathering tools that allow for the collection of personal information of users and distributing such information to outside parties ("Senate," 2008). The House rules have no similar provision but prohibit commercial and campaign related use. The House rules do require a notice to users that they are exiting the official House website with a disclaimer that neither the member nor the House is "responsible for the content of linked sites ("House," 2009)." A review of House sites often found this disclaimer missing. Commercial advertising also can often be found on congressional Facebook pages, although the provider will block them upon request by a member.

[8] In January 2009, YouTube created separate Senate and House hubs for official congressional YouTube channels accessible through an online map of the United States. The hubs are at http://youtube.com/senatehub and http://youtube.com/house-hub. In May 2010, Facebook launched a similar aggregator page for congressional Facebook at http://www.facebook.com/congress?v=app_244855997751#!/congress?v=app_244855997751. At press, Twitter had not created a similar site, although an aggregator site has been established by the online advocacy group Tweet Congress at http://tweetcongress.org/.

[9] The Senate feed is at http://twitter.com/SenateFloor and the House feed is at http://twitter.com/housefloor.

[10] The Congressional Research Service study in August of 2009 found that 158 members had Twitter accounts. The study found that 54% of House Republicans and 10% of Senate Republicans had joined Twitter compared to 27% of House Democrats and 9% of Senate Democrats (Glassman, Straus & Shogun, 2009). Another study by a Washington public affairs firm of Twitter use in November 2009 found House Republicans were outstripping their Democratic colleagues by a factor of four in terms of Twitter followers (Senak, 2010). In March 2009, TubeMogul released data from its track of congressional YouTube channels that showed eight of the top 10 channels belonged to Republicans, with Republicans registering 4.9 million views at the time compared to 4.3 million for the Democrats (Rowland, 2009).

[11] In April 2010, the House Republicans held a *New Media Challenge,* followed by the Democrats' *Member Online All Star Competition* in June.

[12] Analyzing more than 6,000 Twitter posts of members as of September 2009, the study found that 53% of posts were informational releases much like those issued to old media. Another 27% announced locations of congressional activity, such as appearances in the home districts. The study found only 7% of the *tweets* involved direct communication with constituents. Congress members were found rarely to *re-tweet*, a form of interactivity, and made little use of *hashtags* to mark the subject matter (Golbeck, Grimes & Rogers, 2010).

[13] The CMF received 260 responses to an online survey distributed widely to congressional offices. On a cautionary note, the survey was not random, and no response rate was reported. Although possibly skewed by self-selection, 72% said social media allowed Congress to reach people who were not reached before and only 7% disagreed with that view; 59% said social media was worth the time spent on it and 10% disagreed, and 55% said the rewards outweighed risks, while 14% disagreed. Three-fourths of the respondents said Facebook and YouTube were very or somewhat important in communicating a member's views to constituents. Half said the same for Twitter. The majorities shrunk, however, when asked how useful the

platforms were in understanding the views of constituents. Two-thirds of the staffers said Facebook was useful in that regard, but only four in ten said Twitter was useful in assessing constituent views and a third of the staffers found YouTube useful in hearing from constituents.

14   At the time of the data collection, there were two vacancies in the House, and four senators and 31 House members were not active in social media. So the study covered the remaining 498 members of the 533-voting-member Congress who had some presence on one of the three platforms. Fifty-two congressional organizations – committees and caucuses – also had a presence on one of the three platforms but were excluded from the quantitative portion of the study because of difficulties in categorizing and creating a known universe.

15   The daily tracking data used in the study originates with TubeMogul's database that was periodically updated through October 2009 with new congressional channels. One of the authors updated it again in July 2010 and downloaded each individual track for inspection. Prior to July 2010, there is a 4.6 million view difference between the total daily tracked data for the 111th Congress and the cumulative total. How these lost data distribute over time is impossible to know. Some lost data predate 2009 and some lost data result from gaps between the time a channel was launched and time it was inserted in the TubeMogul analytic. The result is that the two-year track of congressional YouTube views could undercount the volume of viewership for the first 18 months compared to the final six months when the database was finalized. Analysis of the lost data found the Republican channels were missing 2.2 million views and the Democratic channels were missing 2.4 million views.

16   Cumulative views of videos on a channel were found to be the best measure of audience size. Although several other YouTube metrics are available, including channel views, subscribers and comments posted, those were found to be very small compared to the actual number of views of the videos. Using cumulative data also means some traffic to the channels predates the 111th Congress. The amount of earlier traffic, however, is likely to be relatively small given that there were only a handful of early adopters. For example, Pelosi was the first adopter of YouTube, registering 4.1 million cumulative views in July 2010 on her four-year-old channel. Half of those views pre-date the 111th Congress. Pelosi, however, would appear to be an anomaly; the study found only seven other members with long-time channels with sizeable pre-2009 audiences; These seven members registered 6.5 million cumulative views, but only 8% of those views predated 2009.

17   RSS (Really Simple Syndication) feeds are web tools that allow the publishing of frequently updated online content, such as blog posts or news releases.

18   The ACU rated members on 25 votes on conservative issues and the study used the average score on a scale of 0 to 100. Similarly, the ADA rated members on 20 votes on liberal issues and the study used the average ADA score on scale of 0 to 100. The 2009 ACU ratings were available for all but four members in the sample. The 2009 ADA ratings were available for all but 12 members in the sample. Democrats in the sample averaged 6.8 on the ACU and 90.9 on the ADA scales, while Republicans averaged 90.6 on ACU and 9.3 on ADA. The range for Democrats on ACU was from 0 to 72, while on ADA the Democratic range was 20 to 100. The range for Republicans

on ACU was 48 to 100, while on ADA the Republican range was 0 to 65.

[19] The *n* for senators is small and gets even smaller when controlling for party (55 Democrats and 41 Republicans). Also, the differentiation among senators is less than the differentiation among House members with senators ranking disproportionately in the top two tiers of the index.

[20] Other examples of well-known partisans in the 111th Congress who made our Stars list but are not members of their party's top echelon: South Carolina Republicans Sen. Jim DeMint and Rep. Joe Wilson, Rep. Tom Price of Georgia, Sen. James Inhofe of Oklahoma; Democrats Rep. Alan Grayson of Florida and Rep. Tom Perriello of Virginia, both of whom were defeated in 2010.

[21] It is unclear why a similar pattern did not emerge clearly among senators, although the statistical analysis was hampered by a small *n* of senators with available ADA and ACU ratings (38 and 37 Republicans and 56 and 55 Democrats, respectively). Republican senators who are Stars did score 11 points better on the conservative ACU scale than Laggards, but Strivers and Muddlers showed no differentiation. The Republican senators showed a similar pattern on the ADA ratings, but for both indices the correlations were negligible, although correctly positive ($p = .055$) on the ACU but incorrectly positive on ADA ($p = .01$). There was no discernible pattern among Democratic senators, which incorrectly showed positive correlation with ACU ($p = .150$) and a correct positive correlation with ADA ($p = .115$). In their Digital IQ study of senators on social media, Galloway and Guthrie (2010) reported a relationship among Republican senators to their voting records but found none among Democratic senators.

[22] Several other legislators also have become social media stars by dint of personal involvement. Democrat Rep. Edward Markey of Massachusetts built a substantial audience on YouTube by actively engaging in media production, including filming while presiding over a committee and once interviewing YouTube co-founder Chad Hurley on the virtues of congressmen using YouTube (Markey, 2007). One of the first members to make a splash in the news by using Twitter was Republican Rep. John Culberson of Texas who supplied minute-by-minute tweets of a Republican protest over energy policy in August of 2008 (Nylen, 2008). But maintaining the personal commitment can be a challenge and Culberson became disillusioned with the platform declaring there were "a lot of trolls on Twitter" and that he had become "sick and tired of it (Lovley, 2011)."

[23] Members of Congress seem to enjoy some immunity from copyright challenge by television providers. Their videos, for whatever reason, appear to fly under the radar of YouTube's software recognition technology that allows television providers to routinely eliminate infringing content posted by others (May, 2010, pp. 503-4). The review of YouTube channels found a few examples of copyright enforcement but they were rare. One example of copyright enforcement on a member occurred in December 2009 when Viacom struck a video by Sen. James Inhofe (R-Okla.) containing an excerpt of the *Daily Show* that drew more than 200,000 views.

[24] The YouTube track was clearly influenced by Roger's one video on health care that went viral. However, when Rogers was dropped from the analysis the pattern of YouTube views with the timing of the health care debate persisted.

Chapter 15
i–Government:
Interactive Government Enabling Civic Engagement and a New Volunteerism

Linda-Marie Sundstrom
California State University- Long Beach, USA

ABSTRACT

This research is intended to introduce a new concept of Interactive Government (i-Government), provide an overview of current practices, and offer recommendations for development and implementation. i-Government is the use of smartphone applications to: a) connect citizens with resources; b) engage citizens in collaboration; c) empower citizens as volunteers; and d) enable citizens to serve as watchdogs. Smartphone applications enable government agencies to provide citizens with information and resources anytime (24/7), from anywhere. This anytime, anywhere feature, combined with smartphone technology such as a camera, GPS/location detection service, and an Internet browser, allows citizens to interact with government by accessing information and providing real-time data. Citizens become a new type of volunteer force, who serve as sensors in the community, and who provide information on anything from potholes, to graffiti, to suspicious activity. Because smartphones are always on, government agencies can directly contact citizens who are also willing to serve their community.

DOI: 10.4018/978-1-4666-0318-9.ch015

INTRODUCTION

The basis for Interactive Government (*i*-Government) is the 2007 introduction of Apple's iPhone, the first smartphone with widespread distribution that combined a phone, camera, Personal Digital Assistant (PDA), and Internet connectivity, with a user-friendly browser, touch screen, GPS/location detection service, multi-media capabilities, and many other technology features. Developers utilized this powerful mobile technology to develop software applications (apps) for use with the iPhone (and later, other smartphones such as Android) that utilized the advanced technology for games, entertainment, productivity tools, news, social networking, and much more. By 2010, government applications were being developed to enable citizens to quickly and easily connect with government agencies *anytime,* from *anywhere.*

This article explores the progression of government interaction with citizens from the use of Electronic Government (E-Government) to Mobile Government (M-Government) to the advent of Interactive Government (*i*-Government). It provides a survey of current *i*-Government applications that fall into several categories including applications that a) connect citizens to government resources; b) engage citizens in collaboration with government agencies; c) empower citizens as volunteers; and d) enable citizens as watchdogs. Additionally, the article presents information on turn-key solutions being used in several cities, implementation successes, and challenges of actual start-up operations. This initial exploration of the current uses of *i*-Government applications is intended to provide a base upon which practitioners and researchers can begin an evaluation of the effectiveness of this interactive technology which is intended to connect, engage, and empower, citizens as sensors in the community.

BACKGROUND

E-Government

Electronic Government (E-Government) has been a practice since the 1990s, where federal, state and local government agencies apply Information and Communication Technologies (ICTs), such as basic Internet applications, to deliver government services, engage citizens, and improve efficiencies (Trimi & Sheng, 2008). E-Government began as a way for government information and services to be available to the public 24/7 through the Internet. During the period known as Web 1.0, these types of websites included information such as: a) how to access government services; b) hours of operations; and c) ways to obtain and/or pay for information, such as obtaining copies of birth certificates, paying property taxes, and filing for permits and licenses. E-Government provided a means to make services more convenient for the citizens and reduce the cost of services provided by the government agencies. Recent research done by CitySourced, a smartphone application platform developer, estimated that walk-in services (a citizen walking into a government building to obtain services) costs a government agency approximately $9 per contact, whereas an online, web-based self service transaction can result in costs to the government agency as low as $0.24 to $0.65 per contact (K.Daradics, personal communication, 2011).

E-Government to M-Government

E-Government focused on computer-based internet applications to connect citizens with government agencies. This connection was available whenever the citizen was logged in to his/her computer. M-Government utilized text messages to disseminate time-sensitive information from government agencies to citizens mobile phones. Unlike computer-based internet services, mobile phones provided a means to reach citizens *anytime* or *anywhere* since most citizens carried a mobile phone with them throughout the day which was *always on*. Mobile Government (M-Government) used mobile technology, such as standard featured cell phones and Personal Digital Assistants (PDAs), such as a Blackberry-type device, to provide a limited range of government services to citizens (Zefferer, 2011). In 2002, M-Government services primarily included using Short Message Service (SMS) text messages. These included one-way communication (text messages) from the government agency, which were sent to the citizen's cell phone. For example, during a critical California electricity shortage, text messages could be sent to citizens asking them to conserve energy, or loyal blood donors could be contacted when blood banks ran low on certain blood types. These services worked on an "opt-in" model, where the user elected to have the government contact him/her in specific instances. Although cell phones were beginning to be equipped with text message capabilities, cameras, and limited Internet access (primarily to receive email, download ringtones, and download games), these earlier models were not equipped with browsers that made Internet usage easy to use.

Beyond E-Government – Beyond M-Government: With the introduction of Apple's iPhone in 2007, the basic Internet services of E-Government were suddenly combined with the mobility of M-Government in one device. In addition to Internet services that provided access *anytime*, and the mobility of a handheld device that provided access *anywhere*, the iPhone introduced additional powerful, interactive advancements in mobile technology including an easy-to-use Internet browser, GPS/location detection devices, cameras, multi-media capabilities and other technology that enabled a new collaboration between citizens and their government. (Note: For the purpose of this article, the term Global Positioning System (GPS) will refer generically to the location detection component of a cellular phone which may be derived from a satellite, or by a combination of

satellites, wi-fi hotspots and cellular towers used to pinpoint the geographic location of the device.)

M-Government to *i*-Government

Interactive Government *(i*-Government) utilizes smartphone mobile technology combined with custom software applications to a) connect citizens with resources; b) engage citizens in collaboration; c) empower citizens as volunteers; and d) enable citizens as watchdogs. *i*-Government utilizes free applications designed specifically for smartphones or other mobile devices such as iPads or tablets. These applications can be downloaded onto the smartphone and accessed *anytime* the citizen wants to connect with his/her government agencies, from *anywhere*. Citizens do not have to wait until they have access to desktop or laptop computer – they only have to tap the screen of their smartphone to obtain a vast array of resources at their fingertips. Applications have been designed to connect citizens with resources (e.g., displaying hours of operation, locations of resources, emergency service information, etc.) For example, with a smartphone application, a*nytime,* and *anywhere* citizens would be able to find locations of sandbag distribution centers in the event of a possible flood. Additionally, with the power of the GPS location device inside the phone, the application could immediately pinpoint the citizen's location and provide him/her with turn-by-turn directions to route the citizen to the nearest distribution location. Additionally, since smartphones have multi-media capabilities, citizens can view audio and video clips to learn what to do in an emergency, such as shelter in place. Because applications can be downloaded and stored on the phone, many features can remain operational even if there is no electricity, no operational phone lines, and no Internet access. Other applications have been designed to engage citizens in collaboration by reporting community issues directly to the government agencies. For example, if a citizen sees graffiti in the neighborhood, a tap on the smartphone screen can bring up a program that allows the citizen to take a photo of the graffiti and send it immediately to the city. The city will receive the photo, along with longitude and latitude data to pinpoint the exact location of the graffiti. This information can then be routed internally to the public works department to automatically create a work order ticket, and simultaneously be routed to law enforcement to determine if the graffiti may be gang related.

In 2007, Apple Inc. introduced its first iPhone, which changed the landscape of the smartphone market by adding a new dimension to the cell phone. In 2008, iPhone's competitor, Android, was released with similar features and used similar app programs to run a variety of functions on the phone. Whether an iPhone, Android, or other type of operating systems (OS), smartphones are not isolated to particular demographic groups. It was recently reported that by November 2010, 28% of the cell phone users had smartphones and the number was even higher among those who were younger. Among those who acquired new cell phones in the preceding six months, 41% of all purchases opted for smartphones over a standard feature phone. Additionally, smartphone owners were more diverse than standard phone ownership (Table 1). Seventy-six percent of people who purchased standard feature phones were white, compared to only 62% of those who purchased smartphones. Therefore, applications utilizing Smartphone technology have the potential of reaching a large and diverse citizen population.

Historically, in order for citizens to convey their concerns to a government agency, it required attendance at a city council meeting, a trip down to city hall, or a phone call in hopes of being connected to the right department. Additionally, in order for the city to discover neighborhood issues, it meant sending staff in the field to survey areas for a variety of concerns such as potholes, graffiti, broken street lights and other community-related issues. However, *i*-Government applications transform every citizen into a volunteer

Table 1. Smartphone ownership third quarter 2010

Race/Ethnicity	Feature Phones N=40,938	SmartPhones N=13,242
White	76%	62%
Hispanic	9%	19%
Black/African American	8%	10%
Asian/Pacific Islander	4%	6%
Other	3%	3%
Total	100%	100%

Source: Nielsen Wire: http://blog.nielsen.com/nielsenwire

sensor who can provide vital communication information to a government agency. Rather than government employees having to locate community problems, the citizens can quickly and easily report concerns within their own neighborhoods. The easy-to-use smartphone applications drastically reduce the time, and streamline the process for citizens to report issues. Within a few seconds, and a tap of the screen, a pothole can be reported to the city, along with a photo of the pothole and the longitude and latitude information. The internal city system can be programmed to automatically generate a work order and dispatch employees to repair the pothole. Since a photo can accompany the report, workers can know the severity of the situation which can enable them to bring appropriate tools and supplies out to the field to reduce trips back and forth to gather enough supplies. The ease of use of the applications permits new ways to enable interactive government, resulting in collaborative efforts between citizens and their government to work together to improve communities. The phrase, "Every Citizen a Sensor" (Tumin & Wasserman, 2008, p. 11) reflects the spirit and practice of *i*-Government applications.

i-GOVERNMENT TO CONNECT AND ENGAGE CITIZENS

By 2010, Interactive Government (*i*-Government) applications were becoming more widespread in the United States, especially at the city and county levels of government. Free applications could be downloaded onto a smartphone provided an innovative way for citizens to interact with government agencies. This section provides overview of several *i*-Government applications throughout the United States that are intended to a) connect citizens with resources; b) engage citizens in collaboration; c) empower citizens as volunteers; and d) enable citizens as watchdogs. *i*-Government utilizes applications, which are generally free for citizens to download, and are designed specifically for smartphones. *i*-Government applications are intended to do more with less resources, while still meeting the desire for citizens to connect with government. The purpose of this section is to begin classifying the types of smartphone applications available that promote interaction between citizens and government, explore the current options already in existence, and begin to look at ways applications may be used in the future. This section will close with recommendations that should be considered by government agencies that are exploring the possibility of utilizing a smartphone application in the future.

i-Government Connecting Citizens with Resources and Information

One-Way Information in Portable Format

The Office of Emergency Management in Orange County, Florida developed an application that citizens can download onto their smartphones to help them prepare for a disaster. The application is called OCFL Alert and has four sections including a) alerts about weather conditions and evacuation/shelter-in-place advisories; b) locations to pur-chase shelters, tarps, sandbags, water, and ice; c) events being promoted by the Office of Emergency Management; and d) a Frequently Asked Questions (FAQs) section. The intent of this application is to provide citizens with emergency information, and since many of the maps, addresses and phone numbers are downloaded and stores on the phone, citizens are able to access the information even if the phone lines and Internet connections are not functioning (McKenna, 2011). This type of application is an information-only application. It is a convenient way to get information to citizens that can be accessed even if the electricity is not working (a situation which would make desktop computers not operational). The mobility of having the information in a handheld device has the potential to keep vital information easily available to citizens, even during an emergency.

Information Utilizing GPS and Citizen Input

Another example of an information-type application that combines the dissemination of information with the power of a GPS locator on the smartphone, is Philadelphia's iCondomPhilly application. Philadelphia is in the top 10 U.S. cities for sexually transmitted diseases, and this application is intended to provide information to encourage the use of condoms and provide information on where to find them. Citizens in Philadelphia can start the application and by tapping the button labeled "Find Nearest" the application will identify the exact location of the citizen and route him/her to the nearest condom dispenser in the area. This application is part of a larger application called iCondom which provides the same information for New York City and Washington, D.C. (Martinelli, 2011). As in this example, each government agency does not necessarily have to create their own applications from scratch. Some applications used in other areas can be easily tailored to fit the needs of similar regions. Additionally, the government agency may not need to enter all the information by themselves. In this example, the city asks locations that distribute condoms to input and update the location information. Therefore, the government application merely facilitates communication from the citizens to available resources that may help to solve a public health issue, with little time or maintenance effort on the part of the city staff.

i-Government Engaging Citizens in Collaboration

Development and Implementation of i-Government Applications

In order to implement a smartphone application, a city can select from a variety of ready-made, third-party, turn-key solutions that can be customized for their regional needs. Companies such as CitySourced, GoRequest, SeeClickFix, Nixle, and Tip411, have set up systems in a variety of cities that process GPS data, photos taken on the scene, and data input by the citizens. These elements are combined into customized categories and integrated into the city's work order system.

In 2010, the City of Glendale introduced their application using a CitySourced platform (with an ESRI GIS component to process GPS data received from a smartphone) to obtain information from citizens and integrate the requests into their internal system. The request is then routed to the right department and right staff member (K.Daradics, personal communication, 2011). The City of Colorado Springs uses the GoRequest platform to enable citizens to report a variety of community issues including abandoned vehicles, barking dogs, parks and trail maintenance, potholes, broken sidewalks, streetlight, traffic signals and signs, among other issues (Smith, 2010). Within seconds, the citizen is able to open the application, select the appropriate category, obtain data (e.g., snap a photo) and send the request to the city. GPS information (which pinpoints the exact location of the report), along with the date

and time of the request are automatically added to the data which is received by the city. Cities that have successfully implement *i*-Government applications reported that the application a) gave the public a real-time method to report problems; b) provided an application that was free for the citizens to download and use; c) provided a way for citizens to easily and quickly submit a photo with their concern; d) enabled concerns to be reported anonymously; and e) pinpointed the exact geographic location of the problem. Citizens did not have to call city hall during busy business hours, or leave a voice mail after hours, and the citizen could check on the status of their report and track the progress.

Challenges with Application Integration

To reduce Information Technology (IT) overhead for internal government services, some cities selected third-party application platforms that were advertised to be simple, turn-key systems that could provide a seamless application integration solution. Although many third-party vendors appear to have successfully accomplished this task, some cities have experienced challenges with this approach. One reported concern was that, despite the city's efforts to publicize the application, citizens were unaware of the application's availability and/or were unaware of the limited scope of issues that could be reported. Citizens did not appear to be satisfied with the pre-determined categories, such as categories to report a pothole, broken streetlights, etc. They would try to use categories, like pothole repair, to report things like "woman screaming" rather than calling 911. Some cities experience problems integrating the application with their in-house IT system. In some cases, one person was assigned to manually route the reports to various departments because the automated routing feature did not work properly. Some struggled with knowing which department was responsible for each report. Cross-departmental reports resulted in neither department taking the responsibility for the report and resulted in complaints (which should have been resolved in a matter of days) remaining open for weeks (K. Alexander, personal communication, 2011). Turn-key systems require coordination and integration into existing systems and processes. If interoperability within a government is strained prior to implementation, the chances of a smooth implementation can be dramatically decreased.

i-Government Empowering Citizens as Volunteers

Citizen Volunteers as First Responders

New Volunteerism results when citizens provide feedback, information, data and services to a government agency via an application on their smartphone, or respond to a request made by a government agency on their smartphone without any compensation to the citizen. In 2011, San Ramon Valley, California Fire Protection District released an *i*-Government application that notifies people who are trained in CPR if someone nearby is having a heart attack. If a person is having a cardiac emergency in a public location such as a restaurant, park, business or government building, individuals who have downloaded the application and have opted to receive notifications are alerted to where CPR is needed if they are within walking distance of the emergency. In the past, anyone who knew CPR and was willing to help a fellow citizen in need, had to be in the right place at the right time. This application expands the possibilities for help to arrive even before the fire department arrives at the location. In the first three months after it was released, nearly 500 people downloaded the application (Hickey, 2011).

Citizens Volunteering Smartphone Data to Improve Neighborhoods

Many cities have created applications that allow citizens to report potholes, but the City of Boston is trying to automate the process through citizens' smartphones. An application called Street Bump is currently being designed to use the smartphone's accelerometer to detect the pothole, and the GPS data to pinpoint the exact location. The citizen will help the city create work orders for problem areas without requiring the person to manually report potholes through the application. The phone would be placed on the dashboard, and if the car runs over a pothole, the application will detect it and automatically generate the work order. The city is currently receiving help from a variety of high tech institutes to further develop the application so that the phone can accurately detect the difference between a pothole, a speed bump, railroad tracks, sewer grates and other types of objects. Microsoft, MIT and others are also working to solve this issue, with varying degrees of success. Although the final solution may be somewhere in the future, this is an example a new type of volunteerism. Rather than volunteering time or money, citizens may be volunteering their smartphone data to help improve the city (Dillow, 2001).

i-Government Enabling Citizens as Watchdogs

Citizen Watchdogs Reporting Fraud and Abuse

In 2011, Philadelphia's City Controller released the Our Philly WatchDog application enabling citizens to quickly and easily report fraud, waste and abuse. If citizens observe a city worker "goofing off" they can report it using the application. Citizens can also send photos or videos anonymously, along with the complaint. Additionally, city employees can use the application to report abuses within the city anonymously, and use the whistle-blower protections afforded employees. The application is reported to have cost $5,400 to develop (Lucey, 2011). This low up-front cost is anticipated to generate a large return on investment.

Citizen Watchdogs Reporting Suspicious and Criminal Activities

Eye on Laredo was released in 2011 to enable Texas residents to report crime or suspicious activity from their smartphones. The local sheriff indicated that this application is the 21st century upgrade of the traditional neighborhood watch program (Martinelli, 2011). Other applications, such as Eyes and Ears on Kentucky (released in 2011) and iWatch Dallas (released in 2010) enable citizens to report any suspicious activities that could be linked to terrorism, along with any suspicious items or objects. However, the American Civil Liberties Union (ACLU) claims that suspicious activity reporting (SAR) programs can result in reporting common activities such as taking pictures or drawing diagrams. The ACLU believes these programs will increase the probability that innocent people will be stopped by the police and have their personal information entered into databases (Rich, 2011). In order to balance public safety and individual privacy concerns, data collection and usage policies must be further developed.

Recommendations

Interactive Government (*i*-Government) applications are intended to a) connect citizens with resources; b) engage citizens in collaboration; c) empower citizens as volunteers; and d) enable citizens as watchdogs. As government agencies begin the decision making process to determine if they will develop and implement a smartphone application, there are several things they should consider.

- Traditional website vs. smartphone application: Government agencies must first look at the type of interactions with citizens they are hoping to achieve with a smartphone application. If the intent of the interaction is to provide information (e.g.,

the hours of operation that the local hazardous waste facility accepts household products) then adding that information to a city website may be more effective rather than building an application. Since smartphone users have access to the Internet through a browser, they are still able to access information on standard websites. If the intent of the interaction is to notify citizens of emergencies and/or events, then possibly sending a text message that can reach both standard feature phones and smartphones would provide the best coverage as opposed to developing an application. However, if the interaction with the citizen requires the government agency to receive data, obtain a photo, pinpoint the location of the citizen, then a smartphone application that incorporates a camera function and/or the GPS location function might be more appropriate. Lastly, if the interaction requires that citizens have access to information that can be stored on their smartphone in the event of power outages, phone line interruptions and/or Internet interruptions, a smartphone application that easily downloads information to the phone itself may be more appropriate.

- Cost of development: Although stand alone smartphone applications may be low-cost items (e.g., less than $5,000) to create, turn-key solutions with full system integration into a government agency's back office work order system can be quite costly. Turn-key solutions can provide a custom front-end application that is viewed by the citizens, and integrated with the internal government systems to automatically route requests to the appropriate department, automatically email a response to the citizen that the problem is being reviewed, track the work order internally, and notify the citizen when the work is complete. However, if the government agency's internal systems do not have interoperability (e.g., the public works system is not compatible with the police department's system), integration may prove more of a challenge, which can result in longer implementation time and increased development costs.

- Cost of maintenance: The system maintenance of the new applications over the long-term may prove timely and costly. As platforms expand from the iPhone to the Android and beyond, and as updates to operating systems get released, applications must be continually updated (Towns, 2010). Unlike installing computers and software in an office that will continue operating even if new operating systems or software versions are released, smartphone applications built for older operating systems may cease to function as soon as they are updated. A sustainability plan must be put in place to provide updates and revisions to the applications to ensure they continue to work as the smartphone operating systems continue to grow and evolve at a rapid pace.

- Cost of personnel: Personnel costs and workload may need to be considered, not only for the development and maintenance of the application, but also for potential workload increases due to the ease of citizen reporting. Although research is limited in the area of service calls, there is a possibility that the number of service request could increase with the implementation of a smartphone application. For example, if a person noticed a pothole on the way to work, and needed to wait to find a way to report the issue by phone or through the internet once they were at work, requests received by the local government agency may be limited. However, if the process could be done in 30 seconds with a smartphone app, the service order volume could potentially increase, resulting in the need

for additional staff to field the requests or increase burden on current workloads. These hidden costs may not be apparent until implementation is complete, but could potentially make-or-break the success of a project.

- Verifying data integrity: Government agencies can verify the integrity of data such as graffiti and potholes because the citizen will usually provide a photo which is sent along with longitude and latitude data and the time of day the request was made. However, if a citizen is using a smartphone to anonymously report suspicious activity that does not contain photos, the credibility of the report may come into question. Additionally, the application needs to distinguish between duplicate reports to track the data accurately. Lastly, the system, or administrative personnel must develop procedures to deal with erroneously submitted information. For example, if a citizen uses the application to report suspicious activity, but the narrative indicates that he/she is merely upset with a neighbor for not taking in the trash cans off the streets, procedures need to guide the appropriate actions so that the error can be administratively addressed by the staff. Some systems that are not fully integrated may require manual routing by staff. Clear policies and procedures need to be developed for those instances, so that success of the citizen interaction is not dependent on one person who intuitively knows how to route reports through the system. Analysis of data generated by the system will be meaningless if data integrity is not insured.

- Provide citizen feedback: Manual or automated systems need to be put in place to ensure that citizens know, in a timely manner, that the request was received. Additionally, the citizen interaction should include a way to track the request, and a way for citizens to know when the problem or issue has been resolved.

- Considering the digital divide: Additionally, consideration should be given to the options available to those who will not or cannot own a smartphone. Traditional reporting channels may need to be maintained for reporting all the same information that can be done with a smartphone application. Portions of the population may not own smartphones due to financial concerns, or who cannot or will not learn the technology. Additionally, those people who choose to be *off-the-grid* (avoid technology where government agencies can track their whereabouts) may be hesitant to report any incidents where the government agencies can track their precise location, time of day, and incident reported. For any of these populations, traditional reporting methods via phone, mail, or internet reporting may need to remain a viable option.

- Advertise to the public: Lastly, if a government agency implements a smartphone application, it must be widely publicized to the citizens, and they need to know the intended application of the software. A marketing outreach plan should be developed and launched after the go-live test period has concluded. It is important to reach as many citizens as possible with a high frequency rate. A one-time announcement or a single flyer put in with the water bill may not be enough exposure to reach the majority of local residents.

FUTURE RESEARCH DIRECTIONS

The technological and communication improvements made possible by *i*-Government applications, also raise a number of questions that have not yet been explored. Directions for further research include issues of privacy with regards to GPS location data being transmitted, and privacy issues related to people reporting suspicious activity. Questions regarding social equity and equal access to services may require additional research. Currently, with the higher price of smartphones and the higher cost for phone service to support the Internet connectivity, applications may be more readily available to higher socioeconomic groups, and may be unavailable to low-income populations. Additionally, since smartphone applications are intended to make it easier for citizens to interact with the government, the question arises as to a possible increase in reports and workload for government agencies. Pre and post implementation data should be collected to determine if the number of citizen interactions increased or decreased, and if the automated systems increased or decrease government workload. More research needs to be done on the cost/benefit analysis of the implementation of a variety of smartphone applications in a variety of categories to further determine long-term viability. Finally, more research should be conducted to determine citizen awareness of the applications, perceived usability and benefits, and satisfaction levels of the citizens in each community.

CONCLUSION

As technology continues to rapidly evolve, smartphone applications and smarter mobile technology, such as iPads and tablet PCs, will enable more and more government interaction with citizens. Applications are beginning to link citizen reports with tracking features on social networking sites, like Facebook, where neighbors can unite to track issues of concern to groups of people in a community. But the keys to successful engagement lie, not only with the technological advancements, but with the focus on developing functional applications that solve a community problem, and not create applications for the sake of technology alone. When developing *i*-Government applications, government agencies need to address system and process integration, develop strong policies and procedures to institutionalize the operation, account for development and maintenance costs, monitor changes in the number of citizen complaints/reports, track changes in workload for staff, and monitor response times and closure rates for work orders. *i*-Government is enabling citizens to interact in a meaningful and powerful way with their government, and has the potential to prioritize community concerns, streamline communication and workflow between citizens and their government, and enable a new sense of volunteerism to improve communities throughout the country.

REFERENCES

Dillow, C. (2011, February 10). Boston's 'Street Bump' app tries to automatically map potholes with accelerometers and GPS. *Popular Science.* Retrieved from http://www.popsci.com/technology/article/2011-02/bostons-street-bump-app-will-use-accelerometers-gps-automatically-log-pothole-complaints

Hickey, K. (2011, March 23). Fire department's iPhone app can help save lives. *Government Computer News Magazine.* Retrieved from http://gcn.com/articles/2011/03/23/iphone-app-cpr-alerts-san-ramon-valley.aspx

Lucey, C. (2011, April 20). iSpy: City controller unveils program for mobiles to report bad city workers. *Philly.com.* Retrieved from http://articles.philly.com/2011-04-20/news/29451458_1_iphone-app-report-fraud-app-store

Martinelli, N. (2011). Does crime reporting app create digital vigilantes? *Cult of Mac.* Retrieved from http://www.cultofmac.com/does-crime-reporting-app-create-digital-vigilantes/89207

Martinelli, N. (2011). Public health app helps find condoms on the go. *Cult of Mac.* Retrieved from http://www.cultofmac.com/public-health-app-helps-find-condoms-on-the-go/90043

McKenna, C. (2011). County iPhone app to put disaster resources at residents' fingertips. *Emergency Management Magazine.* Retrieved from http://www.emergencymgmt.com/disaster/County-iPhone-App-Disaster-Resources-033011.html

Nielsen Wire. (2010). *Mobile snapshot: Smartphones now 28% of U.S. cellphone market.* Retrieved from http://blog.nielsen.com/nielsenwire/online_mobile/mobile-snapshot-smartphones-now-28-of-u-s-cellphone-market/

Rich, S. (2011, April 13). Suspicious activity report is now mobile – In Kentucky. *Government Technology.* Retrieved from http://www.govtech.com/public-safety/Suspicious-Activity-Reporting-Mobile-in-Kentucky.html

Smith, J. (2010). SpringsGov.com request for city services goes mobile. *City of Colorado Springs.* Retrieved from http://www.springsgov.com/news.aspx?newsid=710

Towns, S. (2010, June 7). Government "apps" move from cool to useful. *Governing Magazine.* Retrieved from http://www.governing.com/columns/tech-talk/Government-Apps-Move-from.html

Trimi, S., & Sheng, H. (2008). Emerging trends in m-government. *Communications of the ACM, 51*(5), 53–58. doi:10.1145/1342327.1342338

Tumin, Z., & Wasserman, R. (2008). *311: The next wave. Nine imperatives for leadership of 311-enabled government.* Retrieved from Harvard University, Kennedy School of Government website http://www.innovations.harvard.edu/cache/documents/1285/128521.pdf

Zefferer, T. (2011). *Mobile government: E-government for mobile societies.* Secure Information Technology Center, Version 1.0, Austria. Retrieved from http://www.a-sit.at/pdfs/Technologiebeobachtung/mobile_government_1.0.pdf

KEY TERMS AND DEFINITIONS

App: Shortened version of the term APPlication referring to software programs specifically designed to be downloaded to a smartphone.

E-Government: Electronic Government (E-Government) utilizes web-based internet applications to provide information and deliver government services through the use of personal computers and other stand alone computer devices.

GPS: Global Positioning System (GPS) using satellites to pinpoint the exact location of a GPS-enabled device. For iPhones, GPS refers to the location detection component of the cellular phone which may be satellite generated or a combination of satellites, wi-fi hotspots and cellular towers to pinpoint the location of the device.

i-Government: Interactive Government (*i*-Government) utilizes smart device mobile technology combined with custom applications to a) connect citizens with resources; b) engage citizens in collaboration; c) empower citizens as volunteers; and d) enable citizens as watchdogs.

M-Government: Mobile Government (M-Government) uses mobile technology, such as standard feature cellular phones and Personal Digital Assistants (PDAs) to provide a limited range of government services such as one-way communication (text messages) sent from a government agency to a citizen's cellular phone.

New Volunteerism: Citizens working to provide feedback, information, data and services to a government agency via an application on their smartphone, or responding to a request made by a government agency on their smartphone without any monetary compensation to the citizen.

Smartphone: A cellular phone with advanced computing and graphics capabilities that enable it to run an Internet browser, utilize GPS location services, and run applications (apps) designed specifically for mobile phones such as the iPhone and Android.

Compilation of References

Abdallah, S., & Khalil, A. (2009). Web 2.0 and e-governments: An exploration of potentials & realities in the Arab world. *Proceedings of the European and Mediterranean Conference on Information Systems*, Izmir, Turkey.

Ackerman, S. (2011, January 14). Tweet away, troops: Pentagon won't ban social media. *Wired*. Retrieved from http://www.wired.com/dangerroom/2011/01/tweet-away-troops-pentagon-wont-ban-social-media/

ADA Today. (2010). 2009 Congressional voting record inside. *Americans for Democratic Action, 65*(1).

Agranoff, R. (2007). *Managing within networks*. Washington, DC: Georgetown University Press.

Agranoff, R., & McGuire, M. (2001). Big questions in public network management research. *Journal of Public Administration: Research and Theory, 11*(3), 295–326.

Ahmed, N. (2003). *An overview of e-participation models*. New York, NY: United Nations Division for Public Administration and Development Management.

Ahuja, M., & Carley, K. (1999). Network structure in virtual organizations. *Organization Science, 10*(6), 741–757. doi:10.1287/orsc.10.6.741

Aikins, S., & Krane, D. (2010). Are public officials obstacles to citizen-centered e-government? An examination of municipal administrators' motivations and actions. *State and Local Government Review, 42*(2), 87–103. doi:10.1177/0160323X10369159

Air Force Public Affairs Agency/AFPAA. (2010). *New media and the Air Force*. Retrieved from http://www.af.mil/shared/media/document/AFD-090406-036.pdf

Akdere, M., & Roberts, P. B. (2008). Economics of social capital: Implications for organizational performance. *Advances in Developing Human Resources, 10*(6), 802. doi:10.1177/1523422308325007

Albert, A., & Passmore, E. (2008). Public value and participation: A literature review for the Scottish government. [online] The Work Foundation. Retrieved July 17, 2011, from http://www.scotland.gov.uk/Publications/2008/03/17090301/0

Alcock, P. (2004). Participation or pathology: Contradictory tensions in area-based policy. *Social Policy and Society, 3*(2), 87–96. doi:10.1017/S1474746403001556

Altheide, D. L. (1996). *Qualitative media analysis*. Thousand Oaks, CA: Sage Publications.

Anderson, D. M. (2003). Cautious optimism about online politics and citizenship . In Anderson, D., & Cornfield, M. (Eds.), *The civic Web* (pp. 19–34). Lanham, MD: Rowman and Littlefield Publishers Inc.

Anderson, S. E., & Harris, J. B. (1997). Factors associated with amount of use and benefits obtained by users of a statewide educational telecomputing network. *Educational Technology Research and Development, 45*(1), 19–50. doi:10.1007/BF02299611

Arellano, N. E. (2008). Canada embarks on major Web 2.0 initiative. *ITBusiness*. Retrieved March 30, 2011, from http://www.itbusiness.ca/it/client/en/home/news.asp?id=48569

Argyres, N. S. (1999). The impact of Information Technology on coordination: Evidence from the B-2 "Stealth" bomber. *Organization Science, 10*(2), 162–180. doi:10.1287/orsc.10.2.162

ARMA International. (2009). *Generally accepted record-keeping principles*. Retrieved from http://www.arma.org/garp/garp.pdf

Army, U. S. (2009). *Army public affairs handbook, version 2.0*. Fort Meade, MD: Army Public Affairs Center.

Arnstein, S. (1969). A ladder of citizen participation. *Journal of the American Institute of Planners, July*.

Äström, J. (2004). *Digital democracy: Ideas, intentions and initiatives in Swedish local government* (pp. 96–115). Routledge ECPR Studies in European Political Science.

Asur, S., Huberman, B., Wang, C., & Szabo, G. (2011, February). *Social media: Persistence and decay.* Social Computing Lab, Hewlett Packard Labs Palo Alto, CA. Retrieved from http://www.scribd.com/doc/48665388/Trends-in-Social-Media-Persistence-and-Decay

Austin, E., & Callen, J. (2008). Reexamining the role of digital technology in public administration: From devastation to disclosure. *Administrative Theory & Praxis, 30*(3), 324–341.

Auty, C. (2005). UK elected Members and their Weblogs. *Aslib Proceedings: New Information Perspectives, 57*(4), 338–355.

Bachmann, R., Knights, D., & Sydow, J. (2001). Special issue: Trust and control in organizational relations. *Organization Studies, 22*(2). doi:10.1177/0170840601222007

Baker, P. M. A., & Panagopoulos, C. (2004). Political implications of digital (e-) Government . In Pavlichev, A., & Garson, D. G. (Eds.), *Digital government: Principles and best practices* (pp. 78–96). Hershey, PA: Idea Group Publishing.

Baker, W., Addam, H., & Davis, B. (2005). Critical factors for enhancing municipal public hearings. *Public Administration Review, 65*(4), 490–499. doi:10.1111/j.1540-6210.2005.00474.x

Bandura, A. (1969). *Principles of behavior modification*. New York, NY: Holt, Rinehart and Winston.

Bandura, A. (1977a). *Social learning theory*. Englewood Cliffs, NJ: Prentice-Hall.

Bandura, A. (1989). Human agency in social cognitive theory. *The American Psychologist, 44*(9), 1175–1184. doi:10.1037/0003-066X.44.9.1175

Bannister, F. (2005). The panoptic state: Privacy, surveillance and the balance of risk. *Information Polity: The International Journal of Government & Democracy in the Age, 10*, 65–78.

Barabasi, A. (2002). *Linked: The new science of networks*. Cambridge, MA: Perseus Publishing.

Barabas, J. (2004). How deliberation affects policy opinions. *The American Political Science Review, 98*(4), 687–701. doi:10.1017/S0003055404041425

Barber, B. (1998). Three scenarios for the future of technology and strong democracy. *Political Science Quarterly, 113*(4), 573–589. doi:10.2307/2658245

Barber, B. (1999). Three scenarios for the future of technology and strong democracy. *Political Science Quarterly, 113*(4), 573–589. doi:10.2307/2658245

Barber, B. (2000). *A passion for democracy*. Princeton, NJ: Princeton University Press.

Barber, B. (2001). The uncertainty of digital politics: Democracy's uneasy relationship with Information Technology. *Harvard International Review, 23*, 42–47.

Barney, J. (1991). Firm resources and sustained competitive advantage. *Journal of Management, 17*(1), 99. doi:10.1177/014920639101700108

Baron, R. M., & Kenny, D. A. (1986). The moderator-mediator variable distinction in social psychological research: Conceptual, strategic and statistical considerations. *Journal of Personality and Social Psychology, 51*(6), 1173–1182. doi:10.1037/0022-3514.51.6.1173

Bearman, T. C., Guynup, P., & Milevski, S. N. (1985). Information and productivity. *Journal of the American Society for Information Science American Society for Information Science, 36*(6), 369. doi:10.1002/asi.4630360605

Becerra, M., & Gupta, A. K. (2003). Perceived trustworthiness within the organization: The moderating impact of communication frequency on trustor and trustee effects. *Organization Science, 14*(1), 32. doi:10.1287/orsc.14.1.32.12815

Becker, S. A. (2004). E-government visual accessibility for older adult users. *Social Science Computer Review, 22*(1), 11–23. doi:10.1177/0894439303259876

Becker, T., & Slaton, C. (2000). *The future of teledemocracy*. Westport, CT: Praeger.

Bekkers, V. (2007). Modernization, public innovation and information and communication technologies: The emperor's new clothes? *Information Polity: The International Journal of Government & Democracy in the Information Age, 12*(3), 103–107.

Benhabib, S. (1994). Deliberative rationality and models of democratic legitimacy. *Constellations (Oxford, England), 1*(1), 26–52. doi:10.1111/j.1467-8675.1994.tb00003.x

Bennett, W. L. (2007). *Changing citizenship in the digital age*. OECD/INDRE Conference on Millennial Learners. Retrieved August 1, 2011, from http://spotlight.macfound.org/resources/Bennett-Changing_Citizenship_in_Digital_Age-OECD.pdf

Bennett, W. L. (2008). Civic learning in changing democracies: Challenges for citizenship and civic education . In Dahlgren, P. (Ed.), *Young citizens and new media: Learning and democratic engagement*. New York, NY: Routledge.

Berman, E. M. (1997). Dealing with cynical citizens. *Public Administration Review, 57*(2), 105–112. doi:10.2307/977058

Berman, J., & Mulligan, D. K. (2003). Digital grass roots, issue advocacy in the age of the Internet . In Anderson, D. M., & Cornfield, M. (Eds.), *The civic Web* (pp. 77–96). Oxford, UK: Rowman and Littlefield Publishers Inc.

Berntzen, L., & Winsvold, M. (2005). Web-based tools for policy evaluation. In *E-Government: Towards Electronic Democracy . Proceedings, 3416*, 13–24.

Bertot, J. C., Jaeger, P. T., & Grimes, J. M. (2010). Using ICTs to create a culture of transparency: E-government and social media as openness and anti-corruption tools for societies. *Government Information Quarterly, 27*(10), 264–271. doi:10.1016/j.giq.2010.03.001

Bertot, J. C., Jaeger, P. T., Munson, S., & Glaisyer, T. (2010). Social media technology and government transparency. *Computer, 43*(11), 53–59. doi:10.1109/MC.2010.325

Bertot, J., Jaeger, P., & Simmons, S. (2010). Using ICTs to create a culture of transparency: E-government and social media as openness and anti-corruption tools for societies. *Government Information Quarterly, 27,* 254–271. doi:10.1016/j.giq.2010.03.001

Bertot, J., Jaeger, P., Simmons, S., & Shuler, J. (2009). Reconciling government documents and e-government: Government information in policy, librarianship, and education. *Government Information Quarterly, 26,* 433–436. doi:10.1016/j.giq.2009.03.002

Bianchi, T., & Cottica, A. (2011). Harnessing the unexpected: Public administration interacts with creatives on the Web. *European Journal of E-Practice, 9,* 82–90.

Blecker, T., & Newman, R. (2000). Interorganizational knowledge management: Some perspective for knowledge oriented strategic management in virtual organizations . In Malhodra, Y. (Ed.), *Knowledge management and virtual organizations* (pp. 63–83). Hershey, PA: Idea Group Publishing.

Blogger Home Page. (n.d.). *Free weblog publishing tool from Google*. Retrieved from www.blogger.com

Bloomberg Newsweek. (2011, June 6). *Not just the Facebook revolution*, (pp. 63-66).

Boehner, J. (2009, July 1). *Bloodhounds* [Video file]. Retrieved from http://www.youtube.com/watch?v=tl_q0afUl0E&feature=player_embedded

Bohman, J. (1996). *Public deliberation: Pluralism, complexity, and democracy*. Cambridge, MA: MIT Press.

Boulton, A. (2010). Just maps: Google's democratic map-making community? *Cartographica, 45*(1), 1–4. doi:10.3138/carto.45.1.1

Bovens, M., & Zouridis, S. (2002). From street-level to system-level bureaucracies: How information and communication technology is transforming administrative discretion and constitution control. *Public Administration Review, 62,* 174–184. doi:10.1111/0033-3352.00168

boyd, d. (2005). Sociable technology and democracy. In J. Lebowsky & M. Ratcliffe (Eds.), *Extreme democracy Lulu.*

Boyd, d., Golder, S., & Lotan, G. (2010). Tweet tweet retweet: Conversational aspects of retweeting on Twitter. *43rd Hawaii International Conference on System Sciences-HICSS-43* (pp. 1-10).

Boyd, D. M., & Ellison, N. B. (2008). Social network sites: Definition, history, and scholarship. *Journal of Computer-Mediated Communication, 13*(1), 210–230. doi:10.1111/j.1083-6101.2007.00393.x

Boyle: The belle of the Web (2009, December 29). *The New Orleans Times-Picayune,* p. C1.

Brainard, L., & McNutt, J. G. (2010). Virtual government-citizen relations: Informational, transactional or collaborative? *Administration & Society, 42*(7), 836–858. doi:10.1177/0095399710386308

Brainard, L., & McNutt, J. G. (2010). Virtual government-citizen relations: Old public administration, new public management or new public service? *Administration & Society, 42,* 836–858. doi:10.1177/0095399710386308

Brandyberry, A. A., Li, X., & Lin, L. (2010). *Determinants of perceived usefulness and perceived ease of use in individual adoption of social network sites.* Paper presented at the AMCIS 2010, Paper 544.

Breindl, Y., & Francq, P. (2008). Can Web 2.0 applications save e-democracy? A study of how new Internet applications may enhance citizen participation in the political process online. *International Journal of Electronic Democracy, 1,* 14–31. doi:10.1504/IJED.2008.021276

Bremmer, I., & Keat, P. (2009). *The fat tail: The power of political knowledge for strategic investing.* New York, NY: Oxford University Press.

Brewer, G., Neubauer, B., & Geiselhart, K. (2006). Designing and implementing e-government systems: Critical implications for public administration and democracy. *Administration & Society, 38*(4), 472–499. doi:10.1177/0095399706290638

Brinck, T., Wood, S., & Gergle, D. (2001). *Usability for the Web: Designing web sites that work.* San Francisco, CA: Morgan Kaufmann.

Brock, C. (2010). *Testimony of Carol Brock, Certified Records Manager on behalf of ARMA International.* Retrieved from http://democrats.oversight.house.gov/images/stories/Hearings/Information_Policy/06.17.10_Electronic_Records/061510_IP_Carol_Brock_061710.pdf

Brody, C. E. (2009). Catch the tiger by the tail: Counseling the burgeoning government use of social media. *The Florida Bar Journal,* (December): 52–58.

Brown, M., Sr. (2011). *Social networking and individual performance: Examining predictors of participation.* Unpublished Ph.D., Old Dominion University, United States -- Virginia.

Bryan, C., Tsagarousianou, R., & Tambini, D. (1998). Electronic democracy and the civic networking movement in context . In Tsagarousianou, R., Tambini, D., & Bryan, C. (Eds.), *Cyberdemocracy: Technology, cities, and civic networks* (pp. 1–17). New York, NY: Routledge.

Bryer, T. A. (in press). Public participation in regulatory decision making: Cases from Regulations.gov. *Public Performance and Management Review.*

Buckley, J. (2003). E-service quality and the public sector. *Managing Service Quality, 13*(6), 453–462. doi:10.1108/09604520310506513

Burke, N., Chomitz, V., Rioles, N., Winslow, S., Brukilacchio, L., & Baker, J. (2009). The path to active living: Physical activity through community design in Somerville, Massachusetts. *American Journal of Preventive Medicine, 37*(S62), S386–S394. doi:10.1016/j.amepre.2009.09.010

Burnett, R., & Marshall, P. (2003). *Web theory* (pp. 108–115). New York, NY: Routledge.

Butler, D. (2007). Agencies join forces to share data: US to create a universal database of all its research results. *Nature, 446*(7134), 354. Retrieved April 12, 2011, from http://www.nature.com.mutex.gmu.edu/nature/journal/v446/n7134/full/446354b.html

Cammaerts, B. (2009). Civil society participation in multistakeholder processes: In between realism and utopia . In Stein, L., Kidd, D., & Rodriguez, C. (Eds.), *Making our media: Global initiatives toward a democratic public sphere* (pp. 83–101). Cresskill, NJ: Hampton Press.

Campbell, D. T., Stanley, J. C., & Gage, N. L. (1966). *Experimental and quasi-experimental designs for research*. Chicago, IL: R. McNally.

Cantwell, P. (2011). When telework really isn't: GSA's closure of telework centers raises a question. *Federal Computer Week Online*. Retrieved April 12, 2011, from http://fcw.com/articles/2011/03/03/telework-centers-are-not-true-telework-paul-cantwell-argues.aspx

Cappel, J. J., & Huang, Z. (2007). A usability analysis of company websites. *Journal of Computer Information Systems*, *48*(1), 117–123.

Carafano, J. (2011). Understanding social networking and national security. *Joint Forces Quarterly*, *60*, 78.

Carmel, E., & Harlock, J. (2008). Instituting the third sector as a governable terrain. *Policy and Politics*, *36*(2), 155–171. doi:10.1332/030557308783995017

Carr, D., & Halvorsen, K. (2001). An evaluation of three democratic, community-based approaches to citizen participation: Surveys, conversations with community groups, and community dinners. *Society & Natural Resources*, *14*, 107–126. doi:10.1080/089419201300000526

Carrizales, T. (2008). Functions of e-government: A study of municipal practices. *State and Local Government Review*, *40*(1), 12–26. doi:10.1177/0160323X0804000102

Carrizales, T. (2008). Functions of e-government: A study of municipal practices. *State and Local Government Review*, *40*(1), 12–26. doi:10.1177/0160323X0804000102

Cartwright, D., & Atkinson, K. (2009). Using computational argumentation to support e-participation. *IEEE Intelligent Systems, Special Issue on Transforming E-government and E-participation through IT*, *24*(5), 42-52.

Cascio, W. F. (2000). Managing a virtual workplace. *The Academy of Management Executive*, *14*(3), 81–90. doi:10.5465/AME.2000.4468068

Castells, M. (2000). *End of millennium: The rise of the fourth world: Capitalism, poverty and social exclusion*. Oxford, UK: Blackwell.

Castells, M. (2007). Communication, power, and counter-power in the network society. *International Journal of Communication*, *1*, 238–266.

Center for Digital Government. (2010). *Digital government achievement awards*. Retrieved from http://www.centerdigitalgov.com/survey/88

Central, C. I. O. (2006). *Intellipedia: The intelligence Wikipedia*. Retrieved April 12, 2011, from www.ciocentral.org/.../intellipedia-the-intelligence-wikipedia/

Cerulo, K. A. (1990). To err is social: Network prominence and its effects on self-estimation. *Sociological Forum*, *5*(4), 619–634. doi:10.1007/BF01115394

Cetron, M., & Davies, O. (2008). *Fifty five trends now shaping the future*. Washingon, DC: Proteus USA. Retrieved from http://www.carlisle.army.mil/proteus/docs/55-future.pdf

Chadwick, A. (2003). Bringing e-democracy back in: Why it matters for future research on e-governance. *Social Science Computer Review*, *21*(4), 443–455. doi:10.1177/0894439303256372

Chadwick, A. (2006). *Internet politics: States, citizens and new communication technologies*. Oxford, UK: Oxford University Press.

Chadwick, A. (2011). Explaining the failure of an online citizen engagement initiative: The role of internal institutional variables. *Journal of Information Technology & Politics*, *8*(1), 21–40. doi:10.1080/19331681.2010.507999

Chambers, S. (1996). *Reasonable democracy: Jurgen Habermas and the politics of discourse*. Ithaca, NY: Cornell University Press.

Chandler, J. A. (2001). *Local government today* (3rd ed.). Manchester, UK: Manchester University Press.

Chang, A.-M., & Kannan, P. K. (2008). *Leverage Web 2.0 in government. IBM Center for the Business of Government*. Washington, DC: Government Printing Office.

Chatterton, P., & Style, S. (2001). Putting sustainable development into practice? The role of local policy partnership networks. *Local Environment*, *6*(4), 439–452. doi:10.1080/13549830120091725

Chen, D. Y., Huang, D. I., & Hsiao, N. I. (2003). The management of citizen participation in Taiwan: A case study of Taipei city government's citizen complains system. *International Journal of Public Administration*, *26*(5), 525–547. doi:10.1081/PAD-120019234

Chen, D. Y., Huang, D. I., & Hsiao, N. I. (2006). Reinventing government through on-line citizen involvement in the developing world: A case study of Taipei City Mayor's E-mail Box in Taiwan. *Public Administration and Development*, *26*, 409–423. doi:10.1002/pad.415

Chiang, I., Lin, C., & Wang, K. M. (2008). Building online brand perceptual map. *Cyberpsychology & Behavior*, *11*(5), 607–610. doi:10.1089/cpb.2007.0182

Chicago Metropolitan Agency for Planning. (2011). Retrieved April 4, 2011, from http://www.cmap.illinois.gov/

Chowdhury, S. (2005). The role of affect- and cognition-based trust in complex knowledge sharing. *Journal of Managerial Issues*, *17*(3), 310–326.

Christakis, N., & Fower, J. (2009). *Connected: The surprising power of our social networks and how they shape our lives*. New York, NY: Little, Brown, and Company.

Chung, K. S. K., Hossain, L., & Davis, J. (2007). *Individual performance in knowledge intensive work through social networks*. Paper presented at the 2007 ACM SIGMIS CPR Conference on Computer Personnel Research: The Global Information Technology Workforce, St. Louis, Missouri, USA.

Chun, S. A., Shulman, S., Sandoval, R., & Hovy, E. (2010). Government 2.0: Making connections between citizens, data, and government. *Information Polity*, *15*, 1–9.

CIA. (2009). *Intellipedia celebrates third anniversary with a successful challenge*. Retrieved April 12, 2011, from https://www.cia.gov/news-information/featured-story-archive/intellipedia-celebrates-third-anniversary.html

Cisco Blog. (2009). *Ideas for state/local leaders: Fix my street*. Retrieved April 4, 2011, from http://blogs.cisco.com/localgov/fix_my_street/

City of Kirkland. Washington. (2009). *More people, more places, more often: A plan for active transportation*. Retrieved February 13, 2011, from http://www.ci.kirkland.wa.us/depart/Public_Works/Transportation___Streets/Active_Transportation_Plan.htm

City of Reno. (2011). *Social media policy*. Retrieved April 4, 2011, from http://www.reno.gov/index.aspx?page=2142#Facebook

Clawson, J. (2009). *Level three leadership*. Upper Saddle River, NJ: Pearson.

Clift, S. (2003). E-democracy: Lessons from Minnesota . In Anderson, D. M., & Cornfield, M. (Eds.), *The civic Web* (pp. 157–165). Oxford, UK: Rowman and Littlefield publishers Inc.

Clinton, H. (2011). *Internet rights and wrongs: Choices & challenges in a networked world. Remarks*. Retrieved April 4, 2011, from http://www.state.gov/secretary/rm/2011/02/156619.htm

Clinton, W. J. (1996). *Executive Order 13011 of July 16, 1996*. Retrieved from http://www.cio.gov/documents/federal_it_jul_1996.html

Coco, A., & Short, P. (2004). History and habit in the mobilization of ICT resources. *The Information Society*, *20*, 39–51. doi:10.1080/01972240490269997

Cohen, L. S. (2010). *6 ways law enforcement uses social media to fight crime*. Retrieved July 30, 2011, from http://mashable.com/2010/03/17/law-enforcement-social-media/

Cohen, S., & Eimicke, W. (2001). The use of the Internet in government service delivery . In Abramson, M. A., & Means, G. E. (Eds.), *E-government 2001* (pp. 9–43). Oxford, UK: Rowman and Littlefield.

Coleman, S. (2004). Whose conversation? Engaging the public in authentic polylogue. *The Political Quarterly*, *75*(2), 112–120. doi:10.1111/j.1467-923X.2004.00594.x

Coleman, S., & Gøtze, J. (2001). *Bowling together: Online public engagement in policy deliberation* [online]. London, UK: Hansard Society.

Comfort, L. K., & Naim, K. (2006). Inter-organizational coordination in extreme events: The World Trade Center attacks, September 11, 2001. *Natural Hazards*, *39*(2), 309–327. doi:10.1007/s11069-006-0030-x

Compaine, B. M. (Ed.). (2001). *The digital divide: Facing a crisis or creating a myth?* Cambridge, MA: MIT Press.

Congressional Management Foundation. (n.d.). Retrieved April 5, 2011, from http://www.cmfweb.org/

Conservative.org. (2009). *Ratings of Congress.* American Conservative Union [Online archive]. Retrieved from http://www.conservative.org/congress-ratings/

Consultation Institute. (2009a). *Glossary.* Retrieved August 26, 2011, from http://www.consultationinstitute.org/resources/glossary/glossary-c/

Corburn, J., & Bhatia, R. (2007). Health impact assessment in San Francisco: Incorporating the social determinants of health into environmental planning. *Journal of Environmental Planning and Management, 50*(3), 241–256. doi:10.1080/09640560701260283

Cornfield, M. (2003). Adding in the Net: Making citizenship count in the digital age . In Anderson, D., & Cornfield, M. (Eds.), *the civic web* (pp. 97–119). Oxford, UK: Rowman and Littlefield Publishers Inc.

Council, C. I. O. (2009). *Guidelines for secure use of social media by federal departments and agencies.* Washington, DC: Federal CIO Council ISIMC NISSC Web 2.0 Secuirty Working Group. Retrieved from http://www.cio.gov/Documents/Guidelines_for_Secure_Use_Social_Media_v01-0.pdf

Craglia, M. (2004). Cogito ergo sum or non-cogito ergo digito? The digital city revised. *Environment and Planning B, 31*(1), 3–4. doi:10.1068/b3101ed2

CrisisCommons Home Page. (n.d.). *A crowdsourcing app specializing in connecting and coordinating resources during crisis response scenarios.* Retrieved from http://crisiscommons.org/

Crosby, N., Kelly, J. M., & Schaefer, P. (1986). Citizen panels: A new approach to citizen participation. *Public Administration Review, 46*(2), 170–178. doi:10.2307/976169

Curtin, D., & Meijer, A. (2006). Does transparency strengthen legitimacy? A critical analysis of European Union policy documents. *Information Polity, 11,* 109–112.

D'Agostino, M. (2009). Securing an effective voice for citizens in intergovernmental administrative decision making. *International Journal of Public Administration, 32*(8), 658–680. doi:10.1080/01900690903000054

D'Agostino, M., Schwester, R., Carrizales, T., & Melitski, J. (2011). A study of e-government and e-governance: An empirical examination of municipal websites. *Public Administration Quarterly, 35*(1), 3–25.

Dalton, R. (2004). *Democratic challenges, democratic choices: The erosion of political support in advanced industrial democracies.* Oxford, UK: Oxford University Press.

Danziger, J. N., & Andersen, K. (2002). Impacts of Information Technology on public administration: An analysis of empirical research from the golden age of transformation. *International Journal of Public Administration, 25*(5), 591–627. doi:10.1081/PAD-120003292

Data.gov. (n.d.). *United States government.* Retrieved April 5, 2011, from http://www.data.gov

Datamasher. (n.d.). Retrieved April 5, 2011, from http://www.datamasher.org

Davidow, M. (1995). *A conceptual framework of customer communication handling and management.* Paper presented at the Marketing and Public Policy Conference. Atlanta, GA, US.

Davidow, W. (2011). *Overconnected: The promise and threat of the Internet.* Harrison, NY: Delphinium Books.

Davis, A. (2010). New media and fat democracy: The paradox of online participation. *New Media & Society, 12*(5), 745–761. doi:10.1177/1461444809341435

Davis, F. D. (1989). Perceived usefulness, perceived ease of use, and user acceptance of Information Technology. *Management Information Systems Quarterly, 13*(3), 319–340. doi:10.2307/249008

Davis, F. D., Bagozzi, R. P., & Warshaw, P. R. (1989). User acceptance of computer technology: A comparison of two. *Management Science, 35*(8), 982. doi:10.1287/mnsc.35.8.982

Davis, T. R. V., & Luthans, F. (1980). A social learning approach to organizational behavior. *Academy of Management Review, 5*(2), 281–290.

Dawes, S. (2008). The evolution and continuing challenges of e-governance. *Public Administration Review,* (December): S82–S106.

Dawes, S., Cresswell, A., & Pardo, T. (2009). From "need to know" to "need to share": Tangled problems, information boundaries, and the building of public sector knowledge networks. *Public Administration Review, 69*(3), 392–402. doi:10.1111/j.1540-6210.2009.01987_2.x de Kool, D., & van Wamelen, J. (2008). Web 2.0: A new basis for e-government? *3rd International Conference on Information and Communication Technologies: From Theory to Applications (ICTTA)*, (pp. 1-7).

Dedrick, J., Gurbaxani, V., & Kraemer, K. L. (2003). Information Technology and economic performance: A critical review of the empirical evidence. *ACM Computing Surveys*, *35*(1), 1–28. doi:10.1145/641865.641866

Deehr, R., & Shumann, A. (2009). Active Seattle: Achieving walkability in diverse neighborhoods. *American Journal of Preventive Medicine*, *37*(S62), S403–S411. doi:10.1016/j.amepre.2009.09.026

Defense Science Board/DSB. (2009). *Understanding human dynamics*. Washington, DC: Office of the Undersecretary of Defense for Acquisition, Technology, and Logistics.

Dekker, K., Volker, B., & Lelievelet, H. (2010). Civic engagement in urban neighborhoods: Does the network of civic organizations influence participation in neighborhood projects. *Journal of Urban Affairs*, *32*(5), 609–632. doi:10.1111/j.1467-9906.2010.00524.x

Deloitte. (2009). *Integrating health and human services delivery: Making services citizen-friendly*. Retrieved April 12, 2011, from http://www.deloitte.com/view/en_US/us/Industries/us-state-government/Big-Issues-in-Government/improving_human_services/63ae11eef03a4210VgnVCM100000ba42f00aRCRD.htm

Department of Defense. (2000). *DoD records management program*. Retrieved from http://www.defense.gov/webmasters/policy/dodd50152p.pdf

Department of Defense. (2007). *Department of Defense privacy program*. Retrieved from http://privacy.defense.gov/dod_regulation_5400.11-R.shtml

Department of Defense. (2010). *Directive-type memorandum (DTM) 09-026 – Responsible and effective use of Internet-based capabilities*. Retrieved from http://www.dtic.mil/whs/directives/corres/pdf/DTM-09-026.pdf

Department of Defense. (2011). *Department of Defense info*. Retrieved from http://www.facebook.com/home.php#!/DeptofDefense?sk=info

Department of Defense. (n.d.). *About the Department of Defense*. Retrieved http://www.defense.gov/about/

Department of State. (2010). *5 FAM 790: Using social media*. Retrieved from http://www.state.gov/documents/organization/144186.pdf

Department of State. (n.d.). *A short history of the Department of State*. Retrieved http://history.state.gov/departmenthistory/short-history/origins.

DeSantis, G., & Monge, P. (1999). Communication processes for virtual organizations. *Organization Science: Special Issue: Communication Processes for Virtual Organizations*, *10*(6), 693–703.

Dess, G., Rahsheed, A. M. A., McLaughlin, K., & Preim, R. (1995). The new corporate architecture. *Academy of Management Review*, *9*(3), 7–20.

Dholakia, N., & Kshetri, N. (2002). The global digital divide and mobile business models: Identifying viable patterns of e-development. In S. Krishna & S. Madon (Eds.), *Proceedings of the Seventh IFIP WG9.4 Conference*, (pp. 528–540). Bangalore, India.

Di Gennaro, C., & Dutton, W. (2006). The Internet and the public: Online and offline political participation in the United Kingdom. *Parliamentary Affairs*, *59*(2), 219–313. doi:10.1093/pa/gsl004

Dillow, C. (2011, February 10). Boston's 'Street Bump' app tries to automatically map potholes with accelerometers and GPS. *Popular Science*. Retrieved from http://www.popsci.com/technology/article/2011-02/bostons-street-bump-app-will-use-accelerometers-gps-automatically-log-pothole-complaints

DiNucci, D. (1999). Fragmented future. *Print*, *53*(4), 32.

Dirks, K. T., & Ferrin, D. L. (2001). The role of trust in organizational settings. *Organization Science*, *12*(4), 450. doi:10.1287/orsc.12.4.450.10640

Disposal of Records. 44 U.S.C. § 3301. (2006).

Dobson, N., & Gilrow, A. (2009). From partnership to policy: The evolution of active living by design in Portland, Oregon. *American Journal of Preventive Medicine*, *37*(6S2), S436-S444.

Dollner, J., Kolbe, T. H., Liecke, F., Sgouros, T., & Teichmann, K. (2006). The virtual 3D city model of Berlin – Managing, integrating, and communicating complex urban information. *Proceedings of the 25th International Symposium on Urban Data Management,* Aalborg, Denmark, 15-17 May 2006.

Doyle, A. (2003). *Certificates, monitoring, & firewall working group on Information Systems and services.* Retrieved April 12, 2011, from http://wgiss.ceos.org/meetings/wgiss16/Monday/Doyle_Grid_Toolkit.ppt

Drapeau, M., & Wells, L. (2009). *Social software and security: An initial net assessment.* Washington, DC: National Defense University. Retrieved from http://www.dtic.mil/cgi-bin/GetTRDoc?AD=ADA497525

Dryzek, J. (2000). *Deliberative democracy and beyond: Liberals, critics, contestants.* Oxford, UK: Oxford University Press.

Dryzek, J. S. (2002). *Deliberative democracy and beyond: Liberals, critics, contestations. Oxford Political Theory.* Oxford, UK: Oxford University Press.

Dutton, W., Guerra, G., Zizzo, D., & Peltu, M. (2005). The cyber trust tension in e-government: Balancing identity, privacy, security. *Information Polity: The International Journal of Government & Democracy in the Information Age, 10,* 13–23.

Dvorak, P., & Landers, P. (2011). Japanese plant had barebones risk plan. *The Wall Street Journal.* Retrieved July 30, 2011, from

Eastin, M. S., & LaRose, R. (2000). Internet self-efficacy and the psychology of the digital divide. *Journal of Computer-Mediated Communication, 6*(1).

Eggers, W. D. (2005). *Government 2.0: Using technology to improve education, cut red tape, reduce gridlock, and enhance democracy.* Lanham, MD: Rowman & Littlefield Publishers.

ElectionMap. (2008). *United States electoral map, election 2008.* Retrieved April 5, 2011, from http://www.mapmash.in/election_map.html

Eliasoph, N. (1998). *Avoiding politics: How Americans produce apathy in everyday life.* New York, NY: Cambridge University Press. doi:10.1017/CBO9780511583391

Elwood, S. (2006). Critical issues in participatory GIS: Deconstructions, reconstructions, and new research directions. *Transactions in GIS, 10*(5), 693–708. doi:10.1111/j.1467-9671.2006.01023.x

Endenburg, G. (1998). *Sociocracy: The organization of decision-making.* Delft, The Netherlands: Eburon.

Environmental Information Exchange Network. (2010). *Return on investment.* Retrieved on May 2, 2010, from http://www.exchangenetwork.net/benefits/roi.htm

Environmental Protection Agency. (2010). *Central data exchange benefits.* Retrieved on May 2, 2010, from http://www.epa.gov/cdx/benefits/index.htm

Environmental Protection Agency. (2010). *Privacy and security notice.* Retrieved from http://www.epa.gov/epafiles/usenotice.htm

Environmental Protection Agency. (2011). *EPA comment policy.* Retrieved April 4, 2011, from http://www.epa.gov/epahome/commentpolicy.html

Erickson, C. L., & Jacoby, S. M. (2003). The effects of employer networks on workplace innovation and training. *Industrial & Labor Relations Review, 56*(2), 203. doi:10.2307/3590935

European Commission. (2010). *Digital agenda for Europe.* Retrieved April 3, 2011, from http://ec.europa.eu/information_society/digital-agenda/index_en.htm

Farrar, C., Fishkin, J. S., Green, D. P., List, C., Luskin, R. C., & Levy Paluck, E. (2010). Disaggregating deliberation's effects: An experiment within a deliberative poll. *British Journal of Political Science, First View,* 1-15.

Fearn-Banks, K. (2007). *Crisis communications: A casebook approach.* New Jersey: Lawrence Erlbaum.

Federal Computer Week. (2009). *Top 10 agencies with the most Facebook fans.* Retrieved from http://fcw.com/articles/2009/09/14/government-facebook-friends-list.aspx

Federal Computer Week. (2011). *12 telework centers shuttered: GSA cuts funding to telework centers.* Retrieved April 12, 2011, from http://fcw.com/articles/2011/03/02/12-telework-centers-shuttered.aspx

Federal Web Managers Council. (2011). *Types of social media*. Retrieved from http://www.howto.gov/social-media/social-media-types

Federal, C. I. O. Council. (2009). *Guidelines for the secure use of social media by federal departments and agencies*. Retrieved from http://www.cio.gov/Documents/Guidelines_for_Secure_Use_Social_Media_v01-0.pdf

Ferber, P., Foltz, F., & Puhliese, R. (2005). The Internet and public participation: State legislature web sites and the many definitions of interactivity. *Bulletin of Science, Technology & Society, 25*(1), 85–93. doi:10.1177/0270467604271245

Ferguson, S. (2000). *Researching the public opinion environment: Theories and methods* (pp. 180–182). Thousand Oaks, CA: Sage.

Ferriero, D. S. (2010). *Guidance on managing records in Web 2.0/social media platforms*. Retrieved from http://www.archives.gov/records-mgmt/bulletins/2011/2011-02.html

Ferrin, D. L., & Dirks, K. T. (2003). The use of rewards to increase and decrease trust: Mediating processes and differential effects. *Organization Science, 14*(1), 18. doi:10.1287/orsc.14.1.18.12809

Ferrin, D. L., Dirks, K. T., & Shah, P. P. (2006). Direct and indirect effects of third-party relationships on interpersonal trust. *The Journal of Applied Psychology, 91*(4), 870–883. doi:10.1037/0021-9010.91.4.870

Ferro, E., & Molinari, F. (2010). Framing Web 2.0 in the process of public sector innovation: Going down the participation ladder. *European Journal of E-Practice, 9*, 20–34.

Field, J. (2003). *Social capital*. London, UK: Routledge.

Fien, J., & Skoien, P. (2002). I'm learning… How you go about stirring things up- in a consultative manner: Social capital and action competence in two community catchment groups. *Local Environment, 7*(3), 269–282. doi:10.1080/1354983022000001642

Finholt, T., & Olson, G. M. (1997). Laboratories to collaboratories: A new organizational form for scientific collaboration. *Psychological Science, 8*(1), 28–36. doi:10.1111/j.1467-9280.1997.tb00540.x

Fishkin, J. S. (1997). *The voice of the people: Public opinion and democracy*. New Haven, CT: Yale University Press.

Fitch, B., & Goldschmidt, K. (2005). *Communicating with Congress: How Capitol Hill is coping with the surge in citizen advocacy*. Congressional Management Foundation [Report]. Retrieved from http://www.cmfweb.org/index.php?option=com_content&task=view&id=63

Flaherty, D. H. (1984). The need for an American privacy protection commission. *Government Information Quarterly, 1*(3), 235–258. doi:10.1016/0740-624X(84)90072-8

Florino, D. (1990). Citizen participation and environmental risk: A survey of institutional mechanisms. *Science, Technology & Human Values, 15*(2), 226–243. doi:10.1177/016224399001500204

Floyd, P. (2010). *Social media and the U.S. military*. Interview with Neal Conan, National Public Radio, March 16, 2010.

Foley, P., & Alfonso, X. (2009). E-government and the transformation agenda. *Public Administration, 87*(2), 371–396. doi:10.1111/j.1467-9299.2008.01749.x

Forbes, R. (2009, May 6). *Our Judeo-Christian nation*. Retrieved from http://www.youtube.com/watch?v=dpQOCvthw-o&feature=player_embedded

Ford, C. (2011). Twitter, Facebook, and ten red balloons. *Homeland Security Affairs, 7*, 1–7.

Fountain, J. E. (2001). *Building the virtual state: Information Technology and institutional change*. Washington, DC: Brookings Institution Press.

Fowler, S. W., Lawrence, T. B., & Morse, E. A. (2004). Virtually embedded ties. *Journal of Management, 30*(5), 647–666. doi:10.1016/j.jm.2004.02.005

Franks, P. (2010). *How federal agencies can effectively manage records created using new social media tools*. Retrieved from http://www.businessofgovernment.org/sites/default/files/How%20Federal%20Agencies%20Can%20Effectively%20Manage%20Records%20Created%20Using%20New%20Social%20Media%20Tools.pdf

Frantzich, S., & Sullivan, J. (1996). *The C-SPAN revolution*. Norman, OK: University of Oklahoma Press.

Friedman, J. (2011). *Personal interview.*

Frontline SMS Home Page. (n.d.). *A free, large-scale text messaging solution for NGOs and non-profit organizations.* Retrieved from http://frontlinesms.com

Fyfe, T., & Crookall, P. (2010). *Social media and public sector policy dilemmas.* Institute of Public Administration of Canada. Retrieved March 30, 2011, from

Galbraith, J. (1973). *Designing complex organizations.* Reading, MA: Addison-Wesley.

Galloway, S., & Guthrie, D. (2010, August 18). *Digital IQ: U.S. Senate.* L2: A Think Tank For Digital Innovation. Retrieved from http://l2thinktank.com/research/u-s-senate-2010/

Galusky, W. (2003). Indentifying with information: Citizen empowerment, the Internet, and the environmental anti-toxins movement . In Mccaughey, M., & Ayers, M. D. (Eds.), *Cyberactivism: Online activism in theory and practice* (pp. 195–208). New York, NY: Routledge.

Gambetta, D. (1988). *Trust: Making and breaking cooperative relations.* New York, NY: B. Blackwell.

Gang, S. (2005). Transcending e-government: A case of mobile government in Beijing. *The Proceedings of the First European Conference on Mobile Government.* Brighton, England.

Gant, D. B., & Gant, J. P. (2003). Enhancing e-service delivery in state government . In Abramson, A. M., & Morin, T. L. (Eds.), *E-government 2003* (pp. 53–80). Oxford, UK: Rowman and Littlefield.

Garrett, R. K. (2009). Politically motivated reinforcement seeking: Reframing the selective exposure debate. *The Journal of Communication*, *59*, 676–699. doi:10.1111/j.1460-2466.2009.01452.x

Garson, G. D. (1995). *Computer technology and social issues.* Hershey, PA: Idea Group Press. doi:10.4018/978-1-87828-928-5

Gastil, J., Black, L. W., Deess, E. P., & Leighter, J. (2008). From group member to democratic citizen: How deliberating with fellow jurors reshapes civic attitudes. *Human Communication Research*, *34*(1), 137–169. doi:10.1111/j.1468-2958.2007.00316.x

Gates Foundation. (2011). *Social media for social good.* Retrieved April 3, 2011, from http://www.gatesfoundation.org/foundationnotes/Pages/alyssa-milano-101015-social-media-social-good.aspx

Gellman, R. M. (1994). An American privacy protection commission: An idea whose time has come… again. *Government Information Quarterly*, *11*(3), 245–247. doi:10.1016/0740-624X(94)90043-4

General Accounting Office. (2001). *Electronic government: Challenges must be addressed with effective leadership and management.* Retrieved August 11, 2005, from http://feapmo.gov/links.asp

Gentzkow, M., & Shapiro, J. M. (2010, September 21). Ideological segregation online and offline. *Chicago Booth and National Bureau of Economic Research.* Retrieved from http://faculty.chicagobooth.edu/jesse.shapiro/research/echo_chambers.pdf

Geraghty, A., Seifert, W., Preston, T., Holm, C., Duarte, T., & Farrar, S. (2009). Partnership moves community towards complete streets. *American Journal of Preventive Medicine*, *37*(S62), S420–S427. doi:10.1016/j.amepre.2009.09.009

Gessner, G. H., Volonino, L., & Fish, L. A. (2007). One-up, one-back ERM in the food supply chain. *Information Systems Management*, *24*(10), 213–222. doi:10.1080/10580530701404561

Ghoring, N. (2010, March 1). U.S Defense Department Oks social networking. *PC World.*

Gibson, R.K., & Lusoli, W., 7 Ward, S. (2005). Online participation in the UK: Testing a contextualised model of Internet effects. *British Journal of Politics and International Relations*, *7*(4), 561–583. doi:10.1111/j.1467-856X.2005.00209.x

Glassman, M. (2007, December 5). *Franking privilege: Historical development and options for change.* Congressional Research Service, RL34274. Retrieved from http://www.fas.org/sgp/crs/misc/RL34274.pdf

Glassman, M., Straus, J., & Shogun, C. (2009, September 21). *Communication: Member use of Twitter during a two-week period in the 111th Congress.* Congressional Research Service, R40823. Retrieved from http://www.fas.org/sgp/crs/misc/R41066.pdf

Golbeck, J., Grimes, J., & Rogers, A. (2010). Twitter use by the U.S. Congress. *Journal of the American Society for Information Science and Technology, 61*(8), 1612–1621.

Goldfinch, S. (2007). Pessimism, computer failure, and Information Systems development in the public sector. *Public Administration Review, 67*(5), 917–929. doi:10.1111/j.1540-6210.2007.00778.x

Goldschmidt, K. (2011, July 26). *Communication with Congress: Perceptions of citizen advocacy on Capitol Hill.* The Partnership for a More Perfect Union at the Congressional Management Foundation. Retrieved from http://www.congressfoundation.org/projects/communicating-with-congress/social-congress

Goldschmidt, K., & Ochreiter, L. (2008). *Communicating with Congress: How the Internet has changed citizen engagement.* Congressional Management Foundation [Report]. Retrieved from http://www.cmf-web.org/index.php?Itemid=50&id=64&option=com_content&task=view

Goldsmith, S., & Eggers, W. D. (2004). *Governing by network: The new shape of the public sector.* Washington, DC: Brookings Institution Press.

Goldstein, A. P., & Sorcher, M. (1974). *Changing supervisory behavior.* New York, NY: Pergammon.

Gomez-Feliciano, L., McCreary, L., Sadowsky, R., Peterson, S., Hernandez, A., & McElmurry, B. (2009). Active living Logan Square: Joining together to create opportunities for physical activity. *American Journal of Preventive Medicine, 37*(S62), S361–S367. doi:10.1016/j.amepre.2009.09.003

Gong, Y., Teng, A., & Galic, I. (2011). Integration of geospatial Web services with the 311 call center operations. *ESRI Federal User Conference Proceedings 2011,* Washington, DC.

Gooberman-Hill, R., Horwood, J., & Calnan, M. (2008). Citizens' juries in planning research priorities: Process, engagement and outcome. *Health Expectations, 11*(3), 272–281. doi:10.1111/j.1369-7625.2008.00502.x

Goodchild, M. (2008). Spatial accuracy 2.0. *Proceedings of the 8th International Symposium on Spatial Accuracy Assessment in Natural Resources and Environmental Sciences,* Shanghai, China, June 25-27, 2008.

Goodchild, M. (2007). Citizens as sensors: The world of volunteered geography. *GeoJournal, 69,* 211–221. doi:10.1007/s10708-007-9111-y

Goodwin, B. (2008). *Matrix of Web 2.0 technologies.* Retrieved February 2011, from http://www.gsa.gov/portal/content/103597

Gorla, N. (2008). Hurdles in rural e-government projects in India: Lessons for developing countries. *Electronic Government, an International Journal, 5*(1), 91-102.

Government 2.0 Taskforce. (n.d.). *Australia.* Retrieved April 5, 2011, from http://gov2.net.au

Government 2.0. (n.d.). *Best practices wiki.* Retrieved April 5, 2011, from http://government20bestpractices.pbworks.com/w/page/10044431/Canada

Government Accountability Office. (2003). *Privacy act: OMB leadership needed to improve agency compliance.* Retrieved from http://www.gao.gov/new.items/d03304.pdf

Government Services Administration (GSA). (2009a). *GSA social media handbook.* Retrieved from http://www.gsa.gov/graphics/staffoffices/socialmediahandbook.pdf

Government Services Administration (GSA). (2009b). *GSA Social media policy.* Retrieved from http://www.gsa.gov/graphics/staffoffices/socialmediapolicy.pdf

Government Services Administration (GSA). (2009c). *GSA promotes best practice for citizen service.* Retrieved from http://www.gsa.gov/portal/content/103597

GovLoop. (2011). Retrieved April 4, 2011, from http://www.govloop.com

Grabowski, M., & Roberts, K. (1999). Risk mitigation in virtual organizations. *Organization Science, 10*(6), 704–721. doi:10.1287/orsc.10.6.704

Grant, G., & Chau, D. (2004). Developing a generic framework for e-government. *Journal of Global Information Management, 13*(1), 1–30. doi:10.4018/jgim.2005010101

Grayson, A. (2009, September 30). *Rep. Alan Grayson on the Situation Room.* Retrieved from http://www.youtube.com/watch?v=3H3gND4M9HA

Green, D., & Roberts, G. (2010). Personnel implications of public sector virtual organizations. *Public Personnel Management, 39*(1), 47–57.

Greene, R. W. (2000). *GIS in public policy: Using geographic information for more effective government.* Redlands, CA: Esri Press.

Grey, C., & Garsten, C. (2001). Trust, control and post-bureaucracy. *Organization Studies, 22*(2), 229–250. doi:10.1177/0170840601222003

Griggs, B. (2010, July 21). U.S. not getting broadband fast enough, FCC says. *CNN.* Retrieved August 15, 2010, from http://www.cnn.com/2010/TECH/web/07/20/fcc. broadband.access/index.html

Grimes, M. (2006). Organizing consent: The role of procedural fairness in political trust and compliance. *European Journal of Political Research, 45,* 285–315. doi:10.1111/j.1475-6765.2006.00299.x

Grönlund, Å. (2010). Ten years of e-government: The end of history and a new beginning. In M. A. Wimmer, J.-L. Chappelet, M. Janssen, & H. J. Scholl (Eds.), *Proceedings 9th IFIP WG 8.5 International Conference, EGOV 2010, LNCS 6228,* Lausanne, Switzerland, August/September 2010, (pp. 13-24). Springer.

Groper, R. (2004). Digital government and the digital divide . In Pavlichev, A., & Garson, G. D. (Eds.), *Digital government: Principles and best practices* (pp. 291–305). Hershey, PA: Idea Group Press.

Gross, G. (2006). US intelligence community's wiki aids info sharing. *Infoworld.* Retrieved March 30, 2011, from http://www.infoworld.com/t/applications/us-intelligence-communitys-wiki-aids-info-sharing-673

Gross, G. (2007). U.S. House member gets Second Life. *Computerworld.* Retrieved March 30, 2011, from http://www.computerworld.com/s/article/9007218/

Grossman, M. B., & Kumar, M. J. (1979). The White House and the news media: The phases of their relationship. *Political Science Quarterly, 94*(1), 37–53. doi:10.2307/2150155

GroundCrew Home Page. (n.d.). *A group organization and dispatching application.* Retrieved from http://groundcrew.us/

Gulick, L. H. (1936). Notes on the theory of organization. In L. Gulick & L. Urwick (Eds.), *Papers on the science of administration* (pp. 3–35). New York, NY: Institute of Public Administration. Fedorowicz, J., Gogan, J., & Williams, C. (2006). *The e-government collaboration challenge: Lessons from five case studies.* Arlington, VA: IBM Center for the Business of Government.

Gursakal, N., Oguzlar, A., Aydin, Z. B., & Tuzunturk, S. (2009). Measuring trust in an intra-organisational context using social network analysis. *International Journal of Management and Enterprise Development, 6*(4), 494–512. doi:10.1504/IJMED.2009.024238

Gutmann, A., & Thompson, D. (1996). *Democracy and disagreement.* Cambridge, MA: Harvard University Press.

Habbo Hotel. (n.d.). *A social networking website aimed at teenagers.* Retrieved from www.habbo.com/

Habbo Hotel. (n.d.). *Where else?* Retrieved April 5, 2011, from http://sulake.com/

Hacker, K. L., & van Dijk, J. (2000). What is digital democracy? In Hacker, K. L., & van Dijk, J. (Eds.), *Digital democracy: Issues of theory and practice* (pp. 1–9). Thousand Oaks, CA: SAGE.

Hamamoto, M., Derauf, D., & Yoshimura, S. (2009). Building the base: Two active living projects that inspired community participation. *American Journal of Preventive Medicine, 37*(S62), S345–S351. doi:10.1016/j.amepre.2009.09.025

Hanabusa, C. (2011, June 14). *One minute floor speech.* Retrieved from http://www.youtube.com/user/rephanabusa#p/u/7/3_deCQwOiPI

Hansen, D. L., Shneiderman, B., & Smith, M. A. (2011). *Analyzing social media networks with NodeXL insights from a connected world.* Burlington, MA: Elsevier.

Hansen, H., & Salskov-Iversen, D. (2005). Remodeling the transnational political realm: Partnerships, best-practice schemes, and the digitalization of governance. *Alternatives: Global, Local . Political, 30*(2), 141–164.

Hardy, H., Shimizu, N., Strzalkowski, T., Liu, T., Zhang, X., & Wise, G. B. (2002). Cross-document summarization by concept classification. *SIGIR 2002: Proceedings of the 25th Annual International ACM SIGIR Conference on Research and Development in Information Retrieval, August 11-15, 2002, Tampere, Finland* (pp. 121-128).

Harris, T., & Weiner, D. (1998). Empowerment, marginalization and community-integrated GIS. *Cartography and Geographic Information Systems, 25*(2), 67–76. doi:10.1559/152304098782594580

Hart, K. (2009, November 19). On technology. *The Hill,* p. 12.

Harvey, P. (2009). Between narrative and number: The case of ARUP's 3D digital city model. *Cultural Sociology, 3*(2), 257–276. doi:10.1177/1749975509105534

Hatala, J. P. (2006). Social network analysis in human resource development: A new methodology. *Human Resource Development Review, 5*(1), 45. doi:10.1177/1534484305284318

Hatala, J. P., & Fleming, P. R. (2007). Making transfer climate visible: Utilizing social network analysis to facilitate the transfer of training. *Human Resource Development Review, 6*(1), 33. doi:10.1177/1534484306297116

Hatala, J. P., & Lutta, J. (2009a). Managing information sharing within an organizational setting: A social network perspective. *Performance Improvement Quarterly, 21*(4), 5. doi:10.1002/piq.20036

Hatala, J. P., & Lutta, J. G. (2009b). Managing information sharing within an organizational setting: A social network perspective. *Performance Improvement Quarterly, 21*(4), 5. doi:10.1002/piq.20036

Havaria Information Services Alerts Map. (n.d.). *National Association of Radio-Distress Signaling and Infocommunications (RSOE), Budapest, Hungary*. Retrieved March 30, 2011, from http://hisz.rsoe.hu/alertmap/

HealthMap. (n.d.). *Global health, local information*. Retived April 5, 2011, from http://healthmap.org/

Heeks, R., & Bhatnagar, S. (1999). Understanding success and failure in information age reform . In Heeks, R. (Ed.), *Reinventing government in the information age: International practice in IT-enabled public sector reform* (pp. 49–74). London, UK: Routledge. doi:10.4324/9780203204962

Heeks, R., & Davies, A. (Eds.). (1999). *Reinventing government in the information age: International practice in IT-enabled public sector reform*. London, UK: Routledge. doi:10.4324/9780203204962

Heikkila, T., & Isett, K. R. (2007). Citizen involvement and performance management in special purpose governments. *Public Administration Review, 67*(2), 238–248. doi:10.1111/j.1540-6210.2007.00710.x

Heintze, T., & Bretschneider, S. (2000). Information Technology and restructuring in public organizations: Does adoption of Information Technology affect organizational structures, communications, and decision making? *Journal of Public Administration: Research and Theory, 10*(4), 801.

Hendaoui, A., Limayem, M., & Thompson, C. W. (2008). 3D social virtual worlds: Research issues and challenges. *IEEE Internet Computing, 12*(1), 88–92. doi:10.1109/MIC.2008.1

Hendrix, W. H. (1984). Development of a contingency model organizational assessment survey for management consultants. *Journal of Experimental Education, 52*(2), 95–105.

Hickey, K. (2011, March 23). Fire department's iPhone app can help save lives. *Government Computer News Magazine*. Retrieved from http://gcn.com/articles/2011/03/23/iphone-app-cpr-alerts-san-ramon-valley.aspx

Higgs, G., & Turner, P. (2003). The use and management of geographic information in local e- government in the UK. *Information Polity, 8*(3-4), 151–165, 1570–1255.

Hindess, B. (2000). Representative government and participatory democracy . In Vandenberg, A. (Ed.), *Citizenship and democracy in a global era* (pp. 33–50). Houndsmill, UK: MacMillan Press Ltd.

Hinson, C. (2010). Negative information action: Danger for democracy. *The American Behavioral Scientist, 53*(6), 826–847. doi:10.1177/0002764209353276

HLWIKI Canada. (2010). *Mashups in medicine*. Retrieved April 5, 2011, from http://hlwiki.slais.ubc.ca/index.php/Mashups_in_medicine

Ho, A. T.-K., & Ni, A. (2004). Explaining the progressiveness of e-government: A case study of Iowa county treasurers' offices. *American Review of Public Administration, 34*(2), 164–180. doi:10.1177/0275074004264355

Hodge, N. (2010, March 1). Will the Pentagon finally get Web 2.0? *Wired*. Retrieved from http://www.wired.com/dangerroom/2010/03/will-the-pentagon-finally-get-web-20/

Holden, S., & Millett, L. (2005). Authentication, privacy, and the federal e-government. *The Information Society, 21*(5), 367–377. doi:10.1080/01972240500253582

Holzer, M., & Kim, S. T. (2008). *Digital governance in municipalities worldwide, a longitudinal assessment of municipal web sites throughout the world*. The E-Governance Institute, Rutgers University, Newark; & The Global e-policy e-government Institute, Sungkyunkwan University.

Holzer, M., & Manoharan, A. (2009). Tracking the digital divide: Studying the association of the global digital divide with societal divide, in e-government development and diffusion. In Sahu, G. P., Dwivedi, Y. K., & Weerakkody, V. (Eds.), *Inhibitors and facilitators of digital democracy* (pp. 54–63). Hershey, PA: IGI Global. doi:10.4018/978-1-60566-713-3.ch004

Holzer, M., Manoharan, A., Shick, R., & Stowers, G. (2008). *US municipalities e-governance survey 2008: An assessment of municipal websites. E-Governance Institute*. Newark: Rutgers University.

Holzer, M., Melitski, J., Rho, S.-Y., & Schwester, R. (2005). *Restoring trust in government: The potential of digital citizen participation. IBM Center for the Business of Government*. Washington, DC: Government Printing Office.

Hooper, M. (2008, July 8). House rules on Web advertisements put video-sharing member offices in bind. *Congressional Quarterly Today*.

Horrocks, I., & Bellamy, C. (1997). Telematics and community governance: Issues for policy and practice. *International Journal of Public Sector Management, 10*(5), 377–387. doi:10.1108/09513559710180600

Hosmer, L. T. (1995). Trust - The connecting link between organizational theory and philosophical ethics. *Academy of Management Review, 20*(2), 379–403.

House Committee on House Administration. (2009). *Member's handbook* (pp. 44–45).

Howard, M. (2001). E-government across the globe: How will "e" change government? *Government Finance Review, 17*(4), 6–9.

Howard, T. J., & Gaborit, N. N. (2007). Using virtual environment technology to improve public participation in urban planning process. *Journal of Urban Planning and Development, 133*(4), 233–241. doi:10.1061/(ASCE)0733-9488(2007)133:4(233)

Hsiao, N., & Huang, D. J. (2005). *The feasibility of e-democratic government: The perception of public officials' behavior*. Paper presented at the 5th Political and Information Science and Technology Academic Conference at Fo Guang University, Ilan, Taiwan. (in Chinese)

Huberty, J., Dodge, T., Peterson, K., & Balluff, M. (2009). Activate Omaha: The journey to an active living environment. *American Journal of Preventive Medicine, 37*(S62), S428–S435. doi:10.1016/j.amepre.2009.09.024

Hudson-Smith, A. (2007). Digital urban – The visual city. *UCL Centre for Advanced Spatial Analysis Working Paper Series*, Paper 124. London, UK: UCL.

Hudson-Smith, A. (2008). The visual city. In Dodge, M., McDery, M., & Turner, M. (Eds.), *Geographic visualization: Concepts, tools, and applications* (pp. 183–196). London, UK: Wiley & Sons. doi:10.1002/9780470987643.ch9

Huff, L., & Kelley, L. (2003). Levels of organizational trust in individualist versus collectivist societies: A seven-nation study. *Organization Science, 14*(1), 81. doi:10.1287/orsc.14.1.81.12807

Hui, G., & Haylarr, M. (2010). Creating public value in e-government: A public-private-citizen collaboration framework in Web 2.0. *The Australian Journal of Public Administration, 69*(1), 120–131. doi:10.1111/j.1467-8500.2009.00662.x

Human Capital Institute. (2010). *Social networking in government: Opportunities & challenges*. Human Capital Institute and Saba. Retrieved March 30, 2011, from http://www.hci.org/files/field_content_file/SNGovt_SummaryFINAL.pdf

Igbaria, M., & Tan, M. (1997). The consequences of Information Technology acceptance on subsequent individual performance. *Information & Management, 32*(3), 113–121. doi:10.1016/S0378-7206(97)00006-2

Information Technology Management and Reform Act of 1996. 40 U.S.C. §11313. *(2006).*

Innes, J. E., & Booher, D. E. (2004). Reframing public participatory strategies for the 21st century. *Planning Theory & Practice, 5*(4), 419–436. doi:10.1080/1464935042000293170

Institute for Local Government. (2010). *Social media and public agencies: Legal issues to be aware of.* Retrieved July 30, 2011, from http://californiacitynews.typepad.com/files/technology-legal-issues.pdf

Intellipedia. (n.d.). *United States intelligence community.* Retrieved March 30, 2011, from www.intelink.gov

Interactive Traffic Map. (n.d.). *Ottawa, Canada.* Retrieved April 5, 2011, from http://ww.traffic.ottawa.ca

International Telecommunication Union (ITU). (2009). *Measuring the information society–The ICT development index.* Place des Nations, CH-1211 Geneva Switzerland. ISBN 92-61-12831-9 Retrieved March 30, 2011, from http://www.itu.int/ITU-D/ict/publications/idi/2009/index.html

Irvine, W., & Anderson, A. (2008). ICT (information communication technology), peripherality and smaller hospitality businesses in Scotland. *International Journal of Entrepreneurship Behaviour and Research, 14*(4), 200–218. doi:10.1108/13552550810887381

Irvin, R. A., & Stansbury, J. (2004). Citizen participation in decision making: Is it worth the effort? *Public Administration Review, 64*(1), 56–65. doi:10.1111/j.1540-6210.2004.00346.x

Issa, D. (2010, May 15). *Issa gets real with Bill Maher* [Video file]. Retrieved from http://www.youtube.com/watch?v=0TgKflkVfOE&feature=player_embedded

Ivancevich, J. M., Konopaske, R., & Matteson, M. T. (2008). *Organizational behavior and management* (8th ed.). New York, NY: McGraw-Hill/Irwin.

Iyengar, S., & Hahn, K. S. (2009). Red media, blue media: Evidence of ideological selectivity in media use. *The Journal of Communication, 59*, 19–39. doi:10.1111/j.1460-2466.2008.01402.x

Jaeger, P. T., & Bertot, J. C. (2010). Transparency and technological change: Ensuring equal and sustained public access to government information. *Government Information Quarterly, 27*(4), 371–376. doi:10.1016/j.giq.2010.05.003

Jaeger, P. T., McClure, C. R., & Fraser, B. T. (2002). The structures of centralized governmental privacy protection: Approaches, models and analysis. *Government Information Quarterly, 19*(3), 317–336. doi:10.1016/S0740-624X(02)00111-9

Jensen, J. L. (2003). Virtual democratic dialogue? Bringing together citizens and politicians. *Information Polity, 8*, 29–47.

Jin, L., Wen, Z., & Gough, N. (2010). Social virtual worlds for technology-enhanced learning on an augmented learning platform. *Learning, Media and Technology, 35*(2), 139–153. doi:10.1080/17439884.2010.494424

Johnston, P., Craig, R., Stewart-Weeks, M., & McCalla, J. (2008) *Realising the potential of the connected republic: Web 2.0 opportunities in the public sector.* Cisco Internet Business Solutions Group. Retrieved March 30, 2011, from http://s3.amazonaws.com/connected_republic/attachments/11/Government_2.0_WP_REV1126_NobelDraft.pdf

Joint Chiefs of Staff/JCS. (2005). *Public affairs.* Joint publication 3-61. Retrieved from http://www.fas.org/irp/doddir/dod/jp3_61.pdf

Jones, S. (2003). *Encyclopedia of new media*. Thousand Oaks, CA: Sage Publications.

Jorgensen, D., & Klay, E. (2007). Technology-driven change and public administration: Establishing essential normative principles. *International Journal of Public Administration, 30*(3), 289–305. doi:10.1080/01900690601117770

Jou, C. T., & Humenik-Sappington, N. (2009). *GIS for decision support and public policy making*. Redlands, CA: Esri Press.

Joyce, P. (2002). E-government, strategic dependent and organizational capacity . In Milner, E. M. (Ed.), *Delivering the vision-public services for the information society and the knowledge economy* (pp. 157–171). London, UK: Routledge.

Jung Yun, H., & Opheim, C. (2010). Building on success: The diffusion of e-government in the American states. *Electronic . Journal of E-Government, 8*(1), 71–81.

Jun, K.-N., & Weare, C. (2010). Institutional motivations in the adoption of innovations: The case of e-government. *Journal of Public Administration: Research and Theory, 21*(3).

Kakabase, A., Kakabadse, N. K., & Kouzim, A. (2003). Reinventing the democratic governance project through Information Technology? A growing agenda for debate. *Public Administration Review, 63*(1), 44–60. doi:10.1111/1540-6210.00263

Kamarck, E. C., & Nye, J. S. (Eds.), *Governance.com: Democracy in the information age* (pp. 141–160). Washington, DC: Brookings Institution Press.

Kampen, J. K., & Snijikers, K. (2003). E-democracy. A critical evaluation of the ultimate e-dream. *Social Science Computer Review, 21*(4), 491–496. doi:10.1177/0894439303256095

Kaplan, A. M., & Haenlein, M. (2010). Users of the world, unite! The challenges and opportunities of social media. *Business Horizons, 53*(1), 59–68. doi:10.1016/j.bushor.2009.09.003

Kaplan, A. M., & Haenlein, M. (2011). The early bird catches the news: Nine things you should know about micro-blogging. *Business Horizons, 54*(2), 105–113. doi:10.1016/j.bushor.2010.09.004

Karan, K., & Khoo, M. (2009). Mobile diffusion and development: Issues and challenges of m-government with India. In J. S. Petterson (Ed.), *Proceedings of 1st International Conference on M4D 2008, General Tracks*, Karlstad University Studies, (p. 61).

Kearnes, I., Bend, J., & Stern, B. (2002). *E-participation in local government*. London, UK: IPPR. Retrieved April 15, 2011, fromhttp://www.ippr.org.uk/members/download.asp?f=%2Fecomm%2Ffiles%2Fe_ participation_in_local_government.pdf

Keeton, P., & McCann. (2005). Information operations, STRATCOM, and public affairs. *Military Review*, (November-December): 83–86.

Keniston, K., & Kumar, D. (2004). *Experience in India: Bridging the digital divide*. Thousand Oaks, CA: Sage Publications.

Kennedy, A. (2010). Using community-based social marketing techniques to enhance environmental regulation. *Sustainability, 2*, 1138–1160. doi:10.3390/su2041138

Kent, M. L., & Taylor, M. (1998). Building relationships through the World Wide Web. *Public Relations Review, 24*(3), 321–334. doi:10.1016/S0363-8111(99)80143-X

Kettering Foundation. (1989). *The public's role in the policy process: A view from state and local policy makers*. Dayton, OH: Kettering Foundation.

Kim, C., & Holzer, M. (2006). Public administrators' acceptance of the practice of digital democracy: A model explaining the utilization of online policy forums in South Korea. *International Journal of Electronic Government Research, 2*(2), 22–48. doi:10.4018/jegr.2006040102

Kim, J. (2006). The impact of Internet use patterns on political engagement: A focus on online deliberation and virtual social capital. *Information Polity, 11*(1), 35–49.

Kim, S., & Lee, H. (2006). The impact of organizational context and information technology on employee knowledge-sharing capabilities. *Public Administration Review, 66*(3), 370–385. doi:10.1111/j.1540-6210.2006.00595.x

King, C., Feltey, K., & Susel, B. (2008). The question of participation: Toward authentic public participation in public administration . In Roberts, N. (Ed.), *The direct age of citizen participation* (pp. 383–400). Armonk, NY: M.E. Sharpe. doi:10.2307/977561

King, S., & Cotterill, S. (2007). Transformational government? The role of Information Technology in delivering citizen-centric local public services. *Local Government Studies, 33*(3), 333–354. doi:10.1080/03003930701289430

Kirlin, J. (1996). What government must do well: Creating value for society. *Journal of Public Administration: Research and Theory, 6*(1), 161–185.

Kirlin, J., & Kirlin, M. (2000). Strengthening effective government-citizen connections through greater civic engagement. *Public Administration Review, 62*, 80–85. doi:10.1111/1540-6210.62.s1.14

Klijn, E., & Koppenjan, J. F. M. (2002). Rediscovering the citizen: New roles for politicians in interactive policy making. In McLaverty, P. (Ed.), *Public participation and innovations in community governance* (pp. 141–163). Burlington, MA: Ashgate.

Koehler, I. (2011). *Speak out Sutton!* Retrieved July 30, 2011, from http://socialgov.posterous.com/speak-out-sutton

Kraidy, M., & Mourad, S. (2010). Hypermedia space and global communication studies lessons from the Middle East. *Global Media . Journal, 9*, 1–19.

Kramer, R. M. (1996). *Trust in organizations: Frontiers of theory and research*. Thousand Oaks, CA: Sage Publications.

Kubicek, H. (2005). Scenarios for future use of e-democracy tools in Europe. *International Journal of Electronic Government Research, 1*(3), 33–50. doi:10.4018/jegr.2005070103

Kumar, N., & Vragov, R. (2009). Active citizen participation using ICT tools. *Communications of the ACM, 52*(1), 118–121. doi:10.1145/1435417.1435444

Kumar, S., Chhugani, J., Kim, C., Kim, D., Nguyen, A., & Dubey, P. (2008). Second Life and the new generation of virtual worlds. *Computer, 41*(9), 46–53. doi:10.1109/MC.2008.398

Kurland, N. B., & Egan, T. D. (1996). Participation via the Net: Access, voice and dialogue. *The Information Society, 12*(4), 387–406. doi:10.1080/019722496129369

Kushchu, I., & Borucki, C. (2004). *Impact of mobile technologies on government*. Mobile Government Lab. Retrieved August 19, 2010, from http://www.mgovlab.org

Kushchu, I., & Kuscu, H. (2003). From e-government to m-government: Facing the inevitable. *The Proceedings of European Conference on E-Government*, Trinity College, Dublin.

Kuttan, A., & Peters, L. (2003). *From digital divide to digital opportunity*. Lanham, MD: The Scarecrow Press, Inc.

Kuzma, J. (2010). Asian government usage of Web 2.0 social media. *European Journal of E-Practice, 9*, 69–81.

Kwon, O., & Wen, Y. (2010). An empirical study of the factors affecting social network service use. *Computers in Human Behavior, 26*(2), 254–263. doi:10.1016/j.chb.2009.04.011

Lambright, K. T., Mischen, P. A., & Laramee, C. B. (2010). Building trust in public and nonprofit networks: Personal, dyadic, and third-party influences. *American Review of Public Administration, 40*(1), 64–82. doi:10.1177/0275074008329426

Lambrinoudakis, C., Gritzalis, S., Dridi, F., & Pernul, G. (2003). Security requirements for e-government services: A methodological approach for developing a common pki-based security policy. *Computer Communications, 26*(16), 1873–1883. doi:10.1016/S0140-3664(03)00082-3

Lampe, C., LaRose, R., Steinfield, C., & de Maagd, K. (2011). Inherent barriers to the use of social media for public policy informatics. *The Innovation Journal: The Public Sector Innovation Journal, 16*(1). Retrieved April 10, 2011, from http://www.innovation.cc/scholarly-style/lampe_social_media_v16i1a6.pdf

Lane, C., & Bachmann, R. (1998). *Trust within and between organizations: Conceptual issues and empirical applications*. New York, NY: Oxford University Press.

Lasden, M. (1981). Turning reluctant users on to change. *Computer Decisions, 13*(1), 92.

Latar, M., Asmolov, G., & Gekker, A. (2010). *State cyber security*. A working paper in preparation for Herzliya Conference 2010. Lauder School of Government, Diplomacy, and Strategy. Retrieved from http://www.herzliyaconference.org/_Uploads/3035Newmediafinal.pdf

Leaman, A., & Bordass, W. (2000). Productivity in buildings: The killer variables . In Clements-Croome, D. (Ed.), *Creating the productive workplace*. London, UK: E & FN Spon.

LeRoux, K. (2009). Paternalistic or participatory governance? Examining opportunities for client participation in nonprofit social service organizations. *Public Administration Review*, *69*(3), 504–517. doi:10.1111/j.1540-6210.2009.01996.x

Levy, J. (2011). *Gov't FB pages: Allow fans to post or not? Government 2.0 Beta*. Retrieved April 4, 2011, from http://levyj413.wordpress.com/2011/03/09/govt-fb-pages-allow-fans-to-post-or-not/

Levy, M. (2001). *E-volve-or-die.com: Thriving in the Internet Age through e-commerce management*. Indianapolis, IN: New Riders.

Lewis, J. (1985). *The birth of EPA*. Retrieved from http://www.epa.gov/history/topics/epa/15c.htm

Lewis, N., & Mawson, C. O. S. (1964). *The new Roget's thesaurus*. New York, NY: G. P. Putnam's Sons.

Li, F., & Betts, S. (2003). Between expectation and behavioral intent: A model of trust. *Allied Academies International Conference. Academy of Organizational Culture, Communications and Conflict Proceedings, 8*(1), 33.

Lips, M. (2007). Does public administration have artifacts? *Information Polity: The International Journal of Government & Democracy in the Information Age, 12*(4), 243–252.

Livingstone, S., Bober, M., & Helpser, E. J. (2005). Active participation or just more information? Young people's take-up of opportunities to act and interact on the Internet. *Information Communication and Society, 8*(3), 287–314. doi:10.1080/13691180500259103

Lord, C. (2006). *Losing hearts and minds*. Westport, CT: Greenwood.

Lovley, E. (2011, February 28). Social media not so hot on the Hill. *Politico*. Retrieved from http://www.politico.com/news/stories/0211/50299.html

Lowndes, V., Pratchett, L., & Stoker, G. (2001). Trends in public participation: Part 1- Local government perspectives. *Public Administration, 79*(1), 205–222. doi:10.1111/1467-9299.00253

Lucey, C. (2011, April 20). iSpy: City controller unveils program for mobiles to report bad city workers. *Philly.com*. Retrieved from http://articles.philly.com/2011-04-20/news/29451458_1_iphone-app-report-fraud-app-store

Lüfkens, M. (2011). *How world leaders use social media: Why the @WhiteHouse doesn't follow @BarackObama & other idiosyncrasies*. Retrieved July 30, 2011, from http://www.briansolis.com/2011/05/how-world-leaders-use-social-media-why-the-whitehouse-doesn't-follow-barackobama-and-other-idiosyncrasies/

Luhmann, N. (1988). Familiarity, confidence, trust: Problems and alternatives . In Gambetta, D. (Ed.), *Trust: Making and breaking cooperative relations*. New York, NY: Basil Blackwell.

Lukensmeyer, C., & Boyd, A. (2004). Putting the "public" back in management: Seven principles for planning meaningful citizen engagement. *Public Management, 86*(7), 10–15.

Luskin, R. C., Fishkin, J. S., & Jowell, R. (2002). Considered opinions: Deliberative polling in Britain. *British Journal of Political Science, 32*(3), 455–488. doi:10.1017/S0007123402000194

Luttner, M., & Day, M. (2003). *Electronic records and document management system*. Retrieved from http://epa.gov/records/policy/erdms-memo.htm

Macintosh, A., & Whyte, A. (2006). *Evaluating how e-participation changes local Democracy*. eGovernment Workshop '06 (eGov06) [online], September 11 2006.

Macintosh, A., Robson, E., Smith, E., & Whyte, A. (2003). Electronic democracy and young people. *Social Science Computer Review, 21*(1), 43–54. doi:10.1177/0894439302238970

Macintosh, A., & Whyte, A. (2008). Towards an evaluation framework for e-participation. *Transforming Government: People . Process & Policy, 2*(1), 16–30.

Maguire, D. J. (1991). An overview and definition of GIS . In Maguire, D. J., Goodchild, M., & Rhind, D. W. (Eds.), *Geographic Information Systems: Principles and applications* (pp. 9–20). London, UK: Longman/Wiley.

Mahler, J., & Regan, P. M. (2010). Implementing virtual collaboration at the environmental protection agency . In Garson, G. D., & Shea, C. (Eds.), *Handbook of public Information Systems* (3rd ed.). Boca Raton, FL: Taylor and Francis.

Mahrer, H., & Krimmer, R. (2005). Towards the enhancement of e-democracy: Identifying the notion of the middleman paradox. *Information Systems Journal, 15*(1), 27–42. doi:10.1111/j.1365-2575.2005.00184.x

Majchrzak, A., Rice, R. E., Malhotra, A., King, N., & Ba, S. (2000). Technology adaptation: The case of a computer-supported inter-organizational virtual team. *Management Information Systems Quarterly, 24*(4), 569–600. doi:10.2307/3250948

Makadeo, J. (2009). Towards an understanding of the factors influencing the acceptance and diffusion of e-government services. *Electronic . Journal of E-Government, 7*(4), 391–401.

Manoharan, A., & Carrizales, T. (2010). Technological equity: An international perspective of e-government and societal divides. *Electronic Government: An International Journal, 8*(1), 73–84. doi:10.1504/EG.2011.037698

Manz, C. C., & Sims, H. P. Jr. (1981). Vicarious learning: The influence of modeling on organizational behavior. *Academy of Management Review, 6*(1), 105–113.

Marketwire. (2009). *Social networking and reputational risk in the workplace.* Retrieved March 30, 2011, from http://www.marketwire.com/press-release/Proofpoint-Inc-1027877.html

Markey, E. (2007, May 10). *YouTube CEO Chad Hurley & Rep. Ed Markey discuss Web video* [Video file]. Retrieved from http://www.youtube.com/watch?v=Fx1r8u_cmfs

Martinelli, N. (2011). Does crime reporting app create digital vigilantes? *Cult of Mac.* Retrieved from http://www.cultofmac.com/does-crime-reporting-app-create-digital-vigilantes/89207

Martinelli, N. (2011). Public health app helps find condoms on the go. *Cult of Mac.* Retrieved from http://www.cultofmac.com/public-health-app-helps-find-condoms-on-the-go/90043

Mason, B., & Dragicevic, S. (2006). Web GIS and knowledge management systems: An integrated design for collaborative community planning . In Balram, S., & Drageicevic, S. (Eds.), *Collaborative Geographic Information Systems.* Hershey, PA: IGI Global. doi:10.4018/978-1-59140-845-1.ch014

Masrom, M. (2007, 21-24 May 2007). *Technology acceptance model and e-learning.* Paper presented at the 12th International Conference on Education, Sultan Hassanal Bolkiah Institute of Education, Universiti Brunei Darussalam, Universiti Teknologi Malaysia City Campus.

Matisoff, D. C. (2008). The adoption of state climate change policies and renewable portfolio standards: Regional diffusion or internal determinants? *Review of Policy Research, 25*(6), 527–546. doi:10.1111/j.1541-1338.2008.00360.x

May, A. (2010). Who tube? How YouTube's news and politics space is going mainstream. *International Journal of Press/Politics, 15*(4), 499–511.

May, A. (2009). The preacher and the press: How the Jeremiah Wright story became the first feeding frenzy in the digital age . In Johnson, D. (Ed.), *Campaigning for the Presidency 2008* (pp. 78–101). New York, NY: Routledge.

Mayeda, A. (2010). *You have a friend request from Ottawa: Feds to expand use of social media,* PostMedia News. Retrieved March 30, 2011, from http://www.canada.com/technology/

Mayer, I., Edelenbos, J., & Monnikhof, R. (2005). Interactive policy development: Undermining or sustaining democracy? *Public Administration, 83*(1), 179–199. doi:10.1111/j.0033-3298.2005.00443.x

Mayer, R. C., Davis, J. H., & Schoorman, F. D. (1995). An integrative model of organizational trust. *Academy of Management Review, 20*(3), 709–734.

Mayfield, R. (2007). *Twitter tips the tuna.* Retrieved April 5, 2011, from http://ross.typepad.com/blog/2007/03/twitter_tips_th.html

Mayfield, T. (2011). A commander's strategy for social media. *Joint Forces Quarterly*, *60*, 79–83.

Mayhew, D. (1974). *Congress: The electoral connection*. New Haven, CT: Yale University Press.

Mazman, S. G., & Usluel, Y. K. (2009). The usage of social networks in educational context. *World Academy of Science . Engineering and Technology*, *49*, 404–408.

McAllister, D. J. (1995). Affect-based and cognition-based trust as foundations for interpersonal cooperation in organizations. *Academy of Management Journal*, *38*(1), 24–59. doi:10.2307/256727

McCarthy, L., & Yates, D. (2010). The use of cookies in Federal agency web sites: Privacy and recordkeeping issues. *Government Information Quarterly*, *27*(3), 231–237. doi:10.1016/j.giq.2010.02.005

McCaskill, D. (2009, April). *Why I Tweet*. Tumblr.com [Personal blog]. Retrieved from http://clairecmc.tumblr.com/post/100898280/why-i-tweet

McCollum, B. (2009). *Advisory legal opinion AGO 2009-19*. Retrieved from http://coralsprings.org/fb/Advisory%20Legal%20Opinion%20-%20Records,%20municipal%20facebook%20page.pdf

Mccreedy, M., & Leslie, J. (2009). Get active Orlando: Changing the built environment to increase physical activity. *American Journal of Preventive Medicine*, *37*(S62), S395–S402. doi:10.1016/j.amepre.2009.09.013

McDermott, P. (2010). Building open government. *Government Information Quarterly*, *27*(4), 401–413. doi:10.1016/j.giq.2010.07.002

McEvily, B., Perrone, V., & Zaheer, A. (2003). Introduction to the special issue on trust in an organizational context. *Organization Science*, *14*(1), 1. doi:10.1287/orsc.14.1.1.12812

McKenna, C. (2011). County iPhone app to put disaster resources at residents' fingertips. *Emergency Management Magazine*. Retrieved from http://www.emergencymgmt.com/disaster/County-iPhone-App-Disaster-Resources-033011.html

Mclaverty, P. (2002). Is public participation a good thing? In McLaverty, P. (Ed.), *Public participation and innovations in community governance* (pp. 185–198). Aldershot, UK: Ashgate Publishing Ltd.

McLaverty, P. (2010). Participation . In Bevir, M. (Ed.), *Handbook of governance*. London, UK: Sage.

Meadows, V. (2007-2008). Versatile bureaucracy: A telework case study. *Public Management*, *36*(4), 33–37.

Mechling, J. (2002). Information age governance: Just the start of something big? In

Mehta, M. D., & Darier, E. (1998). Virtual control and disciplining on the Internet: Electronic governmentality in the new wired world. *The Information Society*, *14*(2), 107–116. doi:10.1080/019722498128917

Mergel, I., Schweik, C., & Fountain, J. (2010). *The transformational impact of Web 2.0 technologies on government*. Retrieved from http://ssrn.com/abstract=1412796

Merriam-Webster, Inc. (1986). *Webster's ninth new collegiate dictionary*. Springfield, MA: Author.

Messenger, T. (2009, March 16). McCaskill is all a-Twitter about politics in new age. *St. Louis Post-Dispatch*, p. A3.

Metropolitan Council of Governments. (2011). Retrieved from http://www.mwcog.org/

Microsoft Popfly. (n.d.). *A platform used to create mashups*. Retrieved from http://www.popfly.com/

Miles, D. (2010). *New policy authorizes social media access, with caveats*. American Forces Press Services.

Millard, J. (2010). Government 1.5- Is the bottle half full or half empty? *European Journal of ePractice, 9*. Retrieved December 15, 2010, from http://www.epractice.eu/files/European%20Journal%20eprractice%20Volume%209.3_1.pdf

Millard, J. (2010). Government 1.5 – Is the bottle half full or half empty? *European Journal of E-Practice*, *9*, 35–48.

Miller, E., & Scofield, J. (2009). Slavic Village: Incorporating active living into community development through partnerships. *American Journal of Preventive Medicine*, *37*(S62), S377–S385. doi:10.1016/j.amepre.2009.09.023

Miller, L. (2008). E-petitions at Westminster: The way forward for democracy? *Parliamentary Affairs*, *62*, 162–177. doi:10.1093/pa/gsn044

Millich, G. (2008). Mich. police bust up party promoted on Facebook. [Radio transcript]. *NPR: All Things Considered* [Online]. Retrieved July 30, 2011, from http://www.npr.org/templates/story/story.php?storyId=89441570/

Milward, H. B., & Provan, K. G. (2006). *A manager's guide to choosing and using collaborative networks*. Arlington, VA: IBM Center for the Business of Government.

Milward, H. B., & Snyder, L. O. (1996). Electronic government: Linking citizens to public organizations through technology. *Journal of Public Administration: Research and Theory*, *6*(2), 261–275.

Mitchell, D. (1995). *From MUDs to virtual worlds*. Retrieved March 30, 2011, from http://web.archive.org/web/20051113010438/research.microsoft.com/research/scg/papers/3DV.htm

Mitra, A. (2001). Marginal voices in cyberspace. *New Media & Society*, *3*(1), 29–48.

Mnjama, N., & Wamukoya, J. (2006). E-government and records management: An assessment tool for e-records readiness in government. *The Electronic Library*, *25*(3), 274–284. doi:10.1108/02640470710754797

Molinari, F. (2010). On sustainable e-participation. *Proceedings of the IFIP ePart2010 Conference*, Lausanne (Switzerland).

Montgomery County. (2011). *MCDOT storm operations*. Retrieved from http://www5.montgomerycountymd.gov/snowmap/

Moon, M. J. (2003, January 6-9). *Can IT help government to restore public trust? Declining public trust and potential prospects of IT in the public sector.* Paper presented at 36th Annual Hawaii International Conference on System Sciences. Big Island, Hawaii. Retrieved from http://csdl2.computer.org/persagen/DLAbsToc.jsp?resourcePath=/dl/proceedings/&toc=comp/proceedings/hicss/2003/1874/05/1874toc.xml&DOI=10.1109/HICSS.2003.1174303

Moon, J. (2002). The evolution of e-government: Rhetoric or reality? *Public Administration Review*, *62*(4), 424–433. doi:10.1111/0033-3352.00196

Moon, M. J. (2002). The evolution of e-government among municipalities: Rhetoric or reality? *Public Administration Review*, *62*(4), 424–443. doi:10.1111/0033-3352.00196

Moon, M. J. (2004). *From e-government to m-government? Emerging practices in the use of mobile technology by state government. E-government Series*. Washington, DC: IBM Center for the Business of Government.

Moon, M. J. (2005). Linking citizen satisfaction with e-government and trust in government. *Journal of Public Administration: Research and Theory*, *15*(3), 371–391.

Moon, M. J., & Bretschneider, S. (2002). Does the perception of red tape constrain IT innovativeness in organizations? Unexpected results from simultaneous equation model and implications. *Journal of Public Administration: Research and Theory*, *12*(2), 273–291.

Moon, M. J., & Welch, E. W. (2004). Same bed, different dreams? A comparative analysis of citizen and bureaucrat perspectives on e-government. *Review of Public Personnel Administration*, *25*(3), 243–264. doi:10.1177/0734371X05275508

Morgenson, F. III, Van Amburg, D., & Mithas, S. (2010). Misplaced trust? Exploring the structure of the e-government-citizen trust relationship. *Journal of Public Administration: Research and Theory*, *21*(2).

Morgenson, F. III, Van Amburg, D., & Mithas, S. (2011). Misplaced trust? Exploring the structure of the e-government-citizen trust relationship. *Journal of Public Administration: Research and Theory*, *21*(2), 257–283. doi:10.1093/jopart/muq006

Morgeson, F., & Mithas, S. (2009). Does e-government measure up to e-business? Comparing end user perceptions of U.S. federal government and e-business web sites. *Public Administration Review*, *69*(4), 740–752. doi:10.1111/j.1540-6210.2009.02021.x

Mossberger, K., Tolbert, C. J., & Stansbury, M. (2003). *Virtual inequality: Beyond the digital divide*. Washington, DC: Georgetown University Press.

Muhlberger, P. (2005). *Democratic deliberation and political identity: Enhancing citizenship*. International Society of Political Psychology 28th Annual Scientific Meeting. Toronto, Ontario.

Muhlberger, P. (2007). *Report to the Deliberative Democracy Consortium: Building a deliberation measurement toolbox.*

Muhlberger, P. (2011). (Manuscript submitted for publication). Stealth democracy: Authoritarianism and democratic deliberation. *Political Psychology.*

Muhlberger, P., Stromer-Galley, J., & Webb, N. (2011). *Public policy and obstacles to the virtual agora: Insights from the deliberative e-rulemaking project.* Information Polity.

Muhlberger, P., & Weber, L. M. (2006). Lessons from the Virtual Agora Project: The effects of agency, identity, information, and deliberation on political knowledge. *Journal of Public Deliberation, 2*(1), 1–39.

Mutz, D. C. (2006). How the mass media divide us . In Pietro, S. N., & Brady, D. W. (Eds.), *Red and blue nation? Characteristics and causes of America's polarized politics* (*Vol. 1*, pp. 223–248). Washington, DC: Brookings Institution Press.

Mysociety. (2011). *About us.* Retrieved April 15, 2011, from http://www.mysociety.org/about/

Nakata, C., Zhu, Z., & Kraimer, M. (2008). The complex contribution of Information Technology capability to business performance. *Journal of Managerial Issues, 20*(4), 485.

NASA. (2008). *About AstroBiology.* Retrieved on April 13, 2011, from http://astrobiology.nasa.gov/about-astrobiology/ accessed 3-27-2011

NASA. (2011). *Kepler: Search for habitable planets.* Retrieved on March 27, 2011, from http://kepler.nasa.gov/Mission/QuickGuide/

National Archives and Records Administration. (2001). *Frequently asked questions about records management in general.* Retrieved from http://www.archives.gov/records-mgmt/faqs/general.html

National Archives and Records Administration. (2005). *NARA guidance on managing Web records.* Retrieved from http://www.archives.gov/records-mgmt/pdf/managing-web-records-index.pdf

National Archives and Records Administration. (2010). *A report on federal Web 2.0 use and record value.* Retrieved from http://www.archives.gov/records-mgmt/resources/web2.0-use.pdf

National Environmental Policy Act of 1969, 42 U.S.C.A. § 4331. *(1969)*

National Policy Consensus Center. (2002). *Partnering program saves ADOT millions.* Retrieved February 16, 2011, from http://www.policyconsensus.org/casestudies/docs/AZ_transportation.pdf

National Policy Consensus Center. (2003a). *Bryan Park interchange- Richmond, Virginia.* Retrieved February 16, 2011, from http://www.policyconsensus.org/casestudies/docs/VA_bryanpark.pdf

National Policy Consensus Center. (2003b). *Colorado shortgrass prairie case study.* Retrieved February 16, 2011, from http://www.policyconsensus.org/casestudies/docs/CO_shortgrass.pdf

National Policy Consensus Center. (2003c). *Florida strategic intermodal system.* Retrieved February 16, 2011, from http://www.policyconsensus.org/casestudies/docs/FL_intermodal.pdf

National Policy Consensus Center. (2003d). *Martin Luther King Jr. Boulevard reviatalization- Portland, Oregon.* Retrieved February 16, 2011, from http://www.policyconsensus.org/casestudies/docs/OR_mlkBlvd.pdf

National Policy Consensus Center. (2003e). *Sacramento transportation and air quality collaborative case study.* Retrieved February 16, 2011, from http://www.policyconsensus.org/casestudies/docs/CA_AirQual.pdf

National Policy Consensus Center. (2003f). *Utah 3500 South partnering agreement.* Retrieved February 16, 2011, from http://www.policyconsensus.org/casestudies/docs/UT_3500south.pdf

National Policy Consensus Center. (2003g). *Washington-Oregon strategic plan for I-5 corridor.* Retrieved February 16, 2011, from http://www.policyconsensus.org/casestudies/docs/WA_OR_stratplan.pdf

National Policy Consensus Center. (n.d.a). *Negotiating transportation rules in Oregon.* Retrieved February 16, 2011, from http://www.policyconsensus.org/casestudies/docs/OR_transportation.pdf

National Policy Consensus Center. (n.d.b). *Case study: Florida DOT gains consensus on state transportation plan*. Retrieved February 16, 2011, from http://www.policyconsensus.org/casestudies/docs/FL_trans.pdf

National Policy Consensus Center. (n.d.c). *Mediating a highway dispute in Florida*. Retrieved February 16, 2011, from http://www.policyconsensus.org/casestudies/docs/FL_highway.pdf

National Science Foundation. (2008, May). *Beyond being there: A blueprint for advancing the design, development, and evaluation of virtual organizations, final report from Workshops on Building Effective Virtual Organizations*. Retrieved on April 13, 2011, from http://www.ci.uchicago.edu/events/VirtOrg2008/VO_report.pdf

Nelson, B. (2010, May 20). *Never before seen footag*. Retrieved from http://www.youtube.com/watch?v=EXTcM2ntlkM

Neuendorf, K. (2002). *The content analysis guidebook* (pp. 9–23). Thousand Oaks, CA: Sage Publications.

New media (2010, March). *The state of the news media 2010*. The Project for Excellence in Journalism, Pew Research Center. Retrieved from http://stateofthemedia.org/2010

New Media Age. (2009). *Talk to Frank launches anti-cannabis activity on Habbo*. Retrieved March 30, 2011, from http://www.nma.co.uk/news/talk-to-frank-launches-anti-cannabis-activity-on-habbo/41819.article

Newell, E. (2010). Homing in on telework. *Government Executive, 42*(11), 33–40.

Newell, S., & Swan, J. (2000). Trust and inter-organizational networking. *Human Relations, 53*(10), 1287–1328.

Newman (Ed.), *Remaking governance, peoples, politics and the public sphere* (pp. 119-138). University of Bristol: The Policy Press.

Newman, J. (2005). Participative governance and the remaking of the public sphere. In J.

News coverage index. (2010, July 1; 2011, July 1). *The Project for Excellence in Journalism*, Pew Research Cente. Retrieved from http://www.journalism.org/by_the_numbers/datasets

Nielsen Wire. (2010). *Mobile snapshot: Smartphones now 28% of U.S. cellphone market*. Retrieved from http://blog.nielsen.com/nielsenwire/online_mobile/mobile-snapshot-smartphones-now-28-of-u-s-cellphone-market/

Norris, D. F. (2010). E-government 2020: Plus ça change, plus c'est la meme chose. *Public Administration Review, 70*(Supplement), S180-S181. McDermott, P. (2010). Building open government. *Government Information Quarterly, 27*(X), 401–413.

Norris, D. F., & Moon, M. J. (2005). Advancing e-government at the grassroots: Tortoise or hare. *Public Administration Review, 65*(1), 64–75. doi:10.1111/j.1540-6210.2005.00431.x

Norris, D., & Moon, J. (2005). Advancing e-government at the grassroots: Tortoise or hare? *Public Administration Review, 65*(1), 64–75. doi:10.1111/j.1540-6210.2005.00431.x

Norris, P. (2001). *Digital divide: Civic engagement, information poverty, and the Internet worldwide*. Cambridge, UK: Cambridge University Press.

NYC.gov. (2011). *Announcing the road map for the digital city: A plan to make NYC the nation's leading digital city*. Retrieved July 30, 2011, from http://www.mikebloomberg.com/index.cfm?objectid=f994fba2-c29c-7ca2-fbee94bd47bd91a3

Nyhan, R. C. (2000). Changing the paradigm: Trust and its role in public sector organizations. *American Review of Public Administration, 30*(1), 87–109. doi:10.1177/02750740022064560

Nylen, L. (2008, September 29). Hill explores Net's worth. *Congressional Quarterly Weekly*, p. 2550.

O'Reilly, T. (2005). *What is Web 2.0: Design patterns and business models for the next generation of software*. O'Reilly Media. Retrieved August 24, 2011, from http://www.oreillynet.com/pub/a/oreilly/tim/news/2005/09/30/what-is-web-20.html

O'Reilly, T. (2007). What is Web 2.0: Design patterns and business models for the next generation of software. *Communications & Strategies, 65*, 17-37. Retrieved from http://ssrn.com/abstract=1008839

O'Reilly, T., & Battelle, J. (2009, October). *Web squared: Web 2.0 five years on.* Paper presented at Web 2.0 Summit, San Francisco, CA. Retrieved from http://www.web2summit.com/web2009/public/schedule/detail/10194

O'Reilly, T. (2010). Government as a platform. In Lathrop, D., & Ruma, L. (Eds.), *Open government: Collaboration, transparency, and participation in practice.* Sebastopol, CA: O'Reilly Media.

Obama, B. (2009). *Memorandum for the heads of executive departments and agencies: Transparency and open government.* Retrieved from http://www.whitehouse.gov/the_press_office/TransparencyandOpenGovernment/

OFCOM. (2010). *Communications market research report.* Retrieved April 11, 2011, from http://stakeholders.ofcom.org.uk/market-data-research/market-data/communications-market-reports/cmr10/

Office of Citizen Services and Innovative Technologies and the Federal Web Managers Council, USA. (n.d.). Retrieved March 30, 2011, from http://www.howto.gov

Office of Personnel Management. (2011). *Status of telework in the federal government: Report to the Congress. A Guide to Telework in the federal government.* Retrieved on April 13, 2011, from http://www.telework.gov/Reports_and_Studies/Annual_Reports/2010teleworkreport.pdf

Office of Personnel Management. (n.d.). *A guide to telework in the federal government.* Retrieved on April 13, 2011, from http://www.opm.gov/pandemic/agency2a-guide.pdf

Office of the Chief of Public Affairs/OCPA. (2011). *U.S. Army social media handbook.* Washington, DC: Pentagon. Retrieved from http://www.carlisle.army.mil/dime/documents/Army%20Social%20MediaHandbook_Jan2011.pdf

Offstein, E. H., Morwick, J. M., & Koskinen, L. (2010). Making telework work: Leading people and leveraging technology for competitive advantage. *Strategic HR Review, 9*(2), 32–37. doi:10.1108/14754391011022244

Omishakin, A., Carlat, J., Hornsby, S., & Buck, T. (2009). Achieving built-environment and active living goals through Music City Moves. *American Journal of Preventive Medicine, 37*(S62), S412–S419. doi:10.1016/j.amepre.2009.09.005

Ong, C. S., & Wang, S. W. (2009). Managing citizen-initiated email contacts. *Government Information Quarterly, 26,* 498–504. doi:10.1016/j.giq.2008.07.005

O'Reilly, T. (2005). *Web 2.0: Compact definition?* Retrieved March 30, 2011, from http://radar.oreilly.com/archives/2005/10/web-20-compact-definition.html

Orr, J. (2008, October 19). Lawmakers now a click closer to constituents: Congressmen allowed to post on Internet sites after rule reversal. *Houston Chronicle,* A.16.

Orr, K., & Mcateer, M. (2004). The modernisation of local decision making: Public participation and Scottish local government. *Local Government Studies, 30*(2), 131–155. doi:10.1080/0300393042000267209

Orszag, P. R. (2010). *Guidance for agency use of third-party websites and applications.* Retrieved from http://www.whitehouse.gov/sites/default/files/omb/assets/memoranda_2010/m10-23.pdf

Osimo, D. (2008). *Web 2.0 in government: Why and how?* Institute for Prospective Technological Studies (IPTS), JRC, European Commission, EUR 23358. Retrieved from http://ipts.jrc.ec.europa.eu/publications/pub.cfm?id=1565

Osimo, D. (2008). *Web 2.0 in government: Why and how?* JRC Scientific and Technical Reports. Office for Official Publications of the European Communities, European Communities. EUR 23358 EN.

Osimo, D. (2010). Hype, hope or reality? *European Journal of E-Practice, 9,* 2–4.

Ostling, A. (2010). ICT in politics: From peaks of inflated expectations to voids of disillusionment. *European Journal of E-Practice, 9.*

Ostrom, V. (1989). *The intellectual crisis in American public administration.* Tuscaloosa, AL: The University of Alabama Press.

Otenyo, E. E., & Lind, N. S. (2004). Faces and phases of transparency reform in local government. *International Journal of Public Administration, 27*(5), 287–307. doi:10.1081/PAD-120028811

Otis, B. (2007). *Factors in social computing related to worker productivity.* Unpublished Capstone Report, University of Oregon, Portland.

O'toole, T., Marsh, D., & Jones, S. (2003). Political literacy cuts both ways: The politics of non-participation among young people. *The Political Quarterly*, *74*(3), 349–360. doi:10.1111/1467-923X.00544

Paden Noble Consulting. (2010). *Smart political social media use changes Newark, NJ election.* Retrieved July 30, 2011, from http://www.padennoble.com/politics/darrin-sharif-newark-political-social-media

Pallis, G., Zeinalipour-Yazti, D., & Dikaiakos, M. D. (2011). Online social networks: Status and trends . In *New directions in Web data management* (*Vol. 331*, pp. 213–234). Heidelberg, Germany: Springer Verlag. doi:10.1007/978-3-642-17551-0_8

Paperwork Reduction Act of 1995. 44 U.S.C. §3502. *(2006).*

Paperwork Reduction Act of 1995. 44 U.S.C. §3504. *(2006).*

Parameswaran, M., & Whinston, A. B. (2007a). Social computing: An overview. *Communications of the Association for Information Systems*, *19*, 762–780.

Parameswaran, M., & Whinston, A. B. (2007b). Research issues in social computing. *Journal of the Association for Information Systems*, *8*(6), 336–350.

Parent, M., Vandebeek, C. A., & Gemino, A. C. (2004). Building citizen trust through e-government. Retrieved from http://csdl.computer.org/comp/proceedings/hicss/2004/2056/05/205650119a.pdf

Parnes, A. (2011). *White House press pool losing scoops to Twitter.* Retrieved July 30, 2011, from http://www.politico.com/news/stories/0611/58161.html

Parvez, Z. (2008). E-democracy from the perspective of local elected members. *International Journal of Electronic Government Research*, *4*(3), 20–35. doi:10.4018/jegr.2008070102

Parvez, Z., & Ahmed, P. (2006). Towards building an integrated perspective of e- democracy in practice. *Information Communication and Society*, *9*(5), 612–632. doi:10.1080/13691180600965609

Parycek, P., & Sachs, M. 2010. Open government – Information flow in Web 2.0. *European Journal of E-Practice, 9.*

Pasely, J. (2001). *The tyranny of printers: Newspaper politics in the early American republic, Jeffersonian America.* Charlottesville, VA: University Press of Virginia.

Patterson, G., & Sprehe, J. T. (2002). Principal challenges facing electronic records management in federal agencies today. *Government Information Quarterly*, *19*(10), 307–315. doi:10.1016/S0740-624X(02)00108-9

Pattie, C., Seyd, P., & Whitely, P. (2003). Civic attitudes and engagement in modern Britain. *Parliamentary Affairs*, *56*, 616–633. doi:10.1093/pa/gsg106

Paul, C. (2011). *Strategic communication: Origins, concepts, and current debates.* Santa Barbara, CA: Praeger.

Pavlichev, A., & Garson, D. G. (Eds.). (2004). *Digital government: Principles and best practices.* Hershey, PA: Idea Group Press.

Peled, A. (2001). Centralization of diffusion? Two tales of online government. *Administration & Society*, *32*(6), 686–709. doi:10.1177/00953990122019622

Pelosi, N. (2009, January 13). *Speaker Pelosi presents Capitol cat cam.* Retrieved from http://www.youtube.com/watch?v=wtOW1CxHvNY&feature=player_embedded

Perry, R. (2006). Diffusion theories. In E. F. Borgatta & R. J. V. Montgomery (Eds.), *Encyclopedia of sociology* (2 ed., Vol. 1, pp. 674-681). New York, NY: Macmillan Reference USA.

Perry, C. (2010). Social media and the Army. *Military Review*, (March-April): 63–67.

perspectives-on-social-media-the-vancouver-riots

Peters, T., & Waterman, R. (1982). *In search of excellence: Lessons from America's best-run companies.* New York, NY: Harper & Row.

Pina, V., Torres, L., & Royo, S. (2007). Are ICT's improving transparency and accountability in the EU regional and local governments? An empirical study. *Public Administration*, *85*(2), 449–472. doi:10.1111/j.1467-9299.2007.00654.x

Pirog, M. A., & Johnson, C. (2008). Electronic funds and benefits transfers, e-government, and the winter commission. *Public Administration Review*, (December): 103–114. doi:10.1111/j.1540-6210.2008.00982.x

Pirog, M. A., & Johnson, C. (2008). Electronic funds and benefits transfers, e-government, and the winter commission. *Public Administration Review*, (December): S103–S114. doi:10.1111/j.1540-6210.2008.00982.x

Pivato, M. (2007). *Pyramidal democracy.* Retrieved from http://mpra.ub.uni-muenchen.de/3965/1/MPRA_paper_3965.pdf

Plautz, J. (2009, September 3). Mike Rogers, YouTube sensation? *NationalJournal.com.* Retrieved from http://healthtopic.nationaljournal.com/2009/09/mike-rogers-you-tube.php

Plocher, D. (1999). The digital age: Challenges for records management. *Government Information Quarterly*, *16*(1), 63–69. doi:10.1016/S0740-624X(99)80016-1

Plough, A., & Krimsky, S. (1987). The emergence of risk communication studies: Social and political context. *Science, Technology, & Human Values, 12*(3), 4-10. doi:01622439/87/03/07/j.sthv.2011.02.04

Plowman, D. A., Solanksy, S., Beck, T., Baker, L., Kulkarni, M., & Travis, D. V. (2007). The role of leadership in emergent, self-organization. *The Leadership Quarterly*, *18*, 341–356. doi:10.1016/j.leaqua.2007.04.004

Polat, R. K. (2005). The Internet and political participation. Exploring the explanatory links. *European Journal of Communication*, *20*(4), 435–459. doi:10.1177/0267323105058251

Politwitter. (n.d.). *A Canadian non-partisan political twitter & social media aggregator & directory.* Retrieved April 5, 2011, from http://www.politwitter.ca

Pool, I. (1983). *Technologies of freedom.* Cambridge, MA: Harvard University Press.

Power, A. (2002). EU legitimacy and new forms of citizen engagement. *Electronic . Journal of E-Government*, *8*(1), 45–53.

Powner, D. A. (2009). *National archive: Progress and risks in implementing its electronic records archive initiative.* Retrieved from http://www.gao.gov/new.items/d10222t.pdf

Pratchett, L. (1999). New fashions in public participation: Towards greater democracy? *Parliamentary Affairs*, *52*(4), 616–633. doi:10.1093/pa/52.4.616

Preece, J., & Shneiderman, B. (2009). The reader-to-leader framework: Motivating technology-mediated social participation. *AIS Transactions on Human-Computer Interaction*, *1*(1), 13–32.

Price, V., & Cappella, J. N. (2002). Online deliberation and its influence: The electronic dialogue project in campaign 2000. *IT & Society*, *1*(1), 303–329.

Public printing and documents. 44 U.S.C. § 2901. (2006).

Public printing and documents. 44 U.S.C. §3601. (2006).

Putnam, R. (2002). Bowling together. *The American Prospect, 13*(3). Retrieved April 1, 2011, from http://prospect.org/cs/articles?articleId=6114

Putnam, R. (2000). *Bowling alone: The collapse and revival of American community.* New York, NY: Simon and Schuster.

Putnam, R. D. (1993). *Bowling alone.* New York, NY: Simon & Schuster Paperbacks.

Quinn, S. (2002). *Knowledge management in the digital newsroom.* Oxford, UK: Focal Press.

Rainer, R. K., Cegielski, C. G., Splettstoesser-Hogeterp, I., & Sanchez-Rodriguez, C. (2011). *Introduction to Information Systems*, 2nd ed. John Wiley & Sons, Canada, Ltd. ISBN: 978-0-470-67888-6

Rainey, H. (2009). *Understanding and managing public organizations.* San Francisco, CA: Jossey-Bass.

Raja, S., Ball, M., Booth, J., Haberstro, P., & Veith, K. (2009). Leveraging neighborhood-scale change for policy and program reform in Buffalo, New York. *American Journal of Preventive Medicine*, *37*(S62), S352–S360. doi:10.1016/j.amepre.2009.09.001

Ranzinger, M., & Gleixner, G. (1997). GIS datasets for 3D urban planning. *Computers, Environment and Urban Systems*, *21*(2), 159–173. doi:10.1016/S0198-9715(97)10005-9

Reagans, R., & McEvily, B. (2003). Network structure and knowledge transfer: The effects of cohesion and range. *Administrative Science Quarterly*, *48*(2), 240–267. doi:10.2307/3556658

Records management by the archivist of the United States and by the Administrator of General

Reece, B. (2006). E-government literature review. *Journal of E-Government*, *3*(1), 69–110. doi:10.1300/J399v03n01_05

Regan, P. M. (1986). Privacy, government information and technology. *Public Administration Review*, *46*(6), 629–634. doi:10.2307/976229

Regio, M. (2002). Government virtual service networks. *Proceedings of the 35ᵗʰ Hawaii International Conference on System Science IEEE*. Retrieved on April 13, 2011, from www.hicss.hawaii.edu/HICSS_35/HICSSpapers/PDFdocuments/ETEGV04.pdf

Rethemeyer, R. K. (2007). The empires strike back: Is the Internet corporatizing rather than democratizing policy processes? *Public Administration Review*, *67*(2), 199–215. doi:10.1111/j.1540-6210.2007.00707.x

Rhodes, J., Lok, P., Hung, R. Y.-Y., & Fang, S.-C. (2008). An integrative model of organizational learning and social capital on effective knowledge transfer and perceived organizational performance. *Journal of Workplace Learning*, *20*(4), 245. doi:10.1108/13665620810871105

Rich, S. (2011, April 13). Suspicious activity report is now mobile – In Kentucky. *Government Technology*. Retrieved from http://www.govtech.com/public-safety/Suspicious-Activity-Reporting-Mobile-in-Kentucky.html

Ritchie, D. (1991). *Press gallery: Congress and the Washington correspondents*. Cambridge, MA: Harvard University Press.

Roberts, N. (2004). Public deliberation in an age of direct citizen participation. *American Review of Public Administration*, *34*(4), 315–353. doi:10.1177/0275074004269288

Rogers, M. (2009, July 16). *Congressman Mike Rogers' opening statement on health care reform in Washington, DC*. Retrieved from http://www.youtube.com/watch?v=G44NCvNDLfc&feature=player_embedded

Rohlinger, D., & Brown, J. (2009). Democracy, action and the Internet after 9/11. *The American Behavioral Scientist*, *53*(1), 130–150. doi:10.1177/0002764209338791

Roof, K., & Glandon, R. (2008). Tool created to assess health impacts of development decisions in Ingham County, Michigan. *Journal of Environmental Health*, *71*(1), 35–38.

Roof, K., & Maclennan, C. (2008). Tri-county health department in Colorado does more than just review a development plan. *Journal of Environmental Health*, *71*(1), 31–34.

Roof, K., & Oleru, N. (2008). Public health: Seattle and King County's push for the built environment. *Journal of Environmental Health*, *71*(1), 24–27.

Roof, K., & Sutherland, S. (2008). Smart growth and health for the future: Our course of action. *Journal of Environmental Health*, *71*(1), 28–30.

Rosenbaum, B. L. (1978). New uses for behavioral modeling. *The Personnel Administrator*, 27–28.

Rose, W. R., & Grant, G. G. (2010). Critical issues pertaining to the planning and implementation of e-government initiatives. *Government Information Quarterly*, *27*(1), 26–33. doi:10.1016/j.giq.2009.06.002

Rouse, L. J., Bergeron, S. J., & Harris, T. M. (2007). Participating in the geospatial Web - Collaborative mapping, social networks, and participatory GIS . In Scharl, A., & Tochtermann, K. (Eds.), *The geospatial Web*. London, UK: Springer. doi:10.1007/978-1-84628-827-2_14

Rousseau, D. M., Sitkin, S. B., Burt, R. S., & Camerer, C. (1998). Not so different after all: A cross-discipline view of trust. *Academy of Management. Academy of Management Review*, *23*(3), 393. doi:10.5465/AMR.1998.926617

Rowland, K. (2009, March 20). GOP bests its rival for YouTube views. *Washington Times*. Retrieved from http://www.washingtontimes.com/news/2009/mar/20/gop-bests-its-rival- for-youtube-views/

Rowley, J. (2004). Online branding. *Online Information Review*, *28*(2), 131–138. doi:10.1108/14684520410531637

Roy, J. (2003). The relational dynamics of e-governance: A case study of the City of Ottawa. *Public Performance & Management Review*, *26*(4), 391–403. doi:10.1177/1530957603026004006

RSOE EDIS. (n.d.). *Emergency and disasters information and monitoring services, hosted by the National Association of Radio-distress Signalling and Infocommunications*, Retrieved April 5, 2011, from http://hisz.rsoe.hu/alertmap/index.php?lang=eng

Rushen, A. (2011). *Personal interview*.

Sabatini, F. (2009). Social capital as social networks: A new framework for measurement and an empirical analysis of its determinants and consequences. *Journal of Socio-Economics*, *38*(3), 429–442. doi:10.1016/j.socec.2008.06.001

Saebø, Ø., Rose, J., & Skiftenes, F. L. (2008). The shape of e-participation: Characterizing an emerging research area. *Government Information Quarterly*, *25*(3), 400–428. doi:10.1016/j.giq.2007.04.007

Safko, L., & Brake, D. K. (2009). *The social media bible: Tactics, tools, and strategies for business success*. Hoboken, NJ: John Wiley & Sons.

Saglie, J., & Vabo, S. I. (2005). *Online participation in Norwegian local politics- The rise of digital divides?* Lokalpolitisk deltakelse,14th Nordic Political Science Association (NOPSA) Conference, 11 –13 August 2005.

Sako, M. (1992). *Prices, quality, and trust: inTer-firm relations in Britain and Japan*. Cambridge, UK: Cambridge University Press. doi:10.1017/CBO9780511520723

Samuel, A. (2011). *10 challenging perspectives on social media & the Vancouver riots*. Retrieved July 30, 2011, from http://www.alexandrasamuel.com/world/10-challenging-

San Francisco Department of Public Health. (n.d.). *Health, traffic and environmental justice: A health impact analysis of the Still/Lyell Freeway Channel in Excelsior District*. Retrieved December 8, 2010, from http://www.sfphes.org/HIA_PODER.htm

Sanford, C., & Rose, J. (2007). Characterizing e-participation. *International Journal of Information Management*, *27*(6), 406–421. doi:10.1016/j.ijinfomgt.2007.08.002

Sauerbier, R. (2010). Social networking . In Grant, A., & Meadows, J. (Eds.), *Communication technology update and fundamentals* (12th ed., pp. 292–304). New York, NY: Elesevier. doi:10.1016/B978-0-240-81475-9.50020-7

Scavo, C., & Shi, Y. (2000). The role of Information Technology in the reinventing government paradigm: Normative predicates and practical challenges. *Social Science Computer Review*, *18*(2), 166–178. doi:10.1177/089443930001800206

Schacter, J. (2010). Digitally democratizing Congress? Technology and political accountability. *Stanford Law Journal* [Paper], No. 1565645.

Schaper, N. (2010). Entrepreneurial insurgency: Republicans connect with the American people . In Lathrop, D., & Ruma, L. (Eds.), *Open government: Collaboration, transparency and participation in practice* (pp. 5376–5562). Sebastopol, CA: O'Reilly Media Inc.[Kindle edition]

Schasberger, M., Hussa, C., Polgar, M., McMonagle, M., Burke, S., & Gegaris, A. (2009). Promoting and developing a trail network across suburban, rural, and urban communities. *American Journal of Preventive Medicine*, *37*(S62), S336–S344. doi:10.1016/j.amepre.2009.09.012

Schierholz, S. (2011). *Personal interview*.

Schlosberg, D., Zavetoski, S., & Shulman, S. (2007). Democracy and e-rulemaking: Web-based technologies, participation, and the potential for deliberation. *Journal of Information Technology & Politics*, *4*(1), 37–55. doi:10.1300/J516v04n01_04

Schweiger, D. M., Sandberg, W. R., & Ragan, J. W. (1986). Group approaches for improving strategic decision making: A comparative analysis of dialectical inquiry, devil's advocacy, and consensus. *Academy of Management Journal*, *29*(1), 51–71. doi:10.2307/255859

Schwester, R. (2010). Socio-demographic determinants of e-government adoption: An examination of major U.S. cities. *Journal of Public Management and Social Policy*, *16*(2), 21–32.

Sclove, R. (1995). *Democracy and technology*. New York, NY: Guilford Press.

Scott, D. (2010). *The new rules of marketing and PR*. Hoboken, NJ: John Wiley and Sons.

Scott, J. (2000). *Social network analysis: A handbook*. London, UK: SAGE Publications.

Scott, J. (2006). E" the people: Do U.S. municipal government web sites support public involvement? *Public Administration Review*, *66*(3), 341–353. doi:10.1111/j.1540-6210.2006.00593.x

Scott, J. K. (2006). 'E' the people: Do U.S. municipal government web sites support public involvement. *Public Administration Review*, *66*(3), 341–353. doi:10.1111/j.1540-6210.2006.00593.x

Second Life Home Page. (n.d.). *A free 3D virtual world where users can socialize, connect and create using free voice and text chat*. Retrieved from http://secondlife.com/

Segrest, S. L., Domke-Damonte, D. J., Miles, A. K., & Anthony, W. P. (1998). Following the crowd: Social influence and technology usage. *Journal of Organizational Change Management*, *11*(5), 425. doi:10.1108/09534819810234841

Senak, M. (2010, January). Twongress: The power of Twitter in Congress. *Fleishman-Hilliard*. Retrieved from http://www.eyeonfda.com/files/twongress-white-paper-final-1-14-10.pdf

Senate Committee on Rules and Administration. (2008, September 19). *U.S. Senate Internet services usage rules and policies*. Retrieved from http://www.senate.gov/usage/internetpolicy.htm

Serrat, O. (2010). *Social media and the public sector*. Retrieved March 30, 2011, from http://www.asiandevbank.org/documents/information/knowledge-solutions/social-media-and-the-public-sector.pdf

Services. 44 U.S.C. § 2904(b). (2006).

Shachtman, N. (2009, July 30). Military may ban Twitter, Facebook as security "headaches." *Wired*.

Shangapour, S., Hosseini, S., & Hashemnejad, H. (2011). Cyber social networks and social movements. *Global Journal of Human Social Science, 11*(1)

Shapiro, D. L., Sheppard, B. H., & Cheraskin, L. (1992). Business on a handshake. *Negotiation Journal*, *8*, 365–377. doi:10.1111/j.1571-9979.1992.tb00679.x

Shark, A. (2010). Behind the curve. *American City & County Magazine*. Retrieved July 30, 2011, from http://americancityandcounty.com/technology/web-business-intelligence-201007/

Shear, M. D. (2011, June 16). House Democrat writes with GOP as editors. *The New York Times*, p. A24.

Shelley, M. C., Thrane, L., Shulman, S., Lang, E., Beisser, S., Larson, T., & Muttiti, J. (2004). Digital citizenship: Parameters of the digital divide. *Social Science Computer Review*, *22*(2), 256–269. doi:10.1177/0894439303262580

Sheng, H. & Trimi, S. (2008). M-government: Technologies, applications and challenges. *Electronic Government, an International Journal, 5*(1), 1-18.

Shetzer, L. (1993). A social information processing model of employee participation. *Organization Science*, *4*(2), 252. doi:10.1287/orsc.4.2.252

Shiang, J. (2002). Digital democracy . In Shiyi, L. (Eds.), *Popular government* (pp. 69–91). Taipei, Taiwan: Open University Press. (in Chinese)

Shim, D., & Eom, T. (2009). Anticorruption effects of information communication and technology (ICT) and social capital. *International Review of Administrative Sciences*, *75*(1), 99–116. doi:10.1177/0020852308099508

Shiode, N. (2001). 3D urban models: Recent developments in the digital modeling of urban environments in three-dimensions. *GeoJournal*, *52*, 263–269. doi:10.1023/A:1014276309416

Shipan, C. R., & Volden, C. (2008). The mechanisms of policy diffusion. *American Journal of Political Science*, *52*(4), 840–857. doi:10.1111/j.1540-5907.2008.00346.x

Shirky, C. (2008). *Here comes everybody*. New York, NY: Penguin Books.

Shirky, C. (2008). *Here comes everybody: The power of organizing without organizations* [Kindle edition]. New York, NY: Penguin Press.

Shirky, C. (2010). *Cognitive surplus*. New York, NY: Penguin Books.

Shirky, C. (2011). The political power of social media. *Foreign Affairs (Council on Foreign Relations)*, *90*, 28–41.

Sieber, R. (2006). Public participation and geographic Information Systems: A literature review and framework. *Annals of the Association of American Geographers. Association of American Geographers*, *96*(3), 491–507. doi:10.1111/j.1467-8306.2006.00702.x

Silicon Republic–Innovation. (2011). *Dublin councils launch 18-hour open data challenge*. Retrieved July 30, 2011, from http://www.siliconrepublic.com/innovation/item/22301-dublin-councils-launch-18-h/

Silicon Republic-Strategy. (2011). *The open data movement will be the people's choice.* Retrieved July 30, 2011, from http://www.siliconrepublic.com/strategy/item/21784-the-open-data-movement-will/

Simmons, J. (1978). *The fairness doctrine and the media.* Berkeley, CA: University of California Press.

Sindelar, J., Mintz, D., & Hughes, T. (2009). The past is prologue: The Obama technology agenda. *Public Management, 38*(4), 24–27.

Sipior, J. C., & Ward, B. T. (2005). Bridging the digital divide for e-government inclusion: A United States case study. *The Electronic . Journal of E-Government, 39*(1), 137–146.

Six Apart. (6A). (n.d.). *Home page - Blog hosting service.* Retrieved from www.sixapart.com

Small, S., & Strzalkowski, T. (2009). HITIQA: High-quality intelligence through interactive question answering. *Journal of Natural Language Engineering: Special Issue on Interactive Question Answering, 15*(1), 31–54.

Smith, A., & Rainie, L. (2010). *8% of online Americans use Twitter.* Washington, DC: Pew Internet and American Life Project, Pew Research Centre. Retrieved from http://pewinternet.ord/Reports/2010/Twitter-update-2010.aspx

Smith, G. (2005). *Beyond the ballot: 57 democratic innovations from around the world.* ISBN: 0955030307.

Smith, J. (2010). SpringsGov.com request for city services goes mobile. *City of Colorado Springs.* Retrieved from http://www.springsgov.com/news.aspx?newsid=710

Smith, B., Fraser, B. T., & McClure, C. R. (2000). Federal information policy and access to Web-based federal information. *Journal of Academic Librarianship, 26*(4), 274–281. doi:10.1016/S0099-1333(00)00128-2

Smith, G. (2009). *Democratic innovations: Designing institutions for democratic governance.* Cambridge, UK: Cambridge University Press. doi:10.1017/CBO9780511609848

Snellen, I. (2002). Electronic governance: Implications for citizens, politicians and public servants. *International Review of Administrative Sciences, 68*(2), 183–198. doi:10.1177/0020852302682002

Snellen, I. T. M., & Thaens, M. (2008). From e-government to m-government . In Pennella, G. (Eds.), *European cases, administrative innovation and growth* (pp. 211–256). Formez, Italy: Gianni Research.

Snyder, B. (2011). *Facebook facial recognition: Why it's a threat to your privacy.* Retrieved July 30, 2011, from http://www.cio.com/article/684711/facebook_facial_recognition_why_it_s_a_threat_to_your_privacy

Snyder, W. M., Wenger, E., & Briggs, X. D. (2003). Communities of practice in government: Leveraging knowledge for performance. *Public Management, 32*(4), 17–21.

Southern California Association of Governments. (2011). Retrieved from http://www.scag.ca.gov/

Sprehe, T. J. (2000). Integrating records management into information resources management in U.S. government agencies. *Government Information Quarterly, 17*(1), 13–26. doi:10.1016/S0740-624X(99)00022-2

Sprehe, T. J. (2005). The positive benefits of electronic records management in the context of enterprise content management. *Government Information Quarterly, 22*(2), 297–303. doi:10.1016/j.giq.2005.02.003

Stanley, J., & Weare, C. (2004). The effects of Internet use on political participation: Evidence from an agency online discussion forum. *Administration & Society, 36*(5), 503–527. doi:10.1177/0095399704268503

Starr, P. (2004). *The creation of the media: Political origins of modern communications.* New York, NY: Basic Books.

Steeves, V. (2008). If the Supreme Court were on Facebook: Evaluating the reasonable expectation of privacy test from a social perspective. *Canadian Journal of Criminology and Criminal Justice, 50*(3), 331–347. doi:10.3138/cjccj.50.3.331

Steinfield, C., DiMicco, J. M., Ellison, N. B., & Lampe, C. (2009). *Bowling online: Social networking and social capital within the organization.* Paper presented at the Fourth International Conference on Communities and Technologies, University Park, PA.

Sterling, R. (2005). Promoting democratic governance through partnerships? In Newman, J. (Ed.), *Remaking governance, peoples, politics and the public sphere* (pp. 139–158). University of Bristol: The Policy Press.

Stewart, K. (2007). Write the rules and win: Understanding citizen participation game dynamics. *Public Administration Review*, *67*(6), 1067–1076. doi:10.1111/j.1540-6210.2007.00798.x

Stowers, G. (2004). *Measuring the performance of e-government*. Washington, DC: IBM Endowment for the Business of Government.

Streib, G., & Navarro, I. (2006). Citizen demand for interactive e-government: The case of Georgia consumer service. *American Review of Public Administration*, *36*(3), 288–300. doi:10.1177/0275074005283371

Stromer-Galley, J., & Muhlberger, P. (2009). Agreement and disagreement in group deliberation: Effects on deliberation satisfaction, future engagement, and decision legitimacy. *Political Communication*, *26*(2), 173–192. doi:10.1080/10584600902850775

Stroud, N. J. (2011). *Niche news: The politics of news choice*. New York, NY: Oxford University Press.

Sunstein, C. (2010). *Social media, Web-based interactive technologies and the Paperwork Reduction Act*. Retrieved from http://www.whitehouse.gov/sites/default/files/omb/assets /inforeg/SocialMediaGuidance_04072010.pdf

Sunstein, C. (2007). *Republic.com 2.0*. Princeton, NJ: Princeton University Press.

Sunstein, C. (2009). *Going to extremes: How like minds unite and divide*. New York, NY: Oxford University Press.

Susanto, T., & Goodwin, R. (2010). Factors influencing citizen adoption of SMS-based E-government services. *Electronic . Journal of E-Government*, *8*(1), 55–70.

Swanstrom, T. (2009). Breaking down silos: Transportation, economic development and health. In S. Malekafzali (Ed.), *Healthy, equitable transportation policy: Recommendations and research*. Retrieved March 2011, from http://www.policylink.org/site/apps/nlnet/content2.aspx?c=lkIXLbMNJrE&b=5136581&ct=8439979

Szalay, A., & Gray, J. (2001). The world-wide telescope. *Science*, *293*(5537), 2037–2040. doi:10.1126/science.293.5537.2037

Talpin, J., & Wojcik, S. (2010). Deliberating environmental policy issues: Comparing the learning potential of online and face-to-face discussions on climate change. *Policy & Internet, 2*(2).

Tan, S., & Wong, O. (2006). Location aware applications for smart cities with Google Maps and GIS tools. *Proceedings of the Fourth International Conference on Active Media Technology (AMT06)*, Brisbane, Australia.

Tapscott, D. (1997). *The digital economy: The digital economy: Promise and peril in the age of networked intelligence*. London, UK: McGraw-Hill.

Taylor-Smith, E., & Lindner, R. (2010). Social networking tools supporting constructive involvement throughout the policy-cycle. In *Proceedings of EDEM 2010 - Conference on Electronic Democracy, May 7-8, 2010, Danube-University Krems, Austria*. Vienna, Austria: Austrian Computer Society.

Tenbrink, D., McMunn, R., & Panken, S. (2009). Project U-Turn: Increasing active transportation in Jackson, Michigan. *American Journal of Preventive Medicine*, *37*(S62), S329–S335. doi:10.1016/j.amepre.2009.09.004

The City of New York. (2011). *Road map for the digital city: achieving New York City's digital future*. Retrieved July 30, 2011 from http://www.mikebloomberg.com/NYC_Digital_Roadmap_05162011.pdf

The National Public Toilet Map (the Toilet Map). (n.d.). Retrieved April 5, 2011 from http://www.toiletmap.gov.au/

Thomas, I., Sayers, S., Godon, J., & Reilly, S. (2009). Bike, walk, and wheel: A way of life in Columbia, Missouri. *American Journal of Preventive Medicine*, *37*(S62), S322–S328. doi:10.1016/j.amepre.2009.09.002

Thompson, G., & Wilkinson, P. (2009). Set the default to open: Plessy's meaning in the twenty-first century and how technology puts the individual back at the center of life, liberty, and government. *Texas Review of Law & Politics*, *14*(1), 48–89.

Thompson, J. (1967). *Organizations in action*. New York, NY: McGraw Hill.

Tichenor, P. J., Olien, C. N., & Donahue, G. A. (1970). Mass media flow and differential growth in knowledge. *Public Opinion Quarterly*, *34*(2), 159–170. doi:10.1086/267786

Tolbert, C., & Mossberger, K. (2004). *The effects of e-government on trust and confidence in government.* Retrieved from http://knowlton.osu.edu/ped/Egov/TolbertMossbergerOSU1.pdf

Tolbert, C., & Mossberger, K. (2006). The effects of e-government on trust and confidence in government. *Public Administration Review, 66*(3), 354–369. doi:10.1111/j.1540-6210.2006.00594.x

Toregas, C. (2001). The politics of e-gov: The upcoming struggle for redefining civil engagement. *National Civil Engagement, 90*(3), 235–240. doi:10.1002/ncr.90304

Towns, S. (2010, June 7). Government "apps" move from cool to useful. *Governing Magazine.* Retrieved from http://www.governing.com/columns/tech-talk/Government-Apps-Move-from.html

Transportation Research Board (TRB). (2010a). *Colorado Step Up environmental collaboration supported by Web-based technology.* Strategic Highway Research Program 2, Case Studies in Collaboration. Retrieved February 16, 2011, from http://onlinepubs.trb.org/onlinepubs/shrp2/SHRP2_CS_C01_CO-STEP-UP.pdf

Transportation Research Board (TRB). (2010b). *Maricopa County, Arizona: Regional transportation plan.* Strategic Highway Research Program 2, Case Studies in Collaboration. Retrieved February 11, 2011, from http://onlinepubs.trb.org/onlinepubs/shrp2/SHRP2_CS_C01_Maricopa.pdf

Transportation Research Board (TRB). (2010c). *Wasatch Front Region, Utah: Regional transportation plan.* Strategi cHighway Research Program 2, Case Studies in Collaboration. Retrieved February 16, 2011, from http://onlinepubs.trb.org/onlinepubs/shrp2/SHRP2_CS_C01_UT-Wasatch.pdf

Transportation Research Board (TRB). (2010d). *Binghamton metropolitan transportation study.* Strategic Highway-Research Program 2, Case Studies in Collaboration. Retrieved December 12, 2010, from http://onlinepubs.trb.org/onlinepubs/shrp2/SHRP2_CS_C01_NY-Binghamton.pdf

Transportation Research Board (TRB). (2010e). *CALTRANS: Corridor systems management plan: Using performanc emeasures to conduct analysis and make decisions.* Strategic Highway Research Program 2, Case Studies in Collaboration. Retrieved November 22, 2010, from http://onlinepubs.trb.org/onlinepubs/shrp2/SHRP2_CS_C01_Caltrans.pdf

Transportation Research Board (TRB). (2010f). *Colorado US-285: Foxton road to Bailey - Using a context sensitive solutions approach to highway capacity.* Strategic Highway Research Program 2, Case Studies in Collaboration. Retrieved Novemer 23, 2010, from http://onlinepubs.trb.org/onlinepubs/shrp2/SHRP2_CS_C01_Colorado.pdf

Transportation Research Board (TRB). (2010g). *Grand Rapids Michigan: US-131 S-curve replacement, collaborative design and construction closure of central urban access.* Strategic Highway Research Program 2, Case Studies in Collaboration. Retrieved November 22, 2010, from http://onlinepubs.trb.org/onlinepubs/shrp2/SHRP2_CS_C01_Michigan.pdf

Transportation Research Board (TRB). (2010h). *I-69 Trans-Texas corridor study: Using GISST, TEAP, Quantm, SAM, and ProjectSolve technologies.* Strategic Highway Research Program 2, Case Studies in Collaboration. Retrieved November 23, 2010, from http://onlinepubs.trb.org/onlinepubs/shrp2/SHRP2_CS_C01_Texas.pdf

Transportation Research Board (TRB). (2010i). *Idaho's transportation vision.* Strategic Highway Research Program 2, Case Studies in Collaboration. Retrieved December 12, 2010, from http://onlinepubs.trb.org/onlinepubs/shrp2/SHRP2_CS_C01_Idaho.pdf

Transportation Research Board (TRB). (2010j). *Illinois Prairie Parkway project: Developing comprehensive transportation system improvements using an in-depth screening process.* Strategic Highway Research Program 2, Case Studies in Collaboration. Retrieved November 23, 2010, from http://onlinepubs.trb.org/onlinepubs/shrp2/SHRP2_CS_C01_Illinois.pdf

Transportation Research Board (TRB). (2010k). *NJ-31 integrated land use and transportation plan.* Strategic Highway Research Program 2, Case Studies in Collaboration. Retrieved December 12, 2010, from http://onlinepubs.trb.org/onlinepubs/shrp2/SHRP2_CS_C01_NJ-31.pdf

Transportation Research Board (TRB). (2010l). *Oregon I-5/ beltline interchange: Structured decision making using community values as performance measures.* Strategic Highway Research Program 2, Case Studies in Collaboration. Retrieved December 12, 2010, from http://onlinepubs.trb.org/onlinepubs/shrp2/SHRP2_CS_C01_Oregon.pdf

Transportation Research Board (TRB). (2010m). *Puget Sound region, Washington: Regional TIP policy framework and Vision 2040 - Using paint the region to evaluate scenarios.* Strategic Highway Research Program 2, Case Studies in Collaboration. Retrieved December 12, 2010, fromhttp://onlinepubs.trb.org/onlinepubs/shrp2/SHRP2_CS_C01_Washington-PugetSound.pdf

Transportation Research Board (TRB). (2010n). *Sacramento region, California: Blueprint Project.* Strategic Highway Research Program 2, Case Studies in Collaboration. Retrieved December 12, 2010, from http://onlinepubs.trb.org/onlinepubs/shrp2/SHRP2_CS_C01_Sacramento.pdf

Transportation Research Board (TRB). (2010o). *US-24: New Haven Indiana to Defiance, Ohio; The 9-step transportation development process.* Strategic highway Research Program 2, Case Studies in Collaboration. Retrieved November 22, 2010, from http://onlinepubs.trb.org/onlinepubs/shrp2/SHRP2_CS_C01_Ohio-Indiana.pdf

Transportation Research Board (TRB). (2010p). *Woodrow Wilson Bridge in Maryland and Virginia: FHWA leads the planning process for bridge redesign.* Strategic Highway Research Program 2, Case Studies in Collaboration. Retrieved November 22, 2010, from http://onlinepubs.trb.org/onlinepubs/shrp2/SHRP2_CS_C01_WilsonBridge.pdf

Traunmüller, R. (2010). Web 2.0 creates a new government. In . *Proceedings of EGOVIS, 2010,* 77–83.

Trimi, S., & Sheng, H. (2008). Emerging trends in m-government. *Communications of the ACM, 51*(5), 53–58. doi:10.1145/1342327.1342338

Trimi, S., & Sheng, H. (2008). Emerging trends in m-government. *Communications of the ACM, 51*(5), 53–58. doi:10.1145/1342327.1342338

Tseng, D. I. (2003) *E-government's influence on administrative governance: A case study of economic department's international trade bureau.* Doctoral dissertation in Public Administration at National Chengchi University.

Tumblr Home Page. (n.d.). *A microblogging platform.* Retrieved from http://www.tumblr.com/

Tumin, Z., & Wasserman, R. (2008). *311: The next wave. Nine imperatives for leadership of 311-enabled government.* Retrieved from Harvard University, Kennedy School of Government website http://www.innovations.harvard.edu/cache/documents/1285/128521.pdf

Turner, A. J. (2006). *Introduction to Neogeography. O'Reilly Short Cuts Series.* Sebastopol, CA: O'Reilly Media.

Twitter Home Page. (n.d.). *A social networking and microblogging platform.* Retrieved from http://twitter.com/

Tyler, T. R. (2006). *Why people obey the law (illustrated edition.).* Princeton University Press.

United Nations Development Program. (1999). *Human Development Report 1999.* New York, NY: United Nation Development Program/Oxford.

United Nations Human Development Report. (2009*). Overcoming barriers: Human mobility and development.* Retrieved April 2, 2010, from http://hdr.undp.org/en/reports/global/hdr2009

United Nations Public Administration Network (UNPAN). (2008). *Global e-government survey: From e-government to connected governance.* Division for Public Administration and Development Management. Retrieved March 16, 2010, from http://www.unpan.org/egovkb/global_reports/08report.htm

United States Department of Commerce. (1999). Falling through the net: Defining the digital divide. Washington, DC: United States Department of Commerce. Retrieved November 12, 2007, from http://www.ntia.doc.gov/ntiahome/fttn99/FTTN.pdf

United States Department of Commerce. (2000). *Falling through the net: Toward digital inclusion.* Washington, DC: United States Department of Commerce. Retrieved November 12, 2007, from http://search.ntia.doc.gov/pdf/fttn00.pdf

Ushahidi Home Page. (n.d.). *An open-source crowdsourcing and information democratizing application.* Retrieved from http://ushahidi.com/

Vajjhala, S. P. (2006). Ground truthing policy: Using participatory map-making to connect citizens and decision makers. *Resources, 162,* 14–18.

Van De Belt, T., Engelen, L., Berben, S., & Schoonhoven, L. (2010). Definition of Health 2.0 and Medicine 2.0: A systematic review. *Journal of Medical Internet Research,* 12(2). Retrieved February 12, 2011, from http://www.jmir.org/2010/2/e18/

van de Bunt, G. G., Wittek, R. P. M., & de Klepper, M. C. (2005). The evolution of intra-organizational trust networks: The case of a German paper factory: An empirical test of six trust mechanisms. *International Sociology, 20*(3), 339–369. doi:10.1177/0268580905055480

Van Dijk, J. (2006). *Network society.* London, UK: Sage.

van Dijk, J. A. G. M. (2005). *The deepening divide: Inequality in an information society.* Thousand Oaks, CA: Sage Publications.

Vandermerwe, S. (1987). Diffusing new ideas in-house. *Journal of Product Innovation Management, 4*(4), 256. doi:10.1016/0737-6782(87)90029-4

Venkatesh, V. (2000). Determinants of perceived ease of use: Integrating control, intrinsic motivation, and emotion into the technology acceptance model. *Information Systems Research, 11*(4), 342. doi:10.1287/isre.11.4.342.11872

Verma, N., & Ornager, S. (2005). *E-government toolkit for developing countries.* Retrieved August 5, 2010, from http://www.unescobkk.org/fileadmin/user_upload/ci/documents/UNESCO_e-Govt_Toolkit.pdf

Virtual Policy Network. (n.d.). *Best practice forum 235: Virtual worlds and public diplomacy in the digital age.* Department of Business, Innovation, and Skills, UK Government. Retrieved March 30, 2011, from http://www.virtualpolicy.net/_downloads/igf09/ukgov_tvpn-igf09-vw_publicdiplomacy.pdf

Vogelstein, F. (2007, October). Saving Facebook. *Wired,* 188-193.

Volonino, L., Sipior, J. C., & Ward, B. T. (2007). Managing the lifecycle of electronically stored information. *Information Systems Management, 24*(3), 231–238. doi:10.1080/10580530701404637

Von Haldenwang, C. (2004). Electronic government (e-government) and development. *European Journal of Development Research, 16*(2), 417–432. doi:10.1080/0957881042000220886

Waldo, D. (1952). Development of theory of democratic administration. *The American Political Science Review, 46*(1), 81–103. doi:10.2307/1950764

Walfoort, N., Clark, J., Bostock, M., & O'Neil, K. (2009). ACTIVE Louisville: Incorporating active living principles into planning and design. *American Journal of Preventive Medicine, 37*(S62), S368–S376. doi:10.1016/j.amepre.2009.09.007

Wallis, J. (2005). Cyberspace, information literacy and the information society. *Library Review, 54*(4), 218–222. doi:10.1108/00242530510593407

Wangpipatwong, S., Chutimaskul, W., & Papasratorn, B. (2008). Understanding citizen's continuance intention to use e- government website: A composite view of technology acceptance model and computer self-efficacy. *Electronic . Journal of E-Government, 6*(1), 55–64.

Warren, C. (2010, March 16). How PR pros are using social media for real results. *Mashable.com.* Retrieved from http://mashable.com/2010/03/16/public-relations-social-media-results

Warshaw, P. R., & Davis, F. D. (1985). Disentangling behavioral intention and behavioral expectation. *Journal of Experimental Social Psychology, 21*(3), 213–228. doi:10.1016/0022-1031(85)90017-4

Wasserman, S., & Faust, K. (1994). *Social network analysis: Methods and applications.* Cambridge, UK: Cambridge University Press.

Watershed. (2011). *Media sandbox: The hills are evil.* Retrieved April 1, 2011, from http://www.mediasandbox.co.uk/category/overlay-media/

Waugh, D. (2011). *Personal interview.*

Weare, C. (2002). The Internet and democracy: The causal links between technology and politics. *International Journal of Public Administration, 25*(5), 659–691. doi:10.1081/PAD-120003294

Webb, N. Hepple, M., & Wilks, Y. (2005). Dialogue act classification based on intra-utterance features. *Proceedings of the AAAI Workshop on Spoken Language Understanding.*

Webb, N., & Ferguson, M. (2010). Automatic extraction of cue phrases for cross-corpus dialogue act classification. *Proceedings of the 23rd International Conference on Computational Linguistics (COLING-2010).* Beijing, China.

Weber, L. M. (2002). *A survey of the literature on the Internet and democracy.* Paper presented at the Prospects for Electronic Democracy Conference, Carnegie Mellon University, September 20-22, Pittsburgh, PA.

Weiner, A. (2010, February 24). *Ever met a Republican not owned by the insurance industry?.* Retrieved from http://www.youtube.com/watch?v=KBqtyvn7OVw

Weiner, D., Harris, T. M., & Craig, W. J. (2002). Community participation and geographic Information Systems . In Craig, W. J., Harris, T. M., & Weiner, D. (Eds.), *Community participation and Geographic Information Systems* (pp. 3–16). New York, NY: Taylor & Francis.

Weinger, M., & Barr, A. (2011, July 7). McCotter finds friends on Hill. *Politico.* Retrieved from http://dyn.politico.com/members/forums/thread.cfm?catid=1&subcatid=1&threadid=5642494

Weiss, H. M. (1978). Social learning of work values in organizations. *The Journal of Applied Psychology, 63*(6), 711–718. doi:10.1037/0021-9010.63.6.711

Welch, E. W., & Wong, W. (2001). Global information technology pressure and government accountability: The mediating effect of domestic context on website openness. *Journal of Public Administration: Research and Theory, 11*(4), 509–538.

Wellman, B., & Haythornthwaite, C. (2002). *The Internet in everyday life.* Blackwell Publishing. doi:10.1002/9780470774298

West, D. M. (2008). *Global e-government survey.* Retrieved March 16, 2010, from http://www.insidepolitics.org/

West, D. (2004). E-government and the transformation of service delivery and citizen attitudes. *Public Administration Review, 64*(1), 15–28. doi:10.1111/j.1540-6210.2004.00343.x

West, D. M. (2004). E-government and the transformation of service delivery and citizen attitudes. *Public Administration Review, 64*(1), 15–27. doi:10.1111/j.1540-6210.2004.00343.x

West, D. M. (2004). E-government and the transformation of service delivery and citizen attitudes. *Public Administration Review, 64*(1), 66–80. doi:10.1111/j.1540-6210.2004.00347.x

White House Blog. (March 17, 2011). *Sunshine, savings, and service.* Retrieved April 1, 2011, from http://www.whitehouse.gov/blog/2011/03/17/sunshine-savings-and-service

Wiebe, J., Wilson, T., & Cardie, C. (2005). Annotating expressions of opinions and emotions in language. *Journal of Language Resources and Evaluation, 39*(2-3), 165–210. doi:10.1007/s10579-005-7880-9

Wikipedia Home Page. (n.d.). *The free encyclopaedia.* Retrieved from http://www.wikipedia.org/

Willem, A., & Buelens, M. (2007). Knowledge sharing in public sector organizations: The effect of organizational characteristics on interdepartmental knowledge sharing. *Journal of Public Administration: Research and Theory, 17*(4), 581–606. doi:10.1093/jopart/mul021

Williams, D. (2006). On and off the 'Net: Scales for social capital in an online era. *Journal of Computer-Mediated Communication, 11*(2), 593–628. doi:10.1111/j.1083-6101.2006.00029.x

Wills, D., & Reeves, S. (2009). Facebook as a political weapon: Information in social networks. *British Politics, 4*(2), 265–281. doi:10.1057/bp.2009.3

Wilshusen, G. C. (2010). *Challenges in federal agencies' use of Web 2.0 technologies.* Retrieved from http://www.gao.gov/new.items/d10872t.pdf

Wilson, D. (1999). Exploring the limits of public participation in local government. *Parliamentary Affairs, 52,* 246–259. doi:10.1093/pa/52.2.246

Wojcik, S. (2008). *The three key roles of moderator in online discussions. The case of French local governments' forums*. Politics: Web 2.0: An International Conference, hosted by the New Political Communication Unit, Royal Holloway, University of London, April17-18, 2008.

WordPress Home Page. (n.d.). *A semantic personal publishing platform.* Retrieved from http://wordpress.com

Working in Canada (WiC). (n.d.). *Government of Canada.* Retrieved April 5, 2011, from http://www.workingin-canada.gc.ca/content_pieces-eng.do?lang=eng&cid=1

Wright, S. (2006). Electrifying democracy? 10 years of policy and practice. *Parliamentary Affairs, 59*(2), 236–249. doi:10.1093/pa/gsl002

Wu, C. J., & Isaksson, K. (2008). *Participatory mapping as a tool for capturing local perspectives on cultural landscapes*. Stockholm, Sweden: KTH – School of Architecture and the Built Environment.

Wu, M. (2002). *SPSS statistics and application*. Taipei, Taiwan: Song Gang Press. (in Chinese)

Wyld, D. C. (2007). *The blogging revolution: Government in the age of Web 2.0. E-Government Series*. IBM Center for the Business of Government.

Xie, B., & Jaeger, P. T. (2008). Older adults and political participation on the Internet: A cross cultural comparison of the USA and China. *Journal of Cross-Cultural Gerontology, 23*(1), 1–15. doi:10.1007/s10823-007-9050-6

Yahoo. Pipes Home Page. (n.d.). *A platform used to create mashups.* Retrieved from http://pipes.yahoo.com/pipes/

Yang, G. (2009). Online activism. *Journal of Democracy, 20*(3), 33–36. doi:10.1353/jod.0.0094

Yang, K. (2005). Public administrators' trust in citizens: A missing link in citizen involvement efforts. *Public Administration Review, 65*(3), 273–286. doi:10.1111/j.1540-6210.2005.00453.x

Yang, K., & Callahan, K. (2005). Assessing citizen involvement efforts by local governments. *Public Performance & Management Review, 29*(2), 191–216.

Yang, K., & Callahan, K. (2007). Citizen involvement efforts and bureaucratic responsiveness: Participatory values, stakeholder pressures, and administrative practicality. *Public Administration Review, 67*, 249–264. doi:10.1111/j.1540-6210.2007.00711.x

Zack, M. H., & McKenney, J. L. (1995). Social context and interaction in ongoing computer-supported management groups. *Organization Science, 6*(4), 394. doi:10.1287/orsc.6.4.394

Zefferer, T. (2011). *Mobile government: E-government for mobile societies.* Secure Information Technology Center, Version 1.0, Austria. Retrieved from http://www.a-sit.at/pdfs/Technologiebeobachtung/mobile_government_1.0.pdf

Zillig, L. P., Herian, M., Abdel-Monem, T., Hamm, J., & Tomkins, A. (2010). Public input for municipal policymaking: Engagement methods and their impact on trust and confidence. *ACM International Conference Proceeding Series: Proceedings of the 11th Annual International Digital Government Research Conference* (Vol. 292, pp. 41-50).

Zimmer, M. (2008). Preface: Critical perspectives on Web 2.0. *First Monday, 13*(3).

Zucker, L. G. (1986). Production of trust: Institutional sources of economic structure . In Staw, B. M., & Cummings, L. L. (Eds.), *Research in organisational behaviour* (*Vol. 8*). Greenwich, CT: JAI.

About the Contributors

Kathryn Kloby, Ph.D. is an Assistant Professor in the Department of Political Science and Sociology at Monmouth University. She teaches courses at the graduate and undergraduate levels in public policy, public administration, and research methods. She is the Director of the Master of Arts in Public Policy Program. After earning her doctoral degree at Rutgers University-Newark Campus, she continues to publish research in the area of public sector performance measurement, accountability, citizen participation, and e-government.

Maria J. D'Agostino is an Assistant Professor of Public Administration at John Jay College of Criminal Justice, CUNY, department of Public Management, where she teaches Public Administration for the graduate and undergraduate programs. She holds a PhD in Public Administration from Rutgers University. Her research interests include gender and public administration, volunteers and nonprofits, and citizen involvement.

* * *

Mohamad G. Alkadry is an Associate Professor of Public Administration at Florida International University. He received his Ph.D. from Florida Atlantic University (2000) and his Master's of Public Policy and Public Administration from Concordia University in Quebec (1996). Dr. Alkadry's work appears in *Review of Public Personnel Administration, International Journal of Organizational Theory and Behavior, Public Administration Review, Administration and Society, Journal of Education Finance, Social Work in Health Care, Public Productivity and Management Review, Public Administration and Management, Public Administration Theory and Praxis*, among other journals. His research interests include administrative responsiveness, race and gender relations. Dr. Alkadry's practitioner experience includes service as a senior research associate at the Center for Urban Redevelopment and Empowerment (Florida Atlantic University) and as a Value-for-Money (performance) Auditor with the Office of the Auditor General of Canada (Ottawa). Dr. Alkadry has authored several community and professional studies in areas of governance and public management.

Christopher F. Arterton is Professor of Political Management at The George Washington University's Graduate School of Political Management, where he served as Dean from 1987 to 2010. Previously, he was a Professor at Yale University for ten years, teaching in both the Political Science Department and the School of Organization and Management. Dr. Arterton's research, years of teaching, and his considerable experience as a consultant on American public opinion make him an expert on the strategic environment of American political leaders -- an area which encompasses the news media and communications technology generally, political strategy and tactics, public opinion, and ethics and leadership in politics. He has written four books on these topics. He received his Ph.D. in Political Science from the Massachusetts Institute of Technology.

Hugo Asencio is a Doctoral candidate in Public Administration and Public Policy at Auburn University. He teaches undergraduate courses in American National Government in the Department of Political Science and Public Administration at Auburn University, Montgomery campus. His main research areas focus on public service ethics, leadership, organizational culture and behavior in public organizations, corruption and anti-corruption, e-government and Information Technology, and comparative public administration and policy.

Anteneh Ayanso is an Associate Professor of Information Systems at Brock University at St. Catharine's, Canada. He received his Ph.D. in Information Systems from the University of Connecticut and an MBA from Syracuse University. He is Certified in Production and Inventory Management (CPIM) by the Association for Operations Management through APICS. His research interests are in data management, business analytics, electronic commerce, and electronic government. His articles are published in leading academic journals such as *Communications of the AIS, Decision Support Systems, European Journal of Operational Research, Government Information Quarterly, Journal of Database Management, International Journal of Electronic Commerce, Information Technology for Development, Journal of Computer Information Systems,* among others. In addition, he has contributed chapters to several books and published in proceedings of major international conferences in Information Systems and related fields. His research in data management has been funded by the Natural Sciences and Engineering Research Council of Canada (NSERC).

Lamar Vernon Bennett is an Assistant Professor of Public Administration in the School of Business, Public Administration and Information Sciences at Long Island University-Brooklyn. Dr. Bennett holds a Ph.D. in Public Administration and Policy from The American University School of Public Affairs and a Master's of Public Administration from Rutgers University–Newark, School of Public Affairs and Administration. Dr. Bennett's research interests include: e-government, citizen participation in local government, public administration pedagogy, and urban public management.

Susan Bergeron is an Assistant Professor in the Department of Politics and Geography at Coastal Carolina University. Susan holds a Ph.D. and M.A. in Geography from West Virginia University, an M.A. in History from Syracuse University, and a B.A. in History frm Duke University. Her research interests include immersive simulation and 3D landscape reconstruction, geovisualization, the development of digital city models for small municipalities and rural areas, GIScience and the humanities, and geospatial technologies in education. Susan has worked on several GIS and geovisualization projects with NGO organizations, including the Monongalia County Solid Waste Authority. Susan has co-authored book chapters on Web 2.0 and the Geospatial Web, and GIS and geovisualization in the humanities.

Michael A. Brown Sr. is an associate specializing in strategic communications with Booz Allen Hamilton in Norfolk, Va. He earned his Doctorate in Public Administration and Urban Policy, International Business, from Old Dominion University, VA. His dissertation topic is "Social Networking and Individual Performance: Examining Predictors of Participation." He holds three leadership positions in the Public Relations Society of America (PRSA) and has been consistently successful at managing high-level programs, planning and influencing organizational procedures and policies, and building positive corporate images and reputations. He has a solid reputation as an expert at influencing public policy, establishing rapport, motivating employees, and building relationships with stakeholders and customers. He is a Senior Manager skilled in all aspects of public relations and public affairs, including social media. His interests are public relations, organizational change, and leadership development.

Tony J. Carrizales is an Assistant Professor of Public Administration at Marist College and Editor-in-Chief of Journal of Public Management and Social Policy. His research interests include diversity in the public sector, the digital divide, and e-governance.

Colleen Casey is an Assistant Professor in the School of Urban and Public Affairs at the University of Texas Arlington. She teaches courses that address network and collaborative models of governance, including theory of public organizations and development and advanced public organization theory. Her recent funded research includes a grant to develop and conduct a survey of municipalities to explore public and private collaborations in the formulation, implementation, and delivery of housing policy objectives and a project focused on organizational collaboration and decision making between the public health and transportation planning communities. In addition to publishing in a number of refereed journals, she was recently affiliated as a visiting scholar with the Federal Reserve Banks of Dallas and Atlanta in the Community and Economic Development Division, where she was responsible for working with key community development stakeholders.

Tammy Esteves has been a graduate faculty member with Troy University for ten years and has also taught courses for The Presidio Graduate School, NC State, Virginia Commonwealth University, the University of Richmond, Christopher Newport University, and Indiana State University. She brings both practical and academic experience to the profession, preferring the moniker, "pracademic." Her practical experiences include roles as Training Coordinator, Human Resources Director, Community Services Coordinator, Development Coordinator, and Interim Executive Director for a women's shelter. She also volunteers with the USCG in the areas of contingency preparedness, and exercise planning. Her main research interest is in the field of crisis informatics, with further interests in the areas of leadership and sustainability in communities and organizations, particularly as is impacted by disasters, and the role of social media in facilitating that sustainability. She has published articles/chapters on ethics, hazard mitigation, and sustainability in the journals *Public Integrity, PA Times*, and *The Public Manager*, and books "Natural Hazards Mitigation" and "Public Administration in Transition."

Kenneth L. Hacker (Ph.D, University of Oregon) is a Professor of Communication Studies at New Mexico State University. He conducts research in political communication, new media networking, and national security and communication. With Jan van Dijk, he is working on new edited volume concerning network society and democracy. He is also the public affairs officer for a volunteer state military unit in his state.

Deniz Zeynep Leuenberger is an Associate Professor of Political Science/Public Administration, the Co-Coordinator of the BSU Center for Sustainability, and the Program Director for the Center for Legislative Studies' Global Civic Leadership and Education Program at Bridgewater State University in Bridgewater, MA. She is also the founding MPA Chair of the Sustainable MPA Program at Presidio Graduate School in San Francisco, CA. Dr. Leuenberger is also the immediate past Faculty Director of the Institute for Regional Development at BSU. She is the co-author, with John R. Bartle, of the book "*Sustainable Development in Public Administration.*" Dr. Leuenberger has recently published articles/chapters on sustainable development, strategic planning, budgeting, and caring labor in the journals *Administrative Theory and Praxis*, *Public Works and Management Policy*, *State and Local Government Review*, *PA Times*, the *Public Manager*, and in the books "*Comparative Public Budgeting: A Global Perspective*" and "*Women in Public Administration Theory and Praxis.*"

Jianling Li is a Professor of Urban Planning at the University of Texas, Arlington, where she teaches transportation planning, planning techniques, research methods, and Geographic Information Systems. Li has thirty years of working experience on transportation planning and policy research. Her recent research focuses on organizational collaboration for transportation planning and the impacts of transportation planning and policies on travel behavior, health outcomes, and social equity. Her research projects have received millions of dollars of funding from the federal, state, regional transportation agencies, and local governments. She has published and presented numerous papers in various refereed journals and national and international conferences.

Barbara L. MacLennan is a graduate student in the Department of Geology & Geography, Eberly College of Arts & Sciences, at West Virginia University. Barbara holds an M.A. in Political Science from West Virginia University, and an M.S. and B.S. in Journalism from the Perley Isaac Reed School of Journalism, West Virginia University. Barbara is a Certified Solid Waste Association of North America Recycling Systems Professional and is recipient of the 2010 Journal of Solid Waste Technology & Management Roy F. Weston Award for contributions by a professional to the field. Barbara has worked with a number of NGO organizations, and was Outreach & Grants Coordinator for the Monongalia County Solid Waste Authority. She has presented on solid waste and environmental decision making, public participation and Civic 2.0, and geovisualization, and is the author of several contributions to the forthcoming Sage publication: Encyclopedia of Consumption and Waste.

Julianne Mahler is a Professor of Government and Politics in the Department of Public and International Affairs at George Mason University. Her research centers on organization theory, especially organization culture and learning. She has also conducted research on the organizational uses of new information and communications technologies and has authored a number articles and chapters on the political and administrative effects of e-government. Recently she published "Organizational Learning at NASA: The Challenger and the Columbia Accidents" with Maureen Casamayou at Georgetown University Press. She earlier coauthored "Organization Theory: A Public Perspective" with Harold Gortner and Jeanne Nicholson. She has served as Director of the MPA program and the Graduate Program in Political Science at George Mason University. She earned her Ph.D. in Political Science at the State University of New York at Buffalo and her B.A. from Macalester College.

Aroon Manoharan is an Assistant Professor of Public Administration at the Department of Political Science, Kent State University. His research interests include e-governance, online civic engagement, and public performance reporting. He holds a Ph.D. in Public Administration from the School of Public Affairs and Administration, Rutgers University–Newark.

Albert L. May is Associate Professor of Media and Public Affairs at George Washington University, where he directed the Journalism Program from 1998 to 2005. His has written on media coverage of online politics and political journalism, including media case studies on the Jeremiah Wright controversy, the Swift Boat Veterans for Truth, and Hurricane Katrina. He joined the faculty of the School of Media and Public Affairs in 1997, after 23 years as a political reporter and editor at the *Atlanta Journal-Constitution, the Raleigh News and Observer.* and the *Arkansas Democrat-Gazette.* Among his honors are a Nieman Fellowship to Harvard University and the George Washington University's Morton A. Bender Teaching Award. He holds an M.A. degree from the University of Missouri School of Journalism.

Darryl Moyers is a recent graduate from Brock University in St. Catharines, Canada. He received his Honours Bachelor of Business Administration Degree with a double concentration in Marketing and Information Systems in June 2011. His research interests include social media and Web design best practices, as well as how technology can be applied to the business environment to encourage process change and organizational improvement.

Peter Muhlberger is a Research Assistant Professor and Director of the Center for Communication Research in the College of Mass Communications at Texas Tech University. He received his Ph.D. in Political Science from the University of Michigan. Dr. Muhlberger designed and directed research on Carnegie Mellon University's Virtual Agora Project, a National Science Foundation (NSF) funded grant project investigating the political, social, and psychological effects of computer-mediated deliberative democracy and community. He was also principal investigator on the Deliberative ERulemaking Project, a NSFfunded project to apply natural language processing and multilevel deliberation to federal agency online rulemaking. Dr. Muhlberger has authored multiple academic papers on the political psychology and communication aspects of online democratic deliberation.

Danielle Newton has taught and worked as a writing and communication specialist for organizations such as the American Lung Association, the California Institute for Rural Studies, and Green River Community College. A recent graduate of the MFA Program in Writing and Literature at Bennington College, Danielle has taught in multiple higher education settings, including Deganawidah Quetzalcoatl University, California's tribal college. She has also contributed to academic conferences and publications focused on issues such as social media, ethnic studies, creative writing and literary theory. A published author, Danielle created and directed the online writing center for the MBA and MPA programs in Sustainable Management at Presidio Graduate School. She is also an Editor for *Ginger Post Press* and an Assistant Editor for the *Fifth Wednesday Literary Journal.*

Jennifer StromerGalley is an Associate Professor in the Department of Communication at the University at Albany, SUNY. Her research interests include: the uses of communication technology and its implications for democratic practice, mediated political campaign communication, and deliberative democracy. Her research has appeared in the *Journal of Communication, Political Communication, Journal of Computer Mediated Communication,* and *Journal of Public Deliberation.* She has been involved in grant funded projects on: e rulemaking, identifying social rules in small group online discussion, and predicting real world characteristics of people based on virtual world communication and behavior.

Linda-Marie Sundstrom is a U.S. State Department Fulbright Scholar who has taught graduate Public Administration in Ukraine. She is a full-time faculty member and the Director of the Bureau of Government Research and Service in the Graduate Center for Public Policy and Administration at California State University, Long Beach. She has a Bachelor's Degree in International Business and Marketing from Cal Poly in Pomona, a Master's in Public Administration from California State University, San Bernardino, and a Doctorate in Public Administration, with emphasis in Nonprofit Organizations, from University of La Verne. Prior to teaching in academia, she was a Senior Analyst in the Executive Office for one of the largest counties in California, where she evaluated, developed, and implemented complex projects that crossed departmental and jurisdictional boundaries. She was also a grant writing consultant for government agencies, nonprofit organizations, educational institutions, and tribal governments.

Elizabeth Tait is a research fellow in dot.rural RCUK Digital Economy Research Hub at Aberdeen University where she researches the socio-economic impact of digital technology in rural areas. Previously she worked as a Researcher and Lecturer at Robert Gordon University where she was also awarded a PhD in 2010. Her main research interest is in how ICTs can be used to increase participation in formal and informal politics.

Guang-Xu Wang, Ph.D. is an Assistant Professor of Public Management and Policy in the Department of Public Administration and Management at the National University of Tainan, Taiwan. Dr. Wang's current research interests include social network analysis, networks and public governance (including issues related to public collaborative management), policy analysis and management, institutional theory, and health care policy, and recent research focuses on the use and integration of social network analysis methodology into public management and policy issues. His recent publications can be found in not only top-tier Chinese journals in Taiwan but also English journals such as *International Review of Administrative Sciences (IRAS), Asian Social Science, Journal of Politics and Law*, and *Journal of Public Administration and Policy Research.*

Nick Webb is a Visiting Assistant Professor in the Department of Computer Science at Union College. His research encompasses a range of natural language processing applications, including information extraction, question answering, and dialogue systems, and he has served as Principal Investigator of several NSF- and EU-funded projects. His Ph.D. research at the University of Sheffield, UK centered on multilingual dialogue processing, specifically the analysis of transcribed human-human speech corpora using statistical techniques to build dialogue act recognition systems.

Hua Xu is an Assistant Professor in the Department of Political Science & Public Administration of Auburn University at Montgomery, Alabama. He teaches graduate courses in Public Administration and Public Management, Organizational Theory and Behavior, Public and Non-Profit Budgeting and Financial Management, and Area Studies. His main research areas include public finance, public budgeting and financial management, e-government and Information Technology, public performance management, research methodology, public affairs education, administrative ethics, and comparative public administration. His work has appeared in *Public Administration Review, Journal of Public Budgeting, Accounting, and Financial Management* (forthcoming), *State Tax Notes, Journal of Public Affairs Education,* and the "Handbook for Research Methods in Public Administration." He worked at U.S. Farm Credit Administration and conducted research on financial regulatory system for U.S. Congressional Research Service. He also worked at the State Council Leading Group Office for Poverty Reduction and Development in Beijing, China.

Nancy Van Leuven is currently the Global Civic Education and Leadership Fellow for the Center of Legislative Studies at Bridgewater State University in Massachusetts. Formerly a core faculty member at Presidio Graduate School in San Francisco, CA, she is an award-winning Professor for online teaching and studies how social media affects global public and private communications for stakeholder engagement and crisis strategies. Dr. Van Leuven has recently presented and published on issues of strategic planning and international development, including co-authoring several communication textbooks as well as articles in *Journal of Women, Politics, and Policy, World Congress on Communication for Development,* and *Journal of Global Mass Communication.* A former GO-MAP honoree at the University of Washington, she also researches topics about equity, education, and the environment.

Staci M. Zavattaro received her Ph.D. in Public Administration from Florida Atlantic University and currently is an Assistant Professor of Public Administration at the University of Texas at Brownsville. Her research interests include the intersection of public administration and public relations, public administration theory, and communication theory. She also has degrees in Journalism and Political Science from the University of Florida. Her research appears in *Administrative Theory & Praxis* and *Employee Responsibilities and Rights Journal.*

Index